PENGUIN BOOKS

# THE PENGUIN HISTORY OF MODERN SPAIN

'This book is impressively researched an[...]
will rightfully become the standard surv[...]
the English language' Gerard [...]

'A detailed survey of political, economic an[...]
many of the trends, tensions and power players that have influenced the
course of Spain's modern era' Sarah Watling, *Spectator*

'Compelling ... Impressively for a book that covers a long and
tumultuous era, Townson makes space for recent research, much of
which will be new to the general reader ... An up-to-date history of
modern Spain is a mammoth task, but one which Townson is well
placed to attempt' Dr Mercedes Peñalba-Sotorrío, *History Today*

'Nigel Townson's compelling analysis of twentieth-century Spain
combines a deep knowledge of European history with the novelist's
eye for the telling detail' Professor Michael Seidman,
University of North Carolina

'Townson provides an engaging and accessible account of Spain's
tumultuous twentieth century. Convincingly dismantling the myth of
Spanish exceptionalism, he shows that the lights and shadows of
modern Spanish history can only be properly understood in the broader
European context. This is a compelling and even-handed book'
Julius Ruiz, Edinburgh University

'A veritable tour de force, this account of Spain's long twentieth century
is a model of clarity, organization and economy alike, whilst at the
same time offering interpretations that are as bold as they are original'
Professor Emeritus Charles J. Esdaile, FRHistS, University of Liverpool

'Nigel Townson's book provides a marvellous overview of more than
one hundred years of Spanish history. It is based on wide-ranging
research, original in approach and accessible in style' Professor
Tom Buchanan, University of Oxford

'A splendid study, a true magnum opus. This is absolutely the best
history of twentieth-century Spain in either language' Professor Stanley
Payne, University of Wisconsin-Madison

'Brings an objectivity to the story of Spain's journey ... that is as
refreshing as it is intelligent ... Townson is a leading historian
of the country' Simon Heffer, *Daily Telegraph*

# NIGEL TOWNSON

# The Penguin History of Modern Spain

*1898 to the Present*

PENGUIN BOOKS

PENGUIN BOOKS

UK | USA | Canada | Ireland | Australia
India | New Zealand | South Africa

Penguin Books is part of the Penguin Random House group of companies
whose addresses can be found at global.penguinrandomhouse.com.

First published in Great Britain by Allen Lane 2023
First published in Penguin Books 2024
002

Printed and bound in Great Britain by Clays Ltd, Elcograf S.p.A.

The authorized representative in the EEA is Penguin Random House Ireland,
Morrison Chambers, 32 Nassau Street, Dublin D02 YH68

A CIP catalogue record for this book is available from the British Library

ISBN: 978-0-141-98421-6

www.greenpenguin.co.uk

MIX
Paper | Supporting
responsible forestry
FSC® C018179
www.fsc.org

Penguin Random House is committed to a
sustainable future for our business, our readers
and our planet. This book is made from Forest
Stewardship Council® certified paper.

*For Marta*

# Contents

# List of Photographic Credits

1. p. 15 Blasco Ibáñez being mobbed at election time. Matteo Omied /Alamy,https://www.alamy.com/blasco-ibez-en-las-calles-de-valencia-el-da-de-las-elecciones-nuevo-mundo-14-de-septiembre-de-1905-image219375932.html?irclickid=yq3xA4RKrxyNRuIRF20F-x4rUkA1FDwWrymuyoo&utm_source=77643&utm_campaign=Shop%20Royalty%20Free%20at%20Alamy&utm_medium=impact&irgwc=1

2. p. 75 Antonio Maura and King Alfonso XIII. Cartagena Histórica 22/2008, p 34. Editorial Áglaya, Cartagena 2008 (PDF)

3. p. 78 The children of striking workers being fed at the socialist headquarters in Madrid. (1920-09-29). "Los pobres niños hambrientos de Riotinto". Mundo Gráfico (465). ISSN 1579-847X

4. p. 101 Miguel Primo de Rivera at Alhucemas with José Sanjurjo and Francisco Franco. Alto Vintage Images / Alamy, https://www.alamy.com/alhucemas-franco-primo-sanjurjo-image214444515.html?irclickid=yq3xA4RKrxyNRuIRF20F-x4rUkA14YXerymuU80&utm_source=77643&utm_campaign=Shop%20Royalty%20Free%20at%20Alamy&utm_medium=impact&irgwc=1

5. p. 108 Female workers at an Ericsson factory near Madrid. UtCon Collection/Alamy,https://www.alamy.com/english-ericsson-established-a-factory-in-getafe-in-1924-the-picture-shows-the-workshop-interior-1924-ericsson-history-spain-telefonaktiebolaget-lm-ericsson-image352478242.html?irclickid=yq3xA4RKrxyNRuIRF20F-x4rUkAyhIRfrymuUco&utm_source=77643&utm_campaign=

Shop%20Royalty%20Free%20at%20Alamy&utm_medium=impact&irgwc=1

6. p. 132 Clara Campoamor. Photograph from Diario16, distributed under a CC-BY-SA-4.0 license, https://commons.wikimedia.org/wiki/File:Clara-Campoamor.jpg

7. p. 171 Arrested Asturian workers. Photographer unknown, Narodowe Archiwum Cyfrowe

8. p. 223 Insurgent troops on the outskirts of Madrid. Photographer unknown, Narodowe Archiwum Cyfrowe

9. p. 243 Two girls watching out for air raids. Zip Lexing / Alamy, https://www.alamy.com/children-during-the-madrid-bombing-image259743367.html?irclickid=yq3xA4RKrxyNRuIRF 20F-x4rUkA145RvrymuU80&utm_source=77643&utm_campaign=Shop%20Royalty%20Free%20at%20 Alamy&utm_medium=impact&irgwc=1

10. p. 257 A primary school in 1940. Photo by Madruganya, licensed under the Creative Commons Attribution-Share Alike 3.0 Unported license, https://commons.wikimedia.org/wiki/File:Salvador_Mart%C3%ADnez_Surroca.jpg

11. p. 284 Franco meeting Himmler in Madrid. Bundesarchiv, Bild 183-l15327/ photographer: unknown

12. p. 355 Prince Juan Carlos and dictator Francisco Franco. Photographer unknown, National Archives of the Netherlands / Anefo, 922-4913

13. p. 383 The Communist Party's May Day celebration of 1978. Photo by Luis Bartolomé Marcos, licensed under the Creative Commons Attribution-Share Alike 4.0 International license, https://commons.wikimedia.org/wiki/File:Madrid,_1%C2%BA_de_Mayo_1978_03.jpg?wprov=srpw1_11

LIST OF PHOTOGRAPHIC CREDITS

14. p. 407 Tejero takes the Cortes by storm. Manuel Barriopedro/AP

15. p. 456 The '15-M' protest movement in Madrid. Photo by Dani
L.G, distributed under a CC BY 2.0 license, https://www.flickr.
com/photos/dntrotamundos/https://www.flickr.com/photos/
dntrotamundos/

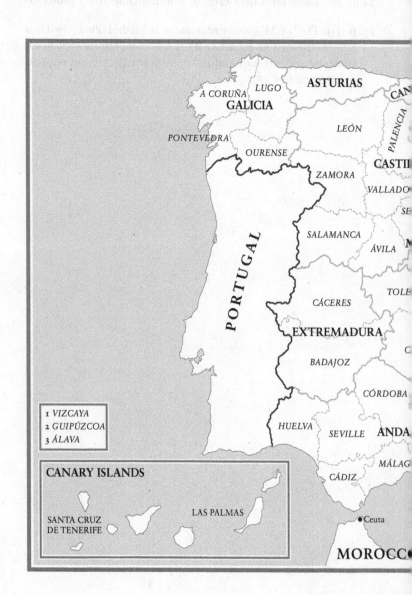

ASTURIAS

GALICIA
A CORUÑA   LUGO
PONTEVEDRA
OURENSE
LEÓN
PALENCIA
CASTI
ZAMORA
VALLADO
SE
PORTUGAL
SALAMANCA
ÁVILA
M
TOLE
CÁCERES
EXTREMADURA
BADAJOZ
CÓRDOBA
1 VIZCAYA
2 GUIPÚZCOA
3 ÁLAVA
HUELVA   SEVILLE   ANDA

CANARY ISLANDS
MÁLAG
CÁDIZ
•Ceuta

SANTA CRUZ
DE TENERIFE
LAS PALMAS

MOROCC

# Acknowledgements

I am extremely grateful to those colleagues who took the time and trouble to comment on one or more chapters of the book: José Álvarez Junco, Óscar Bascuñán Añover, Julio de la Cueva, Tim Rees, Julius Ruiz, and in particular Michael Seidman, who read virtually all the chapters. None are responsible, alas, for the remaining errors and omissions. I am indebted to Tim Rees and Michael Seidman for their bibliographical suggestions. Thanks, too, to David Mathieson for showing me around the Civil War battle sites in the Madrid area with humour and enthusiasm. My father, Duncan Townson, not only surveyed the entire text with his habitual diligence, but also constituted an unstinting source of advice and encouragement. My elder children, Sonia and Oscar, furnished support, interest, and feedback, while baby Alicia played her part by being a bundle of joy. I am also grateful to Chloe Currens at Penguin for her editorial scrutiny, guidance, and succour, as well as to my copyeditor, Richard Mason, for his painstaking revision of the text. My greatest debt is to Marta for bearing the overwhelming brunt of the care for our baby daughter, for her invaluable assistance in relation to the history of women in Spain, for commenting with incisiveness on each and every chapter, and for her unwavering support, encouragement, and love.

Nigel Townson, April 2022, Madrid

# Introduction

The year 1898 is known by Spaniards as the 'Disaster'. In the Spanish-American war of that year, Spain lost its last major colonies – Cuba, the Philippines, and Puerto Rico – to the United States of America. What had been a 'splendid little war' for the United States could scarcely have been more devastating to the pride and prestige of the defeated, as Spaniards now came to the realization that their nation was no longer a great power.[1] 'What bitterness! What disillusionment!' exclaimed the Nobel prize-winning scientist and physician Santiago Ramón y Cajal, 'we believed we still had a glorious empire but it turns out that we are nothing'.[2] The shame and humiliation were especially acute as Spain had lost the colonies just as other European powers were glorying in their far-flung empires. The Spaniards' patriotic bravura of the *ante bellum* period, when the Americans had been ridiculed as 'adventurers' and 'barbarians' bereft of 'a history', promptly gave way to a self-flagellatory culture of intense pessimism. The Spanish 'race' was denounced as decadent and its 'character' dismissed as unfit for the demands of the modern world by the Spanish themselves. The literary and intellectual 'Generation of 1898' set about analysing the so-called 'Spanish problem' – the nation's dizzying drop from imperial grandeur to insular irrelevance – in pitiful tones of self-loathing. 'Where is the bomb that destroys the wretched clod of Spain?' bemoaned the playwright and novelist Ramón del Valle-Inclán. 'Spain,' he lamented, 'is a grotesque deformation of European civilization.'[3] This grievous sense of inferiority was not only to haunt Spaniards for most of the twentieth century, but also to shape profoundly the debate about their country and its place in the world.

Following the 'Disaster', Spain appeared to lurch from one failed regime to another in the quest for 'regeneration'. The Restoration (1875–1923) was a monarchical regime 'without a pulse' as one premier put it.[4] It proved unable to undertake fundamental reform, in particular the transition from an elitist liberal system to a democratic one, despite being increasingly challenged by the opposition of republicans, socialists, anarcho-syndicalists, and regional nationalists. The First World War only served to highlight the country's marginal status as it remained neutral throughout. By then, the regime was staggering from one ministerial crisis to another – governments lasted an average of five months between 1914 and 1923 – and was incapable of solving the 'social question' as manifested in the violent unrest of the 'Bolshevik Triennium' (1918–20) and the gangster-style warfare that characterized the conflict involving workers and industrial bosses in Catalonia between 1919 and 1923. The coup d'état of General Miguel Primo de Rivera in September 1923 ('it is not an act of indiscipline to save the Motherland,' he explained) ruptured the Restoration regime in an effort to forge, in the dictator's own words, 'a new Spain' that would be rooted in 'the revolutionary work that the health of Spain, the march of time, and the decline of everything around us demands'.[5] Still, this authoritarian essay in regeneration, like the Restoration regime before it, signally failed to solve the 'Spanish problem'.

King Alfonso XIII, who had trampled on his own constitution by backing Primo de Rivera (or 'my Mussolini'), was eventually forced into exile and the Second Republic was swept into being on 14 April 1931 on a wave of euphoria.[6] Following the turmoil of Alfonso's reign, the nascent republican regime was welcomed by most sectors of society as the long-awaited panacea to the nation's ills. Nonetheless, the country's first democracy proved unable to fulfil the enormous expectations placed in it, imploding into civil war only five years later. The victory of the military insurgents in the Civil War of 1936 to 1939 condemned Spain to a very different kind of regime: a dictatorship. While post-war Western Europe basked in unimagined prosperity and political freedom, Franco's Spain had to endure widespread misery and brutal repression. And while an increasingly secular Western Europe looked forward to an era of international cooperation and individual tolerance, Catholic Spain harked back defiantly to the global, warmongering empire of Charles V, the scourge of the Reformation, and Franco's hero-from-history, the implacable Philip II. For supporters of the regime, the tourist slogan that did so much to promote the idea of Spanish singularity – 'Spain is Different' – was a source of patriotic pride, but for many Spaniards it was a source of shame and disgust as it publicized the contrast between dictatorial Spain and democratic Europe. Only in the 1960s and 1970s did Spaniards feel that the chasm which separated them from Western Europe was closing, largely as a result of unprecedented economic growth and the transition from dictatorship to democracy in the late 1970s. Full convergence with the West was finally achieved with Spain's entry into NATO and the European Community in the mid-1980s, along with the country's spectacular sporting success, culminating in the football World Cup triumph of 2010. Certainly a measure of self-disgust returned to haunt Spaniards with the onset of the economic crisis in 2008, but this was not experienced as another 'disaster', as the slump had hit all of Southern Europe.

Spaniards' long-standing sense of failure was the product not only of comparisons with other nations, but also of an awareness of the way in which foreigners viewed them. For centuries, Spain was stigmatized by condescending, derogatory, and often damning stereotypes. Throughout the Islamic occupation from the eighth to the fifteenth centuries, the Iberian peninsula, with its intermingling of Christians, Jews, and Muslims, was viewed as a strange, oriental 'Other'. This exotic image gave way to a new hegemonic narrative in the early sixteenth century with the eruption of the Spanish Empire. Taking their cue from the Inquisition, the conquest of the Americas, and Charles V's belligerent championship of the Counter-Reformation, Protestant and Jewish enemies of Spain unleashed what was arguably the first political propaganda campaign in history: the 'Black Legend'. The propagandists branded Spaniards as 'unusually cruel, avaricious, treacherous, fanatical, superstitious, cowardly, corrupt'.[7] This nefarious reputation was not to be challenged until the Romantic movement rebranded Spain in the eighteenth and nineteenth centuries. The Romantics, who came above all from Britain, France, and the United States, were seduced by a country that appeared to fulfil their yearning for a pastoral society unblemished by the evils of industrial capitalism, secularization, and the destruction of tradition. In many ways, the Romantic take on Spain represented a reconfiguration of the Black Legend: what had previously been condemned as religious fanaticism was now praised as a pure and committed faith, and what had once been lambasted as insufferable pride and haughtiness was now revisited by the Romantics as a paradigm of personal integrity and honour. At long last, Spain had acquired a positive image, though even the Romantics still regarded the country as fundamentally inferior.

Both the Romantic myth and the Black Legend remained potent ideas throughout the twentieth century. On the outbreak of the Civil War in 1936, foreigners, who had difficulty in making sense of a country that had scarcely hit the headlines since 1898, readily drew on the two stereotypes. Famously, Ernest Hemingway celebrated 'the only good people left in Europe' and a nation that was 'unspoiled and unbelievably tough and wonderful'.[8] By contrast, a British diplomat considered the Spaniards 'a race of blood-thirsty savages'.[9] For supporters of the Republic, the rebels, much in line with the Black Legend, were religious bigots and pitiless sadists, while for the sympathizers of the insurgents, the republicans also exhibited many Black Legend traits in their assault on 'Christian civilization'. With the victory of the rebels in 1939, Spain was subject to two contrasting, yet mutually reinforcing, stereotypes. On the one hand, the Franco dictatorship was typified in thoroughly contemporary terms as a 'fascist' state. On the other hand, it was often characterized according to the stereotype of the Black Legend as a regime of inquisitorial vindictiveness, wanton cruelty, and religious zealotry. The dictatorship fought back by, ironically, drawing on another foreign-inspired stereotype: the Romantic myth. Foreign tourists were lured to the beaches of the Mediterranean by the bucolic allure of sand, sea, and blue skies. Undoubtedly mass tourism did convince many visitors that a 'new Spain' was emerging from the shadow of the Civil War, but this was powerfully offset by prevailing images of the 'fascist' and 'old Spain', as illustrated by the Amnesty International campaign of the 1960s that enjoined tourists to 'Have a good time – but remember, Amnesty for Spain's political prisoners.'[10] If the Franco dictatorship is viewed as the high point of Spanish exceptionalism in the twentieth century, then the subsequent transition to democracy has constituted its polar opposite: the first time in the modern era that Spain has been lauded as a model worthy of universal imitation, as consecrated by Samuel Huntington's *The*

*Third Wave: Democratization in the Late 20th Century*. Nonetheless, for most of the past century Spain has been regarded not only as marginal to mainstream Europe, but also as 'different' or 'peculiar'.

Historians have often agreed with this assessment. Certainly the post-Civil War generation of scholars judged Spain to be a land apart. As one of the foremost historians of twentieth-century Spain, Santos Juliá, recalls, 'we had been formed with the idea that the history of Spain was an anomaly, a failure. This was the starting point.'[11] This narrative of failure, so reminiscent of the soul-searching after the Disaster of 1898, was forged in the 1940s and 1950s by historians such as Pierre Vilar and Jaime Vicens Vives. Vilar's *History of Spain*, first published in 1947, swiftly acquired canonic status amongst non-Francoist historians. It portrayed the history of modern Spain as a series of lamentable shortcomings. Spain's original sin, according to Vilar, was its alleged failure to launch an industrial revolution. This diagnosis was upheld by scholars in the 1960s and 1970s, for whom the economic landscape had been littered with failure: the 'failure in industrialization', the 'failure' of the banking system, and the 'failure' in economic planning, as crystallized in Jordi Nadal's study of 1975, *The Failure of the Industrial Revolution in Spain*.[12] Intimately linked to the stillborn industrial revolution was the aborted bourgeois revolution. Vilar upbraided the Spanish bourgeoisie for failing 'to carry out the revolution that would transform it into the hegemonic class'.[13] Once more, the historians of the 1960s and 1970s concurred, maintaining that the bourgeois revolution had been 'frustrated' and that those bourgeois elements which did emerge had been 'co-opted by the aristocracy'.[14]

Inevitably, this narrative of failure profoundly shaped research on the twentieth century. Early twentieth-century Spain was portrayed as a backward, agrarian society divided between a rapacious, self-serving elite and the impoverished masses. The period was subject to scant research and even less debate, often being presented as little more than a backdrop to the turbulent events of the 1930s. According to this Manichean scheme, the tensions of the 1930s were largely the result of the class struggle between the poverty-stricken masses and a reactionary oligarchy. The Civil War itself was seen, to its credit, as the first anti-fascist struggle, but the collapse of republican democracy into fratricidal slaughter, the perceived savagery of the conflict, and the idea that it was 'a paupers' war', also served to confirm Spain's pre-modern status.[15] But worse was to come. The dictatorship of General Franco, founded upon the ruins of the Civil War, was viewed as a fascist aberration that stood in monstrous, almost surreal, contrast to Western Europe. There could be no denying the fact: Spain was different.

All of this changed with the transition to democracy in the 1970s. The opening up of the archives, the axing of state censorship, and the liberalization of higher education freed scholarship from the incubus of the Francoist State. The enormous expansion of the universities in the 1980s also meant that there were more historians than ever. However, the history boom was not just a question of supply, but also of demand: after years of Francoist propaganda and lies, people were desperate to discover the truth about the 1930s and the subsequent years. The result was an avalanche of congresses, seminars, public debates, journals, and books, as well as intense media interest. This has dramatically altered the nature of the historical work on Spain. First, Spanish historians have carried out extensive research on every single decade of the twentieth century. By contrast, foreign historians, especially British ones, have remained largely transfixed by the Civil War and its immediate reverberations, partly for commercial reasons and partly because the Romantic myth of the Civil War as 'the last great cause' has proved perennially seductive. Second, Spanish historians have striven to unravel the past not only by looking at the economy, society, and culture in addition to political history, but also by drawing on a range of methodologies. Again, the contrast with foreign scholars is striking, as many of the latter are still strongly wedded to the rarefied realm of high politics.

The Spanish-led research of the last forty years has transformed our knowledge and understanding of Spain in the twentieth century. The first third of the century, to take one example, is no longer seen as a time of economic stagnation, social immobility, and political polarization, but rather as one of constant growth, social change, and even political pluralism. Indeed, hardly a period or topic of Spain's twentieth century has been left untouched. Wide-ranging research on the Republic, the Civil War – 3,000 books were published on it between

1975 and 1995 alone – the dictatorship, and the Transition has produced a much richer and more rounded picture of the last century. The sway hitherto exercised by foreign scholars has been greatly diminished as a result of the avalanche of work produced by Spanish scholars. The overwhelming bulk of this historical writing has been published in Spanish and, to a much lesser extent, in Catalan, Galician, and Basque, but only a fraction of this vast output has found its way into English. Accordingly, a principal goal of this book is to provide an accessible and up-to-date synthesis of this ground-breaking research for an English-speaking audience.

The wave of post-Francoist studies has either reformulated or simply discredited the narrative of failure. The debunking of this discourse has been due in part to the rise of comparative history, the pioneers being the economic historians of the 1980s and 1990s. Instead of taking the major powers as their point of comparison (both Raymond Carr and Jordi Nadal, for instance, took England as their yardstick), they placed the evolution of the Spanish economy within a much broader context. They discovered that Spain was not a case of 'failure, stagnation and backwardness', but one distinguished by 'sustained growth', and that it could be regarded as a laggard only in relation to the leading European economies.[16] Indeed, within the setting of Southern Europe, the Spanish economy surpassed the performance of all bar Italy. In short, the comparative method revealed that the narrative of economic failure was a myth. Much the same occurred with, say, the dominant narrative on the struggle for female suffrage: a defeatist discourse was inverted as a result of comparison with the suffragette movement in other nations.

Still, few areas of modern Spain have been subjected to a comparative analysis, least of all the entire twentieth century. Yet only by comparing Spain with the rest of Europe can its place within the arc of modern European history be established. The aim of this book is not to write the story of Spain as a self-contained narrative focused almost exclusively on the nation state, but rather to position it in relation to the much broader reality of Europe. Pertinent to this task is an appreciation of Spain's transnational dimension. No European country of the twentieth century can be understood without taking into account its extraterritorial traits, such as economic globalization, the spread of ideas and ideologies, or the impact of transnational bodies and accords. Only by framing the trajectory of twentieth-century Spain in relation to Europe and the transnational can it at last be integrated into the mainstream narrative of European history.

A final aspiration of *The Penguin History of Modern Spain* is to capture the lives of contemporary Spaniards. It is one thing for historians to try to make sense of the past, and another to examine how that past was lived. By drawing on the testimony of shopkeepers, peasants, soldiers, industrial workers, lawyers, and many other men and women, I hope to do justice to Spain's tumultuous twentieth century as it was experienced not just by those at the apex of society, but also by those at its base.

# I

## The 'Disaster' of 1898 and the 'Regeneration' of Spain, 1898–1914

On 1 May 1898, Admiral George Dewey of the US Pacific Fleet led a squadron into Manila Bay in the Philippines to confront a Spanish squadron under Admiral Patricio Montojo. While most of Dewey's ships were steel cruisers with armour-plating, Montojo's vessels enjoyed no such protection. Indeed, his biggest ship, the *Castilla*, had a wooden hull. Nor did the Spaniards have anything to match the fire-power of the Americans' eight-inch guns. Beginning at 5.40 a.m. with Dewey's laconic order, 'You may fire when you are ready', the battle was soon over.[1] The Spanish squadron was blown to smithereens. Some 161 Spaniards were killed, 210 wounded, and all ships lost. Not one American died. It was, in short, 'one of the most one-sided naval combats in history'.[2] Yet worse was to follow. The Americans also coveted the Spanish colony of Cuba, the Jewel of the Caribbean. Two months later, they blockaded the port of Santiago de Cuba, which harboured the best ships of the Spanish fleet under Admiral Pascual Cervera. Unlike Montojo's vessels, these all had armoured hulls, though their decks and upper parts were made of wood. On 3 July, at 9.35 a.m., the Spanish ships attempted to breach the American block-ade, Cervera's aide, Captain Víctor Concás, having espied an opening. As the Spanish flotilla headed for the gap, Cervera gave the order to fire. Concás would later recall this as 'the signal that four centuries of glory were ended'. '"Poor Spain," I said to my noble and beloved admiral.'[3] Once the Spanish ships reached open water, the sleeker and fleeter American vessels hunted them down. One by one, the Spanish vessels were either sunk or ran aground. Their flagship, the *María Teresa*, was one of those that ran to ground, but Cervera managed to swim ashore, crawling half-naked onto a beach. In all, 323 Spaniards died, 151 were wounded, and the entire squadron was destroyed. By contrast, the Americans suffered one fatality and three impaired ships. The Spanish-American War of 1898 had cost Spain 'an army, a fleet, and an empire'.[4] 'We have lost everything,' reported Cervera to Madrid. Still, it had been 'an honourable disaster'.[5]

## REGENERATING THE NATION

'Such was my enthusiasm when war was declared, thinking that we would win,' exclaimed María de Echarri Martínez in her diary in late September.[6] Scion of a family dynasty of bankers and lawyers in Madrid, María was a passionate nationalist who was convinced that the 'Spanish lion' would savage the 'Yankee pig' in the war of 1898.[7] Her disillusionment in defeat could scarcely have been greater. 'Such was my confidence! How many mistakes I made! And how great has been my disappointment!' she lamented – 'everything has been lost except honour'.[8] María's reaction to the so-called 'Disaster' (*Desastre*) epitomized the outrage and disgust that engulfed the urban educated classes in the wake of the naval debacles at Manila Bay and Santiago de Cuba. Indeed, the public fury over the loss of the islands of Cuba, Puerto Rico, and the Philippines was incomparably greater than that over the loss of the vast American colonies between 1810 and 1825, despite the fact that those of 1898 constituted only a fraction – less than 5 per cent in territorial terms – of the original empire. The reason for this apparent paradox lay in the contrast between the embryonic national consciousness of the early nineteenth century and the more mature one of the late nineteenth century. In the 1810s and 1820s the colonies were seen as the personal property of the king and their loss as a matter for the monarch. By the 1890s, the idea of national sovereignty – as opposed to the divine sovereignty of absolutism – had achieved sufficient traction for substantial sectors of Spanish society to regard the forfeiture of the colonies in 1898 as a *collective* failure, not just that of the monarch. Thus the very prospect of war with the 'barbarians' of the United States – a nation 'without cohesion and without history' – had provoked protests in Madrid, Barcelona, Málaga, Valencia, and Zaragoza, spreading later to other parts of the country.[9] On 1 May, the day that news of the navy's capitulation at Manila Bay in the Philippines first reached Madrid, demonstrators, mainly soldiers and upper middle-class civilians, called for the resignation of the government.

Spain's decline as an imperial power had been identified even before the 'Disaster' as 'the Spanish problem', but was now transformed from a stream of anxious musings into a lacerating cascade of national self-criticism, as reflected in works on *The National Problem*, *On the National Disaster and its Causes*, and *The Psychology of the Spanish People*. This spawned a literary genre that would reinvent itself remorselessly for at least the next half century. Still, national trauma as a result of military catastrophe was far from exceptional within late nineteenth-century Europe. Obvious parallels can be found in the case of France, humbled by Prussia in 1870–71, or Italy, humiliated by Abyssinia in 1896, the first rout of a European army by an African one in the modern era. Earlier, Russia had been convulsed by calamity in the Crimean War of 1853–6, as it would be later by defeat at the hands of Japan in 1904–5. On a lesser scale, Portugal suffered a national setback in 1890 when Belgium and Britain thwarted its dream of a transcontinental African empire, while Greece's crushing loss at the hands of the Ottoman Empire in the 'Thirty Days War' of 1897 – 'the greatest of the national humiliations of the nineteenth century' – also provoked a sustained period of soul-searching.[10] The problematic imperial progress of the Southern European nations gave rise during the late nineteenth century to the idea, derived from Social Darwinism, that the 'Latin races' of the south were inherently inferior to those of the north or to those peoples of Anglo-Saxon origin such as the Americans. Italians were anguished by their 'weak' national character and by their 'inferiority' to other nations.[11] Many Spaniards feared in the aftermath of the 'Disaster' that the origin of their national 'decadence' was racial, and in particular that their Arab blood had made them one of the 'inferior races'.[12]

The self-pitying and pessimistic literary 'Generation of 1898' saw Spain as a world away from Britain's confident *Britannia*, France's bold *Marianne*, or the United States' forthright *Uncle Sam*. On the contrary, Spain was personified in the *Mater dolorosa*, the crushed and doleful figure of the Virgin Mary in mourning for her dead son. The antimodern and ineluctably Romantic outlook of the 'Generation of 1898' was vividly illustrated by its most prominent figure, the trim-bearded academic and writer Miguel de Unamuno, who sought solace in Spain's traditional virtues. For Unamuno, Spain may have lacked the materialistic know-how and thrust of the United States or Europe, but its human and spiritual qualities, as reflected in *Don Quijote* and Catholic mysticism, ultimately made it superior. Such self-serving arguments echoed those of thinkers from other powers in decline, such as Feodor Dostoevsky in Russia.

Spain's response to the 'Disaster' has invariably been equated with the 'Generation of 1898'. Often overlooked, however, is the fact that 1898 also provoked a stirring nationalistic reaction that defied the racial determinism of the Social Darwinists and the condescension of foreigners – epitomized in Lord Salisbury's damning characterization of Spain as one of the 'dying nations'[13] – through a collective commitment to 'patriotic regeneration'. The land was swept by a Regenerationist fever, with proposals ranging from freethinkers, Freemasons, and anarchists to socialists, republicans, liberals, conservatives, and Carlists, not to forget those of agronomists, feminists, bishops, military men, scholars, and others. Despite the bewildering variety of programmes, they all agreed on one thing: the urgent need for far-reaching reform. At last, Spain began to face the future, refusing to take refuge in the imperial glories of the past. The spirit of Regenerationism was so pervasive that it permeated everyday life: a novel of the time featured a cobbler who advertised 'The Regeneration of Footwear'.[14]

Nonetheless, many Spaniards in 1898 shared neither the patriotic fervour of the Regenerationists nor the dismay of well-to-do urbanites such as María de Echarri Martínez. The leader of the Conservative Party, Francisco Silvela, judged that the war did not produce the slightest change in the 'life or customs or entertainment' of the popular classes.[15] Indeed, commentators were shocked by the general indifference to the 'Disaster'. When news of the Manila Bay calamity reached Madrid, people attended the Sunday bullfight as if nothing had happened. The reaction in the rural areas, where the overwhelming majority of Spaniards still lived, was 'non-existent'.[16] This was symptomatic of a much broader reality. 'Throughout Spain there were many more who worked in silence, concerned only with the bread of every day,' observed Miguel de Unamuno, 'than those bothered with public events.'[17]

Poverty, isolation – nearly half of the country's 9,200 *pueblos* or villages and small towns were inaccessible by road as late as 1910 – and the illiteracy of two out of every three Spaniards all contributed to this indifference. The fact that for most rural Spaniards identity was not shaped by the written language meant that they tended overwhelmingly to associate their community with a locality, not the nation. Despite the dearth of national sentiment, the war *did* nonetheless have an impact on the rural areas. The draft had made the war deeply unpopular as it deprived peasant families of the labour of their able-bodied young men. Moreover, the outbreak of war in May 1898 had adversely affected the value of the peseta, which, together with a run of bad harvests since 1896, had pushed up the price of bread. Riots followed in much of the country. In Asturias, Castile-La Mancha, and Soria, the republican daily *El País* related, the riots assumed 'extremely grave proportions', with the 'sacking of businesses and homes, assaults on factories, sacks of wheat slashed opened, scattering the precious wheat on the floor, and a population in hostage to the rioters who release prisoners from the jails and burn the town hall'.[18] 'Half of Spain' was afflicted by 'extremely grave disorders', the liberal broadsheet *El Imparcial* claimed, imploring the government to ban the export of wheat 'so that we avoid, on top of the civil war and the war abroad, a social war in each province, in each town, in each village and even in each hamlet'.[19] The very demands of the daily struggle in 1898 helps explain why most Spaniards were either indifferent to or simply unaware of the 'Disaster'.

## THE RESTORATION POLITICAL SYSTEM

Regenerationist thinkers were adamant that the principal cause of the 'Disaster' was the political system established upon the restoration of the Bourbon monarchy in 1875. The architect of the so-called 'Restoration' system was the able, sardonic, and forceful Antonio Cánovas del Castillo, affectionately known as 'the Monster'. His paramount objective was to eliminate the political instability of the earlier nineteenth century, a period characterized by war, military uprisings, civil wars, revolution, and fitful governance. The new political order was based on two premises. The first was that the army had to be removed from politics. The uprising of Colonel Rafael del Riego in 1820 in support of the liberals in their struggle against the absolutists had set a precedent for military involvement in politics. The subsequent dependence of the liberals on the army meant that numerous prime ministers were generals, not politicians, and that the most popular public figure in Spain between the 1830s and 1870s was General Baldomero Espartero. Hardly surprisingly, the army, not parliament, came to be seen as the supreme national institution. However, Cánovas del Castillo brought the political protagonism of the military to a close by granting it control of the colonies and the ministerial portfolio for the armed forces. The second pillar of the Restoration system was the *turno pacífico* or 'peaceful rotation' in power of the two monarchist parties, the Conservatives under Cánovas del Castillo and the Liberals under Práxedes Sagasta. This was a 'peaceful rotation' because it was based on a pre-electoral agreement between the dynastic parties as to how the seats in parliament would be divided up. In other words, the elections were rigged, a cynical arrangement which was regarded as a necessary evil by its beneficiaries. Indeed, Cánovas del Castillo regarded the new political order as the best possible solution in the circumstances, convinced that a country like Spain was not yet ready for the politics of mass participation.

The most vociferous denunciation of the Restoration political system was made in *Oligarchy and caciquismo*, a book edited by the Aragonese lawyer, indefatigable reformer, and foremost Regenerationist, Joaquín Costa. *Oligarchy and caciquismo* lambasted the system for its self-serving elitism, its denial of mass politics, and its electoral subterfuge. The chief villain of the book was the *cacique*, a word of Caribbean origin which denoted a local 'boss' or 'enforcer' (the phenomenon was therefore known as *caciquismo*). Bereft of any legal or institutional standing, the *cacique* had to arrange the general election in accordance with the will of the politicians in Madrid. This was achieved by a range of stratagems, including the granting of favours, the buying of votes, the falsification of the electoral roll, the breaking of ballot boxes, and sometimes coercion. It has been widely assumed that *caciquismo* was peculiar to Spain, but this is a myth. Throughout nineteenth-century Europe, electoral malpractice was the norm, not the exception. Portugal, Italy, and Greece all harboured systems which were very similar to *caciquismo*. However, to frame this in terms of

Southern Europe tends to reinforce the idea that it was backward in relation to the north. In reality, the elections in Northern Europe were plagued by ballot-rigging, influence-peddling, and physical intimidation for much of the century. In Britain, one of the most liberal states, the 1868 general election between Gladstone and Disraeli was held to be 'as corrupt as its predecessors', and it was not until the Corrupt Practices Act of 1883 that a substantial difference was made to 'the workings of the electoral system'.[20] Similarly, the first country in the world to introduce modern political parties, the United States of America, held falsified elections throughout the nineteenth century.

The *cacique* was not just an electoral enforcer, though. He acted as a broker or intermediary between the state and the public at large, obtaining jobs, contracts, legal rulings, draft exemptions, tax breaks, and so on in return for an individual's personal loyalty or some other type of recompense. This was an arrangement rooted in the exchange of favours between a 'patron' and a 'client', patronage constituting a face-to-face relationship, whereas clientelism involved greater numbers and therefore a more elaborate mechanism. By exploiting his access to the public administration and the corridors of power, a *cacique* was able to exercise considerable clout at the provincial or local level. An outstanding example is the network built up by the Count of Romanones in the province of Guadalajara. Having established his electoral stronghold there (which returned him sixteen times between 1888 and 1923), the Count proceeded to extend his control over the entire province, 'as arbiter and director of municipal and provincial politics, as intermediary between the inhabitants of the area and the central institutions of the state, and, in short, as almost absolute master of the public administration'.[21] As one minister put it, in Guadalajara the Count was 'owner and lord of lives and properties'.[22] Far from being an aberration, the *cacique* was symptomatic of the patronage or clientelistic relations that imbued Spanish society as a whole. Again, Spain was no exception in this regard. Virtually all European societies of the nineteenth and early twentieth century were to a greater or lesser degree permeated by patronage or clientelistic relations, especially in those distinguished by weak administrative, legal, and political institutions.

# A BACKWARD COUNTRY?

The Regenerationist thinkers also insisted that Spain lagged far behind 'Europe', as evidenced by the country's bloated agricultural economy, skeletal state, impoverished culture, and venal politics, all of which had produced a people who were, in Costa's exasperated words, 'ignorant mules and stupid'.[23] This modernizing narrative of abject failure, repeated ad nauseam until not long ago by historians, was rooted in an implicit contrast with Britain, Germany, and above all France. Equating 'Europe' with the three leading powers obviously ignores the larger continental picture, which included not just the 'Big Three' but also the many other countries that made up Northern, Central, Eastern, and Southern Europe. If Spain is placed in the context of Europe as a whole, a very different picture emerges. Of course, Spain's own path to modernization was 'peculiar', but so was that of the other nations.[24] Thus the trajectory of Italy during the nineteenth and twentieth centuries has often been regarded as 'deeply flawed' or 'exceptional', but comparison shows that it has been 'distinctive without being exceptional'.[25] In other words, no two nations follow exactly the same route, as each is shaped by its own unique set of circumstances. In sum, Spain pursued its own path to modernization, while sharing much in common with the rest of Europe.

Between 1800 and 1910 the Spanish economy achieved 'sustained growth' at 1.14 per cent a year.[26] The cornerstone of its dominant sector, agriculture, was cereal, which managed to keep pace with the rising population, while there was also increasing diversification, resulting in a vibrant export sector, based mainly on wine, olives, nuts, and fruit, which did much to keep the trade balance in the black. The traditional image of nineteenth-century Spanish agriculture as backward and stagnant – feverishly promoted by the Generation of 1898 – is belied not only by its growth (estimates range from between 0.61 and 0.77 per cent a year between 1800 and 1900), but also by its 'market realignment'.[27] Industry grew too, especially during the latter decades of the nineteenth century, when production soared at 3.23 per cent per annum between 1860 and 1900.[28] The leading sectors were textiles, metallurgy, mining, and railways. Mining surged in the 1860s and 1870s thanks to foreign companies, above all British ones such as Rio Tinto. Indeed, Rio Tinto's sprawling copper operation in the Spanish southwest was the biggest in the world, helping mining become the most vigorous sector of the national economy in the decades prior to the First World War. Also in foreign hands was the construction of the railways, a national network having been created between the 1840s and 1880s. Too impoverished to undertake large-scale mining or the building of railways, the nineteenth-century state did at least ensure the establishment of a rudimentary national market.

Economic expansion was reflected in greater urbanization, which doubled between 1860 and 1900. This was especially pronounced in the two main industrial centres: Bilbao soared from 32,734 residents in 1877 to 83,306 in 1900, while Barcelona rocketed from a population of 248,943 in 1877 to 533,000 by 1900. Madrid's population rose steeply too, from 397,816 inhabitants in 1877 to 539,835 in 1900, its demographic surge propelled by the building sector, the banks, and domestic service. Overall, the Spanish population grew at 0.55 per cent per annum during the nineteenth century, which lagged behind the countries of Northern Europe but was comparable to those in the south. Equally, life expectancy, at 35 years in 1900, was far below that in the north (in England and Wales it stood at 48.5 years), but was similar to much of Southern and Eastern Europe. Hardly surprisingly, educational provision in Spain was poor, as illustrated by the fact that 56 per cent of the adult population was illiterate in 1900, which was significantly higher than in Northern Europe, but similar to many countries in the south and lower than most in the east (in Russia illiteracy was as high as 81 per cent).

As in many other European countries, sluggish industrialization and the relative dearth of work on the land precipitated mass emigration around the turn of the century. Over 2.5 million Spaniards abandoned their homeland in search of work between 1885 and 1913, 1.5 million of them permanently (8–9 per cent of the entire population), though this was dwarfed by Italy, which saw 10.74 million people emigrate between 1881 and 1910.

In reality, Spain displayed the same basic modernizing trends as other European countries during the nineteenth century. It therefore fits 'within the broader European model of economic development, which included rising incomes and health indicators, industrialization, a favourable balance of foreign trade, and food production keeping up with population growth'.[29] In comparison with Eastern Europe, Spain was ahead of the modernizing arc, while sharing most in common with the countries of 'Southern Europe'. Within the latter, Spain was far from a late developer, only being outpaced – and not always – by Italy. Admittedly, these nations differed a good deal amongst themselves, but 'probably' no more than the Western European nations, 'and certainly not as much as those of Eastern Europe, where contrasts are especially extreme'.[30] Within Europe as a whole, Spain was, in short, a middling performer, not a success, but certainly not a 'failure' or a 'laggard'.

## REACTING TO THE DISASTER: THE ANTI-DYNASTIC FORCES

When news of the sinking of the Spanish fleet in Santiago de Cuba reached Valencia, a republican paper in the city reported that 'rebellious groups with a defiant attitude and shouting long live the republic' took to the streets, turning over trams and shouting anticlerical slogans while awaiting the 'glorious appearance' – that is to say, the general who would save Spain.[31] Over the next few days, the newspaper left a blank space on its front page in anticipation of the military hero who would fill the void by overthrowing the monarchy and replace it with a republic. The republicans were not the only ones to put their faith in the army. Public opinion held the politicians, not the soldiers, responsible for the debacle of the 'Disaster'. The hour of the army had arrived. 'The country seeks the right man,' noted a journalist, 'and when he appears it will stand by him.'[32] Conservative Party leader Francisco Silvela was prepared to back General Camilo García de Polavieja, the former Capitan General of Cuba and the Philippines, while another prominent Conservative, Francisco Romero Robledo, looked to General Valeriano Weyler, 'The Butcher of Cuba'. The fact that republicans and monarchists alike turned to the army at a time of national crisis revealed not only the continuing strength of the nineteenth-century praetorian tradition, but also the very weakness of the political system that had been designed to make it irrelevant. Polavieja enjoyed the greatest support for an uprising, but he refused to act without the consent of the Regent, the backing of public opinion, and the undivided loyalty of the army. The uprising never took place.

Vilified as the monarchist parties were, the anti-dynastic forces did not offer a credible alternative. To an important extent this was because they, like the monarchists, had clamoured for war. The republicans, the main opposition, were 'as nationalistic, militarist, colonialist and even as racist as the monarchists'.[33] Moreover, the failure of the anti-dynastic forces to take advantage of the government's catastrophic handling of the conflict reflected their own desultory state. The republicans, who constituted a hodgepodge of weakly articulated local, regional, and national parties, were consumed by doctrinal disputes and procedural matters of no interest to the general public. 'The same conversation groups, the same committees, the same casinos. A wretched life, listless, inward-looking,' as one exasperated activist put it.[34] In the 1896 general election the republicans did not even take part, due to 'an awareness of their weakness'.[35] Yet the socialists were of even less importance. Neither the *Partido Socialista Obrero Español* (PSOE) (Spanish Socialist Workers' Party), nor its trade union organization, the *Unión General de Trabajadores* (UGT) (General Union of Workers), founded in 1879 and 1888 respectively, could be regarded as truly national entities. In the 1898 general election the socialists failed – yet again – to elect a single deputy to the Spanish parliament or Cortes, while at the municipal level it had just nine councillors amongst the country's 9,200 local councils. The UGT had fared not much better, having recruited only 6,154 members by 1896. The other main working-class force, the anarcho-syndicalist movement, was in a still more parlous state. During the 1890s the anarcho-syndicalists had been in thrall to radicals who had pursued a strategy of 'propaganda by deed', that is, terrorism. The major bombings of 1893 and 1896 in Barcelona, along with the 1897 assassination of the Restoration's founding father, Antonio Cánovas del Castillo, had precipitated a blanket repression of the movement, which left the anarcho-syndicalists in 'a profound lethargy', their groups disbanded and their press shut down 'almost entirely'.[36] It was no coincidence that there had been no large-scale strikes or labour conflicts in Spain since the early 1890s. The anti-dynastic cause was further undermined by the mutual hostility that characterized relations between the republicans, socialists, and anarcho-syndicalists. Illustrative of the weakness of the opposition was the fact that in the wake of the 'Disaster' it was in no position to bring down the government or force an election.

## THE CATALYST FOR CHANGE:
## THE CHAMBERS OF COMMERCE
## AND AGRICULTURE

Small wonder, then, that the first mass mobilization against the government came from outside the political system altogether. In November 1898 over ninety representatives of the Chambers of Commerce met in the Aragonese capital, Zaragoza, at the behest of the mirror manufacturer Basilio Paraíso. The following February the Agrarian Chambers also met in Zaragoza, this time on the initiative of Joaquín Costa, the chief cheerleader for Regeneration. Both sets of Chambers saw themselves as representatives of the 'neutral mass', the middling classes excluded by the political system, and as men of upright endeavour who stood in damning contrast to the privileged and parasitical political class. They called for lower taxes, a much-reduced budget, and the overhaul of the public administration. The agitation of the commercial and industrial sectors reflected the extent to which the Restoration was out of touch with urban Spain, but the fact that many property-owning peasants were also disenchanted was indicative of how unrepresentative it had become. On the other hand, the opposition of the Chambers was undermined by their own incoherence, as they clamoured for budget and tax cuts while demanding greater public investment. Not surprisingly, they lacked a common strategy: while the Chambers of Commerce sought to become an economic lobby, the Agrarian Chambers aimed to found a political party that would establish, in Costa's words, an 'authentically national government'.[37]

The first government committed to Regeneration was that of the Conservative Francisco Silvela in March 1899. Few monarchist politicians were more appreciative of the need for far-reaching reform than the urbane, cultivated, and somewhat languorous Conservative leader. Acutely aware that 'unfortunately a real electorate does not exist' and that the Restoration governments were divorced from public opinion by an 'unfathomable abyss', he declared resoundingly that 'my only thought is to head, with the greatest possible speed, towards the Regeneration of the country'.[38] This was given tangible shape by the creation of two new ministries: Public Instruction and Agriculture, Industry and Commerce. Costa's modernizing fix of *school and pantry* – that is to say, education and the economy – seemed to be on the march. Nonetheless, the overriding priority of the government was the state's desperate financial plight following the loss of the colonies and the cost of the war, as 43 per cent of the budget had been consumed in 1898 by the interest payments on the national debt. When the foreign banks questioned the solvency of the Spanish state, the perilous prospect of a deficit loomed. The energetic and resourceful minister of the economy, Raimundo Fernández Villaverde, overhauled the tax system and cut public spending in an effort to curb the debt and balance the budget. The resulting tax hikes infuriated the Chambers of Commerce, especially in Catalonia, the region hit hardest by the colonial debacle. The Chambers responded to the tax rises by closing shops and businesses throughout Spain on 26 June 1899, above all in Barcelona, where regionalist sentiment induced the Chambers to demand a special financial regime like the Basque one. The protest in the Catalan capital climaxed with a tax strike, but the government's response was unyielding: businesses were embargoed, their owners jailed, and non-payment of tax was declared an act of sedition. All resistance was over by 18 November. In an effort to relaunch their campaign, the Chambers of Commerce and Agriculture created the National Union political party early in 1900. The problem was that Fernández Villaverde's economic policy was fast gaining traction. He not only achieved a budget surplus of 52 million pesetas in 1900 – the first in decades – but also rescued the state from bankruptcy. The shutdowns and the tax strike had failed. By this stage, Costa had become thoroughly disillusioned with the 'neutral mass', denouncing his fellow Spaniards as 'madmen, donkeys and cowards' and the politicians as 'public enemies'. Spaniards were still in their political infancy, he concluded, and required an 'iron surgeon' in order to 'haul the nation from the captivity in which it groans'.[39] The National Union won just two seats in the 1901 general election, collapsing shortly afterwards through infighting.

## THE ERUPTION OF THE MASSES

The National Union had signally failed to realize its goals, above all the creation of a governmental alternative to the two monarchist parties. Nonetheless, the protracted protest of the Chambers of Commerce and Agriculture had been instrumental in fuelling the national debate over Regeneration and in rallying shopkeepers, artisans, traders, and farmers. Indeed, the Chambers had demonstrated that the key to opening up the elitist Restoration system lay in the mobilization of the masses. The National Union may not have secured its objectives, but it did act as a powerful spur for other forces, most notably the republicans. Given the staid and hidebound nature of their ageing national leadership, it was no surprise that the reawakening of the republican movement took the form of a local insurgency. This first erupted in Spain's third-biggest city, Valencia. The Valencian republicans mobilized both the working and the middle classes and thus managed to elect a deputy to the Cortes in 1898, to defeat the monarchists in the general election of 1900, and to win control of the city council in 1901. The Valencian republicans had shattered the mould of Restoration politics by routing the monarchists. This was no momentary triumph: they were to win five general elections in a row and to run the city council for all but four years until the coup d'état of 1923. In the process, the republicans in Valencia created the first modern political party in Spain.

The key to the republicans' triumph in Valencia was their populism; that is to say, the mobilization of different social classes by means of a demagogic discourse centred on a charismatic leader. Populism broke with the cultivated, somewhat aloof idiom of republicanism by adopting a colloquial, sometimes vulgar, discourse that was built upon a highly moralistic, Manichean world view which pitted the 'people' (good) against the 'privileged' or 'rich' (bad): 'all of us against a few'.[40] The charismatic leadership was furnished by the stocky, bearded figure of Vicente Blasco Ibáñez, a politician and novelist in his early thirties. Born in the central Market district of the city, home to tradesmen, shopkeepers, and craftsmen, there could be no doubt that Blasco, as he was known, was one of the people. 'These are my people,' he would remind his audiences, 'amongst them was I born.'[41] As one of the people, he was gregarious and down to earth, fraternizing with the public on the streets, in the railway stations, and at the local party centres. Still, as a leader, he was, like his hero, Victor Hugo, larger than life. In perpetual motion, Blasco published regular polemics in the newspapers, gave rousing speeches, dashed off novels, and fought duels (nearly dying in one of them). His dramatic escape from the police in a smugglers' boat bound for Algeria further burnished his legend, as did his incarceration for protesting against the Cuban war and the survival of two attempts on his life. When he arrived at the Valencia train station he would be greeted by as many as 2,000 enraptured supporters, while the dying wish of one republican veteran was to be buried with a portrait of his

The bearded Blasco Ibáñez, in the centre of the picture,
being mobbed at election time

leader. The bohemian Blasco was, in short, 'a politician loved and idolized by his people and by his voters'.[42] Such was his centrality to the movement that the republicans in Valencia were known not by the name of the party, but simply as *blasquistas*. It was entirely fitting that the first major literary success of this iconoclastic republican, *La Barraca*, should have been published in the watershed year of 1898.

The political ascendency of the *blasquistas* owed much to their newfound demagogic discourse, especially its anticlericalism. The Catholic Church was blasted by the republicans as anti-liberal, anti-democratic, and anti-modern, the antithesis of everything they stood for. It was even denounced as anti-Spanish. The *blasquistas* objected to the appointment of Father Nozaleda as Archbishop of Valencia in 1904 on the grounds that he had been responsible in his capacity as the Archbishop of Manila for the defeat of the Spanish forces in the Philippines in 1898. As Blasco himself roared in the Cortes, 'Father Nozaleda will be able to go to Valencia, will enter the city, but he will enter amongst cannons and bayonets'.[43] For the *blasquistas*, republicanism represented progress, science, modernity, secularism, and individual liberty, while Catholicism embodied superstition, obscurantism, submission, irrationality, and authoritarianism. The Church was not merely a symbol of Spain's *atraso* or backwardness, but its chief cause. No wonder that anticlericalism was the lodestar of *blasquismo*.

The mobilizing discourse of *blasquismo* was complemented by a new type of party organization. The amorphous, often inactive, parties of notables of the nineteenth century gave way to a structured party of masses that was rooted in the politics of engagement and perpetual agitation. Party members now paid dues and took orders from the *casinos* or local centres. Nearly all the neighbourhoods of Valencia had a casino, some even had two or three. In stark contrast to the monarchist, Catholic, worker and erstwhile republican centres, the casinos were an 'original creation' because they were a focus for daily socialization (invariably housing a bar, a restaurant, and a games room); for education (providing talks on 'progressive' individuals such as Charles Darwin, Jean-Baptiste Lamarck, and the social question, as well as containing a library); and for politics, as republican figures, including Blasco himself, regularly addressed the casinos. They also constituted the link between the grassroots and the city hall, relaying debates, informing members of new measures, and, if necessary, mobilizing them at short notice to defend republican positions. Finally, and crucially, the casinos were also the party's electoral enforcers, as they scrutinized the electoral roll, manned the polling stations, monitored the count, and in general ensured that no irregularities were committed by the dynastic forces. Another nerve centre of the new party machine was its paper, appositely named *El Pueblo* (The People). This not only informed and enlightened its readers, but also acted as a propaganda mouthpiece, fought the party's corner in public debates, and, in conjunction with the casinos, mobilized the rank and file when required. The fact that it sold as many as 10,000 copies daily in 1910 was a measure of its importance as a 'nexus of unity and activism'.[44] The rupture with the fledgling parties of the nineteenth century was radical indeed. 'We have created in Valencia,' *El Pueblo* boasted, 'an incredibly powerful and disciplined republican party like no other in Spain.'[45]

Critical to the rise of the *blasquistas* was their ability to reach beyond the traditional middle-class heartland of the republican movement to the working class. This was made possible not just by rhetorical appeals to the people, to anticlericalism, and to the material benefits of modernity, but also to a real engagement with the needs of the working class. Between 1899 and 1903 the *blasquistas* revived most of the workers' trade associations, as well as introducing new forms of working-class politicization, such as the *Casa del Pueblo* (House of the People) or workers' centre. It is often assumed that the *Casa del Pueblo* was a socialist initiative, but this was in fact introduced into Spain by Blasco Ibáñez following a visit to a socialist centre in Belgium. Thus the first *Casa del Pueblo* in Spain was built in Valencia in 1902 with the help of a 4,000-peseta donation from the republican city hall. 'I'm a worker just like you,' Blasco declared on its inauguration.[46] The *blasquistas'* hold over the working class ended once exclusively working-class organizations began to appear, such as *Solidaridad Obrera* (Worker Solidarity) in 1907. Nonetheless, many workers continued to vote for the republicans, partly because most of them were anarcho-syndicalists and therefore had no political representation of their own, and partly due to lingering personal and ideological sympathies.

The *blasquistas* knew not only how to seize power, but also how to consolidate it, dominating the Valencian city council between 1901 and 1911 and then again between 1915 and 1923. Once in office, they strove to realize their secular vision of progress by reforming the town centre ('it's rare to find a street without a house being built,' noted a local newspaper), by supplying electricity to neighbourhoods, by funding lay schools, and by boosting the public health system, above all through improvements in the sewage system and the supply of water.[47] Public health was of particular importance to the *blasquistas* as it demonstrated the benefits of modern science – central to their vision of 'progress' – and in this they were strikingly successful: infant mortality in the city dropped from 175.5 per thousand in 1902 to 110.2 per thousand in 1910. Cultural policy was also designed to boost the secular and humanitarian values of the republicans at the expense of Catholicism. Streets hitherto bearing the names of kings, queens, and saints were renamed after scientists, artists, and republicans. Thus 'Saint Francis' became 'Victor Hugo', while 'Saint Ferdinand' gave way to a republican revolutionary, 'Ruiz Zorrilla'. In the same spirit, the town hall declared the 300th anniversary of the publication of *Don Quijote* as a landmark in the 'progress of the human spirit'.[48] It also expressed its solidarity with the first tribute held in Spain to Charles Darwin, while organizing the country's first ever music competition.

No sooner had the *blasquistas* conquered the city hall than the fight was taken to the Catholics. One week after taking control of the municipality in January 1902, the *blasquistas* withdrew public funding for the Festival of Saint Vincent the Martyr. They then tried to tax the ringing of church bells but were vetoed by the monarchist-appointed mayor. Confrontations with the Church hierarchy were positively relished by the *blasquistas*: the public polemic of 1904 over the appointment of Archbishop Nozaleda was followed in 1906 by one with Archbishop Guisasola over his rejection of civil marriage, the city council flagging its dissent by declaring him *persona non grata*. These culture wars had a violent dimension. In the frequent clashes between republicans and Catholics for control of the public space lethal fights sometimes broke out. A clash in 1901 killed two people and another in 1904 saw a brace of young congregationists die. Not that Blasco disavowed the use of violence. In February 1904, following a police charge against republican protestors outside the Cortes, he declared before the chamber that 'I've come to the session with an eight-bullet Brookings', and warned the minister of the interior that 'no policeman will hit me again because the next one that does I will shoot, and I hope all the citizens of Madrid would do the same'.[49]

## THE REPUBLICAN
## REVIVAL IN BARCELONA

The upsurge of the republican cause was not limited to Valencia alone. In Spain's second-largest city, Barcelona, a process of republican renewal was also under way. The key figure here was a man by the name of

Alejandro Lerroux, who possessed a backstory that was even more col-
ourful and risqué than that of Vicente Blasco Ibáñez. Born in 1864 to
a poorly paid army veterinary surgeon, Lerroux joined – and then
deserted – the army as a teenager. Attracted to radical politics, he acted
as a go-between during the republican uprising of General Manuel Vil-
lacampa in 1886 before establishing himself in Grub Street as a radical
journalist. Brash, broad-shouldered, and bristling with energy and
charm, the audacious, moustached Lerroux undertook sensationalist
press campaigns in favour of the downtrodden while fighting duels to
defend his honour. In 1897 his newspaper, El País, achieved a nationwide scoop by publishing first-hand accounts of those tortured at the
Montjuich prison in Barcelona over an anarchist bombing of 1896.
This established Lerroux's name in Catalonia, especially amongst the
working class, and provided him with a base for his own political ambitions. In the 1901 general election Lerroux's republicans, together with
the Lliga Regionalista de Catalunya (Regional League of Catalonia),
destroyed the turno pacífico in Barcelona. Like Blasco before him,
Lerroux did not so much rejuvenate a moribund republican scene as
reinvent it: the new republicanism built up a mass movement that
attracted both the working and the middle classes through a stirring
demagogic discourse centred on anticlericalism, signalling a radical
rupture with the remote and elitist parties of notables that were often
crippled by ideological hair-splitting and procedural disputes. To an
even greater extent than Blasco, the pull of Lerroux at the hustings
depended on an appeal to the male working class. He rejected the
educated language of the older generation of republicans for a crude,
emotional, and anti-intellectual discourse that was blatantly machista,
exhorting the republican youth in one article to 'lift up the habits of the
nuns and turn them into mothers'.[50]

The purpose of this populist discourse was to replace the traditional
republican oratory with one that not only mobilized people but also
got them to act on their ideological convictions. 'It's not the time for
speeches,' Lerroux declared in the celebrations of the 'Jubilee of the
Revolution' in 1901, 'but for acts that demonstrate the vitality of
ideas.'[51] Thus Lerroux's support, like Blasco's, depended not just on his
rousing rhetoric, but also on his capacity to change things. He built up
a mainly working-class movement in Barcelona by relying not so much

on the circles and committees that constituted the core of the old parties as on trade unions, consumer cooperatives, lay schools, summer camps, and other initiatives. One example was the 'Popular Picnic', which gathered together hundreds of families on the slopes of the Montjuich hill in a spirit of republican *fraternité*. Like the *blasquistas*, the *lerrouxistas* had a *Casa del Pueblo* (House of the People) built for the workers, which included a café, a billiards room, a theatre, a library, and a clinic. They also had a bakery opened, along with a co-operative that provided insurance, pension schemes, and legal aid. Such ventures not only fostered a more participatory and supportive politics, but also a broader and more inclusive one, as many of them involved women and children. All of this gave a considerable boost to civil society in Barcelona. The incorporation of families was a means of 'avoiding opposition within the very homes of the affiliates', as well as 'forming future defenders of the cause and counteracting the influence of the Church'.[52] In both Barcelona and Madrid the *lerrouxistas* went a step further by creating women's groups, the Red Ladies and the Radical Ladies. These female activists were as anticlerical as their male counterparts, one woman declaring at a public meeting that 'the influence of religion has to be eliminated because it will shackle us, and rather than be fresh meat for these vultures I'd prefer to die.'[53] The activism of women made republicanism even more of a family affair. According to one observer:

> ... they were women completely identified with the ideas of their husbands or fathers, who admire the same heroes, read the same newspapers, and comment on political affairs out loud in front of the family. They usually go to the republican festivals, symbolic broaches pinned to their breasts or their heads adorned with a ribbon in the colours of the republican flag.[54]

The Red Ladies and the Radical Ladies offered women the space to develop politically, with leading suffragists such as Carmen de Burgos and Consuelo Álvarez emerging from their ranks. However, neither the Red Ladies nor the Radical Ladies lasted more than a few years. Of the other forces on the left, the anarcho-syndicalists had no women's group at all, but the socialists did, first in Bilbao in 1904 and then in Madrid in 1906. Lasting until 1927, the Women's Socialist Group of

Madrid 'transformed socialist political culture, providing a space for an active female leadership', as shown by the prominence within the socialist movement of women such as Virginia González, Juana Taboada, and the García Pérez sisters, Claudina and Luz.[55] In addition, the socialists alone defended female suffrage, though little was done in practice to realize this goal until the 1930s. A certain effort was made by the right to counteract this politicization of women, above all through the establishment of a women's group within the Conservative Party in 1908 and the formation of two Catholic trade unions for women in 1909, one of which was co-founded by the diarist María de Echarri Martínez.

Once the *lerrouxistas* seized control of Barcelona city hall in 1905, they were able to exploit its funds (lacking the independent means of the monarchists and their privileged access to the state administration) not only for their own political activities and extensive clientelage networks, but also to bring public services under municipal control and to improve working conditions for council workers. Thus a minimum wage and an eight-hour day were introduced, both of which were extremely progressive measures by contemporary European or any other standards. These policies, together with the other services provided by the party, were pioneering endeavours insofar as they effectively created an embryonic welfare state that drew on public and private capital alike – a strikingly modern concept. Such social reformism lent credibility to the idea that the republicans represented an alternative vision of state and society, while highlighting the manifest shortcomings of the monarchist regime.

Despite the resounding electoral success of the new republicans, they nonetheless thought of themselves as *revolutionaries*, especially Lerroux, for whom 'it's not the time to conjure up speeches, but to raise barricades; it's not arguments that we need, but rifles.'[56] He therefore took over the mantle of the nineteenth-century republican leader Manuel Ruiz Zorrilla, for whom the republic could only come about through violence. Still, until Alfonso XIII came of age in 1902, the greatest hope of the republicans was that the sickly prince would die as a child. Once he assumed the throne in 1902, the republicans were convinced that his assassination would bring the entire Restoration order to its knees. 'If the king disappears,' as one republican put it, 'the revolution is made.'[57]

Thus a popular insurrection would take advantage of the turmoil following the death of the king to usher in a republic.

Regicide as the key to the unlocking of the Restoration order was an article of faith for much of the left. Like the republicans, the anarchists believed that 'the death of the king will be the revolution in Spain'.[58] This simplistic strategy was not as far-fetched as it may seem given that many monarchs in Europe, including the German Kaiser, the Russian Tsar, and the Austrian Emperor – like the Spanish king – were the most powerful and symbolic figures within their respective societies. As late as 1914, 'the monarchs were still the cornerstone of civil society and politics'.[59] In the case of Spain, the French ambassador wrote, the monarchy was 'the only solid thing in this country'.[60] This explains why the anarchist educationalist Francisco Ferrer Guardia, an ally of Lerroux who furnished him with funds over many years, provided the republicans with the money for an assassination attempt on Alfonso XIII in Paris in May 1905. Despite exploding right under the king's car, the bomb did no more than kill a horse. An even more daring bid was made at the time of Alfonso's wedding to Victoria Eugenie of Battenberg, the granddaughter of Queen Victoria in May 1906. As the carriage bearing the king and queen passed along the Mayor Street of central Madrid, a republican by the name of Mateo Morral threw a bomb at it, killing no fewer than twenty-three people and leaving another hundred injured. Yet neither the king nor the queen was hurt. Once again, the funding for the attack came from Ferrer Guardia, while Lerroux, who aimed to launch a popular uprising in Barcelona had the bomb succeeded, was heavily involved, or, as one biographer notes, 'he's in everything. But he knows nothing.'[61] The failure of these efforts to kill the king may have discredited the strategy of regicide, but they did not alter the fundamental faith of the republicans in the transformative power of political violence.

## LIMITS TO THE NEW REPUBLICANISM

Undoubtedly the republicans did much more to politicize the workers during the early twentieth century than either the anarchists or the socialists. Even in Madrid, the home of the socialist movement, there were nearly three times more working-class republican affiliates (2,067) in 1904 than socialist ones (762). The inter-class nature of the republicans' discourse did much to galvanize the urban middle classes, too. A measure of the republicans' capacity to rouse the urban electorate is provided by the surge in participation in Barcelona: in 1901 Lerroux had needed 5,000 votes to get elected, but in 1905 he required seven times more – 35,000.

There were nonetheless grave limitations to the new republicanism. Blasco Ibáñez and Lerroux both tried to export their municipal model to other parts of Spain, the *blasquistas* at a congress in Valencia in 1906 and the *lerrouxistas* at a congress in Zaragoza the same year. That both initiatives failed miserably underlined the specificity of the political and social conditions in the two cities. Lerroux also strove to consolidate his support amongst the working class in Barcelona by setting up a republican trade union in 1907, but this folded too once the workers formed their own organization the same year, Worker Solidarity. This is not to deny that other cities, mostly ports such as Málaga, Cádiz, La Coruña, and Gijón, which, like Barcelona and Valencia, were connected to the wider world, witnessed a republican resurgence after the Disaster.

Blasco Ibáñez and Lerroux endeavoured to give national expression to their combative brand of republicanism by founding, together with the journalist Rodrigo Soriano, the Revolutionary Federation in December 1901. Nonetheless, the new republicans still paid deference to the older republicans, as the Federation joined the Republican Union, established in March 1903 under the leadership of the aged Nicolás Salmerón, a president from the First Republic of 1873. The new-found unity of the republicans secured them thirty-six seats in the 1903 general election, but the latent divisions within the Union, along with a major rupture over the Catalan question in 1907, resulted in its collapse in 1912. Although the new republicanism had manifestly failed to forge a national movement capable of challenging the Restoration order, it had transformed Spanish politics. Anticlericalism had been the foremost feature of the new mass politics and would remain the dominant political issue for the first decade of the twentieth century. It did immense damage to the dynastic parties by creating a major breach not only between the Liberals and Conservatives, but also within the Liberal Party.

## DYNASTIC ANTICLERICALISM: THE LIBERALS

The rallying of public opinion through an appeal to anticlericalism was not the prerogative of the republicans alone. The cause was also taken up by the Liberal Party, partly to deflect attention from its stewardship during the 'Disaster' and partly to compete more effectively with both the Conservatives and the republicans by demonstrating its commitment to Regeneration. The Liberals had therefore protested at the ultra-Catholic bent of Silvela's Conservative Cabinet of 1899, especially at the inclusion of the Marquis of Pidal and General García de Polavieja (the 'Christian General'), and criticized its pro-Catholic measures, including the strengthening of religious instruction in state schools. Following Silvela's fall from power in 1900, anticlericalism remained at the forefront of public debate as a result of the play *Electra*, premiered in January 1901. Penned by Spain's most celebrated writer, the progressive Benito Pérez Galdós, the play concerned a girl, Electra, who was made to enter a convent against her will. The drama at once caught and magnified the anticlerical spirit of the times, packing theatres across the land as streets echoed to the cry of 'Down with the Jesuits!' Cakes, sweets, and even watches were decorated with the visage of Electra, while Galdós became the most fêted man in all of Spain. The public outcry was made greater still by the court case of December 1900 concerning Adela Ubao, a girl who had entered a convent against her parents' will. The trial was symbolic of the national divide: the Conservative Antonio Maura assumed the defence of the Church while the republican Nicolás Salmerón led the prosecution. Outside the courtroom, demonstrators called for 'death to reaction', members of the clergy were insulted in the streets, and Catholic schools had stones hurled at them. Salmerón's triumph in the trial naturally boosted the anticlerical cause while placing an even greater onus on the Liberal Cabinet formed in early 1901 – the 'Electra Government', as it was dubbed – to deliver on its anticlericalism.

The Liberals, however, were themselves too divided over the religious question to make any meaningful progress. Their lack of consensus was reflected in the distinctly uninspiring nature of their showpiece reform: a law on associations which would include the religious orders. Even this relatively mild initiative was enough to split the Cabinet, the leading anticlerical, José Canalejas, resigning from the government in 1902 on the grounds that 'I will always defend my banner, my convictions, my thought against all and above all.'[62] Such was his belief that anticlericalism was the key to Regeneration that he took the unusual step for a monarchist politician of holding a series of mass meetings in defence of his position. The Liberals proved unable to resolve their differences: neither the government of 1903 nor that of 1905 was able to break the deadlock.

## THE CATHOLIC REVIVAL

The clerical question also reshaped and reinvigorated a mass movement that has received little attention, but which was one of the most formidable of all: Catholicism. Late nineteenth-century Spanish Catholics, under the influence of sister movements in France, Belgium, and Italy, were the first activists to adopt many of the features of modern mass politics, such as the commemoration of symbolic dates, the creation of youth organizations and socialization in local centres, activities later aped by their opponents, whether republicans, socialists, or anarchists. The threat posed by anticlericalism after 1898 radicalized and mobilized Catholics in ever greater numbers. An early sign was the hundreds of plaques put up throughout the country to the Virgin and the Sacred Heart of Jesus during the summer of 1899. The consecration in 1901 of the Sanctuary of the Virgin at Covadonga in Asturias – the supposed starting point for the Reconquest of 'Spain' from the Muslims – was a metaphor of the need to re-Catholicize Spain. A further symbolic triumph for the Church was the construction, starting in 1902, of a colossal church on the Tibidabo mountain that overlooks the city of Barcelona. The increasing mobilization of Catholics was also reflected in the foundation of Catholic Action in 1903, soon the most active and influential of all lay Catholic organizations. A special effort was made to spread the faith in the most hostile setting of all, the urban arena, with the foundation of schools, hospitals, orphanages, asylums, and seminaries. The resurgence was further fuelled by a flood of new Catholic publications, ranging from pamphlets and news-papers to devotional manuals and the lives of saints, as well as the mass production of religious images.

An illustration of the vigour of the Catholic revival was the founda-tion in 1901 of the Catholic League in Valencia, which was a direct result of the ineffectual opposition of the monarchists to the *blasquis-tas*. Convinced that 'the great mass of the Valencian people, the immense majority, virtually all, are sensible, educated and profoundly religious', the League soon established Catholic circles, newspapers, propaganda meetings, and electoral committees, as well as Catholic cooperatives, farmers' associations and women's groups.[63] For the Catholics, this was nothing less than 'a great struggle between negation and affirma-tion, between truth and error, between revolution and order, between anarchy and the traditional principles and eternal foundations of soci-ety'.[64] The League's mission was therefore the city's material and moral salvation from 'the Jacobin domination, the wrongs so great that we suffer not only in the religious and moral order but also the economic, while a terrible future awaits us'.[65] If the *blasquistas* dreamed of creat-ing a 'republic' of Valencia, then the Catholics aspired to a 'Catholic Valencia'.[66]

A similarly combative form of Catholic mobilization unfolded in the province of Vizcaya in the Basque Country. This was a stronghold of the religious orders, a position that was further boosted in 1901 by the arrival of nearly 1,500 French clergy who had been expelled by the Third Republic. Between the 'Disaster' of 1898 and the First World War, the province was the scene of an 'active cultural war' between the Catholics and the anticlericals that was 'constant and diversified'.[67] The placing of Sacred Heart plaques around the city of Bilbao in 1899 was an early source of conflict. The inauguration of Pérez Galdós' *Electra* in the city in March 1901 intensified the stand-off: while posters in Bilbao called on Catholics to 'Defend Yourselves!', the rapture of the anti-clericals led one newspaper to exclaim that the city had never seen 'such an enthusiastic liberal demonstration'.[68] Tensions between the two sides came to a head with the mass pilgrimage to the Virgin of Begoña, the province's patron saint, on 11 October 1903. A 'pitched battle' took place in Bilbao with 'sticks, knives and shots' being deployed. Around 100 people were either wounded or arrested and one person, a gardener at the Jesuit University of Deusto, was killed.[69] This violent showdown, acclaimed by Catholics as the 'Glorious Day', marked a watershed in the relations between the two camps, 'the unease' being 'constant' thereafter.[70] In 1906 the anticlericals and Catholics took to the streets once again over the Liberal government's bill of associations. While 60,000 Catholics gathered in Bilbao to impugn the proposed measure, 4,000 anticlericals held a meeting in defence of the initiative, one republican speaker going so far as to declare belligerently that 'the dagger, the revolver, the knife, anything goes in order to finish off the clergy'.[71] Hatreds were reignited in 1910 by a Catholic campaign against lay schools. A 'great crusade' against the schools was called for by a provincial deputy for Guipúzcoa. In the same spirit, the Jesuit Remigio Vilariño proclaimed that:

> We are entering a phase of perpetual war, in which we have some battle or other every day. Our enemies are everywhere ... if we want to preserve the faith, a daily, incessant, constant struggle is necessary, of all of us against them everywhere and in everything, because everywhere they speak against us, they persecute us, they harass us, they impede us, they want to finish us off.[72]

Later that year the Catholic community went on the offensive once more, this time in protest at the so-called 'Padlock Law' of the Liberals, which forbade the creation of new religious orders in Spain for at least the next two years. *La Gaceta del Norte* exhorted Catholics:

> For religion and the Pope. Long live Pius X! Onwards! Struggle and die. This is our banner. Struggle to save the faith. Die to seal with blood our character as Christians. Die for Christ to save Christ from the godless persecution.[73]

The rising tide of anticlerical agitation during the first decade of the twentieth century had therefore been met by a new and militant Catholicism, which had replicated the mobilizing stratagems of Catholic movements in other Western European countries. Catholic populism was not a purely defensive movement, as it possessed its own vision of regeneration, which was naturally very different to that of the liberals and the left. In Catholic eyes, the decline of Spain as a great power began with the introduction of rationalism and the subsequent assault on faith, a process that was enormously intensified by the Napoleonic invasion of 1808. The French foisted liberalism on the Spanish people, which fostered even more destructive 'isms': republicanism, socialism, and anarchism. For the Catholic Church, liberalism was a foreign ideology that was completely alien to the history, spirit, and values of Spanish society. In sum, liberalism was the antithesis of Spanishness, the nemesis of the nation. Not surprisingly, one of the most popular books amongst Catholics during these years was *Liberalism is Sin* by Félix Sardá y Salvany. Spain's redemption lay in a return to the Catholic faith and the re-establishment of national unity: only in this way would the motherland become a great, imperial power once more. The Catholic cause was, however, undermined by the lack of consensus between the monarchist parties on the religious question.

## THE CHALLENGE OF CATALANISM

Yet another political force to be relaunched in the wake of the Disaster was the Catalan regional movement. The loss of the colonies, especially Cuba, hit the textile sector above all, which was concentrated overwhelmingly in Catalonia: the province of Barcelona alone boasted 1,237 of Spain's 1,563 textile factories. Up to 1898 the Catalan bourgeoisie had defended its interests by means of the Conservative Party. After 1898 the bourgeoisie had initially sought to follow the same path by placing its hopes in General Camilo García de Polavieja, who had appeared sympathetic to its plight. Not only did this come to nothing, but also the fiscal reforms of Fernández Villaverde in 1899 provoked a large-scale revolt by the industrial and commercial sectors of Barcelona.

By this point, the Catalan bourgeoisie was thoroughly alienated by Madrid's historic incompetence and in particular by its crass insensitivity to the needs of one of the few industrialized areas in the country. During the last quarter of the nineteenth century Barcelona had expanded enormously (its population of 533,000 in 1900 being just shy of Madrid's) and had become a stylish and avant-garde metropolis, as reflected in the Modernist architecture of figures such as Lluís Domènech and Antoni Gaudí. Indeed, the brilliant young artist Pablo

Picasso had fled Madrid for Barcelona in 1901 because he found the capital too staid and conservative. Yet the Catalan metropolis was often treated by Madrid like any other provincial capital, even though the overwhelming majority were not only much smaller – one had as few as 15,000 inhabitants – but also cultural backwaters. Accordingly, the Catalan bourgeoisie recast their cause in regionalist terms. After first emerging as a cultural movement in the 1870s, Catalanism had become more politically oriented in the 1880s. In 1892 the Principles of Manresa called for Catalan to be the only official language, for positions in the public sector to be reserved for Catalans alone, and for the establishment of a Catalan parliament that would elect a regional government. In the meantime, 'national' symbols such as the flag and the anthem were created, while Catalan history, especially the rebellion of 1640 against Castile and the War of the Spanish Succession of 1701–13, was rewritten as an unceasing struggle for Catalan liberty in the face of Castilian oppression.

In the wake of 1898, the backing of businessmen such as the sophisticated lawyer and financier Francesc Cambó, famous for his art collection, transformed the regionalist movement by furnishing it with an organizational and monetary muscle which it had hitherto lacked. The multitude of Catalan associations were fused into the *Lliga Regionalista de Catalunya* (Regional League of Catalonia) with Cambó as a key figure. In the 1901 general election, the *Lliga*, along with the republicans, trounced the monarchists in Barcelona. It was the greatest triumph to date of a Catalanist party. Neither the Conservatives nor the Liberals would ever again win in the Catalan capital. Madrid had lost control not only of the nation's second-biggest city, but also of one of the most prosperous regions of Spain. In short, the emergence of Catalan regionalism, which drew to a greater extent than the republican movement on the urban middle and upper classes, represented yet another challenge to the Restoration status quo.

The contrast with Basque nationalism could scarcely have been greater. The Basque movement arose under the visionary figure of Sabino de Arana as a reaction to the loss of the region's *fueros*, or local rights, in the civil war of 1872–6, and to the influx of workers from outside the region into the industrial areas of Vizcaya, especially Bilbao and its environs. In many ways, Basque nationalism represented a reconfiguration of the ultra-Catholic, anti-liberal, and anti-modern Carlist movement (which defended the right of Carlos de Borbón to occupy the throne). Arana founded the *Partido Nacionalista Vasco* or PNV (Basque Nationalist Party) in 1895 and invented a new name for the nation (*Euskadi*), as well as a flag, an anthem, and a motto, 'God and the Ancient Laws', a reworking of the Carlist cry of 'God and the *Fueros*'. Clearly the reactionary, intensely Catholic, and anti-modern Basque nationalist movement was very different to its Catalan counterpart.

## THE ASCENDANCY OF
## THE URBAN WORKING CLASS

The last movement to be rejuvenated by the 'Disaster' was the organized working class. During the late nineteenth century the language of class had begun to gain traction – the noun 'proletarian' was incorporated into the dictionary of the Royal Academy in 1884 – along with rituals, symbols, and forms of mobilization that spoke directly to the working class, such as the annual demonstration in defence of the eight-hour day (first held by the socialists in 1890) and the general strike (first launched in Bilbao in 1892). For the rest of the decade there had been no strikes or labour disputes of note, but in the wake of the 'Disaster' there was an upsurge in labour agitation, beginning with protests in El Ferrol and Valencia in 1899. The first three years of the new century saw scores of strikes, including in major cities such as Madrid, Barcelona, and Bilbao. Many of these disputes were orchestrated by the anarcho-syndicalists, who, with the turn of the century, abandoned 'propaganda by deed' as their principal weapon of revolutionary class warfare for the French-inspired general strike. This reached a peak with the general strike of February 1902 in Barcelona, which brought 80,000 workers out on to the streets as factories shut down, trams came to a halt, newspapers failed to appear, and the first bomb in five years exploded in the Catalan capital. Rather than negotiate, the authorities sent in the army. Barricades sprang up, looting spread, and there were numerous violent clashes as hundreds of workers were arrested, over forty injured, and twelve killed.[74] The number of arrests was so great that battleships had to be deployed as prisons. Once the strike ended, 1,500 workers were fired and martial law was imposed for several months. The collapse of the strike and the harsh repression left the anarcho-syndicalist movement at a low ebb for the next five years. As late as 1910, metallurgy workers were still reluctant to join a union 'in view of the terrible ghost of those weeks of tremendous privations for the family'.[75]

The socialist movement was much more circumspect. Its founder and leader, the supremely cautious if highly respected Pablo Iglesias, often portrayed as a secular saint, condemned the anarchists in general as 'the irresponsible' and the 1902 Barcelona strike in particular as an 'irresponsible movement, without a clear objective'.[76] By contrast, the socialists viewed the strike weapon, in Iglesias' words, as one that 'is used with tact, with judgement, after having exhausted all possibility of agreement', as shown by the successful socialist-backed miners' strike in Vizcaya in 1903. Still, socialist progress amongst the workers was painfully slow and uneven: in 1900 the PSOE had only 6,000 members and in 1908 even fewer, while the UGT's 32,778 members of 1902 had dropped to around 30,000 five years later. In many parts of the country socialist support was negligible or non-existent. When Pablo Iglesias visited Córdoba in July 1900 he was met in a café by twelve workers and two or three 'distinguished republicans'.[77] Later that year, the seventeen members of the Córdoba party contributed nine pesetas towards the cost of Iglesias' journey to a congress in Paris. By comparison with many other Western European socialist parties, the PSOE was a distinctly marginal force. By 1910 the French and Italian parties had dozens of deputies, while membership of the British and German trade unions ran into the millions. The biggest of the European socialist parties, the German Social Democratic Party, won 3 million votes in the 1903 general election, returning 110 deputies in 1912, more than any other party. The paltry progress of Spanish socialism was comparable to that of the Portuguese Socialist Party. Founded in 1875, it failed to elect a single deputy to parliament until 1911, while only a fraction of Portuguese workers were affiliated to a trade union at the turn of the century. In Spain, less than 5 per cent of workers were members of a trade union. Many labourers belonged to a so-called 'resistance group', but these were highly localized in nature and not integrated into broader trade-union structures. Even in Barcelona, the most militant city, affiliation was limited by the fact that most workers were employed in very small enterprises. Indeed, numerous workers still regarded their trade identity as more important than their class one, as shown by their mobilization in Alicante, Barcelona, Gijón, Málaga, and other cities by the inter-class discourse of the republicans. The weakness of the trade unions was reflected in the abiding strength of traditional forms of protest, such as mob attacks on property or anti-tax and food riots. The anarcho-syndicalists and socialists were nonetheless able to draw on the mutual-aid societies, food cooperatives, cultural societies, presses, and lay schools that already existed in order to build up their own organizations. Thus, Worker Solidarity was created by anarcho-syndicalists, socialists, and radical republicans in 1907 through the merger of worker societies and small independent trade unions.

## PEASANT PROTEST

Urban protest in the aftermath of the 'Disaster' has long been contrasted by Regenerationists and historians alike with the apathy and inertia of rural areas, reinforcing the idea of an abyss separating the modernizing city from the dormant countryside. While it is true that the 'Disaster' had a limited political impact on rural Spain, recent research has demonstrated that this Manichean view of urban versus rural Spain not only fails to comprehend 'peasant logic', but has also ignored myriad acts of 'pre-modern' resistance, transgression, and mobilization because they did not form part of the labour movement's 'modern' repertoire of protest.[78] Peasants, especially the most vulnerable ones, were prepared to accept the patronage of the *caciques* as long as they guaranteed their economic and social survival, not least because protest involved risk. The *caciques* provided access to the labour market and acted as mediators in relation to municipal power, whether as regards exemptions from military service, the assessment of a person's local taxes, the issuance of identity cards, or the dispensation of charity. In return, the peasant was expected to vote for the *cacique*'s candidate at election time, or at least to abstain, while outwardly accepting the legitimacy of their power and position. The arrangement did not make the peasant a passive recipient of the *cacique*'s largesse, as this was a relationship that was constantly contested and renegotiated. However, the clientelistic nature of their symbiotic relationship did ultimately reinforce the dominant social order. It also meant that the peasants did not view elections in terms of national party programmes and policies, but rather as an optimal time to extract concessions of a purely local and individual nature from the *caciques*. In the province of Ciudad Real, for example, candidates would travel the length and breadth of the villages and towns during election time promising, say, to improve roads, provide running water, or even bring the railway to the locality. In the general election of April 1907, the Count of Valdelagrana gave the workers of Villanueva de los Infantes a total of 1,000 pesetas so that 'they can help themselves in cases of illness'.[79] The leading Liberal politician the Count of Romanones, who controlled the entire province of Guadalajara, would hand out letters of recommendation, loans, and certificates of poverty during election time. This was why it was so difficult for non-dynastic parties, who did not form part of the local political and institutional order and did not possess the economic resources of the monarchist politicians, to appeal to the peasants. As the *Diario de la Mancha* asked incredulously of a speech given by the national republican leader Melquíades Álvarez in Tomelloso (Ciudad Real) in 1907, 'But what did he say of substance? What did he commit himself to? What guarantees did he offer the district for its prosperity and greater glory?'[80] Any non-dynastic force that managed to establish itself within a rural locality was invariably regarded as a threat to the status quo. The attacks of the mayor of Argamasilla de Calatrava (Ciudad Real) in 1911 on the local branch of the Radical Republican Party were denounced before the Cortes by its leader, Alejandro Lerroux. The mayor's actions, he explained, were prompted by the fact that 'his leadership, his hegemony, the monopoly in terms of social influence which he exercises, in a word, his *caciquismo,* was at risk'.[81]

If the local elite did anything to endanger either the livelihood of the peasants or their communal identity, then protests were likely, taking the form mostly of riots, assaults on the local tax collector, arson attacks, and other violence. A leading grievance of the peasantry was the loss of common lands. These often constituted a vital resource for the poorer peasants, allowing them to graze their cattle, plant crops, and hunt game, as well as to collect fruit, firewood, fertilizers, and building materials. Common lands first came under attack in the eighteenth century, but in the nineteenth century the process was greatly accelerated as a result of the liberals' goal of converting all land into private property. Incursions on these long-held collective rights were fiercely resisted not only because they accentuated social inequality within the rural world, but also because they eroded the cohesion of communities. A second major grievance was the consumer tax, which accounted for between 87 and 100 per cent of municipal income in Castile-La Mancha between 1876 and 1905. The 'complex and arbitrary' manner in which the tax was collected caused widespread resentment.[82] In 1892 there were sixty-six riots against the consumer tax in twenty-four different provinces, prompting *El País* to speak of a 'civil war'.[83] Often linked to protests over the consumer tax was the rise in the price of bread and other basic necessities. On 3 July 1897, for example, the provincial capital of Albacete was engulfed by a riot in which men, women, and children armed with 'sticks, picks and other instruments' burnt down the tax office and all its collection posts, the police proving impotent in the face of 'the thousands of people rioting'.[84] Riots could also erupt as a result of an assault on traditional communal notions of social justice, law and order, or proper governance. The fining of a group of men in the village of Noblejas (Ciudad Real) for gambling in 1910 led to a full-scale riot involving 2,000 people. In all of these cases, protest was the means by which the peasantry influenced the distribution of local resources and the organization of the community.

## ORGANIZING THE RURAL WORKERS

There was one agrarian region of Spain which had seen the emergence of an organized labour movement in the nineteenth century: Andalusia. The Federation of the Workers of the Spanish Region, founded in 1882, managed to set up 218 local groups with 57,934 members in just one year. Revolutionary in aim, but reformist in practice, the Federation was nonetheless seen as a threat by the landowners. The government claimed that the *Mano Negra* (Black Hand), a secret society, was not only linked to the Federation of the Workers of the Spanish Region, but also aimed to 'overthrow the government and destroy the Spanish state'.[85] The authorities took advantage of four murders carried out by members of the *Mano Negra* to assail the Federation, carrying out hundreds of arrests. In reality, the assassinations were an internal affair of the *Mano Negra* (relating to violations of its code), while historians agree that 'nothing indicates' that the society was connected to the Federation.[86] Still, the government crackdown resulted in nine executions and dozens of deportations and jail sentences, some of those convicted remaining behind bars for nearly thirty years.

The memory of the Federation's trade-union example lived on in the provinces of the south. In 1901 there were agrarian strikes in Badajoz, Cádiz, and Seville. The following year Cádiz and Seville experienced stoppages. In 1903 there was a wave of anarchist strikes in Seville and Cádiz, which spread, for the very first time, up the Guadalquivir valley to Córdoba. In 1904 there was another burst of strike activity in Andalusia. By this stage, agrarian associationism had taken hold in other parts of the country. A rash of new associations appeared in 1903 and 1904 in the two Castiles of central Spain, Castile-La Mancha boasting seventy-four associations with 12,000 members by the end of 1904. In contrast to Andalusia, few of these groups were explicitly ideological in outlook, though many of them were influenced by anarchist or socialist ideas. Their priority was the material and moral well-being of their members. As the labourers' association of Villalpando (Zamora) declared, its objective was 'to do without all spirit of schooling, whether religious or political. Its sociological creed being that the emancipation of the workers should be the work of the workers themselves, it is proposed that this society practise the most perfect solidarity as regards the defence of work.' More broadly, the association sought its 'moral and material improvement until it had achieved the desired and complete emancipation'.[87] The 'powerful and unique weapon' of the association undoubtedly enhanced the workers' organizational and strategic effectiveness, while investing them with a new sense of purpose.[88] As the Institute of Social Reforms, an official advisory body created in 1903, observed, the agricultural worker 'clings to the association with the anxiety of a drowning man to a piece of wood, which spreads and propagates in a marvellous fashion in the Castilian fields, bringing hope for the future to their miserable workers, tempering their current anxiety for regeneration'.[89] Nevertheless, the new worker associations did not simply replace traditional forms of direct action, but endured alongside them for a considerable period, as shown by the wave of food riots which exploded in 1920, above all in Badajoz, Ciudad Real, and Toledo. Consequently, the working-class identity which the labour movement was struggling to construct co-existed uneasily alongside the traditional one of the community.

The new-found hope generated by the associations found expression in the wave of strikes which erupted in six wheat-growing provinces of the two Castiles between February and July 1904 – the first such outbreak in the regions' history. The strikes were not organized at the regional or provincial levels, but unfolded on an individual basis at the local level. Illustrative of the labourers' aspirations was the set of demands presented by the 400-strong 'Emancipation' association in the village of Madrigal in the province of Ávila: higher pay, better food, the right to association, preference to be given to local hands, a rest on bank holidays, and a more abundant supply of basic goods. 'Not accepting these conditions,' the association declared bluntly, 'we see ourselves out of necessity dying of hunger in the street.'[90] What led the labourers to strike was a run of bad harvests together with the rise in the price of basic goods, above all bread. In its report of October 1904 on the agricultural situation in the two Castiles, the Institute of Social Reforms denounced the wages of the agricultural labourers as 'derisory salaries'. 'For this reason', it commented, the labourer 'eats badly, lives in rooms lacking all hygiene, his clothes are notoriously insufficient, being, then, much more exposed to illness and death than he who finds himself in other circumstances. His education is virtually nil due to the fact that he needs, in order to augment the scarce incomings with which he is able to provide himself, to employ his children in manual tasks when they are still of school age.'[91]

Many of these strikes achieved short-term wage hikes, but there was a belligerent backlash from the authorities, in tandem with the landowners and the Civil Guard, which resulted in arrests, trials, jailings, and 'all types of arbitrary acts'.[92] The repression in Andalusia was even harsher, which, along with the lack of work, left few associations active by 1906. The overall decline of the workers' associations was reflected in the fact that officially there were only nineteen agricultural strikes in all of Spain between 1905 and 1910. However, the peasantry had acquired a 'new spirit of independence'.[93] During the extensive drought of 1905, which was fiercest of all in Andalusia, many peasants did not give in to the resignation of old but demanded bread from the local councils and work from the landowners.

## DEFUSING THE 'SOCIAL QUESTION'

The fitful rise of the organized working class across urban and rural Spain was nevertheless sufficient to alarm Conservatives and Liberals alike, who euphemistically referred to its emergence as the 'social question'. Both parties agreed that reform was required in order to stave off revolution, resulting in a raft of laws during the first decade of the twentieth century that were designed to defuse the 'social question', ranging from the Law on Labour Accidents (1900) and the Law on the Work of Women and Children (1900) to the creation of a work inspectorate (1906), the first state-pension scheme (1908), and a strike law (1909). Legislating for reform was one thing, enforcing it was quite another, as shown by the travails of the work inspectorate. This was established in 1907, but as late as 1921 there were only ten regional inspectors and forty-five provincial ones for a national workforce of over seven million people. Prior to the First World War the labour legislation was barely applied in the urban areas and not at all in the rural ones. In theory, the legislation concerning female employment was relatively advanced, but in practice abuses were 'constant'.[94] In the agricultural, food, and textile industries, where many women worked, the extremely low level of union affiliation along with the abundant supply of labour meant that female workers were 'at the mercy of the bosses'.[95] Despite a school-leaving age of twelve and the law of 1900 concerning female and infant labour, children under fourteen and even ten were commonly found working in factories and workshops. At the municipal level, the Local Social Reform Juntas were designed to assist in the application of the labour legislation, but in reality they were characterized by their 'total inefficacy'.[96] Nationwide, the inspectors carried out 9,057 visits in 1909 and reported 32,108 breaches of the law, but few of these infringements were punished, as both the local authorities and the courts looked the other way. In Zaragoza, the capital of Aragón, 60,000 complaints were filed by the inspectorate up to 1911, but none of these infractions were acted upon, as a result of the studied negligence of the courts, the mayor, and even the civil governor. In 1918, Spain became the first country in the world to introduce the eight-hour day, but, once again, the law was widely ignored. Not surprisingly, the inspectors 'hardly had any means at their disposal, the number of their civil servants was ridiculous, their work met obstacles everywhere, detected infractions were almost never punished, the social reform juntas did not supersede the status of phantasmagorical organisms, and, to cap it all, not even the neutrality of the inspectors themselves was guaranteed in all cases'.[97] In short, the letter of the law was almost completely divorced from its enforcement. Far from solving the 'social question', the flood of labour legislation during the early years of the twentieth century discredited the Spanish state even further in the eyes of its supposed beneficiaries, as it did next to nothing to alleviate workers' lives, which were generally characterized by pitiful pay, long hours, irregular employment, and wretched conditions.

## REGENERATING
## THE POLITICAL SYSTEM

The political challenge thrown down by the mobilization of the masses in the aftermath of the 'Disaster' had been acknowledged by the Conservative governments of 1902–3 and 1903–4. Prime Minister Silvela aspired in 1902 to overcome the 'immense popular rejection' of politics by mobilizing the 'neutral masses' and holding a clean general election.[98] He promised, in short, a 'revolution from above'.[99] There were nonetheless a number of obstacles to opening up the Restoration order. At the national level, the unifying leadership of the founding fathers of the two parties, Antonio Cánovas del Castillo (Conservative) and Práxedes Sagasta (Liberal), did not long outlast their deaths in 1897 and 1903 respectively. Silvela maintained a certain unity within the Conservative Party after Cánovas del Castillo, but upon his retirement in 1903 the party informally divided into two, the followers of Raimundo Fernández Villaverde and those of Antonio Maura. Upon Sagasta's death, the Liberals split into three factions. The personalized divisions within the two parties made it more difficult than ever to reach an agreement on reform. At the local level, an unforeseen change in the electoral districts exacerbated the parties' fragmentation. Since the late nineteenth century more and more rural districts had come under the sway of a sole *cacique*, the most salient example being the Count of Romanones in Guadalajara province, where 'not a leaf falls ... without the authorization of the Count'.[100] The proliferation of these personal fiefdoms diminished the capacity of the government to influence not just the individual candidates, but the election result itself. Furthermore, the autonomy acquired by these districts reinforced the clientelistic networks that underpinned the party factions, thereby undermining national policy-making still further in favour of purely local interests. In addition, the monarchists were placed on the defensive by the electoral success of the non-dynastic forces in the urban arena, making them even less inclined to change. Thus the ascendancy of factionalism and the growing autonomy of rural and urban districts alike made the question of electoral reform increasingly unappetizing. The perils of change were highlighted by the 1903 general election. Less controlled than usual due to Silvela's initiative, the election permitted the republicans to win thirty-five of the 400 seats. Even a group as small as this, thanks to the parliamentary procedures first drawn up in the 1830s, could effectively block all legislation. The consternation within monarchist ranks at being held hostage by the republicans was such that Silvela resigned from politics, having failed in his quest for regeneration.

Another major obstacle to the reform of the political system was the breach between the dynastic parties over the religious question, which made collaboration on other issues much more difficult. The Liberal reforms of 1906 in favour of public education and civil marriage outraged the Catholic Church, which regarded the Liberals as little less than Jacobins bent on replicating the anticlerical agenda of the French Third Republic. Consequently, the Cortes debate of 1906 on a bill designed to subject the religious orders to the law on associations provoked a momentous Catholic backlash, as manifested in public meetings, special religious services, and nationwide protests, as well as countless petitions and newly formed Catholic Leagues. The campaign climaxed with the extraordinary declaration of the Cardinal Primate in 1907 that to vote Liberal was a sin. By contrast, the attitude of the Church to the Conservative Party was wary but collaborative, an agreement being reached with the Vatican by the Conservative government of 1904 whereby all monasteries, convents, and other ecclesiastical centres were protected from closure. In the meantime, the Catholic community continued to extend its reach over civil society. In 1908, Father Ayala founded the *Asociación Católica Nacional de Propagandistas* (ACNP) (National Catholic Association of Propagandists), which soon established itself as an effective elitist vehicle of indoctrination and mobilization. The launching in 1910 of *El Debate*, a quality Catholic daily which drew on the latest print technology and journalistic techniques, underlined the sophistication and modernity of Catholic propagation. The growing societal presence of the Catholic community made it even less likely that the Liberals and Conservatives would supersede their differences over the religious issue.

A final obstacle to reform was King Alfonso XIII, who had come of age on reaching his sixteenth birthday in 1902. Unlike his father, Alfonso XII, who had adopted a low profile, the young Alfonso was determined to be a major player in Spanish politics, an ambition that was greatly facilitated by the Constitution of 1876. This not only made him head of state and commander-in-chief, but also the ultimate arbiter of the executive, legislative, and judicial branches of government. The monarch appointed and dismissed ministers, convoked and dissolved the Cortes, and approved or vetoed parliamentary bills, as well as nominated the mayors of all the cities and many towns, in addition to having the last word on the selection of judges. Clearly Alfonso's powers violated the separation of powers. Furthermore, national sovereignty resided not in the people, but was shared between the monarch and the Cortes. In other words, this was a constitutional monarch who enjoyed many of the attributes of an absolute one. As if this were not enough, the break-up of the dynastic parties enhanced the king's political leverage by allowing him to play one faction off against another.

In sum, the young Alfonso emerged as the pivotal figure within Restoration politics.

Thanks to the Constitution of 1876, the king was entitled to approve all public-sector appointments, allowing him to build up extensive networks of patronage and clientelism. He made a point of personally choosing the officers not only for his Household Guard, but also for the Army of Africa, which allowed him to create his own military power base. The fact that the king took advantage of the Constitution to establish his own networks naturally conferred legitimacy on clientelistic practices. Management of the networks reinforced Alfonso's political interventionism by involving him closely in the state administration, as well as by providing him with a highly personalized perspective on public affairs that would strongly shape his performance as king.

The most unsettling aspect of Alfonso XIII's approach to public affairs was his unabashed attachment to the army. Educated by priests and generals, he invariably dressed in military uniform in public, as well as much preferring the youthful company of soldiers, with their penchant for hunting, drinking, and womanizing, to that of the relatively staid and elderly politicians. An early sign of Alfonso's predilection for the military was his appointment of the Chief of the General Staff in December 1904 without consulting either Prime Minister Maura or any of his ministers. Such a move was unconstitutional, but the king forced the prime minister's resignation rather than back down. The incident was deeply disturbing, as it showed that Alfonso, who had acted in a petulant and hubristic manner, placed military above civilian power and, critically, regarded himself as above the Constitution.

## THE ARMY RE-ENTERS POLITICS

The gravity of the king's high-handed approach was brought home by the ¡Cu-cut! incident of 25 November 1905. That night 300 army officers in Barcelona ransacked the Catalan publications *La Veu de Catalunya* and *¡Cu-cut!* for satirizing the army and the national flag, this being the first major intervention of the army in politics since 1875.

Far from upbraiding the officers, the captain-generals applauded their vandalism, while the army itself demanded that all offences against the Motherland and the armed forces be placed under military jurisdiction. At the Cabinet meeting the next day, the king not only praised the officers, but also urged them to continue with their rebellion, thereby disavowing the Liberal prime minister, Eugenio Montero Ríos. Faced with a clear-cut choice between civilian and military power, Alfonso had unequivocally come down on the side of the army. This was his 'first major betrayal of the façade of civil supremacy that had been the crowning achievement of the Canovite system'.[101] The discredited prime minister was replaced by fellow Liberal Segismundo Moret, who appeased the army by appointing as minister of war Agustín Luque, the captain-general of Seville, who had publicly rejoiced at the action of the Barcelona officers. His Cabinet then proceeded to pass the so-called Law on Jurisdictions in March 1906, which not only converted the military courts into the arbiters of Spanish nationalism, but also boosted the militarization of public order, a paradoxical measure given that the disorder which had given rise to the law had been caused by the army.

The ¡Cu-cut! incident marked a turning point in the history of the Restoration as it ruptured the founding pact between civilian and military power. Abandoned by the king, the politicians had set the perilous precedent of rewarding military insubordination, which not only made them dependent on the army, but also legitimized the use of political violence. In short, a fundamental shift in power had taken place. The king's ambition to become a Spanish-style Kaiser had led to a grave violation of the Constitution, further tainting the Spanish state and the rule of law.

The political instability resulting from the rise of factionalism, the schism over the religious question, the ascendancy of independent electoral districts, and the interference of army and king were plain to see. Between December 1902 and January 1907 there were ten different governments, seven different prime ministers, and over a hundred ministers. Many of these Cabinet reshuffles were dubbed 'oriental' as they took place within the Royal Palace that dominates the Oriental Square, an indication that the king was heavily involved. There were no stable governments during this period, and the Cortes was closed for lengthy stretches. There were, admittedly, both Liberal and Conservative politicians who remained determined to regenerate Spain, however not only were their parties more fragmented than ever, but they also had to contend with the destabilizing interventions of the king and army, as well as the mounting challenge of mass politics.

That challenge soon took a new and unexpected turn. The ransacking of the Catalan publications in November 1905 had been widely applauded outside Catalonia as the regionalists were seen by many Spaniards as separatists. Nonetheless, that same month the republican leader Nicolás Salmerón declared his backing for the regionalists. During early 1906, as the bill on Jurisdictions was first debated and then passed, this support crystallized into an alliance, Catalan Solidarity. This caused a major schism within the republican movement, as many republicans opposed the regionalists, foremost amongst whom was Alejandro Lerroux, a fervent Spanish nationalist and political rival of the Catalan *Lliga*. By the end of 1906, the republicans had split into two camps: the *solidarios* (supporters of Solidarity) and the *antisolidarios* (enemies of Solidarity). They were to face off in the general election of April 1907, which culminated in an extraordinary triumph for Catalan Solidarity, as it secured forty-four of the region's forty-seven deputies. The breach between the *solidarios* and *antisolidarios*, as highlighted at the Republican Union congress in June 1907, proved unbridgeable. The Catalan question had effectively destroyed the Republican Union.

# THE 'REVOLUTION FROM ABOVE' OF ANTONIO MAURA

For nearly a decade after the 'Disaster' of 1898 next to nothing was achieved by the monarchist politicians in terms of political regeneration. The electoral map, *caciquismo*, the rigged results – all stayed the same. The prospect of reform was made bleaker still by the crumbling of the two dynastic parties, the sprouting of autonomous electoral districts, the political meddling of the king, and the challenge posed by the anti-dynastic forces. Still, the Conservative Cabinet of 1907 under Antonio Maura broke with a string of governments by launching the first truly Regenerationist administration. A successful lawyer from Mallorca (the prosecutor in the high-profile Ubao trial of 1900), the haughty and patrician Maura was nonetheless the first to admit that there was a gulf between the Cortes and the citizenry, as 'the vast majority of the Spanish people have no interest, they do not intervene at all in political life'. It was therefore necessary to 'reintegrate into political life the great popular masses and reinforce the political body with them'.[102] He aimed to create parties that were rooted in public opinion, not electoral fraud: 'I do not believe that the parties are a bad thing, what I deplore is that they do not exist.'[103] He proposed to 'dismantle *caciquismo*' by overhauling the electoral system and rejuvenating local government.[104] The reform of municipal and provincial government, he hinted, might result in the emergence of regional bodies, which suggested a possible solution to the Catalan question. Other goals included greater state support for the economy and the Catholic Church, but the overriding objective was the regeneration of the political system. This was to be Maura's 'revolution from above'.[105]

The new government subjected the Cortes to a blizzard of bills. At the forefront of its Regenerationist agenda was the reinforcement of the economic nationalism which had defined state policy since the protectionist tariff of 1891. A new tariff of 1906 had provided the Spanish industrial sector with the greatest protection in Europe, but in 1907 Maura introduced the Law for the Development of Industry, which was designed to offset the weak domestic market by granting industry tax breaks and other exemptions. Indeed, Spain stood out because of 'the intensity and extent to which they turned to these measures of assistance for the industrial sectors'.[106] Additional reforms included the Law for the Protection of the National Economy (1907), which encouraged the formation of major companies with Spanish capital, and the Law for Naval Construction (1908), which made good the naval losses of 1898 by ordering the construction of thirty-four warships, as well as by refurbishing the Cartagena and El Ferrol naval yards.

Above all, Maura's was the first post-1898 government to undertake meaningful political reform. The Electoral Law of August 1907 was designed to create a more representative and participatory political system by making voting obligatory and by having a candidate elected automatically if there were no others (a measure embodied in article 29). The law failed, however, to have the desired effect. On the contrary, it made the *caciques* even greater protagonists of the electoral process, article 29 in particular legalizing the practice of pre-electoral pacts. A further problem was that the electoral map was unchanged, so rural areas continued to hold sway over urban ones, that is, the monarchists' in-built hegemony remained intact. Complementing the Electoral Law was the bill on Local Administration, presented to the Cortes in May 1907, which aimed to undercut *caciquismo* by bolstering local government, in particular by giving it greater control over education, law and order, public works, and health. The proposed law also raised the prospect of appeasing Catalan sentiment via the creation of regional institutions. However, the bill was opposed by the Liberals and the republicans, who were both extremely wary of decentralization. After 127 days of attritional debate involving 400 articles, 1,387 amendments, and 2,950 speeches, the bill was abandoned. In any case it is doubtful that the envisaged reform would have achieved its objectives, as it lacked the necessary financial provisions.

This defeat over the Local Administration bill was swiftly followed by an even more damaging one for the Maura government. The bill for the Repression of Terrorism, set before the Cortes in January 1908, targeted anarcho-syndicalist terrorism by proposing to shut down the movement's newspapers and make the propagation of anarchist ideas illegal. By this stage, relations between the Conservatives and Liberals had deteriorated drastically. In the general election of April 1907, the Conservatives had reserved for themselves 253 deputies, while leaving the Liberals with only seventy-four. This oversized Conservative majority was designed to appease the multiple factions within the party, but it effectively broke with the *turno pacífico* by failing to ensure a respectable minority for the Liberal Party. Maura had therefore quelled the turmoil within his own ranks, but at the cost of alienating the Liberals. Opposition leader Segismundo Moret now reached out to the republicans in an effort to block the Conservative bill on terrorism. Alarmed by Maura's authoritarianism and protective of the anarchists (many of whom still voted for republican parties), the republicans welcomed the Liberal offer. A joint rally was first held in Madrid in May 1908 to the cry of 'Against Maura and His Power'.[107] This unprecedented alliance between monarchists and republicans, known as the Left-wing Bloc, forced Maura to withdraw his bill, making the breach between the two dynastic parties greater than ever.

## THE CONSEQUENCES OF
## THE 'TRAGIC WEEK'

Relations between the Liberals and Conservatives sank to a new low with the revival of Spain's imperial ambitions. In 1904, France and Spain had reached a secret agreement, consolidated at the Algeciras Conference of 1906, which established their joint tutelage over the Sultanate of Morocco. Spain acquired a mountainous strip in the north that bordered the Mediterranean. Not only was this area vastly inferior to the French domain in terms of size and resources, but it was also home to the Rif tribes, which had long sought their independence from the Sultanate. The Spaniards had held two coastal enclaves, Melilla and Ceuta, since the sixteenth and seventeenth centuries respectively, but as soon as their army and mining companies began to explore the Rif, they came under attack from the tribesmen. These exchanges climaxed with the massacre of colonial troops at the Wolf's Ravine on 27 July 1909, which left 150 Spaniards dead and over a thousand wounded. The Maura government had already decided to call up the reserve in response to the worsening situation, but the dispatch of recruits to Morocco brought back painful memories for many Spaniards of the colonial wars of the 1890s. The embarkation of troops from the port of Barcelona prompted a city-wide general strike on 26 July. Lacking any clear direction, the protest degenerated into violence as shops, businesses, and other properties were ransacked and pillaged. The main target of the protest was the Catholic Church, the embodiment of reaction for the popular classes. By the end of the week-long rampage, twenty-one of the city's fifty-eight churches and thirty of its seventy-five convents had gone up in flames, while 104 civilians and eight Civil Guards lay dead. No wonder that these events have been known ever since as the 'Tragic Week'.

Outraged by the extreme disorder and above all by the onslaught on the Church, Maura suspended the right of association, forbade public meetings, and held a barrage of summary trials. In total, 1,700 people were charged, of whom seventeen were sentenced to death. Amongst them was the anarchist Francisco Ferrer Guardia, who, thanks to his inheritance from a wealthy French lover, had founded

46

the Modern School, a pedagogical movement of international renown. The sweeping and arbitrary bent of the repression was clamorously condemned both at home and abroad. A wave of demonstrations took place outside Spain: one held in Paris attracted over 20,000 people. The protests did enormous damage to Spain's international standing, as they drew powerfully on the Black Legend, the slanderous stereotype from the sixteenth century according to which Spain was a land of clerical fanatics and bloodthirsty reactionaries. Despite the demonstrations, five people, including Ferrer – who, in reality, had not been involved in the planning of the Tragic Week – were executed on 13 October 1909.

The hardline repression of the anticlerical atrocities in Barcelona provoked a ferocious backlash against the aloof and authoritarian prime minister. A public campaign of '¡Maura no!' erupted, involving both the liberal and left-wing press, demonstrations, meetings, and parliamentary attacks on the prime minister. Typically, Maura dismissed the campaign as 'the turbine in the sewer', but the king, unnerved by the international outcry and fearful that the Liberals would swerve even further to the left, withdrew his support from the Conservative leader, who resigned on 21 October 1909.[108] Maura was livid that the Liberals had betrayed the Conservatives by allying with the non-dynastic opposition, that the king had given in to the '¡Maura no!' campaign, and that he had been thwarted from completing his 'revolution'. He thereupon declared his 'implacable hostility' to the Liberals, which appeared to bring the *turno pacífico* to an end.[109]

While the monarchists had never been so divided, the opposition had never been so united. If anticlericalism had provided the non-dynastic opposition with a shared discourse, the '¡Maura no!' campaign had given them a common cause, the republicans and socialists coming together in 1910 to form an electoral alliance, the Republican-Socialist Conjunction. The political landscape had therefore been redrawn by the colonial conflict in Morocco. The war also created a breach within the army itself, as the peninsular army resented the Army of Africa for its combat promotions, its access to wartime funds, and its growing prestige. Accordingly, the paradox of the Moroccan colony was that it had offered Spain the chance for national redemption in the wake of the 'Disaster', but had created instead a political and military maelstrom.

The formation of the Republican-Socialist Conjunction led to the election of the first ever socialist to the Cortes, Pablo Iglesias, in 1910. That same year the UGT was restructured, trade-based associations being replaced by single unions for an entire industry, which gave rise to powerful new entities, such as the Asturian Miners' Union and the Metallurgical Union of Vizcaya. More momentous still was the foundation in 1910 of the first national organization for the anarcho-syndicalists, the *Confederación Nacional del Trabajo* or CNT (National Confederation of Labour). Initially claiming 20,000 affiliates, half of them in Catalonia, the CNT was far from a truly national body, but it did at least provide the anarcho-syndicalists with an overarching framework. The restructured trade unions were further strengthened by new strategies, as shown by the Barcelona general strike of 1911, in which the CNT and UGT – in contrast to 1902 – joined forces. Another novelty was the targeting of essential public services, as initiated by the railway strike of 1912. As in other areas of civil society, the Catholic community was not to be denied, establishing the Catholic Free Unions in 1912 and the National Catholic-Agrarian Confederation in 1916, which brought together peasants from small and medium-sized holdings.

## LIBERAL REGENERATION

The so-called 'long government' of Antonio Maura had been divisive, damaging, and ultimately self-destructive, but it had also set a new benchmark for Regenerationist drive and determination. The cultivated, engaging, and relatively progressive Liberal José Canalejas, appointed prime minister in 1910, was set on governing with the same reformist vim and vigour as Maura. 'I represent,' he claimed, 'the European spirit, the desire for regeneration so that Spain can be the same as other nations, and not live in the eighteenth century.'[110] Oddly, Canalejas' reform agenda did not include the political system. On the contrary, he restored the *turno pacífico* by abandoning the Left-wing Bloc and by fixing the 1910 general election so as to satisfy not only the competing Liberal factions, but also the Conservative Party. He then set out his programme of regeneration.

Inspired by the 'new liberalism' in England, Canalejas sought to turn the state into a powerful agent of modernization. The first area of reform was education. Many Liberals believed that politics should be the reserve of an informed elite so long as the mass of Spaniards had not yet acquired the necessary education. Schooling was therefore seen not just as a necessary complement to economic and social modernization, but also as a means of preparing the populace for participation in politics. Primary education was improved by raising teachers' salaries, upgrading work conditions, providing the schools with more books, and expanding the inspectorate. Higher education was also given a considerable boost. In 1907 the Liberals had created the Junta for the Extension of Scientific Study and Research, which not only funded study-abroad programmes for scholars, but also gave rise to a cluster of research and other academic centres, so that by the 1920s Spain at last had a scientific community that formed part of the international scene. The educationalists behind this transformation of higher education were virtually all acolytes of the progressive *Institución Libre de Enseñanza* (Open Institute of Education), which had also played a key role in the foundation and development of the Institute of Social Reforms. In the second place, Canalejas aimed to tackle the 'social question' by bettering 'the health and life of the workers'.[111] A raft of laws were passed, including a ban on female night work, a maximum working day in certain industries, and the obligatory provision of contracts for apprentices, but the problem, as ever, was that of enforcement. A law of 1912, for example, banned night work for women. The local authorities and courts combined to reduce the efforts of the inspectorate to uphold the reform to a 'dead letter'.[112]

The final area targeted by Canalejas for state action was the Catholic Church. Although a devout Catholic himself – he even had a chapel installed in his home – he had long understood that the prerogatives of state and Church were not one and the same thing, distinguishing between 'the rightful sphere of the state and the rightful sphere of the Church'.[113] Indeed, his Cabinet resignation of 1902 was over the religious question. His principal grievance concerned the unbridled expansion of the religious orders and other Church communities. The problem, as he contended before the Cortes, was the clergy, not Catholicism per se. The sale of Church lands in the nineteenth century had drastically reduced the number of monastic communities, but under the Restoration these had risen sharply. Indeed, there were twice as many nuns in 1910 as in 1868, and five times as many monks. A bill designed to prevent the foundation of new convents and religious houses was presented to the Cortes in July 1910. The Catholic community reacted to the so-called 'Padlock Bill' with a nationwide campaign of protest in the press and on the streets. Within the Cortes the opposition included not only the Conservatives but also the right wing of the Liberal Party. The bill was consequently modified, the final version stipulating that if a new Law of Associations was not passed within the next two years, then the measure would lapse – which is exactly what happened. The Liberal administration did at least empower the Protestants – in accordance with the Constitution of 1876 – to display signs of their faith in public, in spite of yet another strident Catholic campaign in protest. In short, Canalejas realized little of his anticlerical agenda, but in the process he further damaged relations with the Conservatives.

The fidelity of the prime minister to the progressive nineteenth-century programme of 'laicism, the draft and the consumer tax' was reflected in two further reforms: a tightening up of the exemptions from military service and the abolition of the hated consumer tax. A final reform underlined Canalejas' statesmanship. Despite the Liberals' vehement opposition to Maura's bill on Local Administration, once in power he presented a bill in May 1912 for the creation of the *Mancomunidad de Cataluña* (Community of Catalonia). This was rejected by many Liberals as anti-Spanish, but the proposal was nonetheless passed into law five months later. As a result the Liberal government created the first regional Catalan institution of the modern era.

The Regenerationism of Canalejas came to an abrupt halt on 12 November 1912. On that day an anarchist by the name of Manuel Pardiñas was pacing up and down Madrid's central square, the *Puerta del Sol*, as he waited for the carriage of Alfonso XIII to pass by. He intended to commit an act of 'propaganda by deed', just as another anarchist had shot and killed Antonio Cánovas del Castillo fifteen years earlier. As the king was delayed, Pardiñas began looking around him when he espied an alternative target: José Canalejas, who was peering into the window of a bookshop. Seconds later, Pardiñas carried out his 'deed' and the prime minister lay dead.

## THE END OF THE *TURNO PACÍFICO*

The assassination of José Canalejas removed the linchpin that had held the Liberal Party together. Infighting between the factions of Segismundo Moret, the Count of Romanones, and Manuel García Prieto engulfed the Romanones government of 1913, which eventually fell due to the opposition of García Prieto. The elimination of Canalejas from the political scene also ruptured the *turno pacífico* of the two dynastic parties. In October 1913 the king asked the Conservative Antonio Maura to form another government, but he refused unless the Liberals apologized for their unholy alliance with the republicans. As the Liberal apology was not forthcoming, Eduardo Dato agreed to form the new Conservative government. Viewing this as an act of betrayal, Maura abandoned the party along with his supporters, as did Juan de la Cierva, the two factions acting thereafter as independent parties. The fracturing of the Conservatives and Liberals signalled the death knell of the *turno pacífico*, this being replaced by shifting coalitions of factions, which naturally made governance more difficult than ever.

The splits within the parties and the emergence of faction-based coalition governments greatly complicated relations between the Cabinet and the Cortes, making the passing of legislation extremely problematic. After 1914, the budget had to be systematically extended due to a lack of support in the Cortes, while numerous tax bills had to be abandoned for the same reason. The closure of parliament consequently became ever more frequent, the Dato administration of 1913 to 1915 only keeping the Cortes open long enough to fulfil its minimal obligations. For the king, the factionalism of the dynastic parties made divide-and-rule easier still, thereby accentuating his political interventionism. The relative stability of the Maura and Canalejas administrations across 1907–12 fast became a distant memory: between 1914 and 1923 the average government lasted a mere five months. Last, but not least, Canalejas' death brought monarchist regeneration to a shuddering halt. No government thereafter enjoyed sufficient support or stability to carry out major reforms. On the contrary, the fragmentation of the system would be 'total', the Conservative Party 'morally broken', and the Liberal Party made 'virtually useless' by faction-fuelled feuding.[114]

The rallying cry of Regeneration in the aftermath of the Disaster of 1898, reflected in the call for schools, roads, dams, administrative decentralization, and political reform set much of the modernizing agenda for the early twentieth century. At the same time, Regeneration-ism revealed the very stark limits to the Restoration system. The only determined reformist governments were those of Antonio Maura and, to a lesser extent, José Canalejas, but they both suffered premature ends and both fell way short of their own expectations, being hampered by the rise of factionalism, by the clientelist clans that undergirded their parties, by the lack of resources of the Spanish state, and by their own basic unwillingness to open up the political system. The challenge thrown down by the republican, socialist, and regionalist parties in the aftermath of the 'Disaster', with their local centres, mass membership, party newspapers, public meetings, popular demonstrations, and con-stant campaigning was never taken up by the dynastic parties, which remained small, often inactive, assemblages of notables. Maura did appreciate the need to extend political participation, but his vision remained hidebound. He aimed to integrate the so-called 'neutral masses', which he equated with conservative, Catholic opinion, not with the working class or the liberal middle class. In other words, he intended to incorporate like-minded subjects, not critical ones, and cer-tainly not anti-dynastic ones. Not even José Canalejas, the former republican and most reform-minded of the Liberals, ever seriously considered toppling the *turno pacífico*, making his stance the most incoherent of all. Having claimed to personify 'the liberal and demo-cratic spirit of Spain', he did little once in power to advance these objectives in political terms.[115] Ultimately, the monarchists were unwill-ing to channel the interests of a society that was increasingly urban, secular, and vibrant by opening up the Restoration system, even though the political straitjacket of the status quo generated ever greater social and political tension. Monarchist immobilism represented the triumph of *caciquismo* over citizenship, of patrimonialism over participation, of elitism over empowerment. In sum, a short-sighted, self-interested, and indolent political class signally failed to rise to the challenge of mass politics.

Regenerationist thinkers such as Joaquín Costa were right to criticize the Restoration political order, but they were wrong to stigmatize its economy and society as backward and stagnant. Spain's agrarian-based economy was unquestionably underdeveloped in relation to the countries of Northern Europe, but it was still more advanced than most countries in Eastern and Southern Europe. In European-wide terms, the Spanish economy was a middling one, which made it representative of the continent rather than backward. It was never stagnant, the influx of colonial capital following the 'Disaster' accelerating a process of modernization and diversification which had been underway since the early 1890s. Society, too, was on the move, as shown by falling death rates, rising life expectancy, expanding urbanization, and growing trade union affiliation. Despite the vicissitudes of national politics, by the early 1910s Spain was on the cusp of far-reaching economic and social change, a development which would be greatly accelerated by the First World War.

# 2

# Modernization and the Challenge of Mass Politics, 1914–1923

No sooner did the First World War break out than Spain declared 'the strictest neutrality'.[1] As the prime minister, the Conservative Eduardo Dato, explained in a letter, the country lacked 'material resources and adequate preparation for a modern war', while its commitments of 1907 and 1912 to Britain and France 'are limited to Morocco'. The only circumstance in which Spain would abandon its neutrality would be 'if we were directly threatened by foreign aggression or by an ultimatum'.[2] Indeed, Spain was not only extremely ill-prepared in military terms for a European war, but it was also not bound to the treaties of the warring nations. It may have been excluded from the potential spoils of victory, but Dato nonetheless hoped to turn neutrality to Spain's advantage. 'Would we not render a better service to both sides,' he asked rhetorically, 'by sticking to our neutrality so that one day we could raise a white flag and organize a peace conference in our country which could put an end to the current conflict?'[3]

## A NATION DIVIDED

Belligerent or not, Spain was deeply affected by the war. All sides agreed in 1914 that neutrality was the best option, but as the war unfolded, public opinion became bitterly divided, as was made patent in the press, parliament, and public meetings, though most Spaniards, especially those in rural areas, remained indifferent to the conflict. At the outset of hostilities there was overwhelming support for the German cause amongst the pillars of the Establishment, including the court, the aristocracy, the Catholic Church, and the army. The army's adherence was determined by admiration for the Prussian army, resentment at Britain's continuing hold on Gibraltar, hostility to the long-term enemy, the 'degenerate' French, and loathing for the Allies' sympathizers in Spain, the antimilitaristic (and therefore unpatriotic) left.[4] Politically, the Conservative Party, the ultramontane Carlist movement, and most Liberals were firm supporters of the Central Powers. Socially, the landed elites, the Catholic community, and conservative sectors in general also declared themselves *germanófilos* (supporters of Germany). For these groups, the tradition, order, authoritarianism, and religiosity of the Central Powers stood in welcome contrast to the destructive example of the anticlerical and antimilitaristic French Third Republic, the self-proclaimed heir of the Revolution that had spread the toxic virus of liberalism amongst the peoples of Europe. Not all *germanófilos*, however, were conservative. There were some liberals, especially academics who had spent time in Germany, such as the philosopher José Ortega y Gasset, who were, in the words of the historian Rafael Altamira, 'sons of Germany on account of [studies in] philosophy, the judicial sciences, pedagogy, history, linguistics, the experimental methods, medicine'.[5] From the perspective of the Central Powers themselves, neutrality was the best possible option in the Spanish case. They sought to consolidate this position by means of an aggressive propaganda campaign within Spain, which included the bribery of government officials and the buying up of conservative, republican, and even anarcho-syndicalist newspapers and journals. They also attacked Allied interests in Spain, whether through the construction of a peninsula-wide spy network, the undermining of companies supplying the Allies through the manipulation of anarcho-syndicalist groups, and even, with the connivance of Spanish colonial authorities, the launching of insurgent groups within French Morocco.

By contrast, support for the Allied cause was far slower to coalesce. Sympathy was evident amongst the republicans, socialists, the urban professional classes, and the intelligentsia, for whom the Allies represented liberty, democracy, and progress, the paradigm here being republican France, not monarchist Britain. There was also a certain sympathy for the Allied cause amongst the industrial sectors of Asturias, the Basque Country, and Catalonia. The most prominent *aliádofilo* (Allied supporter) on the left was the republican leader Alejandro

Lerroux, but his stance found little favour amongst the popular classes, which, given the 'unwanted and misunderstood' colonial war in Morocco, dreaded the idea of further bloodletting, though this did not prevent an anti-war mob from nearly lynching him.[6] The only major monarchist politician to back the Allies was the Count of Romanones, who, days after the official declaration of neutrality, published an anonymous article entitled 'Fatal Neutralities', in which he argued that non-bellicose support for the Allies would benefit Spain both economically and in terms of its empire in Africa; but he remained an isolated case. In any case, support for the Allies was tempered by the realization that a declaration of war would have disastrous consequences for Spain. Thus the Reformist Party, founded in 1912 by the acclaimed orator and lawyer Melquíades Álvarez as a progressive inter-class force that appealed above all to the urban middle classes, limited its support for the Allies to 'all the moral support that they deserve in this conflict'.[7] Sympathy for the Allies was at least buoyed by the widespread assumption that Alfonso XIII, who was married to a granddaughter of Queen Victoria (Victoria Eugenie of Battenberg), was on the side of the Allies.

The first pro-Allied manifesto was not launched until March 1915. Supporters of the Allies tended to view the conflict through the prism of national politics, equating *germanofilia* and Spain's 'strict neutrality' with the political status quo at home, while identifying the Allied cause with domestic democratic and liberal reform; a manifesto of July 1915 claimed that the goals of the Allies coincided with 'the deepest and most inescapable political interests of the nation'.[8] The conflict between supporters of the Allies and those of the Central Powers could be seen as a 'new manifestation' of the clash between the 'Two Spains' – the liberal, progressive Spain versus conservative, Catholic Spain – which had characterized Spanish politics since the Napoleonic Wars.[9] On returning to power in December 1915, the pro-Allied Count of Romanones officially maintained Spain's neutrality, while exploiting diplomatic back channels in an effort to reach an agreement with the Allies. In early 1916 he tried to persuade France to hand Tangiers over to Spain, confiding to his emissary that 'our fate is inevitably linked to that of France and Britain ... Tangiers is not only the key to the control of the Mediterranean but also to the pacification of our Protectorate in

Morocco'.[10] The French, however, refused to take the bait, as Spain had nothing tangible to offer in return.

## THE ECONOMIC AND
## SOCIAL IMPACT OF THE WAR

While neutrality served to curb the ideological fallout from the First World War, the economic and social repercussions of the conflict were immediate and far-reaching. Neutrality allowed Spain to avoid the destruction of war, while supplying the many needs of the belligerents on both sides. Spiralling wartime demand resulted in unprecedented industrial profits. Large-scale iron and steel concerns, textiles, light metals, and especially mining and Basque shipping recorded exceptional profits, as well as many smaller enterprises. Mining output, for example, soared in value from 462 million pesetas in 1914 to 1,387 million in 1918. For the first time ever, the Catalan textile industry became a prime exporter to Europe, the value of its cotton sales on the continent rising steeply from 53.3 million pesetas in 1913 to 138.4 million in 1915. One Catalan textile manufacturer recalls these years as 'a prodigious dream, in which all the business deals were smooth and prosperous, all ending in a real orgy of profits ... In that period of our exporting fever we felt confidence in our capacity to conquer the entire world.'[11] The region which did best out of the war was the Basque Country, especially its industrial heartland, Bilbao. The city, exulted one observer in 1918, 'is today one of the most flourishing cities in Spain, and I will even say in Europe. One sees life and exuberance wherever one looks. Businessmen stride about in bustling preoccupation. Trucks and automobiles are constantly racing through the streets.'[12]

Wartime capital accumulation enabled the creation of new industries, such as in electrical goods or Spain's first aeronautical manufacturer, *Hispano Aviación*. Some products, such as alcohol, were exported en masse for the very first time. Not even agriculture, often seen as backward and stagnant, was left behind. Up to 1917 agricultural production grew by 27 per cent, exports climbing from 402 million pesetas in 1915 to 533 million in 1916. The cumulative surge in exports allowed Spain to record its first positive trade balance in modern times, gold reserves at the Bank of Spain rocketing from under 350 million pesetas in 1914 to just over 2,000 million in 1917.

The boom in industry and mining sucked in record numbers of workers. Jobs in the transport sector multiplied by over a third between 1914 and 1918, in mining and textiles they almost doubled, and in the metallurgical sector they trebled. Anxious not to interrupt production, employers granted hefty wage rises. Miners in Asturias saw their pay soar from 5.5 pesetas a day to 9.47, while the wages of Catalan workers rose by 20–50 per cent. The wartime economy produced a major realignment in the working population: the industrial sector rose from 15.82 per cent in 1910 to 21.94 per cent in 1920, services from 18.18 per cent to 20.81 per cent (as reflected in the doubling in the number of bank branches across 1914–20), while agriculture declined from 66 per cent of the active population to 57.5 per cent in the same period. These shifts translated into even greater urbanization, Madrid's population growing by 12 per cent between 1914 and 1919, Barcelona's and Bilbao's by 10 per cent.

Nationwide, the percentage of people living in cities of more than 100,000 inhabitants increased from 9.01 per cent in 1910 to 12.5 per cent in 1920, and those in towns of 10,000 or more from 35 to 39 per cent.

Yet this is far from the whole story. While some industries benefited hugely from the war, many others did not. The movement of goods and raw materials was severely impeded by the shortcomings of the railway and road networks at home and by the disruption abroad, especially the shortage of shipping. Industries that foundered during the war included the building trade, food conservation, lumber, and the agricultural export sector. Despite the boom in Catalan textiles, the same sector in Aragón, Navarre, Granada, Seville, and the Balearic Islands saw output drop as production materials such as dye could not be acquired. The situation became even graver with the Central Powers' maritime blockade of both the Allied and Mediterranean countries in February 1917. One export that suffered grievously because of the shortfall in shipping was the orange sector in the east of Spain. The number of boxes of oranges passing through the port of Valencia in 1917 was 1.5 million less than in 1913. Similarly, the province of Castellón exported 30 per cent fewer oranges than before the war, the impact of which was 'utterly ruinous'.[13] The devastation of the orange industry in the east was so great that it did not return to its pre-war export levels until 1924. In fact, the agricultural economy as a whole declined from mid-1917 onwards as a result of transportation difficulties, the lack of fertilizer from abroad, and Britain's sudden drop in imports. In general terms, the industrialized north and northeast of the country – Asturias, the Basque Country, and Catalonia – did well out of the war, but many other regions, including Andalusia, Extremadura, and the east did not.

Inflation hit living standards hard as it outstripped wages. A working-class family of five in Asturias, for example, spent 4.46 pesetas on its basic needs in 1914, but by 1918 it had to pay 8.51 pesetas. Nationwide, wages increased by 25.6 per cent during the war, but prices soared by 61.8 per cent, so real wages actually dropped by one-fifth between 1914 and 1920. The wartime rise of 67.7 per cent in the price of basic foodstuffs in the cities generated widespread social misery, bread riots becoming commonplace from 1915 onwards. Demonstrations also took place, such as the multitudinous protest in Seville on 11 February 1915 demanding 'Bread and Work'. 'In Spain there is nothing but hunger,' exclaimed a Liberal deputy before the Cortes in November.[14] The surge in strikes from 212 in 1914 to 463 in 1918 was caused above all by wages being outstripped by inflation. The flood of rural workers into the cities in search of jobs exacerbated an already difficult situation, as there had been substantial pre-war migration. Competition for jobs was made more desperate still by plummeting emigration (from nearly 200,000 in 1912 to just over 50,000 in 1915), and the initial return of many workers from abroad, fleeing from hostilities, mainly in France. Mass unemployment was only partially offset by the expansion in industry. The widespread suffering reached its peak during the winter of 1917–18. In Madrid the lack of coal resulted in the supply of electricity being cut between 9 p.m. and 6 a.m. and the trams running at half-speed. The capital also saw a sharp rise in muggings, robberies, infant mortality, and destitution as 28,000 beggars crowded the central streets. The distress was compounded by the ostentatious consumption of the entrepreneurs, speculators, and black-market operators, who 'drove large motor cars, dressed lavishly, paraded gilded women, patronized the cocktail lounges that were then appearing in Spain, and in general made themselves odious to a hard-pressed and puritanical proletariat'.[15] Indeed, urban working-class housing, already overcrowded and often squalid, deteriorated still further. 'You have to see it to believe it,' reported one eyewitness from Bilbao, 'hundreds and even thousands of wretches live crowded into bedrooms or rooms where 6, 8 and 10 people or more of both sexes are gathered together in horrible moral and sanitary confusion.'[16] The mining town of Mieres in Asturias was even said to be 'without doubt the dirtiest, most unhygienic, and most uninhabitable in Europe'.[17]

Local authorities struggled to tackle the deprivation by distributing bread and even money to mobs of hungry people, as well as by opening soup kitchens. In the Cortes, a Liberal deputy called on the government not only to tackle the extensive hunger, but also to adopt measures 'against the hoarders and people who live like parasites from the rise in the price of living'.[18] The central authorities, however, did little. The divisions within the Liberal Cabinet of 1915–17 partly explain its ineffectual response, not least its inability to establish an inflationary barrier between Spain and the nations at war, the 'great political failure' of 1916.[19] Not only did the government fail to control prices, but it also permitted the export of food, raw materials, and manufactures that were essential to domestic living standards. Prime Minister Romanones promised aggrieved trade-union leaders in June 1916 and again in November to undertake ameliorative measures, but he did nothing. The same went for the orange producers of Valencia. In 1917 the mayor of Valencia informed the prime minister that 'there is no market for the crop, ruin is certain and the misery will produce disorder'.[20] Nonetheless, the delegation of orange producers that travelled up to Madrid returned empty-handed, the collapse of the market provoking the emigration of over 65,000 workers, mostly to France.

Similarly catastrophic was the situation in the province of Almería, down the Mediterranean coast from Valencia. In September 1916, 300,000 barrels of grapes, Almería's main product, could not be shipped out, due to the maritime disruption. This, a local deputy explained before the Cortes, would have a devastating effect on the province:

As the autumn advances, and above all the winter, there are extremely acute crises due to the lack of work. If the greatest source of income for these peasants, workers and property-owners is suddenly cut, not only will Almería be seized by hunger, but emigration, which has affected 44 per cent of the total number of peasants, will become mass emigration.

The lame response of the government was that 'it is taking steps'.[21] Fruit growers in the Canary Islands were also unable to export their produce, in this case due to the German submarines that lurked outside their ports. As a senator from the Islands informed the Chamber on 9 December 1916, 'imports and exports have been completely suspended and this will result in the ruin and economic disaster of the region. Logically, the paralysis of the ports has produced the paralysis of work.'[22] Clearly the government had no answer to the mounting economic and social strife.

There was one major exception to the Liberal government's laissez-faire approach. Inspired by the interventionist example of the British Liberals, the goatee-bearded minister of finance from Castile-León, Santiago Alba, presented a far-ranging bill of 'national reconstruction' before the Cortes in 1916. In keeping with the spirit of Regeneration, he advocated large-scale public spending on schools, reservoirs, and irrigation schemes, proposing to finance the schemes by means of a 25–40 per cent tax on the wartime profits of the Basque and Catalan industries, as well as by cutbacks in the public sector and a clampdown on tax evasion. Presented to the Cortes on 3 June, the bill on 'excess' profits was vehemently opposed by Catalan business, already aggrieved by Madrid's refusal to contemplate the creation of a tax-free port in Catalonia or to subsidize exports. The *Lliga* leader Francesc Cambó assailed Alba's bill for not taxing the wartime profits of the agrarian interests which the minister represented. The Catalan-led opposition forced the withdrawal of the bill on 11 July.

Mass deprivation had a desultory effect on the trade unions, the socialist UGT slipping from 150,000 members in 1913 to around 110,000 in 1916, by which point the anarcho-syndicalist CNT had no more than 15,000 members. The economic distress created by the war brought the two unions together, the Pact of Zaragoza of July

1916 marking their first national agreement. Calling for the control of inflation and the creation of jobs, they held a number of joint meetings, culminating in the general strike of 18 December 1916, the first in Spanish history. Despite the strike's success – Madrid came to a virtual standstill – the government continued with its policy of 'suicidal inhibition', in the words of one union boss.[23]

## CONTESTING NEUTRALITY

The last year of relative peace for the Restoration regime was 1916. The following year a wave of revolutionary expectation swept the left, the ultimate cause of which was the war. It was the inflation caused by the war that provoked the protest of the workers; it was the ideological clash over the war that made the Spanish left anti-monarchist and pro-republican; and it was the war-induced Russian Revolution of March 1917 that did so much to fuel anti-monarchist and pro-Allied feeling in Spain. It was also the war that, thanks to the upsurge in the economy, relaunched Catalan nationalism, infusing it with a new *raison d'être* and militancy. The war was, one socialist observed, 'the one terrible reality that superimposes itself on everything ... and diminishes every other fact'.[24]

Despite the riots, demonstrations, strikes, and pleadings of the opposition, the Romanones' government undertook no effective measures against either inflation or unemployment. The national strike of December 1916 did not impress the government, for which the agitation of the working class was more a question of law and order than a matter requiring reform. The final straw for the workers was the closure of the Cortes on 27 February 1917. Following a meeting of 5 March between the UGT and CNT, the unions called for a permanent strike in three months' time that would bring the Restoration system down: no longer content to hold mere labour protests, the exasperated workers were now looking to overthrow the regime. Predictably, the government did not attempt to defuse the situation by, say, negotiating with the unions, but instead arrested hundreds of their members for 'sedition'. The government's unyielding stance aside, the trade-union strategy suffered from two major defects. First, both the UGT and CNT remained small and weakly structured, especially the anarcho-syndicalist organization. Second, the two trade unions had divergent goals. The CNT was busily amassing arms and bombs in the conviction that an uprising in Catalonia would topple the Restoration regime and bring about libertarian communism. By contrast, the socialists, who rejected an insurrection as unrealistic, aspired instead to overthrow the status quo through collaboration with the republicans, Reformists, and sympathetic army officers. For the socialists, the next stage on the road to the dictatorship of the proletariat was the establishment of a bourgeois republic, not a leap into the revolutionary void.

Working-class mobilization over the social and economic crisis was bolstered by the political campaign against Spanish neutrality. During the early months of 1917 the German blockade of Spanish waters reached its zenith, the declaration of unrestricted submarine warfare of 1 February coming as a severe shock to Spanish public opinion. Many *aliádofilos* (Allied supporters) felt that Spain was losing touch with the democratic and liberal currents represented by the Allies and that diplomatic relations with Germany should be severed in protest at the submarine siege. 'Interventionist' sentiment – which, in reality, contemplated no more than a policy of benevolent neutrality towards the Allies – was further boosted within republican and liberal circles by the fall of the Romanov dynasty in Russia in March, for this sharpened the war's ideological profile as one of democracy versus autocracy. Pro-Allied and anti-monarchist sentiment was further spurred by the entry of the United States of America into the war on 2 April 1917, reaching a new peak of indignation on 9 April with the German sinking of the Spanish steamer the *San Fulgencio*. For the pro-Allied prime minister, the Count of Romanones, 'the crucial moment has arrived. The sinking of the *San Fulgencio* has been the final straw . . . The note to Germany will be the first and fundamental step.'[25] A note of protest was seen by the Liberal premier as the prelude to the axing of diplomatic ties, but Romanones' own party voted the proposal down, prompting his resignation on 19 April. The king's opposition to the note, regarded by the left as a 'betrayal', made it clear, along with the incoming government's staunch defence of neutrality, that Alfonso XIII was on the side of the Central Powers, not the Allies. Many on the left finally realized that neutrality had, in fact, been a pro-German policy. The result was a growing convergence between the republicans, Reformists, and socialists, while the tone of the pro-Allied camp became increasingly republican, even revolutionary.

The campaign against neutrality climaxed with a mass meeting in the Madrid Bullring on 27 May 1917. The republicans, Reformists, and intellectuals who addressed the crowd did not call for a declaration of war, but for an end to strict neutrality, and for the 'moral intervention' of Spain on the side of the Allies.[26] After all, these were the nations that provided the Spanish left with its template for regeneration and whose victory in the war would – it was expected – unleash far-reaching democratic change within Europe. Indeed, the war in Europe was seen as the Spanish struggle writ large. As the republican leader Alejandro Lerroux put it, 'left and right, progress and reaction, justice and despotism – that is for me the problem contained in this war'.[27] Fellow republican Roberto Castrovido called for the victory of 'democracy, justice, and peace' over 'reaction, imperialism, militarism, clericalism', exclaiming that 'the war is a revolution, and here we must make our own'.[28] Pointedly held on the king's birthday, the meeting amounted to an ultimatum for Alfonso XIII: either he backed the democracies or he risked losing his throne, the writer and intellectual Miguel de Unamuno declaring that he would no longer support the monarchy 'if it insists on neutrality at all costs. The king can be useful; but he is not indispensable, much less irreplaceable.'[29] Although the socialists did not take part in the meeting – refusing to share a platform with 'bourgeois' politicians – they did nonetheless share its vision of the war as a transcendent struggle between the forces of progress and reaction.

## THE RISE OF THE JUNTAS

Paradoxically, the first move against the status quo was undertaken not by the anti-Restoration opposition, but by a pillar of the Establishment: the army. In late 1916 infantry officers throughout the peninsula began to form 'Juntas of Military Defence', or *Juntas de Defensa Militar*. Like other members of the middle class, the officers had been badly hit by the scarcities, inflation, and profiteering of the war, their mouthpiece *La Correspondencia Militar* complaining bitterly that the middle class was 'unhappy, helpless' and 'sees its situation grow daily worse without glimpsing any hope of relief'.[30] Unlike the workers, the officers could not go on strike, which only heightened their sense of grievance. Still, they organized themselves into juntas once it became clear that the army was to be reformed, neutrality having drawn attention to its unpreparedness for war. A wide-ranging bill was introduced by the minister of war, General Agustín Luque, in September 1916, which was partly designed to reduce the extraordinary excess of officers – one for every seven soldiers – by over 3,000. Having been passed by the Senate, the bill reached Congress on 3 December 1916, spreading panic amongst the ranks of the infantry officers. The emergence of the juntas was motivated, too, by a change in the system of promotions. After the Liberals came to power in December 1915, the traditional system, by which promotions were generally carried out in accordance with seniority, began to fall apart. The chief culprit of this unravelling of the system was the king, who, anxious to safeguard the Crown by securing the personal loyalty of the officer corps, had shown increasing favour not only towards those officers who had ingratiated themselves with the court, but also the leading *africanistas*, that is, those officers serving in the Moroccan war who had risen rapidly up the ranks on account of their combat merits. In other words, the officers who formed the juntas were not concerned with the wretched state of the Spanish army, but with their own status and material welfare.

The first junta emerged in Barcelona under the leadership of the ambitious and impressively moustached Colonel Benito Márquez. Such was the indignation amongst the officers that by the end of 1916 juntas had been established in every part of Spain except Madrid and the Moroccan Protectorate. Their objectives were to derail the military reform bill, eliminate royal favouritism, and reinstate promotion by seniority. 'Personal matters obsess them ... promotions and rewards, yes,' noted Alejandro Lerroux, 'skills, material, laboratories, organization, no.'[31] In stark contrast to the revolt of 1905, the rebellious officers of 1916–17 acted independently of their superiors, an entirely new and radical departure.

Two governments of early 1917 made an irresolute attempt to disband the juntas until Alfonso XIII, unnerved at his inability to control the situation, intervened. On 28 May the minister of war, acting on the instructions of the king – not those of the Cabinet – ordered the arrest and court martial of the protagonists of the Barcelona Junta, which by now had become the Superior Junta of the Infantry, the representative of all the juntas. The juntas were too organized, too determined, and too aware of their own power by this stage to be intimidated by the king or Cabinet. Accordingly, the Superior Junta issued an ultimatum on 1 June which called for the release of its leaders, for the legalization of all the juntas, and for the reinstatement of promotion by seniority. If the Junta leaders were not released within twelve hours, 'the army' would be obliged to intervene, that is, launch a coup d'état. The government's stand-off with the juntas had created a perilous situation, especially as the imprisoned officers had the support of garrisons throughout the land. Fearful of alienating the officer corps at a time of mounting social and political agitation – the pro-Allied meeting in Madrid had taken place just days before, on 27 May – Alfonso XIII caved in. Acting of his own volition once again, the king had the officers released. The triumph of the juntas was reflected in Benito Márquez's boast that the monarch 'does not free us, we free ourselves. He can be thankful that we leave him in Madrid.'[32] Having been disavowed by the monarch, the Liberal premier Manuel García Prieto resigned on 11 June. The very next day a Conservative government under Eduardo Dato approved the statutes drawn up by the juntas. The juntas were now, noted the Count of Romanones, 'the masters of Spain'.[33]

The officers' defiance of king and Cabinet, together with the vaguely Regenerationist lexicon of their manifestos, made a profound impact on the opposition. While most officers were concerned only with their personal prospects, the leaders of the Superior Infantry Junta aimed to carve out an independent political role for the army within the state. This was to deny the paramountcy of civilian rule, but the political opposition confused the self-serving ambition of the Junta with a commitment to sweeping, even revolutionary, change. Captivated by the sheer bravura of the juntas and their aura of Regeneration, the left imagined that the army, as in pre-Restoration Spain, had once again become the ally of progressive politics, prepared to collaborate in the task of removing the monarchy, resurrecting the republic, and regenerating the motherland. Thus the Reformist leader Melquíades Álvarez heralded the rebellion of the juntas as 'the beginning of a national renovation'. 'If Spain wishes to be saved,' he declared resoundingly:

> It is necessary that the revolution follow its course, and that the Army join with the people in order to build a new regime, which shall be founded on respect for the sovereign will of the nation and shall have as its only ideal the regeneration and progress of the country.[34]

More cautiously, the socialists hoped that the juntas were not just 'anti-oligarchical' but 'democratic'.[35] Less guardedly, the republican boss Alejandro Lerroux offered to break their leaders out of jail with 800 of his men. Consequently, the juntas had not only infused the republicans, socialists, and Reformists with renewed hope and vigour, but also appeared to have created a window of opportunity for the reconstruction, if not overthrow, of the Restoration regime.

# THE ASSEMBLY OF PARLIAMENTARIANS

The constitutional crisis provoked by the juntas and the rising revolutionary sentiment of the left convinced the main Catalan party, the *Lliga Regionalista de Catalunya* (Regional League of Catalonia), that the moment had come to strike against the Restoration order. The wartime boom, which had greatly enhanced the industrial sector in Catalonia, Asturias, and the Basque Country, had already convinced the wealthy financier and *Lliga* leader Francesc Cambó that the time was ripe to challenge the political hegemony of the landed and financial elites in Madrid. He aimed to create a wide-ranging coalition that would transform the country not by revolutionary means, but by calling a constituent Cortes, which, under the guidance of a 'national coalition government', would provide greater autonomy for Catalonia, shift power from Madrid's landed and financial oligarchy to the industrial and commercial classes, and democratize – not abolish – the monarchy.[36] The 1 June manifesto of the juntas was seized upon by Cambó as the turning of the tide. The *Lliga* responded with its own manifesto on 14 June in which the juntas' revolt was implicitly criticized as 'in truth a pacific *pronunciamiento* [military uprising]', but justified on the grounds that it represented 'a cry of sincerity, a living reality, because the problem which it raises is the constitutional problem'.[37] 'The falling of the Defence Juntas' sword on the Cabinet table,' the manifesto continued, 'was accompanied by the sympathy of those who hope to see opened up, and opened up wide, the path of the great constitutional reforms.'[38] The goal would be a 'federative' constitution as 'the protean or federal state . . . is the normal modern state, the most common, of the leading peoples'.[39] At a meeting of Catalan deputies and senators on 5 July the *Lliga* leader called on the juntas' 'explosion of patriotism' to be harnessed to the regeneration of Spain, while imploring the government to reopen the Cortes as a constituent body.[40] Otherwise, the *Lliga* would summon an 'Assembly of Parliamentarians'.[41] Five days later, Cambó wrote to the head of the Superior Junta of the Infantry, Benito Márquez, urging the army to 'liberate the whole of Spain from a political system that, if it persisted, would lead Spain to her perdition'.[42] Clearly, Cambó's strategy was designed to steer a third way between the intransigence of the monarchists and the radicalism of the left, that is, engineer a political revolution that would avert a social one.

Fearing that opening the Cortes might spark a revolution, Prime Minister Eduardo Dato dismissed the *Lliga*'s proposal out of hand, while condemning the proposed Assembly of Parliamentarians as a 'truly seditious act'.[43] Nonetheless, the Assembly went ahead in Barcelona on 19 July. The bulk of its sixty-eight representatives were Catalans, but it also included republicans, Reformists, and socialists from outside the region. Once again, a plea was made to the juntas to join the 'profound renovation' of the nation rather than limit themselves to 'a sterile act of indiscipline'.[44] The linchpin of Cambó's plan was the Conservative leader Antonio Maura. The *Lliga* leader assumed that Maura was supportive of the Assembly because he was sympathetic to the cause of Catalan autonomy and because he had pursued a 'revolution from above' during his government of 1904–7. Cambó envisaged that Maura would act as a bridge to the juntas, lend legitimacy to the *Lliga*'s 'national' movement, and constitute 'a help in containing the pressure of the left', as 'the greatest risk consisted of being overrun by the forces of the left'.[45] Indeed, at a meeting with Benito Márquez shortly before the Assembly, Cambó offered to abandon the left in exchange for the support of the juntas and the king for a federal state, but neither party was interested. Worse still, neither Maura nor his followers attended the Assembly. In reality, Cambó's venture was overly ambitious from the outset. On the one hand, it was extremely unlikely that Maura, who had been appalled by the Liberal-republican pact of 1907–9, would join a coalition that included not only republicans but also socialists. In any case, Maura was not prepared to defy the government or place the Crown in jeopardy, while he had nothing but contempt for the industrial and commercial sectors, dismissing the Assembly as 'subversive' and a 'marketplace'.[46] This refusal to engage with the representatives of industry and commerce in reshaping the Restoration regime was arguably his biggest single failure. For their part, the juntas regarded an Assembly without Maura as a factious gathering of separatists. On the other hand, it is next to impossible to see how the *Lliga*'s left-wing allies could have collaborated with Maura, as they reviled him as a reactionary. Cambó's vision of a coalition that stretched from the socialists to the *mauristas* was, in short, an illusion.

## THE REVOLUTIONARY STRIKE

By the time the Assembly of Parliamentarians met in Barcelona on 19 July the socialists and anarcho-syndicalists were convinced that the monarchist state was so weak and isolated that they would be able to topple it with ease. This conviction was strengthened by the revolutionary currents that had been rippling across Europe, such as in Russia, Germany, and Italy. The two movements therefore decided to organize a revolutionary strike which would force the king to abdicate and install a provisional government. According to the strike manifesto, the new government would hold 'sincere elections for a constituent Cortes which would undertake, in complete liberty, the fundamental problems of the country's political Constitution'.[47] Until this had been achieved, the unions stressed, 'the Spanish workers' movement is absolutely committed to maintaining the strike'.[48] Accordingly, this was a political, not a social, revolution, the aim being the establishment of a 'bourgeois' republic. The strike manifesto made it clear that the socialists and anarcho-syndicalists coincided with the Assembly of

Parliamentarians on everything except 'a fundamental change of political regimen'.[49] A Revolutionary Committee had already been formed on 5 June under the socialist Pablo Iglesias, the republican Alejandro Lerroux, and the Reformist Melquíades Álvarez, with the unofficial support of the anarcho-syndicalist CNT. The 16 June manifesto of the Committee, issued just two days after the *Lliga*'s, called on 'all the left' to ensure the 'triumph of popular sovereignty'.[50] It appeared that all the opposition forces were coming together at just the right time.

The revolutionary strike, however, did not go as planned. By instigating a railway stoppage for 10 August, the Conservative government compelled the unions to bring the general strike forward in an act of solidarity. The timing of the strike, as the socialist leader Julián Besteiro admitted at his trial, 'was not the one we would have desired but that which was imposed by the government'.[51] Indeed, the socialists had still not secured the definitive backing of the republicans, the Reformists, or anti-establishment officers in the army (which was considered vital to the strike's success), while contact had not even been established with the *Lliga*. The stoppage would arguably have been more effective if it had coincided with the Assembly of Parliamentarians back in July, the socialist ideologue Luis Araquistáin judging that this was a 'missed psychological moment' which permitted the government to pass from the defensive to the offensive.[52] Once Melquíades Álvarez discovered that the strike had been brought forward, he rushed down from Oviedo in Asturias to Madrid in order to stop it, but to no avail, not least because it took him several days to locate the Strike Committee.

Initially, the revolutionary strike triumphed in numerous cities, including Madrid, Barcelona, Bilbao, Valencia, and Oviedo. It had virtually no impact on the countryside, though it broke new ground insofar as there was a woman on the Strike Committee, Virginia González (who has been almost entirely written out of the history books). Women also played a prominent role in Madrid's street protests. Police agent Vicente Camarero was informed that in the north of the city 'a numerous group of women was stoning the Urquijo silver factory'. On reaching the location he was surprised to find:

A group of no less than five hundred women including a few men stoning the aforementioned factory. So I arrested the leader, Teodora Martín Sangal, and others. The former resisted arrest violently, having her sent to the police station with much effort in the company of two guards, from where she was transferred to prison.[53]

In the nearby working-class quarter of Cuatro Caminos:

The women of Santa Engracia Avenue, on their own, without letting a single man join their groups, pulled up the telephone and telegraph posts, putting them on the tram tracks and, as if this were not enough, lying their children down on the rails, attacking the trams frenetically, destroying them and making the drivers and guards flee.[54]

Other women tried to get office workers and managers at the tram station in Cuatro Caminos to join the strike, but, according to one eyewitness, 'one of the bosses threatened various women with a revolver' and 'one of them fired a shot from inside the station'. The women responded by throwing 'stones, breaking the windows of a number of trams'.[55] The extensive involvement of women in the strike – forty-two ended up in jail – makes the 1917 strike 'a landmark in the participation of women in the protest movements of Madrid'.[56]

Yet the strike was blighted by a slew of failings. The Strike Committee's instructions failed to reach many areas, communication between the different regions was extremely poor, and, once the Strike Committee was arrested by the police on 15 August (at, appositely enough, 13 Disillusionment Street), its replacement had little idea what to do. The strike was also gravely undermined by the sharply divergent objectives of the two unions. The CNT launched an uprising in Barcelona independently of the Strike Committee in Madrid, and, judging by its July manifesto, rejected the socialist goal of establishing a republic. The socialist UGT was itself deeply divided over the strike, some members failing to second it (including a majority of railway workers), whereas others, including the combative Virginia González, viewed it as an opportunity for a full-blooded revolution. A final ambiguity was that the strike was ostensibly peaceful, but many protesters deployed violence, one of the principal organizers later admitting that preparations had involved 'the acquisition of arms'.[57]

The strike was further undermined by the lack of political allies, both the republicans and Reformists refusing to back it because a revolutionary coalition had still not been consolidated. Nor was the strike seconded by either the *Lliga* or the Assembly of Parliamentarians, the Catalan party in particular being horrified by the upheaval. The Strike Committee had anticipated that a section of the army would intervene on its behalf, but this proved misplaced: the juntas participated with gusto in the crackdown, as they were repelled by the revolutionary goals of the workers. Indeed, the repression of the strike was vigorous and often bloody. In Barcelona, the CNT insurrection was crushed by 12,000 troops, and in Bilbao and Oviedo the army soon quashed all resistance. In Madrid, a demonstration at the Model Prison in support of the strike was put down at a cost of eight dead and thirteen wounded, while the protest in Cuatro Caminos soon reached a terrible climax. According to an eyewitness, there was first 'a ferocious cavalry charge', which caused 'sabre wounds and abundant damage'.[58] Two machine guns then opened up, so 'everyone saved themselves as they could, seeking refuge in the doorways or nearest street or shop'.[59] This was followed by 'a terrifying silence, a calamity that was so lugubrious and so terrible that one didn't hear anything other than the continuous chattering of the machine guns and the unceasing volleys in all directions'.[60] The onslaught left nine dead and 'numerous' wounded.[61] The strike in the capital was over by 18 August. Nationwide, the workers' attempt at regime change had resulted in 80 dead, 150 injured, and 2,000 behind bars. All the members of the Strike Committee were sentenced to life imprisonment, except Virginia González, as the military court refused to believe that a woman was on the Committee.

Rather than reaffirm the anti-Restoration movement, the strike actually had the opposite effect. Relations between the organized working class and the republicans-cum-Reformists were heavily soured by the lack of solidarity of the 'bourgeois' parties. Even the two unions drew apart, the anarcho-syndicalists reiterating their apoliticism while the socialists reverted to parliamentary politics. For the Catalan regionalists of the *Lliga*, the workers' uprising in Barcelona had intensified their fear of revolution, a fear which would be hugely magnified by the Russian Revolution two months later. Small wonder that the *Lliga* now viewed the army, for all its antipathy to the Catalan cause, not as an enemy but an ally. Further, at a meeting of the Assembly of Parliamentarians on 30 October, the Catalan regionalists chose not to exploit the political crisis of the monarchy by agitating for constitutional reform in collaboration with the other opposition parties. On the contrary, they abandoned the meeting in order to answer the summons of the king to join the government. The *Lliga* therefore betrayed the left and the cause of constitutional reform in order to defend its own interests from within the system.

The crisis of 1917 failed to change the political system because the triumvirate of forces in opposition to the government lacked a common programme. The aims of the juntas were not those of the Assembly, those of the Assembly were not those of the trade unions, and those of the trade unions were not those of the juntas. The lack of ideological, strategic, and tactical affinity doomed both the Assembly of Parliamentarians and the trade unions, though not the juntas. The defenders of the dynastic status quo may not have been especially able or flexible in the exercise of power, but they knew how to *stay* in power, such as by triggering the revolutionary strike prematurely and deploying the juntas against it. The crisis had exposed the naivete of the left's lingering attachment to the nineteenth-century *pronunciamiento* model, by which part of the army would rise up in support of its cause. In reality, the army had had no compunction in suppressing the revolutionary strike.

In stark contrast to the Assembly of Parliamentarians and the workers' movements, the juntas were to emerge from the crisis of 1917 stronger than ever. In the aftermath of the strike, they realized not only that their role in the repression had lost them the goodwill of the public, but also that Prime Minister Eduardo Dato had used them for his own ends. This only made them even more determined to establish themselves as the arbiters of national politics. On 23 October the juntas demanded that Alfonso XIII dismiss Dato, which he duly did four days later (the second Cabinet to be overthrown by the juntas in a matter of months). They subsequently ensured that Juan de la Cierva was made minister of war in the expectation that he would pass a law in defence of their corporate interests. In short, the 1917 crisis had reinforced the military at the expense of civilian power. National politics was now forged not only within the Cortes, Cabinet, and court, but also within the army barracks.

The government formed on 3 November, once again under the Liberal Manuel García Prieto, was nonetheless intent on reasserting civilian control over the army while pursuing political reform. The immediate political crisis had been overcome by incorporating the *Lliga* into the government, but the constitutional question remained very much alive. The government called a general election for 24 February 1918, which, at the insistence of the *Lliga*, would not be prearranged by the minister of the interior, the first time ever under the Restoration. Opposition leaders speculated that a parliamentary majority in favour of constitutional change might be returned, but this was wishful thinking. The republicans, Reformists, and socialists made some headway in the urban arena (the PSOE achieving a 'moral victory' by electing the jailed members of the Strike Committee), but the results merely underlined the enduring strength of the monarchists' clientelistic networks, as they won the great majority of seats.[62] The Cortes was now divided more or less evenly between the Conservatives and the Liberals, though each party was subdivided into three factions, ensuring that there would be no stable majority.

The government's foremost priority remained the dissolution of the juntas. The first step had been taken in December 1917 with the expulsion of the politically ambitious Benito Márquez from the Superior Junta of the Infantry. The next step was to satisfy the corporate demands of the juntas by means of a new military law, which the minister of war, Juan de la Cierva, judged would enable the government to dissolve them. Promisingly, *La Correspondencia Militar* lauded the minister as 'one of the most serious, sensible, and prestigious figures of Spanish political life'.[63] Better still, the military bill met the expectations of the juntas by raising salaries, increasing the number of officers, and regulating promotions by strict seniority, whether in peace or war. In effect, the proposed reform sacrificed the modernization of the Spanish army on the altar of the bloated officer corps. De la Cierva attempted to buttress the bill by having the king pass it by decree before it was presented to the Cortes, but this disregard for parliament led the two *Lliga* ministers to resign, causing the government to fall on 19 March.

Only the threat of abdication by Alfonso XIII ensured the formation of a new Cabinet, the so-called 'National Government' of Antonio Maura, who returned to power after nine years in the political wilderness. In

Conservative premier Antonio Maura and King Alfonso XIII

reality, the Maura administration was not national at all: like its predecessor, it excluded the forces of the left. Again, like the García Prieto government, the overriding objective of the Maura Cabinet was the reform of the army, that is, the passing of De la Cierva's decree by the Cortes, which was finally achieved on 29 June 1918. Far from pacifying the army, the Military Reform Law had the contrary effect. First, it intensified 'the serious divisions' between the senior and junior officers.[64] Second, the reform, despite constituting the first major military overhaul of the twentieth century, completely ignored the colonial forces, the one section of the Spanish army that was actually at war. The Army of Africa was embittered by its exclusion, the impact on its morale being 'devastating'.[65] The colonial newspaper *El Telegrama del Rif* reported that the colonial officers 'seeing themselves alone, without incentives, without justice being done to their deeds, perhaps passed over by favouritism, give up and turn into furious critics'.[66] Third, the law had disbanded the juntas, but they soon began to re-emerge at the local and provincial levels, as the junior officers felt that their interests were best defended by themselves rather than by their superiors. The Military Reform Law of 1918 therefore had two unintended, but far-reaching, consequences. Not only did it encourage political activism in the barracks, but it also left the army more, not

less, divided. Before these issues could be addressed, Maura's government, which was riven by internal rivalries and resentments ('let us
see how long the charade lasts,' the prime minister commented gloom-
ily at its outset), collapsed on 18 November.[67] Neither the García
Prieto nor the Maura government had therefore been able to resolve
either the military or the constitutional question.

The ongoing crisis of the dynastic parties lay to an important extent
in their very nature. Establishing an undisputed leader within a party of
notables which lacked the structures and procedures that generally
characterized a mass party was enormously complicated, not least
because gaining the support of different factions within a party was
often not a matter of ideology or policy but a question of satisfying the
material interests of the clientelistic networks underpinning each one. A
prime example of the sway exercised by these networks is provided by
the story of the Liberal premier, Manuel García Prieto, the key figure in
a five-family clan in the northern province of León that was prominent
in both the legal profession and politics. Through its privileged access
to the central administration, the García Prieto clan built up an immense
clientele in the province, which enabled it not only to become a stake-
holder in much of León's economy, but also to exercise a virtual
stranglehold over the Liberal politician's electoral district. In other
words, support for a leader at the national level depended to a considerable extent on his ability to gratify the needs of the party's networks
at the local level. For example, many Liberals switched allegiance from
the Count of Romanones to García Prieto once the former fell from
power in April 1917 not on ideological grounds but because the latter
was more likely to become the next Liberal prime minister, that is, to
provide access to the central administration for their clientage networks. Equally, addressing the interests of myriad networks in relation
to a particular policy or bill was an extremely tortuous business. Such
were the conflicting interests within the monarchist camp that not one
complete budget was passed between 1914 and 1920, while the Cortes
was closed for lengthy periods in order to avoid divisive and inconclusive debates. Since 1914 a much-reduced version of the *turno pacífico*
(the alternation in power of the two dynastic parties) had been kept
afloat by the Count of Romanones and Eduardo Dato, but the events
of 1917 finished off the *turno* for good, as well as splintering the two

monarchist parties irremediably. Thereafter, neither the Liberals nor the Conservatives governed as a party, but only by means of a single faction or faction-based alliances, the exception being Maura's 'National Government' of 1918, which lasted a mere seven months. Inevitably, this cratering of the dynastic landscape resulted in even greater political instability and even poorer governance, the average Cabinet between the outbreak of the First World War in August 1914 and the coup d'état of September 1923 lasting less than six months.

## THE 'BOLSHEVIK TRIENNIUM' (1918-20)

The so-called 'Bolshevik Triennium' of 1918-20 was launched by an anarcho-syndicalist congress in Seville in May 1918 that represented 30,000 workers from the southern agrarian provinces of Cádiz, Córdoba, Jaén, Málaga, and Seville. The strikes and other disturbances which followed over the next two years were partly a response to the worsening economic situation, but mainly to the triumph of the Bolshevik Revolution in Russia. A notary who regularly gave talks to rural workers later related that 'all conversations inevitably ended up being about the Russian theme. If one spoke of sowing, the question immediately arose: What do they sow in Russia? Does it rain much? How much does a *fanega* of land produce? ... Whereabouts is Russia? Is it far? How many days would it take to get there walking? Russia was an obsession, they didn't stop talking about it.'[68] The American writer John Dos Passos, who was visiting Spain at the time, noted that 'Russia has been the beacon flare'.[69] The Russian Revolution was of interest, however, for one reason alone: the seizure of land. 'If we want land,' the anarcho-syndicalists proclaimed, 'we have to do the same as the Russian Bolsheviks.'[70] However, the call of the anarcho-syndicalists for the revolutionary seizure of land was contradicted by their reformist demands for higher wages, the abolition of piecework, a ban on outside workers, and so on. The socialists were more moderate still, a congress of April 1919 targeting the eight-hour day, the end of piecework, and the setting up of arbitration committees. Further, the protagonists of the protests were not so much the landless labourers as small property-owners. Thus the workers' centre at Bujalance (Córdoba) welcomed 'all those who work, in any kind of labour, even if they are property-owners'.[71] In the same vein, the socialist congress of April 1919 agreed that small property-owners should be accepted as members of the workers' centres. Consequently, the agitation of these years was shot through with ambiguity.

The epicentre of the two-year struggle was the province of Córdoba, which was dominated by the anarcho-syndicalists but included many socialists. The Córdoba strike of March 1919 resulted in crop burnings, estate invasions, assaults on landowners' homes, and bloody clashes with the Civil Guard. Women played a salient role in the disturbances, a number of them being killed or wounded by the Civil Guard. In some towns, including sizeable ones such as Aguilar and Montilla, Bolshevik-style 'republics' were declared. Unrest erupted not only in other parts of Andalusia, but also in Aragón, Extremadura, and the east. In the province of Valencia, streets and squares were renamed 'Lenin', 'Soviets', and 'The October Revolution'.[72] Following the massive strike of May 1919 in the province of Córdoba, the army was called in, 20,000 troops occupying the towns and villages, closing down the workers' centres and arresting their leaders. The continued presence of the army ensured that the 'Bolshevik Triennium' was extinguished altogether in 1920.

The children of striking workers being fed at the socialist
headquarters in Madrid

## THE LABOUR WAR IN CATALONIA

To the industrial workers of Catalonia, the events of the Bolshevik Triennium and the wave of optimism that had greeted the end of the First World War were both a source of inspiration, but once again the greatest impact was made by the Russian Revolution. 'For a majority,' recalled the CNT leader Manuel Buenacasa, 'the Russian Bolshevik was a demi-god ... The splendour of the Russian conflagration blinded us.'[73] During the early post-war period, the Catalan CNT skyrocketed from 107,096 members in late 1918 to 345,000 by the end of 1919. Nationally, the CNT claimed to have around 700,000 members. The movement was also made more cohesive and centralized by the introduction of the *sindicato único* (single union) in the summer of 1918, by which the dispersed and highly autonomous craft unions were replaced by a single union for each regional industry.

The new-found power of the CNT was revealed in the strike launched on 5 February 1919 against the Barcelona Traction, Light and Power Company, popularly known as *La Canadiense* (The Canadian), which was vital to the life of the city as it supplied energy to homes and industry alike. The catalyst for the strike was the dismissal of eight workers for protesting at wage cuts, but its *raison d'être* was company recognition of the CNT. The stoppage spread to other electrical workers, then to those in the gas, water, and textile industries, all of which brought Barcelona almost to a standstill. The city was plunged into darkness, making it seem like 'the end of the world'.[74] The Captain-General of Barcelona, General Lorenzo Milans del Bosch, tried to break the strike by conscripting workers between the ages of twenty-one and thirty-one, but mass resistance thwarted the ploy at a cost of 3,000 jailed. The strike lasted forty-four days, the longest in Spanish history. It ended on 17 March thanks to a deal brokered by the government. The outcome was an unprecedented triumph for the CNT, as all its principal demands had been met: the eight-hour day, a wage rise, no strike reprisals, and the release of nearly all those arrested. For CNT moderates Ángel Pestaña and Salvador Seguí the victory was viewed as an important step in the construction of a structured, disciplined, and effective syndicalist movement.

The triumph of the moderates was, however, short-lived. The juntas, with the complicity of the local authorities, refused to release the imprisoned workers. Their defiance of the government played into the hands of the CNT radicals, who compelled the union to respond with a general strike on 24 March. This was the 'greatest tactical error' the organization could have made, its leader Manuel Buenacasa later recognized.[75] Martial law was declared and the army, together with the *Somatén* (an 8,000-strong civilian paramilitary force), took to the streets with cannon, cavalry, and machine guns. By 14 April the workers had been defeated. Everything that had been won as a result of the *Canadiense* strike was lost on account of the general strike.

The backlash against the CNT was far from limited to the defeat of the general strike. The bosses of Catalan industry reacted at the congress of the Employers' Federation in August 1919 to the establishment of the CNT's 'single unions' not only by strengthening their own organization, but also by falling under the sway of its most reactionary elements, the so-called 'Bolsheviks of order'.[76] Still, that same month negotiations were initiated between the employers and the CNT, but they broke down four months later. The rupture was attributed 'exclusively' by the civil governor to the 'conduct of the employers', whom he regarded as 'stubborn men, of profoundly retrograde opinions ... who wished to smash the Syndicalist organization and remould it to their desire and caprice'.[77] A lockout of 200,000 workers swiftly followed, which lasted until 26 January 1920, the longest of the post-war period. The Conservative minister of the interior was astounded by the 'short-sightedness' of the employers and the 'hard, unjust, provocative, and disruptive egoism' of most of them, having to listen 'day after day to adherents of law and order who would not obey the decrees of the government'.[78] The determination of the industrial bosses to destroy the CNT was fervently shared by the juntas, which backed them up by regularly defying the orders of the government. More serious still, the juntas would bring down those governments which they considered too conciliatory towards the workers, as in April 1919 and January 1920. As a result, the Liberals were effectively excluded from power by the juntas between 1919 and 1921.

The commitment of the captains of industry and the juntas to a solution by force exacerbated the schism within the anarcho-syndicalist movement between the revolutionary anarchists and the reformist syndicalists. For moderate leaders such as Salvador Seguí and Ángel Pestaña, the *raison d'être* of the CNT was the creation of a powerful trade union, but for radicals such as Buenaventura Durruti and Juan García Oliver, who were gripped by a 'mystical and apoca-lyptic idealism', the organization had to take the fight to the industrial bosses, the army, and the state in order to ignite a mass revolutionary uprising that would obliterate them all.[79] From this perspective, the syndicalists had more in common with the socialist UGT than with their anarchist colleagues. Even so, the fault line between the two camps within the CNT should not be overdrawn, as syndicalists were known to finance, protect, and even direct terrorist groups. As a result, the political violence of the anarcho-syndicalists was no longer restricted to the isolated acts of the pre-war 'propaganda by deed' but had become a core feature of the movement.

The origin of the mafia-like violence, or *pistolerismo* (gunslinging), that engulfed Barcelona between 1919 and 1923 lay in the CNT. Even today, there are historians who maintain that the employers' associa-tions, not the anarcho-syndicalists, started the shooting, but in reality it was the CNT *pistoleros* or gunmen who first targeted employers, policemen, judges, politicians, and non-CNT workers during the summer of 1918. Indeed, the very word 'anarcho-syndicalist' became synonymous – admitted one CNT leader – with '*pistolero*, evildoer, outlaw, and habitual delinquent'.[80] The violence greatly radicalized the conflict, especially once the employers, too, turned to hired guns. Counter-terror groups were initially formed under the aegis of the German adventurer and spy, the 'Baron' von Koenig, and of the erst-while Barcelona police chief, Manuel Bravo Portillo, the first victim of these groups being the boss of the Textile Workers' Union, Pablo Sabater ('The Bull'), on 19 July 1919. The violence of the employers escalated still further with the backing of the military governor, Gen-eral Severiano Martínez Anido, who not only endorsed the strategy, but even urged the civilian authorities to assassinate the anarcho-syndicalists and their republican lawyers. 'Peace will be restored,' Martínez Anido told the civil governor, 'if you order the shooting of . . . Salvador Seguí, Luis Companys [a republican lawyer], Angel Pestaña', and others, to which the civil governor retorted, 'Señor Military Governor, I am the civil governor, but I am not an assassin.'[81]

The increasing grip of the gunmen on the CNT provoked a massive haemorrhaging of workers from the movement and the formation of the *Sindicatos Libres* (Free Unions) in October 1919. Denouncing both the 'tyranny' of the employers and 'the most abject, hateful, and criminal despotism' of the CNT, the Free Unions, which claimed to have 175,000 members by July 1922, unleashed a long and bloody struggle against their former colleagues.[82] In other words, this was not just a class war between the 'bourgeoisie' and the 'proletariat', but a 'proletarian war', above all between the CNT and the Free Unions, though socialist, Catholic, and other workers fought the anarcho-syndicalists too.[83] Once Martínez Anido became the civil governor in October 1920, he pursued the 'definitive pacification' – that is, a dirty war – as the overriding goal of an alliance that comprised the employers, the juntas, the police, and the *Lliga*.[84] The Free Unions also collaborated with Martínez Anido and the employers, but the traditional image of them as mere puppets of both greatly underestimates their autonomy of action.

During Martínez Anido's two years as civil governor, the government lost control of the situation. 'I hardly talk with the government,' the general boasted to the press, 'all responsibility is mine. The government has not tried to give me instructions.'[85] High-profile victims of the gangster-style warfare included the secretary-general of the CNT, Evelio Boal, the chief CNT moderate, the gifted Salvador Seguí – a victim of 'the barbarous struggle he had tried to stop' – the Archbishop of Zaragoza, and the Conservative prime minister Eduardo Dato.[86] The violence of the CNT nonetheless declined sharply following the economic crisis of late 1920. Indeed, the slump, together with the unrelenting repression of Martínez Anido and the street warfare with the Free Unions, crippled the anarcho-syndicalist movement. By 1923 the CNT had lost two-thirds of its members.

One of the most enduring myths of these years is that the CNT was the principal victim of the sanguinary struggle, but recent research debunks this long-standing claim. Between January 1917 and the coup d'état of September 1923 there were 981 casualties of the political violence in Barcelona, of whom 267 died. Of the 558 whose political or trade-union identity is known, just over one-third were from the CNT, but two-thirds were victims *of* the CNT. Even during the offensive of Martínez Anido, the CNT suffered 140 casualties, but inflicted 160.[87] In other words, the foremost protagonist of the violence was the CNT – not the employers, the juntas, the police, or the Free Unions.

## ANUAL AND THE QUESTION OF RESPONSIBILITIES

The final death agony of the Restoration arguably began with yet another military disaster, this time at the hands of tribesmen from the Rif mountains in eastern Morocco. From the outset, Spain's colonial war in Morocco had been deeply unpopular, as shown by the anti-war uprising of 1909 in Barcelona, the so-called 'Tragic Week'. In 1914 over a fifth of those called up deserted. Popular antipathy to the war made governments reluctant to pursue the 'pacification' of the Protectorate with conviction. Accordingly, in 1919–20 the peninsular army received over three times more money from the Exchequer than the embattled army in Morocco. In a letter to the minister of war in February 1921, the High Commissioner for the Protectorate, General Dámaso Berenguer, painted a pitiful picture of the forces under his command, describing how the rifles required calibrating, the machine guns were inoperable, the handful of planes lacked munitions, the medical service was denuded of supplies, and the soldiers were often made to eat cold rations, sleep in the open, and were protected in winter by nothing more than a poncho. In the summer of 1921, General Manuel Fernández Silvestre nonetheless undertook the conquest of the eastern part of the Protectorate, which was controlled by tribes from the Rif mountains under the charismatic leadership of Abdel Krim. Urged on not only by General Berenguer, but also the king, Fernández Silvestre advanced rapidly, if not recklessly, towards the east. He established an 80-kilometre front line that lay nearly 100 kilometres from his base at Melilla, the intervening territory being dotted with 'blockhouses', or fortified positions. The vulnerability of this strategy was exposed on 22 July 1921, when the forces under Abdel Krim attacked Fernández Silvestre's position at Anual. The tribesmen, wrote an army doctor, 'came down the hills like avalanches, rose up from ravines and stream-beds', and attacked a column that was 'retreating in confusion and discord'.[88] The Spanish troops were overrun. Fernández Silvestre himself committed suicide. The blockhouses then fell one by one, the great majority of their defenders being butchered by the Rifian irregulars (in one case only 37 out of 604 men survived). The entire eastern zone except for the enclave of Melilla was now under Abdel Krim's control. Around 10,000 Spanish soldiers had been slaughtered in eighteen days. The army's mopping-up operation laid bare the savagery of the fighting. Sergeant Arturo Barea later recalled in his autobiography *The Forging of a Rebel* that:

> The marches through the sandy waste land of Melilla, the outpost of the desert, did not really matter, nor the thirst and the dirty, salty, scanty water, nor the shots and our own dead, warm and flexible, whom we could put on a stretcher and cover with a blanket; nor the wounded who groaned monotonously or screamed shrilly. All that was not important, it lost its force and proportion. But the other dead: those dead we were finding when they had lain for days under the African sun which turned fresh meat putrid within two hours; those mummified dead whose bodies had burst; those mutilated bodies, without eyes and tongues, their genitals defiled, violated with the stakes from the barbed wire, their hands tied up with their bowels, beheaded, armless, legless, sawed in two – oh those dead![89]

The unpopularity of the Moroccan war, its geographical proximity, the loss of so many lives in so few days, and the fact that the defeat echoed not only the Italians' humiliation at Adowa in 1896 (which destroyed their dreams of an Abyssinian empire), but also the 'Disaster' of 1898, ensured that the debacle had a devastating impact on Spanish public opinion. For the parliamentary spokesman of the Socialist Party, the portly and pugnacious Indalecio Prieto, Anual was the site 'where our prestige has been destroyed, where we have been subjected to the greatest and most profound humiliation and shame that Spanish history records'.[90]

A clamour now arose for the military and political 'responsibilities' of Anual to be met, for the troops to be repatriated, and for the 700 men and 400 women and children who were being held hostage by the rebels to be ransomed. 'Responsibilities' became the clarion call of 1921, just as 'regeneration' had been that of 1898 and 'renovation' that of 1917. A vociferous and morally charged campaign in favour of 'responsibilities' was launched by the socialists, republicans, and Reformists, as the traditional antimilitarism of the working class fused with the new-found anti-war sentiment of the middle class. The shift in public opinion converted the Cortes into a tribune of the people as the anti-establishment deputies laid siege to the government. The Cabinet under Antonio Maura tried to chart a middle course between the imperatives of the army – foremost amongst which was the reconquest of the lost territory – and the exigencies of public opinion. The army was temporarily appeased by the renewal of military operations in September 1921, but then infuriated by the government's refusal to bankroll an all-out war. Public opinion reached a crescendo of indignation during the winter of 1921–2 over the plight of the hostages, especially as the government was unwilling to meet the terms of Abdel Krim. Even the monarchist daily *ABC* joined the chorus of denunciation. Bereft of support and divided over the war, the Maura Cabinet resigned in March 1922. The new administration under the Conservative José Sánchez Guerra was immediately thrown on the defensive by the release in April 1922 of General Juan Picasso's Report on the defeat of Anual. Although Maura had striven to prevent Picasso from examining 'the accords, plans, and orders of the High Commissioner', the report still constituted a shocking indictment of the corruption and incompetence of the Army of Africa.[91] The socialist spokesman Indalecio Prieto claimed theatrically that such was 'the magnitude of the catastrophe' that he read the report 'crying on to the pages'.[92] Despite Sánchez Guerra's strenuous efforts to limit the impact of the Picasso Report, Berenguer resigned as High Commissioner. Unable, like Maura, to satisfy the demands of both the army and public opinion, Sánchez Guerra stood down in December 1922.

The new government under the Liberal Manuel García Prieto marked a watershed in Restoration politics due not only to the unprecedented scope of its reform programme, which ranged from religious liberty, reform of the Cortes, and the introduction of proportional representation, to a raft of social, fiscal, agrarian, and army reforms, but also to the inclusion of the non-dynastic Reformist Party. The Liberal-left coalition vowed to take civilian control of the labour conflict in Barcelona and the Moroccan Protectorate. Above all else, the García Prieto administration presented itself as the 'champion' of responsibilities, a cause which had attracted huge support, as shown by the 200,000-strong demonstration held in Madrid on 10 December 1922.[93] Initially, the coalition made promising progress. The Protectorate came under the purview of the Ministry of Foreign Affairs, which was headed by Santiago Alba, who not only appointed the first civilian High Commissioner, but also worked hand in hand with the Bilbao shipowner and republican Horacio Echevarrieta to secure the release of the remaining 326 prisoners of war (a ransom of 4.27 million pesetas being paid). Both of these civilian initiatives were considered an affront by the army, making relations between the political and military authorities tense from the outset. However, the government then backtracked on its agenda. Little of the reform programme was carried out, the issue of responsibilities was left in limbo, and the pursuit of religious toleration was abandoned once the opposition of the Church, the king, and the Catholic community was aroused. The Reformist Party's departure from the government over the religious climbdown meant that the Liberal-left coalition had collapsed after only four months in power.

In the general election of April 1923, the Liberals won 203 seats and the Conservatives 108, but the strength of anti-dynastic sentiment was shown by the fact that – despite the extensive electoral manipulation of the monarchist *caciques* – the Reformists won twenty deputies, the republicans eleven, and the socialists seven. The García Prieto administration staggered on, but the departure in May of the minister of war, Niceto Alcalá-Zamora, over the halt in military operations in Morocco and the failure to declare martial law in response to the rising violence in Barcelona, outraged the army. The government also enraged the left-wing opposition by putting off the question of responsibilities, as shown by the appointment of a parliamentary commission which would not report back to the Cortes until after the summer recess. More determined than either the Maura or Sánchez Guerra administrations to stand up to the military, the García Prieto government was nonetheless still fearful of provoking an all-out confrontation with the army.

## THE LURCH TOWARDS
## AUTHORITARIANISM

The emergence of a more militant strain of Spanish nationalism made relations between the Liberals and the army even tenser. This was a product not only of the nationalist fervour which had gripped Europe during the First World War, but also of the Catalan challenge to Spanish centralism and the escalating threat of working-class revolution. In strident contrast to the pre-war liberal nationalism, the new current was unabashedly combative, Catholic, and counter-revolutionary. Some conservative ideologues were attracted to contemporary forms of nationalism such as fascism, but most sought inspiration in the past, especially the National Catholicism of the late nineteenth century. This re-imagining of the nation was not embodied in a particular movement or party; it was sanctified by the state. In 1918 the 12 October was declared a national holiday, the *Fiesta de la Raza* (Holiday of the Race). Officially, this commemorated Columbus' 'discovery' of the Americas, but the date was also celebrated as the day when Saint James received a vision from the Virgin Mary as she sat atop a pillar, otherwise known as *el Pilar* (the Pillar). In short, 12 October became both a secular *and* a Catholic celebration, a means of merging the nation's identity with Catholicism. The ascendancy of Catholic nationalism reached a peak with the dedication of Spain to the Sacred Heart of Jesus. A massive monument to the Sacred Heart was erected south of Madrid at Cerro de los Ángeles – the geographic heart of Spain – and inaugurated on 30 May 1919 by the king himself. Dressed for the occasion in military attire and accompanied by the entire Cabinet, which gathered round an altar draped with the national flag, Alfonso XIII consecrated Spain to the Sacred Heart of Jesus. The symbolism of the ceremony was unequivocal: the Spanish nation was defined by the monarchy, the Catholic faith, and the armed forces.

The king's embrace of an ardently Catholic and counter-revolutionary nationalism reflected his belief, greatly strengthened by 'the sinister effects of the Russian Revolution', that the future of his dynasty lay not in liberal parliamentarianism, but in authoritarianism.[94] 'Parliaments are convoked and dissolved,' he bemoaned in a speech of 1921, 'without anything useful being achieved.'[95] The post-war crisis of liberalism in Europe and the fall of several dynasties, including the Romanovs, increasingly convinced him that the will of the people ultimately resided in *his* person and that the Constitution was little more than a wearisome shackle upon his dynastic calling. The final straw was the parliamentary debate over Anual, especially the claim by the outspoken socialist spokesman Indalecio Prieto that 'the Crown' bore responsibility for the military disaster.[96] No doubt the king was painfully aware that the Greek King Constantine I abdicated in 1922 following defeat at the hands of the Turks. During the summer of 1923, Alfonso XIII, having suggested to the minister of war earlier in the year that he undertake a coup d'état, defended the need for a 'transitory dictatorship', and even contemplated setting up a National Defence Junta under his own direction.[97] The Conservative politician Antonio Maura nevertheless persuaded him that the Bourbon dynasty's interests would be best served if an authoritarian solution was left to the army: if the monarchy broke with the Restoration settlement, the result would be an 'inevitable suicide'.[98]

Yet another clash over operations in Morocco brought the tensions between the Liberal government and the military to a climax. In August 1923 the Cabinet ordered the army to withdraw its exposed front line, an initiative that was welcomed by public opinion but resented by the army as an affront to its honour and a betrayal of the 'supreme and true interests of the Motherland'.[99] The stand-off was the greatest test so far of the Liberals' commitment to the supremacy of civilian rule, but the vehement opposition of the military, together with the mounting unrest in Barcelona, proved too much for the government. It not only allowed the army to renew its advance, but also mobilized another 20,000 troops for the Protectorate. The government's humiliating climbdown marked the death knell of its reform programme. Ultimately, the Liberals had been unwilling to challenge the military ascendancy established since 1917.

The uneven struggle for supremacy between the civilian and military authorities was finally resolved by the coup d'état of General Miguel Primo de Rivera on 13 September 1923. The government's ineffectual response to the small and far from secret conspiracy was a measure partly of its lack of will and partly of its isolation, as public opinion had lost faith in the Restoration system and few officers were prepared to defend it. Revealingly, García Prieto himself reacted to the coup by praising Primo de Rivera as 'a new saint' for having 'relieved me of the nightmare of governing'.[100] Even so, the great majority of the officers, including six of the eight captain-generals, did not immediately declare for Primo de Rivera, as they awaited the response of the king. In reality, the key figure in this drama was Alfonso XIII, not just because he was the commander-in-chief, but also because the supreme loyalty of most officers was to their monarch. Alfonso had judged, as already made clear during the summer, that his throne was best secured by means of a dictatorship. Accordingly, on 15 September he dissolved the Cortes and appointed Primo de Rivera as prime minister. By breaking with the Constitution of 1876, the king effectively became a hostage of the military, as his throne was likely to be at threat if the army withdrew its support. The fateful decision brought to an end nearly fifty years of constitutional government, marking a turning point in modern Spanish history. By taking the authoritarian high road, the king did not allow the constitutional regime to resolve its own problems, but placed both the Crown and the country at the mercy of the military. The coup thereby resurrected the politics of the pre-Restoration order by legitimizing the use of force as a means of regime change. This response to the post-war crisis of liberalism was nonetheless far from exceptional, as numerous European countries, including Hungary, Italy, Portugal, Poland, and Yugoslavia opted, like Spain, to reject liberal parliamentarianism in favour of right-wing authoritarianism.

Since the emergence of the juntas in 1916 there had been a constant tug of war between the civilian and the military authorities, but by the time of the Anual disaster in 1921 the dynastic politicians had become too dependent on the army to change the relationship. Even though Anual made reform 'unavoidable', the monarchist politicians were impeded by the opposition of the army and by their lack of popular support.[101] In any case, they were too protective of their own interests and too fearful of the masses to undertake meaningful change. The response of the Restoration political elites to the double-headed challenge of the military and mass politics had been hesitant and often hapless, as they continued to defend their right to rule despite their manifest incapacity to do so.

# 3

# The Dictatorship of Primo de Rivera, 1923–30

The fact that Primo de Rivera's *putsch* of 1923 provoked hope or indifference rather than outrage was indicative of the discredit into which the Restoration system had sunk. It also highlighted the despair, demoralization, and disarray of the anti-Restoration forces: the CNT was exhausted, the republicans were at a low ebb, and the socialists 'peculiarly passive'.[1] The anti-dynastic opposition was too divided to furnish a united response and too weak to provide an effective one. Neither the socialists nor the anarcho-syndicalists backed the strike organized by the Communists in Bilbao in protest at the coup, reflecting their ambiguous or antagonistic attitude towards the parliamentary regime. By contrast, the Catalan regionalists, a huge swathe of conservative opinion – the right-wing press had been calling for a dictatorship for nearly a year – and even leading liberal organs such as *El Liberal* and *El Sol* championed the coup, much as they had the juntas in 1917. As the disillusioned liberal philosopher José Ortega y Gasset wrote in *El Sol*:

> The system of equilibrium had been broken in 1917; a new one to replace it had not been created. May God grant that it now be achieved, with the coming of a Spain more noble and fertile than the old and ruinous Spain.[2]

The new regime soon dealt with the brace of forces that had in large measure brought it into being: Catalan regionalism and revolutionary anarchism. Anarcho-syndicalist violence was sharply curtailed and in May 1924 the CNT was outlawed, its leaders were arrested, newspapers closed, and activists hounded. Over the next seven years the movement hardly stirred beyond a crepuscular clandestinity. Despite the support of the Catalan regionalists for the coup, the Catalan flag was prohibited, the *Mancomunidad* (regional authority) dissolved, and use of the Catalan language increasingly restricted. But the main target of Primo de Rivera's ire was the liberal parliamentary regime of the Restoration, the coup being justified in terms of 'the clamorous call of all those who, loving the Motherland, do not see any other salvation for her but to free her from the professionals of politics, who, for one reason or another, present us with a panorama of misfortunes and immoralities that began in the year 1898 and threaten Spain with an imminent, tragic, and dishonourable end'.[3] The two monarchist parties were banned, the Cortes closed down, constitutional rights suspended, and a system of strict censorship implemented. Government was now embodied in a Military Directorate, with the army occupying all the civil governorships.

## A FASCIST REGIME?

The visit of Primo de Rivera and the king to Mussolini's Italy in November 1923 indicated that fascism might become the template for the nascent regime, not least because Alfonso XIII regarded the general as 'my Mussolini', while expressing approval of Italy's 'wise and virile form of government'.[4] Primo de Rivera found much to admire in the Italian dictatorship, being fond of drawing parallels between the two regimes: both were a reaction to the Bolshevik Revolution, both aimed to replace the 'old' state with a 'new' one, and both viewed the 'new state' as highly centralized and corporativist, that is, one in which society is organized by means of corporate groups that are subordinate to the state.[5] Many of the panegyrists of the dictatorship, such as Ramiro de Maeztu, José Pemartín, and José María Pemán, looked to fascism for inspiration. They were convinced that it would invert the centuries-old inferiority of Southern Europe in relation to the north. 'The pachydermic peoples of the north,' cried Pemartín, 'can only contemplate, once again, with their vitreous and lymphatic eyes the triumph' of the south, as shown by 'the revival of art, science, action, politics, and life of the eternal Mediterranean civilization'.[6] Certainly there were borrowings from Italian fascism: the *Organización Corporativa Nacional* or OCN

(National Corporative Organization) that pursued the fascist dream of superseding the struggle between capital and labour; a much more active economic role for the state, including the establishment of monopolies such as the telephone company *Telefónica*, the petroleum company CAMPSA, and the national airline *Iberia*; and the creation of a single, official party, the *Unión Patriótica* or UP (Political Union). Nonetheless, these similarities were often limited: the workers who participated in the National Corporative Organization were not fascists but mainly from the socialist UGT, who, in contrast to Italian workers, retained the right to strike; state intervention in the economy and state-manufactured monopolies did not distinguish fascism alone; and the Patriotic Union was not made up of fascists, but authoritarian Catholics and the followers of the Conservative politician Antonio Maura, or *mauristas*. Nor did the Patriotic Union brandish a fascist ideology, as indicated by the fact that its motto, 'Motherland, Religion, Monarchy', was a reworking of the Carlist slogan. The diffuse doctrine of the Patriotic Union aimed to appeal, as the regime's future minister of finance José Calvo Sotelo noted, to 'a wide variety of people who held disparate, albeit basically right-wing, ideologies', while the party's meetings and other activities were propaganda exercises designed to mollify the masses rather than mobilize them fascist-style.[7] Even more importantly, the *primoverista* state was neither secular nor totalitarian, the Catholic Church being a revered ally, not an adversary, its spiritual and moral teachings being enthusiastically endorsed by the Military Directorate. Indeed, the new regime drew far more on the fervently Catholic and counter-revolutionary nationalism of the war and post-war years than fascism.

The new regime was powerfully inspired by the post-1898 rhetoric of regeneration, Primo invoking the reformer Joaquín Costa's most authoritarian solution to Spain's modernizing ills, that of the 'iron surgeon' who would forge a new Spain.[8] Still, as Primo made plain, the 'theoretical generator' and 'guiding spirit' of his regime was Antonio Maura and his 'revolution from above'.[9] Indeed, the dictatorship can be seen as a redoubtable reconfiguration of the authoritarian tendencies that had sprung up in the aftermath of 1898 and had sprouted exponentially during and after the First World War. But the Primo regime marked a new departure for the extreme right, and in certain ways anticipated both the fascist Falange of the 1930s (a party headed, appropriately enough, by Primo's son, José Antonio) and the Franco dictatorship, especially during its early years. Many of the key ideological and doctrinal tenets of the two movements were to be found in 'Primoriverism': the rejection of liberalism and parliamentarianism, along with the intellectual rationale for the demonization and destruction of democracy; the myth of the Communist peril, Primo and Franco alike justifying their uprisings against constitutional regimes on the grounds of an 'imminent' Communist coup; the permanent and self-serving threat of a 'Masonic-Soviet' plot, or, in the case of Franco, the 'Judeo-Masonic-Communist' one; and the exclusionary idea of the 'Anti-Spain', of which the 'internal' enemy was a core element. Primo also reacted against the concept of the 'party', which, like Franco, he associated with liberalism, preferring to call the Patriotic Union an 'anti-party'. Furthermore, Primo regarded the middle classes, just as Franco did later, as the bedrock of his regime, idealizing them as 'a highly stable social element in their family life, in their dedication to work, and in their romantic faith in the future and prestige of the Motherland'.[10] More than two decades before Franco, Primo even presented himself as a 'sentinel of the West', a principled defender of Christian civilization against the pagan 'oriental despotism' of Bolshevism.[11]

He was backed by the king, who similarly insisted that parliamentary liberalism was unequal to the task of defending 'the actual order of things against the Soviet idea'.[12] And Primo's Patriotic Union or 'anti-party' represented an abrupt breach with the Restoration parliamentary right, as shown by its meetings, parades, and ideology. In contrast to the Restoration right, it was a 'national movement', which not only rejected regionalist sentiment such as Catalanism, but also aimed to reduce the monarchy to a secondary, even purely ceremonial, role.[13] For the Patriotic Union, the supreme figure was not Alfonso XIII but Primo de Rivera, the father of the nation, whose unremitting exertions were designed to liberate the people from the strife of politics. 'People of Spain, your president is vigilant while you are asleep,' as one publication put it.[14] Like so many other features of the dictatorship, the Primo de Rivera personality cult was later an inspiration to Franco. In sum, the regime of Primo de Rivera was not fascist, but it did constitute a new and radical departure for the Spanish right.

## NATIONALIZING THE MASSES

One of the most novel features of the dictatorship was that it made the most serious and sustained effort so far to nationalize the Spanish masses. National symbols were emblazoned on public buildings, the only flag permitted was the Spanish one, and civil servants were made to work in Spanish alone, not Basque, Catalan, or any other regional language. In the discourse of the dictatorship, the motherland – rather than the monarchy or Catholicism – was the key identifying element, that is, sovereignty was considered to reside above all in the nation, which in Primo's thinking was embodied in the state as its permanent representative organ. Thus the single party was called the Patriotic Union, as opposed to the Monarchist or Catholic Union, while the official newspaper was titled *La Nación* (The Nation). Heritage sites were now dubbed 'national' monuments and the thousands of schools constructed under the dictator were 'national' centres of learning where the pupils were instructed in the 'national' language and inculcated with the 'national' glories. In everyday life, nationalist imagery proliferated as never before, adorning stamps, banknotes, sweet papers, almanacs, and so on. The exalted *españolismo* (Spanish spirit) of the dictatorship was reflected in the high-profile *Fiesta de la Raza* (Festival of the Race) each year and in the international exhibitions held in Barcelona and Seville in 1929, both of which were centred upon a *Plaza de España* (Spanish Square). In striking contrast to the old liberal vision, this resurgent nationalism was not self-pitying and angst-ridden, but proud, populist, and triumphalist.

The new brand of nationalism also reimagined the relationship with South America by virtue of 'Hispanism', according to which Spain, the 'mother country', was the spiritual and cultural leader of the so-called 'Hispanic race'. This commonwealth of the Spanish-speaking peoples was first given expression by the king in a speech before the Vatican in November 1923 in which he exalted Spain's role 'in discovering the New World and creating twenty nations on the American continent'.[15] Hispanism was greatly boosted three years later when the four airmen of the *Plus Ultra*, which included the younger brother of Francisco Franco, Ramón, crossed the Atlantic

Ocean the year before Charles Lindbergh. Hailed as a heroic example of 'Iberian vitality', the feat implicitly echoed Columbus' achievement of over 400 years earlier. A further triumph for the cause of Hispanism was the Ibero-American Exhibition of 1929 in Seville, which was at once a celebration of Spanish and Hispanic identity.

Integral to this vigorous new nationalism was Catholicism. The mutual fervour that distinguished the relationship between the dictatorship and the Church anticipated the later alliance between the Church and state under Franco. The tone was set by the king, who, in his ultramontane address before the Vatican in November 1923, portrayed Spain as the 'soldier of Religion, that of the unfailing defender of the Catholic Church', prepared even to undertake a new crusade.[16] The spirit of rational inquiry was rejected by the Primo de Rivera regime for the moral and religious certainties of Catholicism, as shown by a decree of February 1924 calling for the dismissal of any teacher who imparted doctrines 'offensive towards religion'.[17] The Church reciprocated wholeheartedly, lauding Primo – as it later did Franco – as 'the saviour of the Motherland' and as 'the illustrious Caudillo [leader] of our Spain'.[18] No wonder that the Church thrived under the dictatorship, the number of religious communities soaring by nearly 400, the Catholic orders amassing over 900 professional and other colleges, while Catholic associations of a different type also prospered, such as the landowners' Confederación Nacional Católico-Agraria or CNCA (National Catholic-Agrarian Confederation), which claimed over 600,000 members in the 1920s.

Catholicism also inspired the regime to involve women in politics. At the outset of the Restoration, the ultra-conservative Carlist movement had included the female ballot in its programme. Much later, in 1919, the Conservative minister Manuel Burgos y Mazo drew up a bill which granted the vote to all women aged twenty-three and over, but the government fell before the proposal could be discussed in the Cortes. The overriding motive for the bill was to act as a counter-revolutionary measure by offsetting the influence of socialism on women. Under Primo, the Municipal Statute Law of March 1924, drawn up by the ambitious young ex-maurista, the Galician lawyer José Calvo Sotelo, enfranchised women over twenty-two who were either economically independent and single or else widows. Like the Burgos y Mazo bill, this was designed to counteract the advance of socialism and other revolutionary currents. As the Statute was never applied, Primo proceeded to designate at least seven mayoresses and seventy-eight women councillors (the figures are incomplete), six of whom served on the Madrid city council.[19] Even so, the women were generally appointed to insignificant localities and always dealt with public hygiene, education, and health, domains that conformed to the profoundly conservative ideal of Catholic womanhood.

## INTEGRATING THE WORKERS

Catholic corporatism, which drew heavily on the papal encyclical *Rerum Novarum* of 1891, was central to Primo de Rivera's social doctrine. The dictator defended a 'just society' based on a 'Christian' balance between rich and poor and on 'a harmonious association between Capital and Labour' that would make revolution unnecessary.[20] Clearly the 'new state' was the ideal instrument for this feat of social engineering, Primo explaining to the head of the International Labour Office that only 'a democratic dictatorship such as the one that presently rules Spain ... can reorganize the social and economic life of the country without the class bias'.[21] An additional motive was that the working class, 'the most important sector in the life of the country', was essential to his plans for its 'transformation and aggrandizement'.[22] Primo was nevertheless quick to distinguish between the 'bad' workers, such as the anarcho-syndicalists and the Communists, and the 'good' ones, such as the Catholics and socialists.[23] In particular, the dictator aimed to integrate or 'nationalize' the socialist UGT, but only so long as it kept to trade unionism, renouncing the political struggle. The socialist movement itself was split over collaborationism, party leaders Indalecio Prieto and Fernando de los Ríos protesting vigorously at Francisco Largo Caballero's acceptance of a position on the regime's Council of State in October 1924. The critics of collaborationism were nonetheless routed at a meeting of the Socialist Party's Executive Committee on 10 December 1924 by fourteen votes to five, the National Committee declaring that Largo Caballero's decision had been 'absolutely correct and as scrupulous as is the norm in such a beloved companion'.[24] In protest, Prieto resigned from the Executive Committee.

The UGT joined the dictatorship's National Corporative Organization, whose linchpin was the *comités paritarios* (arbitration committees) founded in November 1926, which negotiated working conditions and disputes. Each committee was made up of an equal number of workers and employers, the swing vote lying with the chair, a state appointee, who usually sided with the workers. Nationwide, 652 arbitration committees were set up, involving 320,000 workers and 100,000 employers, the network allowing the UGT to extend and consolidate its presence at the expense of its arch-rival, the now illegal CNT, in places like Andalusia and Castile-La Mancha. Socialist expansion under the dictatorship also benefited, though to a far lesser extent, from the ban on the Communist Party, which only had 500 militants nationwide in 1925. In contrast, the UGT boasted a record 235,000 members by 1928. Socialist involvement in the regime was not limited to the arbitration committees alone. Socialists also participated in local government, in the provincial administration, and in national economic and social planning councils, such as the Council of National Economy and the Comptroller Council of Accounts, while Largo Caballero, the chief architect of collaborationism, joined the Council of State. Its unholy alliance with Primo not only converted the UGT into the largest working-class organization in Spain, but also furnished it with a 'clear juridical personality', for which the trade union, insisted one socialist leader, should 'praise the Dictatorship'.[25] This essay in state participation was to strongly shape the movement's trajectory under the Second Republic of the 1930s, as it expected not only to govern at the national level, but also to benefit from the spoils of power.

The incorporation of the socialists into the dictatorship was based on the traditional corporative principles of social-Catholicism – not those of fascism, the social doctrine of which was still in its early stages – which had been modernized by Pope Leo XIII (r. 1878–1903) and the *Partito Popolare* (Popular Party) in Italy. One of the key tenets of social-Catholicism was the autonomy of the unions, something which was out of the question for fascism, Mussolini replacing all the independent unions with state-controlled syndicates. Undoubtedly the collaboration of the UGT with the dictatorship was facilitated not only by its corporativist outlook, but also by a corresponding disregard for the values of 'bourgeois' democracy. The fact that the socialists were able to form a purely circumstantial alliance with the dictatorship was arguably a major mistake by Primo: had the regime established state syndicates it might have secured greater support from – or at least control over – the workers.

The one area which was off bounds to the arbitration committees was agriculture. The quest for a 'just society' and 'a harmonious association between Capital and Labour' did not, it seems, apply to the biggest sector of the economy. Intense lobbying by landowners' associations, such as the National Catholic-Agrarian Confederation, which denounced the arbitration committees as a socialist Trojan horse, led Primo – who, in any case, shared many of their prejudices – to ignore the landless labourers. Thousands of rural farmworkers left the UGT as a result. Nor did the regime help the tenant farmers, this also being due, one association claimed, to 'the pressure of the big landowners who were being protected by the Dictatorship'.[26] Small and medium-sized landowners cried out for greater credit facilities, but the response of the regime was disappointing. In terms of the rural economy as a whole, little was done to improve productivity, with the exception of hydraulic schemes. The regime's much-vaunted vision of a 'rural awakening' was simply not matched by its policies.[27]

## CACIQUISMO REBORN

Indeed, the rousing rhetoric of the dictatorship was often at odds with reality. A prime target of Primo's wrath was *caciquismo*, symbolic of everything that was ruinous about the Restoration. A start was made with an all-out assault on the stronghold of the *cacique*, local government, with all 9,254 local councils being summarily replaced on 1 April 1924. However, the new councils were made up overwhelmingly of members of the Patriotic Union, *La Nación* later admitting that 'only in very few cases ... can people exercise public functions who are not members of the Patriotic Union'.[28] Small wonder that by 1927 the party boasted as many as 1.7 million members. In the northwestern region of Galicia, the rural provinces of the centre and south, and the Canary Islands, the Patriotic Union tended to be run – ironically – by former Conservative and Liberal *caciques*, now fully paid-up members of the Patriotic Union. In Primo's home province of Cádiz, to take just one example, the first Patriotic Union chief was the ex-*maurista* Luciano Bueno. Thus the *caciquismo* of the monarchist parties was replaced to a considerable extent by that of the Patriotic Union. *Caciquismo* was also to be extirpated by means of 1,400 'governmental delegates', army officers who not only had to oversee the change in local government, but also to ensure that the anti-*cacique* campaign was a success. The delegates interfered constantly in local life, building up their own networks of influence in the process. As Calvo Sotelo observed, many established a 'domain that they governed at their whim'.[29] Like the Patriotic Union, the governmental delegates did not so much destroy *caciquismo*, as reshape it to their own ends. His rhetoric notwithstanding, Primo acted as a Restoration *cacique* writ large, distributing favours, jobs and other perks and privileges on a huge scale amongst his friends, relatives and cronies.

Primo also lambasted multi-employment (*empleocracia*) and patronage/clientelism (*enchufismo*) in the public sector, but his huge expansion of the central bureaucracy, which included scores of new regulatory bodies, increased rather than decreased such practices, as reported on regularly by the press: one public employee, for example, held as many as eighteen different posts. As the Supreme Court of the Treasury noted in 1928, there were also a 'growing number of expense accounts, compensations, gratuities and other kinds of emoluments which, without really having the character of a salary, are being received by officials, both civilian and military'.[30]

The regime displayed an utter contempt for the law, despite's Primo's promise to re-establish 'the independence of the judiciary', appointing judges in an arbitrary fashion and banishing critics of the regime with no consideration for the law.[31] The influential academic and writer Miguel de Unamuno, who dubbed the dictatorship a 'regime of illegal fines', was exiled to the Canary Islands for a private letter in which he censured Primo for intervening in a court case on behalf of a prostitute.[32] Even more bizarrely, the Marquis of Cortina was banished for expressing his disapproval of a shipping tax in the far from sensationalist publication *Actualidad Financiera* (Finance Today). It seems that the dictatorship revelled in its arbitrariness: a decree of May 1926 empowered the government to adopt exceptional measures even if they were 'incompatible with the law', while another of October 1926 permitted it to ignore the judgments of the supreme court.[33] At heart, the regime regarded the rule of law as an impediment and an irritant. 'A dictatorship ought never,' as Primo candidly put it, 'to be accountable for breaches of the law: this would contradict its very essence.'[34]

## THE 'PACIFICATION' OF MOROCCO

General Primo de Rivera's popularity reached its zenith with the pacification of the Moroccan Protectorate. Not for nothing was the General granted in 1925 the prestigious Grand Award of Saint Fernando and the Grand Cross of Naval Merit, the citation claiming in the overblown rhetoric of the regime that 'every difficulty has been overcome by the iron will, the serene courage, the prodigious intelligence, the insuperable military competence of General Primo de Rivera', who had managed to succeed in 'the most arduous enterprise ever carried out by a colonial army'.[35] Spanish imperialism in northern Africa was not motivated by material gain – no major economic group lobbied the government for a more vigorous colonial policy – but a question of national pride, international recognition, and Social Darwinian self-esteem. As the king explained in an interview:

> To abandon the fight would be tantamount to the suicide of the white race, it would mark the beginning of the expulsion of the white man from North Africa, a severe blow to western civilization, that would certainly have repercussions in all other colonies … Spain cannot afford to be the first to fold the flag of the white race in Africa.[36]

Nonetheless, Primo's initial purpose in Morocco was to seek negotiations with the insurgents, just like the discredited civilian governments before him, but during a visit to the Protectorate in the summer of 1924 his abandonist tendencies were given a galvanic jolt. At a banquet offered by the Legion, Lieutenant Colonel Francisco Franco toasted the dictator with the words, 'as we want the honour of Spain to come before the convenience of the government, the Legion awaits your words with anxiety and concern.'[37] In other words, a 'dishonourable' or defeatist policy might place Primo's regime in jeopardy. By September 1924, he appeared to have come to terms with the *africanista* line, declaring resoundingly that 'there is no other way in Morocco than to fight until the enemy is defeated ... otherwise, as a race we should be losing our virility, and as an army our prestige.'[38] However, the calamitous retreat of the army from its forward positions in the west in late 1924, which included the loss of over 180 posts and up to 15,000 casualties, led Primo once again to entertain ideas of abandonment. The Spanish were saved from further humiliation by the proposal of the French, whose territory was now under attack from Abdel Krim (43 of their 66 frontline posts had been lost in three months at a cost of 2,000 casualties), to undertake a joint operation in order to quash the rebels of the Rif. A Franco-Spanish force, involving the first combined air and navy operation in history, landed at Al Hoceima Bay on 5 September 1925. This force eventually defeated Abdel Krim in August 1926. 'We can and should be proud,' proclaimed an exultant Primo, 'of being a sublime race, a vigorous people, a well-organized and well-governed

The dictator Miguel Primo de Rivera at Alhucemas.
To his left is José Sanjurjo and to his right a youthful Francisco Franco

nation.'[39] The General Order of 10 July 1927, which brought the war to an official end, declared portentously that the nation 'prodigally, has shed its blood and its moral energies to maintain the legacy of pride and valour left us by our ancestors, the conquerors of the world'.[40] The dictator had achieved something which no government since 1909 had done: the pacification, with honour, of the Protectorate. The ghost of Anual had finally been laid to rest.

The triumph in the Protectorate encouraged Primo to undertake an ambitious foreign policy that was designed to resurrect Spain's status as a world power. His first goal was to incorporate the international city of Tangiers into the Spanish Protectorate. The second was to acquire a permanent seat for Spain on the Security Council of the League of Nations. 'Spain, glorious Spain,' exclaimed Primo in a typically florid outburst, 'the mother of one hundred nations, cannot afford to sit in the gallery of the world theatre, not even in the stalls. She needs to have a seat in the box.'[41] In both cases, the dictator gravely overestimated Spain's real power and influence. Neither a Franco-Spanish conference of February 1927 nor a conference comprising Spain, Britain, France and Italy in March 1928 secured Tangiers for the Spanish. Primo's plea for a Security Council seat on account of Spain's 'history, its size, the number of its inhabitants . . . and because of the race that it represents', along with his claim to speak in the name of Spain's South American 'daughters', fell on deaf ears, prompting him to abandon the League of Nations altogether in September 1926.[42] In early 1928, Spain returned shamefacedly to the League, Primo's quest for greater international recognition having been a complete failure.

The rapturous reception that greeted the pacification of Morocco also emboldened Primo to substitute the Military Directorate with a Civilian one in December 1925; to cast aside, in other words, the provisional solution of an impromptu army administration for the permanent one of a new regime. 'After a century of misgovernment,' the dictator explained to one newspaper, 'we need at least half a century of strong government.'[43] He was aiming, in other words, to replace the Constitution of 1876 with one of his own. His concern was not just to secure the legitimacy of his regime, but also to establish a position for himself that was independent of the king. He had already sought to consolidate his own standing through the creation of the Patriotic Union, through the extension of the *Somatén* – a Catalan middle-and upper-class militia force – to the entire country, and through his nationwide propaganda tours. He now took a further step by organizing a (rigged) national plebiscite in September 1926 which sanctioned his decision to set up a National

Assembly. However, the king, wary of any potential threat to his own constitution, did not sign the decree convening the National Assembly until September 1927. The principal task of the new body was, as Primo made clear, 'a new constitutional structure for the country', which would mark the foundation of a 'new Spain' by overthrowing 'a legal tyranny, more fallacious and cruel than any recorded by history'.[44] Personally, he believed that sovereignty should reside not in the people but in the state, that the army should not be subordinate to any other body (including the monarchy, nation, or people), and that 'all the activities of national life should be organized along corporatist lines.'[45] Most tellingly of all, he made no comment on the future role of the monarch.

## ECONOMIC REGENERATION

Primo was as anti-liberal in the economic sphere as he was in the political, defending the virtues of corporativism and interventionism against 'ruinous competition'.[46] He took the economic nationalism pursued since the 1890s to new heights by exalting a policy dubbed by the Catalan daily *La Vanguardia* as a 'Spanish-Monroe doctrine – Spain for the Spaniards' and by converting the state into a major interventionist force for the very first time.[47] The aim of Primo's 'economic independence' or self-sufficiency was embodied in the regime's ferocious protectionism, its tariffs being the second highest in Europe after the Soviet Union, a typical slogan exhorting Spaniards to 'Write on Spanish paper with Spanish ink!'[48] Interventionism was resolutely championed by Primo on the grounds that 'in the economic sphere, the government, with all its organs and advisory bodies, is the board of directors of the nation, and it should never allow either ravings or ambitions and egoism to impose themselves. Rather, it should see to it that everybody marches according to the rules.'[49]

Big business was the priority of the new state. First, a number of major industries were created; in 1927, the airline *Iberia*, the petroleum company CAMPSA, and the telephone company *Telefónica*, were all founded. Second, substantial concessions and subsidies were granted to existing companies, such as the airline company *Loring*, which obtained a monopoly on air transportation within Spain, and the Hispano-Portuguese Society for Electric Traction, which, along with the Portuguese government, cornered the concession for the exploitation of the falls on the Duero river. The most polemical concession of all was that concerning the monopoly on the tobacco trade in Morocco, which was granted to the infamous smuggler from Mallorca, Juan March, which was justified by Primo on the grounds of the Mallorcan's 'patriotic and charitable endeavours'.[50] Such a closed system of state subsidies and concessions was a veritable breeding ground for favouritism and corruption. Small wonder that the president of *Loring* was Primo's personal friend, General José Sanjurjo, that the president of the Hispano-Portuguese Society for Electric Traction was Horacio Echevarrieta (who had secured the release of hundreds of Rifian hostages), or that two figures connected to *Telefónica*, Count Güell and the Marquis of Comillas, were key allies of Primo in Catalonia. Just about every monopoly, noted *El Financiero*, involved 'an abuse of expenses, gratuities and an accumulation of posts and salaries'.[51] The dictatorship's lack of accountability and transparency did much to foster a symbiotic relationship between big business and the state that was characterized by patronage, paybacks, and other forms of corruption.

A central pillar of Joaquín Costa's Regenerationist vision had been a far-ranging programme of public works, especially the construction of roads, reservoirs, and schools. The extraordinary budget of July 1926 of 3,539 million pesetas was designed to do just that, financing public works and other state ventures for the following ten years. This was welcomed not just by industrialists and bankers, eager to invest the capital which they had accumulated since 1914, but also by the socialists, who saw the chance both to generate employment and to extend their reach amongst the workers. A total of 9,455 kilometres of road were built, including the first *nacional* or trunk roads, while the entire railway network was upgraded at a cost of 1,300 million pesetas, the volume of freightage increasing by 38 per cent between 1923 and 1928. Greater exploitation of the country's water resources, by companies such as the Hispano-Portuguese Society for Electric Traction, extended electrification and the land available for irrigation. However, the only major success of the Hydraulic Confederations set up in 1926 was in Costa's home region, Aragón, where irrigation systems were installed for over 70,000 hectares of land, while the existing systems in another 109,000 hectares were improved. The dictatorship also invested heavily in the construction of public buildings, above all schools, of which 8,000 were completed.

The financing of public works was achieved not only by means of the extraordinary budget of 1926, but also by making the tax system more extractive. For Primo, there had to be an 'egalitarian tax system which some might call democratic and others even Bolshevik'.[52] The problem, finance minister José Calvo Sotelo noted, was that 'tax evasion is a plant to be found in all areas of Spanish life.'[53] Calvo Sotelo aimed to introduce a progressive income tax, to tax luxury goods heavily, and to launch a vigorous campaign against tax evasion, which 'flourishes in the four cardinal points of the peninsula'.[54] Not all of this proved possible, but at least the revenue from direct taxation, the burden of which fell largely on the middle classes, rose 49 per cent and that from indirect taxation 44 per cent.

Economic growth under the dictatorship averaged an impressive 5.5 per cent per annum, the result not just of the favourable international context, but also of the state's highly interventionist policies. Virtually all areas of industry and commerce prospered under the regime. Productivity in industry and the mines grew by 38 per cent, the output of electrical energy rose by 120 per cent, the profits of the insurance companies soared 166 per cent in just five years (as opposed to a return of 36 per cent during the ten years prior to the dictatorship), and the number of savings banks increased by a third in order to accommodate 1.5 million new savers. By contrast, agricultural productivity, which enjoyed little public investment and underwent no major technological change, remained a hostage to the vagaries of the climate. From a base of 114.5 in 1923, agricultural productivity fluctuated constantly over the next five years, reaching a high of 127.1 in 1927 and a low of 89.8 in 1928.

## SOCIAL AND CULTURAL CHANGE

The spectacular overall growth of the national economy in the 1920s brought far-reaching social change. Under Primo, Spain was transformed from a predominantly agrarian workforce to one that was based mainly on the industrial and service sectors. During the 1920s the proportion of the active population that worked in agriculture plummeted from 57.3 per cent to 45.5 per cent, while those employed in industry increased from 21.9 per cent to 26.5 per cent and those in the service sector rose from 20.8 per cent to 27.98 per cent, thereby expanding enormously both the urban working and middle classes. The boom explains in large measure why these were years, in *El Socialista*'s words, of 'social peace'.[55] The general stability of urban working-class wages was a major factor, though there were marked differences between the skilled and unskilled, between one industry and another, and between one region and another, the more industrialized areas such as Asturias, the Basque Country and Catalonia generally doing better than others. The relatively steady wages, the impact of the arbitration committees, and the involvement of socialist workers in the central, provincial, and local administration – together with the repression of the anarcho-syndicalist and Communist movements – explains why the 952 strikes of 1922–23 gave way to just 636 stoppages between 1924 and 1928, though it should be noted that 'political' strikes were banned under the dictatorship.

Social change was also a direct outcome of the dictatorship's reforms. Expenditure on education rose by 58 per cent between 1920 and 1929, as 8,000 primary schools were built and attendance at school increased by 22.9 per cent. Starting from a low threshold, the regime spent 98 per cent more on social benefits and 200 per cent more on the health services, while encouraging private charities to expand their activities. Not surprisingly, the death rate dropped from 23.5/1,000 in the 1910s to 19/1,000 in the 1920s, while the birth rate, which stood at 34.5/1,000 in the 1900s, fell during the 1920s to around the European average at 29.2/1000. Similarly, the investment in education was reflected in the biggest drop in illiteracy – 8.7 per cent for men and 9.15 per cent for women – before the 1960s. Finally, over 260 million pesetas was invested in cheap housing, which, while falling way short of the regime's promise of 'a house for every Spaniard', represented a huge improvement on the eight million pesetas spent between 1913 and 1923.

A hallmark of the age was increasing urbanization, a result of the shift from an agricultural to an industrial and service-based economy. In the 1920s, towns of over 10,000 grew by over 2 million people, while the population of the provincial capitals rose by nearly a third.

During the same years, Madrid acquired many of the features of a 'modern' city, as reflected in the opening of an underground system, the construction of the New York-style avenue of the *Gran Via*, the erection of striking art deco edifices such as the *Círculo de Bellas Artes* (Fine Arts Centre), and the start of work on the Barajas airport in 1929. Urbanization transformed leisure into a mass industry. Under Primo, radio broadcasting was launched, its fare of music, talks, plays and comment soon becoming a feature of Spaniards' daily life. An increasingly popular form of entertainment in the 1920s was film, the number of cinemas more than doubling between 1914 and 1929, while any city or town worth its salt boasted a 'Monumental' cinema. The hysteria that greeted the visit to Spain of Douglas Fairbanks and Mary Pickford in 1924 was indicative not only of Hollywood's popularity, but also of the creeping Americanization of Spanish culture. The very first form of mass entertainment in Spain was bullfighting, which enjoyed something of a golden age in the 1910s. The following decade, its popularity remained high, the charismatic figure of Juan Belmonte transforming the appeal of *la corrida* (the bullfight) not only with his novel skills, but also his intellectual interests, which helped attract the educated middle classes. The 1920s, as in many other European countries, also saw the development of sport as mass leisure. Football quickly established itself as the sporting spectacle par excellence, large stadia being built in Barcelona in 1922 and in Madrid in 1924, followed by the launch of the professional Football League in 1928. By the late 1920s, boxing and cycling had also caught the public's eye, Paulino Uzcudun's victory over the German Max Schmeling for the heavyweight title of Europe in 1926 being a national event. Clearly the emergence of different professional sports reflected on the new-found urban quest for 'modern' leisure pursuits.

Gender relations were also altered by urbanization within certain class limits. The burgeoning presence of women within the workforce, the decrease in fertility rates, and the impact of foreign modes and mores, produced, at least within sectors of the middle and upper urban classes, a new kind of woman, one whose greater independence and boldness were reflected in the driving of a car, smoking in public, or presence at dance halls and bars without a chaperone. The *Felices Veinte* or Roaring Twenties were a time of great cultural change,

Female workers at an Ericsson factory near Madrid

too, as illustrated by the Iberian Artists' Exhibition of 1925 or the emergence of the so-called 'Generation of '27', which included such path-breaking talents as the poet and playwright Federico García Lorca, the poet Rafael Alberti, and the painter Salvador Dalí. Despite its own deeply traditional social and cultural values, the Primo de Rivera dictatorship oversaw the emergence of a 'new Spain', one that was increasingly urban, hedonistic, and individualistic.

Throughout these years Primo remained a generally popular figure, his appeal resting on his bluster, bonhomie and reputation as a bon-vivant, together with his boundless showmanship, and, above all, his seemingly artless candour, all of which made him highly personable and approachable, in stark contrast to the often aloof and elitist monarchist politicians. Army sergeant Arturo Barea came across the dictator at an Andalusian *bodega* in central Madrid 'lolling in a wicker armchair', accompanied by 'a dark, gypsy-like woman'.[56]

## THE DECLINE AND FALL OF PRIMO DE RIVERA

By 1929, however, Primo had lost the goodwill of huge swathes of Spanish society. Small-scale industry and commerce, along with the agricultural export sector, were alienated by the high tariffs which protected big business and the monopolies. The president of the Chambers of Commerce and Navigation in Valencia lambasted protectionism for aiding 'in an excessive and unjust way the powerful interests that have been monopolizing our economy for a long time' and for causing 'the ruin of our international commerce'.[57] These very same sectors were also estranged by the laws that favoured the large corporations, a deputy at the National Assembly criticizing one such measure as benefiting only 'those who have the right relations, power, means, contact with the authorities'.[58] On the other hand, the entire business community was antagonized by the dictatorship's labour policy, especially the arbitration committees, partly because of their expense and partly because they were skewed in favour of the workers. Despite the committees being denounced as 'a state within the state', the minister of labour, Eduardo Aunós, refused to axe them, on account of their 'labour of pacification', pointing out that the strike level in 1928 was the lowest since 1905.[59]

Also disillusioned by the dictatorship were the professional classes: the teachers by their pitiable salaries and by the burgeoning presence of the Church within the schools; the engineers by the likelihood of a major slump in public works; and the lawyers by the regime's 'hatred for the law'.[60] Nor was much support forthcoming from the intellectuals, which was hardly surprising given Primo's long-standing scorn for them ('I feel a mixture of pity and contempt for these gentlemen'), even those, such as the high-profile philosopher José Ortega y Gasset, who had abetted the regime by praising the virtues of a robust executive and a weak parliament.[61] Amongst Primo's most fervent supporters in September 1923 was the Catalan bourgeoisie, but by 1929 relations between them had greatly soured. Though gratified by the sky-high tariffs and the vertiginous fall in worker conflict – there were a mere three deaths from labour clashes between 1923 and 1928 – by 1929 Catalan big business was nonetheless mightily aggrieved by the regime's labour policy, by its anti-regionalism, and by the exchange rate, which hit textile exports hard. Indeed, the Catalan leader Francesc Cambó now declared that the best solution to the political situation was the establishment of a democracy.

More seriously still, Primo had lost the allegiance of the army. The key issue, as during the pre-dictatorial years, was the question of promotions. By siding in 1924 with the *africanistas* in defending promotion by merit, Primo dismayed many peninsular soldiers. The order of June 1926 making promotion by merit obligatory, together with a severe reduction in the size of the army (it had shrunk by nearly a third by 1930), and the outright favouritism which – ironically – distinguished new promotions, made the situation far worse, as reflected in the military support for the *Sanjuanada* uprising of 1926 (which resurrected the nineteenth-century alliance between the army and the liberals) and a revolt planned for September 1927 (which resulted in the arrest of 200 officers). Worst of all, the imposition of merit-based promotions led the prestigious Artillery Corps, which had abided by a system of promotion by seniority since 1891, to confront the regime, most notably in the attempted coup d'état of July 1928 and the rebellion of the former Conservative premier José Sánchez Guerra in January 1929 (the artillery officers involved were viewed by Primo as 'buds of Bolshevism').[62] The drastic decision to disband the Artillery Corps in February 1929 did immense harm to Primo's standing not only within the army, but also with the king.

The sweeping loss of confidence in the regime among the business community, the professional classes, the intellectuals, the Catalan regionalists, and the army explains why a relatively minor issue such as the student protest at a decree permitting the establishment of two private Catholic universities – thereby ending the public monopoly on higher education – did so much damage to the reputation of the dictatorship. Primo's decision to suspend the decree in September 1929 only made matters worse, as the students sensed his vulnerability. Their riots and demonstrations throughout the winter of 1929–30, which also drew on the persecution of liberal academics and the closure of the Central University in Madrid, would form the agitated backdrop to Primo's rule until the very day of his resignation. Meanwhile, more and more sectors of Spanish society were turning to republicanism, not so much out of ideological affinity but as a channel for their economic and social grievances. Even some conservatives, including a number of generals, reckoned that a republic of order, along the lines of the Third Republic in France, might be preferable to the stumblings of the dictatorship-cum-monarchy. The political malaise and plummeting public confidence precipitated a currency crisis in 1928 that became ever worse in 1929, the peseta dropping from 31.16 to the pound sterling in February 1929 to 34.3 in June before sinking to 40 in January 1930. 'The fall in the peseta,' judged Calvo Sotelo, 'was due above all to the political factor; that is to say, the uncertainty of the future.'[63]

What finally brought the Primo de Rivera dictatorship to its knees was the toxic confluence of the loss of public confidence, the currency crisis, and the spectacular implosion of the regime's constitutional project. The National Assembly published its draft constitution in July 1929, according to which sovereignty lay in the state, not the nation ('the people' were not even mentioned), half the Cortes would be elected by universal suffrage and the other half appointed by the monarch and a number of corporations, while the king would not only ratify legislation and initiate constitutional reform, but also preside over the executive, appointing and dismissing ministers as he saw fit. Having nominated the bulk of the National Assembly's members, Primo was taken aback at the prerogatives envisaged for the monarch, complaining to Gabriel Maura, son of the Conservative politician, that 'one of the errors of the old politics was to let the king play too big a role.'[64] Despite the unwillingness of the National Assembly to reduce the monarchy to a merely ceremonial and symbolic role, Primo defended the proposed constitution as 'the emblem of our illusions and our hopes'.[65] Still, it was overwhelmingly rejected by public opinion, including the extreme right. He later reflected that his biggest single blunder in power had been the failure to anchor his regime at the earliest possible opportunity in a constitution.

A major setback to Primo's constitutional plans had been the refusal of the socialists to join the National Assembly in the summer of 1929. Only a year earlier, in July 1928, the XII Congress of the UGT had voted in favour of collaborationism by the staggering margin of 5,064 votes to 740. The radical shift in stance was not economically motivated – there was no upsurge in labour unrest or unemployment in 1929 – but political in nature. The socialists realized that the regime had become politically bankrupt, so they hastily withdrew their support in order to avoid, in the words of one leader, 'drowning ourselves politically without any glory whatsoever'.[66] 'The political structure of Spain is about to change,' as the trade-union leader Largo Caballero explained, 'and we must play a principal role ... in that transformation.'[67] In short, the socialists not only wanted to avoid a backlash on account of their collaborationism, but also to be in a position to take advantage of the change in regime. However, in order to protect their dictatorial gains, they decided not to take the fight to the regime, but merely to await its fall.

Primo's demise as dictator was ultimately decided by the king. The failed military and civilian uprising of the Conservative Sánchez Guerra in January 1929, which had been designed to bring about a constituent Cortes, made Alfonso XIII appreciate that the dictatorship might place the future of the monarchy itself in question. Just as he had jettisoned the constitutional regime of 1876 for the sake of his Crown, so he now ditched the dictatorship for exactly the same reason. On 28 January 1930, Primo duly resigned and the dictatorship came to an end.

The least-researched period of modern Spain, the regime of General Primo de Rivera has been the subject of a mere handful of studies, in stark contrast to the avalanche of books on the Restoration, the Second Republic, the Civil War, and the Franco dictatorship. Hardly surprisingly, the regime is often treated as a somewhat irrelevant interregnum, detached from the Restoration before it and the Republic which followed it. Yet this is a mistake. The dictatorship powerfully overlapped with both periods. On the one hand, the Primo regime marked the climax not only of the struggle between military and civilian power, but also of the authoritarian currents that had been in the ascendant since the 1910s. On the other hand, it is impossible to explain the fate of the Republic without taking into account the extent to which authoritarianism replaced dynastic liberalism under Primo, the cause of anti-liberal reaction being further fortified by the privileged treatment afforded to the Catholic Church. Neither is it possible to understand the Republic without appreciating that, on the left, the extremists within the CNT and the corporativists within the socialist movement were both greatly strengthened under Primo. In addition, the dictatorship is important in its own right, as it signalled a rupture with the constitutional regime of 1876, while heavily conditioning the future of the Bourbon monarchy. It also oversaw the leap from an agrarian-dominated economy to an industrial- and service-led one, and its inability to cope with the modernizing expectations of the increasingly urban middle and working classes helps explain not only its fall, but also the subsequent rise of the Second Republic. Like the Restoration before it, the dictatorship was unable to channel effectively the political aspirations and modernizing ideals of the 'new' urban Spain. Finally, the Primo dictatorship is important because it was at once a paradigm and a warning for the regime that replaced the Republic: the Franco dictatorship. Spain's second dictatorship of the twentieth century replicated many features of the first, including much of its authoritarian ideology, its alliance with the Catholic Church, and its fervent defence of economic autarky, while learning a great deal from the failings and foibles of the Primo regime.

The collapse of the dictatorship did not make the subsequent fall of the monarchy inevitable, despite the damage done to the Bourbon brand by its symbiotic relationship with the Primo de Rivera regime. Nonetheless, both Alfonso XIII and the Restoration politicians demonstrated during the course of 1930 and early 1931 that they were still too remote from the realities of modern, urban Spain to provide a solution to the ongoing political crisis. In reality, they were too wedded to the politics of factionalism, dynastic infighting, and clientelism to undertake the type of far-reaching political reform which might have restored the credibility that the king had forfeited by abandoning his own constitution in 1923. The monarch and his advisers also badly miscalculated the national mood by taking over a year to organize a new round of elections. By contrast, the republicans and socialists were much more in tune with the expectations of a modernizing society, being hailed as the saviours of the nation in contrast to the discredited forces of the *ancien régime*. Accordingly, the republican-socialist coalition was able to turn the nationwide municipal elections of 12 April 1931 into a plebiscite on the future of the monarchy. The victory of the dynastic parties in the countryside did little more than confirm the durability of their clientelistic networks. On the other hand, the triumph of the republicans and socialists in virtually all the cities, where the electorate was relatively free, provided a far better gauge of the state of public opinion. Indeed, following the municipal elections, Alfonso XIII found himself completely isolated: neither the Cabinet nor the army nor the Civil Guard would stand by him. Refusing to abdicate, he went into exile. The day he did so, 14 April 1931, the Second Republic was proclaimed – Spain's third regime in less than a decade.

# 4

# The Second Republic, 1931–1933

*Democracy, Reform, and the Ascendancy of the Right*

The day the Second Republic was proclaimed, 14 April 1931, people flooded onto the streets and squares of cities, towns, and villages throughout Spain in jubilant celebration, a fitting finale to the triumph of mass politics over the vote-rigging cronyism of the Restoration. But these joyous scenes masked widely differing expectations within the camp of the victors, which ranged from socialists, republicans, anarcho-syndicalists, and Basque and Catalan nationalists, to recent converts to the republican cause. The scenes also belied the ambiguous or openly antagonistic attitude of many sectors, including the military, the Catholic community, landowners, monarchists, revolutionary anarchists, and the Communists, who took to the streets crying 'Down with the Republic! *Viva* the Soviets!'[1] The vote of 12 April 1931 had signalled, above all else, a repudiation of the monarchy. Accordingly, the overriding challenge facing the new regime was to convert the anti-monarchist movement into a pro-republican one by giving effective political expression to the far-reaching social and economic changes of the last two decades.

## THE REFORMS OF
## THE PROVISIONAL GOVERNMENT

The provisional government reflected the sheer diversity of the anti-monarchist opposition, as it comprised conservative, centrist, and left-wing republicans and Catalan and Galician nationalists, as well as socialists. Led by the former monarchist minister, the loquacious lawyer and landowner Niceto Alcalá-Zamora, the Cabinet included the hot-tempered Miguel Maura, son of the monarchist titan Antonio Maura, the charismatic Radical boss Alejandro Lerroux, the aloof left-republican intellectual Manuel Azaña, and three socialists: the obdurate trade-union leader with the steely blue eyes, Francisco Largo Caballero, who was appointed labour minister, the combative parliamentary spokesman, Indalecio Prieto, and the cultivated law professor from Granada, the El Greco-like Fernando de los Ríos. Within this government there were, broadly speaking, two visions of the Republic. The first was that of the left-republicans and socialists, who regarded the Republic as the long-awaited opportunity to modernize Spain in their own image following half a century of conservative rule. Like progressives elsewhere in Southern Europe, they aimed to transform the nation by means of state-led, top-down reform. They were driven by the conviction that Spain lagged behind other countries, above all their chief paradigm, France. As the minister of war, Manuel Azaña, explained, 'for us the Republic is ... an instrument of construction, for remaking the state and Spanish society from their foundations to the very top'. 'Maintaining the revolutionary spirit of the government,' he stressed, 'is the only safeguard of the Republic.'[2] Consequently the left-republicans and socialists had a patrimonial and exclusive vision of the regime: if the Restoration and dictatorship had been the fiefdom of the right, so the Republic would be that of the left. However, the left-republicans and the socialists possessed neither a single vision of state and society nor a common programme: for the working-class organizations the priority was socio-economic reform, for the left-republicans cultural and institutional change, and for the Catalan nationalists regional autonomy.

The second vision was that of the moderate republicans, represented above all by the Radical Republican Party. These centrist or centre-right republicans were acutely aware that the anti-monarchist movement of 1930–31 was forged out of a common opposition, but bereft of a common programme. They also appreciated that the pro-republican movement, despite the electoral success of 12 April, was fragmented and weak. Its most broadly based organization, the socialist UGT, was far from nationwide in scope, while the myriad republican parties were highly localized, had little support outside the towns, and lacked authentic national structures. From this

perspective, the anti-monarchist masses had to be won over by showing that the Republic was 'for all Spaniards'. In short, while the forces
of the left sought to republicanize the nation, the moderate republicans sought to nationalize the republic. The moderate republicans did
not repudiate reform per se – the Republic was not 'a final station, but
a point of departure', as Radical leader Alejandro Lerroux put it – but
believed that for the sake of the regime it had to be calibrated according to its social support.[3] The vision of the centrist republicans – in
contrast to the left – was therefore rooted in the politics of compromise and inclusion.

The reformist ambition of the left was especially perilous given the
adverse international context into which the regime was born. The
Spanish Republic was the last in a long line of republics established
over the previous two decades: the Portuguese Republic was created
in 1910, ten more emerged at the end of the First World War (including the German, Austrian, Czechoslovak, Hungarian, and Polish
republics), and in the 1920s republics were founded in Greece and
Albania. However, by the time Spain turned republican in 1931, most
of these regimes had been swept aside by a tsunami of right-wing
authoritarianism: nearly all of Central and Eastern Europe was under
some form of dictatorship, while in Southern Europe not a single
democracy was left except in Spain. In other words, just as Spain was
embracing democracy, most of Europe had already succumbed to
dictatorship – a far from comforting scenario. A further obstacle to
reform in Spain was the Great Depression. The Crash of 1929 had
had an extremely limited financial impact on Spain due to its absence
from the gold standard, the highly protected nature of its economy,
the depreciation of the peseta, and the fact that it possessed the fourth
largest gold reserves in the world. By contrast, the commercial impact
of the Crash was far greater, hitting the export of agricultural goods
such as citruses, olive oil, fruit, and wine hard, as well as that of minerals and their derivatives. Still, it should be remembered that foreign
trade – in contrast, say, to Britain – made a 'modest' contribution to
the economy as a whole.[4]

What made the economic situation considerably worse were developments within Spain itself. Many investors manifested their lack of
confidence in the Republic by withdrawing their capital: between

1 April and 30 June 1931 bank deposits dropped 10 per cent, while private investment in 1931 fell 20 per cent compared to 1926–9.[5] The labour reforms introduced by the socialist minister Francisco Largo Caballero also discouraged investment, as the crisis 'was only going to get worse with a policy that was directly responsible for a notable increase in labour costs at a time when businesses had to deal with a fall in sales and profits'.[6] In addition, the fiscal orthodoxy of the republicans meant that the decline in private investment was scarcely offset by means of a counter-cyclical increase in public spending. Despite the impact of the Great Depression, the gargantuan debt inherited from the dictatorship, and the low tax regime that prevailed in Spain, the republican governments never embraced deficit-spending as a policy or introduced a proper income tax. In short, they never adopted a bold or innovative approach to the economic crisis, though this was no different to nearly all other governments in Europe. As a result, the reform agenda of the republicans and socialists was to be shackled from the outset by their unquestioning adherence to the orthodoxies of a balanced budget and low taxation. As the prime minister himself admitted in December 1931, 'the reformist impulse which the Republic might feel at this time' had to be suppressed in order to obtain a balanced budget 'at all costs'.[7] Thus the Republic embarked on a sweeping programme of reform armed with the exiguous budgetary resources of the Spanish state in the face of a global recession, massive capital flight, and a vast debt.

The raft of reforms which the provisional government passed by decree during the first weeks of the regime at once highlighted the virtues and the vices of its approach. First, Largo Caballero launched a sweeping series of labour reforms: the Municipal Boundaries decree, which banned workers from outside a municipality from being contracted as long as local hands remained idle; the Obligatory Cultivation decree, which compelled proprietors to cultivate their land (thereby preventing lock-outs); the extension of the Law on Labour Accidents from the urban to the rural areas; the eight-hour day; a National Fund to combat unemployment; and the *jurados mixtos* (arbitration boards), a reconfiguration of the *comités paritarios* of the Primo de Rivera regime, the major innovation being that the *jurados mixtos* would now be introduced into the agrarian economy, the biggest employer of all.

These reforms drastically altered the rural status quo by enabling the landless labourers to organize and defend themselves against the land-owners, the resulting shift in the balance of power being reinforced by the thousands of local councils under socialist and republican control.

These far-reaching measures were, however, blighted by two crucial shortcomings: first, they were not part of a broader economic policy, simply being designed to benefit the workers. Whether the employers, who were not privy to the policy-making process, were actually in a position to comply with the new legislation was not taken into account, despite the damage already wrought by the Great Depression. In fact, the 'substantial increase in labour costs' made life difficult for urban and rural employers alike, especially for small and medium-sized enterprises.[8] From this perspective, the labour reforms sharpened, rather than lessened, class conflict. Second, the reform was not intended to improve the situation of workers per se, but specifically that of *socialist* workers. The anarcho-syndicalists were effectively sidelined, as they refused to collaborate on principle with state agencies, opting instead for 'direct action' or face-to-face dealings with the employers. The fallout from the exclusion of the anarcho-syndicalists under the Primo de Rivera dictatorship had been limited by their repression, but under the more open regime of the Second Republic the backlash would inevitably be far greater, especially as the CNT represented about one-half of all unionized workers. The possibility of offering the CNT an alternative means of collective bargaining in order to keep it within the orbit of the new regime was far from illusory. The syndical-ists, who still held sway within the CNT, welcomed the Republic – unlike the anarchists – as 'the first step towards the conquest of civil rights', while regarding the anarchist pursuit of revolution as 'inopportune' in the circumstances.[9] In addition, most of the CNT's members were nei-ther anarchists nor syndicalists, but rather labourers whose prime preoccupation was their job. 'Within the trade unions,' as one activist explained, 'there are a lot of people who are not trade unionists, only a minority of us could be called men of ideas.'[10] Rather than seize this opportunity to integrate the CNT into the Republic, Largo Caballero sought, just as he had done under the dictatorship, to trap the CNT in a 'cul-de-sac', while presenting it 'as a source of agitation' in order to justify its repression.[11]

Largo Caballero's 'violently hostile' attitude (in the words of the French ambassador) towards the CNT was compounded by that of his ministerial colleagues, as none of them – not even the republicans with links to the libertarians – proposed, let alone pursued, a policy of accommodation in relation to the CNT.[12] On the contrary, the government tended to view all anarcho-syndicalists through the same lens, vilifying them as an incorrigible threat to public order ('an organization of gunmen', according to *El Socialista*),[13] their strikes and protests being accordingly suppressed with greater vigour than socialist ones. This was made patently clear by the brutal response of the Civil Guard to a march on San Sebastián by fishermen and women from the port of Pasajes on 27 May, which was held to request the release of the union representatives who had been arrested during the course of a month-long strike. Despite recognizing the 'tragic situation' of the fishermen, the civil governor ordered the Civil Guard to stop the march from entering the city, which it duly did by firing at 'blank range against the protestors', killing eight and wounding over fifty.[14] The same tigerish approach was taken by the government in relation to the nationwide strike at the telephone company, *Telefónica*, in July 1931, where the overwhelming majority of the unionized workers belonged to the CNT's National Telephone Syndicate. Rather than seek a solution to the conflict by negotiating with pragmatic syndicalists such as Joan Peiró or Ángel Pestaña, the government decided that 'the moment [had] arrived to adopt a vigorous policy and fight against the Confederation'.[15] During the repression four prisoners in Seville were shot in cold blood in a vile throwback to the notorious 'Escape Law'; namely, the shooting of prisoners on the pretext that they were 'escaping'. Those responsible included not only the Civil Guard but also the Civic Guard, a body made up of republican and socialist volunteers which had been set up by the government on the grounds that it offered a means of 'keeping the syndicates down'.[16] Following the public outcry over the shootings, the civil governor was replaced, but no one was put on trial for the murders.

A final example of the republican authorities' hard-line stance towards the CNT was their response to its strike in Barcelona in September 1931. This was organized in support of a hunger strike by 'governmental prisoners', that is, prisoners who were being held without charge, of whom the CNT had several hundred. However, when the Local Federation of Syndicates of Barcelona approached the authorities to negotiate the return to work, the civil governor refused to deal 'with a corporation that has placed itself outside the law', and proceeded to pulverize the protest at a cost of fifteen deaths, six severe injuries, and around 300 arrests.[17] Socialist hostility, republican negligence, and governmental brutality combined to weaken the position of the moderate syndicalists within the CNT, while playing into the hands of the anarchists, as shown by their takeover of the CNT's official newspaper, Solidaridad Obrera, in September 1931. The ascendancy of the revolutionaries within the CNT would destabilize the regime not only by losing it the support of much of the organized working class, but also by heightening socio-economic and political tensions as a consequence of their commitment to 'revolutionary gymnastics'.[18]

The government's policy of coercion towards the CNT was complemented by the elaboration of a law that would allow it, as the premier recognized, 'to close the majority (or all) of the syndical centres'.[19] The sweeping Law of the Defence of the Republic of October 1931 defined a wide range of 'acts of aggression against the Republic', including any 'action or expression' that amounted to 'contempt' of the state and its institutions, the spreading of 'news' that might 'disturb the peace or public order', and any strike that did not concern 'work conditions' and did not abide by an 'arbitration or conciliatory procedure'. The law also permitted the minister of the interior to cancel meetings and marches if they were likely to 'disturb the public peace' and to close those centres and associations that engaged in 'acts of aggression against the Republic'.[20] Clearly the principal target of this ferocious fiat, which effectively placed the government above the law, was the CNT, but it was a profoundly counterproductive measure, as it would only strengthen the revolutionaries at the expense of the syndicalists. By December 1931 the situation of the syndicalists was so desperate that they wrote an open letter to the prime minister lamenting that the repression had reached 'inconceivable extremes' in Andalusia and Catalonia, and that the government's hard-line policy had left 'the Confederation outside the law'.[21] It was to no avail.

The second set of reforms pursued by the left concerned the most hazardous area of all: the military. As its trajectory since 1898 had amply demonstrated, the army viewed itself as the national institution *par excellence*, and civilian authority as inherently inferior. Reconciling the army to the demands of a democracy, which would inevitably be greater than those of a regime of notables such as the Restoration, was always going to be a critical test of republican resolve and tact. Deeply influenced by the French Third Republic, the minister of war, the owlish if self-regarding Manuel Azaña, aimed to modernize the poorly equipped and badly paid peninsular army by restructuring it as a small conscript army with well-remunerated officers and high-quality arms and equipment. The Army of Africa would retain its mercenary ethos, based as it was on the Foreign Legion and the Moroccan Regulars (conscripts having failed as a colonial fighting force), but be reduced in size. As a result, the number of divisions was halved, four of the nation's seven military academies, including the one run by General Francisco Franco in Zaragoza, were closed down, and the Army of Africa was scaled back from 57,000 troops to 45,000. Few questioned the need to restructure the peninsular army or to make savings.

Azaña also sought to tackle the long-standing problem of the bloated officer corps. In 1930 there were 163 generals and 21,996 officers for 115,930 soldiers – that is to say, one officer for every nine privates – which was three times the required number. The decree of 25 April 1931, which offered officers early retirement on full pay, aimed not only to reduce the officer corps, but also to 'republicanize' it by encouraging those hostile to the regime to retire, not least by obliging those officers who chose to remain to take an oath of loyalty to the Republic. The offer was taken up by just over a third of the officers, of whom a third were republicans. In reality, the officers were aggrieved not so much by the reduction in the corps as by the corresponding decrease in their prospects of promotion. In any case, a far greater outcry was caused by a decree of June 1931, which called for the decorations, promotions, and rewards of the Primo de Rivera years to be revised. Of the 500 cases reviewed, 346 resulted in a demotion, most of which were *within* a rank, but this retroactive measure infuriated the Army of Africa. It was further outraged by the investigation – against Azaña's wishes – into the Anual disaster and military collaboration with the Primo dictatorship, especially once this led to the creation of a Responsibilities Commission in August 1931 and the arrest of high-profile figures such as Brigadier General Emilio Mola and General Dámaso Berenguer. A further slight from the military point of view was the overthrow of the Law of Jurisdictions of 1906, which deprived the military courts of jurisdiction over civilians who had allegedly insulted the armed forces or the motherland. These initiatives led the colonial army, ill-disposed to the Republic in the first place, to view it as 'vindictive and hostile'.[22] Azaña's somewhat contemptuous attitude towards the army also made the changes seem more sweeping and harmful than they really were. Applying the template of the French Third Republic to Spain was always likely to be extremely problematic given the historical dependence of its elites on the army to uphold law and order and protect private property. Even so, the Azaña reforms constituted the most far-reaching overhaul of the army in more than a century, but, like the labour reforms, they antagonized powerful interests, in this case the armed forces – the one body which, in the modern era, had demonstrated the capacity to overturn a regime.

The third tranche of reforms dealt with education, the most cherished area of reform for the republicans, for whom enlightenment was the key to progress. For the minister of public instruction, the bespectacled former teacher and journalist Marcelino Domingo, 'education [was] above all else.'[23] Despite Primo de Rivera's educational drive, illiteracy in 1930 stood at 32 per cent while 60 per cent of children received no instruction whatsoever.[24] Domingo vowed to 'sow Spain with schools'.[25] A decree of 23 June provided for the building of 27,151 primary schools within five years (of which 7,000 would be completed by the beginning of the next academic year) and the creation of 7,000 new teaching positions. The schools were to be secular, while all Catholic schooling was to cease by 1 January 1932. Like the French Third Republic before it, the Spanish Second Republic was to imbue its pupils with the values of the new regime, the Director of Primary Education, the socialist Rodolfo Llopis, explaining that 'the school must convert the subjects of the Bourbon monarchy into citizens of the Republic'.[26] The campaign to eradicate illiteracy ('all Spain should be able to read,' Domingo insisted) and to reduce the 'cultural chasm' between town and countryside was also evident in the creation of 'popular' and 'summer' universities (for those unable to attend during term time), as well as the establishment of local libraries, 2,000 of which were opened between 1931 and 1933.[27] The greatest fanfare of all was reserved for the 'Pedagogical Missions', which, according to the decree of 29 May 1931, would generate 'the wind of progress and the means to participate in it', meaning that they would bring low and high culture alike to the *pueblos* (small towns and villages), whether in the form of travelling exhibitions, mobile lending libraries, theatre troupes (the best known being that of the gifted poet, playwright, and actor Federico García Lorca), concerts, or puppet and slide shows.[28]

The education budget doubled under the Republic, but this was still not enough to realize the proposed reforms. By October 1932, 2,510 primary schools had been built over the previous two years. By October 1935, a total of 6,752 schools had been completed. Although a notable achievement, this was still nearly 15,000 schools short, as the target set in 1931 was 5,430 schools a year.[29] The glaring disparity between rhetoric and reality inevitably damaged the credibility of the Republic. On the other hand, the proposed closure of Catholic centres – a measure which, it should be noted, the French Third Republic never undertook – incensed the Church, as its schools were not only important in economic terms, but also a vital source of its social and cultural influence. In addition, the removal of crucifixes from state schools in early 1932 was met 'with enormous displeasure' by the Catholic community.[30] Once again, the reform appealed to republicans, but inflamed the sensibilities of a powerful adversary.

The shortcomings to these early reforms not only reflected the determination of the left-republicans and socialists to remake Spain in their own image, but also their lack of experience. Only Prime Minister Niceto Alcalá-Zamora had previously served at the state level (though Largo Caballero had been a member of Primo de Rivera's Council of State), while some ministers had not even been parliamentary deputies before 1931. Symptomatic of the lack of talent was the appointment of the socialist Indalecio Prieto to the Treasury because there was no republican with the necessary expertise, a move which alarmed an already agitated business world.

## THE MAY CHURCH BURNINGS

The Republic confronted its first major crisis within a month of its proclamation in April 1931. On 10 May a monarchist circle in the centre of Madrid played a recording of the royal anthem onto the street outside, which incensed passers-by. Crowds subsequently stormed the offices of the monarchist daily *ABC* and were then beaten back in a typically heavy-handed fashion by the Civil Guard, resulting in two deaths. The next day anticlericals, mostly anarcho-syndicalists and republicans, retaliated by setting fire to a number of religious buildings in the capital, which not only shocked conservative opinion, but also provoked a confrontation within the provisional government. The minister of the interior, the Catholic Miguel Maura, wanted to call out the Civil Guard, but was vetoed by the Cabinet, the Republican Action leader Manuel Azaña provocatively declaring that 'a handful of burning buildings are not worth the life of a single republican.'[31] Law and order in Madrid was finally restored by the army, but it was unable to stop the incendiarism spreading on 12 May to a number of cities in the south. Over a hundred churches and other religious buildings were sacked or torched.

The May church burnings did enormous damage to the Republic. First, they did much to discredit the cause of conservative republicanism, as the two Catholics in the Cabinet, minister of the interior Maura and Prime Minister Alcalá-Zamora (who was 'sickened and angry' at the incendiarism),[32] had been made to look perfidious, while their assurance of a 'Republic of order' had been dealt a devastating blow. Catholic sentiment was to be further wounded by the expulsion of the Bishop of Victoria and the Archbishop of Toledo from Spain for their anti-republican declarations, by the secularization of the cemeteries, by religious instruction being made optional in schools, and by the removal of Christian symbols from state schools, the Church hierarchy expressing its misgivings in a collective letter on 3 June. Second, the disproportionate response of the Civil Guard to the protest outside *ABC* once again highlighted its patent inadequacy as a police force. Prior to the Republic the left had been extremely critical of the Civil Guard, lambasting it as a crude and archaic gendarmerie at the behest of monarchist reaction. In truth, the Civil Guard was neither equipped nor trained for crowd control, its service instructions having remained unchanged since the mid-nineteenth century. Thus its standard firearm, the Mauser rifle, was completely unsuited to the handling of civilian protest, as it was a lethal weapon capable of killing three people with a single bullet. The logical response to the Civil Guard's excesses would have been to redeploy, reform, or even dissolve it. However, the government rejected all three options, republicans and socialists alike showering praise on the Civil Guard as an indispensable institution of state. An escalating cycle of provocation and repression was accordingly set in motion which was to inflict widespread and enduring harm on the Republic.

## THE LOCAL ELECTIONS

At the end of May a new round of municipal elections were held. Unjustly neglected by historians, these elections revealed that the new politics of the Republic had far more in common with the old politics of the Restoration than is generally assumed. On 14 April the republican-socialist coalition had triumphed in the towns and cities, but not in the countryside. In theory, the second round of elections would take place wherever there existed a 'well-found suspicion' that the popular will had been 'falsified and oppressed'.[33] Around 2,000 out of 8,800 councils were selected for new elections, being replaced in the meantime by republican-socialist steering committees. In practice, the elections were rerun not so much in those *pueblos* where there was proof of irregularity, as in those where the republican-socialist coalition stood a good chance of victory. Thus few elections were held in provinces such as Cuenca and Guadalajara where monarchist *caciques* were well entrenched.

The rationale for the May elections was made even more explicit by the performance of the civil governors. Theoretically neutral, the republican civil governors, like the monarchist ones before them, busily promoted the interests of the party which had sponsored them. The *Derecha Liberal Republicana* (DLR) (Liberal Republican Right) governors for Ciudad Real, Cuenca, and Toledo and the Republican Action appointee for Albacete not only bludgeoned local *caciques* to back their parties, but also criss-crossed the provinces in support of their candidates. Many of the steering committees also abused their position by campaigning on behalf of their parties, sometimes even allowing their own members – despite the law – to stand themselves. Such was the pressure of the republican authorities and the general euphoria surrounding the new regime that many of the dynastic candidates of 12 April had switched sides by 30 May. In the case of Albacete, 30 per cent of the republican candidates had stood as monarchists the previous month.

During the early days of the Republic, *caciquismo* was reviled by the socialists as, in the words of *El Socialista*, a 'grave danger' for the regime.[34] The republicans, too, were well aware of the threat posed by the former monarchist fixers. At a meeting of the Radical Party and Republican Action on 27 April 1931 it was claimed that the entry of *caciques* into their parties would end up 'distorting the revolutionary work'.[35] At a Republican Action meeting of 7 June, Manuel Azaña exhorted the republicans to 'crush' the *cacique*.[36] Like the socialists, many republicans regarded the *cacique* as a Trojan horse which might destroy the regime from within. Nonetheless, a great many *caciques* joined the republican parties, most of them signing up to one of the more conservative ones, such as the DLR or the Radical Party. Indeed, the DLR leader and prime minister, Niceto Alcalá-Zamora, was himself a prominent *cacique* in both his home province of Córdoba and the province of Jaén. An illustration of how the *caciques* adapted to the new political landscape is provided by the Ochando family in the province of Albacete. Prominent throughout the Restoration, the Ochandos had controlled one of the province's five electoral districts, that of Casas Ibáñez. Under the dictatorship, they collaborated with Primo de Rivera while maintaining their links with the Liberal Party. Once the Republic was installed, the Ochandos, like many other *caciques* in Castile-La Mancha, joined a republican party, in this case the Radicals, as the priority was to protect their family's interests by keeping in with the powers-that-be.

Neither were the left-republicans immune to the contagion of *caciquismo*. A striking example of the continuity between the Restoration and the Republic is provided by the case of the Radical-Socialist deputy for Zamora, Ángel Galarza. The scion of a Liberal deputy under the monarchy, Galarza received numerous offers during the early days of the Republic from the erstwhile supporters of his father 'to command his electors', while 'intimate friends' of the former Liberal deputy 'offered their unconditional support in order to give shape to a political Galarzism that was able to maintain the old loyalties in exchange for the traditional favours'.[37] In other words, Galarza drew directly and unapologetically on the clientelist networks forged by his father, to the extent that he even used the very same political secretary. Such continuities with the old regime were hardly surprising, as these practices were rooted in relations of deep-seated deference and socio-economic dependency. In any case, the differences between the monarchists and the republicans under the Restoration should not be overstated, as under the monarchy republicans had not only collaborated with *caciques* in the *pueblos* but had even been *caciques* themselves, while their electoral success in the urban arena had drawn on extensive clientelistic networks.

The results of the May municipal elections speak for themselves. In Albacete, Republican Action won nearly 40 per cent of the councillors, while, in Ciudad Real and Toledo, the DLR, which had barely existed in either province before 12 April, won 33 per cent and 45 per cent of the councillors respectively. The official results for the May elections, though incomplete, revealed the efficacy of the provisional government's strategy of 'republicanization', as 80 per cent of all councillors had been scooped up by the republicans or socialists. Local studies indicate that this triumph was even greater than the official results allow: in the province of Seville the monarchists did not win a single one of the 889 seats on offer, while in Albacete, Ciudad Real, and Toledo the republicans secured 77 per cent and the socialists 21 per cent of the 1,223 seats up for election.

The real victor in many instances was, as always, the *cacique*. Many *pueblos* voted, as they did before the Republic, for the government-approved list, the *caciquismo* of the old regime being supplanted by that of the new. In Albacete, participation was highest in those places where the *caciques* were most dominant and lowest where the republicans and socialists held sway. It could be argued that by co-opting monarchist voters and *caciques*, the republican parties strengthened both themselves and the Republic itself by integrating them into the new political order. The evident danger was that the monarchists might use the local parties for their own ends, while diluting, deforming, or even destroying the reforms of the regime. 'The question at heart,' as the Radical Party boss in Murcia wrote to Lerroux, 'is if the Radical Party of Murcia is to be a republican party which can be joined by those that were not before, and who sincerely wish to collaborate in a *republican* manner, or if it is to be the same old *ciervista* party [i.e. of the monarchist Juan de la Cierva] that until now has been dominant with the same *caciques* in each *pueblo* and using identical methods.'[38] The May elections had nonetheless prepared the ground for the republican and socialist parties in relation to the general election in June, as they had boosted their presence in the rural areas and enabled the new civil governors to flex their muscles, thereby shifting the balance of power in the countryside towards the governing coalition.

Another defining feature of the old regime which retained much of its vigour under the new one was the politics of patronage/clientelism. Its continuing vitality under the Republic was no surprise as it permeated virtually every area of Spanish life, making the political to a notable extent personal. The personification of patronage politics was the Radical leader Alejandro Lerroux, who, much like a Restoration-style 'Godfather', spent a substantial part of each day drafting 'letters of recommendation' and meeting people to dispense favours; the French publication *Paris-Soir* claimed that he received hundreds of supplicants a day. By drawing on their experience under the dictatorship, the socialists exploited the public sector for the benefit of party and trade-union members alike, their corporatist labour policy being an institutionalized form of clientelism. Arguably their most adept practitioner in this regard was Manuel Cordero, who found time not only to be a parliamentary deputy, a regional representative, and a councillor for Madrid, but also a board member of the state petroleum company (CAMPSA) and the head of a parliamentary commission, and president of four arbitration boards. In a spirit of selfless public service, Cordero managed to juggle no fewer than fourteen different jobs. Republicans and socialists alike also exploited their control of local councils to extend their spoils system, an objective that had been much facilitated by the overthrow of the monarchist councils in May.

Even high-ranking positions of state were regarded as fair game for the politics of patronage. The minister of public instruction, Marcelino Domingo, recommended 'with the greatest interest' the owner of a shoeshine stall in Madrid as the civil governor of Soria because, astonishingly, he owed him money.[39] 'The first and most urgent task' of the new governor, the minister of the interior later recalled, was to request 1,000 pesetas from the government for a bullfight.[40] Similarly, the left-republican minister for development, Álvaro de Albornoz, endorsed with 'the maximum interest' the proprietor of an antique bookstall as governor of Segovia because he had procured for him 'absolute bargains' over the years.[41] When the bookseller was asked by the minister why he wanted to become a civil governor, he candidly explained that he hoped to help a friend 'establish himself in the main square and open a proper café'.[42]

## THE GENERAL ELECTION

The landslide victory of the republicans and socialists in the general election of June 1931 reflected to a large extent the optimism that still surrounded the regime. Having never won fifty seats in a general election under the Restoration, they now returned over 400 of the 470 deputies for the Constituent Cortes. The PSOE won 117 seats, the Radical Republican Party ninety-four, the Radical-Socialist Republican Party fifty-eight, and Republican Action twenty-six. The leading regional republican parties were the *Esquerra Republicana de Catalunya* (Catalan Republican Left), which gained twenty-six seats, and the *Organización Republicana Gallega Autónoma* or ORGA (Galician Republican Autonomous Organization), which won twenty-one seats. The socialist and left-republican haul, at 247 seats, provided the left with an overall majority. The centre, headed by the Radical Party, constituted the only other major parliamentary block with 152 deputies. Discredited in the eyes of many conservatives by the church burnings and by the governmental alliance with the left, the moderate right of the Liberal Republican Right still won over a million votes, but only returned twenty-seven deputies, as it paid a heavy price for being largely excluded from the republican-socialist slate. Whereas a socialist required 19,000 votes to be elected, a Liberal Republican Right candidate needed as many as 49,000.

The general election was held in accordance with the electoral law of 8 May 1931. It lowered the voting age from twenty-five to twenty-three and created large multi-candidate constituencies, as opposed to small single-member ones, which were easier for the *caciques* to control. The introduction of mass parties, female candidates, and a freer press made the elections far more representative and competitive, and less corrupt, than any ballot under the monarchy. The electoral law also placed a premium on coalitions, as the winning slate would secure 67–80 per cent of the seats in a district as long as it secured 20 per cent of the vote. As a result, huge swings in parliamentary representation resulted from relatively small movements in the vote, this psephological volatility not being offset by the establishment of a second chamber.

Although these were the first mass, relatively clean elections in Spanish history, paradoxically they provided a misleading snapshot of opinion in the country. Disoriented by the sudden fall of the monarchy, disordered by the dissolution of the monarchist parties, and damaged by extensive conservative abstention, the forces of the right were vastly under-represented. While the republican parties presented 608 candidates and the socialists 144, the non-republican right fielded 123, which covered only 40 per cent of the seats; in other words, the ruling parties had won the election before it even took place. In many constituencies the parties of the republican-socialist coalition, bereft of a credible conservative rival, either competed amongst themselves or else picked on the Liberal Republican Right. The forty-one right-wing deputies who were returned to parliament were a pale reflection of conservative opinion.

The electoral triumph of the republicans and socialists was due to an extent to the persistence of practices which had proliferated under the Restoration, such as the partisanship of the civil governors and the electoral machinations of the *caciques*. An example is provided by the sudden ascendancy of Republican Action in Albacete province. In 1930 and 1931 two friends of the Republican Action leader Manuel Azaña, Arturo Cortés and Enrique Martí, had tried to drum up support there for the party, but with little success. Once the Republic was proclaimed, however, people flooded into the party, including a good many monarchists. In the general election, the party won three of Albacete's six deputies, its best result outside Madrid. How does one account for this sudden change in fortune, especially for an urban-based party in a predominantly agrarian province? The answer lies to an important extent in the influence wielded by the civil governor, the state's supreme representative in each province, who in this case was none other than Arturo Cortés. A complementary reason was the entry of local *caciques* into the party, the one for Alcaraz – previously a Conservative – offering 'the district to the minister of war, Manuel Azaña'.[43]

## THE CONSTITUENT CORTES

The Constituent Cortes, which opened on 14 July as a symbolic nod to the French Revolution, immediately brought to the surface the lurking discord within the governing ranks. The very first article of the Constitution provoked a ruction between the socialists and the centre republicans as the former wanted to define the new regime as 'a Republic of workers'.[44] This partisan proposal, denounced as the defence of 'a particular class', was eventually altered to 'a democratic Republic of workers of all classes', but the exchange revealed the extent to which the left tended to identify the regime with its own agenda.[45] Another out-and-out clash took place over the right of the state to confiscate private property, a left-wing proposition which was heavily disputed, above all by the centre-right premier Alcalá-Zamora. The final vote made all property liable to expropriation for 'reasons of social utility', though 'adequate' compensation would be paid.[46] Alcalá-Zamora also defended the creation of a second chamber, as he was convinced that it would enhance the regime's consolidation by acting as a moderating force. Once again, his proposal was voted down by the left, which regarded a senate as a shackle on reform.

One of the most heated issues was the vote for women. Of the three female deputies, two opposed the measure, the left-republican Victoria Kent arguing that 'it is dangerous to give the vote to women', as they needed 'a number of years of cohabitation with the Republic' before being sufficiently prepared to exercise the vote.[47] The socialist Margarita Nelken was also convinced that those women 'who were real lovers of liberty have to be the first to sacrifice their own interest to the progress of Spain'.[48] Most republican deputies felt the same way. The Radical Rafael Guerra del Río made it clear that, like Kent and Nelken, his colleagues were not opposed to the female suffrage per se, but they harboured the fear that 'women will vote with the priests and reaction'.[49] The notion that women were unduly swayed by Catholic priests had first been posited by Catholic politicians in Belgium in 1902. They did this, ironically, in order to dissuade the Socialist Party from supporting the female suffrage, as they feared that the socialists would dominate the women's vote. This canard not only had the desired effect of dissuading the Belgian socialists from pursuing the vote for women, but later spread throughout Europe, acquiring a quasi-mythical status in the process.

The greatest parliamentary proponent of the female suffrage was Clara Campoamor, a lawyer and lifelong campaigner for women's rights who had been elected as a member of the Radical Party. She contended that men, who flocked to take part in the Easter processions, were also susceptible to the influence of the Catholic Church, while rejecting the argument that women were unprepared for the ballot:

> How can one say that women have not struggled and need time, numerous years under the Republic, to demonstrate their ability? And why not the men? Why do men, on the advent of the Republic, have rights, whereas women have to be placed in quarantine?[50]

Clara Campoamor: the architect of the vote in
favour of female suffrage in the Constituent Cortes

Campoamor defended the female suffrage as a universal right, as 'I feel a citizen first and then a woman.' Moreover, by granting women the vote, 'you save the Republic, you help the Republic, attracting and adding this force which anxiously awaits the moment of its redemption'.[51] Similarly, the socialist Manuel Cordero claimed that the female suffrage was not 'a danger for the Republic', but a 'school of citizenship'. 'The only way to achieve maturity for the exercise of liberty,' he insisted, 'is to be able to use it.'[52] The vote for women was passed on 1 October 1931 by 161 votes to 121, with 188 abstentions. The most crucial vote was that of the Socialist Party, as eighty-three of its deputies backed the measure, while most right-wing representatives did the same. The republicans either voted against it or abstained. Thus Spanish women secured the vote at the national level shortly after their British sisters (1928), but long before those in France (1944), Italy (1945), and Switzerland (1971). The Constitution also granted women other basic rights, long denied, such as equality before the law, public sector employment on an equal basis with men, civil marriage, and divorce.

The most contested issue of the entire constitutional debate was reform of the Catholic Church. Anticlerical sentiment amongst the republicans was extremely acute, in large part because Spain lagged in secularizing terms behind not only the Third Republic in France, but also less-developed Catholic countries such as Italy and Portugal. Manuel Azaña's polemical claim before the Cortes that 'Spain has ceased to be Catholic' – by which he meant that the elites had ceased to be predominantly Catholic – reflected this sense of urgency.[53] The decision to separate Church and state – thereby ending an alliance which had endured since the Middle Ages – was a hammer blow to the Catholic Church, but pragmatic leaders within it, such as Archbishop Vidal i Barraquer and the papal nuncio, Msgr Tedeschini, accepted this as inevitable. Still, the Cortes did not stop there. The Church was deprived not just of its public income, but its private sources of wealth too, as it was banned from education and business, and even from occupying buildings that were too large for its personnel. For good measure, the most prestigious order of all, the Society of Jesus, was expelled from Spain on the grounds that its oath of obedience was to 'an authority distinct from the legitimate one of the state', that is, the Vatican.[54] This amounted to a frontal assault on the

Catholic Church, the spokesman of the right-wing minority announcing that 'we will have no other banner of combat than the repeal of the Constitution.'[55] The two Catholics in the Cabinet, Prime Minister Niceto Alcalá-Zamora and the minister of the interior, Miguel Maura, also resigned in protest, leading to the formation of a new government in October 1931 under Manuel Azaña.

The Constitution of December 1931 was a world away from that of 1876, its predecessor. The new *magna carta* recognized popular sovereignty, created a unicameral legislature, separated Church and state, granted women the vote, furnished Catalonia with an autonomy statute, and enshrined in law rights long resisted, such as freedom of conscience, divorce, and civil marriage. In this way, the Constitution did justice to many of the modernizing changes which had overhauled Spanish society during the previous three decades. At the same time, it was a decidedly left-wing constitution. A number of articles presented a wish-list of reforms, such as article 46, which called upon the state to regulate 'coverage for illness, accidents, unemployment, old age, invalidity and death; the employment of women and children and especially maternity leave; the length of the working day and the minimum and family wage; annual paid holidays; the conditions of employment of Spanish workers abroad': in short, a fully fledged social-security system.[56] Such far-reaching reforms were way beyond the reach of the Spanish state, especially given its slavish adherence to fiscal orthodoxy, but they reflected the determination of the left to equate the Republic with its own reformist vision.

The principal shortcoming of the 1931 Constitution was that it did not establish a truly national framework, one that could accommodate the great majority of Spaniards. 'You will not have fulfilled the prime function of a constituent assembly,' as the spokesman for the right, the thirty-three-year-old law professor and journalist from Salamanca, José María Gil Robles, put it, 'which is to forge a constitution which also serves to provide stability for the political institutions of the country.'[57] The sectarian spirit of the left-wing majority had appalled the moderate republicans, too. The leader of the centrist party, the *Agrupación al Servicio de la República* (Group at the Service of the Republic), the high-profile philosopher José Ortega y Gasset, lashed out at the parties of the left for their 'propagandistic spirit' and for regarding themselves as the 'masters of the situation'. 'The Republic is one thing,' he pointed out, 'radicalism is another.'[58] The most destructive feature of all, embodied in article 26, was the onslaught on the Catholic Church. By savaging the Church, the republicans unwittingly provided the disparate forces of the right with a banner to rally around, that of constitutional reform. 'Today, in opposition to the constitution,' as Gil Robles declared, 'stands Catholic Spain.'[59] Rather than integrate the Catholics *into* the new regime, the Constitution had galvanized them *against* it. Given that about half the electorate was Catholic, this was a short-sighted and profoundly counterproductive move, but it reflected the left's conviction that the regime was theirs. The Spanish republicans appeared to have learned nothing from the contrasting experiences of the Portuguese and French republics. The sweeping series of anticlerical reforms passed by the Portuguese First Republic between 1910 and 1911 had provoked a massive Catholic backlash which contributed greatly to its eventual fall, while the French Third Republic of 1870 had held back on the separation of Church and state until 1905. By following the sectarian Portuguese example rather than the more accommodating French one, the Spanish republicans made the task of consolidating the regime far more hazardous than it would otherwise have been.

## THE LEFT IN POWER, 1931-2

The religious debate had also ruptured the Republic's founding pact with the resignation of the two Catholic ministers, thereby shifting the government further to the left. The fact that Manuel Azaña, whose party commanded a mere 5.5 per cent of the seats in parliament, became the new prime minister reflected the fragmented nature of the ruling coalition. Once the Constitution was passed on 10 December 1931, the Radicals tried to force the socialists from office so that they could hold sway over an all-republican Cabinet, but the left-republicans judged that it was vital to keep the socialists in power not only to pass the Constitution's supplementary laws, but also to restrain the powerful UGT. Underlying these strategic concerns was the determination of the left-republicans to establish the ideological credentials of the 'new' republicanism, as opposed to the 'old' republicanism embodied in the more moderate Radicals. Lerroux abandoned the government in the conviction that it would soon fall through its own contradictions and that he would then dominate an all-republican administration. The departure of the Radicals signalled a major fracture within the republican movement. More than any other party, the Radical Party voiced the concerns of the small and middling industrial and commercial sectors that constituted the backbone of the urban economy. In hindsight, an all-republican government, buttressed by a benevolent socialist opposition, would have furnished the regime with greater stability. As it was, the government had been reduced to the socialist working class and the most progressive sectors of the urban middle classes, a narrow social platform from which to launch an ambitious programme of reform, as it was opposed by the bulk of the working class and most of the middle and upper classes.

The uncertainty surrounding the political future was exacerbated by the parliamentary election of the erstwhile monarchist and former prime minister Niceto Alcalá-Zamora as first president of the Republic. Undoubtedly there were a host of reasons for his selection: he was an experienced politician, he would reassure conservative opinion, he was not corrupt, his centre-right party did not represent a threat to the ruling majority in the Cortes, and he was an acknowledged expert in administrative and constitutional law. These advantages, however, were outweighed by Alcalá-Zamora's patent shortcomings. He had not only resigned from the government over the Constitution but would later publish a book that was unequivocally entitled *The Defects of the Constitution*. Thus the person ultimately responsible for safeguarding the Constitution was, in fact, a detractor. This inherently unsatisfactory situation was made worse still by Alcalá-Zamora's own understanding of the presidency. Whether he regarded himself as a monarch in republican guise (hence his nickname of 'Alfonso XIV'), or acted in lieu of a second chamber, or saw himself as a spokesman for Catholic interests, or failed to grasp the dynamics of a democracy, or whether it was a mixture of all four, the vain and petulant Alcalá-Zamora proved to be a highly interventionist president who drove his governments to distraction with his constant meddling and speechifying. ('He is chatty and anecdotal, but he's not a man for conversation.

You can't talk to him about anything interesting,' commented Azaña acidly in his diary.)[60] Far from acting as a moderating force, the Republic's first president proved to be yet another source of instability.

The scale of the challenges facing the Republic was brought home by a number of confrontations at the turn of the year. In December 1931 four Civil Guards were killed at the remote *pueblo* of Castilblanco in the province of Badajoz in the 'Siberia of Extremadura'. The southwestern region of Extremadura was one of the poorest areas of the country, populated by vast estates on which surplus armies of landless labourers toiled. Since the advent of the Republic, the balance of power in the rural areas had shifted against the property-owners as a result of the labour reforms and socialist control of local councils, making relations between the landowners and the workers increasingly fraught, as shown by over eighty agrarian strikes in Badajoz in 1931. In December 1931 a province-wide stoppage was called by the socialist agrarian union, the *Federación Nacional de Trabajadores de la Tierra* or FNTT (National Federation of Land Workers), in protest at the alleged failure of the left-republican civil governor and the Civil Guard to uphold the labour legislation there. In Castilblanco, the strike was supported by a peaceful demonstration, at the conclusion of which a tussle ensued between the villagers and some Civil Guards outside the *Casa del Pueblo* ('House of the People', a local socialist centre). The jittery Guards ended up firing their weapons, killing one man and wounding two others. In a Dantesque explosion of popular fury, the villagers 'with rocks and knives hacked all four Civil Guards to death'.[61] Over the following days, the Civil Guard left more dead and wounded at Zalamea de la Serena, Villanueva, and Oliva de la Serena in Badajoz, at Épila in Zaragoza, and at Jeresa in Valencia, climaxing on 5 January 1932 with a clash at Arnedo in the northeastern region of Logroño. When the owner of a local shoe factory reneged on his promise to rehire some workers, a demonstration took to the streets of Arnedo. As the Civil Guard clumsily dispersed the unarmed protesters, it opened fire, killing eleven people and wounding nineteen. The only punitive measure taken by the government was to demote the head of the Civil Guard, the pot-bellied, moustachioed General José Sanjurjo, to the *Carabineros* (border guards), which soon led him to join an anti-republican conspiracy. These vendetta shootings highlighted not only the brutality of the Civil Guard, but also the impunity with which it continued to act.

Then, on 19 January 1932, a violent strike was launched by the miners of Fígols in Catalonia in protest at their working conditions, quickly spreading to nearby areas. Historians have regarded this uprising ever since as the first of the three great insurrections of the anarcho-syndicalist movement under the Republic, but, as recent research shows, 'the CNT did not direct, plan or organize it'.[62] Indeed, the CNT was caught completely off guard by the uprising, scrambling to claim it as its own by calling for a 'stoppage in all Spain', but only a handful of *pueblos* in Aragón and the east responded. The prime minister rejected the negotiated solution proposed by the Catalan president, Lluís Companys, informing the Cortes instead that he had ordered the army to crush the rising 'immediately', while attributing it quite absurdly to an international conspiracy 'within and without Spain' that involved 'the extreme right'.[63] By 25 January the strike had been suppressed. Astonishingly, no one was killed, this being due to the readiness of the strikers to give themselves up and to the notable restraint of the army commander, General Domingo Batet. The government took advantage of the Law of the Defence of the Republic in order to deport not only miners from the uprising, but also anarchist revolutionaries who had nothing to do with it. Worse still, none of the 118 deportees, who were sent to the pernicious penal colony in Equatorial Guinea, had been subjected to due legal process. The punitive response of the government to the strike played once again into the hands of the anarchists within the CNT, aiding and abetting their takeover of the National Committee in March 1932 and their subsequent triumph at the National Congress the following month. Their ascendancy transformed 'the very essence' of the CNT, as it abandoned 'the path of trade-union struggle' for that of 'insurrectionism'.[64] The government's blinkered strategy had made a bad situation dramatically worse.

A more positive development of 1932 was an enlargement in both men's and women's rights, but especially those of women. Early in the year the Cortes debated the constitutional provisions regarding divorce, for which, judging by a survey carried out by *Heraldo de Madrid* in October 1931, there was considerable public support. The case was most forcibly put in parliament by Clara Campoamor:

Marriage is an accord between two parties. Once this accord is broken, once these parties cannot live together, once the marriage – which is based, in the view of any moderately sensible person, on love and spiritual affinity – does not realize this function, it is nothing more for the married couple than a torture, a source of suffering, and a degradation of the individual in relation to their own social activity.[65]

In accordance with the law of 2 March 1932, a divorce was granted not only if both parties agreed to it, but there were also thirteen instances in which just one of them could legitimately request it. This was an 'enormously egalitarian and progressive' divorce law, one of the most enlightened in the world.[66] Predictably, the right-wing press, which attributed it to 'the dirty passion of unhappy degenerates', foresaw the destruction of the family, but this doomsday scenario proved far-fetched.[67] By the end of 1933 a mere 4,043 divorces had been granted nationwide, a rate five times less than that in France.[68] In a predominantly rural province such as Toledo there were just forty divorces.[69]

In June 1932 the Cortes also approved civil marriage, thereby giving both men and women the option of eschewing the obligations of the Catholic Church. In fact, the civil was placed above the religious marriage, as all those who tied the knot in church had to undergo a civil ceremony too. The most egregious aspects of the Penal Code of 1870 were also overturned in October 1932: the crime of 'adultery' for women and that of *amancebamiento* for men (which meant that for a man to have committed adultery he had to have had an in-house lover or caused a 'public scandal'), as well as that of 'honour' killings in cases of adultery, which – in another example of the Code's double standards – condemned a man to the 'punishment of exile' but a woman to life imprisonment. In addition, a ministerial order of October 1933 changed the Civil Code of 1889 so that neither widows who remarried nor divorcees lost the custody of their children. On the other hand, the 'authority' of the husband was still required for a woman to sign contracts, administer goods, or undertake any other economic activity. An earlier law of November 1931 also obliged married women to secure the permission of their husbands before working. In many cases, labour agreements specified that women would not be offered work as long as men remained unemployed. Small wonder that women earned 47–75 per cent less than men for doing exactly the same job.[70]

Despite securing the vote in 1931, women made little political headway under the Republic. At the national level, the general election of 1933, like that of 1931, returned just three women deputies, while in 1936 there were six. This amounted to just over 1 per cent of all deputies, even though more than 50 per cent of the electorate was female. Women appeared to have fared even worse at the local level. Between 1931 and 1936 the available data show that only sixty-four mayoresses and forty-three female councillors were elected to the nation's 8,800 town halls, considerably less than 1 per cent of all local representatives.[71] Symptomatic of the situation was the fact that when the first female councillor for the city of Valencia, Guillerma Medrano, was presented to Manuel Azaña, he made a gesture of disdain before turning his back on her. Women made more of an impact in the media, as shown by the greater coverage of women and by the emergence of women's magazines such as *Mujeres Libres* and *Ellas*. The values, mentalities, and practices of an overwhelmingly patriarchal society did change under the Republic, but only very slowly. An illustration of how far women had to go is provided by the case of María Lejárraga. A socialist, feminist, intellectual, and parliamentary deputy, she published a staggering array of literary works, plays, librettos, film scripts, and articles, but all in the name of her husband, Gregorio Martínez Sierra.

During the spring and summer of 1932 the republican-socialist government struggled to advance its reformist agenda, partly due to divergences between the parties, especially over agrarian reform and Catalan autonomy, and partly due to the mounting opposition to the government, headed by the Radical Party. Once out of power, Lerroux's Radicals tried to drive a wedge between the left-republicans and the socialists in order to bring about an all-republican government. The keynote of their opposition was its anti-socialism, the party aiming, as the chief focus of urban middle-class discontent, to establish itself as the natural alternative to the republican-socialist administration. In a speech before 40,000 people in Madrid on 21 February 1932, Lerroux claimed that the socialists had created a 'state of alarm' which had to be defused by the formation of an all-republican administration that ruled 'for all Spaniards'.[72] Only by representing all the social classes, he declared, would the regime cease to be 'divorced from the country' or, worse still, end up as a 'dictatorship of a party or the dictatorship of a social class'.[73]

Such opposition gave voice to the anxieties of the middle classes, which were inextricably shaped by the escalating conflict in the provinces between the socialists and the republicans. On the one hand, the socialists decried the republicans' efforts to reduce local taxes and to restrict the application of labour legislation in order to benefit the shopkeepers, industrialists, and landowners who made up much of their social base. On the other hand, the republicans denounced the socialists' endeavours to raise taxes, to exploit the local council and work funds to provide jobs for their own members, to enforce the social and labour reforms through the use of fines and municipal guards, and to dominate local politics by, say, converting town-hall meetings into popular assemblies. In Granada, the socialists had republican labourers arrested on false grounds or shot at them in order to stop them working in the fields. National republican leaders received a flood of complaints from the provinces at the socialists' abuse of municipal power, which estranged centrist and left-republicans alike. 'The Spanish middle class,' a Radical deputy wrote to a colleague, 'has for the time being just about requested a "divorce" from the Republic.'[74] In parliament, Miguel Maura boomed that the abyss separating the Cortes from the country required the regime 'to change direction and undertake a genuinely national labour, one of national reconstruction, within a spirit of republican solidarity'.[75] In July, the Radical leader Alejandro Lerroux went further still, raising the spectre of a military intervention unless the socialists vacated office.[76]

## THE 'SANJURJADA'

One month later, Lerroux's threat became a reality: on 10 August a number of monarchist officers rose up against the government with civilian support. The government was well abreast of the attempted putsch, which was organized 'in view of everyone'.[77] Quickly routed in Madrid, it fared no better in Cádiz, Córdoba, and Granada, but triumphed in the Andalusian capital, Seville, where it was led by none other than General José Sanjurjo, the former director of the Civil

Guard and ally of Miguel Primo de Rivera who was known as 'the Lion of the Rif' for his exploits in Morocco. Having the support of both the local army and Civil Guard units, the general declared a state of war, replaced the local authorities, and proclaimed a dictatorship, while vehemently denouncing the government and the Cortes alike for having brought the nation to the verge of 'ruin, of iniquity and of dismemberment'.[78] Once the other uprisings folded it was clear that the Seville rebellion was doomed, especially as the troops there refused to fight those on their way down from Madrid. The government had initially reacted to the insurrection by backing the socialists' request to arm volunteers from the UGT and the parties of the left, but President Alcalá-Zamora vetoed this paramilitary venture on the grounds that the overwhelming bulk of the army had remained loyal to the Republic and that such a response ran the risk of turning a floundering insurgency into civil war. Sanjurjo fled for the Portuguese border but was seized en route. The so-called *Sanjurjada* had been a resounding failure. The subsequent repression, in accordance with the Law of the Defence of the Republic, was typically excessive: 114 newspapers, including *ABC*, *El Debate*, *Informaciones*, and *La Nación*, were suspended for lengthy terms and 5,000 people were arrested, of whom 142 were deported to the insalubrious environs of Villa Cisneros in the Sahara. Alcalá-Zamora claimed that there was also a 'vigorous purge' of the diplomatic corps, the judiciary, and the teaching profession.[79] At his trial, Sanjurjo was sentenced to death, but he was then reprieved by a government anxious not to create anti-republican martyrs.

There was widespread speculation afterwards as to whether or not Lerroux was involved in the uprising of August 1932. His position was ambiguous, as he had met with Sanjurjo on a number of occasions beforehand, but he had also made a point of informing the government of the conspiracy. However, there is no question that he kept in touch with subversive military elements after the *Sanjurjada*. In March 1933, for example, he received a letter from General Germán Gil-Yuste, who not only excoriated the government as 'an odious socialist dictatorship', but also declared darkly that 'to save Spain a lot of blood has to be spilt', while assuring Lerroux that he could count on his support 'at all times'.[80] More broadly, the crushing of the *Sanjurjada* strengthened the Republic by discrediting the *pronunciamiento* as an instrument of change and by reaffirming the regime's democratic credentials. Prime Minister Azaña welcomed the rebellion as an opportunity to confute the widespread belief that the Republic had survived because the military allowed it.

The defeat of the *Sanjurjada* also brought the long-standing tensions within the main right-wing party, *Acción Popular* (Popular Action), to a head. Originally a lobby group centred on the Catholic daily *El Debate*, Popular Action had mushroomed since its foundation in 1931 into an umbrella organization of regional parties, drawing not only on the redoubtable resources of the Catholic Church, but also those of the agrarian associations, especially the *Confederación Nacional Católico-Agraria* (National Catholic-Agrarian Confederation). Thus the defence of religion and that of property, as crystallized in the party slogan of 'Religion, Motherland, Order, Family, and Property', were inextricably linked. At the Popular Action congress of October 1932 the *posibilistas* (possibilists, those willing to work within the regime) clashed with the Alfonsists (supporters of King Alfonso XIII). The monarchists' defence of their dynastic identity and of the insurrectionary option was rejected by the possibilists as impractical and counterproductive. The Alfonsists duly abandoned the party, which thereby gained in strategic and ideological coherence. Despite the failure of the *Sanjurjada*, the Alfonsists still aimed to overthrow the Republic through an uprising, for which they built up a formidable war chest of 20 million pesetas. They also founded a political party, *Renovación Española* (Spanish Renovation), in January 1933 with a view to contesting the conservative vote with the possibilists. Thus the *Sanjurjada* at once divided and rejuvenated the forces of the right.

Following the *Sanjurjada*, the republican opposition gave way to a demonstrative display of support for the government. When the prime minister called for the confiscation of the land – without indemnification – of all those involved, the Radical deputy leader, Diego Martínez Barrio, rejoined, 'the Radical Party does not hesitate, the Radical Party does not argue, the Radical Party does not hinder.'[81] When the confiscations were extended, however questionably, to the *grandes de España* (the upper tier of the aristocracy), the Radical Party again stood shoulder to shoulder with the government; and when, on 9 September, the bills on agrarian reform and Catalan autonomy were put to the vote, the Radicals, despite their previous obstruction, were again not found wanting. Not only had the opposition been disarmed by the *Sanjurjada*, but also the government's two most important bills had finally been passed. Recent changes in newspaper ownership also brought three national dailies over to the prime minister's side. Victorious and revived, the Azaña administration was at its zenith. At the National Congress of the Radical Party in October, Lerroux – in stark contrast to his speech of 10 July – dwelt on what united, rather than divided, the republicans. 'We cannot,' he declaimed disingenuously, 'be anything other than followers of this government.'[82]

## THE RISE IN OPPOSITION

The honeymoon, however, was soon over. On 8 January 1933 a workers' insurrection erupted in Barcelona which then spread to other parts of the country. Historians of all stripes attribute this – like the Fígols strike the previous year – to the CNT, but, as new research reveals, this ill-coordinated uprising was in fact engineered exclusively by the revolutionary *Federación Anarquista Ibérica*, or FAI (Anarchist Iberian Federation). It was, as the minister of the interior recognized, 'a terrorist movement, organised by the FAI'.[83] The revolutionary call to arms had a sporadic impact in Catalonia, Valencia, and Andalusia, eventually trickling down to the province of Cádiz in the southwest, where, in the *pueblo* of Casas Viejas, local anarchists attacked the Civil Guard post on the morning of 11 January, killing two of its defenders. Later that day a detachment of forty Assault Guards arrived under the command of a Civil Guard captain, Manuel Rojas. He ordered the mud-and-stone shack of a seventy-two-year-old coalman, commonly known as 'Six Fingers', to be set on fire, as the people holed up there had earlier resisted other Civil and Assault Guards, killing one of them. Two people were killed as they fled the burning hovel, while six more perished in the flames, including 'Six Fingers' himself. The *pueblo* was then searched, a seventy-five-year-old man being gunned down while screaming 'Don't shoot! I'm not an anarchist!'[84] Twelve people were eventually rounded up, only one of whom had taken part in the uprising, and, in a chilling climax, were shot dead in cold blood, all but two of them being under twenty years of age. The final toll for the FAI-inspired insurrection of January 1933 was fifty dead and 100 wounded.

Once the Cortes reopened in February, Lerroux seized the moment to assail the government's entire record in a rhetorical tour de force, claiming that it was divorced from 'the national conscience', that its 'political' failure had climaxed in the *Sanjurjada* and its 'social' failure in the slaughter of Casas Viejas. In short, the government had 'failed totally and categorically'.[85] Unmoved by Lerroux's oratorical onslaught, Prime Minister Azaña retorted defiantly that the possibility of an all-republican administration 'does not exist, not even in the thoughts of the republicans', while lauding the alliance with the socialists as 'a fundamental experience of universal historical interest'.[86] Still, a motion of no confidence presented by the opposition nearly brought the government down. At a tumultuous meeting of the Radical-Socialist parliamentary group, numerous deputies called on the socialists to leave office, but supporters of the alliance with the PSOE squeezed home by twenty-one votes to eighteen, with three abstentions. The government had survived, but only just. 'We live,' Azaña noted, 'on a volcano.'[87]

The tragedy at Casas Viejas highlighted a number of major problems for the Republic. It reflected the failure of successive governments to reach a modus vivendi with the syndicalists of the CNT while they still controlled the organization. The uprising also revealed that reform had advanced little in many areas, a good number of peasants in Casas Viejas having abandoned the reformist UGT for the revolutionary CNT the previous year. The massacre underlined yet again not only the excessive violence of the security forces, but also the injustice of the legal system, as the only person to be put on trial for the slaughter of the civilians was Captain Rojas, while twenty-six local people were charged with the killing of the three guards. The bitter irony of the repression is that it was largely the work of the Assault Guard, the force created in 1931 precisely in order to avoid the habitual excesses of the Civil Guard. The prime minister's self-righteous insistence that his administration was neither blameworthy nor responsible – the minister of the interior did not even consider resigning – was an indictment of his government's entire approach to law and order. Most damagingly of all, the calamity of Casas Viejas violated the government's democratic mandate and impugned the Republic's moral authority. Accordingly, 'Casas Viejas' became a byword for the betrayal of the regime's initial idealism. The Azaña administration would henceforth be known as the 'Government of Casas Viejas', a smear that would haunt it to the very end.

A further blow to the government was the eruption onto the political scene in March 1933 of the first mass Catholic party in Spanish history: the *Confederación Española de Derechas Autónomas*, or CEDA (Spanish Confederation of Autonomous Right-Wing Groups). A coalition of diverse regional and provincial groups, the cornerstone of the new party was Popular Action. Upon its launch in March 1933, the CEDA claimed 700,000 members, more than any other party. Its effective mobilization of women – half the Madrid members, for example, were female – was matched only by the Socialist Party. The CEDA adopted the Vatican-inspired doctrine of 'accidentalism', according to which Catholics should judge a regime not by its political form, but by its religious content, that is, the nature of its modus vivendi with the Catholic Church. The emergence of the CEDA not only created a major breach within the middle classes between the religious and anticlerical sectors, but also represented a fundamental challenge to the constitutional order, as the rallying cry of the CEDA was the revision of the Republic's *magna carta*. The fluctuating and often disjointed opposition of the centrist republicans was therefore already in danger of being outflanked and outmuscled by the resurgent non-republican right.

The real nature and aims of the CEDA have been endlessly debated by historians and political scientists alike. Although the leader of the CEDA, the balding if extremely youthful José María Gil Robles, later admitted that 'the immense majority' of its affiliates were 'decidedly monarchist', the restoration of the Bourbon dynasty was not an immediate goal, as the monarchist cause remained intensely unpopular.[88] The primary objective of the CEDA was the revision of the Constitution. Beyond that, it aspired to an authoritarian regime based on corporatist, Catholic principles, which marked a complete break with the liberal parliamentary tradition of the monarchist parties. This rupture with the Restoration was partly caused by the Primo de Rivera dictatorship, partly a reaction to the ardent anticlericalism of the left, and partly a response to wider international currents. The CEDA identified itself with Chancellor Dollfuss's corporatist regime in Austria rather than with fascist Italy or Nazi Germany, its proximity to the Catholic Church and the old elites being too great for it to be considered fascist. Even so, the CEDA aped certain features of fascism, such as the cult of the leader or *Jefe*, the ultra-nationalist youth wing, and the orchestration of high-octane mass rallies. The new conservative confederation was nonetheless distinguished from the explicitly anti-republican right by the Vatican-inspired doctrine of 'accidentalism', by which a regime was to be gauged by its treatment of the Catholic Church, not its political nature. This made it 'possibilist'; in other words, it was prepared to work within the regime rather than to oppose it outright. Nonetheless, the CEDA constituted an elemental challenge to the identity of the Republic, and in particular to the patrimonial vision of the left.

The seriousness of the challenge represented by the CEDA was underlined by the municipal elections of April 1933. These involved just under a quarter of Spain's 81,099 councillors, the bulk of the elections taking place in rural *pueblos*, above all in Aragón, the two Castiles and Navarre, where monarchist *caciques* had invariably held sway before the Republic. It was also the first election in Spanish history in which women exercised the vote. The republicans felt doubly threatened by the revival of the right and the introduction of the female suffrage, *El Progreso* warning that the electoral organization of the right 'is perfect' and that its mobilization of women 'is difficult to counteract on the part of our republican women', as 'the numerical struggle is unequal and the means and resources inferior'.[89] The ruling coalition won 5,048 councillors and the moderate republicans 4,205, but the resurgent right won 4,954 seats, surpassing the centrist republicans and almost overtaking the governing parties. Ominously for the Azaña administration, the opposition parties had secured nearly two-thirds of the local councillors.

The enormity of the Catholic challenge to the government was made clearer still by the public uproar which greeted the bill on Congregations, the purpose of which was to give legislative form to the religious articles of the Constitution. Opposition to the bill drew not only on the Catholic community, which held demonstrations the length and breadth of the country, but also on the parliamentary right, and President Alcalá-Zamora, who, as the final vote loomed, became 'almost insane, tearful, agitated'.[90] The passing of the bill into law on 17 May outraged the Catholic world: the bishops issued a declaration against it, the Pope published a condemnatory encyclical, and the president made his disapproval manifest by refusing to sign the bill until 3 June. Short of dissolving the Cortes, Alcalá-Zamora had done his utmost, as a Catholic, a conservative, and a constitutional revisionist, including colluding with the republican opposition, to derail the bill. He then took advantage of a minor Cabinet reshuffle in June to force the government's resignation in an effort to seek an alternative ruling majority. The president's priority was the removal of Manuel Azaña as premier since their relations, always prickly and distrustful, had reached their nadir with the Law on Congregations, but the ploy failed, so Azaña duly formed his third administration.

Another escalating source of opposition was the organized working class. During the summer of 1933 the economy reached its lowest point under the Republic, unemployment climbing sharply as public works funds dwindled, the emigration of the 1920s gave way to immigration (100,000 workers returning home between 1931 and 1933), and the economic crisis deepened. Rising from 446,263 in June 1932 to 618,946 by the end of 1933, the unemployment, compounded by chronic structural underemployment, hit rural labourers, building workers, and miners hardest. Worse still, the jobless were criminalized by the draconian Law on Idlers and Criminals of August 1933, by which unemployed workers could be held in workhouses for between three and five years, while those caught spreading propaganda – a practice associated above all with the anarchists – could be retained for up to five years. The workers fell back increasingly on the strike weapon, the 435 stoppages of 1932 soaring to 1,046 in 1933. Mounting misery alone does not explain the mass mobilization of 1933. Many workers struck not out of despair, but, on the contrary, in response to rising expectations, urban salaries having risen by one-fifth since 1931 and those of unionized rural labourers by at least a third.

The widespread protest of the workers made the mobilization of the employers inevitable. Under the Republic, urban employers not only revamped existing organizations, but also launched new ones, such as the *Federación Económica de Andalucía*, or FEDA (Economic Federation of Andalusia), based in Seville, the site of an intense rivalry between the CNT, the UGT, and the *Partido Comunista de España*, or PCE (Spanish Communist Party). In early 1933 the city was engulfed by a wave of violence, as the anarcho-syndicalists and the Communists battled one another with guns and bombs. In May, still in the grip of a 'spiral of terror', the Andalusian capital was hit by a public sector stoppage, the mass closure of its shops, and a general strike of both the CNT and PCE.[91] A thousand employers from Seville travelled up to Madrid to protest at the situation, only for the general secretary of the FEDA to be gunned down on 20 May. The employers' chief grievance – the lack of law and order aside – was the labour legislation, especially the arbitration boards, complaining that the latter were inherently biased, that they greatly complicated relations with the CNT, and that they set unrealistic conditions. Agrarian associations, such as the *Confederación Española Patronal Agrícola*, or CEPA (Spanish Federation of Agricultural Employers), also targeted the labour legislation. Negotiations over the new contracts led the CEPA to organize a campaign of protest which culminated in March 1933 with a rally of over 14,000 farmers in Madrid.

The clamour of the rural and urban employers reached its climax in July 1933 with the nationwide congress of the Economic Union. The employers are often portrayed in crude Marxist terms as a monolithic block, but this was far from the case. Thus the congress of the Economic Union was at once a demonstration of the employers' strength and of their weakness: over a thousand associations were represented, but there was little unison between them. Some wanted the arbitration boards to be reformed, others for them to be eliminated altogether; some called for a coordinating committee of the associations, while others demanded a General Union of Employers (thereby aping the structure of the socialist General Union of Workers, the UGT). Following a heated debate, the congress agreed that the arbitration boards should be reformed. It also voted to establish a coordinating committee, as opposed to a centralized body, which reflected the overall lack of agreement. The demands of the employers nonetheless powerfully reinforced the political opposition to the Azaña government, while resonating with the left-republicans. Relations between the socialists and the left-republicans had been difficult if not antag-onistic at the local level for some time, but it was not until the summer of 1933 that the latter questioned the alliance with the Socialist Party at the national level. In July the leading Radical-Socialist dissident, Félix Gordón Ordás, denounced the 'socialist dictatorship' in a high-profile speech in Madrid, the infighting within the party reaching its climax in September with a seismic schism.[92]

The cumulative opposition of the Catholics, the centrist republicans, the CNT, the employers, and an increasing number of left-republicans during 'that turbulent summer' naturally put the socialists on the defen-sive.[93] In any case, socialist disillusionment with the Republic had been growing since the congresses of the PSOE and UGT in October 1932. For the socialists, the Republic existed insofar as it fulfilled their reform-ist agenda, which they 'guaranteed with their governmental presence'.[94] The irregular application of the labour legislation, the hardship engen-dered by the economic crisis, and the mounting opposition from both within and without the governing coalition had all taken their toll on the socialists. For the intensely pragmatic labour minister Largo Cabal-lero, the Republic was not to be defended per se, but as a stepping stone on the road to socialism, this utilitarian approach having already justified collaboration with the Primo de Rivera dictatorship. Indeed, collaboration, whether with a dictatorship or a democracy, all formed part of 'an intelligent tactic', according to El Socialista.[95] The guiding principle of this 'intelligent tactic' was the welfare of the organized working class, which the socialists tended to equate with themselves as a means of denying legitimacy to their rivals. From this perspective, the attitude of the followers of Largo Caballero, or caballeristas, towards the Republic was as instrumental as that of the CEDA. This explains Largo Caballero's disdain for the principles of parliamentary dem-ocracy, as when he declared in February 1932 that if the republicans discarded the socialists before time, 'they would force us to go to civil war'.[96] Eight months later he warned that if the socialists were forced out of power this would be 'suicide for the socialist movement and for the entire Spanish nation'.[97]

His demagogic threats acquired a new menace during the summer of 1933, not least because of the drop in UGT membership: the one mil-lion members of June 1932 had plummeted to a mere 400,000 one year later. On 23 July 1933 in a speech in Madrid, Largo Caballero thundered that if the socialists were removed from office before fulfilling their mission they would seek 'the conquest of power'.[98] This would be achieved by one of two means: either via parliament – the socialists would rule alone following victory in a general election – or via the 'revolutionary' route, which would be pursued if the socialists were unjustly ejected from power or if the government sought to implant 'a dictatorship or fascism'.[99] He was responding in large part to the shift in the UGT's centre of gravity from the urban workers to the more radical rural ones, a product not just of the more polarized situation in the countryside, but also of the relative political inexperience of the landless labourers. Largo Caballero was now acclaimed by the socialist left as the 'Spanish Lenin', a comparison which hardly did justice to the intellectual and organizational prowess of the Russian leader, but reflected the burgeoning disillusionment within the movement's ranks.

## THE GENERAL ELECTION OF NOVEMBER 1933

The tipping point for the government was the elections to the Court of Constitutional Guarantees on 3 September. Fifteen of the Court's members were to be elected by the local councils, but in many provinces the ruling coalition failed to agree on a united candidature. The Radicals won four seats on the Court, the right six, and the left-wing government only five, the outcome leaving it, in Azaña's words, 'worn out, undone, crushed'.[100] President Alcalá-Zamora took advantage of the government's defeat to withdraw his support before calling on Lerroux to re-establish the 'fraternal understanding between all the republican groups'.[101] The Radical leader duly presented an all-republican Cabinet before parliament on 2 October. Had Lerroux assured the Cortes that his government aimed to pass the Constitution's supplementary laws, he might have improved relations amongst the republican parties. Unfortunately, he lacked the necessary foresight, patience, and tact, as he proceeded to criticize the previous administration, to reiterate that the Cortes was divorced from the country, and to conclude by saying that he could not govern with the current chamber. He then requested a vote of confidence from a body in which he had no confidence himself, in all likelihood so that he could fix the general election to the advantage of his own party. The Radical leader's position, as his deputy recognized, was 'evidently false'.[102] Neither the left-republicans nor the socialists backed the government, Lerroux's first administration being over before it had begun. The president then called on the Radical deputy leader, Diego Martínez Barrio, rather than Lerroux, to form an all-republican government that would oversee a general election. Far from being resigned, as Lerroux noted, to 'the discreet abstention and neutrality that corresponded to the head of a republican parliamentary state as guarantees of his impartiality', Alcalá-Zamora was set on a self-serving policy of divide and rule.[103]

The general election that followed in November 1933 is still regarded by many historians as a travesty of a ballot which greatly prejudiced the left, but the most exhaustive research on the subject has shown this to be a myth. In fact, the vote of November 1933 constituted the first clean and democratic general election in Spanish history. This was not only because the government went to great lengths to ensure that the process was fair, but also because – for the very first time – women voted in a national election. The fair play was partly a product of circumstance insofar as this was the first Cabinet in Spanish history which did not have its own slate to defend. The all-republican government could have favoured the cause of the individual parties within it, but it refused to do so. On the contrary, the scrupulous minister of the interior, Manuel Rico Avello, broke completely with tradition by refusing to exercise any form of 'official influence' during the election. 'I have to guarantee the liberty of all,' he declared.[104] If anyone personified the civic and democratic ideals of the Republic, it was the modest and hard-working Rico Avello, a conscientious administrator who was able to collaborate effectively with colleagues of both the left and right, while eschewing the self-righteous sectarianism and ideological breast-beating that plagued the politics of the Second Republic. Crucially, he was supported unreservedly by the prime minister, Diego Martínez Barrio, who announced on national radio the day before the people went to the polls that 'the government is not a belligerent in this struggle. It acts apart from the parties, sometimes against their will, and always independently of the particular interest of each one.'[105] This is not to deny that fraud, bribery, intimidation, and other electoral malpractices took place, above all in Andalusia, Extremadura, Galicia, and Valencia, but this did not affect the overall result. A measure of the election's equanimity was the fact that not only was the minister of the interior defeated – for the first time in history – but so were three of the four Radical-Socialist ministers. Thus the 1933 general election represented 'an enormous step forward in the political life of Spain – the first reasonably honest yet fiercely competitive elections in Spanish history'.[106]

Electioneering in November 1933 had also been transformed by the introduction of three major technological innovations – the radio, mobile film units, and aeroplanes – which made campaigning more accessible, exciting, and national in scope than ever before. The chief beneficiary of these new techniques was the non-republican right, as it possessed greater resources than the other ideological currents. In the province of Ciudad Real, for example, the CEDA not only deployed 'a fleet of automobiles that literally combed all the *pueblos*, taking the candidates, pamphlets and proclamations to the remotest corners', but also two light aircraft, which 'with the name of *Acción Popular* painted on the wings, flew low over the towns and villages, dropping propaganda to the astonishment of their inhabitants'.[107] Nationwide, the CEDA produced ten million leaflets and 200,000 colour posters for the election.

The left won 100 deputies, the centre 177, the non-republican right 152, and the explicitly anti-republican right 44. In party terms, the CEDA came first with 115 seats, the Radical Party second with 101, and the PSOE third with 58, while the national left-republican parties won a mere 13 of the 473 seats between them. The left-wing majority of 1931–3 had crumbled in the face of a rejuvenated right, while the centre had managed little more than to hold its own. No single tendency had secured a majority, so a hung parliament was the outcome. It is often asserted that 'the right' won the general election of 1933, but this was simply not true. Admittedly, the right won more seats than the left or the centre, but it failed to secure a majority. In any case, the forces of the right were profoundly divided, the 'accidentalist' or non-republican right refusing to collaborate with either the anti-republican monarchists or the Falangists.

Why had the Cortes swung so far to the right? The first reason lay in the pendulous effect of the electoral system, which rewarded slight improvements in the vote with huge gains in representation. The second reason is that not only had the republican-socialist coalition of 1931 fallen apart, but the left-republicans and socialists, who had ruled in tandem for two years, committed the cardinal sin of failing to present a united electoral front. This was even more important than in 1931, as the Electoral Law of July 1933 – drawn up, it should be noted, by the left – placed an even greater premium on coalitions than that of May 1931, as the threshold for the majority seats now stood at 40 per cent, up from 20 per cent. The schism within the left was the fault of the socialists, who stood alone in the seriously mistaken belief that they could actually win the election. In Badajoz, for example, socialist rejection of the left-republicans as allies proved to be 'a fatal error'.[108] A third reason was the resurgence of the right, whose paltry presence in 1931 had been transformed by 1933. In fact, the right spent far more on the election than either the left or centre parties. It showered more than one million pesetas on the Madrid campaign alone, while the glossy posters and plane drops of the Asturian campaign left the republicans gasping at the right's 'magnificent' organization.[109] The fact that the forces of the right were much more united than those of the left was yet another major advantage.

The split within the left and the revival of the right are insufficient, however, to explain the electoral outcome. If the reforms of 1931–3 aimed to consolidate the left's social base, they also generated a 'counter-force' that was determined to overthrow them.[110] The fact is that many social and professional sectors, notably the anarcho-syndicalists, Catholics, landowners, urban employers, and the army, had been alienated by the reforms of 1931–3. The left's bludgeoning of the Catholic Church, to take an obvious example, rallied conservatives the length and breadth of the country. Small landowners, for whom wages constituted a big part of their outlay, were alienated by the demands of Largo Caballero's labour reforms. Equally, the heavy-handed repression of the CNT led it to launch a nationwide campaign of electoral abstention. The movement's newspaper, *Solidaridad Obrera*, implored its readers not to vote for the 'new hangman, the new tyrant, a new exploiter, a new bum, a new leach'. 'Voting is for idiots,' it shrieked.[111] Small wonder that abstention was especially high (62.7 per cent) in Cádiz, the province of Casas Viejas, thereby enabling the fascist party, the Falange, to win its one and only seat under the Second Republic, that of its founder, the sleek, articulate, and youthful José Antonio Primo de Rivera, son of the dictator. At the national level, anarchist abstention cost the left 6 per cent of the vote, or around seventy-five seats.[112]

The reforms of 1931–3 had been inspired above all by the French Revolution and in particular the Third Republic (1870–1940). However, the challenges faced by the Spanish Second Republic were far greater than those of the French Third Republic, yet the Spanish republicans, obsessed by the country's relative backwardness, were determined to overcome them in far less time than the French had, despite commanding a much weaker economy. The inevitable result was a sharpening of political, economic, and social tensions, a situation made worse still by the shortcomings of the reforms themselves. A leading example is the Agrarian Reform Law of 1932. Agrarian reform represented the greatest challenge of all, as 99.1 per cent of all holdings were under 20 acres, while 1,000 large estates and 50,000 estates of over 200 acres comprised 35 per cent of all cultivated land. The law of 1932 was intended to address this extreme inequality in ownership, but it proved a major deception, as it was limited to just fourteen provinces while being greatly hampered by its cumbersome bureaucratic procedures. Between September 1932 and December 1933, just 275 peasants a month were settled on a total of 24,203 hectares.

The backlash against the governments of 1931–3 benefited not just the right but also the centre parties. The essential moderation of the centre, epitomized by its slogan 'Liberal Democracy is Us', attracted many urban middle-class sectors, especially the industrial and commercial classes, who were indignant at the sectarian nature of the labour laws. It could be argued, especially in view of the decision of the socialists to go it alone, that the left-wing and centrist republicans should have joined forces. Admittedly, the two camps were divided by the opposition of the centre from 1932 to 1933 and by Lerroux's parliamentary performance on 2 October 1933. But many left-republicans had also been alienated by the socialists, while sharing the centre's close ties with the Freemasons and its antipathy to the right. If only for the sake of the regime which they embodied, the republicans should have made the effort to reach an electoral understanding. A republican coalition, underpinned by an all-republican government, would have been a leading electoral contender, possibly even winning. The failure of the republicans to join forces was a grievous missed opportunity, as it might well have changed the course of the Republic.

Ever since the general election of November 1933, the female vote has been held responsible for the success of the right. This unproven claim rests on the assumption that, as many deputies asserted during the constitutional debate of 1931, the Catholic clergy wielded an undue influence over their female congregation. However, regular church attendance by women was low in much of Spain, especially in the centre and south. In any case, this view of women as passive vessels was offset by the electoral campaign itself, during which the parties competed vigorously for their vote. If the republicans felt threatened by the organizational prowess of the right – a Radical wrote to Lerroux from León that the female suffrage 'frightens me' because the right had a women's group 'in nearly all the *pueblos*' – then that reflected on their own electoral shortcomings.[113] By the time women came to vote on 19 November 1933 they had in fact been widely politicized, so their exercise of the suffrage was not 'an extension of their subordination in the social and economic spheres into the public', but rather a confirmation of their new political status.[114]

Ultimately, the defeat of the left, the stagnation of the centre, and the resurgence of the right was down to the splintering of the far-flung coalition which had ushered in the new regime, as reflected in the alienation of the anarcho-syndicalists, the opposition of the moderate republicans, and the division between the socialists and the left-republicans, in addition to the failure of the left and centre republicans to reach an electoral agreement. Accordingly, the general election debunks the common portrayal of the Second Republic as a Manichean clash between left and right, the result of a tendency to project back onto the regime's democratic years of 1931 to 1936 the polarities of its civil war between 1936 and 1939. As the November 1933 election underlines, the politics of the regime were far more complex than this reductionist narrative allows. In reality, both the left and the right were deeply fragmented. There was also a substantial centre, which has been overwhelmingly ignored by historians until recently, despite being a major player during the Republic's first five years.

Crushing defeat did not stop the left from asserting its patrimonial right to rule. After the first round of voting, the Radical-Socialist minister of justice urged President Alcalá-Zamora to annul the elections by decree, while the Radical-Socialist minister of industry implored him to dissolve the Cortes before it met. Following the second round, Azaña pressed Prime Minister Martínez Barrio to let a left-wing government hold the election anew, while the socialist Juan Negrín lobbied the president to pass a new electoral law which would guarantee victory for the left in a rerun election. In short, the left now rejected the very rules which it had drawn up. Alcalá-Zamora viewed these attempts to invalidate the result as 'coup d'états' and was struck by the opposition's 'mad desire to regain power', while Martínez Barrio also stood firm, telling the left 'to know how to lose'.[115]

The day the Cortes opened, 8 December 1933, the CNT responded to the outcome of the general election by launching 'the social revolution'.[116] Centred on Aragón and La Rioja, the uprising also unfolded in Catalonia, Valencia, Andalusia, Extremadura, and León. The insurgents derailed a number of trains, notably the Barcelona-Seville express at a cost of twenty-three lives. As ever, the CNT was no match for the army and police. In all, eighty-nine people died: seventy-five civilians, eleven Civil Guards, and three Assault Guards.[117] This was 'the most destructive exercise in futility ever undertaken by the CNT'.[118] The experience left the CNT 'broken, dismantled, without newspapers or journals'.[119] At the beginning of 1934 there were 15,000 CNT members in jail and anarcho-syndicalist branches had been closed down throughout the country. By February 1935 the organization had lost 600,000 members in just three years, the National Committee of the CNT estimating that the organization was 'condemned to death'.[120] Little wonder that the CNT launched no insurrections following the fiasco of December 1933 until the summer of 1936.

# The Second Republic, 1934–1936

*Revolution, Reaction, and Polarization*

On 19 December 1933, Prime Minister Alejandro Lerroux presented a centrist, Radical-dominated government to the Cortes, which depended for its survival on the parliamentary support of the right-wing, Catholic CEDA. The purpose of the alliance, he explained, was 'to nationalize the Republic, to consolidate the Republic, to reconcile, within the law of the Republic, all Spaniards', so that 'the Motherland and the Republic' would be one.[1] This alliance of the centre and right is often presented as a betrayal of the Republic, as the Radicals allegedly sought to advance the CEDA's 'fascist' agenda in exchange for privileged access to the illicit spoils of the public sector. From this perspective, the centre acted as a mere marionette of the right. Certainly the two parties made an odd couple. The CEDA was authoritarian in aspiration, it opposed the Constitution and most of the reforms of 1931–3, and it judged a regime not by its political form but by its treatment of the Catholic Church. By contrast, the Radical Party was liberal-democratic, it backed the Constitution and many of the reforms of 1931–3, and it had always defended the republican form of government. Last, but not least, the CEDA was largely a creation of the Catholic Church, whereas the Radical Party harboured more Freemasons – avowed antagonists of the Church – than any other party, its deputy leader, Diego Martínez Barrio, being the Grand Master of the Grand Spanish Orient, one of the two main Masonic organizations. As the CEDA leader José María Gil Robles noted of the Radical premier Alejandro Lerroux, 'an abyss separated me from his ideology'.[2]

The two parties nonetheless shared a number of common goals: the protection of private property, the defence of law and order, the revision of the labour legislation, an amnesty for the insurgents of August 1932, and their opposition to the socialist movement. In pragmatic terms, the Radicals could not form a parliamentary majority without the support of the non-republican right. They also saw this as an opportunity to realize their goal of 'a Republic for all Spaniards' by integrating the main Catholic party. Ultimately, collaboration was made possible by the fact that the CEDA, in contrast to other right-wing movements – the Alphonsists, Carlists and Falangists – was *possibilist*, that is, it was prepared to work within the regime. This was not simply a matter of opportunism but formed part of a broader Catholic strategy. Both the Spanish Church hierarchy and the Vatican agreed that the best means of defending the interests of the Catholic community was not to oppose the Republic, but to collaborate with it, while evaluating it in terms of its modus vivendi with the Catholic Church. Even so, the posture of the CEDA remained 'ambiguous and dangerous', the threat of violence lurking beneath its possibilist stance.[3] If the CEDA was not allowed to govern, warned its leader Gil Robles, 'we shall seek other solutions'.[4] It is nonetheless extremely difficult, if not impossible, to see how the Republic could have been stabilized without the integration of the bulk of Catholics, who, after all, made up half the political community. Such a strategy, had it triumphed, would have driven an insurmountable wedge between the possibilist and anti-republican right, thereby marginalizing the Alphonsists, Carlists, and Falangists. In any case, if the republicans aspired to the consolidation of the Republic, they at least had to make the *attempt* to integrate the possibilist right into it.

## THE DESTRUCTION OF
## THE REFORMS OF 1931-3?

A classic account of the Republic claims that by September 1934 the Radical Party had dismantled 'the majority of the acts of the First Republican Cortes', while 'proceeding to threaten the remainder'.[5] In fact, the only major law to have been overturned by September 1934 was the Law on Municipal Boundaries, which was 'universally unpopular' outside socialist circles.[6] A different question altogether was the non-application of the laws. Many historians contend that, following the November 1933 general election, 'reforms on the statute book were a dead letter', a prime target of this 'reaction by omission' being the labour legislation.[7] Certainly there were provinces, such as Badajoz, Granada, and Jaén, where the landowners interpreted the electoral defeat of the left as an opportunity to violate the labour laws. In February 1934 the socialist spokesman in the Cortes, Indalecio Prieto, claimed that in Jaén the labour legislation had been widely ignored, the landless labourers had been persecuted by the landowners and the Civil Guard, and that as many as 400 workers had been imprisoned since the general election. Recent investigations, however, have questioned this Manichean interpretation. Research on Castile-La Mancha shows that after the election the socialists did indeed lose influence over the arbitration boards, the job centres, the local labour markets, and the civil governors, but the government did uphold the existing labour contracts. As a result, 'until the end of 1934 and even well into 1935 neither the salaries nor the labour legislation nor the dispositions that affected the agrarian reform were altered in a drastic fashion.'[8] Much the same can be said of Andalusia, where 'the government was not prepared to violate the labour contracts in place and even less to let salaries slide.'[9] Thus the contracts of 1934 for the provinces of Seville and Córdoba were even better than those of 1933.

In the towns and cities there was a widespread expectation amongst employers that the Radicals would carry out, in the words of one republican businessman, 'real rectifications', which demonstrated that 'there is room for all social and economic aspirations', not least because shopkeepers, traders, builders, and industrialists constituted the backbone of the party.[10] Their disappointment with the approach of the left-republicans from 1931 to 1933 was absolute. 'What did they do,' asked a left-republican businessman, 'for the benefit of the small employer, of the small industrialist, of the modest farmer, of the small capitalist and, in general, for all the productive and mercantile classes of the country, which in April 1931 gave their votes to the republicans?'[11] In January 1934 the Radicals reformed the arbitration boards so that the president (who held the deciding vote) could not be a trade unionist. Still, the president could not be an employer either, the aim being to make the boards independent. The business community had already been rocked in December 1933 by the decision of the minister of labour, Josep Estadella, to resolve the strike in Madrid's hotels, cafés, bars, and restaurants by arresting members of the employers' association and finding in favour of the workers. The employers were again astonished in February 1934 when the minister came down on the side of the capital's building workers following a six-month-long strike over the forty-four-hour week. Their spirits were somewhat lifted by the defeat of the Madrid print workers in March, but three months later the metallurgical workers won a strike in defence of the forty-four-hour week. Indeed, the struggle between the bosses and the workers in Madrid 'is always settled, during the first year of Radical government and following long strikes, in favour of the workers' claims and against the employers'.[12] Clearly the Radicals were not prepared just to do the employers' bidding, but, on the contrary, were seeking to uphold the law. The business bosses were astonished at the 'lack of political protection', convinced that the Radicals had declared 'war on the employers'.[13]

If the Radical-led administrations up to October 1934 did not halt or destroy the reforms of the Republic's first biennium en masse, then it follows that there must have been a good deal of continuity with the work of the Constituent Cortes. A notable example is agrarian reform. In February 1934 the centre joined forces with the left in parliament in order to stop the right from expelling the *yunteros* (ploughmen) in Extremadura from the untilled land to which they had been given access in accordance with the Intensification of Cultivation decrees. In June 1934 the centre and left again stood up to the right, this time to prevent it from axing the funds of the Institute of Agrarian Reform, which was responsible for executing the Agrarian Reform Law of 1932. Above all, the centrist governments up to October 1934 upheld the agrarian reform by more than doubling the rate of expropriation of the first biennium, settling 700 peasants a month in contrast to the 275 a month of 1932–3.

The governments of the second biennium also passed laws that were entirely in accord with the spirit of the Constituent Cortes. An outstanding example is the Health Coordination Law of June 1934, an important step in the creation of a national health service and the first such law passed by the Cortes since 1857. The Radical Party was lauded by *La Voz Médica* (The Medical Voice) as the 'only one that has focused on modern health with a clear and effective vision'.[14] In particular, the reform addressed the plight of the rural doctors – 'it will release us from misery and slavery' – many of whom had not been paid for years (nationwide arrears standing at 50 million pesetas).[15] The Law was eventually incorporated into a Francoist reform of 1944, lasting as a result until 1967, which made it one of the most enduring reforms of the Second Republic. Despite tackling one of the most neglected areas of state welfare, it has nonetheless been almost completely ignored in the vast literature on the regime. Another illustration of the Radicals' public spirit, which has also been neglected, was the manner in which they celebrated the third anniversary of the Republic. In contrast to the diffuse message of the first two anniversaries, the third was deliberately designed, in the words of its organizer, 'to create national symbols above and beyond the parties and their passions', particularly by focusing on 'the concept of citizenship'.[16]

The spirit of public service of the Radicals was not incompatible, however, with their exploitation of the state spoils system. Just like the left-republicans and socialists before them, the Radicals appointed a multitude of party members to positions in the gift of the authorities. 'They all want jobs, they all ask for posts,' as one deputy wrote to Lerroux.[17] In the same vein, a commission visited the Radical boss in December 1933 to press the claims of party members in relation to a host of high-profile public positions. Radicals were duly appointed to jobs in education, health, labour, and many other areas, while Lerroux himself allegedly had a niece installed at the Geography Institute, another at the Bank of Spain, and a nephew in the civil service. A major source of patronage or clientelism was local government. At a meeting of the parliamentary party on 29 December 1933, the minister of the interior was urged to overthrow more left-wing town councils in favour of centre-right steering committees not only in order to strengthen the party in the provinces, but also to create more jobs for its members. Such was the eagerness of the Radicals to occupy the steering committees that the CEDA leader Gil Robles complained to Lerroux that his party felt 'spurned', as it did not receive its fair share of positions.[18] What did perhaps set the Radical Party apart was their corruption. The admittedly sectarian *El Socialista* accused Radical deputies of taking bribes and Radical authorities of permitting casinos to operate illegally. However, the other parties were certainly not graft-free, as Indalecio Prieto's controversial concession of a government contract to a business partner in 1932 indicates.

## ACCOMMODATING THE RIGHT

The Radicals' vision of 'a Republic for all Spaniards' and their parliamentary dependence on the CEDA made it inevitable they would make concessions to the right. Up to October 1934, these were not only limited in number, but also strictly constitutional in nature. A foremost example is furnished by the policy on religion. When Gil Robles demanded in parliament the 'rectification of the sectarian legislation that has wounded our beliefs so profoundly' in December 1933, Premier Alejandro Lerroux rejoined that he respected the 'conscience of the majority', while making it clear that he would not 'fail the laws'.[19] In other words, he would make adjustments to the existing legislation, but not ignore it. A first test of this policy was the suppression of the clerical budget in 1934. This would leave the poorest clergy destitute, as Prime Minister Azaña recognized in 1932 when he urged the ruling coalition to find 'a way of helping' these priests.[20] However, the left-wing majority refused to countenance any further state support for the clergy. By contrast, the Radicals passed a bill in April 1934 which granted all priests over forty on 14 April 1931 two-thirds of their salary at the time, though these payments were subject to a cap of 16.5 million pesetas. The measure outraged left and right alike. The former criticized it as an inadmissible attack on the 'purity of the republican regime', while the latter lamented that the law was 'far removed' from its own expectations.[21] The uproar nonetheless made it patently clear that the Radical Party, far from being the cypher of the CEDA, was seeking a third way between the intransigence of the left and the imperatives of the right. The same spirit of equanimity guided the government's approach to the highly contentious issue of the replacement of private Catholic schools by secular state ones. During the first biennium, the process of substitution had been blown off course by bureaucratic bungling and, above all, by the woeful shortage of schools, teachers, and money. The Azaña administrations tried, but failed, to overcome these shortcomings, as would the Popular Front governments of 1936. Once in power the Radicals steered a middle course: the Catholic schools were left alone, while the state system progressed in accordance with the existing legislation, a policy which aimed to accommodate all sides. In reality, the upshot was not very different from the de facto situation during the first biennium, as the Church had kept many of its schools open by registering them as educational benefit societies.

The Radical governments' protection of Catholic schooling therefore went hand in hand with a firm commitment to the public school system. Over the summer of 1934 the minister of education, the veteran republican Dr Filiberto Villalobos, drew up a new *bachillerato* (secondary school syllabus) that was based on the plans of the first biennium, to the fury of the right. He also raised the minimum salary of most primary school teachers by 33 per cent, increased the number of inspectors by 17 per cent, and boosted the number of secondary school places by over 300 per cent. Indeed, the governments of 1934 and 1935 spent a higher proportion of the national budget on education (7.08 and 6.6 per cent respectively) than the left-wing administrations of 1932–3. For *El Debate*, the forces of the left 'continued to be the masters of the Ministry of Education'.[22] In reality, the Radical governments struck a truly centrist compromise over education: they found a way of accommodating both the private and public sectors.

A crucial but sorely neglected aspect of the centre's religious policy was the attempt to secure a new concordat with the Vatican. For the Catholics to be integrated into the Republic, it was considered essential to update the agreement which had governed relations between the Spanish state and the Vatican since 1850. Once again, the centre government did not act as a mere emissary of the CEDA, but appointed its own (left-republican) ambassador to the Holy See and excluded the right completely from the talks. Negotiations began in June 1934, but soon stalled because the Spanish government would not contemplate any measure that clashed with the Constitution. The resulting stalemate led the Spanish ambassador to seek a more limited arrangement known as a 'modus vivendi', which would still have done much to reconcile Catholic opinion to the regime. These negotiations also failed, due to the strength of the ultramontane Spanish lobby within the Vatican. Nonetheless, the centre government had demonstrated not only its willingness to incorporate the Catholics into the new regime, but also that it would only do so on a strictly constitutional basis.

By contrast, the Amnesty Law of April 1934 was an ill-judged and damaging concession to the right. The amnesty not only liberated the monarchist rebels of the *Sanjurjada* of August 1932, but also, under pressure from the left, the anarchist insurgents of December 1933. The law was the result above all of intense lobbying by the right, but, in appeasing the army, it made the Republic look weak, as well as lending an implicit legitimacy to the *pronunciamiento* (military uprising) as a route to power. By pardoning extremists from both ends of the political spectrum and by allowing others, such as the extreme right-wing monarchist José Calvo Sotelo, to return from exile, the amnesty unnecessarily heightened political tensions. Its immediate ramifications were far-reaching. The president, Alcalá-Zamora, was so appalled that, in a 'strictly personal decision', he dismissed Lerroux as prime minister.[23] Unlike Azaña, Lerroux was not prepared (as in October 1933) to stand up to the president, so Alcalá-Zamora was able to remove him and appoint yet another Radical as prime minister. This was the bald, bespectacled, and self-effacing Ricardo Samper, who, the president hoped, would make a more amenable premier than his boss. By accentuating the inbuilt fragility of the parliamentary majority, Alcalá-Zamora further destabilized a regime that required the exact opposite. At heart, the president aimed to establish himself as the dominant figure of the centre.

The amnesty was also the final straw for those within the Radical Party who bristled at the alliance with the CEDA. Deputy leader Diego Martínez Barrio had made it clear in January 1934 that the party had to be 'its own successor', it being better to adopt 'a firm position, and be defeated, rather than be directed or humiliated'.[24] As Grand Master of the Spanish Grand Orient, he came under intense pressure from his fellow Freemasons to distance himself from their arch-enemy, the Catholic right, the lodges passing an order in early 1934 by which all those tainted by 'a strategy of approximation to reactionary forces' would be expelled.[25] In May 1934, Martínez Barrio finally abandoned the Radical Party along with eighteen other deputies and around one-sixth of the rank and file, a major blow which left the parliamentary group with fewer representatives than in 1931. The schism made the party more dependent than ever on the right.

## THE TUMULTUOUS SUMMER OF 1934

The government of Ricardo Samper, which was to last from April to October 1934, was to be wracked by instability. This was partly due to the clash within the Cabinet between the doves, such as the prime minister, and the hawks, foremost amongst whom was the thrusting minister of the interior, Rafael Salazar Alonso. Still, the chief cause was the unremitting efforts of both left and right to advance their respective agendas at the expense of the government. Within the parliamentary majority there was a constant tug of war between the Radicals and the *cedistas* over the direction to be taken, a struggle which was greatly fuelled by the determination of the CEDA to realize its programme. In short, the Radicals and the *cedistas* were at once allies and antagonists.

Much of the summer of 1934 was taken up with three high-profile disputes: a nationwide agrarian strike, a protracted confrontation with the *Generalitat* (the Catalan regional government) over its legislative powers, and a prolonged tussle with the Basque authorities over the *concierto económico* (the region's special economic arrangement with the state). In all three cases, Prime Minister Samper, who defended a 'politics of moderation', strove to reach a consensual solution, but on each occasion he was confronted not only by the hawks within his own Cabinet, but also by the opportunistic opposition of both left and right.[26]

The first conflict concerned the threat of a nationwide strike by the socialist agrarian union, the FNTT, on 5 June. The prime minister and the ministers of agriculture and labour worked hard to avoid a strike through negotiation, but their conciliatory efforts were hindered by the combative approach of Salazar Alonso, who banned meetings, arrested union leaders, and opposed the strike on the grounds that the harvest was 'sacred'.[27] In any case, the approach of the FNTT was ambiguous. The strike demands were reformist, but the leadership had declared itself 'for the Revolution', while amongst the rank and file there was a widely held belief that the strike would usher in a social revolution. On 3 June the FNTT suddenly insisted that the harvest terms, including pay, should be extended to the rest of the year, which 'ended any hope for a negotiated settlement'.[28] As the socialist deputy Juan-Simeón Vidarte later admitted, the goal of the FNTT was to demonstrate its 'enormous force' and secure a 'triumph'.[29] The greatest agrarian stoppage in Spanish history, the FNTT strike was nonetheless doomed from the outset, bereft as it was of support from the UGT and from the CNT outside Andalusia. For Vidarte, it was 'a senseless movement which we could not halt'.[30] As a result of the strike, thirteen workers died and thousands were arrested, though the great majority were released in a day or two. The hard-line Salazar Alonso took advantage of the defeat to assail the socialist movement throughout the south, closing party and trade-union branches as well as local papers. The FNTT did not recover until 1936.

The second dispute involved the right of the *Generalitat* to legislate on agrarian affairs. In June the Court of Constitutional Guarantees ruled that the Catalan regional government had had no right to pass a Law on Contracts of Cultivation two months earlier. To defuse the stand-off between Madrid and Barcelona, the president and prime minister offered the Catalan president, Lluís Companys, an easy way out: if the *Generalitat* passed a slightly different version of the law, the government would not contest it. Not only did Companys reject the offer (on the grounds that patriotism did not allow for compromises), but the national forces of the left rallied around the *Generalitat* as a bastion of republican resistance to the unholy alliance of the centre and right. At the same time, the Cabinet hawks and the right insisted that the authority of the state be upheld. Through all of this, Samper maintained his 'spirit of mutual understanding', but the issue dragged on throughout the summer of 1934, taking a tremendous toll on the government.[31]

The final conflict was sparked by the decision of the treasury minister to alter the state's special economic arrangement with the Basque Country. As in the Catalan case, the prime minister sought a negotiated solution, but the socialists and the left-republicans exploited the issue in order to mobilize the local councils against the government. At the same time, the right and Cabinet hardliners exhorted Samper to take a tougher line. Like the Catalan controversy, the Basque dispute dragged on into September, the government having once again been caught between the enmity of the left and the exigencies of the right.

## THE SOCIALIST REVOLUTION OF OCTOBER 1934

The struggle of the Radical government to construct a more inclusive regime was of no consequence to the socialists. In September 1933 they broke with the left-republicans, in November 1933 with the Republic itself, and in January 1934 they drew up a revolutionary programme. An insurrectionary movement had been put in motion in late 1933. On the one hand, socialist propaganda prepared the masses for the uprising by decrying the 'bourgeois' Republic, by highlighting the threat of 'fascism', and by justifying the recourse to violence. The goal of the socialists, proclaimed Largo Caballero in April 1934, was to 'seize political power in a revolutionary manner', that is, 'violently, fighting on the streets against the enemy'.[32] On the other hand, the socialists set about organizing the insurrection itself by training the militias (first approved in 1932), collecting arms and explosives, and securing support from within the army and police forces. The fact is that the socialists had turned their backs on the Republic because they no longer governed it:

> For the socialists it was enough to feel excluded, expelled, from the
> responsibilities of government, to announce their new intentions ...
> they all considered the Republic as their own creature and they all
> believed that they had the right, above and beyond the elections or the
> popular vote, to govern it.[33]

The revolutionary aspirations of the socialists were not shared by their erstwhile left-republican allies. In January 1934, Manuel Azaña told the moderate socialist and law professor Fernando de los Ríos that a socialist uprising with military support was 'chimerical', adding that the socialists would not be backed by the 'country', because 'four-fifths are not socialist'.[34] In short, the enterprise was not only doomed from the start, but would also 'put the Republic and Spain at risk of ruin'.[35] In Azaña's view, the argument that the socialist leadership was merely reacting to the revolutionary impulse of the rank and file was unconvincing, as 'the feelings of the masses can be changed or channelled, and this is the duty of the leaders'.[36] In the meantime, Azaña tried to galvanize the left-republicans by forming a new and broader party, Republican Left, in April 1934, which was a fusion of Republican Action, the Independent Radical-Socialist Party, and the ORGA, the Galician regionalist formation.

The socialists justified the revolution on the grounds that it would prevent the entry of the CEDA into the government. The veto of the Catholic party partly reflected the socialists' sectarian outlook, that is, they simply did not accept that the CEDA, despite winning the election, had the right to join a government of the Republic. Underlying this conceit was the conviction that the CEDA was 'fascist', which framed its Cabinet entry as a rerun of the rise to power of 'fascism' in Germany and Austria. The term 'fascist' was, however, widely abused in the 1930s. Socialist usage of the term was not only indiscriminate – the Falangists and monarchists were 'fascists', so too were the Radicals, the Liberal-Democrats, and Alcalá-Zamora's Progressives – but also a smear, designed to delegitimize opponents and thereby justify the use of violence against them. Exactly the same rationale lay behind the right's use and abuse of the term *rojo* or 'Red'. Few specialists in fascism would today define the CEDA as 'fascist' – it was too close to the Catholic Church and the traditional elites – but the socialists were certainly justified in regarding the Catholic confederation as a potential authoritarian threat. Even so, the *cedistas* posed no immediate threat to the regime, as they occupied a mere three of the thirteen ministerial portfolios. In any case, neither the Radicals nor the president had the intention of facilitating the rise of right-wing authoritarianism. 'Death rather than surrender to reaction,' as Lerroux theatrically put it.[37] The entry of the CEDA into the government on 4 October 1934 was nonetheless the catalyst for a national strike and insurrection by the socialists, an uprising in Asturias of the socialists and anarcho-syndicalists, and a logistically unrelated revolt by the left-republican *Generalitat*, which declared a Catalan state within 'the Spanish federal Republic'.[38]

In Madrid, events were neither as low-key nor as transitory as many historians have averred. The general strike lasted until 13 October, the longest in the capital's history, while socialist militias assaulted the Ministry of the Interior (while the Cabinet was sitting), the Cortes, the residency of the prime minister, and other strategic points. When the British writer Norman Lewis arrived at the Mediodía railway station he encountered 'a pitched battle between revolutionaries and infantrymen', being told that the revolt would result 'in the victory of the Reds', as the 'reactionaries' were 'at their last gasp'.[39] The socialist movement in the capital 'tried to follow or believed it was following the Bolshevik revolutionary model', with militia leaders assuring their 2,500-strong rank and file that 'at the sound of a pistol the army will join the movement'.[40] As in 1917 and 1930, this proved completely misplaced, as military backing was 'very scarce'.[41] According to a socialist report of November 1934, the Madrid uprising resulted in fifty deaths and the jailing of 1,700 party and trade-union members. By contrast, in Barcelona the army brought the rebellion under control in a matter of hours.

In Asturias, the workers launched a full-blown insurrection, seizing control of a third of the region, including the capital, Oviedo. Priests, seminary students, Civil Guards, and other 'rightists' were detained or shot, and in a number of *pueblos* libertarian communism was proclaimed, while the properties and institutions of the 'bourgeoisie' were ransacked and pillaged, including the Bank of Spain in Oviedo, from which over 14.5 million pesetas disappeared, of which 9.5 million was never recovered. Caught off guard by the strength of the uprising, the government called on not only the peninsular army, but also the Army of Africa, its most effective fighting force. Even so, the army, which was under the immediate authority of General Eduardo López Ochoa but overseen from the Ministry of War by General Francisco Franco, struggled to overcome the tenacious resistance of the workers. After all, this was 'the greatest revolutionary insurrection to have occurred anywhere in Europe between the two world wars', with around 90,000 rifles and 30,000 pistols later being confiscated from the revolutionaries.[42] According to the official figures, the October uprisings produced 1,335 deaths, of whom 1,051 were civilians and 284 soldiers or police, while upwards of 15,000 insurgents were imprisoned.[43]

The events of October 1934 highlighted the splintered nature of the

Arrested Asturian workers

opposition to the governing centre-right. Despite the creation of the *Alianzas Obreras* (Workers' Alliances) in 1934, which aimed to bring the socialists, anarcho-syndicalists, Communists, and other working-class forces together in a united front, the socialists had kept their revolutionary preparations largely to themselves. The rebellion was further hampered by the government's dismantling of the socialists' biggest union, the FNTT, in the aftermath of the agrarian strike of June 1934. The absence of the CNT from both the socialist venture – with the notable exception of Asturias – and the Catalan revolt inevitably weakened both. While the left-wing Catalan nationalists had risen up against the state, neither the Basque nationalists nor the national left-republicans had followed suit. Lastly, the socialist venture was further undermined not only by the division between the trade unionists that organized the strike and the militias that planned the insurrection, but also by the lack of a 'coherent and single insurrectionary plan', the uprising eventually being left to provincial and regional entities.[44]

## THE POLITICS OF PERSECUTION

The failure of the October 1934 rebellion was a shattering setback for the left, a vindicatory triumph for the right, and a disaster for the centre. The Radical dream of 'a Republic for all Spaniards' had been hugely discredited and with it the overriding goal of 'centring' the regime through the integration of left and right alike. The excessive and often arbitrary nature of the repression polarized the political climate to an unprecedented extent, ensuring that 'October 1934' would remain the quintessential point of reference until the outbreak of civil war in July 1936. The sheer scale of the revolutionary uprising in Asturias and the counter-revolutionary protagonism of the Army of Africa – which tackled the insurgents in the same pitiless manner as it did a colonial revolt, as illustrated by the beheading of a number of miners – meant that the region suffered the greatest violence. The revolutionaries executed over fifty people, mainly priests, seminary students, and Civil Guards, while the army committed a similar or slightly higher number of atrocities. As a result of the rebellion, thousands of workers were jailed and 'savagely mistreated', many being tortured.[45] Such was the public scandal – it left the Cabinet 'inwardly crushed' – that the most flagrant torturer, Major Lisardo Doval, had to be hurriedly relocated in mid-December 1934.[46] His removal did not halt the abuses, however. Some 564 prisoners in the Oviedo jail denounced the use of torture in a petition which was made public in January 1935. The outcry soon acquired international dimensions, as reflected in the damning verdict of a British delegation that visited Asturias, the press coverage in Argentina (which claimed that Spain had returned to 'the worst times of Fernando VII'), and the campaign of protest in Western Europe, including a play by the young Albert Camus, which drew uncritically on the Black Legend and in particular the idea of 'inquisitorial Spain'.[47] Well aware that 'we enjoyed a very bad world press', as the minister of communications admitted, the government nonetheless did too little too late to remedy the situation, even though the harshness of the Asturian repression did enormous damage to the Radicals' centrist credentials.[48] Just as the reputation of the Azaña administration had been defiled by the calamity of Casas Viejas, so the Radicals were to be haunted for the rest of their days by 'Asturias! Always Asturias!'[49]

The repression in Asturias was the most extreme example of the nationwide crackdown on the left. Party and trade-union branches were closed down and their members persecuted throughout Spain, including many who had taken no part in the October events. The leaders of the Catalan revolt were placed behind bars, the Catalan

Statute was suspended, and even Manuel Azaña was incarcerated on a ship in Barcelona harbour for his supposed involvement. Censorship and states of alarm and prevention remained in force in much of Spain long after they had outlived their usefulness, reflecting a desire, claimed a former Radical deputy before the Cortes, 'to kidnap liberty and pursue politics for the benefit of the governing parties'.[50] Many employers in both the cities and the countryside took advantage of the repression to go on the offensive: arbitration boards ceased to function, existing contracts were ignored, participants in the October uprising were sacked, and prominent activists were persecuted, some even killed. Working conditions in many rural provinces deteriorated as salaries dropped and unemployment rose, though this was not universal, since contracts were upheld in many parts of the centre and south until the summer of 1935. Nationwide, wages in 1935 were slightly lower than in 1932-3, but still higher than in 1931.

A devastating indictment of the landowners' onslaught in those provinces which experienced the greatest socio-economic and political polarization is furnished by the civil governor for Badajoz, Carlos de Luna. 'In synthesis, the situation is this,' he related in a private letter, 'absolute peace, hunger, humility on the part of the poor and arrogance, wretchedness and incomprehension on the part of the majority of the rich', which led him to conclude that 'the obstinacy and the egoism of these ferocious landowners [is] a suicidal approach that will ruin everything that has been achieved'.[51] The prolonged persecution of the left – 8,000 workers remained in jail throughout 1935, while the trials of the revolutionaries carried on into 1936 – invariably generated a climate of extreme tension within the *pueblos* and towns. In Castile-La Mancha, for example, there reigned 'an unbreathable atmosphere within the local communities'.[52]

The decline in working conditions was greatly facilitated by the fact that the Ministry of Labour was now in the hands of the CEDA. Under the watch of the new minister, José Oriol y Anguera de Sojo, the arbitration boards were suspended, the forty-eight-hour week was reinstated in the building and metallurgical industries, and the mediation of the government in labour disputes ceased. In November 1934 the 'abusive strike' decree was passed, by which all strikes had to be strictly work-related, not political. Clearly the watershed in labour relations was not December 1933, when the Radicals came to power, but October 1934.

The government also took advantage of the revolutionary uprising to topple 1,116 local councils, just over 12 per cent of all municipalities. In Badajoz, to take an extreme example, the Radicals came to control 161 of the 163 local councils. This opportunistic and often illegal policy further tarnished the Radicals' much-vaunted claim to represent 'a Republic for all Spaniards'. The exclusion of the socialists from numerous local councils, the suspension of the arbitration boards, and the reduced presence of the socialist deputies in the Cortes greatly restricted the movement's ability to defend its members. On the other hand, the left drew on the common experience of the repression to unify its disparate forces. The first step was taken with the electoral union of the national left-republican parties, as shown by their manifesto of April 1935. The second step, a coalition between the left-republicans and the socialists, proved to be far more difficult, as the insurrection of October 1934 had produced the greatest schism within the movement since 1921 (which had led to the establishment of the Spanish Communist Party). While the moderates under Indalecio Prieto were determined to return to the democratic fold, the socialist left under Largo Caballero was bent on the Bolshevization of the movement. The left-republican convergence was therefore offset by the schism that now afflicted the socialists.

An inevitable corollary of the political and economic backlash was a rise in poverty. In an editorial entitled 'Misery, misery, misery', the Radical mouthpiece *Renovación* decried the plague of child beggars on the streets of Madrid and the widespread suffering in Andalusia, where children were to be found working from 'sunrise to sunset' and where starving peasants robbed olives from the large estates.[53] In early 1935 the civil governor of Madrid estimated that three-quarters of the urban and rural workforce were without employment. 'The people are asking us for bread,' one CEDA deputy informed the Cortes.[54] Yet in Extremadura the poor were shot at by the Civil Guard for stealing the acorns intended for pigs, while security on the southern estates was tightened so that the needy could not steal firewood and olives. By the end of 1935 the Badajoz civil governor Carlos de Luna was imploring the government to oblige 'the rich to fulfil their duties as citizens, imposing by force the most elemental of all: that of charity and love for their fellow man'.[55] Unfortunately, most right-wing deputies thought otherwise, as underlined by their reaction to the reformist vision of the relatively liberal CEDA minister of agriculture, Manuel Giménez Fernández. In December 1934 the stout, moustached law professor from Seville had allowed 25,000 *yunteros* (ploughmen) from Extremadura to continue working untilled land which did not belong to them. He then announced that the ministry aimed to settle 10,000 peasants per annum on expropriated land, the same target as that of the Azaña administration in 1933. A defender of the small farmer, Giménez Fernández lambasted the big landowners for 'regarding the law merely as the best means of preserving their privileges and their wealth'.[56] He also introduced a bill which would have allowed tenant farmers to purchase the land that they had worked for twelve years. The bill was regarded as an affront to the large landowners, Giménez Fernández being branded a 'white Bolshevik' by his own colleagues, while the 'great hostility' towards him led Gil Robles, despite his own social Catholic leanings, to abandon him in parliament.[57] By the time the bill passed in March 1935, the original text had been emasculated, including the elimination of the right of purchase for tenant farmers.

# THE TRIUMPH OF REACTION?

Despite the dismal political and social panorama, the post-October 1934 period was not one of outright reaction. There were two major areas in which the Radicals stood up to the CEDA in a befuddled attempt to defend the centrist ground that they represented. The first concerned the legislative agenda of the CEDA. With the salient exception of agrarian reform, the Radicals repeatedly stymied the often reactionary parliamentary forays of their allies. In January 1935 the CEDA minister of labour presented a bill which would have condemned 'the workers' parties and trade unions to illegality', but the Radicals thwarted this anti-democratic initiative.[58] That same month, Gil Robles put forward a press bill which the Radical deputy Basilio Álvarez excoriated as 'a draconian monstrosity'.[59] Once again, the Radicals blocked the bill. In February a parliamentary commission began to study the CEDA's proposed reform of the electoral system, but the ruling majority, Gil Robles later lamented, 'could not reach a single agreement, not even inside the commission'.[60] In May a bill came before the Cortes which envisaged the expenditure of 65 million pesetas on unemployment by the end of the year. Basilio Álvarez attacked the measure on account of 'the meanness, the limitedness, the reduced level, it's almost ridiculous', while fellow Radical Rafael Guerra del Río panned it for seeking to balance the budget 'at all costs'.[61]

The second line of Radical resistance concerned the death sentences for the rebels of October 1934, which were handed down by the military courts to the Cabinet for approval. Initially prodded by a far-sighted Alcalá-Zamora, a Radical-dominated government over-turned the very first death sentences in October 1934, infuriating Gil Robles to the extent that he informed a number of sympathetic generals that he was disposed to a 'solution by force'.[62] The tug of war over the death sentences climaxed in March 1935 when the Cabinet voted on twenty of them. All seven Radical ministers favoured clemency, prompting their three CEDA colleagues to resign on 3 April. Despite the 1,381 deaths caused by the October 1934 insurrection and the constant clamour of the right for a hard-line approach, the Cabinets of 1934–5 sanctioned just two death sentences – hardly the work of a 'fascist' state.

Rather than succumb to the blackmail of the CEDA's Cabinet withdrawal, Lerroux tried to call its bluff. In accordance with the Constitution, he closed the Cortes for a month and formed a new government, which was very different to its predecessor, as shown by the inclusion of Azaña's former chief of staff and the head of the Institute of Agrarian Reform. Liberated from the clutches of the CEDA, the Radicals took a much more moderate line, most notably by re-establishing the *Generalitat* and by ending martial law on 9 April. The prolonged crisis of March to May 1935 nonetheless marked the tipping point between the Radical Party and the CEDA. Once the Cortes reopened in May, the Radicals' bluff was called, as the right was more determined than ever to advance its position. Accordingly, a new government was formed on 6 May comprising five *cedistas*, including its leader Gil Robles, and only three Radicals, though Lerroux remained premier. The centre had finally been eclipsed by the right. The tenor of the new administration was set by the minister of war, Gil Robles, who appointed the monarchist General Joaquín Fanjul as under-secretary, and another monarchist, General Manuel Goded, as commander-in-chief, while the more cagey conservative General Francisco Franco was made chief of staff. The government also achieved the right's greatest legislative victory of the entire Second Republic: the toppling of the 1932 Agrarian Reform Law in July 1935, an initiative orchestrated by the minister of agriculture, Nicolás Velayos, who, hardly surprisingly, was the biggest landowner in the province of Valladolid. The burgeoning hubris of the right was reflected in Gil Robles' boast at a rally in July that collaboration with the Radicals was 'the guarantee of victory', adding menacingly 'what need do I have of the army in order to triumph?'[63] At another rally he called for the 'total revision' of the Constitution and, against the backdrop of the Italian invasion of Abyssinia, gave vent to his fascist-style delusions of empire, bragging of 'the superiority of our religion, of the superiority of our language, of the superiority of our culture and of our spirit'.[64]

The Radicals nonetheless continued to resist the ambitions of their allies. In July the Cortes voted on whether Manuel Azaña had illegally supplied the Portuguese revolutionaries with arms while he was prime minister. He was found not guilty thanks to the abstention of the Radicals, this being yet another example, in Gil Robles' view, of their 'policy of appeasement of the revolutionary elements'.[65] In any case, the paramount legislative goal for the CEDA was the overhaul of the Constitution. A bill was presented to the Cortes in July which envisaged the revision of forty of the Constitution's 125 articles, which included those on religion, education, the family, private property, the autonomous regions, and the Cortes. Many Radicals were horrified by the sweep of the bill. Small wonder that it got buried in the parliamentary commission headed by the erstwhile premier Ricardo Samper. The ideological divergences within the ruling coalition reflected the lack of a common agenda. Radical resentment at the CEDA's surging ambition made relations even more tortuous. By now, Radical collaboration with the CEDA was, noted Gil Robles, 'not at all enthusiastic', while the stresses and strains within the alliance frequently brought it to the brink of 'rupture'.[66]

The shift in power at the national level intensified the struggle over the distribution of power and patronage at the local level. The CEDA's accumulation of public positions spread dismay amongst the Radical ranks. 'All the posts are for their members,' as one deputy lamented.[67] At the provincial level, the Radical Party's greatest fear was to lose a civil governorship to its ally. The party president in Almería informed Lerroux of the CEDA's 'deplorable game of intrigues and disloyalties' in relation to the civil governor, alerting that this endangered 'all that is organized in our party and, as a result, its future life'. The party's allies were, in fact, 'our worst enemies'.[68] In the same vein, the Radicals of Orense warned Lerroux that if the civil governorship fell into the hands of another party, 'the doors [would be] hermetically sealed against all hope'.[69]

The CEDA's rush to repression, its counter-revolutionary agenda, its demonization of the left, and its relentless determination to undermine its centrist ally vividly showcased the strict limits to its possibilism. Like the socialists, the *cedistas* aimed to create a regime in their own image, conflating their own sectarian ideal with that of the nation. Such a critical standpoint has been condemned for projecting back onto the past the democratic maxims of the present, but the democratic ideal certainly existed in the 1930s – the Second Republic was, after all, a parliamentary regime based on universal suffrage – and it is difficult to see how the regime could have been consolidated by eschewing the politics of compromise and inclusion. Nevertheless, the possibilists of the CEDA merely exploited their rise to power, observed Alcalá-Zamora, 'to persecute enemies, accentuate their conservatism and maintain themselves in power'.[70]

The radicalization of politics in the wake of October 1934 cannot be blamed on a reactionary and revengeful right alone. Matters were made still worse by the manifest failure of the centre to live up to its inclusive ideals. The Radicals may have curbed the bloodlust of the right and derailed much of its legislative agenda, but they did far too little to prevent the polarization of politics, whether in terms of the repression, the employers' offensive, or the victimization of the left. Nor did they resist the temptation to overthrow over a thousand local councils largely for their own benefit. In other words, the considerable demerits of the centrists did much to impede the normalization of national politics. Least blameworthy of all was the left, but its fixation with the repression and often bellicose rhetoric also contributed to the poisoning of national politics.

## THE FALL OF THE RADICALS

The expulsion of the Radical Party from government in late 1935 following a brace of corruption cases, above all the *Straperlo* scandal, is invariably cited as proof of the Radicals' venal pact with the CEDA. In reality, the 'Straperlo' was a sordid affair which reflected badly on the left and right as well as the centre. In 1934 a German by the name of Daniel Strauss had obtained a licence for a roulette-based game called the *Straperlo* by bribing certain members of the Radical Party. However, the police soon halted proceedings on the grounds that this was a game of chance, and therefore illegal. As a parliamentary commission later established, Strauss was a 'skilful conman' who had fled Mexico because of 'various dirty business deals', as well as the robbery of a $3,000 diamond.[71] He was determined to get compensation for his *Staperlo* losses. Despite his unsavoury reputation, he was aided in this by the opposition, above all Manuel Azaña and Indalecio Prieto, who helped bring the matter to the attention of the president. Rather than instructing Strauss to pursue his claim via the courts, Alcalá-Zamora took advantage of the complaint to dismiss Lerroux as prime minister in September 1935 – replacing him with the independent centrist Joaquín Chapaprieta – before bringing it into the public domain by revealing its existence to the new Cabinet. The Cortes debate on 22 October, the launching of a parliamentary inquiry on 23 October, and a damning verdict on 26 October constituted a shattering blow for the Radical Party. The *Tayá-Nombela* affair of late November 1935, which involved a contested compensation payment authorized by Lerroux when he was prime minister, delivered the party's *coup de grâce*.

The graft involved in the *Straperlo* affair was, in the words of the investigating magistrate, 'small change', especially when compared to the Stavisky scandal in France.[72] In January 1934, Serge Stavisky was murdered because the forged bonds which he had floated on the Paris stock exchange had implicated prominent members of the French Radical Party. The affair not only brought down two governments, but also led to a demonstration in which twelve people were killed and over 200 wounded. In Spain, the *Straperlo* case was transformed into a 'huge scandal' thanks to the complicity of the left, the president, and the CEDA, which had rapidly distanced itself from its ally.[73] The motives of the three parties were, however, quite different. The left hoped that the fall of the Radicals would trigger a general election, which would duly return it to power, the insurrectionary option having failed. The CEDA viewed the scandal as an opportunity to cripple the Radical Party, thereby strengthening its own hold on power, especially by making Gil Robles prime minister. Finally, for Alcalá-Zamora, the *Straperlo* scandal was the key to the destruction of the Radical Party, leaving him as the dominant figure of the centre. Still, by sabotaging the only major centrist party, the president did not so much 'centre' the Republic as destabilize it even farther.

On 9 December, Chapaprieta resigned, dismayed by the breaking of the *Tayá-Nombela* scandal and by the lack of support for his economic reforms. Gil Robles was convinced that his hour had finally come, but the president had other plans. He refused to make the CEDA leader prime minister, partly because of the latter's authoritarian proclivities and partly because he did not want the Cabinet to be dominated by one party, so he decided instead to dissolve the Cortes. In a fit of hubris, Gil Robles shrieked at Alcalá-Zamora that his veto of the CEDA would condemn the right to 'violent solutions' and that whether the right or left won the next election 'there was no alternative, unfortunately, to civil war'.[74] The rebuff of Gil Robles led his under-secretary, General Fanjul, to propose a military uprising, but the initiative was stymied by the chief of staff, the circumspect General Franco, on the grounds that the army was not yet sufficiently united.

The two years from late 1933 to late 1935 have been dubbed ever since as the *Bienio negro* or 'Black Biennium', a domestic reworking of the Protestant-inspired myth of the sixteenth-century 'Black Legend'. This has served not only to discredit the governments of 1933–5 for their supposedly reactionary rule, but also to draw a salutary contrast with the *Bienio reformista* or 'Reformist Biennium' of 1931–3. The second biennium was thus the negation of the first, its antithesis. According to this narrative, 'the right' was in power during this period. In reality, all the governments up to October 1934 were centrist ones.

When the non-republican right did enter the Cabinet in October 1934, it occupied only three of thirteen ministries, and when it did finally seize majority control of the government in May 1935, it still failed to obtain the premiership. In fact, the right never held the office of prime minister under the Republic. Another pillar of this interpretation is the claim that the left struggled valiantly during the 'Black Biennium' to defend the liberal and democratic values of the regime, while the centre is viewed as having betrayed the Republic by acting as the 'puppets' of the right in exchange for access to the public spoils system.[75] The upshot was the insidious advance of 'fascism', which eventually provoked the socialists to rise up in defence of the Republic in October 1934. However, this widely accepted narrative not only misconstrues the *raison d'être* of the socialists, but also misrepresents the nature, purpose, and achievements of the Radical-led governments of 1933-5.

## THE GENERAL ELECTION OF FEBRUARY 1936

The new premier was the tall, stooping, shock-haired figure of Manuel Portela, a Freemason and former monarchist colleague of Alcalá-Zamora, now turned republican. His caretaker administration was to oversee the general election on 16 February 1936. Portela was just the man that the president needed. Alcalá-Zamora aimed to fill the void left by the Radical Party with a centrist force that would not only hold the balance of power in the next Cortes, but also be amenable to his own personal influence. Looking much like a Grand Wizard, Portela first brought into being a new party, the Centre Democratic Party, and then set about – 'without a programme, without organization, and without masses' – conjuring up a sizeable parliamentary group by means of official influence, a throwback to the Restoration.[76] In other words, Alcalá-Zamora, with the connivance of Portela, was acting just like a dynastic party boss from the old regime, in direct violation of the democratic principles that underpinned the new regime.

The politics of persecution had slowly brought the fragmented forces of the left together after the uprising of October 1934, but it was far from a straightforward process. In April 1935 the left-republican parties had reached an understanding which met with the support of the socialist moderates under Indalecio Prieto, but not that of the revolutionary left under Largo Caballero. However, the massive out-pouring of support for Manuel Azaña at a series of rallies in late 1935, the crumbling of the Radical-CEDA coalition, and the lack of an alternative strategy eventually brought Largo Caballero round to the idea of an electoral coalition, but on two conditions: first, the other working-class organizations must also be included, which transformed the original alliance envisaged by Azaña and Prieto, as reflected in its new, Communist-inspired name, the 'Popular Front'. Second, the left-republicans would have to govern alone after the elec-tion; that is to say, the alliance was an electoral arrangement more than an effective formula for government. The resulting coalition comprised the Basque and Catalan regional nationalists, a host of republican parties, and a multitude of working-class organizations, including the Socialist Party, the UGT, the Spanish Communist Party, and the Syndicalist Party of the former CNT leader Ángel Pestaña. This was a brittle compact not only because the programme was basically a republican one (and therefore of circumscribed appeal to the workers), but also because the coalition harboured conflicting visions of the Republic. The inherent instability of the Popular Front was heightened by the resignation of Largo Caballero from the execu-tive committee of the PSOE in December 1935. Thereafter, the executive committees of the PSOE and the UGT went their separate ways, the trade unions under Largo Caballero taking their own initiatives, while ignoring those of the PSOE – that is, acting as if they were a political party. From December 1935 the unity of the socialist movement was 'a thing of the past'.[77]

If anything, the right was even more disunited than the left. There was no overarching coalition of right-wing parties, the principal divide being that between the CEDA and José Calvo Sotelo's anti-republican National Block. The CEDA allied with a variety of forces, including the Radicals, the Agrarians, and the Carlists. Bereft of a common programme, the right-wing parties were defined mostly by what they opposed, which explains why the CEDA-led alliance was frequently referred to as the 'Anti-Revolutionary Coalition'. It is often held that the two main electoral alliances – the Popular Front and the

Anti-Revolutionary Coalition – embodied a bipolar battle between the 'Two Spains', but this is misleading insofar as they were extremely fragile constructs, both of which fell apart once the election was over.

The electoral campaign was dominated by 'October 1934' and its consequences, the right and centre highlighting the threat of revolution ('Against the revolution and its accomplices!' being the CEDA slogan), while the Popular Front called for an amnesty for its political prisoners and the readmission of all workers fired for their participation in the revolution. The incendiary nature of the campaign should not disguise the fact that abstention, at 28 per cent, was only slightly less than in the 1933 general election, which indicates that Spanish society was still not as politicized as many accounts claim.

The result was a close-run thing, the Popular Front winning 47 per cent of the vote, the right 46 per cent, and the centre 5 per cent. The left-wing vote had risen 10 per cent since the 1933 general election, in large measure due to the ballots cast by the anarcho-syndicalists, whose prime concern was the release of their political prisoners. The highly partisan performance of the parliamentary electoral commission, together with the rerun elections in Cuenca and Granada in May, both of which were blighted by blatant official interference and intimidation, ensured that the Popular Front won 263 seats, the right 156, and the centre 54. Partywise, the CEDA won 101 deputies, the Socialist Party 88, the Republican Left 85, Republican Union 37, and Portela's Centrists 21. The Communist and fascist movements, which had done so much to destabilize democracy elsewhere in Europe, scarcely registered in the Spanish election: the Communist Party won just 17 of the 473 seats (and this due to its participation in the Popular Front), while the Falange won a mere 46,466 votes, possibly the worst result of any fascist party in Europe.

Clearly the political system was still far from consolidated. The new Cortes was made up of thirty-three parties, of which only eleven won more than ten seats, which meant that the multi-party nature of the Spanish parliamentary system had increased rather than diminished. Revealingly, in each of the general elections the party or parties which had dominated the previous legislature virtually disappeared: in 1931 the monarchists; in 1933 the national left-republicans; and in 1936 the Radicals, who returned only five seats. The fragmented and fractious nature of the Cortes of 1936 was a matter of paramount concern given the extent to which national politics had become polarized over the previous fifteen months and the corresponding gravity of the problems that the new parliament now faced.

## THE REVENGE OF THE WORKERS

The socialist left's veto on the formation of a joint republican-socialist government meant that the electoral victory of the Popular Front did not translate into a government of the Popular Front. While the moderates under Indalecio Prieto defended collaboration with the left-republicans, the radicals headed by Francisco Largo Caballero shunned them in favour of greater collaboration with the Communists, the anarcho-syndicalists, and other working-class forces. As a result, Manuel Azaña formed an inherently weak left-republican government dependent on the ambivalent parliamentary support of the socialists.

If supporters of the centre-right had interpreted the electoral victory of 1933 as a personal triumph over their class enemies, then the workers did exactly the same in 1936, but with even greater fervour. Indeed, the political and social atmosphere in the months leading up to the outbreak of civil war in July 1936 would be profoundly conditioned by the insurrection of October 1934 and its repercussions. The post-electoral change in climate was immediate. The forced liberation of thousands of political prisoners from provincial jails obliged the government to convoke the Permanent Commission of the Cortes on 21 February, and, with the support of the right, pass a general amnesty for all 'political and social crimes' committed since the November 1933 general election. This did not, however, include crimes committed by the army during the repression of October 1934. On the contrary, General Eduardo López Ochoa, the commander in Asturias, was soon arrested along with a number of other officers. On 1 March the government decreed that all workers fired for political motives since the beginning of 1934 should be not only rehired, but also paid compensation.

The resurgence of the left, the re-establishment of the labour laws, and in particular the determination of the workers to exact revenge for the repression of 1934-5 resulted in drastic, often impossible, demands on the urban employers, as shown by the surge in bankruptcies. The increasingly shrill pleas of the employers' associations for the government to address their plight nonetheless fell on deaf ears. In the countryside a wave of land seizures was unleashed in the centre and south in March, reaching a peak in Badajoz when 60,000 peasants grabbed land on the same day, the occupations being legalized *ex post facto*. The land invasions, together with the sweeping Agrarian Reform Law of June, ensured that more land was settled between February and July of 1936 than over the previous five years, while wages 'almost tripled' during the months following the election.[78] However, the labourers were far from satisfied, above all because unemployment, exacerbated by the damage wrought by heavy rains, remained high in many areas.

The government worked feverishly to meet the workers' demands – the minister of agriculture presented five separate bills on 19 April – in the conviction that their leaders would eventually rein them in, as had occurred during the first biennium. This proved an egregious error of judgement. Despite the gains already made, there were 192 agrarian strikes between 1 May and 18 July, nearly as many as in 1932 and about half the total for 1933, the peak year so far. In reality, the FNTT was no longer interested in legal reformism ('co-existence is not possible,' declared its president before the Cortes), calling in June for the immediate expropriation, without compensation, of any land that was not being cultivated.[79] The FNTT's mouthpiece, *El Obrero de la Tierra*, declared that 'we find ourselves in a civil war, latent in some places and manifest in others'.[80] Socialists in Ciudad Real called for a 'revolutionary labour' until 'the bourgeois peasantry is totally destroyed', while in Andalusia the situation was 'revolutionary'.[81] Small wonder that the landowners felt under siege. After suffering a second invasion of his property, one landowner complained to a deputy in a letter of 27 May that 'this is unbearable, if this is not resolved soon we will have to leave the lands.'[82] The lurking fear of the landowners was that left-wing councils would eventually confiscate all private property.

The towns and cities, too, were engulfed by an avalanche of strikes. In May and June alone there were more stoppages than in the whole of 1932 or 1934. A leading example of the workers' bellicosity was the building strike in Madrid. In April the CNT called for a thirty-six-hour week and pay rises of 15–50 per cent, terms that were seconded in May by the UGT labourers. The builders could not comply with these unprecedented demands, so a strike took place on 1 June, mobilizing around 110,000 workers. The Ministry of Labour proposed a compromise of a forty-hour week and wage hikes of 5–12 per cent, but the CNT – unlike the UGT – rejected the plan. When civil war broke out on 17 July the strike was still in force. The excessive claims of the workers had a devastating impact on the economy, rapidly offsetting the recovery of 1934–5. The situation was made worse still by the economic blunders of the left-republican governments, which failed either to pass a budget or to draw up an adequate fiscal policy (the minister of finance resigning in May 1936 for this very reason).

## THE BREAKDOWN OF LAW AND ORDER

The atmosphere of revolutionary expectation was greatly exacerbated by the endemic public disorder. This was the result not only of violent strikes and demonstrations, but also of an abrupt rise in anticlericalism, which ranged from bans on bell-ringing, public rituals, and processions to the mockery, harassment, and physical assault of believers and priests. There was also a swarm of attacks on parish churches, hermitages, and other religious buildings, which included the wrecking of church doors, the smashing of crosses and images, and arson. A group of Catholics from Alcázar de San Juan in Castile-La Mancha lamented in a letter of June 1936 that after the socialists took over the town hall 'they banned Catholic burials and bell-ringing . . . they smashed the Christ figures on the crosses without any of the authorities having intervened so far.'[83] Nationwide, 325 religious buildings were torched and 416 were assaulted and pillaged in a matter of months – more than in the entire previous five years. Catholic opinion was predictably outraged. An even more alarming manifestation of disorder was the shoot-outs between armed gangs of the left and right, mainly involving socialists, Communists, and Falangists. The bulk of this political violence was caused by the left, but the government, dependent on the votes of the socialists, persistently blamed it on 'fascist' provocation. 'Only the right worries me,' declared the minister of the interior.[84] Left-wing workers became ever more defiant. 'From the middle of May until the beginning of the civil war,' recalled former Radical deputy Clara Campoamor, 'Madrid lived a chaotic situation: the workers ate in the hotels, restaurants, and cafés while refusing to pay and threatening the owners ... Even in the light of day and in the centre of the city, small businesses were looted and goods taken, those shopkeepers who protested being threatened with a revolver.'[85]

Violent clashes over land use were also widespread. The most notorious incident took place near Yeste (Albacete) on 29 May. After arresting six labourers for allegedly stealing firewood from private estates, the Civil Guard released the suspects once confronted by a large crowd. As the Guards returned to barracks, they were assailed by around 2,000 people (one Guard dying from a blow to the head with a logging hook). Pandemonium then broke out as the Guards fired at point-blank range into the crowd. Seventeen people were killed and over thirty injured. The tragedy drew attention not only yet again to the manifest incapacity of the Civil Guard to control crowds, but also to the new-found aggression of the peasantry.

The spiralling disorder was greatly enhanced by the actions of left-wing councils. In theory, the government defended the restoration of all those local councils which had been suspended, including the re-establishment of all the councils elected on 12 April 1931, but in practice the socialists seized control of a vast number of municipalities by riding roughshod over the law. In the province of Ciudad Real, for example, where the right had triumphed in 70 per cent of the localities in the general election, the socialists had grabbed fifty-seven of the province's 100 mayorships by June 1936, having never held more than eight before. By this stage, there were practically no centrist or right-wing councillors left in the province. Local public employees, whether administrative staff, bailiffs, gravediggers, watchmen, rural guards, doctors, or chemists were purged in favour of left-wing loyalists, while the municipal police was converted into a 'political police' by the local authorities.[86] The overnight shift in power was symbolized in new street names, such as 'Largo Caballero' and 'The Martyrs of October'.

## THE AUTHORITIES OVERWHELMED

The defiance of the law, the seizure of land, the attacks on the Catholic community, the forced closure of centrist and right-wing centres, and the harassment of local moderate and conservative politicians by means of fines, house searches, and arrests is incomprehensible without taking into account the radicalization of the socialist left, which had been transformed into a 'proto-revolutionary counterpower' that was not prepared to 'submit to bourgeois legality'.[87] In Andalusia, local power 'came to rest on the twin power formed by the local councils and the socialist centres, to the extent that in 1936 the Andalusian *pueblos* started to live a revolutionary situation'.[88] As Azaña noted, 'they do it in order to dominate the Republic via the local councils and to proclaim the dictatorship and the soviet', while 'the republicans protest and the neutral man is absolutely terrified'.[89] The profound change in climate is reflected in a letter of June 1936 by a woman who regretted that her *pueblo,* 'hitherto one of the most peaceful and prosperous in La Mancha', had been 'converted into a wasps' nest of hatred and resentment that will be difficult to eliminate and will perhaps take a violent form soon'.[90] If the consolidation of a democracy is calibrated by the extent to which the legitimacy of its institutions increases over time, then clearly the Second Republic was far from being a stable democratic regime.

The escalating conflict and the breakdown in law and order soon overwhelmed the government. In February, Premier Manuel Azaña was already lamenting that left-wing agitators 'seem paid by our enemies', producing a 'deplorable' impression.[91] In the middle of March he wrote to his brother-in-law of his 'black desperation': 'I think that there have been more than 200 dead and wounded since the government was formed, and I've lost count of the number of places in which they've burnt churches and monasteries.'[92] He was already convinced that:

> ... we're on a downward trajectory because of the persistent anarchy in a number of provinces, because of the calculated disloyalty of the socialist approach in many parts, because of the brutality of one group or another, because of the incapacity of the authorities, because of the foolishness of

the 'Popular Front' in nearly all the *pueblos*, because of the nonsense that some deputies from the republican majority are beginning to say.

'I don't know right now,' he concluded despondently, 'how we're going to bring this under control.'[93] The oft-repeated assertion that the spring of 1936 was no more conflictive than, say, that of 1932 or 1933 is belied not only by the unprecedented magnitude of the land invasions, the strikes, the anticlericalism, and the political violence, but also by the general breakdown in the rule of law.

During the months of February, March, and April the authorities raided Falangist centres for arms, arrested its leadership, and finally banned the party. The government calculated that suppression of the Falange would greatly reduce the violence, but this proved misplaced, as new recruits – many from the CEDA's youth wing – flooded into the now-clandestine party in even greater numbers than before. The government was also well aware of the threat posed by the army. Potential plotters were 'exiled' from the centres of power, but some of these transfers were wholly misguided, such as that of General Emilio Mola, who was sent to the Carlist stronghold of Pamplona in the northeast. Still, by mid-March, fourteen of the twenty-two top positions in the army were occupied by republicans, four by conservatives, and only three by perceived enemies of the regime. The plotting against the Republic had got underway no sooner had the Popular Front triumphed in the general election, but its myriad, uncoordinated strands made it appear no more threatening than the rebellion of August 1932. However, once Mola took over as 'the Director' in April the conspiracy gained enormously in terms of organization and purpose. Such was the incompetence of the government that the chief concern of the conspirators was not the possibility of being discovered by the authorities, but the political divisions within the army.

At a rally of socialist and Communist youth on 5 April 1936 in Madrid, Largo Caballero proclaimed, amidst a profusion of paramilitary uniforms, revolutionary songs, and red flags with Soviet stars, that the working class was marching 'towards the dictatorship of the proletariat, which is the true democracy', in which, 'as in Russia', the regime would not permit 'the opposition of anyone'.[94] In reality, the socialist leader had no revolutionary plan. On the contrary, it appears that his aim was to form a workers' government once the left-republicans had become discredited, thereby fulfilling his traditional goal of achieving socialism either by legal means or in response to an attempted coup d'état. In the meantime he worked hard to increase collaboration with other working-class forces and even to merge with them, always in the belief that he would retain ultimate control. Early in 1936 the UGT absorbed the Communist trade unions and in April the socialist and Communist youth wings fused. That same month Largo Caballero proposed to the CNT that it also merge with the UGT, but the anarcho-syndicalists rebuffed him. Despite this, the two unions, brought together by the struggle over the amnesty and the rehiring of sacked workers, collaborated closely during the spring and summer of 1936, especially in relation to the strikes. As a result, the greatest single fracture within the left following the general election was not so much that between the left-republicans and the workers, as that between the parties and the trade unions. The revolutionary expectation that pervaded the organized working class was illustrated by the CNT's May congress, which focused not on how to realize the revolution, but on the configuration of the future libertarian society. The possibility that the army might revolt did not perturb the FAI, as it would simply 'mobilize and fight it'.[95] Nor was Largo Caballero disturbed by the prospect of a military uprising, declaring in late June that if disaffected soldiers aspired to a coup d'état, 'then let them do it', as the working class 'cannot be defeated'.[96]

## THE SLIDE INTO CIVIL WAR

In May 1936 Manuel Azaña attempted to bolster the government vis-à-vis the organized working class by means of an extremely hazardous political manoeuvre. First, Alcalá-Zamora was removed as president on the grounds that his second dissolution of the Cortes had been constitutionally unwarranted (a contradictory stance since the left had been beseeching him to do just that for two years). Second, Azaña himself became head of state, allowing him to nominate Indalecio Prieto as prime minister in the belief that the socialist leader would re-establish law and order, restrain the revolutionary tendencies of his own movement, and quash the military conspiracy. Predictably, the supporters of Largo Caballero blocked the nomination, thereby wrecking Azaña's plan. Had the energetic and capable Prieto become premier it is possible that 'war would never have broken out'.[97] Instead, Azaña appointed one of his cronies as prime minister, the conceited and unyielding Santiago Casares Quiroga, who was not only infirm, but also, as events would prove, incompetent. On presenting his government, he declared that 'enemies will be smashed and hidden enemies will be searched out to be smashed as well', a stance which was unlikely to ease the rising social and political tension.[98] He also told Indalecio Prieto that he relished the idea that the conspiratory officers would 'rise up in order to nip the rebellion in the bud'.[99] The new premier, as a centrist deputy remarked, was 'a man more apt to touch off a civil war than to restore normalcy'.[100]

By mid-June the national crisis had reached critical proportions. In the Cortes on 16 June the CEDA leader Gil Robles claimed that 269 people had been killed and 1,287 injured over the previous four months. We now know that there were at least 273 deaths from political violence between 31 January and 17 July, which compares unfavourably with the breakdown in democracy in Italy and Austria during the interwar period. In other words, the Spanish Republic of early 1936 probably experienced the worst political violence in Europe. The radical left had gleaned little from the events of October 1934, Indalecio Prieto judging that 'we are going to deserve a catastrophe because of our stupidity', not least because the maximalist discourse of the left had radicalized and united a hitherto divided right.[101] Not that the right was exempt from responsibility, contributing mightily to the polarization of national politics through the harsh repression of 1934–5. Following the defeat of the CEDA's possibilism in the general election, the initiative had passed on the right to the 'catastrophists': the Alfonsine monarchists, the Carlists, and the Falange. Nonetheless, the CEDA, initially led after the election by the moderate and judicious Manuel Giménez Fernández (Gil Robles stepping aside for a while), voted in a meeting of the parliamentary party in favour of the Republic and democracy. Once Gil Robles returned, the CEDA's stance became increasingly hazy, eventually merging with the extreme right as Falangist gunmen took to the streets and the implacable leader of the parliamentary right, the bullfrog-like José Calvo Sotelo, urged the army to rise up. In early July, Gil Robles backed the conspiracy by placing 500,000 pesetas of the CEDA's funds at its disposal.

The profound anxiety within republican circles at the fast-deteriorating situation gave rise to drastic proposals. In May the Republican Left hierarchy reached the painful conclusion that only a dictatorship would restore the state's authority and guarantee the regime's survival. In June the former minister of the interior, the conservative republican Miguel Maura, declared in a series of newspaper articles that over the previous three months there had been a 'total abdication by the state of its most elemental and obligatory obligations, which is to protect the law, the properties and the lives of all the citizens, without any distinction'. In the provinces, he claimed, extremists had governed by means of 'the Jacobite committees of the Popular Front' and the steering committees, a 'veritable Bolshevik plague'. The situation was therefore one of 'absolute anarchy above, uncontrolled anarchy below', the only solution for which was a 'republican dictatorship'.[102]

The crisis was brought to a head by two assassinations. The killing of the Assault Guard lieutenant and committed socialist José del Castillo by right-wing gunmen on 12 July was avenged the following day by the murder of the leader of the opposition, José Calvo Sotelo, at the hands of left-wing police attached to the Ministry of the Interior. The assassination of the leader of the parliamentary opposition by state police was unprecedented in modern Europe. The response of Casares Quiroga was typically crass, as he arrested numerous right-wingers but not the assassins. In any case, the murder of Calvo Sotelo was the final straw for many of the officers who still harboured serious misgivings about a coup d'état, most notably General Francisco Franco. Accordingly, on 17 July 1936, officers rose up in the Moroccan Protectorate against the government.

The envisaged coup d'état of July 1936 was the latest attempt by a part of the army to subordinate the civilian order to the military one, convinced that the armed forces – not parliament – embodied the authentic will of the nation. By this stage the Republic was not so much polarized as paralysed, due to the extensive violence and disorder, the manifest weakness of the government, the virtual absence of the president, and the lack of support from the principal parties on the left and right. On the left, the left-republicans' natural allies, the socialists, were riven by a schism which left them incapable of providing meaningful support. On the right, the CEDA had initially sided with the Azaña administration, but then abandoned the government as it shifted over to the 'catastrophist' right. That said, to defend the government, as many historians still do, on the grounds that it was 'democratically elected', is to ignore the extent to which the authorities of 1936 had failed to uphold law and order or to govern in a democratic manner. On the contrary, their politics of exclusion had alienated not only much of the officer corps, but also swathes of Spanish society, including many Popular Front voters, who by July 1936 feared for their properties and even their lives. As the moderate socialist Indalecio Prieto observed, fascism in Spain 'is nothing in itself', but 'the middle classes, the *petit bourgeois*, who are terrified on a daily basis and without hope of a viable solution, might turn to fascism'.[103]

# 6

# The Civil War, 1936–1939

Well aware that preparations for a coup d'état were afoot, the government nonetheless had no idea when or where it would be unleashed. On 14 July the government's delegate in the city of Melilla in the Moroccan Protectorate was alerted by the Ministry of the Interior that 'military and right-wing elements are preparing an uprising'.[1] He spoke to the regional commander, general Manuel Romerales Quintero, who assured him that 'the forces under his command would not rise up'.[2] On the morning of 17 July the General reassured the delegate that 'nothing is happening ... We can sleep in peace!'[3] Still, in Melilla that very same day, early in the afternoon, the conspirators made their first move. The delegate immediately informed the government. Exasperated by its complacent response, he insisted that 'it's not a kids' game here, but a full-blown insurrection! The thing now is deadly serious. Or does no one get what I'm saying?'[4] At 17:00 hours – the signal for the revolt was 'The 17th at 17.00' – the rebels took to the streets. General Romerales Quintero was taken prisoner ('the bitterest moment of my military career'), while the delegate urgently requested naval and air support, but to no avail.[5] At dusk an edict was read out on behalf of General Francisco Franco which proclaimed that the army 'has been obliged to act on the yearning of the great majority of Spaniards' in order to 're-establish the rule of law under the Republic'.[6] By 21:00 the city was in insurgent hands. By the following morning, the entire Moroccan Protectorate was under the control of the rebels. The coup was under way.

The rebellion spread rapidly throughout the peninsula, its nation-wide reach being testimony to the abject failure of Casares Quiroga's government to contain or suppress it. Had the army been united, the

Republic would have been quickly overthrown, but it was in fact deeply divided. Indeed, the peninsular army was split more or less down the middle: 46,000 soldiers on the republican side and 45,000 on the rebel one, while the 15,300-strong officer corps was divided almost fifty-fifty, the insurgents having a slight advantage. By contrast, the 67,000-strong police forces, including the Civil Guard and the Assault Guard, were largely loyal.

Overwhelmed by the scale of the uprising, the humbled if not humiliated Casares Quiroga resigned late on the evening of 18 July. President Azaña then made the leader of the Republican Union, Diego Martínez Barrio, premier with a view to overcoming the revolt by striking some sort of deal with the insurgents, but his overtures were rejected both by the rebels themselves ('It's late, very late,' General Mola bemoaned) and by the workers who clamoured outside his office for his resignation.[7] Neither Casares Quiroga nor Martínez Barrio released arms to the workers, because they wanted to avoid, in the words of the latter, 'the horrors of a civil war and to save the Constitution and institutions of the Republic',[8] but for many workers the rebellion had to be met by revolution, not rapprochement. In desperation, the president – who cried 'It's late for everything!' – tried to bring all the forces of the Popular Front into the government, but Largo Caballero once again blocked socialist participation in a republican-led administration, as his priority remained – despite the extreme gravity of the situation – the formation of a socialist-dominated government once the republicans had fallen from power.[9] Yet another left-republican Cabinet was therefore formed on 19 July under Azaña's friend and colleague, the bespectacled chemistry professor José Giral. The new premier promptly distributed arms to the workers in order to secure their collaboration in fighting the rebellion, a momentous decision which was to change the entire course of the conflict. Had Giral relied on the loyalist army and police, he might have defeated the rebellion by conventional means and preserved the constitutional order. On the other hand, by arming the workers he created a new and volatile power which might challenge, if not conquer, the state. Acclaimed as 'the people in arms', with romantic echoes of the French Revolution, the 'people' were in fact the workers, above all the trade unionists of the CNT and UGT.

One of the many myths of the Civil War is that the organized working class – in a further echo of the French Revolution – played the decisive role in suppressing the attempted coup d'état. In Seville and Zaragoza, major bastions of the CNT, the workers were outwitted and outgunned by insurgent troops, just as they were in Cáceres and Granada. In Valencia, the army barracks were surrounded by the police and armed workers until loyalist officers won over the troops inside. In Barcelona, the workers played a greater role than elsewhere, building barricades to hamper the movements of the insurgent troops, but the forces of the *Generalitat* – the Civil Guard, the Assault Guard, and the local police under the command of General José Aranguren – were more important still, the last rebel bastion falling to a combination of their artillery fire and the bombs dropped by the air force. According to the *Generalitat*'s head of public order, the army officer Federico Escofet, it is a 'false legend that the CNT-FAI was the decisive factor in the victory against the military rebellion', as even without the CNT's 'moral' and 'material' help, 'we would have achieved our objective: defeat the rebellion'.[10] In Madrid, the conspirators, holed up in the Montaña barracks, were besieged by both the Assault Guard and armed workers, but they were battered into submission by the artillery and air force, whereupon the workers massacred many of those inside, so that in the officers' mess 'dead officers were lying there in wild disorder'.[11] Certainly the mass mobilization of the working class helped ensure that loyalist armed forces did not waver in their resolution, but the workers did not constitute the decisive military force in any of the major cities.

## THE BALANCE OF FORCES

For the insurgent Generals Emilio Mola and Francisco Franco, Madrid was the key to the coup: if the capital was taken, then the revolt was but a short step from victory. In this instance, at least, the Casares Quiroga government had taken the proper precautions before the uprising, transferring numerous loyal forces into the Madrid area. Moreover, once the insurgents failed to take the capital and other major cities such as Barcelona, Bilbao, and Valencia, the attempted coup d'état inevitably became a civil war. At this point, the balance of forces heavily favoured the Republic. Not only did it control almost two-thirds of the national territory, including the most populous cities and regions, but also the two leading industrial areas, the Basque Country and Catalonia, in addition to nearly all the arms and munitions factories, as well as both the Mediterranean and Cantabrian coastlines, vital to international commerce. The Republic also enjoyed a towering financial superiority, the main financial institutions being based in Madrid, Barcelona, and Bilbao, while the Bank of Spain held the fourth-largest reserves of gold in the world. Last, but certainly not least, the Republic retained Madrid, and with it the government, ministries, and other state institutions. The only major advantage of the insurgents was their control of two-thirds of the nation's agricultural land. Such was the Republic's overwhelming superiority that the pugnacious socialist leader Indalecio Prieto mocked the rebels on national radio in early August for their misguided endeavour:

> With the financial resources totally in the hands of the government, with the industrial resources of the nation also totally in the power of the government, the heroism of those who have impetuously risen up in arms against the Republic could acquire legendary status.[12]

At first glance, the Republic appeared to have the upper hand in military terms, too: the peninsular armies were evenly divided, the bulk of the police was loyal, most of the navy was in government hands, and the republican air force had 230 planes in comparison with the rebels' 100. Only four of the twenty-four major generals were involved in the coup, and only two of these had active commands, Francisco Franco and Miguel Cabanellas. However, this ignores three crucial factors. First, forty-four of the leading fifty-three garrisons rose up against the government. Second, just under half the 15,300 officers were in the republican zone, but 4,450 of them were purged, of whom 1,729 went before the firing squad.[13] By contrast, the insurgents' middle-ranking and junior officers not only played a decisive role in the rebellion, but would remain central to their cause (only 258 rebel officers were executed or cashiered), while the lack of adequate officers would be a perennial problem for the republicans. Third, the 34,000-strong Army of Africa was far superior to the peninsular army, as it was battle-hardened, disciplined, and ruthlessly effective.[14] The only problem was how to get it across the Straits of Gibraltar, as the navy was in republican hands.

## SPAIN AND 'ANTI-SPAIN'

Amongst the plotters there was no prior agreement over their political goals, and the death of the conspiracy's figurehead, the monarchist General José Sanjurjo, in a plane crash on 20 July, further complicated matters. The immediate aim was to crush the left and establish an authoritarian regime, General Mola initially calling for a 'republican military dictatorship'.[15] In any case, the insurgents believed themselves to be the embodiment of Spain not only because they represented the national institution par excellence, but also because they gloried in Spain's imperial past, rejected foreign ideologies as alien to the Spanish mentality, and held Catholicism to be integral to the nation's identity, as reflected in their rallying cry of 'for God and for Spain'.[16] Consequently, the rebels saw themselves as the 'Nationalists', whereas the republicans had been seduced by un-Spanish ideas and by a conspiracy of the Jews, Masons, and Communists, 'Internationalists of varying types, but equally anti-Spanish,' as Mola put it.[17] For this reason, the conflict was not a civil war, but, as the right-wing ideologue José María Pemán declared, 'a new War of Independence, a new Reconquest', inspired both by the struggle of 1808–14 against Napoleon and by the centuries-long fight of the Christian kingdoms against the Islamic domain of Al-Andalus.[18] It was therefore ironic, to say the least, that the Nationalists' elite forces were of alien origin – the Spanish Foreign Legion and the Moroccan *Regulares* – and that the 'new Reconquest' was spearheaded above all by Muslims.

Like the rebels, the republicans saw the civil war in nationalist terms, as this lent their cause a greater unity and legitimacy, it being more straightforward to fight a foreign 'other' than a fellow Spaniard. The 'foreign invaders' they were fighting were 'fascists' and 'Moors', or, in the words of *¡Ay Carmela!*, a song popular with the militia:

> We fight against the Moors,
> Mercenaries and fascists
> Ay Carmela, ay Carmela![19]

The insurgents may have been 'men born in Spain', but, a loyalist newspaper explained, their defence of fascism and their commitment to a Church based in Rome meant that they 'renounced any link with the noble ideology of the Motherland'.[20] Thus the republicans, like the rebels, pronounced the war a 'Second War of Independence', or, as the PCE proclaimed, 'a war of national independence against the military colonizing invasion of the fascist imperialism of Germany and Italy'.[21] This was a staple of republican propaganda, as shown by a poem that was read aloud to the troops at the front:

> Spaniards:
> They are taking our land.
> They stain the soil of Spain
> Dirty foreign claws . . .
> Our people counts for nothing.
> Italians and Germans
> Fight over their prey, cut up our meat
> With the swipes of a panther.

Both sides therefore reduced the complex conflict of 1936–9 to a clash between the two dominant visions of the nation – the progressive secular one and the conservative-Catholic one – while discrediting the enemy as the 'Anti-Spain'. The rebels nonetheless gave greater primacy to the nation, as shown by their self-styled status as the 'Nationalists', whereas their opponents defined themselves more prosaically as 'republicans' or 'loyalists'. Like the insurgents, the republicans saw themselves as the defenders of Spain, but they also regarded themselves as the defenders of liberty, equality, progress, and internationalism, juxtaposing traditional national symbols such as the long-suffering mother and the lion alongside international icons like the hammer and the sickle. Whereas the insurgents would downplay the aid they received from Germany and Italy, the republicans would play up the support of the Soviet Union and the sacrifices of the International Brigades. In short, nationalism held a more compelling appeal for the rebels than for the republicans.

## INTERNATIONAL INTERVENTION
## AND NON-INTERVENTION

The balance of power between the republicans and rebels soon shifted as a result of two developments. On 25 July, Hitler received a surprise visit from emissaries of Franco. Two days later, the first Junker-52 transport plane touched down in Spanish Morocco, to be joined over the next two weeks by twenty-five others and fifteen fighter planes. For Hitler, Spain formed no part of his European ambitions, but he viewed the conflict as a chance to stem the spread of Communism and to establish a pro-German regime on France's southern border. Quite independently of Hitler, Mussolini had also decided to back Franco, seeing the war as an opportunity to lure Spain into Italy's Mediterranean orbit as a junior partner. The *Duce* dispatched around forty planes to north Africa over the next month. The German and Italian planes made possible the first airlift of an army in history, which in turn allowed Franco's African troops to undertake the march on Madrid. This was nonetheless a painstaking build-up, as only 1,500 troops were flown to the peninsula during the first two weeks. Had it not been for the disarray of the republican forces, the operation would have failed. Still, Franco's last-minute pleas to both Hitler and Mussolini had saved the uprising from disaster.

The second paradigmatic shift took place as a result of the Republic's request for aid from Léon Blum's Popular Front government in France on 19 and 21 July. The initial impulse of the socialist premier was to meet the request, but the revolutionary turmoil in the republican zone soon provoked a ferocious right-wing backlash within France, Blum managing to send 'no fewer' than thirty-eight planes in early August before calling an official halt to intervention on 8 August (though another fifty-six planes made it to Spain unofficially between 9 August and 14 October 1936).[22] Gravely hampered by the divisions within the government, his own party, and French society at large, Blum was also hindered by France's diplomatic dependence on Great Britain. The Conservative government of Stanley Baldwin wanted to avoid a clash with the fascist powers at all costs, while fearing that a victory of the Republic would facilitate the spread of Communism. In early August the French therefore proposed a non-intervention agreement in the belief that this would help the Spanish government, as it was thought that the Republic could win the war if there was no outside interference. By mid-September, Britain, France, Germany, Italy and Portugal had all signed up to the Non-Intervention Agreement.

Another signatory to the Agreement was the Soviet Union. The Soviets had found themselves on the horns of a terrible dilemma. On the one hand, they were acutely aware that support for the revolutionary regime in Spain would destroy its strategy of 'collective security' – that is, the sought-after alliance with Great Britain and France – by fulfilling the fears of conservatives throughout Western Europe and by justifying the claim of the insurgents that they were defending Spain from a Judaeo-Communist-Masonic takeover. This would leave the USSR more isolated than ever, making it more vulnerable to the German threat. On the other hand, the Soviets did not want to see the French, with whom they still harboured hopes of a military alliance, encircled by fascist powers. Nor did the Soviets want to dismay and disorient the international Communist movement by not standing up to fascism. A final consideration was that Stalin, whose power was still not absolute, was under pressure at home from the revolutionary internationalists or 'Leninists', who diverged from his supremely pragmatic Soviet-centred security policy. Such domestic tensions were made worse still by the call of the exiled dissident Leon Trotsky for international revolution, which, in Stalin's eyes, threatened Moscow's hold on the international Communist movement. As a result, the Soviet Union signed the Non-Intervention Agreement on 24 August (before either Germany or Italy) to underline its commitment to European collective security and in particular its alignment with the Western democracies. It then contradicted this stance by backing the Spanish republic, the aim being to curry favour with Western opinion by taking the fight to fascism (which, in turn, might bring pressure to bear on the Western governments), to protect France's southern flank (while hoping that the French would eventually respond to German aggression in Spain), and, from Stalin's perspective, to strengthen his position at home by demonstrating international solidarity (the war in Spain receiving massive coverage in the USSR). The hope of the Soviets was that the war would be over in 1936–7, allowing them to retire quickly.

Like the Soviets, the Germans, Italians, and Portuguese had not the slightest intention of abiding by the terms of the Non-Intervention Agreement. From this perspective, the agreement was a complete farce, especially as the Non-Intervention Committee in London had no means of enforcing its decisions, but from the standpoint of the signatories it fulfilled the overriding objective of preventing a conflict between the major powers over Spain. The agreement had a profound impact on the loyalist cause by depriving the Republic of the opportunity to make purchases in the major British and French armaments' markets. This proved to be a colossal blow, as the Republic's search for arms elsewhere often proved to be unproductive. Yet another blow was the refusal of the Non-Intervention Committee (following Hitler's lead) to grant the Republic the status of 'belligerent', which prevented its navy from blockading the ports to which German and Italian arms were being sent.

## THE WORKERS' REVOLUTION

The distribution of arms to the workers on 19 July 1936 by the Giral government was the catalyst for a spontaneous grassroots revolution that was to sweep through virtually the entire republican zone. George Orwell famously expressed his awe upon arriving in 1936 in Barcelona, 'where the working class was in the saddle', but a similar scenario played out in cities, towns, and *pueblos* throughout the Republic.[23] The one partial exception was Vizcaya, and, later, the republican zone in the Basque Country once the Catholic *Partido Nacionalista Vasco* or PNV (Basque Nationalist Party) came to power following the passing of the region's Statute on 1 October 1936.

The revolution gave rise to militia controls on the streets and highways; the confiscation of private automobiles, vans, and trucks; the occupation of buildings and factories; the abolition of money in some places (and the corresponding use of vouchers, credit notes, and barter); the ransacking and pillaging of 'bourgeois' homes; the burning of churches and other religious properties; the collectivization of lands and businesses; the workers' control of many public services; and the persecution of the 'enemies' of the revolution, such as Catholics, property-owners, managers, lawyers, engineers, artisans, shopkeepers, and others. Small wonder that the attire of the 'bourgeoisie' soon became taboo, the former Radical deputy Clara Campoamor recalling that:

> Madrid offered an extraordinary aspect: the bourgeois saluting people with the clenched fist and the Communist greeting so as not to arouse suspicion; men in overalls and espadrilles copying the uniform of the militia; women without hats [wearing] used, worn dresses ... [These were] people who humbly asked for permission to live.[24]

The revolution was not a top-down process directed and controlled by a middle-class party elite, as in Russia. It was a bottom-up, highly atomized phenomenon made up of a thrumming multitude of autonomous experiments. In Barcelona, people needed a pass to move from one working-class neighbourhood to another. The sheer variety of revolutionary experiences was bewildering. The extent and type of worker control in industry and the service sector could vary from one locality to another, as did the forms of control or ownership of property, these ranging from 'takeover' or 'intervention' to collectivization, municipalization, socialization and production cartels. Collectives were more extensive in the rural domain than the urban one, 40 per cent of all land being expropriated in the republican zone, of which 54 per cent was organized in collectives, but this varied a great deal according to the region: in eastern Andalusia nearly all the expropriated land was collectivized, in Castile-La Mancha 60 per cent, in the provinces east of Valencia only a third (with only 21 per cent of the land having been expropriated), and even less in Catalonia. There was no template for the revolution. Inspired by vague ideological principles, much of what the workers did was the result of improvisation. The secretary-general of the Central Committee of the Anti-Fascist Militias of Catalonia relates that 'from an organizational point of view it was chaotic – it couldn't be otherwise. Each "secretary" did more or less what he liked.'[25] The anti-political tradition of the anarcho-syndicalists also militated against the 'bourgeois' vices of discipline, hierarchy, and authority. A member of the FAI's Peninsular Committee remembers that 'everybody seemed to be doing whatever came into their heads, without direction – the same fault as always.'[26] The idiosyncrasy of the revolutionary models was also a product of the weakly centralized structure of the two trade unions which dominated the process, the CNT and UGT. An additional reason was that workers from different movements often joined forces. Of the 2,213 agrarian collectives accounted for by the Institute of Agrarian Reform in 1937, 284 were run by the CNT, 823 by the UGT, and 1,106 were joint ventures, with the Communists, the *Partido Obrero de Unificación Marxista* (POUM) (Workers' Party of Marxist Unification), and even the left-republicans also participating.

The revolution was channelled upwards via local revolutionary committees and/or defence juntas. For the protagonists of this process, the overriding reality was the immediate vicinity, the neighbourhood, village, or town. 'Although we were anti-authoritarian,' relates a CNT member from the Barcelona neighbourhood of Las Corts, 'we were suddenly the only authority there. The local CNT committee had to take over the administration, transport, food supplies, health – in short we were running the neighbourhood.'[27] The revolution was a 'fragmented, differentiated, localized' phenomenon where the 'revolutionary committees ignored state power, drove past it as though it were a corpse'.[28] There were nonetheless superior committees or councils at the municipal, provincial, and even the regional level, though their reach and nature varied widely. The only region where the republican authorities sought to reach an institutional accommodation with the revolution was Catalonia. On 22 July, the left-republican *Generalitat* and the CNT established the Central Committee of the Anti-Fascist Militias, the anarcho-syndicalists not daring, as FAI leader and future minister Juan García Oliver later admitted, 'to go for the lot'.[29] In Aragón, the anarcho-syndicalists set up their own Council of Aragón, which was completely independent of the government in Madrid.

For the militant workers, the revolution was often an exhilarating experience, one socialist recalling it as 'dreamlike', while the Central Committee of the Anti-Fascist Militias of Catalonia also operated in 'a mood of hallucinatory exaltation'.[30] For them, it signalled the destruction of the old order and its representatives, the abolition of private property, the assumption of local power, and the imposition of a new collectivist social order, which was not only social and economic in nature, but also political and military. As the newspaper *Claridad*, Largo Caballero's organ of dissemination, put it on 22

August 1936, 'the people no longer fight for the Spain of 16 July, which was still a Spain dominated socially by the traditional castes, but for a Spain in which these castes are definitely obliterated'; that is to say, the war was 'a social war more than a civil war'.[31]

Another product of the revolution was the mass mobilization of women, as they further eradicated the traditional separation between the public and private spheres by participating in a wide variety of activities, ranging from nursing, teaching, and the making of uniforms to driving buses, labouring in munitions factories, organizing the rearguard, building barricades, and even enlisting as militia. The rising expectations of women were captured by the publication *Mujeres Libres* (Free Women), which in 1937 recalled 'the early days of the heroic struggle, during which every man was a hero and every woman the equal of a man'.[32] There were two main women's groups within the republican camp, the Communist-dominated *Agrupación de Mujeres Antifascistas* (AMA) (Association of Anti-Fascist Women), which had 60,000 affiliates and included socialists, republicans, and Basque Catholics, in addition to the anarcho-syndicalist *Mujeres Libres*, which had 20,000 members. The two organizations did not share a common project, principally because the AMA ultimately defended the traditional familial role for women, whereas *Mujeres Libres* advocated their complete emancipation. Only the AMA received governmental support, but this was of limited solace, as the authorities treated all women's groups with 'lack of interest and official reticence'.[33]

The main priority of female activists was the education of other women, above all those who were illiterate, though classes were also given in general culture, commerce, poultry farming, electricity, and mechanics. They published a host of newspapers and magazines, such as *Mujeres Libres*, *Muchachas* (Young Women), and *Trabajadoras* (Working Women), in an effort to tackle female illiteracy. But the entry of women into the workplace was resisted by trade unionists and in particular by skilled workers, while female workers were still subject to occupational segregation and salary discrimination, even in the collectives. Those women who worked as drivers or mechanics or in an arms factory were, in fact, 'exceptional'.[34] Most occupied traditional, often carer, roles, such as helping refugees, orphans, infants, and the wounded, or else working, say, in clothes' shops or canteens or as washerwomen. During the early weeks of the war, a number of women fought as *milicianas*, but not even the women's groups were prepared to challenge the slogan 'The Men to the Front, the Women to the Rearguard'.[35] From September 1936 onwards, women were made to leave the front, and by early 1937 there were very few still fighting. The strength of patriarchal values was illustrated by the fate of the *Generalitat*'s eugenics-driven abortion policy of December 1936, which failed through a lack of support from men and women alike. While the revolution and war did accentuate the public presence and social profile of women, broadening their cultural and professional horizons, the lack of official backing and a common project, together with the almost universal persistence of traditional attitudes, left them far from emancipated.

The Spanish revolution of 1936–9 was probably the most profound and unplanned in modern Europe history, being much greater in both regards than Russia in 1917 or the Béla Kún regime in Hungary of 1919. The amount of land expropriated in Spain was proportionately double that in Russia in 1917–18, while in Hungary the Communist regime's authority over the countryside 'was often nonexistent'.[36] The sheer scale of the Spanish revolution exceeded those in Russia, Hungary, and Finland, as well as the post-Second World War Greek and Yugoslav revolutions during their early stages. Further, the Spanish revolution, unlike all the others, was not dominated by the Communists or their sympathizers, and therefore displayed a greater pluralism. But, as in Russia between March and November 1917, the revolution in Spain gave rise to two competing powers: the republican state and the working-class revolution, a fundamental disjuncture which was to have a far-reaching impact on the war effort.

## THE LIMITS TO THE REVOLUTION

Despite taking over many state functions at the local level, the revolutionaries made no attempt to seize control of the state itself. In Madrid, the workers occupied churches, factories, shops, restaurants, exclusive clubs, up-market hotels, monasteries, mansions, convents, and palaces, along with centrist and right-wing political centres and newspaper offices (amounting to 500 buildings in two weeks), but they did not storm the Cortes, the ministries, the Bank of Spain, the National Palace, or the prime minister's office. In other words, the revolution gravely undermined both the republican state and government, but it did not replace them with an effective alternative, an instrument by which to direct the many thousands of local committees and juntas, above all in relation to the war. This made Spain's revolution *sui generis*: it was at once extremely profound and exceptionally vulnerable.

The vulnerability of the revolution inevitably raises the question as to why the workers did not try to conquer the state. There are a number of reasons. The paradox of the anti-statist tradition of anarcho-syndicalism is that it had devoted little thought to the question of *how* to destroy the state. The general assumption was that by seizing power at the local level and by taking over many of the functions of the central administration, such as policing, taxation, education, transportation, and so on, the state would simply fade away. Symptomatic of this mindset was the fact that none of the anarchist insurrections prior to the war attempted to seize the nerve centres of state power. From this perspective, the anarcho-syndicalists were never in a position to take over the state, the secretary-general of the International Association of Workers adding that the CNT was 'a conglomerate of regional federations without any collective discipline'.[37]

By contrast, the UGT was a much more centralized and bureaucratic body than the CNT, but it was nonetheless 'an organism clearly deficient in centralized power'.[38] Unlike the anarcho-syndicalists, the socialists were not enemies of the state, regarding it instead as the principal tool for the construction of a future socialist order. Like the anarcho-syndicalists, they were far from being in a position to conquer the state, as many of the decisions taken at the national level were left to the individual criteria of the federations, while the myriad unions attached to the UGT enjoyed a great deal of autonomy. Indeed, both the agrarian strike of June 1934 and the revolutionary uprising of October 1934 had revealed the severe shortcomings to the centralization of the UGT. Thus the socialists – like the anarcho-syndicalists – made no attempt to take control of the state during the summer of 1936. Nor did the Communists consider the seizure of power, as this would have violated the 'Popular Front' policy of the Communist International, not to mention the fact that they were far too weak at the time for such a venture. In any case, had the anarcho-syndicalist, socialist, or Communist movement tried to seize power at the highest level it would inevitably have clashed with the other two, not to forget the state's military and police forces. As a result, many revolutionaries were content to leave the state in republican hands.

The strength of revolutionary sentiment should nonetheless not be underestimated. After the Civil War, the anniversary recognized by the CNT was not 18 July, the day of the mainland uprising, but 19 July, the day of the revolution. Accordingly, the CNT had been fighting not for the Republic's 'bourgeois' democracy, but for a revolutionary alternative. If the Republic won the war, the anarcho-syndicalists anticipated yet another civil war, this time between the various 'loyalist' forces. Thus the Chilean diplomat Carlos Morla Lynch was assured by a group of anarcho-syndicalists that 'whatever happens, after the victory, if there is one, there will be a war between socialists and anarchists.'[39] The Communists also expected a showdown if the Republic won the conflict, the Soviet military attaché, Vladimir Gorev, noting that a confrontation with the CNT was 'absolutely inevitable after victory over the Whites'. The struggle, he stressed, 'will be very harsh'.[40]

The revolution has been greatly downplayed by historians ever since. The origin of this neglect lies in the vigorous campaign by the republican government to defend its democratic credentials before world opinion by simply denying the revolution's existence. Many sympathizers of the Republic have repeated this propaganda line – the so-called 'grand camouflage' – for the very same reason: to present the Republic as a parliamentary democracy under assault from fascism.[41] Even scholars of twentieth-century revolution have neglected the Spanish case, partly because of its sheer complexity (not conforming to the Communist template, it cannot be defined in terms of a single paradigm) and partly because it represents a model of failure.

A major shortcoming of the revolution was that it alienated much of the middle classes from the republican cause. In Catalonia, the middle classes had supported regional autonomy under the Republic, rejecting the insurgents' traditional vision of a 'unified' Spain. However, the revolutionaries had not only confiscated their shops, taxis, cars, factories, mills, offices, and workshops, but also placed their lives in jeopardy. Joan Reig, an industrial manager and Catalan nationalist, was appalled by both the rebellion of 18 July 1936 and the revolution which followed. He was horrified by a man at the barber's who bragged of the 'canaries' he executed every night, above all when the killer invited the barber 'to accompany him that night to witness the spectacle'.[42] José Serra, the driver for a CNT death squad, recalls in his diary that 'one of the arrested, before dying, said to us that he didn't know why we were killing him. But we shut him up because our job was to kill and his to die.'[43] As a result, the revolution came to be seen as 'an even greater threat' by the middle classes than the rebellion, the Catalan president Lluís Companys warning the anarcho-syndicalists that 'we shall lose the war for this reason'.[44]

In Madrid, the reaction of the republican middle classes to the revolution was much the same. The repression in the rearguard, especially the murder of moderate republican leaders such as Melquíades Álvarez and Manuel Rico Avello, caused many middle-class republicans to fear a victory of the Republic – 'tomorrow it'll be our turn' – even more than that of the insurgency.[45] A witness to this major shift in opinion was Clara Campoamor:

> Bit by bit, in the eyes of the people [who were] republican but peaceful, liberal but defenders of law and order, democratic but even more fearful of anarchy than dictatorship, the republican government was losing the legitimacy and legality it had won in the elections.[46]

Little wonder, then, that the defenders of the liberal, democratic Republic – the republicans and moderate socialists – 'quickly realized that the outbreak of war meant that they, and their vision of Spain, were finished'.[47] As a result, the struggle was not to re-establish the democratic Republic, but 'to define what would replace it'.[48] Thus the moderate socialist Juan Negrín contended that there was 'no returning to the old parliamentarism', as it would be 'impossible to allow the "free play" of parties, as it existed earlier, for in this way the right might again force its way into power': the only options were 'a unified political organization or a political dictatorship'.[49]

## THE REPUBLICAN TERROR

The failed coup d'état of 17–18 July 1936 triggered not only a revolution in the republican zone, but also a far-reaching terror in both camps. The victims were killed by means of *sacas* (being removed from prisons) and *paseos* (being taken for 'a ride'), their bodies often being dumped by deserted roadsides or left slumped against a cemetery wall, as well as being slaughtered in mass executions. The idea of a 'terror', or wide-ranging murderous repression, stretches back to the French Revolution, reflecting the fear and loathing produced by a deeply polarized situation in which each side strives to enforce its vision of society on the dehumanized 'other'. Terror characterized all the European civil wars of the early twentieth century, whether in Finland, Hungary, or Russia, and, later, in Yugoslavia and Greece. In the case of Spain, the terror or repression of the Civil War (and early Francoism) has been the most controversial historical topic of the last two decades. The dominant narrative as regards the republican zone deviates surprisingly little from the propaganda line taken by the loyalist government at the time; namely, that the terror had little to do with the state, parties, or trade unions, but was largely the work of fascist provocateurs, criminals, and 'uncontrollables' (invariably taken to mean radical anarchists). By contrast, it is held, the terror of the rebel zone was a cold-blooded affair that was carried out in a systematic and centralized manner, which resulted in 'genocide', 'extermination', even a 'holocaust'. However, this bipolar vision of the terror greatly misrepresents its nature.

The claim that the republican repression was the 'spontaneous' result of 'uncontrollables' – 'isolated groups of murky origins' – who managed to escape the control of the state or the revolutionary militia – is a myth.[50] On the contrary, the republican terror was overwhelmingly carried out by the militia, which were made up of 'Communists, republicans, socialists, anarcho-syndicalists, who responded to the military coup with arms, who killed their political and class enemies in the belief that in their elimination lay redemption [and who believed] that the moment of "popular", "revolutionary" justice had arrived.'[51] Generally speaking, the urban militia took their orders from the 'revolutionary tribunals'. In Madrid, for example, there were sixty-seven revolutionary tribunals, of which thirty-seven not only detained, interrogated, and tortured people, but also had them shot; the biggest tribunal was housed at the Centre for the Fine Arts in the very heart of the city. Of the tribunals, 34 per cent were run by the CNT-FAI, 19 per cent by the Communists, 13 per cent by the socialists, 9 per cent by the *Juventud Socialista Unificada* (JSU) (United Socialist Youth), and 21 per cent were joint operations.[52] These were far from clandestine bodies, as they were often lauded by the press. By far the most powerful revolutionary tribunal was the *Comité Provincial de Investigación Pública* (CPIP) (Provincial Committee of Public Investigation), which was established by the director general of security, Manuel Muñoz, on 4 August 1936, and comprised all the forces of the Popular Front as well as the CNT. Indeed, the CPIP was responsible for 'many of the over 8,000 extrajudicial killings that took place in Madrid during the civil war'.[53] Despite being founded by the director general of security, its status as a Popular Front body, and its far-reaching activities, the CPIP only partially centralized the repression in Madrid, as each party or trade union retained its own mechanisms of repression.[54] Every one of the local revolutionary branches, the socialist Arturo Barea noted, had 'its own militia battalion, its own police, its own prison, its own executioners, and a special place for its executions'.[55] However, around 7,000 right-wingers managed to survive the terror by taking diplomatic refuge, most notably at the Chilean Embassy.

In rural areas, the terror was orchestrated by militia forces in conjunction with defence or revolutionary committees, frequently in collaboration with the local and provincial authorities. In the socialist-dominated province of Ciudad Real, which accounted for 2,292 victims, the repression drew not only on the support of mayors, councillors, politicians, trade unionists, and even the provincial authorities, but also on the terror networks in Madrid.[56] If a wanted person was not found in the province itself, local militia would be dispatched to the capital to search the revolutionary tribunals and other centres for the 'fascist'. The mayor and Defence Committee of La Solana, for example, sent militia up to Madrid to locate and arrest the brother of the Count of Casa Valiente and his two sons. They were able to draw on the assistance of the revolutionary tribunal at the Centre for the Fine Arts, the anarcho-syndicalist Athenaeum, the Libertarian Youth, and even the Assault Guards. Once the three men were arrested, they were taken to the outskirts of the capital, encircled by their captors, and gunned down. Another example of the reach of the terror networks is provided by the case of the former Republican Agrarian deputy and vice-president of a national agrarian association, Andrés Maroto. He was arrested in the capital on the order of the La Solana Defence Committee, taken to the revolutionary tribunal at the Centre for the Fine Arts, and then to La Solana, where he was placed at the 'disposal of the mayor as a detainee'.[57] The next day three leading provincial politicians made the effort to travel to the town to witness his execution. In the case of Andrés Maroto 'it was not a case of "uncontrollables", but of the locality's principal leaders and authorities at that time, who acted in collaboration with their equivalents in the capital of Spain and of Ciudad Real, the provincial capital'.[58]

In the eastern provinces:

> All types of armed bands dependent on the committee, party or trade union in each locality began a process of search and capture of the 'rebels', enemies of the ongoing revolution rather than the Republic, peasants opposed to the forced collectivization of their lands, former bosses, priests, council and court employees.[59]

Also active in the repression were the militia columns that passed through an area on their way to the front, such as the so-called Iron Column in the east or the anarchists in Aragón. In short, the terror was not the work of shadowy groups on the margins, but constituted a core function of the revolution: the elimination of the counter-revolutionary enemy. As the councillor for justice in the government of the *Generalitat* and leader of the POUM, Andreu Nin, declared in October 1936, 'we the Marxists are decidedly in favour of revolutionary terror, which we consider indispensable for the victory of the revolution.'[60]

## THE ROLE OF THE STATE IN THE REPRESSION

The republican governments of 1936 are often absolved of any responsibility for the repression, on the grounds that they were too weak to stand up to the revolutionaries. Certainly, the governments did not initiate the terror, but, in keeping with their stance since February 1936, they went to great lengths to appease the working-class movements, paying tribute to the 'virtuous people' and attributing its 'excesses' to fascists or 'uncontrollables'.[61] They also placated the revolutionaries by purging the state administration, the police above all, and by urging all the forces of the Republic to come together in forging a revolutionary anti-fascist state.

The creation of the CPIP had represented an initial attempt to channel and control the terror, but it rapidly became part of the problem, not the solution. Another effort to contain the extrajudicial killings was made following the massacre of at least twenty-seven people at the Model Jail in Madrid on 22 August 1936, the victims including prominent republicans, such as the Liberal Democratic leader Melquíades Álvarez, the erstwhile minister of justice Ramón Álvarez Valdés, and the moderate minister of the interior from 1933–4, Manuel Rico Avello, all of whom, ironically, had taken refuge in the jail as a means of protection. What shocked and appalled national leaders such as José Giral and Manuel Azaña was not only that these men, who had nothing to do with the uprising, were fellow republicans and former colleagues, but that they were also of the same class and standing. President Azaña, who had first cut his political teeth in Melquíades Álvarez's party, reacted to the slaughter by declaring to Martínez Barrio that 'I'm ready to resign' on the grounds that he was not prepared to preside over a 'Republic coerced by assassins'.[62]

The upshot was the formation of the Special Tribunals, commonly known as the 'Popular Tribunals', on 23 and 25 August 1936, which were designed to temper the excesses of the repression by integrating the revolutionary forces into the judicial system. The limited capacity of these tribunals to control the terror led the government to create the Emergency Juries in October 1936, but these achieved little in stemming the wave of extrajudicial killings. What did finally contain the terror was the integration of the revolutionary forces into the government in late 1936, the replacement of the revolutionary committees and defence juntas by local councils, the incorporation of the militia into the People's Army, and a greater focus on the war effort rather than the revolution. By early 1937 the state had largely brought the repression under control, as reflected in the vertiginous drop in extrajudicial killings.

But the terror of 1936 would have been 'impossible without the complicity of state institutions'.[63] A salient example is the fate of the 245 rightists who were being escorted on 12 August 1936 by the Civil Guard on a train from Jaén in the south to the central jail at Alcalá de Henares to the east of Madrid. When the train stopped at Villaverde station on the outskirts of Madrid it was surrounded by anarchist militia under a CPIP commander, who demanded that the fifty Civil Guards withdraw. After consulting with their superiors, the Civil Guards did exactly this, along with a detachment of Assault Guards on duty at the station. The prisoners were then hauled off to a railway siding where the militia executed 193 of them, including the Bishop of Jaén and his sister. Similarly, the nomination of a new civil governor in the province of Ciudad Real in early October 1936 did not prevent 'the killings carrying on for a few months more', resulting in nearly 600 more deaths.[64] Worse still, the republican authorities were directly involved in the repression, as shown by the role of the local and provincial representatives in Ciudad Real.

A prime target of the loyalist terror was the Catholic Church. Many revolutionaries harboured a millenarian belief that the birth of the new order required the destruction of the old, and for them there was no more visible and hated symbol of the *ancien régime* than the Catholic Church. Undergirding this was the desire to replace the traditional faith of the Spanish people with the new secular religions of anarchism, Marxism, or republicanism. In contrast to the months prior to the military rebellion of July 1936, the anticlericals now assaulted not just Church property, but its personnel too, resulting in the most violent wave of anticlericalism in modern European history. Most of the clerical victims were shot but:

> Others were hanged, drowned, suffocated, burned to death or buried alive. On many occasions, victims were tortured, at times in shockingly sophisticated ways. Mockery, insults, blasphemy and coercion to blasphemy were very likely parts of the torture, which could also include forcing the victims to strip naked, beating, cutting, skinning and mutilation. In the cases of mutilation, there was a morbid fixation on

genitalia ... Finally, irrespective of the type of death they had suffered, the corpses of clerics were likely to be dragged through the streets, exposed in public spaces or desecrated in many other ways.[65]

It is often claimed that the republican government was powerless to halt this tsunami of death and destruction, but the authorities made little or no effort to protect Church property or personnel, or to uphold the freedom of worship. On the contrary, the government of November 1936 contained ardent anticlericals, such as the anarchist Juan García Oliver and the socialist Ángel Galarza, whose Ministry of the Interior housed the radio station *Radio Host*, which called on the masses to assault Church property and slaughter the clergy. Accordingly, the Catholic minister Manuel de Irujo sent a memo to his colleagues in January 1937 lambasting 'the conduct of the Republican government, which has not put an end to such acts of violence but permits them to continue', denouncing its approach as 'a system of true fascism'.[66] In short, the government was complicit in the ravages of the revolutionaries. By contrast, in the republican zone of the Basque Country, the Church was protected by the PNV, though only once it came to power in October 1936 after having secured a Statute of Autonomy.

Most major European civil wars were to an extent a 'war on religion'. The civil war within the French Revolution was triggered above all by the onslaught on the Catholic Church, 3,000 clergy being killed and up to 40,000 going into exile, while religious conflict was also central to both the Russian and Finnish civil wars. However, nowhere did anticlerical violence assume the scale of that of the Spanish Civil War, which saw a total of 6,788 ecclesiastics killed. From this perspective, Spain was indeed different.

## THE INSURGENT TERROR

The rebel repression was ultimately directed by the army, but during the early months the Carlist militia in the north and the Falangist militia in the centre and south played prominent roles. In organizing the conspiracy against the Republic, General Mola had warned his fellow rebels that the revolt 'has to be extremely violent' against an enemy which was 'strong and well organized'.[67] All those leaders who did not form part of the 'glorious National Movement' were to be subjected to 'exemplary punishments' in order to 'strangle the rebellious or strike movements'.[68] Terror, in short, was integral to the uprising.

During the early months of the war, the Nationalist terror was not planned in a centralized fashion, for the simple reason that Franco was not named *Generalísimo* until late September 1936. Yet this was by far the bloodiest period, accounting for 50–70 per cent of all victims.[69] Its brutality was the responsibility of the regional commanders, many of whom, such as General Mola in the north or General Gonzalo Queipo de Llano in the south, granted civilian death squads, mostly made up of Carlists and Falangists, considerable leeway. Queipo de Llano was responsible for the sweeping repression in Andalusia, including on 18 August the assassination of the acclaimed poet and playwright Federico García Lorca, probably the most scandalous single murder of the entire Civil War. The terror in the south was made worse still by the Army of Africa, which, once it crossed the Straits of Gibraltar in the late summer of 1936, rampaged through Andalusia and Extremadura, killing both those who barred their way and many in the rearguard. This onslaught by the 'infernal column' under Colonel Juan Yagüe climaxed once Badajoz was taken in August 1936.[70] On 15 August at around three o'clock in the morning, 'practically throughout the city could be heard the volleys of the firing squads that began the slaughter of the prisoners and immediately, echoing these volleys, was a cry of terror and horror that arose from the throats of the prisoners, conscious that their last moment had arrived'.[71] The Badajoz atrocity, which accounted for perhaps 2,000 republicans, soon became an international scandal, smearing the standing of the insurgents abroad.

What united the military leaders was a ruthless determination, greatly reinforced by their experience of the colonial war in Morocco, to secure the rearguard. As a result, the rebel terror was not limited just to the leading politicians and trade unionists, but also embraced those who might revive the cause of the left, including lesser activists, teachers, intellectuals, and Freemasons. The absence of blood crimes was no defence. The left-republican mayor of Palma de Mallorca, Dr Emili Darder, was executed on 25 February 1937 because he had encouraged 'the workers against the bosses' and because 'it is said' that he took part in the Communist uprising against the Republic that was allegedly 'in preparation'.[72] In other words, there was no real case against him, but Darder's republican outlook, together with his political and professional status, made him a potential threat to the new order. Only a fraction of the victims during the early part of the war actually had the opportunity of defending themselves before a military tribunal – principally officers opposed to the rebellion – though such proceedings were little more than a formality. Of the 2,578 people who were killed in the city of Zaragoza in 1936, only thirty-two had received a trial.[73]

## THE TWO TERRORS COMPARED

The republican and rebel repressions had much more in common than is often acknowledged. On both sides the great majority of the executions took place during the early months of the war. Up to 70 per cent of the Nationalists' victims were killed during the first three months of the conflict. The republican terror followed a similar trajectory, as 'the bulk of the killings are recorded for the months of July, August and September 1936.'[74] The logic of the repression on both sides was to crush all resistance, whether real or potential, in the rearguard. In both zones, prisoners were slaughtered as a reprisal for enemy air raids. In the loyalist zone, hundreds of prisoners in Guadalajara, Santander, and Bilbao were butchered in the wake of aerial bombardments, while prisoners held in the rebel jails of Ávila, Granada, Huesca, and Valladolid were subjected to the same treatment after air attacks. Following the bloodfest of 1936, both terrors were increasingly centralized and institutionalized. The extrajudicial excesses of the loyalist zone virtually came to a halt in early 1937, while in the Nationalist zone these would largely cease by the spring, resulting in a dramatic drop in the number of victims in both zones. Thus the insurgents killed 3,028 people in the province of Seville during the first six months of the conflict, but 137 between February and October of 1937.[75] In the republican province of Ciudad Real, there were 1,808 victims in 1936, but only sixty-five in 1937.[76] Lastly, both sides justified their actions 'in the name of the people'.[77]

But the Nationalist repression was less fragmented, more focused, and more deadly than the loyalist one, producing around 100,000 victims in comparison with approximately 50,000 victims of the republicans. This disparity is explained partly by the fact that the rebel repression embraced an ever-expanding territory, while the loyalist one involved an ever-shrinking one, but also by the fact that the Nationalists were slower to bring the extrajudicial killings to a close. The final tally of non-combatant deaths matched that of the combatants, making the rearguard during the Spanish Civil War 'as dangerous as the frontline'.[78]

The dominant narrative on the repression during the Civil War is highly politicized and moralistic, often portraying the Nationalists – in an echo of the Black Legend – as sadistic, pitiless, and inhumane, while absolving the republican government, parties, and trade unions of any major culpability, on the grounds that the loyalist terror was largely the work of criminals, fascist provocateurs, and 'uncontrollables'. Yet this gravely misconstrues the reality of the terror. On the one hand, the parties and trade unions of the Republic were heavily involved in the repression, while the government was complicit at best and actively involved at worst. On the other hand, the Nationalist terror was more extensive than the loyalist one, but it was never so far-reaching as to qualify as 'genocide', 'extermination', or as a 'holocaust', especially when set against the appalling atrocities of Stalinism in the 1930s, such as the Great Terror of 1936–8 or the 'terror-famine' of five million Ukrainians.[79] Nor does the Spanish repression compare with the myriad crimes committed against non-combatants during the Second World War, such as the deaths of three million Soviet POWs at the hands of the Germans, the Allied bombing of Dresden (with up to 25,000 victims), or the Soviets' slaughter of 15,000 Polish officers at Katyn. Above all, the Nazi-inspired killing of nearly six million Jews during the Holocaust has no parallel in Spain. Comparatively speaking, the Spanish terror was 'very artisanal and of a very limited reach'.[80]

## LARGO CABALLERO COMES TO POWER

The revolution had a far-reaching impact on the republican war effort, diverting time, energy, and resources from the military struggle, especially during the early months when most activists threw themselves into the revolution, not the war. Those militia which did engage with the enemy lacked training, experience, equipment, and leadership, as well as displaying a contempt for the martial virtues of discipline and hierarchy, making them no match for regular troops, least of all the Army of Africa, as shown by the latter's lightning advance through the southwest during the late summer of 1936 (432 kilometres being covered in thirty days). Excessive purges of the police and armed forces further complicated the Republic's response. Indeed, the republican armed forces were never able to achieve the relative unity, discipline, and leadership which characterized the rebels, though Franco never achieved complete control of the Nationalist forces, as the wilful General Gonzalo Queipo de Llano, the 'viceroy of Andalusia', maintained his independence virtually until the end of hostilities.

The revolution's unprecedented onslaught on the Catholic Church did much to consolidate support for the Nationalists, while alienating much Catholic opinion abroad from the Republic, such as in Ireland, France, the United States, and Britain. The greatest damage caused by the revolution was in relation to France and Great Britain, as it effectively thwarted the efforts of the French prime minister to help the Republic, while providing the already hostile British government with a hefty additional motive to turn its back on the Spanish regime. 'On no account, French or other,' Prime Minister Stanley Baldwin instructed Foreign Secretary Anthony Eden, 'must you bring us into the fight on the side of the Russians!'[81] Indeed, the 'Russians', not the Germans or the Italians, were seen as the principal threat to British interests. Cabinet secretary Sir Maurice Hankey speculated in a memorandum of 20 July 1936 that 'with France and Spain menaced by Bolshevism, it is not inconceivable that soon we will have to throw in our lot with Italy and Germany.'[82]

In early September 1936 the Giral government resigned. The left-republican administration had signally failed to establish its authority, create a regular army, overcome repeated diplomatic reverses, or stem the headlong advance of the insurgents, the Chilean diplomat Carlos Morla Lynch noting that the government 'does not have the slightest authority'.[83] Despite all this, Giral had assured the Soviet *Pravda* correspondent Mijail Koltsov as recently as 19 August that the Republic would win the war in a matter of 'months, maybe half a year'.[84] The new Cabinet under the revolutionary socialist Francisco Largo Caballero comprised not only radical socialists, but also moderate ones, left-republicans, a Basque nationalist, and the first Communists to join a government outside the Soviet Union and Mongolia. In November 1936 the CNT also entered the executive, making it the first in history to be joined by anarcho-syndicalists and the first in Spain to include a woman, the anarchist Federica Montseny. Both the trade unions and the parties now agreed that the overriding priority was the war, not the revolution, the government declaring that 'all political concerns are subordinated' to victory over the insurgents, the foremost advocate of the pro-war policy being the PCE.[85] This fundamental shift in the outlook of the revolutionaries was due not just to the fact that the Republic was losing the war, but also to the economic chaos engendered by the revolution, the CNT minister of the economy conceding that the economy was collapsing 'in an almost vertical manner'.[86] In sum, both economic and military disaster loomed.

Largo Caballero's primary objectives were to establish a regular army, restore the authority of the state, and bring the revolution under centralized control. Accordingly, the militia were integrated into the army, a new General Staff was formed, and the front was divided into four theatres: Andalusia, the Centre, the North, and Aragón. The newfound *Ejército Popular* (People's Army) adopted the red star as its official insignia, the clenched fist as its salute, and a political commissariat to keep an eye on both the officers and the rank and file. In short, this was a Soviet-style, 'revolutionary' army. State power was reasserted by the de facto restoration of civil governors and the replacement of the revolutionary committees and defence juntas by local councils, which also brought the revolution under a certain control. Re-establishing the authority of the state over the regions was, however, a very different proposition. In Catalonia, the *Generalitat* was intent on pursuing its own policies, while creating its own autonomous army. In the Basque Country, the PNV-led government also turned a blind eye to key initiatives from Madrid, ignored orders from the commander of the Northern Army, and showed little inclination to fight outside the Basque Country itself. The Basque nationalists would later not only sue for a separate peace, but also try to persuade Britain and France to partition Spain.

Both Cantabria and Asturias in the north also went their own way. As Largo Caballero later complained, 'I had to deal with four independent and autonomous fronts ... Such independence and autonomy were a great obstacle for the conduct of the war.'[87] Little wonder, then, that the Republic never secured the single command achieved by the Nationalists in large measure by late 1936. The Republic's military disunity was inextricably linked to its political divisions. At the end of 1936 there were in effect *six* different governments or regional authorities within the republican zone: the central government, the Basque and Catalan governments, the Council of Aragón, and the autonomous administrations in Asturias and Cantabria.

## FRANCO TAKES CONTROL OF THE INSURGENTS

The highly fragmented and contested nature of power in the republican camp stood in contrast to the Nationalist camp. The rebels quickly declared martial law, that is, the military assumed total power. Accordingly, on 23 July General Mola created the Junta of National Defence, made up entirely of military men, to coordinate activities within the insurgent zone. Five days later another edict announced that 'the crimes of rebellion, sedition' would be subject to military jurisdiction; in other words, all those who defied the rebels would be charged with rebellion.[88] This self-justificatory, if not surreal, 'justice in reverse' was an early sign not only of the military's dominance, but also of the rebels' need to establish the legitimacy of their cause.[89] Nonetheless, the unity of the insurgents should not be overstated. The Junta of National Defence was largely powerless. In reality, the Nationalist zone was divided into separate spheres of influence, those of Franco and Mola in the north, and Queipo de Llano in the south.

On 20 September 1936 Franco's troops captured Santa Olalla in the province of Toledo. Over the previous two months the republicans had unsuccessfully set siege to the city of Toledo's massive Alcázar (fortress), where over 1,000 people, including hostages, were holed up under Colonel José Moscardó. Instead of bypassing Toledo and pushing on to Madrid while the capital's defences were still weak, Franco decided to liberate both Toledo and the Alcázar, as he was not only determined to secure his rearguard, but was also well aware of the city's symbolic importance, and therefore its propaganda value. By taking Toledo, the religious capital of Spain, and by lifting the Alcázar's siege, which echoed the exploits of legendary heroes such as the medieval warlord El Cid, Franco transformed himself into the saviour *invictus* of the Nationalist cause. The relief of the Alcázar was re-enacted on film two days later and then shown in cinemas throughout the world, making Franco an international figure overnight, the global personification of the advancing Nationalist armies. The siege of the Alcázar rapidly acquired mythical status within rebel ranks, inspiring acts of heroic defiance by heavily outnumbered detachments at Oviedo, Brunete, Belchite, and Teruel, which contrasted greatly with the defensive performance of republican troops in similar situations.

The Junta of National Defence had made Franco supreme military commander of the Nationalist forces on 21 September so that they could enter Madrid under a single command. Certainly the forty-three-year-old general was an unprepossessing figure: short, stocky, with an incipient paunch, he had a high-pitched voice, which did little for his oratory (the Italian ambassador described his harangues as 'cold and feminine').[90] In person he was reserved if not remote, bereft of charisma, but he was also astute and ambitious. In any case, the decision had not been difficult. The most prestigious figure in the Spanish military, Franco had not only secured the crucial support of Germany and Italy, but also swept up through southwest Spain at the head of the Army of Africa, the insurgents' prize fighting force. On 28 September, following the liberation of the Alcázar, he was made political leader, a decree of 1 October stating that the *Generalísimo* 'will assume all the powers of the new state'.[91] As Franco put it, 'you place Spain in my hands'.[92] The first step in the institutionalization of this 'full, sovereign, unlimited and indefinite power' was the replacement of the Junta of National Defence by the Technical Junta of State, a merely administrative body.[93] A personal dictatorship was already in the making.

## 'THEY SHALL NOT PASS':
## THE DEFENCE OF MADRID

In early November 1936 Franco's army reached the outskirts of Madrid. Convinced that the capital's fall was inevitable, the government fled to Valencia, highlighting its own failure to organize the city's defence. Premier Largo Caballero justified this unheroic and defeatist

Insurgent troops on the outskirts of Madrid

decision on the grounds that the capital was of no strategic value, which left him with a 'black stain' against his name, especially once Madrid, left to a Defence Junta under General José Miaja, then held out against Franco's forces.[94] That Madrid survived the rebel assault was due to the convergence of a number of factors: the defence of the capital was left above all in the hands of the army, the resolute leadership of General Miaja and Colonel Vicente Rojo not only producing an effective system of trenches and fortifications, but also raising morale; the introduction of the first regular troops of the People's Army, which were far superior to the militia; the arrival of substantial amounts of Soviet aid, which provided the republicans with greater firepower, better tanks, and control of the skies; and the deployment of the first International Brigaders, many of whom had prior military experience thanks to the First World War or national service. These developments, along with the fortuitous discovery of the rebel plan of attack on 7 November, allowed the capital to defy the insurgent attack throughout November and December. Once his frontal assault failed, Franco tried to cut off Madrid's lifeline – the Valencia road to the southeast – at the Battle of Jarama in February 1937, during which the 15th International Brigade lost half its men (the 600-strong British contingent suffering 375 casualties on its very first day in action), but was again repulsed. A last attempt to seize the capital was launched in March 1937 from Guadalajara province in the east, but once again the republicans repulsed the Nationalist forces.

Madrid's defiance of 'fascism' between November 1936 and March 1937 – epitomised in the slogan *No pasarán* (They Shall Not Pass) – was to be the republican army's greatest achievement, a defensive triumph which would only be repeated in the case of Valencia in 1938. The fall of the capital would not have ended the war, but would certainly have hastened its conclusion. The Battle of Madrid proved to be a turning point in the Civil War. It shattered Nationalist hopes of a relatively rapid triumph and converted a war of columns into one of attrition, both sides setting about the creation of mass conscript armies in preparation for a lengthy conflict. Accordingly, the successful defence of Madrid not only extended the war, but also made it a very different type of war.

The balance of power within the republican camp subsequently shifted, augmenting the autonomy of the army and bolstering the Communist cause, as the PCE leaders had stayed in the capital in order to undertake 'the great task of defending Madrid'.[95] Their steadfastness, together with the timely arrival of Soviet aid and the Comintern-organized International Brigades, greatly accentuated the PCE's profile, as shown by its growth. In July 1936 the party had fewer than 90,000 members, but by March 1937 it boasted 249,000 and in January 1938 that number had risen to 339,000 (though Palmiro Togliatti, the chief Comintern delegate in Spain from mid-1937, estimated that the 'real number' was a little above 200,000).[96] By contrast, the unseemly flight of the socialist leaders had harmed their standing, especially that of Largo Caballero.

The epic defence of Madrid against the onslaught of 'fascism' – in reality, a coalition of rightist forces – has overwhelmingly obscured the fact that the capital was, at the very same time, the scene of the greatest single massacre of non-combatants of the entire civil war. Between late October and early December 1936 thousands of prisoners were taken from the jails of Madrid in buses and trucks to a cluster of locations to the east of the capital, above all to an area below the hilltop *pueblo* of Paracuellos de Jarama, and shot. Around 2,500 'fascists' lost their lives this way, a large white cross on the hillside, visible today from Adolfo Suárez Madrid-Barajas Airport, marking the site of the killings. Defenders of the Republic have striven to pin the blame for 'Paracuellos' on Soviet agents in an effort to uphold the Republic's democratic credentials, but recent research has debunked this face-saving myth. In reality, the body responsible was the Provincial Committee of Public Investigation or CPIP, which was a 'quasi-state agency'.[97] The twenty-one-year-old Santiago Carrillo, head of public order in Madrid and later leader of the Spanish Communist Party, is often held responsible for the massacre, but he did not order the killings, though he did facilitate them through the provision of political and logistical support.

Historians sympathetic to the Republic frequently claim that the government only became aware of the shootings at Paracuellos and elsewhere after the event, but this is yet another attempt to prop up the regime's legitimacy. At the time two ministers expressed concern at the prison evacuations, one of them, Manuel de Irujo, raising the issue both in Cabinet and with the president, but to no avail. Meanwhile, diplomats soon surmised what was going on, a British Foreign Office official describing it as 'a ghastly tale of ghastly gangsters'.[98] Far from being unaware of the killings, both the minister of justice, the former anarchist gunman Juan Oliver García, and the minister of the interior, the socialist Ángel Galarza, encouraged and defended the assassins, while the prime minister took the propaganda line that the prisoners were merely being transferred to safer jails. The killings were finally brought to an end by Largo Caballero as a result of intense pressure from both within and outside Spain. There is little doubt that the government was complicit in the executions, but its deft cover-up, which drew on figures such as the Communist deputy Margarita Nelken, avoided the scale of the international outcry that greeted the massacre carried out by the Nationalists in Badajoz in August 1936.

Madrid's heroic defiance of the insurgents has also obscured the decidedly unheroic actions of many of its citizens. The navy and air force minister was outraged that employees at the repair centre in Los Alcázares would not work overtime for the sake of the war effort, while an arms firm in Madrid was plagued by the theft of 'machines, tools, and materials'.[99] The president noted that in those public services and industrial ventures which depended on the trade unions 'the quality and the quantity of the work declined. The trade-union haemorrhaging produces a paralysing effect.' The result was 'disastrous for the Republic'.[100] Many people refused to pay either their rent or taxes. Others picked up food on behalf of a collective, but then consumed it themselves. By late 1936 the capital's courts were more occupied with common criminals than with rebel sympathizers. In short, 'examples of everyday egotism abounded'.[101]

# CONSTRUCTING
# THE NATIONALIST 'NEW STATE'

The Nationalists' failure to take Madrid had major ramifications for their cause. Franco turned in early 1937 to the north with a view to dismantling the Republic region by region. The lengthening of the war also persuaded him to undertake the construction of the 'New State' during rather than after the war. The counter-revolutionary state would not merely 'counter' its revolutionary adversity, but respond with a revolution of its own, as Franco was convinced that Spain required a new and modern type of authoritarian regime. One step was the launch of the personality cult of the *Caudillo* (equivalent to *Führer* or *Duce*), which was to reflect Franco's somewhat portentous personal style, as he had come to believe that his role in Spain's future was providential and that he was responsible to 'God and History' alone.[102] Another step was the establishment of a single party. The various political currents within the rebel camp, ranging from Falangists, Carlists, Alfonsine monarchists to *cedistas* and republicans, were forcibly merged in April 1937 into the clunkily named *Falange Española Tradicionalista y de las Juntas Ofensivas Nacionales Sindicalistas* (Spanish Traditionalist Falange of the Juntas of National Syndicalist Offensive), otherwise known as 'the Movement' in order to implicitly identify it with all the forces of the uprising or 'National Movement'. This state-created entity was dominated by the two main sources of volunteers, the Falange, which had approximately 300,000 members by January 1937, and the Traditionalist Communion (or Carlists), which had around 200,000 affiliates by early 1937, making the new party a highly incongruous hybrid, as it combined the most ultra-Catholic, traditionalist, and retrograde movement in Western Europe with the fascistic modernity of the Falange. The execution of the charismatic Falangist leader José Antonio Primo de Rivera in the Alicante jail on 20 November 1936 made Franco's self-anointment as the 'National Leader of the Movement' straightforward, as well as guaranteeing that, in striking contrast to Nazi Germany or fascist Italy, the state controlled the party, rather than the other way around.[103] Leadership during the war was therefore exercised by the military, not the Movement, which imposed order, discipline, and relative unity on the Nationalist camp, in stark contrast not only to other counter-revolutionaries, such as the fatally fractured Whites of the Russian Civil War (1918–21), but also to the republicans, embroiled throughout the war in political infighting and factionalism.

The creation of the *Falange Española Tradicionalista y de las JONS* also involved the integration of the various women's organizations – the *Sección Femenina* (Women's Section) of the Falange, the Carlists' Traditionalist Communion, and the Nazi-inspired *Auxilio de Invierno* (Winter Auxiliary) – into one body, a new-style *Sección Femenina*. All these groups saw themselves as Catholic, patriotic, and traditional, that is, they all accepted the patriarchal paradigm of women as wives, mothers, and carers. Upon its foundation in 1934 the *Sección Femenina* of the Falange had only fifty affiliates, rising to 2,500 by mid-1936, but, in the words of its president, Pilar Primo de Rivera (sister of José Antonio), 'when the bullets started flying women began to join the Falange.'[104] The pre-war *Sección Femenina* had provided support for Falangist prisoners and taken care of the families of those activists who had been killed, but the wartime *Sección Femenina* took on a whole new range of responsibilities, including nursing, making uniforms, acting as pen pals for front-line troops, fundraising, and working on the land, nearly all of which were also done by women in the republican zone. Thousands of women helped with the harvest and other agricultural tasks, an echo of José Antonio's rural ideal, according to which the countryside was the wellspring of tradition. The Winter Auxiliary, founded in November 1936 (and renamed *Auxilio Social* or Social Auxiliary in May 1937), stood out for its capacity to provide for the hungry, whether through soup kitchens in the rear or through the provisioning of areas that had been 'liberated' by the insurgents. Following the fall of Bilbao, for example, the Social Auxiliary sent 1,319 tons of victuals into Vizcaya.[105] A decree of October 1937 enhanced the Social Auxiliary's presence still further by requiring all women aged between seventeen and thirty-five who aspired to a public-sector position or a professional occupation to spend six months in its ranks. The women's groups in the Nationalist zone were not only organizationally and ideologically more united than those in the republican zone, but arguably did more to mobilize women, as the *Sección Femenina* boasted 600,000 members at the end of the conflict.[106] The public profile of women within Nationalist Spain may have been considerably raised during the war, but they achieved this within a profoundly traditional framing of their societal role, forfeiting shortly after the conflict ended all the rights won under the Republic, such as divorce, co-education, and civil marriage.

A major boost for the insurgent cause was the institutional adhesion of the Catholic Church, as manifested in a *Collective Letter* of 1 July 1937 signed by forty-seven bishops. Catholicism proved to be the single most effective unifying element for the diverse forces of the Nationalist camp, ranging as they did from monarchists, Falangists, Traditionalists, Catholics, and conservative republicans to the military. No ceremony in the rebel camp would be complete without the sanctifying presence of the Church. Furthermore, the endorsement of the ecclesiastical hierarchy provided the rising with its greatest source of legitimacy, the Church reframing the conflict in epic historical terms as 'a crusade' in the name of 'religion, the Motherland and civilization'.[107] Imagining the fratricidal conflict as a holy war lent the Nationalist discourse an even greater intolerance and vindictiveness, especially as the Church disavowed the republicans by casting the war as a titanic struggle between, in the words of Archbishop Isidro Gomá, 'Spain and Anti-Spain, religion and atheism, Christian civilization and barbarism'.[108] This may help explain why priests and other religious personnel did so little to defend victims of the rebel repression, in contrast to the far from insignificant number of republicans who aided or protected members of the clergy and lay Catholics. The Church's backing of the insurgents naturally boosted Catholicism as a political and cultural force within the Nationalist camp, thereby heightening the inherent tension between Catholicism and Falangism. The commitment of the Church to the Nationalists did much to rally support amongst not only the Catholic nations, but also influential Catholic minorities in countries such as Great Britain and the United States. Conversely, the Church's benediction did considerable damage to the Republic's reputation abroad.

The first Francoist government was formed in February 1938, replacing the Technical State Junta. Made up mainly of civilians, the Cabinet set about constructing the so-called 'New State', most notably by passing a draconian press law that would endure until 1966 and by laying the foundations of the *Sindicatos Verticales* (Vertical Syndicates) or state-controlled trade unions. Although the New State, in accordance with the programme of the Falange, was declared authoritarian, national-syndicalist, and imperialist, Franco regarded it not only as singularly Spanish, but also as a work in progress, revealing his awareness of the distinct currents within the regime. In the same vein he realized that the dictatorship would never survive as a strictly military regime, which explains why military officers, Falangists, Carlists, Alfonsine monarchists, Catholics, and technocrats were all drafted into the emerging state structures. By integrating these diverse forces into a unified authoritarian framework, Franco set the template for the dictatorship by providing it with a relatively broad base and by furnishing it with different political options.

## THE IMPACT OF FOREIGN AID

The staunchest supporter of the Nationalist cause was Mussolini, for whom the war in Spain was much more important than it was for either Hitler or Stalin. Following the signing of a friendship agreement with Franco in November 1937, Mussolini sent 500 cannon, 700 mortars, 12,000 machine guns, 3,800 motor vehicles, and 130 planes to the insurgents over the next three months. Italian guns thereafter formed the backbone of Franco's artillery corps, while the Italian infantry or

*Corpo di Truppe Volontarie* reached a peak of 49,000 soldiers. Nearly all of this was provided on credit. During the remainder of the war, the Italians played a prominent role in all of Franco's major offensives. They also took a keen interest in the construction of Franco's 'New State', striving to convert the Spanish right from its 'reactionary' and 'clerical' views to the more modern ones of fascism.

Hitler's approach to the Nationalist cause was much more pragmatic than Mussolini's. He had no interest in the Falange, was not prepared to provide ever more aid, and the nature of the Francoist regime was 'a matter of indifference' to him.[109] For Hitler, the *raison d'être* of the Spanish Civil War was to distract the other powers from his rearmament programme and his plans for territorial expansion, while keeping Italy at odds with Great Britain and France. Accordingly, he was not flustered by Franco's time-consuming military tactics, as they suited his own interests. In the meantime, he was determined to extract economic concessions from the Spaniards, especially in relation to minerals, the Germans eventually controlling four major mining companies. On the other hand, German assistance was also provided largely on credit, Franco having to pay for only 18 per cent of it by the end of hostilities.

The Republic's principal backer was the USSR. Soviet help for the Republic had been conditional on the Spanish paying for the aid and bringing the revolution under control. The Largo Caballero government of early September 1936 met these two criteria by attempting to channel the revolution and by sending nearly all the gold of the Bank of Spain to Moscow by the end of October 1936 (worth $630 million). The Soviet arms which reached Spain that same month not only outstripped the military aid hitherto sent by the Germans and Italians, but also included better tanks and planes. Still, by the summer of 1937 the Soviet commitment was wavering. First, the closure of the Mediterranean route to Soviet shipping due to the interference of the Nationalist navy (with the assistance of Mussolini's submarines) made the delivery of arms and other supplies much slower and more costly, as they had to be shipped from Soviet ports in the north and then transported across France. Second, the Japanese invasion of China in July 1937 raised the spectre of a war on two fronts, prompting Stalin to supply arms to the Chinese, which reduced the aid available for Spain. Finally, the Republic's inability to turn the tide of war led the Soviets to see it as a lost cause, a drain on their resources. As a result, Soviet support for the Republic dropped off drastically in late 1937 and 1938, though it never ceased altogether.

Another source of republican aid was Mexico, which, between September 1936 and September 1937, sold arms worth $2.225 million to Spain, with other shipments being made until October or November 1938. The Mexican aid was the most disinterested of all, the Spanish ambassador to France, Luis Araquistáin, recalling that 'of all the intermediaries who offered to help us, the only one that did not rob or swindle us was Mexico. Only the Mexican government ordered its diplomatic agents to place themselves entirely at the disposition of the Spanish Republic, with no further personal or official profit.'[110]

Foreign intervention played a critical role in the Spanish war, as it did in numerous European civil wars. The Béla Kún regime of 1919 in Hungary was toppled by the Romanian army, while the triumph of the Finnish Whites in 1918 was ensured by the intervention of the Germans. Later, Tito's triumph in Yugoslavia in 1945 was sealed by the Soviets, while in the case of the Greek Civil War of 1946-9 American and British backing for the monarchists – along with Stalin's reluctance to supply the Communists – determined the outcome. Many historians judge foreign intervention to have played *the* decisive role in the Spanish war. Certainly, the Nationalists did better out of the military aid provided by the Germans and Italians than the republicans did out of Soviet and Mexican assistance. On the one hand, the quantities of arms involved were comparable: the Nationalists received about 1,500 planes and 350 tanks, while the Republic obtained around 1,100 planes (plus 250 which were made in Spain according to Soviet designs) and 900 tanks and other armoured vehicles. On the other hand, the quality of the armaments was uneven, as the German and Italian supplies were always of a military grade, but not those of the Soviets. German and Italian supplies were also more attuned to the military needs of the insurgents, as well as being acquired overwhelmingly on credit, whereas the arrival of Soviet arms was less timely and often had to be paid for up front. In any case the insurgents made better use of the aid which they received than either the republicans or the Russian Whites, who squandered Allied material by selling it on the black market.

Not that the republicans helped themselves. Multiple purchasing commissions went forth in search of arms on the international market, ranging from representatives of the government, the PCE, the CNT, and the Republican Left of Catalonia party to the Basque government, the *Generalitat*, and other regional committees. While the buyers met 'a wall of blackmail' from officials everywhere, they were also often inexperienced and easily swindled in dealings both with foreign governments and the 'arms dealers, brokers and other go-betweens'.[111] The result was a 'disaster'.[112] Similarly, in October 1936 premier Largo Caballero named as ambassador to the USSR, the Republic's one and only major ally, Marcelino Pascua, a moderate socialist and professor of medicine in his late thirties who had no diplomatic experience whatsoever. Despite the Soviets furnishing the ambassador with a sumptuous building in the heart of the Russian capital, in addition to exceptional access to the Soviet leadership, including Stalin, the republican government sent just one other person, who, in the ambassador's own words, was 'without any experience whatsoever in the matter'.[113] By contrast, the Spanish Embassy in Paris housed thirty-six diplomats, including seven attachés, even though French aid constituted only a fraction of the Soviet assistance. The dearth of diplomats in Moscow not only affronted the Republic's hosts, but also greatly complicated the work of Pascua and his assistant, as they had to undertake tasks normally reserved for specialists, such as those of a military attaché, which probably helps explain why the Republic paid way over the odds for Soviet arms. The ambassador's increasingly desperate entreaties to his government for more staff – he told the prime minister in October 1937 that the situation was 'truly and absolutely shameful' – fell on deaf ears.[114] Indeed, throughout the war the Spanish government 'maintained the Moscow legation on next to nothing, so it never surpassed a minimal level of subsistence'.[115] The upshot was not only a growing distance between the Spanish Embassy and the Soviet authorities, but also, and more seriously, considerable confusion and delay over the arms shipments to the Republic. Such was Pascua's isolation that his chief companion appears to have been a lapdog by the name of 'Barbitas', which became so well known that the Francoist propaganda ridiculed the ambassador on the grounds that 'the only one whom he trusted was his doggy.'[116] In March 1938 the government suddenly reassigned Pascua to Paris, but without replacing him in Moscow. For the last year of the war, the Spanish Embassy in Moscow was 'totally inefficient, incapable of carrying out any serious responsibility in relation to questions of government or the development of the war'.[117]

Much is still made of the support provided for the Republic by the International Brigades, the majority of whom were Communists who had responded to the call of the Communist International. They came from all over the world, especially Europe and North America, totalling 41,000, though there were never more than 30,000 at any one time. Often used as shock troops, they suffered a far higher mortality rate (15 per cent) than the average republican soldier (6 per cent), playing their most important role in 1936–7. By the time they were withdrawn from Spain in late 1938 most of the International Brigaders were in fact Spanish. The Republic also benefited from 3,000 Soviet personnel, including tankmen and fighter pilots. But there has been a tendency to overlook the fact that there were far more foreigners on the insurgent side than on the republican one. In addition to 16,000 Germans, there were 49,000 Italian 'volunteers', most of whom were fascist militia. Many of these militia were replaced by trained soldiers, making the *Corpo di Truppe Volontarie* (Corps of Volunteer Troops) much more effective, even though it was reduced to 30,000 men. There was also a Portuguese Legion of 20,000 men and the 700-strong Irish Brigade under General Eoin O'Duffy, though the latter returned to Ireland in disgrace in June 1937. More importantly still, the Nationalists managed to recruit between 75,000 and 80,000 Moroccan mercenaries. Like the International Brigaders, these were often deployed as shock troops (they suffered a mortality rate of 15–20 per cent), but unlike the Brigaders these were generally experienced, battle-hardened soldiers who had fought in the colonial war in Morocco, which made them amongst the most capable and feared troops of the entire insurgent army. 'The worst blokes we ever came across were the Moors,' as one British Brigader recalled: 'God they were vicious . . . They'd put the fear of God into you.'[118] During the Civil War, Spain's colonial troops, like the British and French imperial forces during the First World War, therefore played a key role. The high esteem in which they were held was reflected in the building of twelve mosques during the war by the

Nationalists in the Moroccan Protectorate and by the organization of pilgrimages to Mecca on the initiative of Franco himself.

## CONTRASTING ECONOMIC PERFORMANCES

The focus on foreign aid has tended to downplay the importance of other factors in the outcome of the Civil War. Vital to the victory of the insurgents were their superior planning, coordination, and logistics. In July 1936 their only major economic advantage was control of two-thirds of the nation's agricultural land, though they later benefited greatly from the fact that most of the $600 million of German and Italian aid was made available on credit, along with trucks from General Motors and petroleum shipments from the Texaco Company. However, the policies pursued by the Nationalists, such as the regulation of exports, foreign exchange, the financial and industrial sectors, as well as of the trade in precious metals and gems, did much to boost their economy. Basic foodstuffs such as wheat were also regulated, while the production of food was facilitated by flexible pricing policies, the provision of incentives, and less looting and pillage than in the loyalist zone. Confidence in Nationalist economic planning was further enhanced by the fixing of the peseta at its pre-war level, which helped keep prices stable until 1938–9. Unlike the republicans, the rebels not only imported relatively little food, but also avoided slaughtering their donkeys, mules, and horses for meat, as these were central to the rural economy.

The result was that the insurgents were able to feed both their civilian population and their armies, which was one of the keys to their victory, especially as the republicans were unable to do the same. Ample food production not only permitted people to work effectively but was also crucial to morale. It also ensured that the rebel army had a far more abundant and varied diet than its republican counterpart. A Nationalist doctor who served in the north claims that soldiers normally received 'a bowl of soup, another of beans and potatoes with pork fat, and a plate of meat. They also had coffee, both at midday and at night.'[119] In fact, a typical daily ration for a Nationalist soldier in 1937 was 200 grams of meat, 60 of oil and 50 of sugar, whereas a member of the Republic's 37th Mixed Brigade in November 1937 received just 20 grams of meat, 40 of oil and 20 of sugar.[120] As a Nationalist quartermaster put it, the feeding and clothing of troops was essential to 'improving their health and spirit'.[121] Rebel troops would in fact taunt the republicans by broadcasting their daily menu over loudspeakers and by displaying samples of their culinary fare. The agricultural efficiency of the insurgents also meant that mules, donkeys, and horses were available to transport arms, food, and other supplies to the front line for an army that was only partially motorized. Indeed, mules were 'Franco's jeeps' and their drivers 'rural proletarian heroes'.[122] An elite Navarrese unit, for example, had 700 mules, which were, one officer noted, 'necessary and irreplaceable'.[123] The ability of the insurgents to raise taxes, along with substantial 'voluntary' donations, allowed them to pay their troops on a regular basis. Thus the twin incentives of 'meals and money' were the principal attraction for the highly valued Moroccan mercenaries.[124] In conclusion, the performance of the Nationalist economy was far better than that of the republican one: it managed to feed both the rearguard and the front, raise taxes, sustain exports, stabilize the currency, maintain consumption, and keep inflation down to 10 per cent a year.

By comparison with that of the Nationalists, the republican economy was a shambles. The disruption and devastation wrought by the revolution together with the political divisions that afflicted the Republic resulted in a profusion of territorial, administrative, and economic fractures. There were no fewer than six different governments or regional authorities during the early part of the war and a bewildering host of overlapping economic agencies, such as state, regional, and anarcho-syndicalist purchasing commissions, which was improvident in the extreme. More chaotic still was the state of the currency. By the end of 1937 over 2,000 different entities had emitted 'approximately ten thousand kinds and denominations of paper money and fifty or so kinds of metallic money', a formidable obstacle to accounting and trade.[125] Inflexible agrarian price controls, designed to placate urban consumers, encouraged both individual and collectivized enterprises to hoard their produce as the value of the republican peseta dropped. Indeed, the peseta had lost 75 per cent of its value by the end of 1937 and was practically worthless a year later (by contrast the Nationalist peseta had lost only 27 per cent of its value by this stage), the loss of confidence in the official currency contributing greatly to the Republic's economic turmoil. Hoarding was further exacerbated by looting. The pillage and wanton destruction of loyalist soldiers in the Sierra de Guadarrama, for example, jeopardized 'any desire of [the] peasants to work for our cause', a commissar's report explained.[126] In June 1937 the Ministry of Defence had to warn its troops that all looting would be severely punished. Agrarian output was also constrained by the fact that the farmers who benefited from the break-up of the big estates were normally content to achieve self-sufficiency rather than produce for the market. The collectives generally went down the same parochial path, one CNT leader denouncing them for their 'permanent egotism'.[127] Thus the agricultural collectives in Valencia acted in a completely autonomous fashion, disregarding both trade union and state directives. Collectives may have worked at a purely local level, but not at a regional or national one. A salutary contrast is provided by the approach of the Chinese Communists during their civil war of 1946 to 1949, as they appreciated that land ownership could not be drastically disrupted while the fighting was in progress, thereby enabling them to supply both 'beans and bullets'.[128]

In 1937 industrial production stood at 60 per cent of the pre-war level, but it plummeted the following year. Most dismaying of all, the Republic struggled to produce arms. By September 1937 the Hispano-Suiza automobile company in Barcelona had not produced a single car, truck, or aeroplane motor since the outbreak of war, the chief of the General Staff claiming that the loyalist arms sector 'was not able to finish a single kind of rifle or machine gun or cannon'.[129] Exasperated trade-union and party officials made strenuous efforts to raise the production of the collectivized farms, factories, and workshops, but the resistance to work was redoubtable, as manifested in absenteeism, pilfering, and sabotage. Such resistance to wage labour was comparable to that during the Russian Revolution or, later, under the Soviet regime and its East European satellites.

The fall in agricultural production was even more calamitous, as the Republic was unable to feed either its cities or its armies, which had a devastating impact on morale. The first signs of scarcity were apparent in Madrid as early as August 1936. On 19 September 1936 the Chilean diplomat Carlos Morla Lynch noted in his diary that in the restaurants 'there was no food to be found. Everything is finishing. The cake shops are deserted.'[130] A month later, 'food is scarce, there's no coal'.[131] In January 1937 the Defence Junta recorded that 'today we can state that the populace hardly eats. Having [military] material will serve no purpose if Madrid dies of hunger.'[132] Over the following months the crisis spread to the entire republican zone. Draught animals had to be slaughtered for meat, which made it increasingly difficult not only to produce and transport food, but also to supply the front line. By the end of hostilities the Republic was on the verge of famine.

Another crucial shortcoming of the Republic's political economy was the failure to collect taxes, the exertions of finance minister Juan Negrín notwithstanding. Throughout the loyalist zone there was not only a widespread refusal to pay rents, but also a 'de facto taxpayer strike'.[133] Fiscal shortcomings meant that soldiers were often paid late, such as the troops in Asturias, who were owed four months' salary in October 1937. The budgetary shortfall prompted the printing of ever more money, which in turn pushed up prices. By the later stages of the war, inflation had skyrocketed to 1,500 per cent. While the relative success of the Nationalists' political economy proved 'essential' to their victory, the economic calamity that engulfed the republicans was a major factor in their defeat.[134]

## THE FALL OF LARGO CABALLERO

At the beginning of 1937 the socialist left had proposed to the Communists that they form a single party. 'We will forge the organ of the revolution,' urged Largo Caballero's mouthpiece *Claridad* on 6 January, 'for Marxist unity, towards the total unification of the Spanish proletariat.'[135] However, the calamitous loss of Málaga in February 1937 quickly soured relations between the two sides, the Communists holding Largo Caballero's chief military mentor, General José Asensio, responsible. The prime minister reacted by putting the unification process on hold and then by lashing out not only at the Communists, but also at the moderate socialists and republicans. By March it appeared that everyone but the anarcho-syndicalists 'speaks badly of Largo

Caballero'.[136] His fixed daily routine further tarnished his credibility both as a wartime premier and as the 'Spanish Lenin', Mijail Koltsov claiming that 'Come what may, Largo Caballero goes to bed at nine o'clock at night and no one dares to wake "The Old Man". If Madrid fell at midnight, the head of government would only find out the following morning.'[137]

Largo Caballero's rupture with the Communists brought the moderate socialists and the PCE closer together. The former criticized the UGT and the CNT for pursuing, 'like a new revolutionary Saturn, the mission of undermining, replacing and devouring the political parties', arguing that they should instead 'limit themselves to their specific mission as the agents of production'.[138] The anarcho-syndicalists responded by calling on the socialist left to form a purely trade-union government, Largo Caballero indeed raising the possibility with the president of 'a government of the two trade unions and, as regards the rest, a sprinkling of the parties'.[139] The parties, however, had other ideas, the PSOE and PCE creating a series of joint working committees in April. At issue was not so much a rerun of the debate over whether the war or the revolution should be prioritized, as a struggle for control of the government.

The stand-off between the parties and the trade unions reached its climax with the outbreak of violence on the streets of Barcelona. On 3 May a detachment of Assault Guards stormed the CNT-held *Telefónica* building on the central Square of Catalonia in an attempt to reassert the regional government's control there. This provoked an armed confrontation between, on the one hand, the CNT and the dissident Communist POUM (which hoped to turn the struggle into revolution), and, on the other, the left-wing Catalan republicans and the Communist-dominated *Partido Socialista Unificado de Cataluña* (PSUC) (United Socialist Party of Catalonia), which aimed to strengthen their position at the expense of the CNT, while eliminating the POUM. The government eventually sent up to 12,000 police and soldiers to quash the fighting, the five-day pitched battle having caused 218 deaths in the Catalan capital and 279 within the region as a whole.

The 'May Days' of 1937 ruptured the uneasy equilibrium within the government, both the Communists and the moderate socialists taking advantage of the conflict to resign. Largo Caballero tried to form a new administration, but ended up completely isolated, alienating even his sole ally, the CNT, which was aggrieved at being offered just two ministries. The collapse of Largo Caballero's government signalled the demise of his twin-pronged strategy since late 1935: on the one hand, the political unity of the socialists and Communists, and, on the other hand, the syndical unity of the UGT and CNT.

## REINVIGORATING THE REPUBLIC: THE NEGRÍN GOVERNMENT

The moderate socialist Juan Negrín, hitherto minister of finance, was chosen as the new premier. A professor of physiology, Negrín was a cultivated and courteous figure of great vitality and purpose, admired by Azaña for his 'tranquil energy'.[140] He was on good terms with all the forces of the Popular Front, as well as the CNT, spoke several languages, and had established a close relationship with the Soviets while finance minister. Clearly Negrín was highly qualified not only to maintain good relations with the Soviets, but also to persuade the Western democracies to bring the war to an end by means of mediation, an objective which the president had pursued without success since late 1936. The new Cabinet signalled the triumph of the parties over the trade unions, as the UGT and CNT rejected the offer of a single portfolio each. The president expected the new administration to provide 'energy, decision, the will to govern, the restoration of normality in public life, the crushing of indiscipline' and to tackle 'soon the chaos of the rearguard'.[141] It was also a relief for him to find that 'now, when I speak with the head of government, I don't have the impression that I'm speaking to a corpse'.[142]

Negrín's war aims were essentially the same as those of Largo Caballero – namely, to organize a regular army, reinforce the authority of the state, enforce public order, and domesticate the revolution – but undertaken with greater urgency and determination. The ongoing formation of the army was robustly pursued, but progress proved slow. According to Palmiro Togliatti's Comintern report of 30 August 1937, the conversion of the militia into a 'genuine, organized army, capable of fighting against a modern army, has not happened yet', while the army itself was 'lacerated' by a 'great many interminable conflicts:

between the old and the new officers, between the anarchists and the Communists, between the nationalists – Basques and Catalans – and the other parties, etc.'[143]

The reassertion of state power was manifested in the dissolution of the CNT's last agrarian stronghold, the Council of Aragón, on 11 August 1937. The Communist commander Enrique Líster was dispatched by the government to dismantle the Council, arrest its leaders, and return collectivized land to its previous owners. Negrín decided to 'totally recover' Catalonia by installing the central government there in November 1937, though the 'hard bargaining' between the state and the regional authorities would persist until the war's end.[144] Meanwhile, the three northern regions of the Basque Country, Cantabria, and Asturias continued to pay little heed to the government's military and other instructions. Little wonder that the republican governments would struggle throughout the conflict to recreate the two main pillars of the war effort – a centralized state and regular army – which the Nationalists had established to a large extent by the end of 1936, though General Queipo de Llano, who ruled Andalusia like an eccentric warlord, would retain considerable autonomy until 1938. Another advantage of the insurgents was that they devoted relatively little time to political debate, internal intrigues, and decision-making. By contrast, the political semi-pluralism of the Republic permitted its parties and trade unions to dedicate an extraordinary amount of time and energy to in-house debates, disputes, and public polemics both between and amongst themselves, as well as to engage in protracted decision-making processes. 'The comrades who lead,' noted Togliatti in late 1937, 'spend entire days debating amongst themselves and with different persons in the ministries, in the army etc. It is a permanent meeting which unfolds without a plan.'[145] Unrelenting politicking and disputations afflicted the central government too, the Cabinet crisis of March–April 1938 causing 'the paralysis of the organs of government for nearly a month'.[146]

Under Negrín a raft of repressive measures were put in motion to exert greater control over the rearguard, reinforce discipline within the army, and suppress the POUM. In June 1937 the socialist minister of the interior, Julián Zugazagoitia, created the *Departamento Especial de Información del Estado* (DEDIDE) (Special Department of State Information) to pursue the so-called 'Fifth Column'. Two months later, Prieto established the *Servicio de Inteligencia Militar* (SIM) (Military Intelligence Service), which dedicated itself to tracking down Nationalist spies, saboteurs, and collaborators, as well as draft dodgers, deserters, anarchists, and *poumistas*. The SIM soon became 'a synonym for extrajudicial brutality'.[147] In addition, a tranche of new courts were set up, including those of Espionage and High Treason and the Special Duty Courts, the latter leading to the resignation of the justice minister due to the lack of constitutional guarantees. Communist hegemony within the security apparatus facilitated repression of the POUM, which was vilified as a critic of Stalin, feared as a Communist rival, and denounced as Trotskyist in order to justify its persecution. The POUM was outlawed in June 1937, its leader, Andreu Nin, being seized in Barcelona by a Soviet agent and three Spanish socialist policemen, tortured, and then killed. Other POUM leaders were condemned to lengthy prison sentences at their trial in October 1938. Following the mass arrests of *poumistas* and other revolutionaries the number of prisoners in Barcelona's Model Prison soared from 801 in January 1937 to 2,053 in April 1938.[148]

By this stage the Republic had established a system of work camps. The first camps were the brainchild of the anarchist Juan García Oliver, who, upon being made a highly improbable minister of justice in November 1936, announced that his first priority was the establishment of 'concentration camps for rebel prisoners, making them work'.[149] Hanging over the entrance to the inaugural camp was a large sign which anticipated that at the entrance to the concentration camp at Auschwitz by urging inmates to 'Work and Not Lose Hope'.[150] At least eight camps were set up by the Ministry of Justice, the biggest being at Albatera (Alicante), which held around 1,000 prisoners by early 1938. The camps were justified as a redemptive contribution to the republican war effort, but 'all types of abuse were committed in them, violence and brutality were habitual, and the bad treatment sometimes ended with the death of the prisoner'.[151] Another series of camps was set up by the army from 1937, the prisoners tasked mainly with digging trenches and building fortifications. Conditions at these disciplinary encampments may have been even worse than those at the campus of the Ministry of Justice, as 'the guards carried out 90 assassinations' at the Turón (Granada) camp in 1938.[152] Worse still were the camps created by the SIM. At Omells de Na Gaia, one of six camps established in Catalonia during the spring of 1938, twenty-one inmates were executed on one occasion for shirking and another thirteen were shot after two escaped. The SIM camps included anarchists and *poumistas*, in addition to International Brigaders who had been caught trying to leave Spain (of whom there were at least thirty at the Concabella camp). One of the foreigners who fled Spain was Eric Blair (aka George Orwell) and his wife Eileen, who were characterized in a security document as 'declared Trotskzists [*sic*]', since Blair had fought with the POUM.[153]

## THE NATIONALISTS TAKE THE NORTH

By the spring of 1937 the Nationalists had turned their attention to the north, where they took advantage of their massive air superiority. On 25 March the town of Durango in the Basque Country was bombed at a loss of around 250 lives and on 26 April the German Condor Legion attacked Guernica, the symbolic capital of the Basques, killing between 200 and 300 people. The latter caused an international furore due to the coverage by foreign correspondents, in particular George Steer of *The Times* (who feared it foreshadowed the aerial bombing of Britain), and was immortalized in Pablo Picasso's painting *Guernica*, which was displayed at the Spanish Pavilion of the Paris World Fair in June 1937 and did much to equate fascism with death and destruction.

The bombing of Guernica highlighted the experimental deployment by the Germans, Italians, and Soviets of their latest weaponry in Spain, making the Spanish Civil War appear as a fateful harbinger of the Second World War. In reality, it was a war of arresting contrasts. Much of the conflict was reminiscent of the First World War, such as the use of heavy artillery barrages and trenches, or of the colonial wars, such as the deployment of fast-moving columns or the last cavalry charges in Western Europe (in Catalonia in 1939). At the same time, the Spanish Civil War was the very first conflict in which the air force played a major role, whether in terms of air-to-ground support, combined operations involving the artillery, air force, and infantry (a strategy exploited by the Nationalists during the northern campaign), or bombing (though not heavy strategic bombardment), while the employment of armoured assaults also anticipated the Second World War. From a purely military perspective, the Civil War was a transitional conflict, looking at once to the past and the future.

Two girls watching out for air raids

To ease the pressure on the north, the republicans undertook a major offensive in July at Brunete, 30 kilometres west of Madrid, an operation which followed a pattern that would become all too familiar: the surprise attack by the republicans initially breached the enemy lines, only for the Nationalists to swiftly call up their reserves and force the assailants back to where they had begun. After the fall of Bilbao in June ('the enemy could have resisted a lot more,' reckoned a Nationalist officer), the defeated Basques were not interested in fighting on for the Republic, as shown by their surrenders at Bilbao and Santoña (though the Basque government carried on from Barcelona), apart from the fact that both Álava and Navarre had sided with the rebels, the Navarrese constituting the Nationalists' greatest single civilian bulwark.[154] The Basques also refused to destroy their heavy industry (and even a munitions depot) before the insurgents took control, thereby providing the enemy with its first significant industrial base. The lack of collaboration between the three republican regions in the north – the Basque Country, Cantabria, and Asturias – and their insubordination vis-à-vis the government made Franco's task considerably easier. By late October 1937 the Nationalists had taken all of the north.

If the defence of Madrid was the first major watershed of the war, the fall of the north was the second, as the Nationalists now controlled most of the population and territory, the main area of heavy industry, the leading pre-war arms industries, and the prime sources of coal and iron. They had also taken 150,000 prisoners, half of whom would be drafted into their army, along with 250,000 rifles and 500 cannon. Despite this 'strategic disaster', the Republic managed to achieve its only major offensive victory of the entire Civil War on 8 January 1938: the seizure of the freezing, wind-swept provincial capital of Teruel in eastern Aragón.[155] Once again, Franco, who never abandoned his front-line troops, called up his reserves, retaking the town by late February. The hope of the republicans that they had finally passed from the defensive to the offensive proved short-lived.

Franco has frequently been criticized for his slow, piecemeal advance during the war, even being accused of dragging the war out in order to crush the left more thoroughly and to consolidate his own power. Franco's strategy was nonetheless entirely consistent with his temperament, his colonial training in Morocco, and the war of attrition that developed from early 1937. Clearly he was neither a swashbuckling strategist nor an inspired improviser, but rather a prudent and painstaking master of logistical detail, which probably explains in large measure why, in contrast to the Russian and Chinese Whites, he never had to retreat. Only once during the Civil War did he take a calculated risk, namely the running of the Republic's naval blockade of the Straits of Gibraltar during the opening days of the conflict. Thereafter, he ensured that his offensives were overwhelmingly risk-free, being well prepared with functional supply lines and communication channels. Thus Franco's unimaginative but methodical approach to warfare was not only well suited to the war of attrition that characterized the Civil War from early 1937, but also stood in stark contrast to the overly ambitious offensives of the Republic, which invariably failed through logistical shortcomings.

## A DEMORALIZED REPUBLIC RESISTS

By the rain-sodden winter of 1937–8 republican morale was at a low ebb. The lack of food, clothing, coal, and transport, together with rampant inflation (in 1938 the Republic issued the first ever 5,000-peseta note), had produced, in the words of General Vicente Rojo, 'defeatism' in the rearguard.[156] In Madrid the average citizen, according to Dr Francisco Grande Covián, received only 1,060 calories a day between August 1937 and February 1939, but required a minimum of 2,131.[157] Antoñita Berges Martín, a working-class teenager at the time, recalls 'extreme hunger'. If the family ate potatoes, 'it was like paradise'. Fish and meat were generally unavailable, though 'my mother sometimes bought horse meat'. The staple food was lentils, but there was 'very little' and the bread was 'very bad'. 'We had a really bad time,' she relates.[158] The writer Gloria Fuertes remembers her wartime in the capital as one of 'hunger, hunger. Madrid began to suffer hunger one month after the war began. Once we survived on a fried egg for three days.'[159]

The army was in a parlous state, too. A commissar in Madrid reported that a quarter of his men had no shoes or boots. By this stage, desertion, largely undertaken for personal, not ideological, reasons, had become a major problem. Of 600 trials which took place in republican Gijón between November 1936 and October 1937, 58.5 per cent concerned desertions, while another 9.5 per cent involved self-mutilation (another means of avoiding combat). In Teruel at the end of January 1938 the insurgents not only captured 2,260 prisoners, but also welcomed 869 deserters. Down in Extremadura eleven members of the 109th Mixed Brigade were killed, twenty-six were injured, and a grand total of 659 'disappeared' between 20 and 24 June 1938.[160] Similarly, the Army of the Centre recorded 'systematic desertions to the enemy' in November 1938.[161] Drastic measures were taken to stem the haemorrhage, such as drafting a male relative in place of the deserter. Self-mutilators might be forced to stay at the front (and die from gangrene) or even be put to death (as reconstructed in Ernest Hemingway's short story 'Under the Ridge'). Not that the Nationalists were immune to either desertions or self-mutilation. Desertion was a 'grave concern' for the insurgents, General Mola's northern army suffering constant abandonments.[162] The stream of desertions did not ease until 1938-9, though self-mutilation became so widespread that in October 1938 Franco, like his opposite number, had to introduce even stiffer penalties for it. Still, the republican loss of Teruel in February 1938 was followed by a major Nationalist offensive in Aragón which aimed to strike at the Valencia region and

Catalonia. Senior officers reported that the republican troops, who were bereft of food, transport, artillery, air support, and 'all kinds of equipment', were gripped by 'collective panic' and 'fled dishonourably'.[163] General Rojo was convinced that most soldiers were 'good for nothing', while Negrín attributed the mass retreat more to 'moral collapse than technical deficiencies'.[164]

The loss of Teruel in February 1938 and the subsequent headlong advance of the rebels through eastern Aragón made relations between the PCE and the PSOE 'intolerable'.[165] In March 1938 the minister of national defence, Indalecio Prieto, announced before the Cabinet that the war could no longer be won, that its continuation served no purpose, and that it should be brought to an end as soon as possible. While the president shared the socialist minister's gloomy prognosis, he discovered during the protracted governmental crisis of March to April 1938 that there was no political alternative to Negrín's policy of resistance. Following Prieto's resignation, Negrín formed a new but broader Cabinet, which included both the UGT and the CNT. The combative spirit of the so-called 'War Government' was reflected in the fact that 'civilian and military discipline became more severe'.[166] The scale of the challenge it faced was highlighted by the Nationalists reaching the Mediterranean at Vinaroz on 15 April 1938, which cut the republican zone in two, a major logistical and psychological blow.

Negrín went on the diplomatic offensive on 1 May by proclaiming his 'Thirteen Points' – an echo of Woodrow Wilson's 'Fourteen Points' – which, it was hoped, would persuade the international community to pursue peace negotiations. He called for the independence of Spain from 'foreign forces', for the establishment of a democratic republic (to be approved in a referendum), for the defence of private property, and for an 'ample amnesty' for all those who aspired to the 'reconstruction and greater glory of Spain'.[167] The only non-negotiable issue was the amnesty, as Negrín feared that a Nationalist victory would, in his own words, unleash 'a reign of terror and bloody reprisals'.[168] The response to the 'Thirteen Points' was extremely disheartening, as neither the British nor the French were prepared to lobby the Germans and Italians in favour of a negotiated end to the war. The watchword of the government thereafter was 'To Resist is to Overcome', that is, to survive until the European powers *did* intervene. The much-trumpeted speech given by Azaña in Valencia on 18 July 1938 in favour of 'Peace, Pity, and Pardon' – an eloquent plea for national reconciliation – also fell on deaf ears, further hardening Negrín's conviction that, as one adviser noted, 'his one remaining diplomatic card lies in military victory'.[169]

The belief that 'the best defence is attack' resulted in the greatest single offensive of the entire war.[170] During the night of 24–25 July 1938 a 80,000-strong republican army crossed the broad expanse of the Ebro river near Gandesa, catching the Nationalists completely by surprise and establishing a huge bridgehead of 20 by 40 kilometres.[171] Both Negrín and the Chief of the General Staff, General Vicente Rojo, judged the offensive as the only possible means of persuading the British and French to mediate on behalf of a 'respectable peace'.[172] However, the rebels' repeated counter-attacks highlighted not only their artillery and air superiority, but also the logistical shortcomings of the republicans, who were eventually pushed back across the Ebro by mid-November. This was, in Franco's view, 'the greatest, hardest, and ugliest battle of the whole war'.[173] The battle had followed exactly the same pattern as the attacks at Brunete, Teruel, and Belchite: an initial republican breakthrough was stymied by the swift deployment of Nationalist reserves, who finally succeeded in forcing the attackers back to their point of departure, at a cost, in this case, of 50,000–60,000 casualties on each side. The complete failure of the Ebro offensive had a profoundly demoralizing effect on not just the loyalist army and government, but also its populace, as it appeared to be the last throw of the military dice. Arguably, a defensive military strategy would have made better use of the Republic's resources and provided it with a greater chance of survival until hostilities erupted in Europe, especially as the conflict was above all a trench war in which defence held the advantage.

In August 1938, Indalecio Prieto accused Negrín of being a crypto-Communist who was acting on the orders of Moscow, a smear which persists even today. In reality, Negrín's war plan met with little dissent. 'There is no alternative,' as he put it to Azaña.[174] Both men understood that unconditional surrender could only be averted if the British and French forwent the passivity of non-intervention for a proactive policy of mediation. However, the last hope of international intervention was dashed at the Munich meeting on 30 September 1938, the day that Britain abandoned Czechoslovakia to Nazi Germany. The British premier, Neville Chamberlain, suggested to Hitler and Mussolini that they, along with the French, should establish an 'armistice' in Spain and try to resolve the 'differences' between the two sides.[175] Hitler objected that Communism had still not been eliminated in Spain and that the two sides were unlikely to agree to a truce, at which point the hapless Chamberlain desisted.

In October 1938 the International Brigades abandoned Spain in a further if fruitless attempt to bring diplomatic pressure to bear on the Western democracies. The Brigaders were given an emotional send-off in Barcelona at which the incendiary Communist orator Dolores Ibárruri, or *La Pasionaria*, told them, 'You are history. You are legend. You are the heroic example of democracy's solidarity and universality.'[176] This has helped consolidate the myth of the International Brigades as idealistic defenders of democracy, their rebranding today by organizations such as the Abraham Lincoln Brigade Association (ALBA) showcasing issues such as the defence of human rights, democratic accountability, and the environment. In fact, most of the volunteers were Stalinists who went to Spain to uphold not democracy but the anti-fascist cause of the Communist International. The non-Communist volunteer Jason Gurney was 'genuinely and sincerely shocked' to be told by fellow Brigaders who were 'dedicated and obsessed Party members' that Communism did not aspire 'to build a world of social justice', as this was mere 'bourgeois idealism'. Indeed, Gurney's 'bourgeois' non-conformity made him 'liable to be regarded as an enemy in my own camp'.[177] As the American volunteer William Herrick put it, 'Yes, we went to Spain to fight fascism, but democracy was not our aim.'[178]

## THE CASADO 'COUP' AND THE WAR'S END

Negrín made a vain last attempt to win over international opinion in February 1939 by reducing the 'Thirteen Points' to just three: an independent Spain, a referendum to decide the future regime, and 'a patriotic labour of reconciliation'.[179] Following the failure of the Ebro offensive, the only party that still defended a policy of resistance was the PCE, which was further isolated by its 'aggression' and 'its attempt to control the republican state', as well as by the disillusionment of a starving populace that yearned for the end of hostilities.[180] The anti-Communist backlash soon reached a crescendo once Franco conquered Catalonia in February 1939. The immediate catalyst was the recognition of the Nationalists by the British and French on 27 February and the resignation of Manuel Azaña as president of the Republic on the very same day. Azaña's resignation was premature, as it damaged the authority and legitimacy of the Republic, while demoralizing its remaining defenders, who still controlled nearly a third of the national territory. The priority, Negrín insisted, was 'to try to save, with honour and a minimal guarantee, the arms and lives of the last defenders of the Republic', which was why he had returned to the Centre zone on 9 February.[181] The events of 27 February were nonetheless the trigger for the 'coup' of Colonel Segismundo Casado, commander of the Centre Army, who formed a National Council of Defence in Madrid on 5 March 1939 which included all the parties and trade unions in the capital except for the Communists. The Council claimed that the Negrín government was no longer the legitimate representative of the Spanish people and that the military – in an ironic reversion to the nineteenth-century praetorian tradition – now constituted the 'legitimate power of the Republic'.[182] Full-scale fighting erupted in the capital between Council defenders and the Communists, but after five days the Communists succumbed at a collective cost of 243 lives and nearly 600 injured.[183] Casado's conceit was that, as a military man and anti-Communist, he was in a stronger position than Negrín to strike a deal with Franco, but he soon discovered that 'with Franco, there was not, nor could there be, any sort of peace settlement other than unconditional surrender'.[184] The so-called 'Casado coup' aborted the possibility of a relatively orderly retreat of loyalist civilians and soldiers to the ports of the Mediterranean, though Casado himself was whisked into exile by a British destroyer. The war therefore ended as it had begun, with a military rebellion against a republican government that was allegedly falling under the sway of Communism. On 28 March 1939 Nationalist troops strolled down Princesa Street in Madrid without encountering the slightest resistance. Four days later Franco issued the last dispatch of the war:

Today, the Red Army captive and disarmed, the Nationalist troops have achieved their ultimate military objectives. The war has ended.[185]

A comparison with other civil wars brings the achievement of the Nationalists into sharper focus. The Spanish case is comparable to the Russian and Chinese civil wars, as they were all wars of attrition between revolutionaries and counter-revolutionaries in relatively underdeveloped countries. What makes the Nationalists unique is that, unlike their Russian and Chinese counterparts, they defeated the revolutionaries. Thus the Nationalists used foreign aid much more effectively than either the Russians or the Chinese because they were more organized and less corrupt. Further, the Spanish counter-revolutionaries greatly outperformed the Russians and Chinese in economic terms by collecting taxes, securing donations, stabilizing the currency, feeding their people, limiting looting, and even providing public services. In military terms, the Nationalists also outshone the Russian and Chinese Whites through their strong leadership, superior logistics, and coordinated strategy. In short, the Spanish counter-revolutionaries 'proved more competent militarily, politically, and economically than their Chinese counterparts under Chiang Kai-Shek or the Russian Whites under a variety of failed generals'.[186]

## THE CIVIL WAR IN PERSPECTIVE

The Spanish Civil War of 1936–9 is still viewed to a considerable extent through the dual prisms of the Romantic myth and the Black Legend. The republican war effort is often glorified as the heroic fight of the Spanish 'people' in defence of a 'democratically elected' government against the threat of international fascism, a struggle symbolized in the anti-fascist rallying cry of No pasarán (They Shall Not Pass). By contrast, the insurgents or 'fascists' are frequently seen as a relatively narrow stratum of 'rich landowners', 'factory owners', 'Catholics', and 'military centralists' whose triumph can be largely attributed to external factors, principally the backing of Nazi Germany and fascist Italy, and the futile attempt of the Western democracies to appease fascism by abandoning the Republic to its fate.[187]

The anti-fascism of the Second Republic, an idea originally endorsed by the Comintern in 1935 and converted into a mainstay of Communist propaganda until the collapse of the USSR in 1991, has had a redoubtable resonance over the years, especially in Western Europe. Still, the dominant anti-fascism of the Spanish regime was not the broad and inclusive anti-fascism of, say, Winston Churchill or Charles de Gaulle, but revolutionary in nature. Accordingly, the Republic was defined after the uprising of July 1936 not so much by a determination to defend its 'democratically elected' government, as by a commitment to revolution, a phenomenon which was to shape the loyalist war effort until the very end of hostilities. The Communist Party of Spain, in accordance with Comintern policy, officially opposed the revolution, but this did not prevent it from playing a major role within the republican camp. It is no coincidence that George Orwell's scything indictment of Stalinism in *Animal Farm* and *1984* was strongly shaped by his personal experience of the Civil War or that Arthur Koestler was sent to Spain as a Comintern collaborator but lost his faith in Communism following 'the nightmare of Spain, with its betrayals, its prisons and its violence'.[188] Nor is it a coincidence that Ramón Mercader, the Spanish Communist who killed Leon Trotsky in Mexico City in 1940 by plunging an ice pick into his skull, was recruited by the Soviets during the Civil War. In other words, the war was not just about the fight against fascism, but also the legacy of Communism.

The revolt of 18 July 1936 was a manifestation not just of the 'opposition of the privileged', but also of small and middling peasants, shopkeepers, artisans, policemen, local businessmen, clerks, journalists, and even workers, the great bulk of whom feared for their livelihoods, their properties, and their religion in the face of what they perceived as a revolutionary threat.[189] Most of these people would not have defined themselves as 'fascist', but as 'conservative', 'monarchist', 'Catholic', or 'traditionalist'. They did not belong just to the upper strata of Spanish society, but represented a substantial swathe of it, which translated into widespread civilian support for the military rebels of July 1936.

The epic narrative of the Civil War has been overwhelmingly shaped by Manichean wartime propaganda and by ideologically charged accounts of the conflict, both of which have given the impression that people on both sides of the divide were passionately committed to their respective causes. However, Herbert L. Matthews, the *New York Times* correspondent in Spain, reckoned that 'only about 20% of the Spanish people – ten on each side – provided the driving force to keep it going'.[190] In the republican zone up to 85 per cent of wage earners only joined a party or trade union *once* war broke out, because in order 'to keep their jobs, housing, health care, and other benefits, they had to possess a membership card', that is, they became party members or trade unionists not for ideological reasons, but for quotidian, pragmatic ones.[191] The sheer scale of the propaganda campaigns in both camps reflected the need to mobilize a society that 'demonstrated lacklustre enthusiasm throughout the conflict'.[192] The proportion of young men volunteering for either side in 1936 was strikingly low: between 1 and 3 per cent in Andalusia and Extremadura, 1 to 7 per cent in Castile-León, and less than 1 per cent in Galicia.[193] Such was the dearth of martial zeal that as early as September 1936 *El Socialista* was already threatening loyalist troops with the 'death penalty for the deserter'.[194] The shortfall in volunteers soon forced the two armies to turn to conscription, but nearly half of all those men called up in 1937 did not actually report to barracks, an astonishing level of absenteeism.[195] In other words, the story of the Spanish Civil War has to a great extent been that of the politically committed minority, not that of the majority who felt caught up in a war that was not of their making.

# 7

# The Early Franco Dictatorship, 1939–1955

*Repression, Hunger, and the New State*

At the military parade held on 19 May 1939 to mark the Nationalists' victory in the Civil War, Franco alerted his supporters to 'the dangers that still lie in wait for our Motherland. The war has finished, but the struggle continues.'[1] Thus the political parties, trade unions, and other manifestations of civil society from the 1930s were banned, while the leaders of the left and many of their supporters were shot, jailed, exiled, fired, and otherwise discriminated against. Not only were the progressive policies of the Second Republic overturned, but Spain's constitutional, parliamentary, and electoral traditions were also jettisoned, resulting in a political rupture that was far deeper than that of Primo de Rivera in the 1920s. Liberalism was vilified as the very antithesis of 'Spanishness' – the 'Anti-Spain' – and the root cause of the nation's decline, degeneration, and downfall. By contrast, the 'New State' stood for order, discipline, hierarchy, Catholicism, Falangism and, above all else, the paramount figure of the *Caudillo* or supreme leader. Small wonder, then, that Franco's 'New State' has often been seen as the high point of Spanish exceptionalism in the modern era.

Within the Europe of 1939, Franco's New State was nonetheless the rule rather than the exception. By then, nearly all of Central and Eastern Europe had succumbed to one form of right-wing authoritarian rule or another: Hungary in 1919, Poland and Lithuania in 1926, Bulgaria, Estonia, and Latvia in 1934, Romania in 1937, and Austria and Czechoslovakia in 1938 following the invasion of Nazi Germany. In Southern Europe not a single democracy survived: Italy had fallen to fascism in 1922, Yugoslavia to a coup in 1928, Albania to 'King' Zog in the same year, Portugal to António Oliveira de Salazar in 1932, and Greece to

General Ioannis Metaxas in 1936. Allied victory in the Second World War has tended to make the triumph of democracy over dictatorship in Western Europe seem inevitable, but in 1939 its prospects were decidedly grim. Democracy clung on to the northern fringes of Europe – Ireland, Great Britain, Belgium, the Netherlands, and the Scandinavian countries – along with Switzerland. It was also alive in France, but in turmoil. By the end of the 1930s, many Europeans were convinced that the solution to the interwar crisis lay in authoritarianism – whether of the left or right – rather than liberalism. If Spain had swum against the tide in the early 1930s by ushering in a democratic republic, by the late 1930s it had rejoined the European mainstream.

# ORDERING THE NEW STATE: THE AUTHORITARIAN COALITION

Spain's New State was developed and ordered by three bureaucratic behemoths: the single party or Movement, the Catholic Church, and the Armed Forces. They all shared a common hostility to liberalism, democracy, Communism, Freemasonry, and secularization, while evincing a common commitment to public order, discipline, hierarchy, Catholicism and, in particular, the unquestionable figure of the *Caudillo*. They effectively took the place not only of parliament, but also of the political parties, trade unions, and other associations from the Second Republic, that is, of civil society. Accordingly, they provided the New State with its political class, its high-ranking officials, and many of the public employees at the national, provincial, and local levels. The only remnants of civil society that were permitted up to the 1960s were pro-regime business groups, cultural associations, bull-fighting fraternities, and sports' clubs.

The Movement, Franco's single party, aspired in theory to control of the state, but in practice had to settle for a subordinate, auxiliary role within it. On the other hand, it gained custody over extensive areas of public life and civil administration, reaching a peak membership of 932,000 in 1942. It acquired a media and propaganda empire, ranging from forty-five radio stations, including National Radio of Spain, to thirty-five dailies, including its mouthpiece, *Arriba*, and the propaganda department at the Ministry of the Interior under the Falangist Dionisio Ridruejo. In the absence of civil society, the Movement was able to regiment substantial swathes of Spanish society through its control of the single student union, the *Sindicato Español Universitario* or SEU (Spanish University Union), membership of which was made compulsory in July 1943, and the Youth Front (*Frente de Juventudes*), which signed up to 1.5 million youngsters for its sports events, summer camps, and excursions. Women were brought into line by the *Sección Femenina* (Women's Section), which was entrusted in a decree of December 1939 with the 'political formation and professional education of the female members', as well as 'to form women in the Christian and national-syndicalist sense'.[2] Women between the ages of seventeen and thirty-five were encouraged to undertake at least six months of social work under the tutelage of the 'Social Auxiliary' section (282,224 women having done so by 1941), the Social Service certificate being required for university titles, driving licences, passports, the exams for permanent public positions (*oposiciones*), and a job in the professions, and in order to receive unearned income.[3] From October 1944 the *Sección Femenina* also trained the teachers who gave classes in 'Household Lessons' in primary and secondary schools. On 30 May 1939 the head of the *Sección Femenina*, Pilar Primo de Rivera, had declared before 11,000 women that 'the only patriotic mission assigned to women is the household'.[4] This regression to the exclusive realms of motherhood and domesticity was reinforced by a long list of measures: the Labour Charter of 1938 had already declared that the state 'will liberate the married woman from the workshop and the factory';[5] in 1941 contraception was criminalized and abortion made illegal; women were excluded from the ranks of the state's legal and diplomatic corps between 1941 and 1943; the Criminal Code was amended in 1944 to raise the sanctions for infanticide and the abandonment of children, while the pre-republican double standard regarding adultery was reintroduced; and, finally, the Labour Agreements Law of 1944 stipulated that women required the authorization of their husbands in order to work. They also needed their husbands' permission to obtain a passport, own a property, open a bank account, and even to cash their own pay cheque. In short, women's rights took a huge step backwards under the dictatorship, which was bitterly ironic given that the leaders of the *Sección*

*Femenina* were everything that women were not supposed to be – highly qualified, independent, and often single (Pilar Primo de Rivera herself allegedly had an airline pilot as a lover for many years).

The Movement not only supplied 30 per cent of the state's high-ranking officials, but also recruited many of its other employees, a 'recommendation' from a Movement boss often helping to secure a public-sector job. It also occupied a great deal of the provincial and local administration, furnishing civil governors, mayors, councillors, and bureaucrats. In addition, the Movement ran the Institute of Political Studies, a source of policy ideas, as well as attracting 'swarms of intellectuals intent on elaborating the theory of the *Caudillo* fused with the people in the nation's imperial destiny'.[6] The Movement was responsible, too, for the regime's rent-a-crowd, mobilizing the masses for official rallies, processions, visits, and other public events, especially those involving the *Caudillo*. Finally, the Movement constituted a keystone of the dictatorship's state-led economy, as it managed the *Organización Sindical Española* or OSE (Spanish Syndical Organization), which, in the words of the *Fuero de los Españoles* (Charter of the Spanish, 1945), integrated 'all the elements which dedicate their activities to the fulfilment of the economic process', namely, the workers, bosses, and technicians.[7] However, the greater freedom of the entrepreneurs (the Chambers of Commerce and Industry and the Chambers of Urban Property, for example, remained autonomous) meant that these 'vertical syndicates' were concerned above all with the control of the workers. Acting 'at the service of the state', they embodied the fascist ideal of superseding the class struggle for the greater good of the regime, their national delegate declaring in 1941 that 'the vertical syndicates are not instruments of class struggle . . . but they are of harmonization and cooperation in the general interest of the Motherland'.[8]

Under the New State the Catholic Church acquired a position of privilege not surpassed 'since the waning days of absolute monarchy', exceeding that of all Churches in Europe, with the possible exception of Ireland.[9] In June 1941 the dictatorship reached an initial agreement with the Vatican whereby Franco was permitted to participate in the election of bishops. In exchange, and until a new concordat was agreed, he vowed not to legislate on matters 'of any interest to the Church without the previous agreement of the Holy See'.[10] Needless to say, all the anticlerical and secularizing legislation of the Second Republic, fore-most amongst which was the separation of Church and state and the elimination of religious education, was promptly overthrown. The state subsidized clerical salaries, provided for the Church's upkeep, and supplied 'substantial additional funding from a variety of government ministries and other official bodies'.[11] Bishops sat in the Cortes, while members of the clergy occupied numerous public sector positions.

The Church was able, through its control of the Ministry of Educa-tion, to establish a monopoly over primary and secondary schooling, which meant not only that children were made to study religion in all its variants – Catholic morality, dogma, and sacred history – but also that private institutions returned with a vengeance. At the end of the 1950s,

A primary school in 1940

73 per cent of primary schools were in the hands of the state, but only 11 per cent of secondary schools, 60 per cent being Catholic and 29 per cent belonging to other private entities.[12] The values imparted in the schools were those of the regime itself; namely, order, discipline, Catholi-cism, Falangism, and adoration of the national saviour, the *Caudillo* (all classrooms displayed a photograph of both Franco and José Antonio Primo de Rivera, the 'Absent One', as well as a cross). Learning was through memorization, thereby fomenting an unquestioning acceptance of the 'truth', not critical analysis or engagement, a lamentable legacy that still blights the Spanish educational system today. At the university level, the Catholic unions, such as the Confederation of Catholic

Students and the Association of Traditionalist Students, were replaced by the Movement-controlled SEU, but the universities were still seen as innately Catholic, the students being subject to Catholic instruction and constituting, according to a law of 1943, a 'theological army that is prepared to battle heresy in order to defend religious unity'.[13] Further, the *Consejo Superior de Investigaciones Científicas* or CSIC (Superior Council of Scientific Investigation), established in November 1939, was placed under Catholic control from the outset, being intended to guarantee that, in the words of the minister of national education, 'national science is emphatically Catholic'.[14] Catholicism, in short, permeated the entire Francoist educational system. Like the Movement, the Church controlled national dailies, such as *Ya*, provincial newspapers, radio stations, and numerous publishers. Additionally, ecclesiastical courts recovered their jurisdiction over matrimonial matters, while the Church also became a censor of books, plays, and films.

The prestige and authority of the Catholic Church under the New State should not be underestimated. Catholicism pervaded not just the educational system, but national culture as a whole, as reflected in the Catholic-inspired dailies, books, plays, radio productions, and films, as well as in the very lexicon of Spanish society, the leftist greeting of '¡Salud!' (Cheers!) being abandoned for 'Adiós' (To God). Liberated from the constraints of the Republic, the Church took to the streets on a massive scale in the form of processions, outdoor Masses, popular missions, and so on. Under the protection of the dictatorship, the Church was able to launch a rechristianization campaign without precedent in modern Spain. A mission in Valencia of the late 1940s, for example, involved 81 centres, 250 missionaries, and 1,500 lay clergy in the 'religious reconquest' of the working and middle classes.[15] Any official act of note required the sanctifying presence of the Church authorities, while any Church ceremony of significance was patronized by the political authorities. Parish priests became the guardians of public morality, especially in the *pueblos* or villages and small towns, where individuals ran a risk if they did not attend Mass on Sunday. Indeed, the Church was the main institutional conduit for sociability in the 1940s and 1950s, especially the local parish. Relations between men and women were once again governed by the strictures of the Church, the Republic's Divorce Law being repealed in 1939, as it was 'radically opposed to the deep religious feeling of Spanish society'.[16] All the divorces and civil marriages that had taken place under the Republic were declared null and void, so the only form of marriage was a religious one. The new-found alliance between Church and state furnished the Catholic faith with a power, presence, and prestige that it had not enjoyed in over a century. Small wonder, too, that the Church revered the *Caudillo* as much as the Movement, except that the Catholics referred to him not as the 'Caudillo', but as the '*Caudillo* of Spain by the Grace of God'.

The third pillar of the New State was the armed forces, the most powerful entity of all, as reflected in the enforcement of martial law until April 1948. The army made sure that the Movement did not dominate public administration, occupying 40 per cent of high-ranking posts itself. It also kept control of internal order, which it upheld in accordance with a whole raft of repressive laws that were updated from July 1936 right up until August 1975. Those accused of rebellion or sedition, including Communists, socialists, anarcho-syndicalists, republicans, Freemasons, terrorists, and other enemies of the New State, were all tried before a military court. The army was also determined to control the economy, a crucial role as Franco built upon the interventionist state of the Civil War in order to create an 'autarkic' or self-sufficient national economy.

During the early years of the regime there were normally six or seven military men in any one Cabinet, though the ever-wary Franco took the precaution of dividing the armed forces between three different ministries – the Army, Air, and Navy – in an effort to reduce the possibility of coordinated action against him. Franco's closest friends and collaborators were often from the military, such as Francisco Franco Salgado-Araujo, his chief of staff, or the beetle-browed naval officer Luis Carrero Blanco, the dictator's doggedly devoted right-hand man from 1941 until his assassination at the hands of ETA in 1973. When Juan de Borbón issued his anti-Francoist Manifesto in April 1945, the dictator's first impulse was to convoke the Superior Council of the Army in order to receive its unconditional support. In short, the armed forces, 'at the direct orders of the *Generalísimo*', were the ultimate guarantor of Franco's power and prestige.[17]

The argument that the New State's triumvirate of sprawling bureaucracies constituted a form of 'limited pluralism' is misleading.[18] During the Civil War, the lines between the army, the Falange, and the Church were somewhat blurred, as a soldier could be an ardent fascist, a fascist might be a fervent Catholic, and a Catholic (including priests and bishops) could give the fascist salute, but under the dictatorship these identities became increasingly differentiated. Certainly the Movement, the Church, and the armed forces competed for both personnel and parcels of power, but they did not offer real choices in the way that independent political parties do. In reality, each of the three forces fulfilled a series of specific functions within the New State, which were to a large extent mutually exclusive. For example, the Movement controlled the trade unions and propaganda, the Church education and public morality, and the armed forces law and order and the economy. The conflicting aspirations of the Church and the Movement were evident to a degree in the realm of ideas, as shown by the clash of the late 1940s and early 1950s between Falangists and ultra-Catholics over the question of the 'essence' of Spain.[19] At heart was a dispute, in the words of the young Falangist and future minister Manuel Fraga, to establish 'if the 18 July was a "revolution" or a "restoration"'.[20] Such debates presented a certain ideological and institutional choice, but one that was narrowly framed by the principles of the 'National Movement', or what the dictatorship itself defined as the 'contrast of opinions – within the unity of the regime'.[21]

All three bureaucracies spawned patronage and clientelist networks that were intimately entwined with the public sector, not least because four-fifths of all positions – following the purge of 'anti-Spaniards' – were reserved in accordance with a decree of August 1939 for Nationalist veterans or relations of the victims of republican terror. Far from being governed by Weberian principles of rationality, defined hierarchies, and clearly delineated responsibilities, the Spanish public sector was distinguished by its very lack of definition and by the corresponding multiplicity of overlapping if not clashing responsibilities, much like fascist Italy and the Soviet Union. The result was that even everyday administrative procedures, such as changing one's address, obtaining a passport, opening a newspaper kiosk, or starting up a business, could swiftly degenerate into a Kafkaesque nightmare of ever-spiralling proportions, unless, of course, one had a relative, friend, acquaintance, or other *enchufe* (literally a 'plug-in' or personal contact) within the bureaucracy. Indeed, the public sector was saturated by a culture of *enchufismo* (patronage/clientelism), with the result that recruitment was often determined not by merit, but by individual relationships, institutional affiliations, or ideological proximity, along with the requisite letter of 'recommendation' from a person of influence. Theoretically centralized and vertically structured, the Spanish bureaucracy was in fact enormously diffuse and involuted, 'so weak and disorganised' in the experience of the British ambassador of the early 1940s, Sir Samuel Hoare, 'as to be often incapable of coherent action'.[22] The ambassador was equally astonished at the 'incredible lack of cooperation' between the ministries, there being 'no bond of Cabinet responsibility', as Franco 'flourished upon division and inaction, an almost inaccessible Buddha'.[23]

## THE CONVULSIONS OF AUTARKY

The organizing principle of the New State's economic policy was state-led autarky (or self-sufficiency), a system inspired by Italian fascism, the Primo de Rivera dictatorship, and the experience of the Civil War, but above all by an ideal of economic nationalism. At the heart of the autarkic vision lay agrarian society, glorified as the quintessence of Spanish values, especially the smallholders, the 'sovereignty of the peasantry' still being lauded in the 1950s.[24] The Labour Charter of 1938 had conjured up heady images of the rural idyll, envisaging the 'beautification of rural life', a 'small plot, vegetable garden or orchard' for each family, and the land 'for those who worked it directly'.[25] The new system fulfilled the state's traditional role of shielding producers from foreign competition while stifling the demands of the workers, but it was also designed to transform the state into the principal motor of economic development, as manifested in the implementation of price controls, the introduction of rationing, the nationalization of leading industries, including mines, railways, and heavy industry, and a convoluted and ever-evolving array of rules and regulations controlling the activity of every single sector. This endeavour to pursue economic reconstruction in the wake of the Civil War by replacing the market with the state bore the indelible hallmark of the army, which clearly believed it could command prices, demand, and supply much as it did its own troops, and marked a radical break in late modern Spanish history. Still, it was an extremely problematic strategy for an economy heavily dependent on external markets for the supply of essential items such as energy, raw materials, and technology, especially given the New State's virtual ban on foreign investment, the Civil War repayments to the Axis powers, and the refusal to make demands on the regime's social base by introducing an effective income tax.

During the post-Civil War years, the combination of the Ministry of Labour's repressive incomes policy and high inflation produced the greatest peacetime drop in real wages in two centuries. In Madrid, for example, the earnings of 1941 were worth half those of 1936, while at the national level real earnings in the 1940s – with the exception of 1944–5 – oscillated between 60 and 70 per cent of those in 1936. Impoverished wages reduced private consumption by a third in comparison with the years of the Republic, which had a major impact on demand. Miserly wages forced workers back on to the land, pushing the proportion of the active population in the primary sector over 50 per cent for the first time since 1930. The counter-revolution in agriculture was evident not only in the poverty-line pay, but also in the return of 6.3 million hectares of land expropriated under the Republic to its original owners. The dearth of capital, machinery, and fertilizers saw the revival of 'the economy of the mule and manual labour'.[26] The reality of the rural world contrasted bitterly with the idealized rhetoric of the regime. Worse still, the New State's pricing policy induced farmers to grow less and to hold back much of what they did produce for sale on the black market, popularly known as the *estraperlo* (after the corruption scandal of 1935). Those best positioned to take advantage of the black market were the larger landowners, as they possessed the resources to hide their crops, to transport them, and to bribe officials, as well as the political contacts to protect their illicit activities. The *estraperlo* was huge business: the black market in bread and wheat actually exceeded the official one, while that in olive oil was almost as big. Little wonder that the *estraperlo* generated immense profits for those landowners, including ministers and civil governors, able to take full advantage of it.

# THE 1940S: THE 'YEARS OF HUNGER'

Black market produce was of poor, unregulated quality and generally about 2.5 times more expensive than the official goods.[27] The devastation in Europe, the inherent shortcomings of autarky, and in particular the sheer scale of the *estraperlo* resulted in the post-war period being dubbed the 'Years of Hunger'. The worst-hit regions were the centre and south. Between May and October 1939 the *Sección Femenina*'s Social Auxiliary provided nearly 33 million meals in the province of Madrid, covering about 16 per cent of the population.[28] During the autumn of 1939, according to the British naval attaché, up to a quarter of Andalusia and Extremadura was at risk of starvation. Upon arrival in Madrid in June 1940, the new British ambassador, Sir Samuel Hoare, wrote to the foreign secretary that 'the day to day conditions of life are impossible', while informing the prime minister that Madrid had 'the atmosphere of a city in a state of siege, no food, fantastic prices'.[29] The year 1941 was even worse than either 1939 or 1940, a British mining official reckoning that in a small Andalusian town of 4,000–5,000 inhabitants four or five people a day were dying from hunger. In a report of January 1941 the General Directorate of Security described the 'general atmosphere' in the country as 'frankly unfavourable and pessimistic', due to the 'growing lack of work, sharpened by the shortage of the most basic foods for the producer', while 'working-class unemployment grows constantly and begging increases in an alarming manner'.[30] By the summer of 1941, hundreds were perishing of starvation in the south, especially in the provinces of Cáceres and Málaga. In Trujillo (Cáceres) and the surrounding villages there were people who lived for months on grass boiled in salt water. Prolonged malnutrition inevitably led to disease and eventually epidemics. On 8 April, 500 cases of typhus were reported nationwide, but by August there were 5,000 cases in Málaga alone. The outbreak of typhus in March and April in Madrid led to at least 1,800 deaths. In the summer of 1941 a commission of the General Directorate of Health in collaboration with the Rockefeller Foundation established that pellagra and other diseases in the provinces of Badajoz and Cáceres were a direct result of malnutrition. Shockingly, they estimated that between

1.7 and 2 million people might die the following winter if urgent action was not undertaken. The Rockefeller Foundation duly sent large quantities of medical aid, while the American Red Cross distributed 2,000 tons of food within a matter of weeks to the areas in greatest need.

Throughout the 1940s the situation remained dire in many parts of Spain. Out of desperation, many women took to prostitution, as suggested by the dramatic rise in cases of syphilis from 65,000 in 1941 to 268,000 in 1947.[31] The regime's Catholic morality notwithstanding, 'Spain seemed,' noted the American writer Richard Wright, 'one vast brothel.'[32] On a visit to the country in 1949 the English Hispanist Gerald Brenan was appalled by 'the terrible poverty and misery one sees in Spain today'.[33] In Madrid, 'every few yards one meets a one-armed or one-legged man.'[34] In Andalusia, he saw women 'dressed in rags that had never been women's clothes – potato sacks, scraps of army blanket, mouldering remains of soldiers' greatcoats – with their legs and faces caked in dirt which they no longer troubled to wash off'.[35] Such abject poverty was not, however, universal. Brenan noted that in Granada the 'signs of great poverty ... were lacking'.[36] In the north, the province of León was affected by food shortages and distribution problems, but the local Falange reported in April 1946 that 'the economic state of the province is good and if things continue as they have until now, the good harvest that is awaited with anxiety will normalize life completely.'[37] However, the economic upturn of the 1950s only gradually turned the tide of squalor and suffering. In the mid 1950s, Richard Wright found the main square in Valdepeñas (in Ciudad Real province) 'packed with children in dirty cotton rags and, as soon as I alighted, they began a whining begging ... Their faces were pocked with sores and their eyes were large, moist, round, and bloodshot.'[38] His time in Spain convinced him that 'Spaniards simply do not get enough to eat.'[39] Paradoxically, it was during the 'Years of Hunger' that Spain saw the highest rise of the twentieth century in life expectancy, as it soared from 47.8 years in 1940–41 to 61.7 years in 1950–51.[40] A major factor was the drop in infant mortality due to 'public intervention in hygiene, public health and the education of mothers in the care of their children', as well as the introduction of more advanced medical techniques, the *Sección Femenina* playing an important role in this process, especially in the rural areas.[41]

Spain's terrible 'Years of Hunger' were far from exceptional. One thing that all Europeans shared in common during the Second World War was 'the ubiquitous presence of hunger'.[42] In Greece, around 250,000 people died from starvation and related ailments during the conflict.[43] Holland underwent its 'Hunger Winter' in 1944–5 when its inhabitants ate sugar beets and even tulip bulbs to survive. The average adult requires 2,500 calories a day to stay fit and healthy, but in 1941 the rations in German-occupied Belgium and France stood at 1,300, those in Norway and Czechoslovakia at 1,600.[44] In Eastern Europe, hunger was deployed as a weapon of mass destruction against its peoples, as the Germans 'intended deliberately to starve them to death'.[45] The daily ration in Poland's principal cities in 1940 was fixed at just 600 calories per day, while in the Ukraine between 70,000 and 80,000 people perished from lack of food in the city of Kharkov alone. The German siege of Leningrad (1941–4) produced a staggering 641,000 deaths from starvation and its associated diseases. After the war, the situation 'in many places' was even worse, food riots being common in Italy, grass being eaten in Berlin, and dead dogs being devoured in eastern Germany. Starving women in Italy offered sex to Allied soldiers in exchange for a tin of food and in Germany for a chocolate bar. In Britain, the last rations were not phased out until 1954, while food consumption per capita in West Germany did not match pre-war levels until 1955/6. As in Spain, severe malnutrition resulted in epidemics, malaria returning with a vengeance to Southern Europe and tuberculosis spreading nearly everywhere.

Economic stagnation in Spain was worsened by the way the organization of industry under the autarkic regime was overseen by the 'military managers' at the *Instituto Nacional de Industria* or INI (National Institute of Industry), established in September 1941 under the direction of Franco's close friend General Juan Antonio Suanzes.[46] Industrial policy encouraged a lack of competition through the establishment of inefficient monopolies and the strengthening of traditional sectors, not least because the company bosses were involved in drawing up the new legislation. Consequently, employers not only paid rock-bottom wages, but had little to worry about in terms of production. Industrial performance was further hampered by the exasperating, often opaque, bureaucracy, which did much to discourage investment and the creation of new businesses and plants. Not surprisingly, it was characterized by 'all types of irregularities and corruption'.[47] Ironically, the regime's dirigiste industrial policy shared more in common with the unwieldy and inefficient Communist regimes of Eastern Europe than with the capitalist ones of Western Europe.

Another failure of autarky was foreign trade, the results of which were 'catastrophic' in the 1940s.[48] Imports per annum in the 1940s were less than half those of 1935 right up until 1948, which had a devastating impact on Spanish industry given its dependence on overseas machinery, spare parts, raw materials, and especially petrol and electricity. Cars, lorries, and buses became almost a rarity, a Catalan businessman relating that during a road trip from Barcelona to Madrid in 1947, a distance of around 400 miles, he saw just two other cars. The alternative means of transport was the railway, but the newly nationalized RENFE provided a dreadful service that became a byword for the gross economic inefficiency of the 1940s. Power cuts reduced industrial output by an estimated 15 per cent, the lack of electricity and petrol proving to be an 'insuperable obstacle' to economic resurgence.[49]

Clearly, autarkic reconstruction in the 1940s was an unqualified disaster, shattering the upward arc of the Spanish economy since the 1840s. Spain's 'Great Depression' took place not so much between 1929 and the mid-1930s as between 1936 and 1950: GDP for 1935 was not matched until 1951, while per capita income for 1935 was not reached until 1953. This pitiful performance compares very unfavourably with the recovery of those Western European nations that had participated in the Second World War, even though the latter was both longer and more destructive than the Spanish Civil War. In order to equal the pre-war peak for GDP per capita, West Germany required three years, France four, and the Netherlands three, whereas Spain needed fifteen years to return to the pre-Civil War maximum. Other Southern European economies also rebounded with a great deal more alacrity than Spain, as Italy and Greece took only four and five years respectively to scale their pre-war peaks. In terms of industrial production per capita, Spain achieved its pre-Civil War maximum after sixteen long years, whereas West Germany took just four years, France six, Great Britain two, Italy four, and Greece five years post-1945. Neutral countries such as Portugal, Switzerland, and Sweden had *doubled* their industrial output per capita by 1950, by which time neutral (or 'non-belligerent') Spain had still not reached its 1935 level.

During the First World War, Spain had taken substantial economic advantage of its neutral status, but during the Second World War it signally failed to do so. The regressive policy of intervention nonetheless did achieve one of the regime's main goals: to exercise even greater control over Spanish society. Exclusion from the Marshall Plan of 1947 and international bodies such as the International Monetary Fund, the World Bank, and the General Agreement on Tariffs and Trade (GATT) obviously placed Spain at a considerable disadvantage compared to other Western European countries, but the autarkic pretensions of the Francoist dictatorship were nonetheless a calamity in their own right, not only setting the Spanish economy back by at least a decade, but also causing widespread misery and poverty. Only with the relaxation of certain controls under the government of July 1951 – rationing, for example, was axed in 1952 – and the introduction of an import-substitution policy did the economy begin to show notable signs of improvement.

## EXPUNGING REPUBLICAN SPAIN

The New State was founded on repression, not reconciliation. Demonized during the Civil War as the Anti-Spain, the republicans' fate during the post-war period was no different. There existed an unflinching belief within Nationalist ranks, sedulously reinforced by the Catholic Church, that their cause was not only right but righteous, a conviction that was steeled by three years of, in Franco's words, 'the heavy weight of the war', in which 'we sacrificed the best' of 'our youth'.[50] Like Oliver Cromwell, Franco believed himself divinely driven, his triumph a providential one, that is, 'historically inevitable'.[51] Such messianic fervour led the Nationalists to treat their military triumph as merely the first step in the elimination of the alien ideas, values, and cabals that they believed had precipitated the nation's decline and degeneration. 'We shouldn't deceive ourselves,' Franco insisted at the victory parade of 19 May 1939, 'the Jewish spirit that permitted the alliance of big capital with Marxism, which knows so much about pacts with the anti-Spanish revolution, is not eradicated in a day, [as it] lives on in many consciousnesses.'[52] Little wonder, then, that the lexicon of Francoist Spain was dripping in the bile of expurgation: the Motherland had to 'liquidate', 'eliminate', and 'purge' the Anti-Spain.

Undergirding the ideological intransigence of the Nationalists lay their commitment to a deeply conservative and hierarchical order, as defended by the Catholic Church, the army, the Movement, and their socio-economic constituency, which ranged from major landowners, bankers, and industrialists to artisans, shopkeepers, local entrepreneurs, small and middling peasants, as well as workers. Accordingly, the regime pursued a vindictive and exclusionary policy vis-à-vis the republicans which divided Spanish society into the victors and the vanquished. 'Our irresponsible enemies', pronounced the Falangist mouthpiece *Arriba*, should be considered 'irredeemable, unforgivable and criminal' and should suffer 'irrevocable exclusion, without which the existence of the Motherland would be threatened'.[53] So-called 'Reds' were even disbarred from sports clubs and other leisure outlets. The politics of fear and loathing were heavily promoted by the regime, national radio forewarning the public on a nightly basis:

> Spaniards, Beware! Spain remains on a war footing against all internal and external enemies, perpetually loyal to her fallen: Spain, with the blessing of God, continues on her way. One, great, free, towards its irrepressible destiny. Up with Spain!!! Long Live Spain!!![54]

Thus the Francoists kept alive a highly partisan and Manichean memory of the Civil War, with the goal of justifying both their illegal seizure of power and their unremitting hold on it. The preamble to the 1969 amnesty for Civil War crimes would maintain the fiction that the conflict was a 'War of Liberation', thereby preserving to the bitter end of the regime the divide between 'Spaniards' and 'Anti-Spaniards'.[55] By oppressing and stigmatizing the vanquished, who constituted around half the populace, the victors ensured their short-term domination, but made it unlikely that they would enjoy long-term legitimacy or majoritarian support. Not that this bothered the regime, as its goal was to quash the social and cultural pluralism of the Republic in favour of more traditional and, for its supporters, reassuring values. In any case, the repressive rather than reconciliatory approach of the Nationalists was no different to that of the winners in, say, the French, Russian, Chinese,

Yugoslav, Greek, or Vietnamese civil wars. By contrast, the American Civil War (1861–5) stands as an exception in the modern era for the limited extent of the North's reprisals against the South and for its pursuit of national reconciliation.

## REPRESSION BY LEGAL FIAT

Unlike the Nazis or the Soviets, the Francoists strove to legitimize their repression by means of an ever-expanding battery of laws. The supremacy of military law had been established by the declaration of martial law in July 1936, which is why it was not derogated until April 1948. The military judged all 'crimes' committed by the republicans during the Civil War, the proceedings still being framed by the concept of 'justice in reverse', that is, by the idea that defending the Republic was, in the words of a military jurist, 'the true rebellion'.[56] This legitimation of the military uprising of 18 July 1936 therefore inverted the roles of the two sides: the rebels were the republicans, not the actual insurgents. Even the republican army was considered illegal post-18 July 1936, ranks acquired during the war not being recognized by Francoist courts. Further, the military assigned itself the investigation of post-war 'public order' violations. Traditionally, the military had often equated political protest and dissent with public disorder, so it is no surprise that Franco's Spain went further still. A decree of March 1939 declared that 'spreading subversive ideas' or clandestine propaganda amounted to 'rebellion', while common crimes, such as armed robbery and black marketeering, were added to the list.[57]

The military's investigation of criminal responsibilities was complemented by its scrutiny of civil responsibilities, as embodied in the Law of Political Responsibilities of February 1939. The new law declared 'beyond the law all the parties and political and social groups that . . . have comprised the so-called Popular Front', as well as 'the separatist organizations and all those which have opposed the triumph of the National Movement', but, in the interests of 'the spiritual and material reconstruction of our Motherland', offered those who had fomented 'the red subversion' the opportunity to 'redeem their guilt', principally by means of indemnifications, starting with the properties of the 'parties, groups, and organizations declared beyond the law'.[58] In effect, this represented a reconfiguration of decrees from September 1936 and January 1937, both of which had given legal sanction to economic expropriations and fines as a means of paying for the war, a policy also undertaken by the Republic. Distinguished by its 'ill-defined catch-all phrases', the law was also highly irregular, partly because it was applied in a retrospective fashion, starting on 1 October 1934 – which meant that people could be punished for their 'subversion' eighteen months before the 'National Movement' even existed – and partly because it castigated the deceased, missing, and underage, as well as transferring a penalty to relatives if the guilty party was already dead.[59] Naturally, the stiffest penalties were imposed on those considered most responsible for the 'Marxist rebellion'. In April 1941 the president of the Republic during the Civil War, Manuel Azaña, was deprived of his nationality and fined the incredible sum of 100 million pesetas – even though he was already dead. Some people were punished by both sides. The conservative politician Cirilo del Río, a Catholic who had backed the uprising of 18 July 1936, had his assets seized during the war by the republicans, but he was then fined after the war by the Francoists for having been a member of the Portela government of 1935–6. Women who were republican activists, or the widows, wives, daughters, or sisters of men on the loyalist side, could be punished by having their properties and other belongings confiscated, between 4 and 8 per cent of the cases investigated in accordance with the Law of Political Responsibilities involving women.

It has been estimated that up to 9.5 per cent of the entire population of Spain fell under the sway of the Law of Political Responsibilities. Research on its application is still limited, but it includes the three Aragonese provinces, where 13,422 cases were tried during and after the war, resulting in 4,953 fines totalling 20.5 million pesetas.[60] Of these, 40 per cent involved accessory penalties, ranging from restrictions on employment (1,986 cases), internal exile (164), external exile (4), and the loss of all assets (17). The case of Asunción Rodrigo Molins illustrates the moralistic and sometimes multiple nature of these verdicts. She was convicted in April 1941 for 'her opposition to the patriotic uprising', for militating in the Unified Socialist Youth and the Council of Aragón, and for 'the scandals in her private life', being condemned *in absentia* to a 3,000 peseta fine, disqualification as a teacher for fifteen years, and exile from her village for the same period.[61] On the other hand, only 18 per cent of the fines in Aragón were paid.[62] Throughout Spain, a mere 12.5 million pesetas had been collected by July 1940. Clearly there were major bureaucratic problems in applying the Law of Political Responsibilities. The Madrid regional court opened 6,629 cases between July 1939 and October 1941, but only completed 17 per cent of them during this time. By mid-1942 another 36,000 cases were pending.[63] Nationwide, the Law of Political Responsibilities had generated 229,549 cases by September 1941, of which 15.69 per cent had been resolved, 38.6 per cent were in process, and 45.7 per cent still pending.[64] An official report estimated that the backlog would stretch forward into 1956. A decree of February 1942 initiated 'the liquidation of political responsibilities' by exempting entire groups, such as rank-and-file members of banned organizations, anyone with assets of under 25,000 pesetas, and those jailed by the military for under six years and a day.[65] The Law was finally rescinded in April 1945, but outstanding cases dragged on until a pardon of 1966, though even then some cases remained active, one not being formally dismissed until 1989!

Republicans also suffered workplace purges. In common with other repressive mechanisms of the dictatorship, these had been initiated during the early months of the Civil War. They were designed partly to castigate those who had opposed the Nationalists during the conflict and partly to 'defend' post-war society from the enemy within by making employment dependent on ideology. It was no coincidence, then, that the purges were undertaken at a time of mass demobilization, the Nationalist armed forces shrinking from 900,000 in the spring of 1939 to 250,000 a year later. In other words, the purges were 'an essential means for the regime to reward its followers'.[66] Accordingly, a decree of August 1939 reserved 80 per cent of all vacancies in the state administration for either former Nationalist soldiers or the relatives of victims of the republican terror. A month later, the same system was applied to the private sector. In this way, clientelism was elevated to the status of an official state policy. Gerald Brenan judged that 'the Spaniards have no sense of equity. They live by a tribal or client system, which makes it a moral duty for them to favour their friends at the expense of the State and to penalize their adversaries. That is the first law of this country, and it was as much observed during the rule of the Republic as it is today.'[67]

A decree of December 1936 obliged all employees in the public sector to demonstrate their loyalty to the National Movement, while another in February 1939 set out the procedure by which they were to be politically vetted. One in five civil servants in the provincial administration of Madrid, for example, lost their jobs.[68] In education, the nation's 60,000 primary school teachers all had to reapply for their positions. Of the 2,600 primary school teachers in Madrid, 72 per cent were readmitted without any sanction, while only 14 per cent were dismissed outright. A study of 20,435 cases in thirteen provinces presents a similar picture, as 75 per cent of the teachers regained their jobs without punishment.[69] Of 373 magistrates and prosecutors nationwide, fifty-three were sacked after the war, that is, less than 15 per cent. The purges in the private sector appear not to have been as drastic as detractors of the dictatorship have often made out, as 83 per cent of architects were readmitted without sanction, while only three lost their jobs in all Spain. Nonetheless, other areas, such as trade and industry, have been little researched, and it is likely that strongly unionized sectors, such as banking and insurance, suffered heavy purges. Finally, the nationalist zeal of the Francoists resulted in the banning of the Basque and Catalan languages. Those caught speaking the two languages were susceptible to fines and even physical assaults, Spanish speakers admonishing them to 'speak in Christian', 'speak the language of empire', or 'not to speak like a dog'.[70]

## PUBLIC ENEMY NUMBER ONE: FREEMASONRY

The Law for the Repression of Freemasonry and Communism of March 1940 attributed 'the loss of the Spanish colonial empire', the War of Independence of 1808–14, the civil wars of the nineteenth century, 'the disturbances' that hastened the fall of the Restoration monarchy and the Primo de Rivera dictatorship, as well as the Civil War of 1936–9 (that is, the attempt to 'convert our Spain into a satellite and slave of the criminal Soviet tyranny') to the Freemasons, and, to a lesser extent, the Communists and their acolytes.[71] In short, the Freemasons were seen as the greatest single threat to the regime.

The idea that the sinister and secretive Freemasons were, in tandem with international Jewry and Communism, plotting a path, in Franco's words, 'to subordinate the Universe to the whim of certain sectarian passions', was a common staple of Catholic anti-liberal thought in Europe in the late nineteenth and early twentieth centuries.[72] Fascists and right-wing authoritarians alike saw them as a malignant threat to their quest for national resurgence, Mussolini banning them in 1925, Hitler doing the same once he came to power in 1933, and Salazar criminalizing them in Portugal in 1935. General Ion Antonescu of Romania later purged his civil service of Freemasons, while the Vichy government in France persecuted them with gusto. In Spain, many on the right were convinced by the 1930s that there existed a 'Judaeo-Masonic-Communist' plot to destroy the nation. No one was more convinced by July 1936 of the perfidious influence of Freemasonry than Franco himself, for whom Freemasonry was:

> The silent struggle, the Satanic machination, the work in the shadows, the centres and clubs from which they dictate orders; the most perverse men of Spain who have sold themselves and come together in order to execute evil at the service of the anti-Spain . . . For this reason, from the first day of our Crusade, our aim was to destroy the parasitic plant of Freemasonry in Spain.[73]

For Franco, 'the Catholic religion and Spain were the targets of international Freemasonry throughout time' and 'all the misfortunes' of Spain's last century and a half were the 'work of Masonic treachery'.[74] Following the UN resolution of 1946 condemning the Spanish regime as 'fascist', he railed against the 'Masonic superstates' and the 'Masonic government' under the pseudonym of 'Jakin Boor' in a series of articles in the Falangist daily *Arriba*, insisting that the resolution was 'inspired by Freemasonry'.[75]

Little wonder, then, that the Law for the Repression of Freemasonry and Communism spawned its own Special Court or that, unlike the dictatorship's other repressive mechanisms, it remained unreformed until its derogation in December 1963. The Special Court was overwhelmingly focused on the Freemasons, as recent research on Madrid shows, where

96.6 per cent of the 677 defendants between September 1941 and February 1945 were convicted of Freemasonry, while only 1 per cent were found guilty of being both Freemasons and Communists, and a mere 0.3 per cent of being just Communists.[76] In other words, 'few if any' Communists in Madrid went before the court that had been set up for the repression of Freemasonry *and* Communism.[77] Nonetheless, the quotidian reality of Freemasonry was a bitter disappointment for the Francoist investigators. Of the 677 defendants, 64 per cent had no political or trade-union affiliation whatsoever, while only 25 per cent were republicans or socialists and a mere 1 per cent were members of the Communist Party – hardly a hive of conspiratorial intrigue.[78] Paradoxically, there were many more Falangists amongst the accused than Communists, including Gerardo Salvador Merino, a member of the Movement's National Council and head of the vertical syndicates, who was sentenced to twelve years and one day in prison (later commuted). This disillusioning scenario led the Special Court not only to pass the minimal sentence in 500 trials, but also to recommend commutation in more than half of these cases. Nationwide, there was a register of 80,000 suspected Freemasons, even though there were only around 5,000 in all of Spain in 1936. The Special Court was wound up in February 1964 as no more Freemasons, potential or otherwise, could be found, but the threat of Freemasonry survived as a permanent feature of the dictatorship's persecutory mania, Franco lambasting the 'Masonic-Communist' conspiracy in his very last speech of October 1975.

## THE GENOCIDE OF THE LEFT?

Following the Civil War, republican soldiers were held in concentration camps while it was established whether they were to be investigated by the military courts for 'crimes' committed during the conflict. The makeshift camps overflowed with prisoners of war (POWs), but they soon emptied: in Madrid province, there were thirteen camps in 1939, but just one in 1940.[79] However, the torrent of detainees then inundated the prison system, the director general of Prisons pointedly informing Franco in October 1940 that only 106,130 of the 242,778 Civil War prisoners had so far been sentenced.[80] Some reduced their sentences by working on the POW worker battalions, first set up in May 1937, of which there were at least 150 in the early 1940s, while others joined the Militarized Penal Columns, established in September 1939. These prisoners toiled on state projects, such as the massive Benthamite jail at Carabanchel, completed in 1944, or were contracted to private firms, such as those which built the Valley of the Fallen, the religious complex in the Guadarrama mountains northwest of Madrid that was centred on Franco's grandiose mausoleum, and which, in 1943, employed 250 prisoners. Some prisoners built reservoirs, irrigation channels, and railway lines, while others worked in mines or reconstructed *pueblos* damaged during the war. The cheap labour benefited not only the big Spanish building companies, but also foreign firms, such as the Anglo-American *Montes de Galicia*. By June 1939 the POW worker battalions had made a 3.1 million peseta profit, while the hiring of prisoners to private firms between 1939 and 1943 generated a gain for the state of 100 million pesetas.[81] The number of prisoners involved in the work brigades should not be exaggerated, though, as there were no more than 12,781 in December 1939.[82]

The vast prison population of 1940 soon shrank. The reason was simple enough: the government decided to roll back the repression by limiting the volume of new accusations, producing fewer punitive verdicts, by securing the early discharge of POWs via the revision of their sentences and the introduction of a parole system. The single most important measure in this process was the new sentencing guidelines issued by Franco in January 1940, while a further order of May 1940 transferred the final verdict on death sentences from the dictator himself to the captain-generals in consultation with the judge advocate, who proved to be 'the biggest obstacle' to the confirmation of death sentences.[83] In Madrid, for example, death sentences constituted 38 per cent of the verdicts handed down by the military courts in 1939, but just 4.5 per cent in 1941.[84] The parole system was activated in September 1939, leading to the staged release of prisoners, culminating in December 1943 with the discharge of all those sentenced up to thirty years in jail (bar those guilty of 'blood crimes'). The steady parole of Civil War prisoners soon affected the work battalions and columns: by 1943 common prisoners had to be deployed in order to make up for the shortfall in political prisoners. Finally, in October

1945 all Civil War prisoners were pardoned, with the exception of those convicted of 'blood crimes'. The nearly 300,000 Civil War prisoners of late 1940 had plummeted to 4,052 by late 1947. By the early 1950s, 'virtually all prisoners' had been released.[85]

The *raison d'être* for the mass release of republican prisoners was not reconciliation, since this would have contradicted the dictatorship's claim to legitimacy. There were practical concerns that the overcrowding of the jails risked epidemics and public disorder, as well as facilitating the organization of clandestine opposition groups. The dominant reason was the absence of a sufficiently powerful ideological motive to expunge the entire left. The Francoists were not driven by the Nazis' racial antagonism or the Soviets' class one, as their 'ill-defined concept of "military rebellion"' could not be equated with the actual elimination of the left, especially given the excessively bureaucratic and diffuse nature of the military justice system.[86] This is reflected in the number of post-war executions. Only two decades ago it was widely maintained that the Franco dictatorship had killed up to 200,000 republicans after the Civil War, but more recent research paints a very different picture. Today, it is generally accepted that between 20,000 and 30,000 republicans were executed during the post-war period, primarily those deemed guilty of 'blood crimes'. However, this figure does not include those who died in the camps and jails of disease or starvation, or those who perished as a result of the wretched working conditions of the labour details, such as the prisoners who died of silicosis in the Valley of the Fallen. It is nonetheless evident that the Franco dictatorship did not pursue a policy of 'extermination' or 'genocide'.

Many scholars view the Francoist repression as essentially unchanged since its inception in July 1936. Certainly there were elements of the war and post-war repression that remained *in situ* until the very end of the dictatorship, such as the sweeping definition of 'criminality' or the prosecution of anti-Francoists for 'rebellion'. Nonetheless, by the early 1940s the dictatorship had given up on the idea of completely obliterating the 'Anti-Spain' from society. On the contrary, the aim was 'to punish, reform, and purge, but not to physically exterminate'.[87] In other words, the repression was not set in stone, but evolved from the very early days of the regime.

Parallels can be drawn with Greece, which, like Spain, suffered a three-year civil war, as a result of which 37,000 people were put on trial, 8,500 condemned to death, and around 3,500 eventually shot. The lesser scale of the Greek repression is explained by the lobbying of the United States, which had heavily backed the government during the Civil War, and by the fact that it took place under a constitutional monarchy, not a dictatorship. By contrast, the infighting within Yugoslavia during the Second World War and the slaughter thereafter probably resulted in a far greater repression than in Franco's Spain, the vengeance of Communist leader and former International Brigader Josif Broz, or 'Tito', accounting for between 100,000 and 250,000 victims.

## NATIONALIZING THE MASSES

Another central feature of the New State was the drive to nationalize the masses, the most fervent and far-reaching in the history of Spain. This followed in the footsteps of Primo de Rivera, but 'dwarfed this on account of its scale and coercive character'.[88] The regime rhetoric of the 1940s and 1950s was steeped in nationalism, but its shrill and sectarian nature limited its appeal to Franco's supporters alone. As Franco himself put it at the victory parade of May 1939, 'you know the meaning of our victory better than anyone: the existence of our Motherland!'[89] Accordingly, the motherland only existed insofar as it embodied the vision of the victors, the parade signalling 'before the world the independence and greatness of Spain', that is, its 'independence' from the Republic or the 'Anti-Spain'.[90] The nationalizing process was manifested in patriotically inspired bank holidays, processions, and parades, odes to the nation, and youth camps, where the new generations were inculcated in the 'greatness of Spain'. Even comics, such as El Guerrero del Antifaz or Roberto Alcázar y Pedrín, were fervently patriotic. The school remained the principal mechanism of nationalist indoctrination, as reflected in an education based on Catholicism, a profound respect for hierarchy and order, and, of course, a 'wholesome and enthusiastic' love of country, which was buttressed by study of 'The Formation of the National Spirit'.[91]

A major conduit for the propagation of nationalist ideas was the cinema, not least because Franco was a keen cineaste. The dictatorship duly promoted films lauding the heroic civilizing mission of imperial

Spain, such as *Jeromín* or *La Leona de Castilla*, or a Manichean and one-sided version of the Civil War, such as *Sin novedad en el Alcázar* or *¡A mí la Legión!* The importance Franco attached to the persuasive powers of the silver screen is revealed by the fact that he found time, while constructing the New State and in the midst of the Second World War, to write a novel about the Civil War that was the inspiration for the film *Raza* (Race), a big-budget production of 1942, the story of which, hardly surprisingly, was that soldiers make nations great, whereas intellectuals and politicians tear them down.

The fatal flaw in the Francoists' nationalizing project is that it was never inclusive or integrative enough to be truly national, as it attracted only conservatives and Catholics. It excluded all enlightened and liberal culture, as this was vilified as foreign in origin, which meant the silencing not just of the cultural 'Generations' of 1898 and 1927 (and the greatest Spanish novelist of the nineteenth century, Benito Pérez Galdos), but also of the previous three centuries of Spanish cultural endeavour. Consequently, the dictatorship took sanctuary as far back as the sixteenth and seventeenth centuries, above all the 'Golden Century' of painters such as Diego Velázquez and playwrights such as Pedro Calderón de la Barca and Lope de Vega. Franco's supreme hero was Philip II, the fervently Catholic and intolerant overlord of Spain's empire in the sixteenth century, which explains the proximity of Franco's Valley of the Fallen to El Escorial, the site of the emperor's monastery-cum-palace, the Pentagon of its day. This ultra-retro reversion to 'that closed, impermeable climate, that isolation from the literary creations or scientific advances of the external world', was 'obsessive and stifling', revealing much about the blinkered mentality of the dictatorship.[92] Only once Ernest Hemingway won the Nobel Prize in 1954 was his work permitted in Spain. As if excluding liberal Spain from the nationalizing project were not enough, the Francoists' insistence on the indissoluble unity of the motherland and the corresponding rejection of regional cultures that aspired to autonomy (or more) also alienated Basque and Catalan Catholics and conservatives, an illustration of how crude, uncompromising, and ultimately circumscribed the regime's nationalizing vision was.

A further shortcoming to the Francoists' nationalizing vision was that it was inextricably bound up with their victory in the Civil War.

'National' monuments such as the Victory Arch in Madrid, the Ministry of the Air (modelled on El Escorial), and the Valley of the Fallen were not national at all, but celebrations of the triumph of one half of the nation over the other half, just like the 'Crosses of the Fallen' – that is, the *Nationalist* fallen – painted on the walls of churches or the Movement's yoke-and-arrows that were situated at the entrance to towns and villages. The centrepiece of the greatest monument of the Francoist era, the Valley of the Fallen, is a Catholic basilica over which looms the highest cross in Christendom, while inside the basilica are a series of chapels dedicated to the military, and, at the end of the longest nave in the world, lies the tomb of José Antonio Primo de Rivera and, until the exhumation of his remains in 2019, that of Franco himself. Under pressure from the Vatican, the dictator had begrudgingly allowed a number of republican Catholics to be interred there, but the monument has never been anything other than a homage to the greater glory of the Nationalist fallen, as underlined by the mass rallies that the regime held outside the basilica to mark the Civil War. Equally, the formidable Victory Arch at the northwest entrance to Madrid (through which, on a clear day, one can allegedly espy the cross of the Valley of the Fallen) does not celebrate victory over a foreign foe, but one over other Spaniards, a palpable and ever-present reminder for republicans of their defeat and subjugation at the hands of the Nationalists.

More broadly, the merging of the dictatorship's discourse on the nation with its propaganda, as illustrated by the fact that the cry of '¡Arriba España!' (Long Live Spain!) was generally preceded by that of '¡Viva Franco!' (Long Live Franco!), further discredited the nationalizing project in the eyes of the vanquished, especially as the *Caudillo* was universally portrayed as the saviour of the motherland following a series of ill-fated regimes. Once the full extent of the crimes of Nazi Germany became known in the aftermath of the Second World War, nationalism in Europe became widely discredited, but it remained crucial to the identity and unity of Francoism, the dictator going so far as to claim in a speech of 1948 that 'God and reason are, despite everything, on the side of Spain.'[93] Franco's assertion that the 'Motherland is like a beautiful boat in which all Spaniards are aboard' notwithstanding, the national discourse, symbols, and rituals of the regime were of little or no appeal to at least half of all Spaniards, being a perpetual nod to their status as losers in the Civil War, further eroding the dictatorship's legitimacy.[94]

## FRANCOISM AS FASCISM?

Many historians still regard Franco's dictatorial New State as fascist. Certainly the personality cult surrounding Franco as the messianic saviour of the nation, or *Caudillo*, fulfilled an essential attribute of fascism. On the other hand, Franco liked being portrayed on horseback, which was closer to the pre-modern world of Catholic heroes such as Santiago the Moorslayer or El Cid – whom he publicly acclaimed as 'the spirit of Spain' – than to that of the modern, uber-revolutionary right.[95] In terms of Spanish politics, Franco was military, conservative, and Catholic in outlook rather than Falangist, as reflected in his vote for the CEDA in 1933 and his attempt to stand as a candidate for the party in 1936. His dictatorship was a personal, not a party one, in which he directed the triad of institutions – the armed forces, the Movement, and the Catholic Church – upon which the regime rested. In short, this was a Caesarist regime – as indicated by its denomination as 'Francoist' or 'Francoism' – based on a coalition of the military, the Movement, and the Church, his title of '*Caudillo* of Spain and of the Crusade, *Generalísimo* of the Armies' reflecting this triple allegiance.[96]

Unlike Mussolini's Italy or Hitler's Germany, the state controlled the party, not the other way around, the symbols and other trappings of fascism notwithstanding. When the Falange tried to develop an autonomous militia, to command the so-called 'Blue Division' (a Falangist outfit that was sent to the Eastern Front), to dominate the upper echelons of the bureaucracy, or to take over the repression, it was knocked back by the army, and, when it attempted to seize control of education, it was outdone by the Catholic Church. When Franco's brother-in-law, a lawyer, minister, and Falangist, the intensely ambitious Ramón Serrano Suñer, presented the *Caudillo* with a bill on the Organization of the State – a type of fascist constitution – Franco simply ignored it, partly due to Primo de Rivera's own disastrous constitutional experience in the 1920s, partly because it might curb his own power, and partly because both the army and the Church objected to it. This is not to deny that the

Movement exercised considerable influence within the media, the propaganda apparatus, the vertical syndicates, and the administration, especially at the provincial and local levels, but it was not the dominant ideological or institutional force within Francoist Spain.

From late 1942 onwards, the Movement became a thoroughly domesticated force, its political power never matching its bureaucratic heft. A symptom of the Movement's subordinate status was the way in which the question of the succession was resolved. The Movement was implacably opposed to the restoration of the monarchy, as this would thwart its long-awaited 'revolution', but the victors in this pivotal struggle were the Catholics and the monarchists, as demonstrated by the Law of Succession of 1947 (and, later, by the Law of the Principles of the National Movement of 1958, as well as the succession of Juan Carlos I). In any case, the doctrine of the Movement was far from purely 'fascist', but deeply imbued with Catholicism. The original Twenty-Six Points of the *Falange Española* stated that 'our movement incorporates the Catholic outlook (a glorious and dominant tradition in Spain)', while the unification decree of April 1937 proclaimed that the single party would return Spain to 'the resolute faith of its Catholic mission'.[97] Similarly, the *Sección Femenina* was called upon to form women 'in a Christian and national-syndicalist sense', while the Law of the Principles of the National Movement of 1958 asserted that the nation 'considers compliance with the Law of God as a badge of honour, according to the doctrine of the Holy Catholic Apostolic Roman Church, the only true faith, inseparable from the national conscience, which will inspire its legislation'.[98]

Those historians who view Francoism as fascism tend to identify the dictatorship with its earliest years, but this is to overlook the fact that the regime changed over time. If the Falange was foremost during the early years, the Catholics were to be the most influential force in government under 'National-Catholicism' between 1945 and 1956 (and, during the 'Years of Development' of 1957–75, the ultra-Catholic Opus Dei). It also neglects the fact that the 'National Movement' cannot be defined in terms of a single typology, because it comprised an amalgam of differing political and ideological currents, making it a hybrid regime, as shown by the syncretic symbolism. An illustration is the high-profile ceremony that took place in the church of Santa

Bárbara in Madrid on 20 May 1939. Wearing the blue shirt of the Falange under the uniform of a captain-general, Franco lay his sword at the feet of the Santo Cristo of Lepanto. He then embraced Cardinal Gomá – personifying the alliance between Church and state – in the presence not only of numerous generals and bishops, but also of the National Council of the Movement. Thus the troika of forces that underpinned the 'National Movement' were all represented in the one ceremony.

Whether the dictatorship was identified as 'fascist', 'totalitarian', or 'National-Catholic' probably mattered little to Franco, so long as his supreme personal power was left untouched. He nevertheless judged it expedient to provide the different sectors of the ruling coalition with a form of representation – misleadingly dubbed 'organic democracy' – in the Cortes. The Francoist Cortes was promulgated in July 1942, its deputies comprising ministers, national councillors of the Movement, members of the vertical syndicates and professional associations, university rectors, mayors, bishops, and others, including those appointed directly by the Head of State himself. However, this was a parliament that not only was stuffed with deferential loyalists, but also had no legislative or policy-making powers of its own, the law of January 1938 on the administration of the state establishing that to the Head of State 'corresponds the supreme legal authority to pass general judicial norms', while the law of August 1939 on the authority of the Head of State added for good measure that 'his orders and resolutions adopt the form of laws or decrees, and they can be passed even though they have not been preceded by the deliberations of the Cabinet.'[99] The success of Franco's Caesarist policy of divide-and-rule is shown by the fact that he never faced an institutional revolt throughout his thirty-seven years in power. Ultimately, power lay with Franco, and Franco alone.

Franco's New State was therefore typical of the right-wing authoritarian regimes of the interwar period insofar as it was not strictly fascist, but drew on powerful traditional elements, such as religion and militarism, alongside fascist 'borrowings'. There were nonetheless striking dissimilarities with the Eastern Europe regimes, as Field Marshal Piłsudski in Poland, King Alexander in Yugoslavia, and Admiral Horthy in Hungary did not break with their pre-existing political systems to the same extent that Franco did, Horthy even tolerating political parties, independent trade unions, and the holding of limited elections. Franco's Spain was closer to corporativist Austria and Salazarist Portugal than to the East European regimes, but even here there were significant divergences. Portugal's *Estado Novo* (New State), for example, was under civilian control, permitted divorce and civil marriage, undertook a less vehement repression (fewer than a hundred people were executed or died in custody or jail in forty-four years), and maintained the facade of a constitutional republic. In sum, within the arc of right-wing authoritarian regimes, Franco's Spain was probably more *sui generis* than most.


## FROM THE AXIS TO THE ALLIES: SPAIN DURING THE SECOND WORLD WAR

Although the regime was not strictly fascist, the approach of war in Europe inevitably strengthened the hand of the Falange, as reflected in the composition of the government of 9 August 1939, which contained five Falangists, including Franco's brother-in-law, the overweening Ramón Serrano Suñer, the most pro-Nazi figure of the political elite. That same year, Franco signed up to the Nazi-led Anti-Comintern Pact alongside Italy and Japan, while abandoning the Anglo-French dominated League of Nations. The period until late 1942 marked the peak of the Falange's ideological and institutional influence, and therefore stands as the high point of fascist fervour of the entire dictatorship, as reflected in its 'totalitarian' discourse and fascist-inspired iconography.

Upon the outbreak of war in September 1939, Spain, as it had done in 1914, declared itself neutral due to a lack of preparedness, but this position was to shift following the lightning series of German victories of 1939–40 in Poland, Denmark, Norway, Belgium, and the Netherlands, culminating in the fall of France in June 1940. Nazi Germany stood as the master of continental Europe, as the subsequent conquests of Yugoslavia, Greece, and Crete merely underlined. Franco's eagerness to align himself with the Nazis' hegemonic 'New Order' was shown by the switch from neutrality to 'non-belligerence' (a less impartial status not recognized in international law) on 12 June 1940 (just two days after Mussolini) and by Spain's military occupation the same month of the international zone of Tangiers in north Africa, which soon became, in the words of ambassador Samuel Hoare, the 'very citadel of German influence in the region of the [Gibraltar] Straits'.[100] Upon arriving in Madrid in June 1940, Hoare had been struck by 'the ubiquitous signs of German influence'.[101] The regime's growing fascistization was also reflected in the nomination of Serrano Suñer – a 'fanatic', according to Hoare – as minister of foreign affairs in October 1940.[102] That very

Franco meets Heinrich Himmler in Madrid.
Ramón Serrano Suñer is to the far right

same month Franco held his one and only meeting with Hitler at a railway station on the French border at Hendaye. The Spanish leader offered to join the German war effort if Hitler not only supplied Spain with food, petrol, and arms, but also granted it territorial concessions in north Africa at the expense of France. The German leader, who found Franco's boorish sermonizing excruciatingly tedious (he later remarked that, 'rather than go through that again, I would prefer to have three or four teeth taken out'), rejected the proposal.[103] At the time, Spain was considered of little strategic importance to Germany, while Hitler did not want to jeopardize collaboration with the Vichy government by dismantling part of its empire or to alarm Mussolini by enlarging the Spanish presence in north Africa, the Italian dictator regarding the Mediterranean as *mare nostrum*. The Spanish case was again put to Hitler by Serrano Suñer at Berchtesgaden in November 1940, but the German dictator remained unmoved.

Despite Hitler's rebuff, Spain did much to support the Axis war effort: the refuelling and repair of Axis submarines and ships in Spanish ports; the protection given to Axis agents who sabotaged British ships; the setting up of German meteorological and observation stations in Galicia and observation posts on both sides of the Straits of Gibraltar; the repatriation of Axis air crews who were forced to land on Spanish soil, but the arrest of British ones; the establishment of a German Consulate-General and spy ring in Spanish-held Tangiers (in contravention of international law); complicity in a far-ranging Axis espionage network; and, finally, the sale of wolfram to Germany, of crucial importance to its war effort. 'By no stretch of the imagination,' as the British ambassador put it, 'could Spanish non-belligerence be regarded as genuine neutrality.'[104] Further, in 1942 the Blue Division was dispatched to the Eastern Front to support the German campaign in Russia. Spain may not have joined the war, but, in Hoare's judgement, it was 'an occupied country in the second degree'.[105] In the meantime, the British and Americans did everything possible to keep Spain out of the war – its entry would have been a major setback for the Allied cause in the Atlantic and above all in the Mediterranean – through the supply of oil and food, the US ambassador reckoning that their 'economic weapon' had a 'telling effect'.[106]

During the first two years of the war the inherent tension between Falangists and monarchists became ever greater. Much of the army elite, along with a substantial part of the Church hierarchy and the aristocracy, favoured a conservative, Catholic monarchy as the final regime form, to which the Falange was vehemently opposed, as this would imperil the longed-for 'national-syndical revolution'. The Cabinet crisis of May 1941 nonetheless underscored the limits to the Falange's power vis-à-vis the armed forces, as Serrano Suñer was replaced as interior minister by Colonel Valentín Galarza, while the new under-secretary of the Presidency, the naval officer Luis Carrero Blanco, soon supplanted Franco's overly-ambitious brother-in-law as his most trusted aide and adviser. Carrero Blanco reflected the hostility of the armed forces towards the Movement when he commented disdainfully that 'it acts in a disorderly fashion' and that it was formed by 'not a few undesirables of all types, whose outrages and lamentable example are what invigorate the whole'.[107] Still, to appease the Movement, three new Falangists were brought into the Cabinet, but these were Franco loyalists opposed to Serrano Suñer, who, in addition, served as a counterweight to the monarchist pretensions of the military. The confrontation between the Falange and the armed forces came to a head in August 1942 following a Falangist attack on a congregation in Bilbao – two grenades were thrown and dozens wounded – which had just attended a Mass presided over by the arch-monarchist and minister of the army General José Varela. The military saw this as an 'attack on the army' and had the pro-Allied General Francisco Gómez Jordana replace Serrano Suñer as minister of foreign affairs.[108] The resounding triumph of the army over Serrano Suñer marked not only the demise of the 'totalitarian' project, but also the domestication of the Falange, as it was now dependent on Franco to defend its positions within the New State. Franco also took advantage of the Cabinet reshuffle to strike a major blow at the monarchists by removing General Varela. Pointedly, it was Varela himself who presented Franco with a letter on 8 September 1943, signed by eight of Spain's twelve lieutenant generals ('old comrades-in-arms and respectful subordinates'), which implored him to ask himself 'if you do not consider, like us, that the moment has arrived ... to delay no longer the return to those genuinely Spanish modes of government that made our Motherland great', that is, restore the monarchy.[109] This show of strength notwithstanding, the monarchists ultimately lacked the necessary courage and cohesion to challenge the *Caudillo*. The British ambassador, who actively promoted a dynastic solution during the Second World War (including the bribery of generals), sourly noted that there were a great many monarchists 'as long as there was no monarch'.[110]

The expulsion of the 'totalitarian' faction from the government in September 1942 ushered in a more ambiguous foreign policy, as Franco strove to improve relations with both the Vatican and the United States. In return, the Americans assured Franco that Spanish possessions in north Africa would be unaffected by 'Operation Torch' (the Allied invasion of north Africa in November 1942) as long as he did not intervene on behalf of the Axis. As the tide turned against the Germans, especially on the Eastern Front, Franco abandoned 'non-belligerence' for neutrality in October 1943, while the Blue Division was recalled. Nevertheless, Spain continued to supply wolfram to the Germans, vital to their armaments' industry, which prompted the Americans to impose an oil embargo on Spain. Franco eventually bowed to Allied pressure, signing a crucial agreement in May 1944, according to which wolfram exports to Germany would be virtually halted, the German Consulate-General in Tangiers closed down, and Hitler's extensive spy and sabotage networks expelled from Spain. The Spanish dictator, who had long held that the Allies could not win the war, admitted in an interview on 6 July 1944 with the US ambassador, Carlton Hayes, that German defeat was now certain, the American noting ruefully that the large autographed photographs of Hitler and Mussolini which he had seen at their previous meeting in July 1943 had been removed 'and only the one of Pope Pius XII remained'.[111] Compliance with the May 1944 agreement was nonetheless far from straightforward. Pro-Nazi sectors within the dictatorship did much to aid and abet the Germans, the British being 'forced to protest almost daily' at the ongoing violations.[112] The Germans still undertook high-handed actions, including the 'brutal abduction' by the Gestapo of the anti-Nazi minister of the German Embassy, Count Heberlein, and his wife, who were then dragged off to Dachau concentration camp.[113] In July 1944 only nineteen of Germany's 220 spies had left Spain, and as late as December 1944 there were still sixty-eight German agents on Spanish soil.[114] Nevertheless, German influence was clearly on the wane, while the export of wolfram to Germany in 1944 was a mere fraction of that in previous years. Indeed, the US ambassador regarded Spain's stance since the agreement of May 1944 as one of 'benevolent neutrality'.[115]

## THE RESURGENCE OF THE REPUBLICANS

The approaching Allied victory in Europe boosted the morale of the outlawed republican opposition, whose clandestine activities within Spain had been severely curbed by the economic devastation and the sweeping repression. Police raids accounted for no fewer than six national committees of the CNT between 1939 and 1944 and seven executive committees of the UGT between 1939 and 1945. The main goal of the CNT during these years was limited to hiding or liberating its activists, to which end a front company was set up, Levantina Fruits, the van driver for which 'spent his entire time moving people all around the country ... comrades who were in danger of being arrested and shot'.[116] Anti-Francoists, whether republican or monarchist, were confident that an Allied victory would bring about regime change in Spain. 'The liberation of Europe,' as the CNT proclaimed, 'has to be the liberation of Spain.'[117] Within the republican camp, the fault lines of the Civil War continued to sour relations not only between but also within the different parties and trade unions, though the principal divide was between the *negrinistas* and the *anti-negrinistas*. The Civil War prime minister Juan Negrín was backed by a section of the socialist movement, a minority of republicans, and the Communist Party (though its support wavered), while the opposition to Negrín was made up of the socialist followers of Indalecio Prieto, the anarcho-syndicalists, and a majority of republicans. Consequently, there were two competing claims to republican legitimacy: namely, the government of Juan Negrín and the Permanent Delegation of the Cortes, which was under the sway of Diego Martínez Barrio, the interim president of the Republic-in-exile. The ongoing dispute between the *negrinistas* and the *anti-negrinistas* did much to damage the international standing of the Republic, while unleashing a bitter struggle within the exile community in both Europe and the Americas.

In mid-1944 the republicans, anarchists, and socialists of the interior managed to form the *Alianza Nacional de Fuerzas Democráticas* or ANFD (National Alliance of Democratic Forces), thereby bringing together all the republican forces inside Spain bar the Communists and the Basque and Catalan nationalists. The creation of the ANFD underscored the greater pragmatism of the forces inside Spain (a response to the unrelenting repression), as those outside Spain had still not formed a government-in-exile. The ANFD's manifesto of October 1944 called for the re-establishment of 'the republican order', but the Alliance was prepared to accept a constitutional monarchy if this was the choice of a constituent Cortes.[118] The very first contacts between the republicans and the monarchists date from 1940, when the Marquis of Castellón met with republican leaders, including Martínez Barrio, in Mexico City. By 1942 the monarchist general Antonio Aranda had reached the conclusion that the collaboration of the left was essential if the heir to the throne, Juan de Borbón, were to replace

Franco. In late 1944 the ANFD held a series of inconclusive conversations with Aranda, General Alfredo Kindelán, and the former foreign secretary, Colonel Juan Beigbeder, as both sides looked to a post-Francoist future in the conviction that the Allies would overturn the dictatorship. Of the Allies, only the British backed the establishment of a constitutional monarchy in Spain with enthusiasm, though they drew a line in late 1944 at direct involvement in Spanish affairs.

In contrast to the Alliance, the Communists, who had little or no faith in the Allies, believed that Franco had to be deposed by force. Towards the end of 1944 the Communists began in earnest to organize *maquis* (guerrilla fighters) within Spain in order to overthrow the dictatorship. Between 1944 and 1946 guerrilla groups emerged 'in practically all the regions', attacking railway lines, electricity grids, and other installations.[119] The *maquis* never threatened the regime militarily, but the latter reacted by 'massively' deploying the Civil Guard, the Foreign Legion, the Moroccan *Regulares*, and the army, adopting measures in many parts of the country 'more appropriate to a country at war'.[120] Cooperation between the resistance networks was still marred by ideological disputes rooted in the Civil War. Thus the Federation of Guerrillas of Galicia-León, established in 1942 as the first disciplined guerrilla group, refused to join forces in 1944 with the Communist-dominated Guerrilla Army of Galicia due to their differences over the ANFD. The same month that the ANFD issued its manifesto, the Communists launched a series of 'invasions' over the Pyrenees, culminating on 17 October 1944 with the storming of the Valley of Aran by between 3,500 and 4,000 *maquis*. The greater numbers and firepower of the army and Civil Guard beat the *maquis* back after ten days of fighting, during which thirty-two members of the security forces and 129 guerrillas were killed, in addition to hundreds being arrested.[121] Both the PCE and the CNT also attempted to set up urban guerrilla groups in Madrid and Barcelona, which not only failed miserably, but also brought down the rest of their respective movements. For example, the Communist guerrilla network in Barcelona was established in early 1945, but in April nearly 200 people were arrested, including 'the entire leadership', along with numerous political and trade-union activists.[122] The upshot was the paralysis of the party branches in Barcelona, Badalona, Lleida, and other centres.

The Catalan Communist Party 'would take years, if not an entire decade, to recover from this failure'.[123]

# FRANCO'S SPAIN AS
# INTERNATIONAL PARIAH

Encouraged by the Allies' Yalta agreement of February 1945 and in particular by British backing for a constitutional monarchy, Juan de Borbón relaunched the monarchist cause in March 1945 by publishing his Lausanne Manifesto. He attacked the dictatorship outright for having been 'inspired from the beginning in the totalitarian systems of the Axis powers, so contrary to the character and tradition of our people'.[124] He went on to defend the establishment of a constitutional monarchy, while endeavouring to appeal both to diehard monarchists – by promising a 'Traditional Monarchy' – and to the republicans, by holding out the prospect of an ample amnesty, 'as many reforms as the interest of the nation demands', and 'a more just distribution of wealth'.[125] He therefore called on Franco to 'abandon power and give way to the restoration of the traditional regime of Spain'.[126]

By this stage, the dictatorship was already scrambling to adapt its ideological discourse to that of the Allies. In November 1944 Franco told the United Press that his regime had nothing to do with fascism, because its defining feature was Catholicism. He also defended the dictatorship as an 'organic democracy', as embodied in the new Cortes of 1942, which included representatives of the military, the Movement, the Catholic Church, and the municipalities. The vulpine foreign secretary, José Félix de Lequerica, repeatedly assured the American ambassador in late 1944 that Spain wished to draw 'much closer' to the United States, to serve as a 'natural bridgehead' between the Americas and Europe, and to undertake 'a very considerable evolution'.[127] Such rhetorical overtures did little or nothing to appease Western public opinion, outraged that the 'fascist' Franco should remain in power following the downfall of his Axis allies, Hitler and Mussolini. Clearly the Spanish dictatorship had much to do to alter perceptions in the wake of its consecration of Hitler's 'New Order'. In June 1945 the regime passed the *Fuero de los Españoles* (Charter of the Spanish), but the exercise of these rights was conditional upon their never 'threatening the spiritual, national and social unity of Spain' – that is, anything which displeased the authorities – while the rights of free speech, association, and habeas corpus, as well as protection against search and entry, could be 'temporarily suspended by the government'.[128] In any case, the Cortes would have to pass the laws 'for the exercise of the rights recognized in this Charter'.[129] A popular joke at the time was that Spaniards had the most rights in the world given that, in addition to the theoretical rights of liberalism, they had the 'right to be arrested', the right to 'liberty on bail', and the right to 'supervised liberty', an apt summary of the state of affairs under the dictatorship.[130] Another so-called 'fundamental law' of 1945 that was designed to give the dictatorship a more benevolent air was the Referendum Law. At first sight this smacked of democratic accountability, but in reality it reinforced the regime's Caesarism, as it established a direct link between the 'Head of State' and 'the Nation' (superior to the 'subjective judgement' of the country's 'leaders'), with Franco himself determining 'the opportunity and convenience' of a referendum.[131] As it happened, 'the opportunity and convenience' of a referendum arose only twice during the course of the next thirty years.

The key to the dictatorship's change in image was its rebranding as a 'National-Catholic' regime. As Franco's right-hand man, Luis Carrero Blanco, explained, 'the Catholic thing' was highly valued in Washington, while 'it is very important now' to create a favourable impression on the Vatican.[132] Thus 'National-Catholicism' became the regime's official brand. A brainchild of the Catholic polymath Marcelino Menéndez Pelayo in the 1880s, 'National-Catholicism' was a riposte to the liberal concept of the nation, thereby furnishing the right with its own discourse on the nation. Thus the Referendum Law defined the dictatorship as 'a regime of Christian co-existence', while the Charter of the Spanish not only stated that 'the profession and practice of the Catholic religion . . . is that of the Spanish state', but also pointedly ignored the Movement.[133] This doctrinal sleight of hand was accompanied by symbolic shifts, such as suppression of the fascist or 'national' salute and Franco's discarding of the Falange's blue shirt.

The most tangible manifestation of the dictatorship's embrace of 'National-Catholicism' was the entry of Catholicism as a political force into the government of July 1945. The key post of foreign secretary, held from 1940 to 1942 by the pro-Nazi Serrano Suñer, was now placed in the hands of Alberto Martín Artajo, a former CEDA deputy and president of the national junta of Catholic Action, an elitist Catholic organization that assiduously prepared its members for public office. Catholics controlled the ministries of Education and Public Works too. By contrast, the Movement was reduced to the portfolios of Labour and Justice and had its secretary-general deprived of Cabinet status. Much like the CEDA in the 1930s, Catholic Action was closely aligned with the Church. Martín Artajo was determined not just to improve Spain's international image, but also to enhance the Church's power within the regime at the expense of its arch-rival, the Movement. The ultimate goal of political Catholicism was restoration of the monarchy as a natural extension of the dictatorship, though this would be a 'traditional' dynasty, not a French-inspired liberal one.

An early move against the Movement was the foundation of the apostolic associations of *Acción Católica Especializada* or ACE (Specialized Catholic Action) in 1947. Like the Movement's vertical syndicates or student union, the bodies of the ACE were designed to help fill the vacuum created by the banning of the autonomous trade unions and other associations of the 1930s. Thus the *Juventud Obrera Católica* or JOC (Catholic Worker Youth) targeted working-class youth, the *Juventud Estudiante Católica* or JEC (Catholic Student Youth) students, and the *Hermandades Obreras de Acción Católica* or HOAC (Workers' Brotherhoods of Catholic Action) workers. The creation of the ACE ended the Movement's monopoly on the affiliation of students and workers. Still, membership of the Movement's unions was obligatory, while that of the ACE's bodies was voluntary. In contrast to the millions of members of the Movement's trade unions, the JOC and HOAC could count in the 1950s on the support of between 150,000 and 180,000 affiliates.

Franco's repackaging of the dictatorship as National-Catholic was designed not only to appease the Allies, especially the British, but also to disarm both Catholic and monarchist opinion, a process that culminated in the transformation of 'the nation into kingdom'.[134] The Law of Succession to the Head of State, passed in June 1947, defined Spain as 'a Catholic, social, and representative state that, in accordance with its

tradition, declares itself a kingdom', being approved in a national referendum four months later.[135] Naturally, Franco ensured that the law was
drawn up on his terms. He was therefore recognized as the '*Caudillo* of
Spain and the Crusade, *Generalísimo* of the Armies', his rule was indefinite, and the choice of successor was his alone.[136] The latter could be
either a king or a regent, which freed Franco from the line of succession, thereby allowing him to dictate terms to Juan de Borbón, now
reduced to the humiliating role of a mere pretender.

The identification of Francoism with National-Catholicism did
little, however, to assuage the post-war antagonism of the Allies. At
the Potsdam Conference of July–August 1945 the United States, the
Soviet Union, and Great Britain agreed to block Spanish entry into the
United Nations. The Soviets wanted to adopt even tougher measures,
but the British in particular lobbied hard to deflect them. Further
divergences between the 'Big Three' prevented the claims of either the
republicans or the monarchists from being recognized. A more cohesive approach was taken by the Americans, British, and French in the
Joint Declaration of March 1946, which called on 'patriotic and
liberal-minded Spaniards' to remove Franco from power, to dissolve
the Falange, and to establish a provisional government, the nature of
the new regime to be decided by the Spanish people.[137] On the other
hand, the Joint Declaration, like the Potsdam Conference, did not
advocate direct intervention in Spanish affairs, while ignoring the
monarchists and republicans alike as a viable alternative.

## THE ANTI-FRANCOIST OPPOSITION: A VIABLE ALTERNATIVE?

Once the war in Europe was over, the republicans had striven to
present a common front in order to bolster their claim as the only
legitimate alternative to the dictatorship. In August 1945 the Republic's institutions were at last reunited in Mexico City. Diego Martínez
Barrio was elected president of the Republic-in-exile by the Cortes,
Juan Negrín duly presented his resignation as premier, and José Giral
was then asked to form a government, which he did to the exclusion
of the Communists and *negrinistas*. The *raison d'être* of the Giral

administration was the re-establishment of the Second Republic. In March 1946 the PCE joined the government-in-exile, making it representative of nearly all the forces of the Republic. The republicans had nonetheless left it far too late to overcome the profound misgivings of the Americans and British, as 'to restore republican legitimacy after 1945 was not a realistic position at all'.[138] The former US ambassador, Carlton Hayes, noted that the opposition was 'too divided, too broken into quarrelsome groups'.[139] Revealingly, a new republican movement, *Acción Republicana Democrática* or ARD (Republican Democratic Action), recognized at its founding congress of 1960 that:

> Our biggest mistake was not having formed a legal instrument of power when Hitler and Mussolini fell from power [which was] capable of displacing and replacing the fascist state. This instrument was absent because rivalries, ambition, stupidity and apathy had conspired to create contradictory and rival juntas, alliances and blocs that cancelled each other out and lacked the intrinsic legal attributes capable of reconciling and bringing together the respective wills in a movement of national liberation.[140]

Had the institutions of the Republic been reunited in 1940 and had Negrín then been presented to the world as the prime minister of a democratic government-in-exile overthrown by fascism, the outcome might have been different, but the deep-seated divisions of the Civil War proved too much.

Despite joining the Giral government in early 1946, the PCE had continued to place its faith in the armed struggle. The Communist Party, as Dolores Ibárruri explained in December 1945, aimed to 'organize the armed struggle and the national insurrection' against the Franco regime, as this 'represents the best way to eliminate it and destroy its roots'.[141] By the summer of 1946 there were between 2,000 and 2,500 guerrillas in rural Spain, parts of the country being declared 'war zones' in 1947 and 1948.[142] The scale of the problem was underscored in April 1947 by the passing of a law that was specifically designed to tackle what the dictatorship termed 'banditry and terrorism'. The guerrillas, despite eventually killing an estimated 1,000 Civil Guards, struggled to make any headway against the regime's security forces.[143] The CNT-linked *Agrupación de Fuerzas Armadas de la República*

*Española* or AFARE (Armed Forces' Association of the Spanish Republic), established in Barcelona in January 1945, was active in Catalonia, Aragón, and the Valencia region, but was soon dealt a major blow by the arrest of seventy activists in Barcelona in April 1945, followed by the mass detention of Aragonese activists in September 1946. Similarly, the PCE's Madrid guerrilla network collapsed in October 1945 following the capture of seventy activists, ten of whom, including the leader Cristino García Granda, were shot in February 1946. By 1947 the guerrilla campaign had reached a 'dead end', especially as the PCE was not prepared to send sufficient supplies of men and arms to take the fight on to another level.[144] In a meeting with Spanish Communist leaders in October 1948, Stalin 'recommended' that they abandon the armed struggle for the organization of the masses, but the PCE nonetheless fought on until total defeat in early 1952.[145]

Strikes also formed part of the repertoire of protest, despite being illegal. In 1946 there was a major stoppage in the textile industry of Barcelona and in 1947 a widely supported strike by metalworkers in the Basque Country, but the biggest stoppage of the early dictatorship was the general strike of 1951 in Barcelona. Starting out as a spontaneous boycott of the trams due to a hike in prices and fuelled by resentment at the lower cost of transport in Madrid, the 300,000-strong strike was notable for being called out by the vertical syndicates, for its regionalist dimension, and for being 'the gesture of a city community'.[146] The authorities were so unnerved by the stoppage that battleships were dispatched to the port of Barcelona and 4,000 marines marched through the streets as a show of strength. However, the strike was not so much an anti-Francoist protest as a dispute *within* the political class of the dictatorship, for the local syndicates had defended the interests of both the workers and the region in opposition to the state. The stoppage also drew on the anarcho-syndicalists, Communists, and HOAC activists who had infiltrated the vertical syndicates, but they were a small minority. 'Entryism' had been pursued by dissident anarcho-syndicalists (it was not CNT policy) since 1947 for a variety of motives, ranging from self-interest and syndical coercion to peer pressure, the desire to aid persecuted comrades, and the conviction that militating within the official unions constituted the best means of defending the interests of the workers. A few anarcho-syndicalists even rose up the ladder of the vertical syndicates to high-ranking positions, such as José Alcaina, who eventually became a deputy in the Francoist Cortes. In any case, anarcho-syndicalists were to operate within the vertical syndicates in 'many places' throughout the dictatorship.[147] On the other hand, the Movement actively encouraged entryism, the national delegate of syndicates, Fermín Sanz Orrio, contending in November 1945 that the workers should be represented:

> By genuine workers of the greatest prestige in each locality ... left-wing but sound workers to whom one can grant a certain confidence, many of whom will be won over by the regime, while the others can oppose [it], which is even convenient.[148]

By contrast, the overtly anti-Francoist opposition was crushed by the efficacy of the dictatorship's security forces. Between 1946 and 1951 a total of 8,324 activists were swept up by the police and army, of whom 7,392 were arrested during the immediate post-war years of 1946–8. By far the most dynamic anti-Francoist force was the Communist Party, which suffered 4,410 arrests, compared to 1,651 for the anarcho-syndicalists (in addition to 419 for the Armed Forces' Association of the Spanish Republic), 525 for the socialists, 519 for the Basque nationalists, and 61 for the republicans.[149] The ANFD folded in 1947 following the detention of virtually the entire national committee and the majority of the regional delegates. The end came for the dissident Communists of the POUM, the Armed Forces' Association of the Spanish Republic, and the republican parties in 1949, the General Directorate of Security crowing in a report that 'the year 1949 can be considered extraordinarily beneficial ... the politico-social delinquency has experienced a notable decline.'[150] Two years later, it congratulated itself on 'the fecund work carried out [that] did so much to shatter the morale of left-wing activists'.[151] With the arrest of the CNT's National Committee in 1952, the movement 'was completely dismantled and did not form another national committee until the autumn of 1960'.[152] The Communist Party recovered more quickly, but in 1959 had a maximum of 2,000 members nationwide.[153]

The isolation of Franco's Spain in the aftermath of the Second World War reached a climax with the resolution of the United Nations'

General Assembly on 12 December 1946, which condemned the regime as 'fascist' and recommended that it be excluded from all UN agencies, a monumental blow to the dictatorship's international standing. The General Assembly called, too, for a diplomatic embargo, all ambassadors being withdrawn except for those of Argentina, Portugal, Switzerland, and the Vatican. Internationally ostracized and reviled, Franco's Spain never seemed more different. On the other hand, the dictatorship had got off relatively lightly, as American and especially British pressure had avoided more stringent sanctions, including an economic blockade. Moreover, the UN had failed to back either the republicans or monarchists as the legitimate alternative to Franco, a grievous setback to both causes.

The UN's refusal to acknowledge the legitimacy of the Second Republic prompted Giral's resignation in January 1947 as head of the government-in-exile. Despite Giral's failure, the new government under socialist Rodolfo Llopis pursued exactly the same unrealistic strategy, ignoring the Joint Declaration in favour of an explicitly pro-republican stance. By contrast, fellow socialist Indalecio Prieto realized that Allied opinion was too divided for the republican cause to prosper, which meant that the rival claims of monarchists and republicans had to be subsumed if the Allies were to be won over. By 1947, Prieto had reached the conclusion that the only option with sufficient support amongst the Americans and British (Stalin having abandoned Spain to the West) was a constitutional monarchy. He also understood that, in the context of the Cold War, the Communists would be excluded from government under such a regime. In August 1947 he won a socialist assembly in France over to his position, which not only provoked the fall of the Llopis government-in-exile (the last of any influence), but also prompted negotiations with the monarchists under the auspices of the British Labour government. The two sides finally signed the Pact of Saint-Jean-de-Luz in August 1948, which called for a peaceful transition to democracy, an amnesty, religious liberty, the exclusion of all totalitarian parties from government, and the international alignment of Spain with the West. Unfortunately for the signatories, the Pact was already a dead letter. The heir to the throne, Juan de Borbón, had met Franco three days earlier, effectively scuppering the negotiations, and the Americans had ditched the British-backed monarchist solution in favour of support for

Franco. The reason for this volte-face was simple enough: the onset of the Cold War.

## THE TURNING OF THE TIDE: THE COLD WAR

Initially, US President Harry Truman had been openly hostile to Franco. He recoiled at the Spanish dictator's support for the Axis and the authoritarian nature of his regime, particularly his persecution of Protestantism and Freemasonry, as the president was both a Baptist and a Grand Master of the Freemasons. The start of the Cold War, however, was to transform the American perception of Franco's Spain, as the epoch of 'American globalism' was unleashed.[154] The American policy of containment, or the so-called 'Truman Doctrine', began with the Greek Civil War between the monarchists and the Communists. The latter were aided by the Communist regimes of Yugoslavia, Albania, and Bulgaria, and, briefly, by the USSR, while the former were backed by Britain. When the overstretched British withdrew in early 1947, the Americans stepped in, Truman pleading with Congress on 12 March to 'support free peoples who are resisting attempted subjugation by armed minorities or outside pressures'.[155] Massive US military and economic aid for the Greek monarchist government inaugurated 'the era of Cold War interventionism', the Americans finally claiming victory in December 1949.[156] The Cold War, as a State Department document of October 1947 made clear, converted Franco's Spain from a political outcast to a geostrategic boon, above all because it controlled the entrance to the 'strategically vital' Mediterranean, thereby vindicating the dictatorship's unrelenting self-promotion as an anti-Communist bulwark and its pursuit since late 1944 of, in the words of its foreign secretary, 'special understandings' with the United States.[157] The American military first visited Spain in 1948, its government provided a $62.5 million loan in 1950, and, amidst much fanfare, a new US ambassador presented his credentials to Franco in 1951. In the meantime, the diplomatic pressure eased as the French reopened their border in 1948, the United Nations overturned its condemnatory resolution in 1950, and relations with the Western democracies were largely normalized through bilateral agreements. A new concordat with the Vatican in August 1953, which reinforced the Catholic Church's privileged position within the Spanish state and society while giving Franco the last word in the election of bishops, further enhanced the regime's international position.

The crowning achievement of Spain's international rehabilitation was the signing of the Pact of Madrid with the United States of America on 26 September 1953. This furnished the Americans with military bases at Torrejón de Ardoz (Madrid), Zaragoza, Morón (Seville), and Rota (Cádiz). The first three were airbases that reported directly to the Strategic Air Command in Nebraska (initially hosting B-47 nuclear bombers), while the last one supported the Sixth Fleet in the Mediterranean. These were theoretically joint ventures, but in practice the Americans kept themselves quite separate. In exchange, Spain received $1,523 million in economic aid over the next ten years and $456 million in military assistance in the form of second-hand hardware and training programmes.[158] American funds made possible the importation of desperately needed primary materials, machinery, and food, especially as Spain had been excluded from the Marshall Plan of 1947, crucial to the economic reconstruction of Western Europe. The inflow of US capital not only covered nearly the entire trade deficit between 1953 and 1956, but also permitted the purchase of fertilizers from abroad, which dramatically reduced food imports from $60 million in 1948-9 to $3 million in 1952.[159]

The Pact was nonetheless a heavy blow to the dictatorship's national pride, as it gave the lie to Franco's boast of 'the independence and greatness of Spain'.[160] Accordingly, the protocol specifying that the United States was not obliged to defend Spain in the event of an attack was kept secret. Still, Spain may have been repulsed by NATO, but it had effectively been integrated into the Western security alliance. Many anti-Francoists felt that, as one man told the American writer Richard Wright, 'their hope for freedom had been betrayed by the pact'.[161] Whether the alliance with the Americans was decisive in the consolidation of Franco's regime is a moot point. Certainly the US was central to its international rehabilitation while providing it with urgently needed economic assistance, but without the collaboration of the Allies it is extremely difficult to see how the opposition could have toppled the dictatorship, let alone have averted another civil war.

Spain's dealings with the United States opened the doors to a host of international bodies, such as the FAO, WHO, UNESCO, the Postal Union, and the International Labour Organization. The process of global integration climaxed with the vote of the UN General Assembly on 15 December 1955 in favour of Spanish entry. Despite having been pilloried by the UN in 1946 as 'fascist', Franco's Spain had redeemed itself nine years later. Thus the supreme achievement of political Catholicism was the international rehabilitation of the dictatorship, its reinvention as 'National-Catholic' having made it less noxious to Western opinion. For the *Caudillo*, this was a towering triumph, especially as it had been achieved without making any political concessions or bringing the restoration of the monarchy any nearer.

The situation of the Franco dictatorship in 1955 was therefore radically different to that ten years earlier. The Cold War had transformed Spain from a political pariah to a geostrategic asset, the 'fascist' outcast giving way to an anti-Communist outpost. Under the protective umbrella of the United States, Spain had not only been integrated de facto into the Western defence system, but had also secured international recognition as a member of the United Nations. A further cause for satisfaction was the upturn in the economy. A partial economic and administrative liberalization of the early 1950s, together with US credit and the demand generated by the Korean War of 1950–53 (Spanish exports leapt 40 per cent during these years), eliminated the black market overnight, and prompted a massive increase in production (the output of electricity, for example, jumped 94 per cent between 1949 and 1952).[162] The crippling stagnation of the 1940s was replaced by the heady growth rate of 4.35 per cent per annum between 1951 and 1958. Not only had the dictatorship been consolidated, but its prospects seemed brighter than at any time since its foundation in 1939. Little wonder, then, that, in his end-of-year message for 1955, Franco boasted that Spain 'finds herself in possession of new, solid political solutions, her own mistress, and [with] a luminous political horizon of her own'.[163]

# 8

## The Late Franco Dictatorship, 1956–1975

### The 'Economic Miracle' and the Rebirth of Civil Society

If 1955 was a time of continuity, even celebration, 1956 was to be a time of change, even crisis, as it marked a tipping point in the history of the dictatorship. The year 1956 saw the eruption of a new opposition, as manifested in the student rebellion of February 1956, the adoption of a policy of 'national reconciliation' by the *Partido Comunista de España* or PCE (Spanish Communist Party), and the emergence of the first workers' commissions (*comisiones obreras*). These opposition forces would transform politics in Franco's Spain, as the latter would no longer be the exclusive preserve of the regime elites, but would necessarily involve engagement with mass movements harbouring a very different agenda. A further fracture of 1956 was the decolonization of Morocco, the 'jewel in the crown' of the Spanish Empire, which dealt a monumental blow to the dictatorship's claims to imperial grandeur. Finally, the escalating threat of economic crisis in 1956 led the regime to abandon its semi-autarkic model for a mainly liberal one engineered by the so-called 'technocrats' of the elitist Catholic organization Opus Dei, a rupture that would not only drastically alter the course of the dictatorship, but also greatly weaken its hold over both state and society.

## THE WATERSHED OF THE REGIME: 1956

The roots of the student rebellion of February 1956 lay in the opening up of higher education to new intellectual and cultural currents by the minister of national education, the liberal Catholic Joaquín Ruiz-Giménez, who aimed to make culture 'truly national'; in other words, one that embraced non-regime as well as regime currents.[1] However, the official students' union, the *Sindicato Español Universitario* or SEU (Spanish University Union), was unable to keep developments under its control, anti-Francoists at the University of Madrid calling in early 1956 for a National Congress of Students 'to give a representative structure to their corporate organization', that is, an independent student union.[2] The fast-mounting tension between Falangists and non-Falangists exploded into violence on 8 February – appositely enough the 'Day of the Fallen Student' – which left a Falangist student dead, accidentally shot by one of his own. The incident resulted in a slew of arrests, the sacking of the rector, Pedro Laín, and the dismissal of both the minister of national education and the minister for the Movement, Raimundo Fernández Cuesta. The clash caused seismic shudders within the upper ranks of the dictatorship not just because it revealed that student loyalty could no longer be relied upon, but also because many of the protestors were scions of Nationalist families. In short, the student rebellion had brought together the off-spring of the victors and the vanquished, both inspired by a vision of 'national reconciliation'. This new narrative, in rejecting the Francoist 'War of Liberation', framed the conflict as a national tragedy that could only be superseded through reconciliation.

It was no coincidence that many of the leaders of the student revolt in Madrid were either Communists or fellow travellers, as the discourse on 'national reconciliation' had been drawn up by the PCE. In 1954 the Communist Party had begun to re-evaluate its anti-Francoist strategy under the influence of a new generation of militants, a shift reflected in the call of Dolores Ibárruri in July 1955 to 'attract to the democratic camp those who want to abandon the Francoist colours, without ask-ing them how they thought yesterday, but how they think today and what they want for Spain'.[3] This rallying cry was given even greater impetus over the next eighteen months by international developments. Spain's entry into the General Assembly of the United Nations in December 1955 did much to discredit the Civil War as a point of polit-ical reference, as it now seemed pointless to attack the regime on the grounds of its illegitimacy. More important still, the exposure of Stalin's crimes in January 1956 by the new Soviet leader, Nikita Khrushchev, together with the Polish crisis of 1956 and the Soviet invasion of

Hungary later that year, led the PCE, like many other Communist parties, not only to concentrate on national concerns at the expense of Soviet ones, but also to pursue a much more autonomous line. In March 1956 Santiago Carrillo, the foremost figure amongst the younger generation of leaders, proclaimed 'the idea of superseding the dividing line of the Civil War, the necessity of elaborating a political perspective without revenge or second acts'.[4] This policy of 'national reconciliation', formally approved by the party in June 1956, was designed to bring the anti-Francoist forces together in defence of a democratic alternative to the dictatorship. The new generation of leaders, which included Carrillo, Fernando Claudín, and the writer Jorge Semprún (the liaison for the Madrid students), eventually seized control of the party in 1959, but 1956 marked the party's move away from the imperatives of Soviet foreign policy towards one that focused overwhelmingly on the anti-Francoist struggle. The call for 'national reconciliation' was even taken up by a sector of the regime. In 1957 the *Unión Española* (Spanish Union), a Catholic-cum-monarchist grouping, was founded by the lawyer Joaquín Satrústegui, who questioned whether 'the foundations of a political regime' could be built on 'a civil war'.[5] 'We believe', he concluded, that 'a civil war is an enormous tragedy on which the future cannot be built'.[6] Accordingly, the members of the *Unión Española* renounced the dictatorship in favour of national reconciliation under a constitutional – as opposed to authoritarian – monarchy.

Another setback for the dictatorship was the abandonment of its prize colony, the Moroccan Protectorate. The insurgents of July 1936 had originally harboured dreams of imperial greatness by extending the Spanish territories in north Africa and by forging a 'special relationship' with the Spanish-speaking or 'Hispanic' peoples of the Americas, but the lack of military muscle, economic resources, and international influence had made this impossible. Worse still, Spain's standing abroad was undermined by the diplomatic isolation of the post-war years and by its subsequent dependence on the United States. The Moroccan Protectorate was 'central to Spanish claims to empire', especially for the army and in particular for Franco (who had spent the best years of his life there as a colonial officer), despite being thinly populated and weakly integrated into the national economy.[7] However, the wave of European decolonization in the wake of the Second World War, together

with Spain's military and material shortcomings, forced the dictatorship to withdraw from the Protectorate in 1956 once the French pulled
out of Morocco. Franco's pro-Arab policy in north Africa and the
Middle East failed to make up for the loss of Morocco, the end of
the Protectorate deeply wounding the dictatorship's *amour propre*.

The year 1956 was also notable for 'the last "full-out" battle' of the
Falange.[8] Having lost out to political Catholicism in the aftermath of
the Second World War, the frustration of the Falange at the postpone-
ment of the 'pending revolution' became ever greater, Pilar Primo de
Rivera calling on the Movement in January 1956 to 'renew itself or
die'.[9] 'Once again,' she warned, 'the attempt at a revolution for all and
within all Spaniards might fail if the Falange does not endeavour to
replace what is outdated with renewed energy.'[10] Certainly there had
been a 'significant' resurgence of the Movement in the early 1950s,
largely due to the promotion of a greater cultural inclusiveness, which
drew on non-regimen figures, such as the intellectuals José Ortega y
Gasset and Miguel Unamuno.[11] The prospect of a monarchist succession
was seen as a major obstacle to the advancement of the 'revolution',
the Falangist leader and minister José Antonio Girón writing to the
*Caudillo* in April 1956 of his 'concern' about 'how we're going to
conserve this after Franco'.[12] The secretary-general of the Movement,
José Luis de Arrese, reacted vigorously to this dilemma by urging
Franco to 'institutionalize' the regime by placing the single party at
the centre of government once again, as opposed to the second-rank
status that had bedevilled it since 1945.[13] He therefore put forward a
new series of 'fundamental' laws, which would define the doctrine of
the state and the powers of the Movement, and separate the roles of the
head of government and the head of state. The proposed reforms craft-
ily diminished the Falangist rhetoric of the Movement while increasing
its power, especially in relation to the post-Francoist future. At heart
lay a bid to leave 'the Movement, not the monarchy, as heir to the
dictatorship'.[14] Predictably, the plan provoked a near-universal outcry
from the other regime elites and in particular from Franco's right-
hand man, the dour Admiral Luis Carrero Blanco. Shortly afterwards,
Arrese was relieved of his position as secretary-general and relegated
in the Cabinet reshuffle of February 1957 to the peripheral Ministry
of Housing. Little wonder, then, that the Law of the Principles of the

National Movement that was passed in May 1958 fell way short of Arrese's aspirations, amounting to a reformulation of the Falange's Twenty-Six Points in terms that were 'as innocuous as possible'.[15] The decline in the fortunes of the Falange was also a product of its inability to control the students and its economic mismanagement. In December 1955 the minister of labour, the populist José Antonio Girón, had proclaimed to the workers that 'now it's the turn of others to endure. The national economy cannot be confused with the particular economy of a privileged group.'[16] He was as good as his word. In March 1956, he raised salaries by 16 per cent and a few months later approved a further hike, which led to spiralling inflation, greatly exacerbating the dictatorship's economic woes.

Indeed, the greatest single challenge facing the dictatorship in 1956 was the economic crisis. The limited liberalization of the early 1950s had generated impressive growth, but as the American aid fizzled out and the import-substitution scheme imploded, the policy shortcomings came to the fore, as manifested in rising inflation, a fast-growing public debt, and an alarming balance of payments deficit. Not only had the semi-autarkic model pursued since 1951 become unsustainable, but it had also become a political necessity for the dictatorship to guarantee economic expansion. In the autumn of 1956 a professor of administrative law, Laureano López Rodó, had presented Carrero Blanco with a highly attractive proposition: the reform of the central administration, making it more efficient, and a new economic policy, which would achieve steady growth without endangering the authoritarian political framework. A tall, balding man with outsized glasses and a supremely complacent demeanour, López Rodó belonged to Opus Dei (the Work of God), a secretive lay Catholic organization founded in 1928 'by divine inspiration' by the Aragonese priest José María Escrivá de Balaguer, whose members sought to realize their apostolic mission through outstanding achievement in the professions.[17] There are parallels here with the elitist ACNP, but Opus Dei had an ethos all of its own, managing to alchemize an ultra-Catholic theology and reactionary politics with a ferocious, Protestant-style work ethic (embodied in Escrivá's spiritual guidebook *El Camino*) and a thoroughly modern regard for the virtues of American capitalism. The so-called *numerarios* such as López Rodó were celibate and lived in residences structured by gender, the women acting as auxiliaries to the men. Opus Dei sought power by stealth, first establishing a bridgehead in the educational system through the support of the minister of national education in the 1940s, José Ibáñez Martín, which led to the foundation of the first all-round Catholic university in Spain in 1952, the University of Navarre in Pamplona. By the end of 1956, López Rodó had persuaded Carrero Blanco to make him technical secretary-general of the Presidency and to entrust him with the reform of the administration, as realized by laws in 1957 and 1958 which were designed to provide the state bureaucracy with greater coordination, streamline certain procedures, and strengthen the Presidency (Franco's governmental department), as well as institutionalizing Carrero Blanco's position as under-secretary of the Presidency.

# THE 'STABILIZATION PLAN' OF 1959

The ascendancy of Opus Dei's besuited 'technocrats' was reflected in the Cabinet reshuffle of February 1957 when members of the society took over the key portfolios of finance (Mariano Navarro Rubio) and commerce (Alberto Ullastres), while the Falangist Girón was sacked and Arrese demoted. The most crucial change was the expansion in the powers of the Presidency, where the axis of Carrero Blanco and López Rodó now held supreme. Carrero Blanco was weary of the confrontation between the Falangists and the political Catholics (a 'disintegrating force'), while being drawn to Opus Dei because it did not form part of the original authoritarian alliance, because – in contrast to Catholic Action – it did not have a troublesome social base, and because Opus Dei members generally favoured an authoritarian monarchist succession in accordance with the Law of 1947.[18] The Cabinet of 1957 therefore marked the rise of the monarchist option 'with force'.[19]

The entry of the Opus Dei technocrats into the government marked a turning point in the history of the dictatorship. Not only was the bureaucracy reformed, but economic policy was transformed, shifting it from the hidebound priorities of autarky to the liberalizing dynamics of international market-led integration. Certainly this radical shift in policy was designed to hitch Spain's wagon to the booming economies of the West, which were basking in the 'Golden Age' of capitalism, including countries in Southern Europe such as Italy and Greece. However, Franco was extremely reluctant to abandon autarky, as it embodied his agrarian ideal and ensured state control of the economy, a central pillar of the regime. Exposing Spain to the international markets and transnational regulatory bodies filled him with dread, as he rightly feared that the dictatorship would lose control over the economy, society, and even its own politics. Still, he was realistic enough to realize that the collapse of the economy might well place the regime – and hence his personal power – in jeopardy, begrudgingly accepting change from without if it preserved his own power within. He made the best of the situation by going to great lengths in a televised address to claim that the new policy was merely a continuation of the old, citing extracts from speeches of the 1940s and early 1950s to the effect that 'our goal' had always been 'economic liberty', as 'the economic life of a people cannot be hermetic and sealed off within its frontiers, but has to be connected with the economic life of other peoples'.[20]

Thus the economy was first integrated into the Organization for European Economic Cooperation (OEEC), the International Monetary Fund (IMF), and the World Bank in 1958, which provided Spain with expert advice and substantial credits. The quid pro quo was the so-called 'Stabilization Plan' of July 1959, which at once stabilized *and* liberalized the economy. Stabilization was to be achieved by bringing inflation under control, by overcoming the public deficit, and above all by avoiding the suspension of international payments. Liberalization involved the removal of numerous regulations, the devaluation of the currency (from 48 to 60 pesetas to the dollar), the reduction of the multiple exchange rates to a single rate, and the opening up of the Spanish economy to foreign capital, credit, and commerce. As the government's Memorandum to the IMF and OEEC of June 1959 explained, 'the moment has arrived to give a new direction to economic policy, with the aim of aligning the Spanish economy with the countries of the Western World and liberating it from interventions inherited from the past'.[21] In sum, the Plan swept aside the national autarkic order and inserted the Spanish economy into the international capitalist order.

# AN ECONOMY TRANSFORMED

The early results of the 1959 Plan were highly promising: inflation was curbed, the deficit disappeared, the trade balance reversed, and in 1960 there was a major influx of capital from abroad, though the initial adjustments also brought about a depression from 1959 to mid 1960. Thereafter the economy boomed. Growth between 1960 and 1974 averaged 7.9 per cent per year in terms of GDP and 6.9 per cent in terms of GDP per capita, the latter a rate seven times greater than that of the previous century.[22] Exports rose 11.5 per cent a year between 1961 and 1973 and imports 12.9 per cent.[23] Worldwide, only Japan surpassed Spain's vertiginous upward arc. Spain would leap from an agrarian-led economy to an industrial and service-based one in a mere fifteen years, Franco presiding over the greatest period of growth in Spanish history. As a result, Franco's Spain 'stepped into the First World and joined the exclusive club of those countries with a per capita income of $2000 dollars or more'.[24]

The prosperity of the second half of Franco's regime permitted Spaniards to commit a far smaller proportion of their earnings to basic expenditures (those on food, drink, tobacco, clothes, and shoes dropped from 70 per cent in 1958 to 47.2 per cent in 1973/4), and a far greater proportion to the enticements of the consumer revolution, spending on leisure, health, communications, and transport rising from a mere 8.3 per cent in 1958 to 23.6 per cent in 1973/4.[25] In 1960 just 1 per cent of households possessed the ultimate symbol of modern-day autonomy and ostentation – the automobile – but only fifteen years later 40 per cent had one. Household ownership of the television, the most prized leisure commodity, also skyrocketed, from only 4 per cent in 1960 to a staggering 85 per cent in 1975. Hardly surprisingly, sales of the labour-saving appliances of domestic modernity – the washing machine and refrigerator – soared too: a fifth of households had the former in 1960 but one-half in 1971, while only 4 per cent of households had the latter in 1960 but two-thirds by 1975. The new-found prosperity generated rising expectations, which did much to dispel the despair and fatalism that had characterized the 1940s and 1950s.

Integration into the Western-style consumer culture was greatly enabled by the spread of department stores, supermarkets, a consumer press, and the professionalization of advertising. By the mid-1960s Spain had the home-grown department store chains of *Galerías Sederías* and *El Corte Inglés* (both modelled on American retailing techniques), and *Sears de España*, part of the US global network. These not only introduced American consumer habits and fashions, but also undermined Francoist social mores, such as by creating 'Youth' departments, which allowed young people to mingle without being chaperoned (a notable innovation given that more than half the population was under thirty by 1971). The first supermarket opened in Madrid in 1957, the sector being dominated in its early days by the Dutch chains VéGé and SPAR, the latter spreading like wildfire from 100 locations in 1961 to 810 by mid-1963.[26] Supermarkets transformed the shopping experience, while making many more foreign products available, thereby accelerating the 'consumption-driven social convergence with Europe'.[27] Western European and American 'coded modernity' was further enhanced by consumer magazines such as *AMA*, while the impact of advertising was revolutionized by the application of US-inspired practices.[28] Risqué adverts challenged social norms, such as that featuring a quasi-dominatrix towering over an enchained man for the Copan trousers' campaign of 1967 ('Copan satisfies').[29] In short, the headlong advancement of mass consumerism did much to foment Spain's social convergence with Western Europe and the United States.

Modernization converted industry and the services sector into the bedrock of the Spanish economy, as the proportion of the active population employed in the primary sector dropped from 39.7 per cent in 1959 to a mere 22.8 per cent in 1972, while industry climbed from 23.5 to 27.8 per cent and the tertiary sector from 36.8 to 49.4 per cent.[30] The number of workers on the land fell from 4.9 million in 1960 to 3 million in 1974, while those in industry rose from 2.6 to 3.6 million.[31] The chief motor of the modernizing process was industry, which by 1974 had reached an unprecedented peak of 35.2 per cent of national output. This was partly because it grew faster than any other sector (10.2 per cent per annum between 1960 and 1973), partly because it received three-quarters of all foreign investment, and partly because it drove the structural changes, due not so much to the shift in employment as to the 'substantial and cumulative' rise in productivity.[32] Traditional industries such as cement, shipbuilding, steel-making, and textiles expanded, while hitherto lesser ones, including the production of cars, plastics, pharmaceuticals, and household appliances, were converted into major concerns. The car industry, for instance, grew at 22 per cent a year between 1958 and 1973.[33] Hardly surprisingly, industrialization spread beyond the traditional heartlands of Barcelona and Bilbao to other cities, such as Alicante, Madrid, Seville, Valencia, and Zaragoza. Also revolutionized during these years was the service sector, which generated 1.5 million jobs in the 1960s and growth of 6.7 per cent a year between 1960 and 1974, principally in tourism, banking, and the public services.[34] By the 1970s, services accounted for nearly 50 per cent of GDP.[35] The emergence of a sizeable and relatively prosperous urban middle class of professionals, managers, and other white-collar employees is inexplicable without taking into account the expansion of industry and services.

The transformation of the economy altered gender relations insofar as female workers were in demand for the expanding industrial and service sectors, thereby leading to a clutch of reforms in the early 1960s that reflected this shift, including equal pay (in theory), full rights to property, and an end to the dismissal of women who married (though they required the permission of their husbands to work). In the meantime, working women were still expected to fulfil their traditional domestic duties. These changes were introduced by the regime on the grounds of economic necessity, not being designed to alter the patriarchal order, despite the repeal of the laws on adultery in 1958.

The rural exodus which resulted from the expansion of industry and the service sector meant that the populace in Andalusia, Aragón, and Galicia hardly increased, while the emptying of some regions, such as Extremadura and the two Castiles, reduced the number of inhabitants. By contrast, Madrid, the Basque Country, Catalonia, and the Balearic and Canary Islands underwent the greatest demographic surge in their history. At the beginning of the liberalization process, the disparities in wealth between the different regions were vast. The three richest areas – Madrid, the Basque region, and Catalonia – had per capita incomes that were 80 per cent of the West European average, while Andalusia, the two Castiles, and Extremadura stood at a mere 40 per cent. Indeed, the disparity in income between Vizcaya in the north and Almería in the south was 'in 1955, slightly greater than that between, for example, Belgium and Algeria or Brazil in 1960', that is to say, it was of intercontinental proportions.[36] The vertiginous growth of the 1960s and early 1970s set in motion a process of convergence, as the most impoverished regions expanded fastest. Thus the Castiles, Galicia, and Murcia were three of the poorest regions in 1959, but they registered the rapidest GDP per capita growth rates of all between 1960 and 1975, though the gaps remained substantial, as the per capita GDP of the richest region, the Balearic Islands, was 2.3 times that of the poorest, Extremadura. While the four most prosperous regions – the Balearic Islands, the Basque Country, Catalonia, and Madrid – enjoyed a GDP per capita income in 1975 that was near or above the West European average, the three most deprived regions – Andalusia, Extremadura, and Galicia – now stood at between 47 and 62 per cent.

Liberalization of the economy did not mean, however, the end of intervention. The *Instituto Nacional de Industria* or INI (National Institute of Industry), the flagship of industrial dirigisme in the 1940s and 1950s, was downsized but continued to command enormous resources. Industrial intervention assumed new forms. The National Industry Act, for example, was replaced in 1963 by the Preferential Industry Act, which favoured those companies considered a priority by the government. Similarly, the 1962 Banking and Credit Act provided financial institutions with greater freedom, but numerous regulations persisted, such as those controlling interest rates or the issue of bonds and shares. A further mechanism of intervention was the French-style Development Plans introduced in 1964, which were designed to coordinate the activities of the public and private sectors. Overseen by López Rodó, the Plans allowed the government to set investment targets, as well as sectorial and territorial goals, but they were more of a hindrance than a help until their elimination in 1975. The joint ventures, to take one example, proved to be a 'very expensive and bad' investment.[37] Intervention took a positive form with the Law on Collective Agreements of 1958, which replaced wage-fixing by the ministries with a process of collective negotiation between employers and workers. The introduction of wage bargaining trans-formed industrial relations by providing the workers with much greater leverage than before.

Clearly the technocrats of Opus Dei were far from indifferent to the economic 'miracle' which had erupted in the United States and Western Europe in the early 1950s, the 'Golden Age' of Western capitalism. On the contrary, Spanish planners aimed to take full advantage of the spectacular expansion of the Western economies, which had not only confounded all expectations but also swiftly fostered a general belief 'in boundless economic growth, backed by full employment and low infla-tion'.[38] The new international framework created by the Bretton Woods Conference (1944), the European Payments Union (1950), and the European Economic Community (1957), together with the far-reaching impact of American aid, technology, investment, and managerial techniques, enabled the Western European economies to grow at unpre-cedented rates. By entering the international economy at such a hugely favourable juncture, Spain was able to profit from massive foreign investment, the explosion of mass tourism, and an unparalleled demand for exports, while its surplus labour was absorbed by the roaring econ-omies of Western Europe, emigrant workers sending home remittances that covered nearly a quarter of the foreign debt. In short, the 'Spanish miracle' owed a colossal debt to the Western 'miracle'.

## THE THREE PILLARS OF THE 'ECONOMIC MIRACLE'

The three principal pillars of the Spanish 'economic miracle' were for-eign investment, emigration (both internal and external), and tourism. The liberalization of the economy facilitated colossal investment from Western Europe and the United States. Between 1959 and 1973 Spain received more than $6.1 billion in foreign capital, an investment that was matched by 'no other in the world', with the exception of the most advanced nations.[39] Two-thirds of the direct investments were made by America, Switzerland, and West Germany, followed by the United Kingdom, France, and the Netherlands. The greatest single investor was the US at 35 per cent of the total. One stimulant to investment was the negotiations with the EEC between 1962 and 1970, which encouraged investment from abroad, while the final agreement, the Preferential Commercial Agreement (1970), not only provided incentives to extra-European multinationals, but also gradually opened up the single market to Spanish industrial goods. The paradox was that the virulently anti-liberal Francoists had ended up embracing the nineteenth-century liberal economic paradigm of foreign capital as the key to economic development.

The booming economies of Northern Europe also sucked in millions of immigrant workers from Southern Europe, as well as from East Germany (up to August 1961), north Africa, and Turkey. A total of 1.12 million Spaniards emigrated to Western Europe between 1961 and 1975.[40] Emigration not only reduced unemployment (absorbing 10 per cent of the active population up to 1973), thereby strengthening the unions back home, but also generated remittances sufficient to cover 23 per cent of the foreign debt between 1961 and 1973. Within Spain, the rapid growth of industry and services produced extensive internal migration, as 4.5 million people abandoned their homes in the 1960s in the search for work.

The main magnet for investment (both foreign and domestic) and for the internal migrants was the tourist industry. Spain enjoyed a host of advantages as a tourist destination for Northern Europeans in particular, ranging from the geographical proximity of its sun, sand, and sea (with more beaches than anywhere in Europe), the low salaries (which guaranteed cheap service), and the market awareness of entrepreneurs and politicians alike. It is often assumed that the growth of mass tourism in Spain was a product of the 1960s boom, but the upgrading of tourism to ministerial status in July 1951 indicates that its potential had already been noted, nearly one million visitors arriving in 1954, two million in 1957, and over four million in 1960.[41] The initial surge in the tourist trade not only helped overcome the regime's international isolation, but by the mid-1950s also provided Spain with its greatest source of foreign currency. As a principal hub of the post-war Western European leisure industry, tourism in Spain was more a cause than a consequence of the 1959 Stabilization Plan, furnishing the regime with 'the strength and confidence to implement major economic reforms'.[42] Further, the 1959 devaluation of the peseta took place at the same time as the deregulation of air charters for package deals in Western Europe, thereby precipitating an even greater avalanche of tourists. By 1960 Spain had surpassed France in terms of tourist volume and by 1964 had even overtaken Italy, the number of leisure-seekers rising to 11 million in 1965, to 21 million in 1970, and then leaping to 31 million in 1972.[43] Between 1961 and 1973 tourism contributed $16,500 million in revenue, enough to cover 77.4 per cent of Spain's trade deficit, while acting as collateral for loans from the World Bank and other international bodies.[44] It also greatly improved the infrastructure of the Mediterranean coast, taking up 53 per cent of the nation's road-building budget in 1965 and prompting the construction of several airports.[45] In sum, the lure of 'Spain is Different', a tourist slogan first launched in the 1940s, actually made Spain less different, as mass tourism did much to bring the Spanish economy ever closer to that of Western Europe, as well as becoming a reference point for the development of tourism in other parts of Europe, South America, and elsewhere.

Agriculture, too, was transformed during these years, despite being displaced as the cornerstone of the economy by industry and the service sector, its contribution to GDP having dropped to 18.5 per cent by 1965. The rural exodus pushed wages up by over five times between 1964 and 1976, while the dearth of workers led to an overnight revolution in production, as fertilizers, fodder, combine harvesters, tractors, and other means were introduced en masse, the number of tractors rocketing from 56,800 in 1960 to 355,000 in 1974.[46] The upshot was that agricultural production rose 5.8 per cent a year between 1960 and 1974, and the focus of production also changed, as more meat and milk-related goods were made available, considerably enriching the Spanish diet.[47]

## REBRANDING THE DICTATORSHIP

Spain's unprecedented economic boom went hand in hand with the rebranding of Franco's Spain as a regime of 'development' – that is, modern, affluent, and 'normal' – especially in relation to the United States. The dictatorship commandeered American public relations firms not only for its political lobbying in the US, but also in order to influence the media, tourist, and entertainment industries there. This soft-power outreach, enthusiastically promoted in the 1960s by Manuel Fraga's Ministry of Information and Tourism and Fernando de Castiella's Ministry of Foreign Affairs, climaxed with the dazzling Spanish Pavilion at New York's World Fair of 1964–5. The $7 million Pavilion, designed by the internationally acclaimed Spanish architect Javier Carvajal, cost even more to make than the Oscar-winning film of 1964, *Mary Poppins*. Lauded by *Life* magazine as 'The Jewel of the Fair', the Pavilion was visited by no fewer than 23 million people and treated to near-universal adulation by the US media, the Spanish daily *ABC* claiming that it had done 'more for Spain's prestige in six months than has been done in many previous decades'.[48] Tourism was central to the dictatorship's soft-power strategy. In fact, the 'initial impetus for developing Spain's modern foreign tourism infrastructure came from American travel industry exhortations and guidance'.[49] In 1953 the Hilton group opened its first European hotel in Spain, the *Castellana Hilton* in Madrid, a home-from-home for American celebrities such as astronauts and film stars. In 1959–60 the Barcelona and Madrid airports were overhauled so that they could accommodate the Boeing 707 and DC-8 jet planes that soon began to ply the route between the United States and Spain. In 1968, 700,000 American tourists travelled to Spain, mostly middle- and upper-middle-class customers who were more interested in the country's culture and heritage sites than in the hedonistic pleasures of its beach life. Spain's peripheral participation in the US space programme, which involved a number of tracking stations, also paid soft-power dividends, as the station at Robledo de Chavela (Madrid) secured the first image of Earth from outer space, while a number of astronauts visited Spain, including Neil Armstrong, Buzz Aldrin – the first moonwalkers – and Michael Collins of Apollo 11, who were paraded through the streets of Madrid.

The most glamorous and high-profile spin-off of the regime's soft-power sell to the United States was the transformation of Spain into a favoured Hollywood film venue in the 1950s and 1960s. Samuel Brontson, producer of such blockbusters as *El Cid*, *55 Days at Peking*, and *The Fall of the Roman Empire*, was, recalls a high-ranking official, 'a very welcome man' (despite being the nephew of Leon Trotsky), as he was 'an American film producer, intelligent, powerful, with money . . . to produce films, made in Spain for the world. And that was the first time that such a thing happened.'[50] The premiere of *Pleasure Seekers* (1964), which projected a beguiling image of Spain as an ideal tourist destination bedecked with historic sites and quaint traditions, was attended not only by the minister of information and tourism, Manuel Fraga, but also by Franco's daughter, the Marchionesse of Villaverde. Sunny, desert-strewn Almería became such a popular Hollywood film location that at one point in 1968 nine films were being shot there simultaneously, while the Almería airport was inaugurated by none other than Franco himself. Little wonder, then, that in 1967–8 Michael Caine shot three films in Spain, while director Sergio Leone's epochal 'Spaghetti Westerns', starring Clint Eastwood, were also largely made in Spain. *The Good, the Bad, and the Ugly* (1966), for instance, was filmed between Rome, Almería, and Burgos, the epic graveyard scene being shot in an unspoilt spot in the latter province (the set having since been painstakingly recreated by film enthusiasts, as recounted in the *Desenterrando Sad Hill* documentary of 2017).

## A NATIONALISM FOR THE TIMES

Economic liberalization, especially as regards mass consumerism and tourism, did much to transform not only the regime's nationalist discourse, but also the very identity of ordinary Spaniards. One of the dictatorship's founding myths was that of national exceptionalism, which contrasted Spain's Christian civilization and traditional forms of representation ('organic democracy') with the West's degenerate and decaying parliamentary democracies. The change in discourse began with the evolving military and economic relationship with the United States. A harbinger of this shift was the remake of Franco's film of 1942, *Raza*. The less stridently titled *Espíritu de una raza* (Spirit of a Race) of 1950 eliminated not only the film's fascist features, but also the less-than-complimentary references to the United States and other democracies. Similarly, with the launching of *el desarrollo* (economic modernization) in the late 1950s, 'Europe' was no longer reviled and repudiated but respected, even admired and emulated. At the forefront of the drive for Europeanization was tourism, the youthful, thrusting, and self-assured minister responsible for it, the professor of political science Manuel Fraga, declaring grandly that the industry was 'Spain's European vocation'.[51] Not for nothing was an ever-closer relationship with the EEC the overriding goal of Spanish foreign policy in the 1960s. Illustrative of this Europeanizing mission was the trumpeting of Spain's first shopping mall as the country's entry into Europe's 'Shopping Centre Common Market'.[52]

Modernization and Europeanization also required that Franco's Spain no longer be seen as different. A state newsreel of 1964 reflected this aspiration to normalcy by declaring that 'Spain is a country open to all and where foreigners feel at home.'[53] Tourist posters after 1962 were far less likely to feature bucolic beaches and folkloric exotica, especially bullfighting and flamenco. Complementing this was the elimination of the slogan 'Spain is Different' from all new poster series after 1961, while the promotional guidebook *Spain is You* (made available in eleven languages), was eager to make clear that 'Spain is not so different'.[54] Exoticism was therefore replaced by regional diversity, that is, pluralism and (implicitly) tolerance, traits not readily associated with Franco's Spain. The more affluent and cultured tourists, many of them Americans, frequented the state-sponsored *paradores* (often reconverted castles, monasteries, and convents), which enjoyed a halcyon age in the 1960s and 1970s. Consequently, the xenophobic defensiveness of the dictatorship's initial years gave way to xenophile sentiments, 'the official contempt for foreign influence of the earlier period disappearing completely in the 1960s'.[55]

## THE SPANISH
## ACHIEVEMENT IN CONTEXT

Starting from a much lower threshold, Spain's spectacular growth rate of 6.9 per cent between 1959 and 1974 even surpassed that of the principal European economies, as France, West Germany, and Great Britain grew at 5.8 per cent, 4.9 per cent, and 2.9 per cent respectively between 1959 and 1970. On the other hand, the proportion of the Spanish populace still working on the land in 1974 was more than double that in France, West Germany, and Britain, while the consumer revolution in Spain was about ten years behind that in the other three countries. If Spain is placed in relation to the centrally planned economies of the Communist bloc, it is apparent that by the late 1960s the Comecon countries 'forsook any real prospect of competing with the West'.[56] In particular, the Communist regimes were ill-disposed and ill-equipped to produce the kind of technological and consumer goods that characterized the West. There were flickerings of consumerist culture, such as the appearance of supermarkets in Poland in the early 1960s, but even the relatively prosperous East Germany could not compete with Spain, only 16 per cent of *middle-income* households owning a car in 1970, though 69 per cent had a television.[57] The most economically innovative Communist regime of all, Yugoslavia, still fell far short of Spain's consumer boom, as only 25 per cent of Yugoslav households had a fridge in 1968 and a mere 3.5 per cent possessed a car in 1970. Finally, if Spanish modernization is compared to Portugal, Italy, and Greece in Southern Europe, it is clear that Spain lagged somewhat behind Italy's 'economic miracle' of 1958–63, but overshadowed the other nations. In short, the economic convergence of Southern with Western Europe was headed by Spain and Italy rather than by Greece, Portugal, Yugoslavia, or Stalinist Albania. The dictatorial nature of Franco's Spain also made it inevitable that it diverged from the dominant Western European model. The absence of independent trade unions ensured that there was no social pact along the lines of the democracies, whereby the workers exercised wage restraint in exchange for the development of the welfare state or the investment of profits in production. Additionally, democratic governments tended to redistribute wealth by means of a progressive income tax, but the dictatorship did not, as this would have harmed its social base.

Indeed, Franco's unwavering defence of 'social justice' proved to be largely rhetorical, designed above all to appease the Falangists and social Catholics, as state provision was woeful, spending on health rising from just 0.9 per cent of the budget in 1945 to only 3.5 per cent thirty years later, that on housing increasing from 1.2 to 3.5 per cent, and that on pensions from 3.9 per cent in 1945 to 5.7 per cent in 1975. The one notable expenditure concerned education, which climbed from a lowly 4.7 per cent in 1945 to 12.5 per cent three decades later.[58] In addition, Spanish workers laboured longer than their

EEC counterparts for less: in 1969 they worked eleven hours a week more for half the pay. A further divergence was that Spain, like Greece, was technologically deficient, as reflected in the pitiful proportion of GNP devoted to Research and Development – 0.27 per cent in 1971 as opposed to the OECD average of 2.4 per cent – a fault line that persists today. Finally, in common with the other countries of Southern Europe, Spain underwent massive emigration, which kept unemployment down, but at the cost of breaking up families and communities. In sum, Spain's modernization at once converged with, and diverged from, that of Western Europe.

Economic liberalization may have been the dictatorship's short-term salvation, but in the longer term it would do much to erode its support, especially as the regime had been designed to marshal a rural, not urban, population. Franco's Spain experienced the same modernizing trends and tensions as the rest of Western Europe, such as the flood of rural immigrants into the cities, pell-mell urbanization, the massifica-tion of the universities, rapid but far-reaching adjustments to the newly liberalized markets, and severe shortcomings in the public services and general infrastructure. The difference lay in the regime's management of growth. Not only was it patently unprepared for the demands of modernization, it was also politically unwilling to address them. Reforms that characterized much of Western Europe, such as the rationalization of the public sector, large-scale infrastructural improvements, and the enormous expansion of the welfare state, were tackled either partially or not at all by the dictatorship. The blatantly inadequate initiatives undertaken by the authorities were further blighted by the rampant corruption that characterized the public administration, not least the designation of contracts, a principal beneficiary being the building companies, which often erected substandard structures. One of the most piratical builders of the age was the Trump-like Jesús Gil, a shame-less self-promoter and arch-Francoist who after the Transition became the corrupt owner of the Atlético de Madrid football club and the mal-feasant mayor of Marbella. In June 1969 an illegally built structure of Gil's in San Rafael de los Ángeles (Segovia) collapsed, killing fifty-eight people and injuring 147. He was jailed, but then pardoned after eight-een months by Franco, which helps explain why he placed a bust of the dictator in Marbella town hall. Clearly the regime was unable to deal with 'the modernity it had itself unleashed'.[59] Little wonder, then, that local residents, workers, students, and professionals mobilized in defence of their interests, often creating new social movements and modes of protest that paralleled those found in Western Europe.

# THE RESURGENCE OF
# ASSOCIATIONAL LIFE

Helter-skelter urbanization, deficient infrastructure, and a dearth of public services generated widespread popular disaffection. The centralized bureaucracy of the Francoist state proved remote and unresponsive, while local government lacked the administrative leverage, money, and drive to defend the interests of its communities. A rise of social protest posed an evident problem for the regime, which responded by allowing a limited measure of participation within the public arena. This took the form of the Law of Associations of 1964, which has received scant attention from historians until recently. The aim of the reform was to channel popular discontent through the revival of associational life, but without crossing the red line of *political* associations. Thus the objectives, membership, and scope of the new associations were left undefined, except insofar as they excluded 'subversive elements'.[60] The 1964 Law spawned a whole new generation of voluntary organizations, with as many being created over the following three years as during the previous twenty-three. Altogether, a thousand associations were formed each year between 1964 and 1974, a good number dealing with the concerns of local residents or the parents of schoolchildren. Despite being set in motion by the dictatorship, the associations tended to adopt basic democratic practices by, say, conducting debates, reaching consensual decisions, holding elections, mounting public campaigns, and lobbying local and other authorities. Launching non-ideological associations in an effort to defuse the urban crisis ultimately proved counterproductive for the regime, as it inadvertently opened up a space for the development of a civil society that was more participatory and pluralistic than anything seen so far under Franco.

The resurgence of associational life in accordance with the 1964 law was boosted by yet another current that had been launched quite separately by the Movement. Starting in 1963, the Movement sponsored the Heads of Household Associations, which formed part of its new discourse on mass participation. Far from drawing on the Movement's totalitarian origins, this discourse aimed, in the words of the secretary-general, to 'populate with uncorrupt voices the national silence' of the previous twenty-five years.[61] Unlike the 1964 law, this was not a reaction to pressure from below, but yet another endeavour by the Movement to raise its political profile – greatly overshadowed since 1945 by its purely bureaucratic role – through the generation of grassroots support. The project of mass mobilization took further shape with the passing of the Organic Statute in 1968. The failure of the Movement to convince Franco of the need for political associations has detracted greatly from its success in persuading the dictator to approve *non*-political ones. Thus the Organic Statute allowed for 'free and spontaneous' associations that would be 'open to their own goals like a multi-coloured fan', though of course such new-found diversity was only admissible insofar as it was ideologically loyal to the dictatorship.[62] The focus on family associations gave way in 1971 to more specialized ones, so that by June of that year there were 2,284 family associations, 134 parent associations, 43 for families with disabled members, 25 for housewives, 20 concerned with consumer affairs, and 11 devoted to domestic workers.[63] The following year, family associations claimed over a million members, and by the time the Movement was dissolved in April 1977 there were 4,521 associations nationwide. The impact of the Movement's initiative, like that of the 1964 law, was to foment the adoption of basic democratic practices, which shows that the 'new discourse of participation could be taken in unintended directions'.[64]

By fostering greater public accountability and participation, the two associational currents eroded the demobilization and deference that had hitherto characterized society under the dictatorship. In boosting civil society, the authoritarian state inadvertently strengthened the popular resistance to it, despite the fact that the associations did not initially form part of the anti-Francoist opposition. Consequently, the associations narrowed the gap between Franco's Spain and the Western European democracies, as underscored by the fact that they later merged into the 'Citizens' Movement' of 1977–9 that did so much to

shape the Transition. Indeed, the Citizens' Movement shows how dictatorial initiatives could morph into the democratic realities of the
post-Francoist era. From this perspective, the social history of the Transition is inextricably bound up with that of the late Franco regime.

## RECALIBRATING THE REPRESSION

The efforts at channelling the aspirations of local residents, families,
and others notwithstanding, the dictatorship kept a vigilant watch
over what it stigmatized as 'subversion'. The university protests and
strikes of the late 1950s prompted a reaffirmation of the regime's
repressive mechanisms with the Law of Public Order of July 1959, a
reiterative catch-all measure prohibiting acts which 'threaten the spiritual, national, political, and social unity of Spain', which 'threaten or
attempt to alter public order', 'collective stoppages', 'demonstrations
and illegal public meetings', or anything which 'altered the public
peace or social co-existence'.[65] In September 1960 the law incorporated a revision of the measures passed in 1943 and 1947 regarding
'military rebellion' and 'banditry and terrorism', but without modify-
ing the criminal offences, so that the distribution of clandestine
propaganda or participation in strikes, illegal meetings, and demonstrations were still considered an act of 'military rebellion'. In other
words, internal security – that is, political dissent – remained in the
hands of the armed forces. This military hegemony made it exceedingly difficult for the accused to rebut the charges brought against
them, as trials were generally held in secret and defence lawyers, who
had to be military officers until 1963, were given little time to prepare
their cases and forbidden from questioning the state's evidence or
cross-examining hostile witnesses.

The repression further intensified as a result of a meeting of 118
Christian democrats, liberals, and socialists, from both within and
without Spain, in Munich in June 1962. Brought together under the
aegis of the European Congress Movement, the exiles and internal
dissidents, many of whom were former Francoists, provided an early
demonstration that the divisions of the Civil War could be overcome,
as crystallized in their joint declaration that Spain should only be

permitted to enter the EEC 'in accordance with the European Convention on Human Rights and the European Social Charter'.[66] The government, which characteristically dubbed the gathering as the 'Munich conspiracy', went into a frenzy, denouncing the participants as 'enemies and traitors' and launching a vitriolic campaign against them, especially the former CEDA leader, now Christian democrat, José María Gil Robles. Franco tried to rebut the claims of the 'conspiracy' by insisting in a speech in Valencia that the Spanish system was 'incomparably more democratic' than 'abroad'.[67]

The government declared a state of exception on 8 June 1962, which was to last two whole years. Under a state of exception, the right of habeas corpus was suspended (so people could be held indefinitely without charge), torture was commonly practised, and right-wing vigilante groups, such as the *Guerrilleros de Cristo-Rey* (Warriors of Christ-the-King), were unleashed, that is, the police, Civil Guard, and paramilitary groups combined to enforce the will of Franco's police state. During the state of exception of 1962–4, the Communist leader Julián Grimau was tried and executed (in April 1963) for crimes committed during the Civil War (the last such case), and a few months later two anarchists were unjustly convicted and executed for a brace of bombings in July 1963. Following the international uproar over Grimau's execution, the dictatorship's reputation was further blackened by a report of the International Commission of Jurists, which denounced the regime for its violations of civil rights and the excessive reach of its military justice system.

For the regime, the 'conspiracy of Munich' had damaged 'the credit and prestige of Spain', a particularly sensitive topic given that Spain had applied for membership of the EEC in February 1962.[68] Clearly the regime was infuriated that the Achilles heel of its 'Europeanization' – political authoritarianism – had been showcased for the entire international community. A further repercussion of the 'Munich conspiracy' was a major overhaul of the repressive structures of the state. In December 1963 the Tribunal of Public Order was created, which not only replaced the Special Tribunal for the Repression of Freemasonry and Communism, but also reduced – for the first time under the regime – the jurisdiction of the military tribunals. Henceforth, most 'political' crimes would be judged by the Tribunal of Public

Order, the latter trying over 2,000 people between 1963 and 1968, the military courts around 1,500 between 1964 and 1968. Even so, the regime was unable to stem the rising tide of protest by students, workers, dissident Catholics, and regional nationalists.

## THE STUDENT REVOLT

During the 1960s student protest spread outwards from the universities of Madrid and Barcelona, becoming virtually universal by 1965, with the popular assemblies, demonstrations, strikes, closure of faculties, and intimidatory police presence becoming common features of campus life. The roots of the student rebellion shared much in common with those in Western Europe and the United States. A quantum-like leap in the number of students and a shortfall in university provision was patent in the Spanish case: from an average of 70,000 enrolled students between 1955 and 1960 to 400,000 between 1970 and 1975, while spending per student stood at a mere $71 in 1965, compared to $400 in the case of Italy and more than $1,000 in Britain, France, and West Germany.[69] Another shared trait was the radicalizing impact of Marxism and the revolutions in the developing world, above all those in Algeria, Cuba, and Vietnam. An internal document of Spain's Ministry of Education contended not only that Marxist ideology attracted the students because it was 'the only one that offers a critically effective instrument and response to capitalist and bourgeois society', but also, somewhat surprisingly, that the appeal of Marxism was partly due 'perhaps to the scarce effectiveness and modernity of the other ideologies (Falange, Christian thought, Movement, Traditionalism, Christian democracy, etc.)'.[70] Finally, the 'revolution' of May 1968 in France had a galvanizing effect on Spanish students, as elsewhere.

The major point of divergence between the students in dictatorial Spain and those in the democratic West was that the overriding goal of the Spaniards was to replace their state-controlled union with an independent one, a basic freedom that was taken for granted by students in the democracies. The primacy of this political goal, together with the deeply entrenched conservatism of Francoist society (a famous photo of Madrid students fleeing from the police in the late 1960s shows them wearing ties and jackets) and the students' lack of economic independence, meant that there was far less of the anti-materialism, the pursuit of alternative lifestyles, and the exploration of free expression, along with the rejection of conventional hierarchies, than in Western Europe. Still, the dictatorship itself was under no illusions whatsoever as to the significance of the student revolt. A government report of June 1957 warned that alienation of the students from the regime would leave 'state and government policy in a vacuum', while a minister of national education warned Franco himself of 'the disastrous consequence of losing the university youth for the regime'.[71] Clearly, the failure to integrate the students within the dictatorship would not only damage its legitimacy, but also condition its very future, as the country's leadership cadres would emerge from the ranks of university graduates.

The approach of the dictatorship to student rebellion oscillated between heavy-handed repression and the semi-conciliatory search for a means of 'channelling' the student protest. In the late 1950s an attempt was made to 'de-ideologize' the official union, the SEU, by involving students in a series of participatory bodies, but the mass entry of anti-Francoists prompted the introduction of much more restrictive membership criteria in 1961, which effectively defeated the object of the exercise.[72] Between 1962 and 1964 the energetic and eloquent head of the SEU, Rodolfo Martín Villa, tried to disarm the disaffected students by means of an extensive process of democratization, but this outraged the regime while generating 'constant struggles' between the SEU and the new delegates.[73] Indeed, unrelenting and uncompromising student opposition to the SEU led to its dissolution in April 1965. As Martín Villa had feared, 'the young have abandoned us.'[74] Having toppled the SEU, the students' next goal was to establish their own, freely elected unions, as achieved in Barcelona in March 1966, when 450 delegates, gathered within the walls of a Capuchin monastery, elected the Democratic Syndicate of University Students. The regime persisted in looking for a way of bringing the students back within the bounds of the dictatorship, the SEU being replaced by 'Professional Associations of Students', but these were either boycotted or hijacked by the students, invalidating them as a mechanism of control.

These ineffectual efforts at 'channelling' the aspirations of the students were combined with repression, especially after 1965. In early 1968 the minister of information and tourism, Manuel Fraga, noted that 'for the moment there's an "armed peace", that is, a police occupation' of the university.[75] Within the government the minister of national education, Manuel Lora-Tamayo, called for conciliatory measures, while the minister of the interior, General Camilo Alonso Vega, demanded 'energetic measures'.[76] Franco himself, who attributed the protests to 'agents of Communism ... in the pay of foreign committees and associations', deplored the 'rebellious atmosphere and disorder' in the universities, remarking in April that if the current minister of national education failed he would be replaced by one who adopted – as Alonso Vega had insisted – 'energetic measures'.[77] In September a new minister of national education claimed that the students 'in their majority are recoverable and can be channelled within the regime', but two months later his ministry set up a military unit to deal with 'subversion'.[78] Shortly afterwards, in January 1969, Enrique Ruano, a student in the Political Science and Economics Faculty at the University of Madrid, fell to his death from a seventh-floor flat during a police search. The ensuing tidal wave of protests ushered in a state of exception that lasted for three months, during which 315 students were arrested. Carrero Blanco justified the state of exception before the Cortes on 7 February on the grounds that the protesters had started with 'the stonings, the turning over of vehicles, the strikes, the unauthorized meetings', but had reached a 'unbearable point' with 'placards insulting the Motherland and head of state, the exhibition of the sickle and hammer, outrages regarding the crucifix and national flag, mistreatment of the work and embarrassing trials of lecturers', adding that the students, who 'haven't studied or been given classes', had become 'poisoned in body and soul'.[79] In his opinion, 'one shouldn't do sport in a church, nor science in the circus, nor politics in the university'.[80] Given that 'subversion' was 'on view for everyone', the government, 'conscious of its duty', had taken the decision 'to end it'.[81] Like Franco, Carrero Blanco's political outlook remained largely frozen in the 1930s, as he believed the dissenting lecturers 'serve Communism and Freemasonry', while the rebellious students were 'agents of subversion', that is, the disturbances were the work of sinister outside forces. Governmental action did much to ensure that the life of the democratic unions was fleeting. Most universities established student unions between 1967 and 1968, but their crippling internal divisions, together with the repression, soon put paid to the movement.

By the time of the Cabinet reshuffle of October 1969, the regime basically regarded the university as a lost cause.[82] The campuses would explode once more in February 1975 with nationwide protests at the death in police custody of a student at the University of Valladolid. By then, higher education had reached an 'unbearable point'.[83] All attempts at 'channelling' student protest had failed, while repression had merely inflamed anti-Francoist sentiment. Clearly this was symptomatic of a wider failure, as it was painfully evident that the aspirations of many sectors of Spanish society could not be accommodated within the framework of the authoritarian regime.

## THE NEW WORKING-CLASS MOVEMENT

Like the students, the embryonic workers' movement of the 1950s pursued objectives already achieved by their Western European counterparts – namely, independent trade unions and collective bargaining – but were denied both by the dictatorship. The Spanish workers were brought a step closer to Western Europe by the Law on Collective Agreements of 1958, which formed part of the economic reform package of the late 1950s. Driven by the new demands of the international market, the regime wanted to ensure that its workers were sufficiently motivated. Wages would no longer be fixed by the ministries, but determined by a process of collective bargaining between the employers and the workers, though this would necessarily take place within the framework of the official union, the *Organización Sindical Española* or OSE (Spanish Syndical Organization). The fixed bonuses of the 1950s gave way to flexible ones that were linked to productivity, the new incentives amounting to one-half of wage packets. Small wonder, then, that by 1964 over three-quarters of the collective agreements contained productivity-linked clauses. By introducing a system of wage bargaining and by replacing the state with the employers as the workers' main interlocutor, the dictatorship transformed industrial relations – 'a new framework for the struggle', according to Marcelino Camacho, the dogged, white-haired leader of the Madrid metalworkers – though it continued to intervene, sometimes limiting wage rises, especially after 1965.[84] The new arrangement nonetheless endowed the workers with a leverage hitherto denied them, while fostering a much closer bond between union activists and rank-and-file workers. The unions were further strengthened by the vertiginous growth of the urban working class in the 1960s and by the emergence of a new generation of manual labourers, untrammelled by the ideological feuds of the 1930s. By 1965, for example, nearly two-thirds of Catalan workers had no memory of the Civil War. The working-class movement of the 1960s and 1970s therefore signalled a profound rupture with that of the 1930s not only in terms of its values and aspirations, but also in terms of the type of collective actions which it undertook. As Marcelino Camacho observed, this was 'a new working-class movement'.[85]

The first major test of the collective bargaining process took place in 1962 in the Asturian coalfields. The structural shortcomings of the mines (especially the poor quality of the coal and its inaccessibility, apart from the fact that coal was losing out to oil), the recession of 1959–60, and the resulting inflation combined to produce a highly conflictive situation, not least because the workers, the civil governor acknowledged, were 'ill-treated by the companies'.[86] The upshot was a strike that spread to all the principal industrial centres, contributing to the declaration of a two-year state of emergency throughout Spain in June 1962. In the case of Asturias, the OSE acknowledged internally that many miners 'live in terrible conditions, spread out amongst the mountains and farmsteads, far removed from the mines, and they have to get there by their own means, in awful conditions'.[87] Despite being heavily repressed, the strikes of 1962 – the most serious since the Civil War – marked the beginning of a new era, as they gave the lie to the Syndical Organization's 'social harmony' and Franco's fabled 'peace'. They also changed industrial relations, as the Law of Collective Disputes of September 1962, which distinguished between 'political' and 'economic' stoppages, constituted an implicit recognition of the right to strike over strictly labour matters. Worker agitation thereafter was to be a persistent and ever-growing feature of life under the dictatorship, while the new dynamic of collective bargaining would increasingly marginalize the OSE, much as the students were to do with the SEU.

Franco predictably viewed the strike movement of 1962 as 'directed and encouraged from the exterior' by Communists and Freemasons, especially the latter, who, he averred, were 'very interested in this strike conflict'.[88] A much more realistic assessment was provided by the Asturian civil governor, who reckoned that the PCE was not responsible for the 'paternity and direction of the work conflicts' but 'takes advantage of a climate of opposition and discomfort'.[89] The most remarkable feature of the new-found labour agitation was the prominent role played by the Catholic clergy and laity. The Catholics and the Communists, remarked the Madrid civil governor in 1964, 'shared the same objectives', the Guipúzcoa civil governor similarly observing that the apostolic associations of Specialized Catholic Action 'work with intensity and control a good part of the youth and mass of workers'.[90] Indeed, the labour movement of the 1960s would above all be the work of an 'alliance between Catholics and Communists that had no precedent in the history of modern Spain'.[91]

By far the most important channel for the workers' grievances was to be the *Comisiones Obreras* or CCOO (Workers' Commissions). One of the very first workers' commissions was formed in the Asturian coalmine of La Camocha by 'workers without affiliation, Communists, socialists, the priest and the Falangist mayor of the working-class neighbourhood of La Camocha'.[92] These commissions were fleeting bodies that were hastily cobbled together for a specific purpose – in the case of La Camocha to defend the workers' coal ration – before disbanding. In the 1960s these provisional commissions gave way to more structured and stable entities. The first to emerge was the Workers' Commission of the metalworkers of Madrid, which was elected by 600 workers in an assembly in September 1964 under the eagle-eyed supervision of the official state union. Consequently, the new commission contained not only Communists and Catholics, but also Falangists, for the OSE initially accepted the need for the commission as a natural outgrowth of the new bargaining process and as a means of channelling workers' grievances. By contrast, the first workers' commission in Barcelona, founded in November 1964, was a clandestine organization. The commissions were therefore at once legal and illegal, the ideal one juggling both activities. As the national leader of the Workers' Commissions from 1967, the pragmatic Marcelino Camacho, explains, 'the catacombs, clandestineness, were the death of the mass movement and for that reason it was necessary to combine in a flexible manner the legal struggle with the extra-legal struggle, that is, the illegal'.[93] By focusing on labour matters, the commissions managed to overcome the deep-seated divisions of the Civil War, bringing together Communists, Catholics, socialists, anarcho-syndicalists, and even Falangists in defence of the workers' interests. As a result, trade-union activists inside Spain were a long way ahead of those outside it, as the exiled leadership of both the UGT and the CNT condemned collaboration with the Communists. Thus the needs of the shop floor 'overrode the ideological divisions so cherished by some of the exiled leaders, living still in the political world of the Civil War'.[94]

## THE IMPACT OF ENTRYISM ON THE OFFICIAL UNION

In an attempt to divide the growing opposition and boost the Movement's support, the secretary-general of the Movement, José Solís, tried to entice the CNT into the vertical syndicate, a revival of the policy pursued in the late 1940s and 1950s. The two sides reached an agreement in November 1965 based on the so-called 'Five Points', according to which the anarcho-syndicalists would enter the state trade union in exchange for the latter's democratic autonomy, while the strike weapon would be replaced by 'another procedure'.[95] Once the conversations became public knowledge in April 1966, the agreement was discussed in Cabinet on 6 May 1966, Carrero Blanco and Alonso Vega denouncing it, along with the technocrats of Opus Dei, for putting at risk the regime's 'principles, its dynamism and its organization'.[96] By contrast, Solís defended the agreement on the grounds that it weakened the opposition while strengthening the official syndicates. Although Franco made clear his discrepancy, the arrangement remained intact. For the CNT, which approved the strategy at the National Meeting of the Regional Organizations in December 1965, this was a golden opportunity to leapfrog the Communists. Unlike the Communists, the anarcho-syndicalists sought to seize control of the syndicates rather than destroy them from within. In reality, the anarcho-syndicalists had been weaponized by the Movement. As one activist noted, the Falange responded to the entryism of Communists by seeking out 'people from the CNT to fight the Communists politically because they knew that the anarchists have always been anti-Communists'.[97] At the National Meeting of 1968 the CNT not only endorsed the policy of entryism, but also divided the movement into a 'legalist' section, which operated within the state syndicates, and a clandestine one. While all the positions on the National Commission of the 'legalist' branch were filled, no one wanted to become secretary-general of the clandestine branch, which remained vacant until 1975. Unquestionably this unholy alliance between the OSE and the CNT explains much about the decline and virtual disappearance of the anarcho-syndicalist movement.

The impact of the very different entryism of the Workers' Commissions was demonstrated by the OSE elections of 1966. These formed part of Solís' ambitious plan to raise the political profile of the Movement by means of a controlled mobilization of the masses, as had been attempted with the launching of the family associations in 1963. Like the Workers' Commissions, the OSE aimed to secure the support of a new generation of workers. The elections were remarkable for appearing to offer the workers a choice between competing candidatures. To support the official slate, Solís – 'the Smiling Face of the Regime' – appeared on television on 23 September 1966, urging the workers to resolve their grievances 'in a brotherly fashion, in open dialogue, freely, like Christians'.[98] 'We look,' he professed, 'not so much to a man's past, as his future, accommodating within the unions all those who dream of a better, juster Spain, and with an even better syndicalism.'[99] In the same apparently liberal spirit, the OSE campaign adopted the slogan of 'vote for the best', while reassuring the workers in Big Brotherly terms that 'our democracy does not discriminate on grounds of sex, race, religious belief or political creed'.[100] In reality, the election was a major gamble for the Movement, which accordingly did everything possible to ensure that its candidates were 'the best', a police report revealing that the syndicate aimed to 'give the impression' that the elections were to be held 'in the most democratic manner', while 'making the greatest possible effort' to ensure that the Workers' Commissions were 'defeated'.[101]

Despite the Movement's behind-the-scenes machinations, the Workers' Commissions won an unexpected number of positions, if still a minority. In the large-scale factories of Barcelona the Commissions' slate 'swept the board', while an official report related that in Vizcaya they 'came first', in Asturias they were 'decisive', and in the Madrid metallurgical industry they 'have triumphed completely'.[102] For Marcelino Camacho, this was 'an important victory'.[103] Undoubtedly the results were a vindication of the CCOO's strategy of entryism, which set alarm bells ringing within the corridors of power. A police report expressed the fear that this was the 'first step in a total transformation of the unions', which might eventually convert them into an 'efficient and powerful institution opposed to the regime', as the fate of the SEU had already demonstrated.[104] Similarly, a report of the Presidency, Franco's governmental department, concluded that the aim of the Workers' Commissions and the Communist Party was to 'eliminate from within the political leaders of the [official] unions and democratize them'.[105] As the civil governor of Asturias pointed out in a report of May 1967, the CCOO, often in 'close collaboration' with the HOAC and JOC, 'represent the broadest and most dangerous platform of the opposition to the regime', especially as they were linked to 'the so-called Democratic Unions of Students', while receiving financial backing from Communist and non-Communist organizations abroad.[106] By this means, the official syndicate faced the terrifying prospect of becoming 'the bastion that is legally deployed to overthrow the Spanish political system'.[107]

Predictably, the regime hurriedly strove to rectify the OSE's massive miscalculation in holding the relatively free elections of 1966 by means of a wide-ranging crackdown on the Workers' Commissions. Over the next year thousands of activists were arrested, or fired, or had their credentials as union delegates or shop stewards revoked by the OSE. This major setback for the CCOO was exacerbated by the economic crisis of 1967, which led to a year-long wage freeze from November and the suspension of all collective negotiations. The Barcelona Commission noted despondently that 'things have changed. The employers and the government have brutally stepped up their respective policies with the intention of snatching our victories from us, and of separating the leaders and the vanguard from the masses.'[108] Thus the workers' offensive of 1962 to 1966 gave way to the dictatorial onslaught of 1967 to 1969, as the Commissions retreated into clandestinity, or, as one activist recalls, a 'den of intrigue'.[109] Hardly surprisingly, the 1969 union elections were cancelled. The aim of the repression, noted Marcelino Camacho, was to 'force us to adopt a clandestine existence, go into exile, or, naturally, abandon the struggle'.[110]

## THE IMPLOSION OF
## THE REGIME'S LABOUR POLICY

Despite this repression, the turn of the decade saw a huge upsurge in labour militancy as a result of collective bargaining, the 491 strikes of 1969 being dwarfed by the 1,595 stoppages of 1970.[111] Following a drop to 616 in 1971, the number of strikes continued to rise year after year, from 835 in 1972 to 931 in 1973, 2,290 in 1974, and 3,156 in 1975. The biggest change of all took place in the building sector, skyrocketing from fewer than twenty disputes a year to nearly 500 in 1970. Thereafter, the building trade constituted the greatest source of labour protest under the dictatorship with the sole exception of the engineering industry. Another major shift was the mounting protest of white-collar workers, a class segment that had grown exponentially as a result of the huge expansion in the tertiary sector. Spearheaded by bank employees, the strikes spread from 1971 to other services, such as health, insurance, and telephone operatives. There were also protests among teachers, lawyers, and civil servants.

The rise in labour protest within Spain reflected a wider pattern of militancy within Western Europe. The economic boom of the 1950s and 1960s had reinvigorated trade-union movements throughout Western Europe, which then reacted resolutely to the inflation that assailed working-class living standards in the late 1960s. For example, the Italian trade unions were very weak in the 1950s, with only 10–15 per cent of the workforce being affiliated, but after 1962 there was an upsurge in labour militancy that culminated in the 'Hot Autumn' of 1969. Similarly, in France, following the torpor of the early years of the Fifth Republic, worker protest built up to the general strike of May 1968. The breach between Franco's Spain and democratic Western Europe nonetheless remained cavernous, as Spanish workers were denied independent unions and subjected to state surveillance and repression. From this perspective the Spanish experience was closer to Portugal under Salazar or Greece under the Junta of 1967–74.

The Franco dictatorship's efforts at channelling the workers' protest, whether through modification of the Penal Code in 1965, the passing of the Syndical Law in 1971, or the strike decree of May 1975, were too little and too late. Indeed, every single one of these timorous changes signalled the triumph of the regime *ultras* or hardliners over the reformists. Overwhelmed by the ever-rising tide of protest, the regime's instinctive response was to resort to repression, especially once Carrero Blanco took effective control of the government in October 1969. Thus a building strike in Granada in 1970 left three workers dead and numerous injured, while a stoppage of 1972 in El Ferrol resulted in two deaths. As Carrero Blanco told the National Council of the Movement in March 1972, 'one has to finish with the strikes completely', or, as a circular of the Ministry of Labour put it, labour conflict 'is always a problem of public order'.[112] One of the most damaging disputes for the dictatorship was the SEAT automobile strike of October 1971 in Barcelona. The SEAT plant was not just the largest in the country, but also the regime's much-vaunted showcase for industrial relations. Founded in 1949, the state-owned company, run by the military and supplied by FIAT, had launched the Mini-like SEAT 600 in 1957, which swiftly became the prize symbol of Spain's 'economic miracle'. The factory occupation of October 1971 was provoked by the sacking of dozens of activists and led to a thirteen-hour pitched battle with the police, who killed one worker and injured many others. The company's failure not only to maintain order, but, more importantly, to reach a collective agreement, greatly tarnished its image and by extension that of the regime. In an effort to limit the damage, the firm's headquarters was transferred from Madrid to Barcelona and the first civilian managing director appointed. No longer a paradigm of industrial relations, SEAT now became a 'model of militancy for the opposition'.[113]

The dictatorship's dull-headed approach to labour disputes not only exacerbated the divisions within the regime, but also further fuelled the resentment of the workers, which in turn boosted the Workers' Commissions. In Catalonia, the police viewed the town of Terrassa as the main focus of 'social rebellion' due to the activities of 'Catholic workers and Communists included within the so-called "Workers'

Commissions", the promoter of numerous demonstrations and gatherings'.[114] Not even the arrest of the Commissions' national coordinating committee in Pozuelo de Alarcón just outside Madrid in June 1972 would quell the ever-rising protest of the workers, the number of strikes climbing to over 2,000 in 1974 and beyond 3,000 in 1975, one of the most expansive strike waves in Europe. The profoundly counterproductive nature of the repression was highlighted in a police report of January 1974: on the one hand, 'never as in recent times was governmental action against the clandestine groups so resolute', but, on the other, the protest kept escalating 'in an alarming fashion'.[115] A sign of the times was the general strike in Baix Llobregat (Catalonia) in July 1974. Not only was the dispute backed by workers of all industries and much of the community, but it was also organized from within the local state syndicate. In other words, the official union in Baix Llobregat no longer served the interests of the Francoist state, but those of the workers themselves. By the early 1970s many employers preferred to negotiate directly with the clandestine unions rather go through the official unions, regarded as increasingly irrelevant. Indeed, in a survey of 1973, 74 per cent of employers defended the establishment of independent trade unions, while only 19 per cent were opposed. Clearly the aspirations not only of many workers, but also of a growing number of entrepreneurs, were at odds with those of the authoritarian regime.

The death-knell of the official syndicates was sounded in the union elections of the spring of 1975. A broad anti-official slate, the Unitary Democratic Candidatures, won a clamorous victory. The results were a thorough vindication of the Commissions' pragmatic policy of mixing clandestine organization and propaganda with entryism, as the infiltration of the official syndicate furnished activists with a degree of legal protection while providing access to the bureaucratic structures that governed arbitration, collective bargaining, and litigation, all of which were of crucial importance. By contrast, the UGT and the clandestine branch of the CNT, both of which rejected entryism, counted for little amongst the workers.

Labour protest nonetheless remained highly fragmented and uneven. The causes of unrest varied according to the industry, and even within an industry; there was not one labour movement but many, as reflected in the overwhelmingly local, sectorial, or regional nature of strikes, while mobilizing workers in favour of political anti-Francoism was far from straightforward. Conventional accounts tend to focus overwhelmingly on the areas of conflict, but much of Spain experienced scant worker protest. In many regions, including Aragón, the Canary Islands, Extremadura, the two Castiles, Galicia, and much of Andalusia, there was little labour agitation in the 1960s and early 1970s. As late as 1972 the civil governor in Almería in Andalusia reported that the province was characterized by 'general political abstention and passivity', in the province of Cuenca 'complete normality' prevailed, while the civil governor in Jaén province claimed that 'absolute normality' predominated except for a handful of disputes in Linares. As late as 1970 the dictatorship was still not challenged 'by the majority of Spanish society'.[116]

## CATHOLIC DISSENT

The greatest paradox of the rising opposition to the dictatorship was the widespread involvement of Catholics. In reality, civil society was restructured under the regime not just by the trade unions, student groups, and neighbourhood and other associations, but also by nonconformist Catholic groups and individuals, both lay and clerical, who challenged the status quo by championing social justice, seeking an accommodation with Marxism, and providing a training ground for activists in the student, worker, women's and other movements, as well as by constituting a substantial source of protest in their own right. At the forefront of the shift in Catholic attitudes was *Acción Católica Especializada* or ACE (Specialized Catholic Action), founded in the aftermath of the Second World War as an outgrowth of the nascent National-Catholic state. The ACE comprised the *Hermandades Obreras de Acción Católica* or HOAC (Workers' Brotherhoods of Catholic Action), which focused on the organization of workers, the *Juventud Obrera Católica* or JOC (Catholic Worker Youth), centred on young workers, and the *Juventud Estudiante Católica* or JEC (Catholic Student Youth), which dealt with students, both in secondary schools and at the universities. These apostolic associations of the ACE enjoyed considerable autonomy under the dictatorship, partly because of the nature of the pact between the Church and state, partly because they were fiercely protected by Archbishop Enrique Plá y Deniel and partly because of the way they were organized. Within the ACE the top-down ecclesiastical control of the past largely gave way to the bottom-up activism of the workers and students themselves, the result being that the associations were much more radical than any traditional Catholic bodies. Meanwhile, the outlook of the ACE's clerical cadres was transformed by their interaction with the workers and students, by the abysmal working and living conditions of the 1940s and 1950s, and by the hard-line repression of the state.

The unprecedented radicalism of the ACE within Catholic circles also sprang from its transnationalism, as the individual associations all belonged to worldwide apostolic movements which furnished the Spanish branches not only with material support, but also with ideas, values, and strategies that were often at variance with those of the Spanish ecclesiastical hierarchy. Another transnational influence during the 1950s was the new tendencies in post-war European theology, especially those emanating from Belgium, France, and West Germany, which were given expression in Spain by the 'National Catholic Conversations'. The ACE in the 1940s and 1950s provided the workers and students with the only relatively free space for debate and organization. While the Movement's vertical syndicates strove to regiment the workers, the HOAC and JOC sought to enable them. Whereas the Movement's student union aimed to imbue its members with its doctrinaire line, the JEC engaged in debate and discussion with clandestine groups.

The upshot was that the apostolic associations developed a momentum all of their own, the HOAC and JOC becoming advocates of the right to strike, press freedom, and even workers' control of industry, which converted them into antagonists of the official syndicates under the Movement. Both the HOAC and the JOC not only backed the strikes of 1951, 1956, and 1958, but also collaborated in the foundation of a host of clandestine unions, including the *Federación Sindical de Trabajadores* or FST (Syndical Federation of Workers), and the *Unión Sindical Obrera* or USO (Syndical Worker Union), the latter being a product of the JOC congress of 1960, which was attended by over 10,000 delegates.

Change within Spanish Catholicism was enormously accelerated by the Second Vatican Council of 1962 to 1965. In an extraordinary attempt to meet the challenges of the modern world, the Council turned the Catholic world upside down. Relations within the Church were transformed by introducing the 'apostolate of the laity', ending the clergy's monopoly on the liturgy, and framing the Church not as the exclusive domain of the clergy, but as that of all believers, 'the people of God'. These far-reaching changes empowered both the clergy and the laity at the expense of the traditional structures and hierarchy. Relations without the Church were radically realigned by a new lexicon of social justice and human rights, a rethinking of the Catholic community that made it compatible with democracy, and by reaching out to other faiths and philosophies, above all Marxism (which gave rise to a combative theological fusion, Liberation Theology). The most radical form of evangelization was that of the worker-priests, banned by Pope Pius XII in 1954, but legalized in 1965 by the Second Vatican Council. More than any other group within Catholicism, the worker-priests demonstrated how to empower the rank-and-file clergy and how to eliminate the barriers between the clergy and the laity. Accordingly, the Church became a champion of the poor and the underprivileged, in both the developing and developed worlds.

In Spain, the Second Vatican Council mobilized Catholics, both lay and clerical, on a scale that dwarfed the activism of the 1940s and 1950s. They became heavily involved in the clandestine trade unions, illegal student groups, neighbourhood associations, and regional nationalist movements, helping to rebuild the civil society that had been crushed by the dictatorship. Not only did Catholic activists establish two trade union movements in the 1960s, but they were also in the vanguard of the main anti-Francoist force, the Workers' Commissions. Having co-founded the Commissions, Catholics played a major role within the organization in the Basque Country, Catalonia, and Madrid in the 1960s, and remained a 'significant' presence at the national level into the 1970s.[117] A Catholic also founded the second biggest student union of the 1960s, the *Frente de Liberación Popular* or FLP (Popular Liberation Front), popularly known as the 'Felipe'. Catholics were involved, too, in the neighbourhood associations.

A worker-priest, Pedro Requena, who was based in the town of Getafe to the south of Madrid, recalls that the local neighbourhood association 'operated from our premises or from our own house ... Anything that boosted the civil fabric, whether neighbourly, trade unionist or political, had to be supported.'[118] José Molina, a Catholic in the Maoist *Organización Revolucionaria de Trabajadores* or ORT (Revolutionary Organization of Workers), helped set up the first neighbourhood association in the working-class area of Vallecas in Madrid. The collaboration of the Church was 'fundamental' because 'it gave us legal cover, because it lent us the churches, because it provided resources'.[119]

Left-wing priests encouraged parishioners to speak out and ask questions, something that neither the educational system nor the Church itself did. Some organized popular assemblies, an overtly subversive act given that even small gatherings required a special permit. Mariano Gamo, a charismatic and courageous worker-priest in the working-class district of Moratalaz in Madrid, held an assembly every Sunday after the main Mass was over. These assemblies, he relates, were 'open to everyone', whether believers or non-believers, and they would 'try to tackle all problems, absolutely all', which ranged from the collapse of a local housing scheme and the celibacy of the clergy to the Soviet invasion of Czechoslovakia in 1968.[120] Even though the assemblies were an unequivocal challenge to the dictatorial order, the police were reluctant to act against them, underscoring the relative autonomy of the Church under Franco. Still, when the assembly discussed the significance of Labour Day in April 1968, the parish church was surrounded by the police, but the assistant bishop then intervened, leading the participants out 'from the front'.[121] The onlookers burst into applause, the priest recalling that 'never have I seen such spontaneous and generous public applause for the bishop'.[122]

The comparatively high number of worker-priests in Spain was inspired partly by the Council, partly by the insalubrious working conditions in many industries, and partly by the patently inadequate infrastructure of many working-class neighbourhoods, a result of the rapid urban expansion of the 1960s. When the priest Pedro Solabarría arrived at the Basque industrial town of Baracaldo in the 1960s, he found:

... a very poor neighbourhood, without water, without electricity, without bathrooms, without roads. The majority of the population were immigrants from the south. All very poor miners. Really hard jobs. There was no postman and no doctor because of the lack of roads. There was only one telephone for 600 people, in a bar. The school was Third-World and without a teacher because of illness. Muddy roads full of puddles.[123]

He took the decision to become a worker-priest, ripping off his cassock before the astonished workers on his first day of manual labour, and remaining one for the next thirty years. Like the workers themselves, worker-priests defended the right to strike, form independent trade unions, and hold mass gatherings of workers, thereby fomenting the egalitarian ideals and participatory practices that informed the construction of social citizenship. Mariano Gamo, the worker-priest from Moratalaz, even put a sign over the entrance to his church that read 'The House of the People of God', which was not only a reference to the Vatican Council's vision of the Church as 'the people of God', but also a subversive nod to the *Casa del Pueblo* ('House of the People'), the name given to a local branch of the socialist movement before the dictatorship.[124] The same priest composed a catechismal song to the music of 'The Internationale', which captured the spirit of the Council:

> Poor of the World
> Join in Fellowship
> Make the Earth the Kingdom of the Lord
> Make the Earth the Kingdom of Love[125]

Gamo was eventually arrested for his activities in 1969 and imprisoned for three years in a jail in Zamora that had been specially created for dissident clergy the year before.

By the 1960s, women within the apostolic associations of the ACE were replacing the discourse of the 1940s and 1950s of 'women for the family' with 'women for society', as members of the Female Catholic Worker Youth and the Female Worker Sisterhood of Catholic Action became involved in the labour struggle and the neighbourhood associations. As early as 1960, Catholic women were being elected as union delegates in accordance with the opposition strategy of entryism, and in 1962 and 1966 they were involved in strikes in Asturias and the Basque Country respectively. They were also active in the neighbourhood associations, the emigrant community, and consumer cooperatives. For Catholic women, a 'new female model' therefore emerged in the 1960s, which, through their experiences in the workplace and neighbourhood associations, evolved in the late 1960s and 1970s into a discourse of 'women for themselves'.[126]

Catholic activism in the rural areas was much more limited, due to the greater control exercised there by the authorities, but efforts were made nonetheless to revive civil society. One example is the *Movimiento Rural de Adultos* or MRA (Rural Adult Movement) in the province of Albacete, which was designed to educate the populace in the countryside in the teachings of the Second Vatican Council. Training centres and schools were set up with the goal of introducing the workers, both male and female, to ideas, values, and practices that contested those of the dictatorship. For example, Popular Culture Courses were run for women by Christian base communities, aiming to 'open the mind and the heart to the world beyond the house and the family'.[127] At covert meetings of the MRA, according to a Civil Guard report, the priests questioned 'the authorities, the official norms, laws and orders, and the regime, in an effort to illuminate the ignorant'.[128] An agricultural cooperative run by priests and Communist activists established a 'dense local network of cultural and social services, while at the same time channelling the most heartfelt social claims of the residents, thereby contributing to a broad anti-Francoist politicization'.[129] Consequently, Catholics in the countryside, like those in the city, strove to rebuild civil society from the bottom up.

## THE BACKLASH OF THE HIERARCHY

Following the death of Archbishop Plá y Deniel in 1968, the long-standing tensions between the ACE and the ecclesiastical hierarchy finally came to a head. Leonardo Aragón, who was European and then worldwide President of the JEC, recalls that in 1967 the bishops at the head of Catholic Action deprived the JEC of:

... any judicial status. The Church ceased to recognize us. But we carried on. We would meet where we could. The situation, as a result, was a much more difficult one, but this occurred in Madrid and at the national level. The JEC practically exploded, disappeared, because they wouldn't accept the type of approach that we had.[130]

In the late 1960s the ACE was not only purged by the ecclesiastical hierarchy, but numerous activists decided to abandon the Church altogether, many joining the secular opposition. Even so, the hierarchy was unable to stem the anti-Francoist tide within the Church, an in-house survey of 1967–70 revealing that half the priests under thirty considered themselves socialist. Clearly the nonconformist currents within the Church had done much to erode the very foundations of the alliance between Church and state that had served both so well since 1939. In September 1971 an unprecedented Joint Assembly was held between the clergy and the bishops, the first time the Church had publicly questioned its relationship with the dictatorship. Two years later the Church finally broke with the regime, its statement 'On the Church and the Community' affirming the right 'of the political community to determine its own constitutional system'.[131] The Catholic Church had been transformed from the guardian angel of the regime to its avowed enemy, a colossal – if belated – blow to the regime, as Catholicism had been the dictatorship's principal source of social and cultural legitimation for over three decades.

The achievement of Catholic activism in Spain is all the more remarkable when placed in relation to that of religious dissidents under the Communist dictatorships of Eastern Europe. Activism under regimes such as those of the USSR and Czechoslovakia was next to impossible during the 1950s and 1960s due to the remorseless repression of the state, while other Churches, such as those of Poland, Hungary, and Yugoslavia, were inclined to quell internal dissent in order to establish a modus vivendi with the Communist regime. Consequently, the quest for a more just society often took a spiritual rather than a political turn. In Hungary, for example, religious radicals registered their protest by underscoring their links with pre-Communist entities, such as the *Regnum Marianum* community, which was devoted to 'youth education and an everyday spirituality'.[132] Even this was banned in 1951 and many of its activists were put on trial in 1961, 1965, and 1971. The far greater autonomy of the Spanish Church therefore allowed its dissidents to achieve far more than their Eastern European counterparts, with the notable exception of the Polish Church in the 1980s.

In overall terms, the opposition of the clergy, workers, students, and association activists was too fragmented and too weak to bring about the regime's fall, especially as it was not backed up by the political parties, the only one with any kind of meaningful organizational presence inside Spain being the PCE. The party void made it difficult to coordinate the disparate forces of anti-Francoism and present a coherent and credible alternative to the authoritarian regime. Nonetheless, the opposition did much to erode the legitimacy of the dictatorship and provide tangible proof that it was widely unpopular. The knock-on effect was the mounting conviction within Spanish society that regime change was inevitable.

## THE RESURGENCE OF REGIONAL NATIONALISM

During the late 1960s and 1970s another opposition force came into its own: Basque nationalism. If Catalan nationalism had been the prime source of regional agitation before the Civil War, it was Basque nationalism that presented the state with its greatest challenge thereafter, though Catalanism remained a powerful cultural presence. The rise of Basque nationalism can be traced to the foundation of *Euzkadi Ta Askatasuna* or ETA (Basque Homeland and Freedom) in July 1959 by young Basques who were frustrated at the passivity of the Basque Nationalist Party in the struggle against the dictatorship. ETA's first violent action (the attempted derailment of a train) took place in July 1961, its first robbery in September 1965, and its first major ideological work, Federico Krutwig's *Vasconia: Estudio dialéctico de una nacionalidad*, was published in 1963. Krutwig, heavily influenced by the French colonial war in Algeria, viewed the fight against the Spanish state as 'a movement of national liberation' against 'the yoke of colonialism', which was 'by definition, a revolutionary ideal'.[133] His political philosophy guided ETA's Fifth Assembly of March 1967, which defined the organization as a 'Basque socialist movement of national liberation', and framed the armed struggle within the Marxist-Leninist tradition.

ETA's first victim was the Civil Guard José Pardines, gunned down at a roadblock on 7 June 1968, followed by the assassination of the police commissioner and notorious torturer Melitón Manzanas on 2 August 1968. The murder of Manzanas had far-reaching repercussions. A state of exception was declared for Guipúzcoa on 2 August, which remained in place until late March 1969. Following Manzanas' death, around 600 Basques were arrested, of whom sixteen were charged in relation to his assassination. The trial took place at a military court in Burgos between 3 and 9 December 1970 in a climate of extreme political tension, as strikes and other protests erupted throughout Spain. A three-month state of exception for the province of Guipúzcoa was declared on 4 December and then extended to the entire country on 14 December. It lasted for six months and saw a total of 1,221 people arrested.

The dictatorship regarded the Burgos trial as an opportunity to showcase its uncompromising defence of national unity, but this stratagem backfired spectacularly, above all because the trial was open to the press, both national and international. The defence lawyers highlighted the use of torture, the flagrant abuses of the military judiciary, and the feebleness of the condemnatory evidence, all of which was highlighted by the international media, as well as the protests, stoppages, and other demonstrations that accompanied the trial. A further setback was the kidnapping of the West German honorary consul in San Sebastián, Eugen Biehl, by ETA on 2 December, which brought even greater pressure to bear on the regime. Of the Burgos 'sixteen', one was acquitted, six were condemned to death, and the other nine were sentenced to 341 years in prison. Both the Vatican and the Catholic hierarchy in Spain pleaded for clemency, and on 24 December Biehl was released unharmed. Franco duly responded on 30 December by commuting the death sentences to thirty years in prison, but it was the dictatorship, not ETA, that had been roundly condemned by international opinion, the trial being a public relations disaster from which the regime would never recover.

ETA itself emerged from the Burgos trial 'confused, broken, and disorganized', though its image had been greatly boosted in the Basque

Country, especially amongst the young.[134] The organization reasserted itself in January 1972 by kidnapping the Basque businessman Lorenzo Zabala after he had fired 154 strikers over a disputed wage claim. This was a new departure for ETA, as it was the first time it had kidnapped someone over a labour conflict (designed to show the workers that the group would protect them in their struggle against capitalism) and the first time it had taken punitive action against a fellow Basque. The success of the kidnapping (the workers were reinstated while Zabala was released) also signalled the ascendancy of a new generation of leaders, who would control the organization into the 1980s. Inspired by the armed insurgency of the Tupamaros in Uruguay and the Palestinian Black September group (which killed six Israeli athletes at the 1972 Olympic Games in Munich), ETA began to cultivate its international links by signing a joint communiqué in February 1972 with the Kurdish Democratic Party and the Palestinian Fatah group, and another with the IRA and the Breton Liberation Front three months later.

On 16 January 1973, ETA carried out its most daring action to date, the kidnapping of the Navarrese businessman Felipe Huarte after he had dismissed striking workers at a plant in Pamplona, part of the extensive commercial and industrial holdings of the Huarte family. This time ETA demanded not only the readmission of the striking workers, but also a $800,000 ransom, which it secured before releasing Huarte on 26 January. The sheer audacity of the Huarte kidnapping was surpassed on 20 December when an ETA commando blew up the car of the prime minister, Admiral Luis Carrero Blanco. 'The intensity of the explosion,' in the words of the police report, 'was such that the heavy Dodge flew up into the air, crashed against the cornice of the Jesuits' building, flew over the roof, and landed on the second-floor terrace that faces the patio.'[135] 'Operation Ogre' was undoubtedly ETA's most acclaimed action, as Carrero Blanco's assassination was widely interpreted by the opposition as making the post-Franco transition from dictatorship to democracy possible. Still, this was not ETA's goal. On the contrary, the armed struggle was designed to advance the cause of Basque independence – not Spanish democracy – by forcing the state to the negotiating table. Having killed just three people in 1973, the organization, which split into ETA (p-m) (political-military) and ETA (m) (military) in November 1974, accounted for fourteen lives in 1974 and another sixteen in 1975.[136]

## ANTI-FASCISM AS INSPIRATION

Only a minority of the opposition groups of the 1960s and 1970s were inspired by the anti-fascist struggle of the Civil War. This was partly because of the lack of political continuity (nearly all the parties and trade unions of the 1930s had either been crushed or exiled), and partly because little was known about the Civil War, as a result of censorship, distrust of the official narrative, the lack of alternative accounts, and the self-censorship that families exercised as a protective measure. Another reason was that by the 1960s a major generational shift had taken place within the opposition. Francisco Pereña of the Popular Liberation Front recalled that 'the Civil War always seemed to me to have been in the Middle Ages'.[137] The most important single reason was that the Civil War was a paradigm of defeat. For Juan Aranzadi, who helped found the Maoist Revolutionary Organization of Workers or ORT, 'the memory of the Civil War and the memory of the political parties in the Civil War and the anti-fascist struggle was, in reality, a memory, or historiographical knowledge, [but] it held very, very little interest'.[138] A parallel can be drawn here with Greece. The Greek left tended to seek inspiration in the uplifting story of the ultimately successful resistance to the Nazi occupation of 1943–5 rather than in the Civil War of 1946–9, which, like the Spanish case, resulted in defeat.

There were nonetheless groups in Spain that *were* inspired by the Civil War, above all those which embraced the 'armed struggle'. The *Frente Revolucionario Antifascista y Patriota* or FRAP (Revolutionary Anti-Fascist and Patriotic Front) – as its name indicates – was inspired by the idea that the anti-fascist fight of the 1930s still continued. Established in 1973, the FRAP aimed to overthrow the dictatorship through violence and establish a revolutionary socialist regime, rejecting the policy of national reconciliation preached by the Communists, on the grounds that 'reconciliation with a regime that after thirty odd years still practises the same fascist behaviour that gave rise to the war is really absurd'.[139] There was even generational continuity with the 1930s, as the honorary president of the FRAP was none other than Julio Álvarez del Vayo, foreign secretary of the Republic during the Civil War. Another far-left group that identified with the anti-fascism of the 1930s was the Catalan *Movimiento Ibérico de Liberación* or MIL (Iberian Movement of Liberation), portrayed in the film *Salvador* (2006) about the life and death of MIL activist Salvador Puig Antich. The militants of the MIL regarded themselves as the heirs of the *maquis*, the 'anti-fascist' guerrilla fighters who had needled the dictatorship for over two decades after the Civil War. At the time the MIL was founded in 1970, recalls one member, 'seven years before they had killed the last maquis. We considered ourselves *maquis*. We had the arms of Sabaté, of Quico Sabaté, the most famous of the Catalan *maquis*. All these arms that we had at the end were from the *maquis* of the Civil War.'[140]

Anti-fascism was nonetheless increasingly displaced by, or combined with, the anti-imperialist politics of the 1960s, the chief source of inspiration being the revolutionary struggles in Algeria, Cuba, Vietnam, and Latin America. This new mode of anti-imperialism or 'Third Worldism' was first adopted in Spain as a response to the 'western imperialism' allegedly exercised by the United States during the Cold War.[141] Francisca Sauquillo, a founder member of the Maoist ORT, relates that 'we understood that the problems of Spain came from the support which it gave to the United States'.[142] This anti-Americanism was placed within a wider context, the Popular Liberation Front being modelled on the 'liberation fronts' which, recalls founder member José Ramón Recalde, had been created 'to fight against the colonial powers'.[143] For the Popular Liberation Front, the model of revolutionary socialism was Cuba, the activist José María Mohedano Fuertes stressing that 'the country that was closest to our utopia was Cuba. What a great mistake ... But yes, it was our dream, our utopia.'[144] By contrast, ETA was motivated by the idea that the Basque Country was a colony not of the United States, but of Spain, as first contended in Krutwig's *Vasconia*. Although the 'Third World' current within ETA had been overthrown by 1970, the colonial paradigm remained central to its thinking.

Some Marxist groups turned to the developing world out of disillusion with the Soviet Union. For Juan Aranzadi and other members of the Maoist ORT, Communist China was the paradigm of revolutionary socialism because this was 'the place where there had been a revolution within the revolution and which had maintained the purity of the revolution'.[145] It was not just that China appeared to offer an untainted form of Marxism, but also that China, as the ORT's secretary-general, José Sanroma, underlines, 'supported the revolutionary movements in the Third World'.[146] Anti-imperialism also appealed because of its internationalism: militants in Spain viewed their struggle as part of a much wider 'anti-imperialist front'.[147] For Sanroma, the ORT was integrated into a 'world revolutionary process', while Manuel Garí of the Popular Liberation Front avers that 'at a global level, I felt part of an anti-imperialist front'.[148]

There was, too, an important transnational dimension to the struggle within Spain. The anti-fascist MIL travelled to France, Belgium, and Italy to collect arms from fellow anarchists. The ORT secretary-general, José Sanroma, took three trips to China between 1975 and 1979, though the interest of the Chinese was disappointedly limited to the establishment of 'a company to enable commerce between the two countries'.[149] The Popular Liberation Front had contacts with 'Cuba, with Algeria, and with Yugoslavia,' recalls José Luis de Zárraga. 'In fact,' he remarks, 'a substantial part of the leaders of the Popular Liberation Front II [1960–62] were trained in Yugoslavia.'[150] Having met Che Guevara in Algeria, the group also secured money and propaganda from the Cubans, though it had hoped for arms. Consequently, anti-imperialism linked the struggles of radicals in Spain with those of the 'Third World' and fostered 'a shared revolutionary outlook that could bind radicals together in both real and imagined forms of solidarity across Europe'.[151]

## THE CULTURAL BATTLE

The rise of opposition movements was paralleled by the emergence across Spain of new aspirations, ideas, and values that increasingly rubbed up against those of the regime. A key catalyst of this process was mass tourism, which brought Spaniards into contact with affluent Northern European workers, who influenced local social and moral values – the bikini had become more or less accepted by the late 1950s – rather than political ones. Emigration to countries such as France, Germany, and Switzerland also altered the mentality of Spaniards by introducing them to different lifestyles, social environments, and political cultures, as well as exposing them to the anti-Francoist opposition (Workers' Commissions, for example, made a concerted effort to reach out to emigrant Spanish workers). The freedom with which Spanish workers abroad could travel back and forth (in contrast, say, to the Greeks or Yugoslavs) ensured that they made a deep impression on their compatriots, the police reporting that the emigrants 'talk of grand things, of fabulous wages. Some have brought [*sic*] their own cars, and ridicule the wages in Spain, dazzling their listeners with imaginary grandeurs. All this is stirring up discontent among the local working class who feel inferior as a result. Insults have even been proffered against the regime and the Unions.'[152] Growing access to the press, radio, cinema, and the dominant medium of television all enhanced awareness of new attitudes and values. Shoddily built estates also stimulated higher expectations by mobilizing local residents in defence of neighbourhood improvement, while the ambitions of many young people were changed by greater educational opportunities in higher education. The spread of new ideas is illustrated by the extent to which Marxism permeated the thought of students, workers, artists, intellectuals, and progressive sectors of the clergy. In short, the sweeping social and economic changes of the late Franco regime profoundly shaped the mentality of Spaniards, wrecking the dictatorship's founding ambition of a depoliticized and deferential society.

Some scholars maintain that by the mid-1950s the dictatorship had lost 'the battle of culture' to a resurgent liberalism, the regime culture having been reduced to a mere 'subculture of the masses' and a 'culture of evasion' that served to 'disguise in some way the failure of its own official culture'.[153] The idea that the dictatorship struggled to stem the rising tide of liberalism by resorting to a mixture of censorship and an 'escapist, evasive subculture' has, nonetheless, been contested as 'scarcely consistent with the capacity for survival of the regime'.[154] After all, the regime still controlled cinema, radio, the press, publishing, and television (launched in 1956), as well as being able to draw on the redoubtable cultural resources of both the Movement and the Catholic Church, which controlled access to myriad grants, subsidies, radio stations, press outlets, and publishers. In reality, the dictatorship never gave up on 'the battle of culture'.

Central to this 'battle' was a shift in the early 1960s in the dictatorship's legitimizing discourse, which was based not so much on its origins – victory in the Civil War – as on its governance or the benefits of 'Franco's Peace', principally modernization. In other words, the regime's legitimacy now rested mainly on its management of the economy rather than its victory in the war, in particular its ability to meet people's material and consumer needs. In this fashion, the new discourse complemented the demands of an increasingly affluent society for more entertainment and leisure, which were especially acute after twenty years of extreme hardship. Taking advantage of its monopoly on newsreels and television, as well as its control of the press, radio, cinema, theatre, and publishing, the dictatorship transmitted a modernizing message of 'peace' and prosperity. This shift in narrative was personified by Franco himself, whose uniformed harangues of the 1940s and 1950s before huge partisan crowds faded to a besuited, becalmed figure, often wearing a trilby, who could be seen inaugurating airports, factories, and reservoirs. The new legitimizing discourse was inherently less ideological and more accommodating than the old one, as it looked to a future of universal well-being rather than a past of fratricidal conflict, though of course the old Civil War narrative reared its head for the anniversary celebrations, such as 1 April (Victory Day), 18 July (Day of the Uprising), and 1 October (*Caudillo*'s Day). The dictatorship nonetheless strove to safeguard its legitimacy by satisfying the material and cultural demands of a mass consumer society. From this perspective, the 'escapist, evasive' mass culture of the dictatorship was a tremendous success, as shown by the popularity of the films of Pedro Lazaga (such as *La ciudad no es para mí* (1965) or *Sor Citroen* (1967)), the light comedies of Alfonso Paso (which were running simultaneously in up to seven theatres in Madrid in the late 1960s), or the radio soaps of Guillermo Sautier Casaseca, which ran from the 1950s to the 1970s. The fact that the popular culture under Franco is often scorned today does not diminish its historical importance. The greatest sporting achievement was in football, above all that of Real Madrid, which won five European Cups between 1956 and 1960 and became a triumphant icon of Franco's Spain, though paradoxically its two best players,

Alfredo Di Stéfano and Ferenc Puskás, were both foreigners. Far from 'culturally helpless', this was a regime that actively sought a broader legitimacy based on commercial culture.[155]

The opening up of culture was accelerated by Manuel Fraga's Press Law of 1966, the greatest liberalizing measure of the dictatorship, which repealed the draconian law of 1938. Despite its many limitations, the Press Law removed prior censorship and the governmental appointment of editors. A handful of publications, such as the journal *Cuadernos para el Diálogo*, founded by ex-minister Joaquín Ruiz-Giménez, the magazines *Destino* and *Triunfo*, and the daily *Madrid*, constantly challenged the boundaries of what was permissible, thereby broadening news coverage and the range of opinions, while fostering a higher-quality journalism. This liberalization of the press had a knock-on effect in publishing, cinema, and the theatre. By the late 1960s, high culture was firmly in the hands of liberalism and, to a lesser extent, Marxism, while anarchist and other radical strains were increasingly tolerated. The historian José Álvarez Junco recalls being stopped by the Civil Guard on a trip back from France in 1965 with a bootload of anarchist texts. Having inspected the material, the Civil Guard simply waved him on. The work of Spanish exiles was also recovered in the 1960s. Thus the internationally renowned director Luis Buñuel not only shot two films in Spain in the 1960s, but also had his work showcased to acclaim in Madrid in 1970. The work of exiled writers such as Francisco Ayala, Max Aub, and Ramón J. Sender became available back home, while Jorge Semprún, a leader of the PCE until 1964, won a Spanish book prize that very same year. A study was even published in Spain in 1968 on the most vilified figure of the Second Republic, Manuel Azaña, penned by the exile Juan Marichal. Yet the regime's cultural policy was far from coherent or consistent, as reflected in the arbitrary closure of theatres, the unpredictable swoops on newspaper offices, or the fact that Buñuel's masterpiece *Viridiana* was presented as the official Spanish entry at the Cannes Film Festival but banned in Spain itself. Moreover, the regime continued to monitor the reading material of the young extremely closely. *Superman*, Spain's best-selling comic, was prohibited in 1964 not only for extolling the virtues of democracy and undercutting Spanish nationalism (the 'American' from the planet Krypton was more popular than the home-bred hero *Capitán*

*Trueno*), but also for making children think that 'they too could change the world', as well as for challenging the dictatorship's patriarchal value system.[156] Thus Clark Kent was excoriated in a report as an 'asexual perversion', not least for 'dressing as a woman' (i.e. donning an apron) in order to cook for a 'super-baby', while 'Luisa' Lane scandalized the Francoist authorities for being a sexually dominant and assertive professional who 'dressed in a manly fashion' (i.e. wore trousers, both literally and metaphorically).[157] In short, both Superman and Lois Lane defied 'gendered stereotypes'.[158] However, the ban was lifted in 1972, as the regime was unable to stem the tide of clandestine copies.

The increasing commercialization of Francoist culture, as profit was prioritized over propaganda, made it less ideological and more popular. Indeed, many of the people who voted for the democratic Constitution in 1978 had preferred the cultural fare of the dictatorship to that of the anti-Francoist alternatives, which tended to be much more ideological. The upshot was that by the 1970s there did not exist a hegemonic culture within Spain, but rather a pluralistic panorama. Ultimately, the dictatorship's liberalization of culture in the quest for greater legitimacy proved counterproductive, as its discourse became wan and ineffectual, with few making the case for Francoism-after-Franco.

## WAS SPAIN DIFFERENT?

Although Spain remained 'different', its economic, social, and cultural convergence with democratic Western Europe in the 1960s and 1970s was undeniable. Far from being immobile and impervious, Spain under Franco was transformed during this period, the drab and inward-looking regime of the early years contrasting starkly with the prosperous and outward-looking one of the later years, to the extent that the dictatorship can be viewed as a 'bifurcated regime'.[159] What is more, the differences between the late Franco dictatorship and the rest of Europe have been overdrawn. After all, the countries of Eastern Europe, comprising East Germany, Poland, Czechoslovakia, Hungary, Romania, and Bulgaria, as well as the Baltic states of Estonia, Latvia, and Lithuania, together with Yugoslavia and Albania in the southeast, were dictatorships, while the constitutional monarchy in Greece was more semi-authoritarian than democratic. Within Southern Europe, Franco's Spain was far from exceptional, as it coincided with the dictatorships of Portugal, Yugoslavia, and Albania, as well as the Greek Junta between 1967 and 1974. Democratic Europe was in fact confined to the original EEC 'Six', in addition to Austria, Switzerland, Ireland, Scandinavia, and the United Kingdom, being delimited not just by geography, but also by its very nature, as the overriding goal up to the 1970s was to strike a balance between conflicting economic and social demands rather than expand democratic practices and rights.

A further shortcoming of democratic Europe was that the leading countries were all beset by periods of grave political turmoil, which sometimes threatened the very regimes themselves. France, for example, was convulsed by the Algerian conflict of 1954–62, which exposed a myth central to French national identity, that of 'its liberating and civilizing mission'.[160] The student revolt of May 1968 in Nanterre and Paris resulted in the occupation of the Sorbonne, attacks on public buildings, a strike by six to seven million workers, and, last but not least, the fall from power of General de Gaulle. French democracy had been rocked to its foundations. Italian democracy also came under serious threat during the 1970s and early 1980s, as it was stricken by terrorism of the extreme left and right, which caused more than 400 deaths. The very future of the Republic appeared uncertain, Italy finding itself in a position that was not so different to Spain, Greece, and Portugal in the 1970s insofar as all of them were struggling to consolidate democracy. In West Germany, extensive student protests and the terrorism of the revolutionary Marxist Red Army Faction (commonly known as the Baader-Meinhof Gang) placed democracy there under severe strain during the late 1960s and 1970s, while British politics were profoundly shaken by the 'Troubles' in Northern Ireland, which claimed about 2,000 lives between 1968 and 1980. It would be wrong therefore to ignore the fact that 'for much of the late Franco period the benefits and resilience of West European democracy were far less evident than hindsight might allow'.[161]

In other respects, however, the divergences between Francoist Spain and Western Europe had become an abyss by the 1970s. The protests of the 1960s led to far-reaching reform in France, Italy, and West

Germany. At the same time, the very nature of democracy was being reconfigured in Western Europe, mostly due to the work of bodies such as the Council of Europe, the European Court of Justice, the European Parliament, and pressure groups such as Amnesty International (founded in 1961 in the United Kingdom thanks partly to the abuses of the Franco regime), which defined and defended international human rights. These rights not only conditioned the relations of European democracies with non-democratic regimes, but also set new standards for admission to the EEC. In other words, Western European democracy had become at once more inclusive and exigent. The breach between Franco's Spain and Western Europe was made wider still by the democracies' far-reaching social reforms in the 1960s and 1970s. Women's rights, for example, were transformed. The contraceptive pill was made available in numerous countries in the 1960s, while abortion and divorce became commonplace in the early 1970s. By contrast, abortion, contraception, and divorce all remained taboo in Spain until the end of the dictatorship.

## A DIVIDED ELITE

By the time Franco died in 1975, the regime was in a state of unresolved turmoil. Ever since the early 1960s the Francoist elites had been broadly divided into *inmovilistas* or hardliners and *aperturistas* or reformists (*apertura* means 'opening up'), but the debate over 'the subversion' – that is, the emergence of widespread opposition – accentuated the breach. For the hardliners, who became known as the 'bunker', the clamour for change had to be met by an uncompromising defence of the dictatorship's fundamental values, as reform would ultimately destroy them. From this perspective, the dictatorship had reached its apogee with the passing of the Organic Law of the State in 1967 and the nomination of Prince Juan Carlos as successor to Franco in 1969. The Organic Law of the State, the last of the 'Fundamental Laws', was regarded by Franco, then seventy-four, as completing the regime's institutionalization, that is, the framework of Francoism-after-Franco. 'The apposite moment has arrived', as the preamble to the law explained, 'to complete the institutionalization of the regime ... born on 18 July

1936', while ensuring 'the loyalty of the highest organs of the state to the Principles of the National Movement'.[162] The Law ratified the monarchy as the form of state, made a distinction between the positions of prime minister and head of state (with a view to the monarchist succession), and reaffirmed the regime's identification with the Principles of the National Movement, 'by their very nature, permanent and unalterable'.[163] It also made the regime's 'organic democracy' less unrepresentative by electing 108 'family' deputies to the Cortes in a corporatist fashion, recognized liberty of conscience in line with the Second Vatican Council (the Fundamental Principles of the Movement obliged the regime to follow Church doctrine), and reaffirmed that the interests of the individual were firmly subordinate to the state. The bill was subjected to only the second national referendum in twenty years, obtaining an implausible 95.86 per cent of the votes, and then passed into law in January 1967, thereby fulfilling its purpose of 'improving the fundamental legislation'.[164] As Franco himself put it, 'the continuity of the National Movement lies in the Movement itself.'[165] The nomination of Prince Juan Carlos in July 1969 as successor to Franco finalized the institutional process so far as the hardliners were concerned.

Prince Juan Carlos and dictator Francisco Franco

For the reformists, the Francoist state had to adapt to the profound economic, social, and cultural changes wrought by economic modernization. Still, this change had to be undertaken in a carefully controlled manner, as suggested by the populist initiatives of José

Solís, secretary-general of the Movement in the 1960s, which sought to guarantee the dictatorship's continuity, albeit in a somewhat different form. One of the boldest reformers was the bustling Manuel Fraga, who, as minister of information and tourism, had fought hard for the liberalizing Press Law of 1966. In his book *El desarrollo político* (Political Development) of 1971, Fraga, clearly looking to his post-Franco career, averred that 'economic and administrative progress is not enough', as most people wanted 'public life to be real, and not rhetorical' and 'political activity' to be 'authentic, whether dealing with the press, elections or associations'.[166] In his view, the goal should be 'a great, real society' which 'includes *all Spaniards*'.[167] Accordingly, Spain 'urgently' required 'a clear commitment to political development', which should not be 'the work of a small group, but the result of a fecund national dialogue', involving 'participation at all levels', so that a 'renovated citizenship' would be able 'to find its own leaders, at all levels: trade union, local, business, national, etc.'.[168] In other words, he was advocating a transition – 'with the limitations and gradualism that are indispensable' – towards a less illiberal regime, but to what extent it would be democratic was not spelt out.[169] Fraga's position fell short of the unequivocal endorsement of parliamentary democracy evinced by former Francoists such as Joaquín Ruiz-Giménez, founder of the liberal journal *Cuadernos para el Diálogo* and lawyer for the Workers' Commissions, and José María de Areilza, erstwhile ambassador to the United States. For most reformists, the whole point of reform was to ensure the survival of the dictatorship following what was euphemistically called the 'successional fact', in other words, the death of Franco.[170] From this perspective, what divided the hardliners and the reformists was not so much the end – some form of authoritarian continuity – but the means. The reformists were nonetheless profoundly disappointed by the Organic Law of the State, as they had hoped that it would introduce greater modernization and a degree of political pluralism, not a 'mere codification and reordering of existing legislation along with some administrative reform'.[171]

The escalating tensions within the upper echelons of the dictatorship were reflected in the MATESA affair of August 1969. This erupted when the Falangist director-general of customs denounced Juan Vilá Reyes, the head of Spain's first multinational, Maquinaria Textil, S.A., for securing substantial export credits without the requisite orders, thanks in large measure to his Opus Dei contacts. Such fraud was common practice under Franco, but the Movement hoped to exploit MATESA's malfeasance in order to strengthen its own position within the regime at the expense of the rival Opus Dei. Extensive press coverage transformed the affair into the greatest financial scandal of the dictatorship. Vilá Reyes was arrested, the company was expropriated by the state, and in October 1969 the government fell. However, the Movement's machinations backfired, as the new government marked a 'complete victory' for the hardliner Carrero Blanco (Opus Dei's guardian angel), for nearly all the key positions were occupied by Opus Dei or ACNP members (or their allies), while the prominent reformists Fernando María de Castiella and Manuel Fraga (a 'dangerous liberal' in Carrero Blanco's judgement) were both sacked.[172]

## THE REGIME FIGHTS BACK: THE GOVERNMENT OF OCTOBER 1969

The new government, which marked a shift to the right, did not represent all the forces of the regime, as a declining Franco had not carried out his usual balancing act, leaving the composition of the Cabinet to Carrero Blanco. Indeed, the *Caudillo*'s most trusted collaborator acted thereafter as de facto prime minister in place of the ailing dictator, a symptom of the dictatorship's incapacity to renew its political cadres outside the economic domain. The so-called 'monocolour government' of October 1969 was notable for reaching a hugely beneficial agreement in 1970 with the European Economic Community, for overseeing exceptional economic growth between 1971 and 1973, and for opening diplomatic relations with both China and East Germany. On the other hand, Carrero Blanco's resistance to change was manifested in the freezing of the political provisions of the Organic Law of the State, most notably the introduction of political associations, the key issue at debate between the hardliners and reformists. Confronted by spiralling strikes, student agitation, and the terrorism of ETA, the de facto premier took a hard line on the anti-Francoist opposition – 'it will be totally dismantled,' he told the

Cortes – as illustrated by the Burgos ETA trial of December 1970, the closure of the *Madrid* daily in November 1971, the arrest of 113 members of the Assembly of Catalonia in October 1973, and the trial of the leaders of Workers' Commissions in December 1973.[173]

The benefits of this unflinching approach were far from obvious. The national and international protests provoked by the Burgos trial in particular had a devastating impact on the morale of the dictatorial elites. The perplexity and pessimism engulfing the regime are illustrated by the extraordinary meeting of the National Council of the Movement in February 1971 to discuss the 'general political situation'.[174] The councillors constantly referred to the rally held in the Oriental Square in Madrid on 17 December 1970 in response to the outcry over the Burgos trial as confirmation of the enduring popularity of the regime. Beneath this veneer of self-congratulation, however, lurked an acute awareness of the dictatorship's lack of international democratic credibility, with Admiral Pedro Nieto Antúnez, erstwhile minister of the navy, pointing out that Spain was 'an isolated nation, a despised regime . . . a country vilified by the international media'.[175] The problem, according to Francisco Labardíe Otermín, was that there existed 'an immense vacuum in official policy', which had resulted in 'grave uncertainty over the future of the Movement itself'.[176] Once again, the Movement was convinced that greater political participation was the panacea to the regime's crisis of 'political development', the report of the Permanent Commission of the Council contending that the regime should consider 'all paths that reflect the plurality and diversity of existing opinions and interests . . . and make them prosper for the common good', that is, introduce political associations.[177] The question, as ever, was what type of associations? The peril, as former secretary-general Raimundo Fernández Cuesta noted, was that associations that 'defend political ideologies will end up as parties, whatever name you give them', which 'would go against' the Fundamental Laws.[178] Indeed, the regime should reject outright the idea that, in the words of one hardliner, 'democratic liberalism is by definition the "norm"' and that all other systems 'are exceptional and therefore temporary'.[179] The Permanent Commission defended the idea of participation 'within the system', even though this was an approach that had been tried and found wanting in the 1966 syndical elections.[180] Worse still, the opposition, lamented Labardíe Otermín, not only had 'definitively lost fear', but was also eyeing up the dictatorship in order 'to assail it and destroy it'.[181] The enveloping sense of doom and gloom was reflected in the prophetic observation of Fernández Cuesta that 'perhaps . . . in the subconsciousness of many lies the conviction that it is inevitable that once Franco disappears, the regime disappears, that their lives are united'.[182]

Carrero Blanco himself admitted to the National Council of the Movement that the regime was on the defensive, declaring before it on 7 March 1972 that 'our youth does not prepare itself in the best interests of the Motherland; the university is not what we would all like it to be; labour relations do not develop in accordance with the peace, justice, and reciprocal loyalty that our doctrine establishes; the morality of the people . . . is not what we would want, it's not the traditional morality of our Motherland.'[183] 'We are at war,' he concluded, the dictatorship still under the cosh of Communism and 'the liberal propaganda that Freemasonry sponsors'.[184] On the other hand, he was aware that if the regime did not evolve towards liberalism, 'we will see ourselves excluded from the European Eden'.[185] His solution, however, was typically unyielding: unity 'in loyalty' and steadfastness 'in our doctrine', in other words, a refusal to open up the regime in any way.[186] Symptomatic of the situation was the resignation in May 1973 of the interior minister, Tomás Garicano Goñi, on the grounds that 'a genuine opening up is necessary.'[187] A month later, the ageing Carrero Blanco was formally designated prime minister, an indication of the regime's lack of internal renewal. Carrero Blanco's assassination by ETA on 20 December 1973 not only deprived Franco of his greatest collaborator (he was seen 'weeping profusely' at a funeral Mass for Carrero Blanco), but also signalled Opus Dei's downfall.[188]

## FLATTERING TO DECEIVE: THE ARIAS NAVARRO ADMINISTRATION

The new prime minister, Carlos Arias Navarro, was another hardliner, having been the military prosecutor during the savage repression of Málaga in 1937. A protégé of the uncompromising minister of the interior Camilo Alonso Vega, he had been the most recent minister of the interior himself, and therefore responsible for Carrero Blanco's security (or lack of it). Yet his presentation of the Cabinet to the Cortes on 12 February 1974 is often held to have heralded an 'authentic opening up' of the Francoist system, as reflected in the press's acclamation of the 'Spirit of 12 February'.[189] According to this narrative, Arias Navarro conjured up a vision of a 'gradual democratization of the regime', but this is highly questionable.[190] Certainly he accepted that the 'adherence' that characterized the 'national consensus' around Franco would have to give way to 'participation'.[191] He also proposed a clutch of reforms: a bill for the direct election of mayors, another to regulate the conflicts of interest of the deputies in the Cortes, a change in the Syndical Law of 1971, and, most importantly of all, a bill on political associations. The latter would nonetheless be designed 'in accordance with the principles and norms of our Fundamental Laws', that is, it did not contemplate a democratization – however gradual – of the system.[192] Arias Navarro was prepared to make only 'limited changes' to ensure the regime's continuity by attracting the support of Francoist reformists and the moderate opposition.[193]

Admittedly, the new administration oversaw the most enlightened press regime so far under the dictatorship, Fraga's former deputy at the Ministry of Information and Tourism, Pío Cabanillas, allowing pro-democracy publications such as *Cambio 16*, *Informaciones*, *Triunfo*, and *Ya* to act as a 'paper parliament'.[194] The government also granted the moderate opposition, ranging from the Christian democrats to the liberals and even the PSOE, a certain liberty. Still, the 'Spirit of 12 February' was almost immediately shattered by the government's splenetic reaction to a sermon on 24 February by the Bishop of Bilbao, Antonio Añoveros, in defence of Basque culture and rights ('an extremely grave attack on national unity', in the Cabinet's view), and by the execution by *garrote vil* on 2 March of the anarchist Salvador Puig Antich, who was convicted, on extremely doubtful grounds, of killing a policeman.[195] The death of Puig Antich prompted the European Parliament to denounce 'the repeated violations by the Spanish government of the basic human and civil rights' that prevented 'the entry of Spain into the European Community'.[196] The government was thrown even further on the defensive by the Portuguese Revolution of 'the Carnation' in April (which appeared to confirm the worst nightmare of the Francoists), the collapse of the Greek Junta in July 1974, and the most sanguinary terrorist act of the dictatorship, ETA's bombing on 13 September 1974 of the Cafetería Rolando in Madrid near the General Directorate of Security, which killed twelve people and wounded eighty.

The reformist spirit of Arias Navarro soon evaporated. Cabanillas was sacked in late October 1974 for his liberalism, prompting a raft of resignations by like-minded officials, such as Francisco Fernández Ordóñez, president of the INI, and Marcelino Oreja, under-secretary at the Ministry of Information and Tourism. The Statute on Political Associations, which had been debated on and off by the regime since the 1950s, was finally passed in January 1975, but proved to be as limited as Arias Navarro had indicated, as it restricted the associations to 'the ideological orbit and organizational control of the Movement'.[197] In reality, the regime had no intention of opening up the channels of political participation in a meaningful fashion. A declaration by Juan de Borbón in June 1975 flagged up the dictatorship's political ossification, declaring that 'the end of absolute power' was near, while backing 'the democratic change that the interest of the nation demands and the Spanish people is asking for'.[198]

Like Carrero Blanco before him, Arias Navarro reacted to the huge wave of strikes (over 2,000 in 1974 and more than 3,000 in 1975), the unrelenting student protests, and the terrorism of ETA and the FRAP with escalating repression, underscoring in a television interview that his government had the means 'to crush inexorably any attempt to subvert or alter the life of the country'.[199] Even the provincial university of Valladolid was shut down in February 1975 following the protests over the death of a student at the hands of the police. On 27 August 1975 the government declared an indefinite state of exception, which was even harsher than those under Carrero Blanco, because all members of the opposition were classified as terrorists, while the role of the military courts was reinforced. In September 1975 five terrorists were executed (two ETA and three FRAP members), despite the domestic and international outcry, which had included pleas for clemency from the European Parliament, the Vatican, and the secretary-general of the United Nations, as well as demonstrations in many European cities and the withdrawal 'for consultation' of the ambassadors of Great Britain,

France, West Germany, Portugal, Italy, and nine other European countries. A defiant dictatorship responded to the international opprobrium as in 1946, by orchestrating a mass rally in the Oriental Square in Madrid on 1 October. In his last public appearance Franco attributed the attacks on the regime yet again to the 'left-wing Masonic conspiracy' in tandem with the 'Communist-terrorist subversion', showcasing the dictatorship's deep-seated political sclerosis.[200]

Clearly Arias Navarro was too much of a diehard Francoist to undertake substantial reform of the political system, underlining in a speech on 15 June 1974 that the *Spirit of 12 February* 'cannot be, nor desires to be, different from the permanent and irrevocable spirit of the regime of Franco from the hour of its foundation'.[201] Ever since the dictatorship had sunk into crisis towards the end of the 1960s, the political agenda had in reality been overwhelmingly dominated by the hardliners at the expense of the reformists. The reformists had achieved some success, such as the Law of Associations in 1964 and the Press Law in 1966, but these merely allowed citizens a little more leeway, rather than providing a genuine framework for the integration of workers, students, local residents, progressive Catholics, and Basque and Catalan regional nationalists into the regime. The mass mobilization of the 1970s brought to the surface the myriad contradictions that characterized the regime: a kingdom without a king that was rejected by the head of the royal family; a Catholic state that no longer enjoyed the support of the Church; an official discourse of 'social justice' that was belied by the paucity of the welfare state; a regime of 'peace' and 'social harmony' that was convulsed by demonstrations, strikes, and terrorist bombings; and a nation state built on centralist 'unity' that had given rise to regional nationalisms to which it had no answer.

Little wonder, then, that the anti-Francoist opposition was already looking to the post-Franco future, the opposition launching two wide-ranging coalitions: the *Junta Democrática* (Democratic Junta), created by the PCE in October 1974, which included the Workers' Commissions, the Popular Socialist Party, and prominent dissidents, and the *Plataforma de Convergencia Democrática* (Platform of Democratic Convergence), set up by the PSOE in July 1975 with the support of the UGT, the Basque Nationalist Party, the Maoist ORT, and others. Both coalitions backed a peaceful 'rupture' with the dictatorship, the

*Junta* calling for a provisional government and a national referendum on 'the definitive form of state', while the *Plataforma* demanded that the break with 'the current regime' should be followed by 'the opening of a constituent process' and that the type of regime should be determined by 'the popular will expressed in elections'.[202]

## THE DEATH OF FRANCO

Franco's Civil War allies, Hitler and Mussolini, both perished in 1945, but the Spanish dictator remained *in situ* for yet another thirty years. The contrast by the 1960s and 1970s between Spain's grim, fascistic dictatorship and the prosperous, permissive democracies of the West appeared grotesque, almost surreal. Who could deny it? Spain was different. Yet in other ways Franco's Spain was not so different. The diplomatic isolation of 1945 had largely been overcome by 1950. Relations with the United States not only led to a military agreement in 1953, which integrated Spain de facto into the Western defence system, but also opened the doors to a host of international bodies, including UNESCO, WHO, and the International Labor Organization, climaxing in 1955 with the General Assembly of the United Nations. Spain's economic integration into the West took place in the late 1950s with its entry into the International Monetary Fund, the World Bank, and the Organization for European Economic Cooperation. The unprecedented boom of the 1960s and 1970s drew the country ever closer to the West not only in economic and social terms, but also in political ones, as new social movements and forms of protest emerged.

In reality, the dictatorship had undergone a momentous change, whether intended or not. The harrowing poverty and economic backwardness of the 1940s and 1950s were largely eliminated by the unprecedented prosperity of the 1960s and 1970s; the spasmodic strikes of the 1940s and 1950s were swept aside by a tidal wave of protest in the 1960s and above all the 1970s; the neo-Traditionalist culture of the 1940s and 1950s was derailed in the 1960s and 1970s by an eclectic scene in which liberal and Marxist artists, actors, directors, musicians, and writers competed with Francoist ones; an unflinching defence of empire during the initial years was replaced by peaceful decolonization after the mid-1950s; the heavily militarized dictatorship of the 1940s and 1950s ended up spending less on the armed forces in relative terms than any other nation in Europe; the mass executions of the early 1940s gave way to less than one political execution a year between 1960 and 1975; and, finally, the administrative and political cadres of the later regime were less ideological and more technocratic in outlook than those of the early years, thereby weakening the cohesion of the dictatorial elites. Franco's Spain not only evolved, but it evolved far more than, say, Fidel Castro's Cuba, Enver Hoxha's Albania, or António Oliveira de Salazar's Portugal. It has even been contended that 'there has never been a personal dictatorship which has changed as much as Franco's did'.[203]

It was fitting that the Spanish Sahara, the last of the nation's African colonies – the continent where the dictator had made his name – was abandoned in October 1975 in the face of the Moroccan occupation (the so-called 'Green March') as Franco himself neared death. In another throwback to the past, he died on 20 November, the same day of the month as the 'Absent One', José Antonio Primo de Rivera. The overriding question now was whether there would be a 'rupture' with the dictatorship or a 'reform' of the regime, that is, whether Spain would become a democracy or remain authoritarian.

# 9

# The Transition

*From Dictatorship to Democracy, 1975–1982*

The death of Franco was not the death of Francoism. Not only were the institutions of the dictatorship, including the Cortes, the Movement, the Councils of State and the Kingdom, the army, the judiciary, and the state and local administration left intact, but also the ultra-Francoists or *inmovilistas* enjoyed a substantial presence in all of them. But, at his coronation on 22 November 1975, Juan Carlos made it clear that change was in the air. On the one hand, the king promised the deputies 'to fulfil and ensure the fulfilment' of the dictatorship's 'Fundamental Laws'.[1] On the other hand, he foresaw a 'new era in the history of Spain', distinguished by 'an effective consensus of national concord', which would usher in a 'free and modern society'.[2] The king aimed to appoint a prime minister in line with his own thinking, but he had to abandon this in order to ensure that his most trusted ally, Torcuato Fernández-Miranda, a badger-eyed *éminence grise* of the dictatorship who had been a key adviser since 1969, became president of both the Cortes and the Council of the Realm, the control of both institutions being vital to the reform of the political system. Given the widespread anticipation of political change following Franco's death, the deep-seated economic recession, and the foreign policy crisis engendered by Morocco's occupation of Spain's Saharan territories, the continuation of Carlos Arias Navarro as prime minister, the 'sphinx without a secret', did not bode well.[3] Indeed, Fernández-Miranda regarded Arias Navarro's premiership as a mere parenthesis during which time he would identify the ideal prime minister for the king.

## THE SEARCH FOR CONTINUITY: THE ARIAS NAVARRO GOVERNMENT

In presenting his Cabinet to the Cortes on 13 December 1975, Arias Navarro pledged himself to 'preserve and continue the gigantic labour of Franco', rejecting the democratic opposition's call for a 'rupture' and a constitutional process.[4] For Arias Navarro, reform was necessary only insofar as it consolidated the monarchy of Juan Carlos I. In unveiling his programme to the Cortes on 28 January 1976, the prime minister lavished praise on Franco, 'undisputed and indisputable *Caudillo* of our people', for his 'unrepeatable magistracy', 'far-sighted prudence', and 'gigantic labour', before explaining that his objective was not to introduce a Western-style democracy, but to construct a 'Spanish democracy', the 'democratic framework for our co-existence' lying in 'our Fundamental Laws'.[5] Accordingly, he aimed to make 'some very limited modifications', so that 'our laws and institutions' would be brought up to date – 'as Franco would have wanted'.[6] The reform would exclude those who threatened 'the sacred unity of the Motherland' and those who defended 'totalitarian Communism' and (paradoxically) 'the dictatorship of a party'.[7] Clearly Arias Navarro's principal audience was not the Spanish people, but the Francoist Cortes ('the legitimate representatives of the Spanish people'), as underlined by the fact that he did not even mention many of the issues of greatest public concern, such as a political amnesty, regional autonomy, the eradication of the state's repressive apparatus, or the calling of a general election.[8] Convinced that between the *inmovilismo* (immobilism) of the Francoist *ultras* and the 'rupture' of the democratic opposition lay a terrain fertile for a 'reformist continuity' – on the grounds that most Spaniards prized law and order above political freedom – the prime minister was determined to pursue not a change *of* regime, but an exceedingly limited change *in* the regime.[9] 'What I want,' he stated in February before a parliamentary commission, 'is to continue Francoism.'[10] Unlike the king, he refused to meet members of the democratic opposition (arguing, predictably, that Franco would not have done so), even though their collaboration was essential to the success of any reformist project. As one minister noted, 'he is not a statesman, he is a Francoist politician.'[11]

The magnitude of the government's breach with the public mood was illustrated by a survey of December 1975, in which only 18 per cent of those polled supported the continuation of the dictatorship, 30 per cent called for an 'evolution' towards a democratic regime, and 29 per cent the establishment of a democratic system 'immediately' – that is, nearly two-thirds of Spaniards aspired to some form of democracy (of the university educated, a mere 4 per cent identified with Franco- ism).[12] The renewal of 2,000 trade-union agreements (two-thirds of the national total) in early 1976 and the general expectation of polit- ical change resulted in the greatest wave of strikes yet seen under the dictatorship (17,371 between January and March, nearly six times more than in the whole of 1975), the opposition believing that this would force the government to negotiate. The main centres of agita- tion were Madrid, Barcelona, and the Basque Country, but there were also strikes in Andalusia, Asturias, Galicia, and Valencia. In Madrid between 400,000 and 500,000 workers downed tools, while in Barce- lona the official union was taken aback by 'endless labour conflicts . . . that are generated in an alarming fashion'.[13] As the civil governor of Barcelona, Salvador Sánchez-Terán, observed, 'if there was a categorical divorce between what was real and what was legal, that was in the world of the trade unions'.[14] The Basque region was the scene of extreme tension, accentuated by the reactivation of both ETA branches, the terrorists assassinating the mayor of Galdácano, the local boss of the Movement in Basauri, and the PNV-linked businessman Ángel Berazadi in early 1976. The worst industrial clash took place in Vitoria on 3 March, when the police killed five strikers and injured more than one hundred, provoking the biggest strike seen in the Basque Country since the 1930s. The police brutality did enormous, arguably irrever- sible, damage to the government's exiguous reformist credentials.

In numerous cities there were also political demonstrations, the principal goal of which was an amnesty for the anti-Francoist prison- ers. For the opposition, and much of Spanish society, an amnesty was an indispensable first step towards a more just and democratic society, but precisely for this reason it was fiercely resisted by the Francoists, as this would bring into question the legitimacy of the dictatorship. There were pro-amnesty demonstrations in Bilbao, Bur- gos, Zaragoza, and many other cities, climaxing on 20 January with a massive protest in Madrid. In the Basque Country and Catalonia the call for an amnesty was inextricably linked to that for autonomy, as demonstrated by the march of 75,000 people in Barcelona on 1 February, a police report noting that the opposition had never achieved such a 'display of force'.[15] The following week another large-scale protest took place in the Catalan capital, organized by the Assembly of Catalonia under the banner of 'Liberty, Amnesty, Statute of Autonomy'. 'The battle of the transition,' noted the civil governor, 'is taking place on the street.'[16]

The governmental backlash against the strikes and protests of early 1976 brought the newly emergent political parties of the opposition closer together. Following the execution of five terrorists in September 1975, the *Junta Democrática de España* or JDE (Spanish Democratic Junta) and the *Plataforma de Coordinación Democrática* or PCD (Platform of Democratic Coordination) issued a joint statement on 30 October 1975 urging the Spanish people to mobilize for the 'effective conquest of fundamental rights and liberties'.[17] The deaths of the five workers in Vitoria in March hastened the merger of the two coalitions, which formed the Democratic Coordination (*Coordinación Democrática*) on 26 March 1976. Popularly known as the *Platajunta*, Democratic Coordination signalled the victory of the reformists over the *rupturistas*, as the Communists abandoned the idea of toppling the government by force in favour of the face-saving formula of a 'negotiated democratic rupture'. Further, the opposition no longer called for a referendum on whether the future regime should be a monarchy or a republic, but merely a 'popular consultation', which might comprise the election of a constituent Cortes or a referendum on the Constitution once it had been drawn up. Certainly the two platforms had been slow to coalesce, but the *Platajunta* provided the opposition with a prominence and purpose that it had hitherto lacked. However, the unity of the *Platajunta* should not be overdrawn, not only because the PSOE and PCE were extremely wary of one another for historical reasons and as left-wing rivals, but also because the new coalition failed to improve relations between the different socialist parties. A final problem was that Democratic Coordination did not represent all the opposition parties, as those in the Catalan *Consell de Forces Polítiques* or CFP (Council of Political Forces) did not join it.

The *Platajunta* soon had to contend with yet another opposition force. In May 1976 the so-called 'Citizens' Movement' emerged, bringing together the neighbourhood, parent, housewife and other associations which had revived civil society in the 1960s and 1970s. Over 10,000 associations were founded between 1964 and 1974 (starting from a base of 2,500), but by 1979 there were nearly 30,000 nationwide.[18] The associations came increasingly together during the transition, as when the 'Zones' Coordinator' organized the first 'Citizenship Week', a 50,000-strong demonstration in the capital in June 1976, and another in the Madrid neighbourhood of Moratalaz in September which rallied 100,000 people to the banner of 'Bread, Work and Liberty'. The latter was acclaimed as a 'Citizenship Demonstration' by *El País*, the centre-left daily founded in May 1976 which soon became the progressive newspaper of record. The growing convergence of the associational milieu represented the appearance of not only a new social actor, but also one with an agenda which was very different to that of the opposition parties. On the one hand, the associations continued to defend their particular interests, as shown by the call of one local neighbourhood bulletin to 'reconstitute the social fabric destroyed by the dictatorship'.[19] On the other, the Citizens' Movement embodied an alternative vision of the transition, which was based on a communitarian model of citizenship, a form of direct democracy that defended active participation as a core principle of democratic practice. As Tomás Villasante declared at the June 1976 demonstration in Madrid:

> We want to say that we fight against the high cost of living, against speculation, for the legalization of our Associations, and a long etc. But we don't stop here. The residents of Madrid and its neighbourhoods pursue without rest all types of actions towards achieving our most important objective: the absolute and total democratization of municipal life.[20]

Consequently, the Citizens' Movement held a view of the transition which diverged not only from that of the government, but also from that of the opposition parties. Both the JDE and PCD were party-driven platforms, but they nonetheless included organizations and individuals from outside, above all at the local level. Indeed, there was a considerable overlap between the two, as many party members were active in the associations. During the early part of the transition the parties and associations therefore occupied more or less the same oppositional space, but once the JDE and PCD began to discuss their merger, the leaders of the PCD demanded that the associations 'should not have a leadership function', as their 'permeability' exposed them to 'the risk of manipulation'.[21] The objections of sectors of the JDE to this party-exclusive plan were ignored in favour of the Communist Party's overriding goal of fusing with the PCD. Thus the nascent Democratic Coordination established that only political parties could form part of the leadership and that non-party organizations had a voice, but not a vote, in the local plenary sessions. The Democratic Coordination insisted, too, that demonstrations of the Citizens' Movement had to be unanimously approved by its members. In other words, the opposition parties defended a liberal form of representative democracy whereby they monopolized political decision-making at the expense of the communitarian participatory model put forward by the Citizens' Movement. Not surprisingly, when the official negotiations between the government and the opposition began in January 1977, the Citizens' Movement was excluded.

The emergence of Democratic Coordination was nonetheless a formidable blow to the government, as it presented a democratic alternative to the dictatorship. As the Eurocommunist Manuel Azcárate wrote in *El País*:

> That socialists and Communists see eye to eye, after 37 years of division, is important in itself. But the coming together within the same political coalition of working-class forces and a substantial part of the Catholic world, of the parties of the left and right, proletarians and capitalists, with the objective (specific, yes, but decisive) of re-establishing democracy, is quite simply an event without precedent.[22]

Limited to small regional groups in the 1960s and 1970s, the socialist movement had been transformed upon the election of the young and charismatic Andalusian Felipe González as leader of the party at the 13th Congress in Suresnes (France) in 1974. Not only did González bring a hard-nosed pragmatism to the socialist movement, but he also managed to secure the ideological and financial backing of Western European social democracy, especially that of the German Social

Democratic Party. In the process González established the PSOE as the leading socialist force in Spain, though it had to compete with the exiled leadership in Toulouse, the Popular Socialist Party of Professor Enrique Tierno Galván, and a host of other socialist entities.

In tackling the opposition, the minister of the interior, Manuel Fraga, drew a distinction between those parties that could be legalized in the not-too-distant future and those which could not, the latter referring above all to the Communists. In Fraga's estimation, legalization of the PCE would have to wait until after the first democratic elections. The aim of this strategy was to divide the opposition, but the creation of Democratic Coordination threatened its basic premise, an exasperated Fraga exclaiming 'they now come out with the popular front. That's an end to tolerance! The authorization of meetings and congresses is over!'[23] On 29 March, true to his word, Fraga had a number of Communist leaders arrested, including the Workers' Commissions' leader Marcelino Camacho, who had become the international personification of the workers' struggle in Spain. A few days later, other Communists were detained, including the film director Juan Antonio Bardem (uncle of the actor Javier Bardem) and the economist Ramón Tamames. Widely criticized for his brazen approach, the defiant Fraga retorted 'they are Communists, and, as a result, I won't let them go.'[24] He nevertheless continued to cultivate the socialists, authorizing the 30th Congress of the UGT in Madrid in April, a major socialist meeting in Barcelona in May, and the 3rd Congress of the Popular Socialist Party in June.

Hardly surprisingly, Arias Navarro soon lost control of his Cabinet, one observer remarking bluntly that the ministers 'don't pay him a blind bit of notice'.[25] By the end of March, the government, which had yet to present any reforms, had lost credibility not only with public opinion, but also with the king. In an interview with *Newsweek* in April, Juan Carlos lambasted the Arias Navarro administration as an 'unmitigated disaster', while underscoring his commitment to 'the freely expressed desires of the people' in an address to the Congress of the United States in early June.[26] Any lingering credibility that the government still enjoyed soon evaporated as a result of the thoroughly retrograde nature of the reforms which it presented to the Cortes in May and June 1976. In May a labour law was passed that maintained the official Syndical Organization while ignoring the claims of all other trade unions and in particular the right to freedom of association. A highly restrictive law of assembly was also approved in May which required an authorization for outdoor gatherings and prior warning for indoor ones. In June the Cortes passed the government's flagship reform, the Law of Political Association, which was ably defended before parliament by the youthful secretary-general of the Movement, Adolfo Suárez. The new law required prospective political parties not only to declare their loyalty to the Francoist institutions, but also to be vetted by the Ministry of the Interior. The regime's blinkered approach was crowned by the refusal of the Cortes on 11 June to alter the Criminal Code so that membership of a political party was no longer a crime, a decision which effectively invalidated the law just passed.

The scant expectations placed in the Arias Navarro administration were completely dashed by its reactionary, ostrich-like stance, which had the opposite effect to the one sought, namely the perpetuation of the dictatorship by means of minimal change. 'There is no reform without continuity,' claimed the prime minister, but he had failed to make them compatible.[27] With the government's 'reform' process stymied and the opposition unable to advance its 'negotiated democratic rupture', both king and country had reached an impasse. The gulf separating the democratic impulse of the head of state from the dictatorial inertia of the head of government had become unsustainable. The only option left was to pursue genuinely democratic reform, as opposed to the oxymoron of Arias Navarro's 'Spanish democracy'. On 1 July, at the behest of the king, the prime minister duly resigned.

## THE RISE OF ADOLFO SUÁREZ

The new prime minister was the relatively unknown Adolfo Suárez, minister of the Movement in the Arias Navarro administration and director of Spanish Television and Radio between 1969 and 1973. His unexpected elevation to the premiership had been engineered by the president of the Council of the Realm, Torcuato Fernández-Miranda, the king having requested a 'tractable' replacement for the unyielding

Arias Navarro.[28] The wily Fernández-Miranda judged that the youth and ambition of Adolfo Suárez, then aged only forty-four, fitted the 'identikit picture' requested by the monarch.[29] In any case, Suárez grasped from the outset that the legitimacy of the monarchy required a much more meaningful democratic project than that of Arias Navarro. The king later revealed that he chose Adolfo Suárez because he was 'young, modern and sufficiently ambitious to want to be the man capable of facing up to the times we were living through'.[30]

Not only the prime minister but also the Cabinet marked a rupture with the previous administration. Half the incumbents were new, the average age of the ministers was under forty-five, and the heavyweight figures of José María de Areilza, Joaquín Garrigues, and the belligerent Manuel Fraga were all gone. This was largely a Cabinet of Suárez's own making, giving it a loyalty, unity, and sense of purpose that contemporaries badly misjudged, as it was widely mocked as a 'government of junior lecturers'.[31] The change in climate was reflected, too, in the abandonment of the dictatorial lexicon (no more 'organic democracy') and the adoption of a much more accessible, if not democratic, style. Much in the manner of President Franklin D. Roosevelt's 'fireside chats', on 6 July Suárez addressed the nation on television from the reassuring setting of his own home, a far cry from the severe formality of Arias Navarro. Showcasing his personable manner and striking good looks, Suárez winningly told his audience that 'the concerns of the nation are my concerns'.[32] He made it clear that the king wanted 'to achieve a modern democracy for Spain' and that, in his capacity as prime minister, he would govern 'with the consent of the governed'.[33] In a further break with the past, he promised 'to respect the adversary and offer them the possibility of collaboration'.[34] He soon met moderate opposition leaders such as José María Gil Robles and Joaquín Ruiz Giménez, and later, in August, the socialist Felipe González and Catalan regionalist Jordi Pujol. Despite these conciliatory gestures, Suárez was careful to keep his distance, not involving the opposition in the construction of the new regime until the new year. These developments were closely followed by the European Parliament and the Assembly of the Council of Europe, both of which provided the democratic opposition with 'an inestimable political support'.[35]

Before becoming prime minister, Suárez had been a loyal servant of the Francoist state. Indeed, he had been regarded as a key figure in ensuring its continuity, having been made president of the *Unión del Pueblo* (Union of the People), a political party created by the Movement in June 1975 in order to perpetuate the dictatorship. As a member of the Arias Navarro government, Suárez had backed a highly restrictive form of democracy, calling for nothing more than the reform of the Fundamental Laws while opposing the dissolution of the Movement. As soon as he became prime minister, however, he took a very different tack. The government programme of 16 July declared resoundingly that 'sovereignty resides in the people', that the administration would work towards 'a democratic system based on the guarantee of rights and civil liberties, on the equality of political opportunity for all the democratic groups, and on the acceptance of true pluralism', and that a general election would be held before 30 June 1977, prior to which a referendum would be held on the 'constitutional reform' that had been carried out.[36] In other words, there was to be a transition to democracy, but this was to be a top-down operation engineered by a Cabinet made up of politicians from the dictatorship.

A few days later, the government had the Criminal Code amended to incorporate not only the legalization of political parties, but also the rights of assembly, protest, propaganda, and association. This changed the political climate overnight, the opposition enjoying a freedom hitherto unknown under the dictatorship. Another paradigmatic shift was the government's responsiveness to public opinion. In Catalonia, the first *Diada* or 'national' day was authorized in nearly forty years, the celebration on 11 September 1976 attracting large crowds. The government also responded to the protests held in cities across Spain during the first half of July in favour of a political amnesty, most notably in Bilbao, where the demonstration numbered around 100,000 people. For most Spaniards, this was the most pressing issue of all, with 67 per cent of people in a survey carried out that month supporting an amnesty. Well aware that the legitimacy of its political project depended on public support, the government issued an amnesty on 30 July for all political prisoners except those convicted of terrorist acts, which meant that between 400 and 500 of the remaining 650 political prisoners were released. In the case of the Basque Country, however, the question remained unresolved, due to the 150 or so ETA militants still in jail. Although 400 Basques had been released upon Franco's death and another 150 as a result of the amnesty of 30 July 1976, demonstrations took place in the region throughout the summer (two people dying in clashes with the police), climaxing with the general strike of 27 September, the anniversary of the execution of two ETA members. Tensions within the Basque region were further exacerbated by a resurgence in ETA violence, the president of the provincial council of Guipúzcoa and his four body-guards being killed on 4 October 1976.

## THE LAW FOR POLITICAL REFORM

The flagship reform of the government was the bill for Political Reform, the first draft of which was drawn up in August 1976 by Tor-cuato Fernández-Miranda. In an effort to contain the fallout from the army, Suárez explained the measure in person to the army chiefs in September, insisting not only that the government would keep a tight rein on the process of political reform, but also that the Communist Party would not be legalized. Even so, the bill provoked the resigna-tion of the vice-president, the ultra-Francoist General Fernando de Santiago, who was replaced by General Manuel Gutiérrez Mellado, a liberal who proved to be a major asset to the government, especially as regards the pacification of the army. While Suárez was trying to neu-tralize the threat from the right, the democratic opposition kept up the pressure from the left. The *Platajunta* and the main regional groups (with the exception of the Catalan Council of Political Forces) had failed to agree on an alternative to the government's reform plan at a meeting in early September, but by late October they had merged to form the *Plataforma de Organismos Democráticos* or POD (Platform of Democratic Bodies). The new coalition declared that 'popular sovereignty will freely decide the new constitution of the state', which indicated that the opposition had given up on the idea of a referendum on the monarchy.[37] In early November the *Plataforma* called on voters to abstain in the projected referendum on the Law for Political Reform on the grounds that the opposition had not been consulted. It then sought to boost its cause by launching a general strike on 12 November

375

involving one million workers, the biggest yet under the dictatorship, but the government kept the public services going while discrediting the stoppage by means of the state-controlled media.

The bill for Political Reform was presented to parliament in October and finally debated in mid-November. In the Cortes, Suárez defended the proposed law on the grounds that it was inspired not only by the 'greatest respect for the existing fundamental legality', but also by an 'awareness of the profound changes which have taken place in Spanish society over the last forty years'.[38] It was therefore necessary 'to adapt our political institutions to the necessities of our modern society and to the profound desires that pulsate within the very being of our people'.[39] Recognition of the need for the political system to adapt to the far-reaching changes within Spanish society was complemented in the preamble to the bill by a reflection on 'our painful modern history'. 'Abstract creations, dreams – however noble they be – extreme attitudes, *pronunciamientos* and impositions, dogmatic sectarianism', the preamble posited, 'not only do not lead to democracy, they destroy it.'[40] Such considerations amounted to a damning indictment of both the Second Republic and the dictatorship. Accordingly, democracy could only be established if it was the 'result of the effort and work of all the Spanish people'.[41]

The overriding objective of the bill was to elect a democratic Cortes that would then proceed to draw up a constitution. It proposed a 350-member Congress and a 248-member Senate (in representation of 'the territorial entities'), both of which would be elected by universal suffrage, though forty-one of the senators would be designated by the monarch.[42] In contrast to the government's programme of July 1976, the Constitution would involve the legislature, not just the executive. Once the Cortes had approved the Constitution, it would be put to a national referendum. The roadmap laid down in the bill effectively derailed the opposition's strategy of a provisional government and a plebiscite on the nature of the regime.

The government claimed that the bill for Political Reform was entirely consistent with its policy of 'reform', not least because it constituted change, in the words of Fernández-Miranda, 'by the law, to the law'.[43] Certainly the bill was passed into law in accordance with Francoist legality (that is, by means of a vote in the Cortes), but rather than involving a reform of the Fundamental Laws themselves, it simply bypassed the Francoist legislation altogether. From this perspective, this was not a *reform* of the dictatorial system, but a break from it. As the ultra-Francoist deputy Blas Piñar observed, 'in truth it's not a reform, it's a rupture, though the rupture wants to present itself without violence and as legal.'[44] Still, as a collaborator of Suárez noted, 'the immense advantage of undertaking the change by respecting legality [was] evident, even if it was only "formally".'[45] The bill was passed in the Cortes by the overwhelming margin of 425 votes to 59, a colossal triumph for the government.

Why, then, did the Francoist Cortes commit collective suicide by voting in favour of the bill, especially given that few of them were democrats? Before the debate took place, each minister lobbied a section of the deputies with a view, in the words of Adolfo Suárez, 'to make them see the unviability of a regressive position', while assuring them that they would not be politically marginalized.[46] Indeed, the minister of the interior, Rodolfo Martín Villa, recalls that 'we did everything bar sleep with them.'[47] In the Cortes, Adolfo Suárez argued that change was unstoppable and that obstruction would only provoke the opposition-inspired 'rupture' which the deputies dreaded. He also promised to respect the government-appointed positions held by many of them in the public administration, the state banks, and nationalized companies such as *Telefónica*, that is, he obliquely threatened them with the loss of lucrative public posts. Finally, he reassured the deputies that the government would retain control of the reform process, just as it had done until then. The receptiveness of the deputies was heightened by the fact that many young, relatively liberal members had entered the Cortes in 1967 and 1971, while some felt that a peaceful end to the dictatorship was more dignified than a last-ditch act of resistance which was doomed to failure.

The forward march of the Suárez government nonetheless produced the first major post-Franco schism within the political class of the dictatorship. In October 1976, Manuel Fraga founded the *Alianza Popular* or AP (Popular Alliance) in protest at the direction taken by the Suárez administration. Headed up by seven prominent Francoists (the 'Magnificent Seven'), the new party justified its creation on the grounds that the government had made 'excessive concessions to revanchist activities, [which] eroded peace and law and order, and undermined national unity', as well as being appalled by the 'crisis of authority at all levels', and the 'unnecessary acceptance of ideas of rupture'.[48] In founding the AP, Manuel Fraga jettisoned the centrist strategy that he had pursued since the early 1970s, partly because Adolfo Suárez had already occupied the centre ground and partly because Fraga saw an opportunity to mobilize what was dubbed 'sociological Francoism', located principally amongst the upper classes, the Catholic middle classes, and the farmers and rural workers. The Popular Alliance served a valuable function insofar as it integrated many Francoists into the democratic regime, the 183 deputies who joined the party playing a vital role in passing the bill for Political Reform, while the new party also strengthened the government's centrist credentials by occupying the space to its right.

The government's control over the process of political reform reached its climax with the holding of the national referendum on the Law for Political Reform on 15 December 1976. The *Plataforma* was divided over the referendum, the most progressive forces, especially the Communists, calling somewhat unconvincingly for abstention, while the Christian democrats, liberals, and social democrats took no official stance. The Citizens' Movement, however, called on its members to abstain, as the government still refused to legalize its umbrella organizations. Faced by the abstentionist campaign of the opposition, Suárez mobilized the redoubtable resources not only of the state media, especially television and radio, but also of the Movement, above all the civil governors, in order to guarantee a mass turnout in favour of the law. The opposition was banned from campaigning, though Suárez astutely permitted the neo-Francoists to defend the 'No' vote on television, as this reinforced the government's moderate image, not least because they claimed that the dictator himself would have voted 'No'. Despite the abstentionist stance of the opposition, participation reached 77 per cent. The government won an overwhelming victory with 94.2 per cent in favour of the reform and 2.6 per cent against it. The referendum also reinforced the position of the king: in a poll of January 1977, 61 per cent favoured a constitutional monarchy as the form of state, while only 22 per cent chose a republic. It marked, too, the first time that women had voted en masse since the Second Republic. The

Suárez government was now at the zenith of its power and popularity. Not only had it disarmed the Francoist hardliners, but it had deftly marginalized the democratic opposition, establishing itself in the process as the chief driver of the transition.

Government success placed the opposition on the back foot. The Platform of Democratic Bodies had reacted on 27 November 1976 by fixing the conditions for the participation of the opposition in the first democratic elections. The so-called 'seven conditions' included the recognition of all political parties and trade unions, a far-reaching amnesty, the dissolution of the Movement, the political neutrality of the state media, and the creation of regional institutions. Hereafter, the overriding political issue was to be the very nature of the democracy that was to be constructed in Spain. This ushered in a prolonged struggle between the opposition, which called for a full-blown liberal democracy, and the government, which defended a more restrictive vision.

That the government saw the still-illegal PSOE as central to the legitimacy of the forthcoming general election was made abundantly clear by its authorization of the party's congress in early December, the first to be held in Spain since 1932. The congress showcased not only the party's programme and leadership, especially the youthful and compelling Felipe González, but also its international credentials, as many of Europe's leading social democrats attended, including Willy Brandt (president of the Socialist International), François Mitterrand, Olaf Palme, and Michael Foot. Acutely aware of the importance of the Socialist International within Western European politics, the government was eager to promote the PSOE, despite its having only 10,000 members at the end of 1976, as the principal force on the left. Indeed, the government's sponsorship helped the PSOE outstrip its rivals, including the PSOE-in-exile, the Popular Socialist Party, and others. The PSOE would further consolidate its position in the build-up to the general election by insisting that other socialist parties merge, rather than ally, with it. At the congress, Felipe González acknowledged not only that Adolfo Suárez had skilfully 'entered the terrain of the opposition', but also that the PSOE would take part in the elections, while calling for a post-electoral 'constitutional commitment' that would ensure the constituent nature of the Cortes.[49] In yet another strategic shift, the PSOE now judged that the drawing up of a constitution would fulfil the terms of the 'negotiated democratic rupture'.

## THE LEGALIZATION OF THE PCE

In contrast to the PSOE, the PCE was viewed by the Suárez Cabinet, in common with all the governments of the dictatorship, as its nemesis. In late September 1976 the minister of the interior had instructed the civil governors that 'including up to the PSOE, personal and institutional tolerance will be shown', but for the PCE 'the intolerance will be both personal and institutional'.[50] During the third quarter of 1976, 1,506 Communist militants were arrested and another 1,263 in the last quarter. It was therefore no surprise that the informal discussions that started up between the government and the opposition in November 1976 did not include the Communists. Even the opposition appeared to harbour an ambiguous attitude towards the PCE, the Socialist Congress of early December fuelling Communist fears that the socialists were willing to take part in the elections without them. Santiago Carrillo therefore seized the initiative by giving a press conference in Madrid on 10 December 1976 in which he effectively warned the government that the exclusion of the PCE from the elections would delegitimize them. 'Liberty is indivisible,' he insisted, 'either it exists for everyone or it's not liberty.'[51] Arrested shortly afterwards, Carrillo was then released a few days later. However, the PCE was excluded from the first round of official talks between the opposition and the government on 4 January 1977, forcing the PCE to negotiate by proxy.

The situation of the PCE was to be transformed by an upsurge in terrorist violence, the extreme left and right alike pursuing a 'strategy of tension' in an effort to disrupt the transition by provoking the intervention of the military. On the far left, the most active group was GRAPO (*Grupos de Resistencia Antifascista de Primero de Octubre*) (Anti-Fascist Resistance Groups of the First of October), which was founded in 1975 by, amongst others, Pío Moa, who later became – in a curious twist – a prominent neo-Francoist historian. In December 1976, GRAPO first kidnapped the president of the Council of the State, the diehard Francoist Antonio María de Oriol, and then, in January, the president of the

Supreme Council of Military Justice, Lieutenant General Emilio Villaes-cusa. Simultaneously, the far right, horrified at the prospect of being marginalized by the new regime, undertook its own campaign of terror with the complicity of members of the security forces. This inadvertent pincer movement reached a climax with Madrid's 'Black Week' of 23–28 January 1977. On 23 January right-wing extremists killed a student at a pro-amnesty demonstration. The next day GRAPO kidnapped Villaescusa, the police killed another student protester, and far-right gunmen assaulted a lawyers' office on Atocha Street in central Madrid linked to the Workers' Commissions and the PCE, killing five people and seriously wounding four others. The victims were lined up against a wall before being shot, a macabre reconstruction of the Civil War repres-sion. Finally, on 28 January, GRAPO assassinated four members of the security forces.

The government tried to prevent the PCE from holding a public funeral for the 'Atocha 5', but to no avail. The peaceful and orderly nature of the burial procession, a 'silent sea of red carnations and raised fists', attended by thousands of people, did much to dispel the image that the dictatorship had assiduously cultivated of the anti-Spanish 'other'.[52] The outpouring of sympathy for the Communists had a tre-mendous impact on public opinion: whereas a poll of October 1976 found only 25 per cent in favour of legalizing the PCE and 35 per cent against, by February 1977, 43 per cent supported the measure and 24 per cent opposed it. The restraint exercised by the Communists at the funeral and the upsurge in support for legalization made a deep impres-sion on Adolfo Suárez. Having first established contact with Carrillo via an intermediary in August 1976, Suárez was increasingly convinced not only that it would be impossible to marginalize the PCE from the future democratic regime, but, even more importantly, that the price of exclusion would be even greater than that of inclusion. The upshot was a six-hour clandestine meeting between Suárez and Carrillo on 27 February 1977 at which the two men established a genuine rapport (Carrillo later remarked that 'we greeted one another like old friends').[53] At the meeting, the Communist leader accepted a democratic monarchy in exchange for the legalization of the PCE, Suárez saying he would do 'everything possible' to achieve it.[54] As a gesture of goodwill, Suárez authorized a 'Eurocommunist Summit' in Madrid in early March.

Attended by the French and Italian Communist leaders, Georges Marchais and Enrico Berlinguer respectively, the summit enhanced the PCE's image as a responsible and restrained force. No doubt Suárez was further reassured by a poll which revealed that only 9 per cent of those surveyed would vote for the PCE.

Sometime after the meeting with Carrillo, Suárez took the decision to legalize the PCE. This was a seismic volte-face given the centrality of the 'Judaeo-Marxist-Masonic plot' to the mythology of the Franco dictatorship and the fact that – in stark contrast to the Jewish people or the Freemasons – the Communists had done more to combat the regime than any other force. Accepting the bête noire that had bedevilled the dictatorship for forty years constituted a traumatic break for many Francoists, but, as Adolfo Suárez later observed, 'the key to the internal and external credibility of the political process was the recognition of the PCE'.[55] The very fact that he took this momentous decision shows not only how unforeseeable and indeterminate the passage from dictatorship to democracy was, but also how far Suárez had come since first being made prime minister in July 1976, as no one would have predicted then that he would later legalize the PCE. In addition, one of the 'great paradoxes' of the transition was that the terrorist attacks of the extreme left and right had the opposite effect to the one intended.[56] Instead of debilitating the political process, they fortified it by increasing the unity of the democratic forces and by drawing the government and opposition closer together, thereby speeding up rather than stalling or subverting change.

The timing of the PCE's legalization – arguably the most critical moment of the entire transition – was carefully calibrated in order to contain the immediate fallout. The announcement was made during Easter Week on Saturday 9 April 1977 in the expectation that many of the principal objectors would be absent from Madrid on holiday. The response of the combative Manuel Fraga was predictably vehement, the leader of *Alianza Popular* denouncing the move as 'an authentic coup d'état, which has transformed reform into rupture and ruined both legality and legitimacy', but the most feared reaction was that of the army.[57] The Superior Council of the Army declared its 'general condemnation' of the initiative, but 'accepts the fait accompli in a disciplined fashion' in defence of 'national interests of a higher order', that is, the monarchy – not the government. It also reminded the government of its 'irrevocable obligation to defend the unity of the Motherland, her flag, the integration of the monarchist institutions, and the good name of the Armed Forces'.[58] Shocked and angered by the measure, the army chiefs had been pacified by the personal intervention of the king and the vice-president, General Gutiérrez Mellado, though the minister of the navy, Admiral Gabriel Pita da Veiga, resigned on 11 April.

The destabilizing effects of the legalization were assuaged by the PCE's immediate declaration of support for the national flag, the constitutional monarchy, and the 'unity of the Motherland', a move that Carrillo regarded as a necessary 'dramatic effect', as it would cause a 'profound impression on the country, capable of diminishing the effect of the military declaration'.[59] Indeed, the legalization of the PCE was now supported in a poll by 55 per cent of Spaniards and opposed by only 12 per cent. On the one hand, the legalization of the

The Communist Party's May Day celebration of 1978

PCE meant that there was no turning back for the Suárez government. There had hitherto existed 'reasons to doubt the sincerity of the government', but the legalization of the PCE gave it an unequivocal democratic credibility.[60] For example, the European Parliament had insisted in 1976 that a non-negotiable condition for the entry of Spain into the EEC was recognition of the PCE. On the other hand, Suárez paid a high price for the initiative, as he earned the enmity of many conservatives, especially amongst the military.

## THE GENERAL ELECTION
## OF JUNE 1977

Legalization of the PCE was not the only paradigmatic shift undertaken by the government between the referendum of December 1976 and the general election of June 1977. On 8 February, following negotiations between the government and the opposition's so-called 'Commission of Nine', the Law of Associations of June 1976 was modified so that the political parties simply had to register themselves rather than be vetted by the state. The situation of the illegal trade unions was also transformed. Back in October 1976, the government, following a series of talks with the clandestine trade unions, had transferred the patrimony, services, and 20,000 public employees of the Syndical Organization to a new administrative branch prior to the body's formal dissolution. Still, a government decree of 4 March only endorsed a restrictive right to strike, while omitting to legalize the clandestine trade unions. Predictably, the measure was heavily criticized by the opposition, prompting the government to pass the Syndical Law on 1 April, which legalized the Communist-dominated Workers' Commissions, the UGT, the USO, and other clandestine unions. In addition, obligatory membership of the Francoist Syndical Organization was legally suppressed in early June. The 'Commission of Nine' also secured a new amnesty on 14 March, which included those terrorists without blood on their hands. The amnesty, together with other conciliatory initiatives, such as recognition of the Basque flag, or *ikurriña*, and a truce with ETA (political-military) on 20 May, failed to ease the tensions within the Basque Country, as shown by the tumultuous pro-amnesty demonstrations in May (during which six people died) and by the kidnapping and later assassination of the businessman and former mayor of Bilbao, Javier de Ybarra, by the other ETA group, ETA (military), a defiant riposte to the government's truce with ETA (political-military).

The 'Commission of Nine' was adamant, too, that the Movement had to be dissolved before the general election was held so that the government could not draw on its extensive resources, as it had done during the referendum. The Movement's General Secretariat and National Council were disbanded by decree on 1 April, the party's 7,000 public employees, like those of the Syndical Organization, being absorbed by the general administration to avoid fuelling resentment. Suárez nonetheless ensured that the Movement's media empire, which employed 4,500 people and encompassed thirty-nine dailies, ten magazines, forty radio stations, and the *Pyresa* news agency, remained under his control. One reform over which the opposition was able to exercise little influence was the Electoral Law of 14 March 1977. The government purposely over-represented the rural provinces in order to favour conservative interests, its chief negotiator later admitting that 'hectares counted for ... more than the citizens'.[61] Thus in Soria in northeast Spain 34,636 votes would elect a deputy, whereas in Madrid 139,569 were required. The law obliged the electorate to choose a party list rather than an individual candidate, which not only bestowed an enormous power of patronage on the national leaders (who drew up the lists), but also provided them with a surgical means of eliminating dissent, as non-conformists could be simply cut from the lists. Despite the Constitution later declaring that the 'internal structure and functioning' of the political parties 'should be democratic', the system of 'closed lists' has greatly stifled debate and dissent within them.[62] Small wonder that the 'Commission of Nine' was the principal driver of political reform during this period, as it constantly challenged the government's more circumscribed vision. The transformation wrought by the government under the watchful eye of the opposition was reflected in the resolution of the European Parliament of 22 April 1977, which formally acknowledged that the prime minister had fulfilled his promise of democratic reform. Following Suárez's first official trip to Bonn that same month, deputy premier Alfonso Osorio claimed that 'the government has now won the political battle in Europe.'[63]

The general election of 15 June 1977 was the first democratic election to be held in Spain since 1936. Numerous parties took part, ranging from the extreme left to the extreme right via a cluster of centrist formations, along with the main left-wing parties, the PSOE and the PCE, and the dominant force on the right, the AP, in addition to a host of regionalist entities, such as the Basque Nationalist Party and the *Convergència Democràtica de Catalunya* or CDC (Democratic Convergence of Catalonia). Very few women were to be found in leadership roles, the *Izquierda Democrática* (Democratic Left party) of the former Francoist minister Joaquín Ruiz-Giménez being an exception with four female members on its executive committee. In all, 5,359 candidates (of whom only 708 were women) contested the 350 congressional seats, while 938 (of whom just thirty-nine were women) competed for the 207 senatorial ones. Adolfo Suárez stood for the *Unión de Centro Democrático* or UCD (the Union of the Democratic Centre), the origin of which lay in the *Partido Popular* or PP (Popular Party) created by José María de Areilza, Pío Cabanillas, and José Pedro Pérez Llorca in June 1976. The Popular Party aimed to become the linchpin of an electoral coalition called the 'Democratic Centre', but the entire enterprise was taken over in May 1977 by Suárez and renamed the *Unión de Centro Democrático*, incorporating Catholic, liberal, social-democratic, and even 'independent' (i.e. Falangist) strands. This was a centrist, catch-all formation that placed a premium on the politics of consensus, thereby aspiring to counteract the potential polarization of the electorate into antagonistic blocs. Like the incumbent government, it was led by those who, a future UCD minister noted, 'had not participated in the civil war', who 'shared the desire to prioritize the future over the past', and who therefore 'coincided with ample sectors of the left'.[64] Unlike the PSOE, the UCD was a coalition rather than a party, as Suárez did not yet insist on the merger of the numerous groups within it. As the coalition's campaign manager, Leopoldo Calvo Sotelo, remarked, Suárez 'relied more on himself, his charisma, his mastery of television, his exuberant friendliness, than on the supportive base of a political organization'.[65] Despite the dissolution of the Movement, the party drew heavily on its former personnel, mobilizing civil governors, provincial leaders, and local apparatchiks of the dictatorship's single party on behalf of democracy. In addition, seventeen of those who headed the UCD's fifty-one lists were former Francoist deputies, while a third of its successful congressional candidates were 'independents', that is, former members of the Movement. The idea was to ensure, explained one of Suárez's closest collaborators, 'that those who are carrying out the political reform are not excluded from the new political class that is being formed'.[66]

The UCD's links to the erstwhile Movement notwithstanding, Manuel Fraga's *Alianza Popular* was of a different generation, ideology, and outlook, including 183 Francoist deputies on its slate, so that 80 per cent of the party's congressional deputies would be former deputies of the dictatorship. The identification of the party with the dictatorship was heightened by the incorporation of candidates such as the pugnacious intellectual and former minister Gonzalo Fernández de la Mora and even ex-premier Carlos Arias Navarro. It was nonetheless assumed that the AP would achieve 'excellent results'.[67] The principal forces on the left, the PSOE and the PCE, had far more in common with the UCD than the AP. The dominant leitmotif of their campaigns was the democratic nature of their projects, the PCE stressing that 'the Communist vote is a vote for democracy', while the PSOE identified socialism with the 'conquest of liberty and democracy'.[68] The goal, declared Felipe González, was to transform 'our country into a society similar to that of our neighbours'.[69]

Adolfo Suárez was confident of winning an absolute majority, a misplaced optimism strongly shaped by his spectacular triumph in the referendum on the Law for Political Reform. The UCD failed to win a majority, but it did finish first with 165 deputies, while the PSOE came second with 118 seats. Between them, they won 64 per cent of the vote and 81 per cent of the congressional seats, the UCD's support being concentrated in the rural areas and amongst the urban middle classes, while the PSOE's prime constituencies were the skilled working class and the young. What differentiated the support for the two parties was not so much class as religion, as 80 per cent of the UCD's voters were practising Catholics, in contrast to less than 50 per cent of the PSOE's voters. The electoral outcome made it inevitable that the new constitution would be a work of inter-party compromise, partly because the UCD had failed to secure an outright majority and partly because the PSOE had enough deputies to be a major player during the constitutional proceedings. The PSOE was nonetheless the 'moral victor', having established itself as the leading alternative to the UCD.[70]

The electoral system had not only under-represented urban areas, but also penalized those parties with under 10 per cent of the vote. Thus the PCE, with 9.33 per cent of the vote, secured only twenty (5.7 per cent) of the 350 deputies and the *Alianza Popular*, with 8.3 per cent of the vote, returned only sixteen (4.6 per cent) of the congressional seats. Having done so much more than the socialists in the struggle against the dictatorship, the Communists were naturally aggrieved at the electoral outcome, but the result was very much in line with the pre-election polls and similar to that of the Greek and Portuguese Communist parties during their transitions (the Greek Communists won 9.4 per cent of the vote in the first post-dictatorial elections and the Portuguese 12.4 per cent). For Fraga's AP, the election was a catastrophe, indicative of how unpopular the dictatorship had become by the time of the *Caudillo*'s death. That only twenty-one female deputies were returned to the Congress of Deputies, and a mere six female senators, underlines how low a priority was placed by the parties on the role of women in politics.

There was a strong correlation between those families which had voted for the Communists and socialists in 1977 and those that supported the Popular Front in 1936, as well as between those families which had voted for the UCD in 1977 and those that backed the CEDA in 1936. Such trends reflected the extent to which political values were transmitted from one generation to another, but any fears of a return to the politics of the Second Republic were misguided. Only four of the thirty-three parties in the Cortes of 1936 were present in the Cortes of 1977 – the Socialist Party, the Communist Party, the Basque Nationalist Party, and the Republican Left of Catalonia – while there were other major differences between the two elections, such as the disappearance of the anarcho-syndicalist constituency, the republican vote being transferred largely to the socialists (facilitating their success in, for example, Catalonia and Valencia), and above all the fact that the two main parties in 1977 were fully democratic rather than semi-democratic. The reformist PCE of 1977 also provided a major contrast to the revolutionary party of 1936, though it was still led by figures from the 1930s, such as Santiago Carrillo and Dolores Ibárruri. On the other hand, the dissolution of the republican institutions-in-exile on 21 June 1977 was a measure of the legitimacy of the general election of 1977, as well as a further blow to the narrative of the 'Two Spains'.

The success of the UCD and PSOE represented the triumph of moderation over extremism. The majority of Spaniards, repelled by the polarities of the past but fearful of the future, voted for consensual, orderly change. In looking to the future, not the past, they voted for a younger generation of politicians who had not lived through the Civil War, who were not implicated in the repression, and who were the living embodiments of the ascendant middle classes that emerged with the economic modernization of the 1960s and 1970s. Consequently, the youthful, appealing figures of Adolfo Suárez and Felipe González held an allure that those associated with the dictatorship, such as Manuel Fraga and Marcelino Camacho, or with the Civil War, such as Santiago Carrillo and Carlos Arias Navarro, could not match. It was clear that the politicians of the transition had learned a fundamental lesson from the 1930s, as reflected, say, in the preamble to the Law for Political Reform: the politics of intransigence would destroy democracy rather than consolidate it.

The general election of June 1977 had transformed the political landscape. An unelected government that had set the political agenda had been replaced by an elected one that was dependent on a hung parliament. Accordingly, the politics of negotiation and compromise, which had admittedly distinguished the Suárez administration since the referendum, would be even more necessary now. The uncertainty of the future was enhanced by the Cabinet reshuffle after the general election. In exchange for agreeing to the merger of the different parties that made up the UCD, the party leaders – otherwise known as the 'Barons' – were rewarded with positions in the Cabinet, but the policy differences between the Christian democrats, the liberals, the social democrats, and the so-called 'regionalists' meant that the government lacked the cohesion and coherence of its predecessor. Adding to this destabilization was the fact that the government and the Cortes stood as an oasis of democracy within the vast institutional and legal expanse of the dictatorial state. Only those Fundamental Laws that clashed directly with the Law for Political Reform had been overturned, while the armed forces, the police, the judiciary, and the civil service all remained in the hands of Francoist appointees.

## THE AMNESTY

For the regionalists and left-wing parties, it was essential that an amnesty be passed for the political prisoners before the constitutional proceedings could begin. Ever since the 1940s there had been sections of the anti-Francoist opposition that had viewed reconciliation over the Civil War as vital to the reconstruction of democracy in Spain, this becoming official Communist Party policy in the 1950s. The 'radical novelty' of the transition was that this policy was extended to the dictatorship and its political heirs.[71] This approach has been dubbed the *pacto de olvido* (literally, the pact of oblivion), often translated as the 'pact of silence', an implicit reproach of the opposition for not making the Francoists pay for their crimes. In reality, the proponents of reconciliation – the Communists, socialists, and regional nationalists – were driven not by the act of forgetting, but by their very memory of the suffering and loss caused by the Civil War. Accordingly, their aim was to achieve closure by eschewing the hatreds and antagonisms of the past, as a continuation of the seemingly endless saga of the 'Two Spains' would greatly impede the efforts to construct a democracy. After all, those guilty of blood crimes were to be found not only amongst the ranks of the Francoists, but also – if on a much lesser scale – in the ranks of the opposition, foremost amongst whom was the Communist leader Santiago Carrillo, one of those responsible for the massacre at Paracuellos in late 1936. 'How could those who had been killing one another reconcile ourselves,' asked the Workers' Commissions' leader, Marcelino Camacho, who had spent many years in Francoist jails, 'if we did not erase the past once and for all?'[72] 'Erasing' the past therefore involved a conscious effort to avoid a showdown over the Civil War and the dictatorship, as this would cause unforetold, even irreparable, damage to the transition. At heart lay a commitment not to repeat the tragedies of the past, but to focus on the future.

The memory of the war and of the dictatorship therefore went hand in hand with the politics of consensus, allowing the secretary-general of the Communist Party, Santiago Carrillo, to collaborate with the last secretary-general of the Movement, Adolfo Suárez. Indeed, it was this very desire for collaboration that distinguished the post-Francoist transition from all the other regimes in modern Spanish history, as it was based on reconciliation not revenge, consensus not conflict. No doubt the reconciliatory politics of the transition were less dramatic and newsworthy than the turbulent Glorious Revolution of 1868–74 or the tumultuous Second Republic of 1931–9, but they were to prove a far more effective formula for the creation and consolidation of democracy.

By the time the Cortes met in late July 1977, the overwhelming majority of political prisoners had already been released, but not those who had committed 'blood crimes'. The opposition called for the liberation of the remaining anti-Francoists, but it did not aim to put the Francoists on trial – a move that would have been politically untenable, in any case. The UCD, however, was extremely reluctant to pursue the matter. It proposed a highly restrictive measure, but this was vigorously contested by the opposition. An agreement was finally reached following an intense series of negotiations. The amnesty of 14 October 1977 covered all acts up to December 1976, and all those up to 15 June 1977 if carried out in defence of democracy or autonomy; in other words, ETA was included, but not the extreme right. After 15 June 1977, however, ETA was officially a terrorist organization. The only deputies to vote against the bill were from the AP (Fraga denouncing it for giving 'encouragement to the terrorists') and the sole deputy from a left-wing Basque party.[73] For *Fuerza Nueva* (New Force), this represented a 'great betrayal' of the dictatorship, but the party's political irrelevance reflected the exiguous support for the core ideals of Francoism.[74]

## THE MONCLOA PACTS

The most urgent task of the UCD government was to tackle the far-reaching effects of the economic recession that had convulsed Spain since the oil crisis of 1973. The three principal problems were inflation, unemployment, and the balance of payments, inflation having reached 17.5 per cent in 1976 and 42 per cent by mid-1977. During the summer Adolfo Suárez attempted to reach an agreement with the trade unions and the employers' organization, the *Confederación Española de Organizaciones Empresariales* or CEOE (Spanish Confederation of Business Organizations), only established in May 1977. Both the PCE and the Workers' Commissions (or CCOO) eagerly endorsed a pact, as this would raise the party's profile following its disappointing election results, but the PSOE and UGT were little inclined to assist the UCD, their principal rival. A further obstacle to a pact was the scant enthusiasm of the employers. As a result, Suárez abandoned the pursuit of a pact between the employers' organization and the trade unions for one between the political parties. The Communists called for a national government to be formed, but the socialists rejected the proposal outright, as it would only strengthen their two main competitors while weakening the PSOE's projection as the alternative to the UCD. However, once Adolfo Suárez and Santiago Carrillo reached an initial agreement on the need for a political pact to resolve the economic crisis, the socialists had no option but to join them.

Beginning in early September, the negotiations over the so-called 'Moncloa Pacts' were finally concluded on 25 October 1977. The agreement aimed to tackle the crisis by controlling the money supply, reining in public spending, devaluing the peseta, and pursuing wage restraint. The Pacts had an immediate impact insofar as inflation dropped from 26.4 per cent in 1977 to 16 per cent in 1978, the balance of payments deficit was eliminated, and the foreign currency reserves rose from $4,000 million in mid-1977 to $10,000 million by the end of 1978. On the other hand, the pacts failed to prevent unemployment climbing from 6.3 per cent in 1977 to 10 per cent in 1978 or the number of workers on strike rising from 2.3 million in 1977 to 3.6 million in 1978 before peaking at 5.75 million in 1979. Worse still, much of the recovery was to be undone by the oil crisis of early 1979. Nonetheless, the Moncloa Pacts furthered the transition to democracy by underlining the willingness of the parties to reach agreements at a time of national crisis and by fostering a broad consensus over the social market model. It also set a precedent that the UGT and CEOE would follow with their labour agreements of 1979, 1980, and 1981, all of which helped consolidate the new regime by reducing tensions in the workplace. Symptomatic of the new alignment within industrial relations was the calling of the first democratic trade-union elections since the Republic in early 1978, as well as the holding of the first legal May Day celebration since the 1930s, which attracted around one million people in Madrid.

## THE CONSTITUTIONAL DEBATES

While the Moncloa Pacts were being negotiated, the Cortes set about drawing up the new constitution. The UCD had originally aimed to draw up the Constitution on its own terms, the minister of justice remarking before the general election that if the PSOE won more than ninety deputies this would thwart the UCD's ambition 'to draw up the Constitution that we wanted'.[75] Once the party failed to secure a majority in the Cortes, the government sought to have the first draft of the Constitution drawn up by the Ministry of Justice, but the left, especially the socialists, objected that this should be the task of the Cortes. A further initiative to have the draft produced by a team of experts in constitutional law did not prosper either. As a result, a thirty-six-member parliamentary Commission of Constitutional Affairs and Public Liberties was formed which then created a sub-committee of seven members, comprising three UCD deputies, one socialist, one Communist, one representative of the Popular Alliance, and a Catalan regionalist, who represented both Catalan and Basque interests (though the Basques soon withdrew their delegated author-ity). The politics of the transition had suddenly shifted from the open spaces of the streets and squares, the sites of demonstrations, rallies, and strikes, to the closed spaces of committee rooms and the chamber of the Cortes. The secrecy that characterized the deliberations of the subcommittee allowed its members to make the type of concessions and reach the kind of compromises which would have been difficult, if not impossible, in the public arena of the Cortes, a salutary contrast to the constitutional proceedings of the Second Republic.

Once the first draft of the Constitution was finished by late De-cember 1977, over a thousand amendments were presented. The subcommittee then set about processing the amendments, the UCD members forging a tacit alliance with Manuel Fraga of the Popular Alli-ance and the Catalan regionalist Miquel Roca in order to alter the text in accordance with the government's aspirations, which led the PSOE's Gregorio Peces-Barba to abandon the subcommittee in protest on 6 March 1978. Once the Constitutional Commission began to debate the sub-committee's draft in May, a similar scenario played out, as most of the articles were passed by the UCD in alliance with the AP, which together had a majority of nineteen votes to seventeen. By 18 May the PSOE was threatening to leave the Commission, which alarmed Adolfo Suárez, as he did not want the Constitution to be seen as 'right-wing'.[76] As a result, a series of late-night meetings took place between Fernando Abril of the UCD and Alfonso Guerra of the PSOE, which created a 'new constitutional consensus', thereby allowing the deliberations of the Commission to progress more smoothly.[77] The UCD's sudden change of tack, an effort to establish a broader consensus by incorporating the main force on the left, provided yet another contrast to the partisan proceedings of the Second Republic.

The most contentious constitutional question of all was the territorial structure of the new state. The large-scale demonstrations in the Basque Country and Catalonia in favour of autonomy led the government to seek an arrangement that would ease the tensions in both regions before the constitutional debates began. In the Catalan case, the government, anxious not to be outmanoeuvred by the recently formed Assembly of Catalan Parliamentarians, invited the exiled Catalan leader Josep Tarradellas to Madrid for talks in late June 1977, the subsequent negotiations eventually also including the Catalan parties. The upshot was an agreement in late September 1977 by which the *Generalitat* (Catalan government) of the 1930s would be provisionally restored. Tarradellas's jubilant return to Barcelona on 23 October 1977 following thirty-eight years in exile was crowned by his triumphant greeting 'Ja sóc aquí' ('I have returned').[78] Such an outcome had never formed part of the UCD's original plans, but events had resulted in 'an exercise in political engineering which was very characteristic of the Spanish transition, in which reformist and rupturist elements were mixed together'.[79] At Tarradellas's swearing-in as president of the *Generalitat* on 24 October 1977, Suárez acclaimed the accord as a 'victory of the people' that would help 'consolidate the process of democratization of Spanish life', while justifying its pre-constitutional realization as 'something so indisputable and just'.[80] In the Basque case, an agreement was reached whereby a historic economic arrangement would be incorporated into a Statute of Autonomy once the Constitution was completed. The process culminated with the formation of a General Basque Council on 30 December 1977.

The upsurge in regional sentiment was not confined to the Basque Country and Catalonia alone. Demonstrations in favour of autonomy were held in many other parts of Spain in late 1977, such as in Valencia on 9 October. For Andalusia, which had never possessed a strong political identity, autonomy was transformed into the foremost public issue following Franco's death, as reflected in the demonstration of 4 December 1977 in Seville, which attracted around 1.5 million participants. The minister of the regions, Manuel Clavero Arévalo, eagerly pursued a policy of *café para todos* ('coffee for everyone'), despite the conflicting views within the UCD over the autonomy issue. Between January and October 1978 juntas and councils were formed in fourteen regions, ranging from Asturias, Galicia, Castile-León, Navarre, and Aragón in the north to Andalusia, the Levante, Extremadura, Castile-La Mancha, Murcia, and the Canary Islands in the south. The wave of pre-autonomous entities heavily conditioned the constitutional debate on the territorial structure, as the sweeping nature of the process made it almost inevitable that it would be replicated throughout the country. By the time the Constitution was passed it was 'nearly unthinkable' that any of the pre-autonomous bodies would renounce their claim to full autonomy.[81] The virtually nationwide movement in favour of autonomy revealed not only the visceral nature of the backlash against the heavy-handed centralism of the dictatorship, but also a desire to obtain the same regional powers as the Basque Country and Catalonia, which was inflected by a lurking resentment at the idea of the two regions acquiring special privileges.

The constitutional debate over the territorial structure of the state was extremely laborious, not least because the parties, especially the UCD, did not have a clear model in mind. A further complication, recalls Jordi Solé Tura, the PCE's representative on the subcommittee, was that it took place 'in the midst of so many opposing interests, of so many reservations, of so many obstacles. The consensus was in peril on numerous occasions.'[82] The greatest point of contention was the idea that Spain 'is based on the indissoluble unity of Spain', while constituting a 'nation of nationalities'.[83] Manuel Fraga objected in the Cortes that 'one cannot accept more than one "nation": Spain, nor more than one "nationality"', but the liberal monarchist Joaquín Satrústegui retorted that it was an 'urgent necessity' to adapt the state to 'the national and regional plurality of Spain, which is a historical reality'.[84] In a similar vein, the socialist Txiki Benegas averred that 'the greatest liberty of the peoples of Spain' was 'the greatest guarantee of the unity of Spain', this being the only way to tackle 'a problem in Spain [which has been] always badly solved'.[85] Even so, the inherent tension between the 'nation' of Spain and the regional 'nationalities' was never fully resolved, an ambiguity which was born of the compromises that were made. Indeed, the UCD had felt trapped, in the words of the minister of the interior, Rodolfo Martín Villa, between 'the two fires of a Basque and Catalan nationalism with a maximalist approach, and inclined to giving ultimatums, and a left given to emulating the nationalist exigencies'.[86] As a result, the UCD 'had no other option than to try to put on a brave face, subordinating everything to the achievement of the great objective of the moment, which was none other than to give birth to the Constitution'.[87]

There were essentially two models at issue: the creation of a special autonomous status for the 'historic' regions of the Basque Country, Catalonia, and Galicia, or a state organized along federal lines that offered autonomy to all the nationalities or regions. The Constitution eventually offered autonomy to all, though access was via a two-track system. The fast track, embodied in article 151, was basically reserved for those regions that had held a plebiscite under the Second Republic, that is, Catalonia, the Basque Country, and Galicia, while the slow one, outlined in article 143, envisaged full autonomy being achieved after at least five years. Certainly the first Suárez government had never foreseen a 'state of the autonomies', but following the general election of June 1977 democracy and autonomy had become increasingly entwined. Article 148 of the Constitution nonetheless failed to define the powers of the autonomous regions, later a source of considerable conflict.

## THE CONSTITUTION

Many of the constitutional articles were shot through with ambiguity, but this reflected the search for consensus, as the parties generally sought to accommodate one another rather than impose their own criteria. Thus the state was declared aconfessional ('no faith will have a state character'), but would maintain 'relations of cooperation with the Catholic Church'.[88] Recognition of the market economy and the rights of private property were juxtaposed alongside state planning and the confiscation of private property. Free and universal public education was guaranteed, but private education would be partly financed by the state. The death penalty was abolished, but upheld for the armed forces in time of war. The right to life was defined in such a way as to leave the door open to abortion. Determined to avoid a repetition of the baleful political meddling of Alfonso XIII, the left strove to restrict the monarchy's powers (often with the backing of the former Falangist Manuel Fraga), but the head of state still designated the prime minister and remained commander-in-chief of the armed forces. The tendency to prioritize consensus-building over ideological imposition was partly shaped by the unprecedented convergence of monarchy and democracy, partly by the inclusive outlook of the two main parties, and partly by an acute awareness of the damage wrought by the doctrinal dogmatism and divisions of the 1930s. Unlike in the Portuguese transition, the military was not involved in the confection of the Constitution, which was just as well, as none of the three military senators designated by the king voted in its favour. The Constitution of 1978 was unprecedented in modern Spanish history insofar as it did not represent the victory of one group over another. On the contrary, the triumph of the 1978 text lay in the very fact that it embodied a synthesis of divergent ideologies and party programmes.

The new state was defined as 'social and democratic' and framed as a parliamentary monarchy. All Spaniards were 'equal before the law' and could not be discriminated against on grounds of 'birth, race, sex, religion, opinion and any other condition', though the head of state cannot be a woman.[89] The nominal equality of women with men was subsequently developed in a series of laws, and would eventually culminate in the 2007 Law for the Effective Equality of Women and Men. The state was founded on 'the indissoluble unity of the Spanish nation', but 'recognizes and guarantees the right to autonomy of the nationalities and regions which make it up'.[90] In contrast to the Second Republic, a bicameral if asymmetrical Cortes was established, comprising the Congress of Deputies, elected by proportional representation, and the Senate, chosen by a first-past-the-post system that furnished each province with the same number of seats. Relations between the government and parliament were strongly shaped by the experience of the Second Republic, during which the Cortes was seen as a source of instability, so the vote of confidence was designed to be used sparingly. The same desire for stability meant that the Cabinet was 'absolutely dominated' by the prime minister.[91]

A notable aspect of the Constitution was that it addressed one of the principal demands of the Citizens' Movement, namely, participation as a pillar of democratic citizenship. Half a dozen articles defended the right to participate, such as article 27, which states that 'the teachers, the parents, and, in their case, the pupils will intervene in the control and management of all the centres maintained by the administration with public funds', or article 48, which protects the right of young people to participate in 'political, social, and cultural development', while article 129 invoked the right of workers to participate in 'the management of businesses'.[92] Article 87 even allows citizens to initiate legislation through the collection of 500,000 signatures. These rights were dwarfed by the scope of article 9, which commanded the state to 'remove the obstacles' to the full participation of the citizens in 'political, economic, cultural, and social life', that is to say, the state did not just protect participation, it actively encouraged it.[93] The right to participation was complemented by a whole raft of other rights that both defined and guaranteed it. In fact, the rights of citizens composed one of the lengthiest parts of the Constitution, fleshing out the declaration in article 1 that Spain was a 'social and democratic state'. Thus the state recognized that citizens have a right to education, health care, 'dignified and adequate housing', culture, and even 'an environment adequate to the development of a person'.[94] However, this tended to transform the demands of the Citizens' Movement into abstract rights rather than, it can be argued, 'expanding opportunities for active political mobilization and participation'.[95] In other words, the Constitution basically came down on the side of the liberal, rights-based model of democratic citizenship rather than the participatory and communitarian one. Little wonder, then, that the Constitution recognized the right to form trade unions and professional associations, but the request of the Citizens' Movement to 'constitutionalize' the neighbourhood associations was explicitly rejected. Finally, the Constitution overthrew those Fundamental Laws that had not yet been invalidated by the Law for Political Reform, putting a formal end to the dictatorship. In purely legal terms, the transition was over.

The Constitution was passed by the Cortes on 31 October 1978, the Congress voting by 325 votes to six (with fourteen abstentions), and the Senate by 226 to five. Extraordinarily, the deputies of the AP voted at once for and against the Constitution (as well as abstaining), though its National Junta backed the *magna carta* on 30 October 1978 by the admittedly tight margin of forty-eight votes to forty-four. A substantial clerical minority within the Catholic Church rejected the Constitution, the bishops criticizing it for not offering a 'sufficient response to the religious reality of the Spanish', while even the liberal president of the Episcopal Conference, Vicente Enrique Tarancón, was aggrieved that the text had not recognized that 'in Spain we Catholics are a majority'.[96] Some members of the armed forces reacted by entering into conspiracies against the new constitutional order, drawing on the support of ultra-Francoists such as those in *Fuerza Nueva*, which lambasted the Constitution as 'the total and definitive destruction of Spain' for being 'anti-Christian, anti-Spanish, and anti-family'.[97] By contrast, the overwhelming majority of Spaniards approved of the Constitution. In the referendum of 6 December 1978, 88.54 per cent voted in favour and only 7.89 per cent against, though participation, at 67 per cent, was significantly lower than in the referendum of December 1976. In the Basque Country, 55 per cent of the electorate followed the PNV's abstentionist stance (of those who did vote, 69 per cent approved), but in Catalonia both participation and approval were fractionally higher than in the rest of Spain.

The overwhelming support for the Constitution of 1978 gave the lie to the idea that Spain was somehow different to the rest of Western Europe. On the contrary, the Spanish constitutional process was more consensual and less contentious than those elsewhere in Southern Europe. In Portugal, the Constitution of 1976 was blighted by the impositions of the army, which made constitutional reform necessary in 1981, while in Greece the Constitution of 1974 was so powerfully identified with the conservative politician Constantine Karamanlis that the main opposition party, the Panhellenic Socialist Movement (PASOK), would not recognize it until after the party had won the general election of 1981. Further, the Spanish constitutional process was the most participatory, involving three popular consultations: the referendum of December 1976, the general election of June 1977, and the plebiscite of December 1978. Hardly surprisingly, the Constitution of 1978 enjoyed a legitimacy greater than that of any of its predecessors.

## THE GENERAL ELECTION OF 1979

As soon as the Constitution was promulgated, Adolfo Suárez dissolved the Cortes and called a general election for March 1979 in the expectation that he would win an absolute majority. By this stage he had merged the many parties of the UCD coalition into a single, presidential-style party. At its first congress in October 1978, which represented 80,000 members, the party defined itself as 'democratic, progressive, interclassist, and integrative'.[98] To the right, Fraga's support for the Constitution had separated the democratic conservatives from the neo-Francoists, the former Francoist ministers Federico Silva Muñoz and Gonzalo Fernández de la Mora abandoning the party in November 1978. The Popular Alliance's extreme rightism of 1977 was therefore replaced by a more moderate conservatism, as shown by the fact that the liberal monarchist José María de Areilza and the erstwhile UCD vice-premier Alfonso Osorio joined the party. On the left, the PSOE had absorbed the Popular Socialist Party, which was dissolved in April 1978, and merged the three currents of Catalan socialism into one party. Like the UCD, the PSOE was both stronger and more united than at the time of the 1977 general election. Finally, the PCE, which had at last jettisoned Leninism at its congress of April 1978, was convinced that its responsible and temperate role during the constitutional deliberations would benefit it at the ballot box.

The election campaign of 1979 was very different to that of 1977, as the parties now competed openly with one another. For the socialists, the politics of consensus had been consigned to 'the archive of history'.[99] In a television address of 27 February, Suárez resurrected the 'language of fear' of the Catholic right of the 1930s by claiming that the socialists would introduce a collectivist economy, end religious education, allow free and untrammelled abortions, and even dismantle the security forces.[100] What was at stake, he declared resoundingly, was 'nothing more and nothing less than the very definition of the societal model which we aspire to live in'.[101] The politics of national consensus had given way to party politics.

Despite the bellicosity of the election campaign, the results of the two leading parties were very similar to those of 1977, the UCD returning 168 deputies to Congress and the PSOE 121, between them securing 65 per cent of the vote and 83 per cent of the seats. Attracting 10.8 per cent of the vote and twenty-three seats, the PCE did slightly better than in 1977. By contrast, the AP won only 6.1 per cent of the vote and nine seats, seven less than in 1977, indicating that it could not compete with the UCD for the centrist vote. The electoral system had still not been consolidated, not least because the vote for the regional parties rose from 5.5 per cent to 10 per cent. There was also a sharp rise in abstention from 22 per cent to 33 per cent, which has often been attributed to the *desencanto* or disillusionment that spread through Spanish society in 1979, in large measure attributable to the economic depression and the lowering of the voting age from twenty-one to eighteen, many of the 3.5 million new voters taking a limited interest in politics. Finally, women fared even worse than in the 1977 general election, as only nineteen female deputies and six female senators were elected.

On 3 April 1979, Spaniards returned to the polls in order to elect the first democratic local councils since the 1930s, thereby replacing the Francoist councils that had continued *in situ* during the first three years of the transition. At stake were 69,715 councillors in 8,046 municipalities. The political parties were not the only movements that aspired to compete in the local elections. A majority in the Citizens' Movement demanded that the neighbourhood associations should be directly represented in local government. If democracy was not to be 'more than a myth in our country', declared the La Paz association in Madrid, 'each neighbourhood association should collaborate in the election of municipal representatives'.[102] Equally, the San Blas association in Madrid voted to 'collaborate to achieve the full democratic participation of neighbours in the municipal government'.[103] Predictably, most of the parties viewed this goal as an unacceptable intrusion on their control of the political process. The PSOE had already made clear its opposition to association candidates in September 1977 on the grounds that they were 'unrepresentative'.[104] In any case, argued the socialists, the Citizens' Movement had degenerated into a 'strange mixture, from businessmen to housewives'.[105] Underlying this rejection lay the knowledge that other parties on the left enjoyed a greater presence within the associations, but the principal reason was that the socialists' liberal, rights-based view of democracy held that the parties were the true representatives of the people, not collectives that ranged from 'businessmen to housewives'.

In the elections, the UCD came first with 29,614 councillors and the PSOE second with 12,220, but a post-electoral pact between the socialists and the Communists meant that three-quarters of the populace now lived under left-wing councils. The elections did much to consolidate the democratization process not only by bringing local institutions into much closer contact with the concerns of ordinary citizens, but also by transforming the very nature of local government with the incorporation of people, parties, and policies that had little or no connection with the dictatorship. However, it took another six years before the Francoist local government system was overhauled in accordance with the demands of a democratic regime. The 1985 Basic Law on Local Government defended a suffrage based on party lists and determined that the mayor would be elected by the councillors, even though the Constitution offered a choice between 'the councillors' and 'the neighbours'.[106] Accordingly, the reform not only reinforced the political parties' control over local government, but also reflected their top-down vision of democracy, which viewed municipal power as a decidedly low priority.

Following the 1979 local elections, the Citizens' Movement gradually faded away. At the national level, the parties successfully monopolized political decision-making, while at the local level the democratic councils tackled many of the problems that had first given birth to the associations, numerous activists from the Citizens' Movement becoming civil servants in the process. In addition, some councils did introduce participatory mechanisms. Perhaps surprisingly, the Communists were much more receptive to the claims of the Citizens' Movement than the socialists. In the nineteen provincial capitals controlled by the socialists few participatory schemes were introduced, while in the fifty municipalities of more than 50,000 residents that were now run by the PCE, measures were introduced 'of participation or participatory practices'.[107] In any case, the legacy of the neighbour-hood associations can be seen in the neighbourhood committees, which work democratically and lobby the local council for improvements. It has nonetheless proved impossible to institutionalize the mobilization of local residents at the national level. Nonetheless, the Citizens' Movement, which had its origins in the associations of the 1960s and 1970s, did demonstrate that an 'elite-brokered transition' requires a strong and active civil society in order to succeed, as the failure of the transitions in Russia and elsewhere indicate.[108]

## THE DECLINE AND FALL OF ADOLFO SUÁREZ

Following the general election, Suárez bolstered his Cabinet position by replacing nearly all the 'Barons' – the factional leaders within the UCD – with the so-called 'president's men', foremost amongst whom was his close friend Fernando Abril. The aggrieved 'Barons', who still exercised considerable influence, struck back by forcing Suárez to create the Permanent Commission, a *sui generis* body to which they all belonged and which ranked above both the party's Political Council and its Executive Commission. This unstable arrangement was wors-ened by the emergence of a breach between the UCD party base and the parliamentary group, the former being strongly identified with the president and the UCD apparatus, while the latter was closely aligned with the 'Barons', as they chose the candidates for the electoral lists. Paradoxically, progressive institutionalization weakened the UCD by setting the parliamentary group against the provincial and local party.

The resurgence of the 'Barons' crystallized the two quintessential problems of the UCD: factional infighting over parcels of power and a lack of ideological clarity, which was to hamper gravely the execu-tion of the party's reform programme over the next three years. One of the most divisive issues was education. The social democrats and Christian democrats became embroiled in a festering feud over the Statute on Teaching Centres, which was eventually passed into law in

March 1980, but left a bitter legacy, as the social democrats resented the state financing of private schools (most of which were Catholic) without any compensatory concessions. They also clashed heavily over the Law on Divorce, the christian democrats delaying the passing of the bill until June 1981. Factional feuding also led to a long-running confrontation over university reform between 1978 and 1980. These damaging disputes highlighted not only the lack of a common party programme, but also the fact that Adolfo Suárez was providing neither the government nor the party with the required leadership. Frequently absent from the Cortes, invariably secluded behind the walls of the Moncloa Palace, he failed to arbitrate in the constant clashes. His once-renowned capacity for decision-taking appeared to have deserted him, all of which gave rise to the impression that the prime minister had lost his way.

Beyond this, the government faced two principal challenges, the first being Basque terrorism. During the summer of 1978 anti-terrorist policy was transformed by the assassination on 28 June of José María Portell. A Bilbao journalist, Portell had been involved in the most promising effort to date to reach a ceasefire with the most intransigent ETA group, ETA (military). Up to this point the UCD governments had not only dismantled the dictatorship's internal security apparatus, but also striven to secure a ceasefire with both branches of ETA. The death of Portell completely reversed that policy, as reflected in the 'vigorous anti-terrorist legislation' that was now passed, such as the Anti-Terrorist Law of December 1978.[109] The new counter-insurgency approach drew on the expertise of the West German security forces, resulting in the creation of specialized anti-terrorist units, such as that under police commissioner Roberto Conesa in Bilbao. Not surprisingly, the number of ETA prisoners soared (from around 100 in late 1978 to 298 in January 1981), while around 350 members of the terrorist group were put on trial between October 1978 and May 1981. Still, the new policy 'did little if anything to restrain or limit ETA violence', as the number of attacks increased.[110] Having killed nine people in 1977, ETA was to account for the deaths of sixty-seven in 1978, seventy-two in 1979, and eighty-eight in 1980.[111]

Another major challenge for the government was the second oil crisis of early 1979, a result of the Iraq-Iran war, which pushed prices up by 70 per cent. Spain was especially vulnerable to rises in the price of oil, as it imported three-quarters of its energy. The oil crisis brought the economic recovery to a shuddering halt, its most baleful effect being the upsurge in unemployment, which climbed to 12 per cent in 1980 and 15 per cent in 1981. The cost of unemployment benefits, together with that of state pensions, enormously increased the public debt. The workers responded to the slump with 1,789 strikes during the course of 1979. In an effort to keep inflation under control, the UGT signed an Interconfederal Basic Agreement with the employers' association (or CEOE) in July 1979, though the Workers' Commissions refused to back the accord. Further wage-restraint deals were struck between the UGT and CEOE in January 1980 and February 1981, which helped bring inflation down from 16 per cent in 1980 to 14.4 per cent in 1982. The level of labour conflict nonetheless remained high, 1980 registering 1,351 strikes, even though trade-union affiliation had dropped from a peak of 40 per cent of the working population in 1977 to 30 per cent in 1980. The second oil crisis had a devastating impact on the economy, 1979 recording negative growth of −0.1 per cent, which improved to 1.2 per cent in 1980, but then fell back to 0.2 per cent in 1981. Spanish democracy was nonetheless sufficiently solid for the recession not to threaten it, as nearly 80 per cent of those polled in 1978 and again in 1980 remained convinced that 'democracy is the best political system for a country like ours'.[112]

The Suárez government was further weakened by its reverses over the development of the state of autonomies. After the general election, statutes of autonomy were negotiated for both the Basques and the Catalans between their respective assembly of parliamentarians and the Constitutional Commission of Congress, as envisaged in article 151 of the *magna carta*. Both regions obtained marked levels of self-government, including control over education, health, and regional infrastructure, as well as their own police forces and Supreme Court of Justice, while the Basques also recovered their historic economic rights. The referendums for the two regions were held on 25 October 1979, resulting in a resounding triumph for the 'yes' vote in both cases. However, the government was alarmed at the prospect of all the regions demanding the same, so it tried to 'rationalize' the process by reining in Galician claims, but by this stage a 'race for autonomy' was underway.[113]

The front runner was Andalusia. Fearful of having to wait five years for complete autonomy, as required by article 148 of the Constitution, Andalusian regionalists decided, like the 'historic nationalities' of the Basques, Catalans, and Galicians, to pursue autonomy via article 151, which would allow them to achieve full autonomy without delay. The government tried, and failed, to hold back the Andalusian process, prompting the resignation of the minister of the regions, Manuel Clavero Arévalo. He then became head of the campaign of the Andalusian UCD in favour of autonomy, while the national UCD called for abstention. The bewilderment engendered by the UCD's ambivalent stance was exploited by the PSOE, which vigorously backed the campaign for autonomy. In the referendum of 28 February 1980, the 'yes' vote won in all the Andalusian provinces except Almería. The victory of the regionalists was a defeat for the government, a reverse made worse still by the advance of the Basque and Catalan regionalists in the first autonomous elections of 9 March 1980. In the Basque Country, the Basque Nationalist Party won twenty-five seats, *Herri Batasuna* or HB (Popular Unity), the political front for ETA, eleven, the socialists nine, and the UCD only six; while in Catalonia, Jordi Pujol's Convergence and Union obtained forty-three seats, the socialists thirty-three, the Communists twenty-five, and the UCD a mere eighteen. The sky-high abstention in the Galician referendum later that year – 71 per cent – reflected the chaos sown by the government's muddled policy.

The socialists took advantage of the government's divisions to present a vote of confidence in May 1980. Although the government prevailed by 166 votes to 152, the contrast between Felipe González's commanding performance and Suárez's floundering one damaged the prime minister. The UCD was assailed thereafter by the PSOE from the left and the Popular Alliance from the right. The socialists aimed to win over the UCD's social democrats to a 'new majority', while the Popular Alliance tried to attract its conservative sectors in order to manufacture a 'natural majority'. The return en masse of the 'Barons' to the Cabinet in September 1980 brought Suárez's presidential-style rule to an end, further debilitating his position.

During late 1980 the UCD was engulfed by a deepening political crisis due to the economic recession, an escalation in terrorist violence, and rumours regarding a coup d'état, which intensified after the military seized power in Turkey in September. Suárez's increasingly tenuous grip on the UCD suffered a major reverse in October when Miguel Herrero de Miñón – who had recently published a newspaper article in which he had lambasted the prime minister for his 'arbitrary leadership which tries to disguise the irremediable loss of political leadership in the party, in parliament, and in the state' – was elected parliamentary spokesman.[114] For Suárez, this was a 'devastating blow'.[115] Not only the opposition but also a substantial section of the UCD was determined to bring him down. On 26 January 1981 he resigned in the presence of the 'Barons', being replaced by his deputy, Leopoldo Calvo Sotelo. 'At least,' he announced prophetically, 'I leave you with the military problem resolved.'[116]

## THE ATTEMPTED COUP OF 23 FEBRUARY 1981

Late on the afternoon of 23 February 1981, just as the Cortes was voting on the nomination of Calvo Sotelo as prime minister, a detachment of Civil Guards under Lieutenant Colonel Antonio Tejero burst into the chamber and, in the words of the official parliamentary record, 'took over strategic places, threatened the presidency by force and, after an altercation with the first vice president of the government, Lieutenant General Gutiérrez Mellado, ordered everyone to lie down on the ground, bursts of machine gun fire sounding'.[117] While Tejero was taking the

Tejero takes the Cortes by storm

Cortes by force, the tanks of the III Military Region were rumbling onto the streets of Valencia under General Jaime Milans del Bosch. The military uprising brought to an end three years of rumours. Estranged and angered by the transition, the armed forces had been particularly outraged by the terrorism of ETA and the creation of the autonomous communities. The Cabinet resignations of General de Santiago and Admiral Pita da Veiga, the vote of half the twenty-eight military deputies against the bill for Political Reform, the refusal of the military senators designated by the king to endorse the Constitution, and the numerous affronts endured by the minister of defence, Gutiérrez Mellado, at the hands of fellow officers, all attested to the grave disquiet of the armed forces. The paradox is that the exiguous capacity of the armed forces to intervene in the politics of the transition can be attributed to General Franco, who had buttressed his own position as dictator by curtailing their political power. The limited political clout of the military, as highlighted by its negligible influence on the drafting of the Constitution, meant that its opposition often took the form of isolated acts of rebellion, like 'Operation Galaxia', an aborted coup of November 1978 also involving Tejero, which had aimed to seize the Moncloa Palace while the Cabinet was in session and the king abroad.

The '23-F', as it quickly became known, comprised at least two conspiracies. The 'hard' coup under Tejero envisaged, like Operation Galaxia, the overthrow of the government and the creation of a military junta, along the lines of the Greek coup of 1967. By contrast, the 'soft' version, headed by General Alfonso Armada, planned to form a national government under the general that would include all the main political parties. These two contradictory strands were connected by Milans del Bosch, who believed that Tejero would take control of the Cortes so that Armada could establish a national government. The coup was aborted in a very short time, thanks to the failure of the army's elite unit, the Brunete Armoured Division, to join the coup, the refusal of the king to meet Armada, and the lobbying of the eleven captain-generals by Juan Carlos I in his capacity as commander-in-chief, though it was not until 1.20 a.m. on 24 February that he addressed the nation on television to announce its quashing. Unquestionably, the king understood that the legitimacy of his crown depended on the defeat of the revolt, not its triumph. Probably the single most important factor in the collapse of the 23-F was the loyalty of the army to the king (as opposed to the government), partly because he was commander-in-chief and partly because he was the successor nominated by Franco, which did a great deal to make the transfer of loyalties from the dictatorship to democracy possible. As Lieutenant General Guillermo Quintana Lacaci, who played a key role in the suppression of the attempted coup, explained, the king 'ordered me to stop the coup of 23-F and I stopped it; if he had ordered me to assault the Cortes, I would have assaulted them'.[118] In any case, the military was not in a position to undertake a large-scale rebellion, because it lacked an alternative political project, the required leaders, and the necessary social support to carry it out. Thirty-two members of the armed forces and one civilian were put on trial for the uprising, many of the lenient sentences handed down by the military courts later being overhauled by the civilian Supreme Court. Armada, Tejero, and Milans del Bosch all received thirty years in jail.

The military revolt of 23 February 1981 raises the obvious counterfactual question as to what might have happened if the coup d'état had succeeded. The internal divisions within the army would almost certainly have resulted in a confrontation between the loyalists and the insurgents, while the nationwide resistance of the trade unions, the business organizations, and political parties would have brought the country to a grinding halt. In stark contrast to 1936, the rebels would have enjoyed little or no civilian support, not even from the Catholic Church, and none whatsoever from abroad. Though the Americans might not have come to the aid of Spanish democracy (the Secretary of State, Alexander Haig, dismissed the coup as an 'internal Spanish affair', an extraordinary recusal for the supposed leader of the free world), Western Europeans certainly would.[119] Indeed, it is difficult to see how the coup, isolated both at home and abroad, could have succeeded in the long term. Contrary to the intentions of the conspirators, the attempted seizure of power reinforced democratic sentiment, as shown by the millions of Spaniards who took to the streets on 27 February in defence of the new regime, which did much to dispel the disillusionment that had become so widespread since early 1979.

## THE IMPLOSION OF THE UCD

The resignation of Adolfo Suárez and the 23-F had a galvanizing effect on national politics, as Calvo Sotelo's first impulse was to revive the politics of consensus. He found a willing partner in the shape of Felipe González, as the socialist leader appreciated that the government had to be supported at the time of democracy's greatest crisis. The two men first collaborated on the new pact to tackle the economic crisis, the 'National Agreement on Employment' of June 1981, which was backed by the government, the employers' organization, and both the UGT and the CCOO. The unions agreed to a cap on wages in exchange for the creation of 350,000 jobs (800,000 having been lost in the previous two years) and an improved unemployment benefit. The good news was that this was the first time a government had actively participated in the negotiations between the bosses and workers and had been a signatory to the pact. The bad news was that in 1982 another 500,000 jobs were lost, unemployment climbing to 17 per cent.

Calvo Sotelo and González also joined forces over the development of the autonomous communities, as the PSOE leader shared the prime minister's concern that the process had hitherto been 'disorderly and unpredictable'.[120] The pact signed between the government and the socialists on 31 July 1981 allowed the UCD and PSOE to approve the remaining statutes, both agreeing that fast-track access via article 151 of the Constitution should be limited to the four regions where referendums had already been held, while the rest should acquire autonomy via article 143. By the time the Cortes was dissolved on 28 August 1982, only four of the seventeen autonomous communities had statutes pending. The socialists also supported the government's legislation regarding the rights of women. The advertisement of contraception had been decriminalized back in October 1978, but in May 1981 marital equality was established and in July of that year the Civil Code was reformed to regulate marriage, divorce, and separation in a more equitable fashion. Nonetheless, women had a long way to go before achieving absolute equality, as indicated by the long list of laws concerning their rights which have been passed since then.

Cooperation between the two leaders did not, however, extend to the prize foreign policy goal of Calvo Sotelo's premiership: Spanish membership of NATO. As the prime minister explained to the Cortes, he aspired to a foreign policy that was 'European, democratic, and Western, clear and irreversible, far from dreams which could betray an isolationist tendency'.[121] Convinced that Spain's geopolitical position did not allow it to become neutral in the context of the Cold War, a paramount priority was the renegotiation of the Bases Treaty of 1976 with the US (which ended in June 1981), especially as the Americans made it plain that they were not inclined to change the terms of the treaty unless Spain joined NATO. Calvo Sotelo believed that entry into NATO would also help reboot the talks with the EEC – stalled since the summer of 1980 thanks to French president Valéry Giscard d'Estaing – in large measure because many of the NATO signatories were members of the EEC too.

Joining NATO would not only modernize the Spanish armed forces, but also do much to offset their anti-democratic tendencies, not least because the military would be focused on its international obligations rather than on national political developments. Finally, the premier hoped that NATO membership would improve cooperation with the UK over Gibraltar, especially as regards its military use. By contrast, Felipe González believed that Spain should eschew the two Cold War blocs in pursuit of a non-aligned policy, the party calling in its 1979 electoral programme for 'an active neutrality which would supersede the false dilemma of USA–USSR'.[122] In response to the government's pro-NATO stance the socialists took to the streets under the banner of 'No to joining NATO', while González publicly committed the socialists in September 1981 to a referendum on the transatlantic organization. Even so, on 19 October 1981 the Cortes authorized the government by a vote of 186 to 146 to request entry into NATO, Spain becoming its sixteenth member on 30 May 1982. The decision to join NATO in opposition to the left was arguably the most polemical decision taken by a government during the entire transition.

What brought the government down was not the opposition but the UCD's own internal crisis. As Calvo Sotelo later wryly remarked, 'what deafened me then was not the sound of sables, but the noise of the forks of the members of the UCD who met to conspire in expensive restaurants.'[123] The most divisive issue was the Divorce Law of the social democrat Francisco Fernández Ordóñez. Shortly after the law was passed in June 1981, he resigned as minister of justice, dispirited by the bitter infighting over the reform. He later abandoned the UCD in November 1981 along with sixteen other deputies (the leading figures emerging on the slate of the PSOE in the 1982 general election). While the social democrats within the UCD were looking to the left, the conservatives were reaching out to the right. The vehement dispute over the Divorce Law led to the creation of a 'Moderate Platform' in July 1981 with the backing of thirty-nine deputies and thirty-one senators, the aim of which was to create a 'new majority' in combination with the Popular Alliance. The refusal of Calvo Sotelo to countenance an alliance with Fraga's conservative party triggered the departure of Miguel Herrero de Miñón and two other deputies for the Popular Alliance. Following the UCD's calamitous results in the Andalusian autonomous elections of May 1982 (the UCD won just 13 per cent of the vote), twelve deputies left to form the Popular Democratic Party. The greatest blow of all was the abandonment of Adolfo Suárez himself in July 1982, together with twelve other deputies. He did not merely walk out on the party, but created a rival one, the *Centro Democrático y Social* or CDS (the Democratic and Social Centre). For Calvo Sotelo, Suárez had been the linchpin of the UCD, his departure heralding the party's collapse. The main cause of the UCD's downfall was to be its lack of ideological coherence, just as that of the centrist Radical Party under the Second Republic led to a major schism in 1934. By the time the UCD imploded in 1982, the Popular Alliance had ditched much of its neo-Francoist baggage, while the Socialist Party had jettisoned the Marxist discourse of the anti-Francoist struggle. Accordingly, there were now two parties ready and able to occupy the ample centrist space vacated by the UCD. Arguably, the UCD was no longer necessary 'due to the very success of the process which it had driven'.[124]

## THE SOCIALIST TRIUMPH OF 1982

Between the 23-F and the general election of October 1982 the Socialist Party burnished its credentials as a party of government through its collaboration with Calvo Sotelo, while underlining that it was also a force for change through its opposition over NATO and its social-democratic reformism. The absence of factional infighting within the PSOE and the undisputed leadership of Felipe González further strengthened its claim to power by presenting a stark contrast to the UCD. In competing for the centrist space occupied by the latter, the socialists took care throughout 1982 to project an image of moderation, such as by stressing that they would not undermine the market economy or deprive private education of its state subsidies. The socialists' carefully calibrated appeal was first put to the test in their heartland of Andalusia – both Felipe González and deputy leader Alfonso Guerra were from the region, along with one-quarter of the party membership – in the May 1982 autonomous elections. The outright majority obtained in the elections was a resounding vindication of the PSOE's pragmatic approach.

In the general election of October 1982 the PSOE, which campaigned under the slogan of *Por el cambio* (For Change), aimed to take full advantage of the disintegration of the UCD by vowing to tackle outstanding questions, such as the integration of the armed forces within the new constitutional order, while committing itself to a wide-ranging social-democratic project, including the development of the welfare state and the redistribution of wealth. The socialist programme therefore responded to the widespread hope that the transition should constitute not just a political transformation, but a social one, too. Nonetheless, the party that aimed to gain most from the unravelling of the UCD was the Popular Alliance, the cornerstone of the Popular Coalition. On the other hand, the electoral prospects of the PSOE were enhanced by the tumultuous crisis of the Communist Party, one of the gravest in its entire history. At the congress of July 1981, Santiago Carrillo had caused the exodus of a group of reformists from the Central and Executive Committees by allying with the pro-Soviets, which provoked a massive haemorrhage of members. By the time of the 1982 general election, the PCE was in a critical condition, having forfeited much of its prestige from the anti-Francoist years. Felipe González quipped that Santiago Carrillo had achieved in seven years what Franco had failed to do in forty, that is, destroy the Communist Party.

In the face of the economic depression, the terrorism of ETA, the collapse of the UCD, and, above all, the 23-F – the peril of which was underlined by the dismantlement of another military plot in early October – the election campaign was characterized by a ringing endorsement of democracy, as reflected in the mass gatherings (the PSOE's final rally attracting 500,000 people), as well as in a soaring turnout, which, at 79.8 per cent, was nearly 12 per cent higher than in 1979. The election therefore laid the ghost of the *desencanto* or disillusionment firmly to rest by reaffirming the faith of the Spanish people in the democratic process.

The outcome of the general election was an astounding triumph for the socialists, who won 202 deputies, the first democratic majority in Spanish history. The PSOE secured 10.1 million votes, nearly double those of 1979, robbing the UCD of 1.2 million ballots and the PCE of one million, while attracting two million from first-time voters. The other major winner was the Popular Coalition with 107 deputies and 5.5 million votes, three million of which came from the UCD. This was a remarkable turn-about following the disaster of the previous election, but the Popular Alliance remained a long way behind the PSOE. For the PCE, the results were a calamity, the party garnering just 4 per cent of the vote and four deputies. Shortly afterwards, Santiago Carrillo resigned as secretary-general, having dominated the party for over two decades. Predictably, the biggest loser of all was the UCD, which plummeted from 166 deputies in 1979 to just twelve, losing 4.7 million votes in the process. In fact, 'there has never existed such a defeat' in the history of Europe.[125] The party was dissolved not long after. Adolfo Suárez's CDS won 600,000 votes, but only two deputies. Lastly, the extreme left and right were eliminated altogether, *Fuerza Nueva* losing its sole deputy from 1979, while the Basque and Catalan nationalists both consolidated their positions. With the emphatic victory of the PSOE, the transition had reached a milestone in the ongoing process of democratic consolidation, as the regime had been able to generate an alternative government in just six years. This was remarkable given that the post-war Federal Republic of Germany took twenty years and the First Republic in Italy nearly fifty years.

# THE SPANISH TRANSITION:
## A GLOBAL PARADIGM?

The Spanish transition was the first time in the late modern era that Spain was universally acclaimed as a paradigm worthy of emulation, 'rather than the failure to pity or avoid'.[126] The Southern European transitions of the 1970s were regarded as the spearhead of a 'Third Wave' of global democratization, following those of the late eighteenth century and the post-Second World War period. Beginning in Southern Europe, the 'Third Wave' spread to Latin America and Asia, reaching a climax with the Eastern European transitions of the early 1990s. Of these tens of transitions, the Spanish one was applauded as the greatest success. This not only transformed Spain into a 'normal' European country, but also launched it as a 'global model, really as *the* model, for both democratization and consolidation'.[127] The key to the Spanish 'Transition' with a capital 'T' was considered to be the series of agreements, compromises, and pacts reached by its national political elites. A further cause for celebration was the way in which the transition was undertaken 'relatively peacefully', suggesting that it was a smooth, even predictable, process.[128]

This uplifting narrative, however, does a tremendous disservice to the experience of the transition. Far from being a time of peace, these were years marked by attempted coups, sudden shifts in politics, an economic depression, and the bombings, assassinations, and kidnappings by terrorists, resulting in 665 deaths from political violence between 1975 and 1982, far more than during either the Greek or the Portuguese transitions. Ordinary Spaniards recall it as a time of hope, uncertainty, excitement, and fear, as the transition was not a linear process but 'so disconcerting, so on the edge of the abyss always'.[129] Still, by the end of the twentieth century, only the Southern European transitions had been consolidated, many of those in Eastern Europe and elsewhere either faltering or having failed altogether. In the meantime, the very nature of the Spanish transition was being questioned, the elite-brokered model coming under sustained scrutiny. In reality, the Spanish transition was *sui generis* and is explained in terms of not a single factor, but a multiplicity of them, including the economic modernization of the 1960s and 1970s, the rise of civil society, the depoliticization of the armed forces, the mass mobilizations of the 1970s, and the wider international context. The transition is often framed as a narrative of the passage from dictatorship to democracy, but this ignores the vigorous debate that took place over the *meaning* of democracy. Not only did the vision of the political opposition differ substantially from that of the Francoist governments of 1976–8, but there was also a debate among the opposition over the merits of a liberal, rights-based democracy versus a communitarian and participatory model. Even so, the transition in Spain fits well into the pattern of European democratization that advanced 'in fits and starts' between the late nineteenth and twentieth centuries.[130] In other words, Spain was very much an integral part of modern European history, not a peripheral onlooker.

# 10

# Democratic Spain

*Prosperity, Corruption, and International Recognition*

The socialists came to power in late 1982 at an exceedingly difficult juncture. The economy was still deep in recession, the terrorism of ETA was unabated, the sudden collapse of the UCD had shaken the party system, and, not least, Spain's new-found democracy continued to be threatened by the military, as shown by the coup attempt of October 1982. The first socialist government was extremely youthful, the average age of its members being forty-one, lower even than that of Adolfo Suárez's first administration. There were no women, no manual workers, and no socialist dissidents in the Cabinet, which reflected above all the values and aspirations of men from the ascendant middle classes of the 1960s. The PSOE's parliamentary majority brought the transition's politics of negotiation to an end, making it a government 'with power and authority' which sought to satisfy the widespread desire for 'a government that governs'.[1] Its position was further strengthened by the lack of a credible left-wing alternative (given the turmoil within the Communist Party) or a right-wing one (in view of the Popular Alliance's still limited appeal). The socialists therefore found themselves in an excellent position to undertake a sweeping programme of reform. Their overriding goal was to consolidate the nascent democracy, above all by subordinating the military to civilian rule and by completing the system of autonomous communities. They also aimed to make the economy more competitive, while achieving their social-democratic goals of improving the welfare state and public services. The paramount objectives of their foreign policy were to join the EEC and to pursue a non-aligned path in international affairs that distanced Spain from both Cold War blocs.

## RECONFIGURING THE ECONOMY

The most urgent task was to tackle the economic crisis that had dragged on since 1974. Inflation stood at 14 per cent, unemployment at 16.5 per cent (having passed the two million mark), the public deficit had reached 5.6 per cent of GDP, and growth for 1979–82 was a mere 0.5 per cent per annum. The pitfalls of a full-blown Keynesian approach had been highlighted by the experience of the French socialists, whose expansive policy of 1981 had to be sharply reversed in mid-1982. Felipe González himself regarded the French experiment as 'catastrophic' and resolved instead to 'use the market. Encourage the investors.'[2] The PSOE aimed to overcome the recession by reining in inflation and by reducing the trade and public-sector deficits. Through a combination of monetarism and wage restraint, inflation was scaled down to 8.8 per cent by 1985 (the lowest rate since 1972), while the trade imbalance was addressed by devaluing the peseta by 8 per cent (turning a deficit of 2.4 per cent of GDP into a surplus of 1.7 per cent by 1985). Unlike conservative governments in the United Kingdom, West Germany, and Scandinavia, the Spanish administration did not try to reduce the public-sector deficit by cutting back spending and lowering taxes, despite the fact that the welfare state throughout Western Europe was under threat. In pursuing their social-democratic objectives, the socialists took the decision to *raise* both spending and taxes. Public expenditure climbed over the next four years from 36 per cent of GDP to 42 per cent, while taxes grew as a proportion of GDP by 1 per cent a year, so that by 1986 they had reached 36 per cent. The tax increase translated into a one-third rise in spending on education between 1982 and 1986, while one-quarter of the budget was devoted to health, unemployment benefits, and pensions by 1986. Unlike the social-democratic parties in the established Western European democracies, such as the West German Social Democratic Party, the PSOE did not cut back benefits, but, on the contrary, strove hard to build up the welfare state from a very low foundation.

The socialists were not content, however, just to solve the immediate problem of the economic crisis. They also sought to create a more competitive national economy by undertaking extensive structural reforms, ranging from the industrial and financial sectors to the social security system and the labour market, the guiding principle being to down-grade the role of the state in favour of the market. This euphemistically dubbed 'industrial restructuring', introduced by decree in November 1983, affected nearly a third of national industry, especially the iron and steel sectors, shipbuilding, and textiles. The closure of uncompetitive firms produced 80,000 job losses between 1983 and 1987, provoking a wave of strikes in the affected areas, while costing the Exchequer 1.5 billion pesetas. The neo-liberal dimension to the government's economic policy meant that it refused to bail out companies in crisis, the sole exception being *Rumasa*. Employing more than 45,000 people in over 400 businesses and twenty banks, the *Rumasa* group, headed by the flamboyant José María Ruiz Mateos, was expropriated by decree in February 1983 (at a cost of 800,000 million pesetas), largely because the government feared that its collapse would provoke a national financial crisis. Despite its neoliberalism, the government only privatized one nationalized company during this period, the car manufacturer SEAT, which was sold to Volkswagen in 1986.

The UGT, which had become the largest of the trade-union movements in the union elections of 1982, cooperated with the PSOE's economic policy insofar as it backed the wage restraint agreement of 1984, the last of the high-profile pacts of the 1980s between the government, the employers, and the unions (though the CCOO did not take part). On the other hand, the UGT, like the CCOO, was aggrieved by the liberalization of the labour market of 1984 and by the industrial 'restructuring' of 1983, dubbed the 'savage restructuring' by the CCOO leader, Marcelino Camacho.[3] This was hardly surprising, as unemployment, far from dropping by 800,000 as forecast in the PSOE's electoral manifesto, ballooned by a further 825,000 between 1982 and 1986, reaching over three million or 21.3 per cent of the working population, the highest level ever recorded. Clearly the economic adjustment of the socialists' first term in office was undertaken 'above all in relation to employment'.[4] As Camacho noted, 'we continued to be the poor relations of democracy.'[5] The greatest grievance of the unions was the reform of the pensions system in May 1985, which introduced more stringent conditions for its beneficiaries. The disgruntled leader of the UGT, Nicolás Redondo, exclaimed that 'to our great surprise and dismay we have encountered a series of decisions made and policies implemented without our having been previously consulted.'[6] For the head of the CCOO, the PSOE displayed 'no desire for rapprochement and much less to explore avenues for negotiation'.[7] The disenchantment of the unions was understandable insofar as they had waited forty years for a government that represented their interests. By the summer of 1985, Redondo had stopped attending the meetings of the PSOE's Executive Committee, while González failed to appear at the 1 May celebrations of 1985. On 4 June 1985 the UGT joined other trade unions in a protest march – its first against a socialist government – against the reform of the pensions system, but stopped short of backing the general strike of 20 July 1985 or of calling on its members not to vote for the Socialist Party in the general election of June 1986.

## CIVILIANIZING THE MILITARY

Another critical area of reform was the military, especially in light of its disconformity with the transition, as expressed most ominously by the plots of 1978–82. In contrast to the politicians of the Second Republic, the socialists set about bringing the military under civilian control with a prudent and effective strategy. This was illustrated by González's visit in early December 1982 to the headquarters of the most prestigious unit in the Spanish army, the Brunete Armoured Division. Relations between the government and the military were tense not only because the army was wary of the socialists' anti-militaristic (and anti-Francoist) tradition, but also because of the quashed coup attempt in October 1982. The Brunete Armoured Division was especially aggrieved because its commander, General Víctor Lago Román, had been assassinated by ETA in November that year. The visit of the prime minister was therefore well received, marking the beginning of a relationship between the socialists and the military that was to prove 'surprisingly cordial'.[8] The military chain of command was brought under civilian control by means of the National Defence Law of January 1984, which 'ended 110 years of effective autonomy of the military institution'.[9] Meanwhile, the General Plan of Modernization, initiated in 1983, reduced the size of the army, the number of officers dropping from 41,500 to 32,000 in eight years (including the elimination of nearly half the generals), while regular troop numbers fell from 252,000 in 1984 to 169,000 in 1992. As a result, military expenditure decreased from 11.5 per cent of the budget in 1982 to 5.7 per cent in 1992. National service was also reduced to just twelve months in 1985, while conscientious objection was admitted. Finally, the jurisdiction of the military courts was limited to the armed forces alone, their courts having condemned fifty-two civilians as late as 1979 for 'insults to the army' and similar offences. Meanwhile, Spanish membership of NATO not only provided the armed forces with an external rather than internal focus, such as NATO training exercises and humanitarian missions, but also gradually imbued them with the democratic *de esprit corps* that characterized most of their transatlantic allies. Not that disquiet within the armed forces was eliminated altogether, thanks in large measure to the ongoing attacks of ETA. A military plot to blow up the king, queen, and prime minister on the Day of the Armed Forces in June 1985 was aborted by the secret service. Still, arguably the greatest single achievement of the socialist era was the overwhelming acceptance by the military of the supremacy of civilian authority.

## LAUNCHING THE AUTONOMOUS COMMUNITIES

Another key objective of the socialists was to complete the administrative, political, and territorial division of Spain into autonomous communities. By early 1983 the government had negotiated the four remaining statutes of autonomy, resulting in the creation of seventeen autonomous communities in total. In May 1983, elections were held for the thirteen autonomous communities that had not yet gone to the polls. The upshot was that the PSOE controlled twelve autonomous governments and the Popular Alliance three, while regional nationalists governed in both the Basque Country and Catalonia. The protracted wrangles between the central government and the regional authorities over exactly which powers and resources were to be devolved often had to be decided by the Constitutional Court, which resolved 429 disputes between 1983 and 1987. The state eventually transferred to the autonomous communities authority over a considerable range of areas, including education, health, finance, the police, the environment, and urban planning. The shift in budgetary resources from the state to the regions was correspondingly substantial: in 1981, 87 per cent of the national budget was spent by the state, 9 per cent by local bodies, and a mere 3 per cent by the autonomous communities, but by 1985 the state took up 73 per cent of the budget, local entities 12 per cent, and the autonomous communities 14 per cent. In a few years Spain had gone from one of the most centralized states in Western Europe to one of the most devolved. The new arrangement was accepted by all seventeen autonomous territories, bar the Basque Country, as 'a legitimate framework of territorial organization'.[10]

In Catalonia, the victory of Convergence and Unity under the wily populist Jordi Pujol in the autonomous elections of 1980 and 1984 allowed the CiU to develop the regional institutions largely in its own nationalist image, though within the bounds of the Constitution. In the case of the Basque Country, the success of the *Partido Nacionalista Vasco* or PNV (Basque Nationalist Party) in the 1980 autonomous elections permitted it to form a regional government under Carlos Garaikoetxea. Rather than integrating both the nationalist and non-nationalist forces that had backed the Basque Statute of Autonomy within a framework of democratic collaboration, Garaikoetxea opted instead to mobilize the resources of the regional government in the service of a 'nationalism of resistance', which not only rejected the institutions and symbols of the Spanish state, but also brought into question the state's struggle against ETA. Having won a majority in the 1984 autonomous elections, Garaikoetxea was nonetheless ousted as *lehendakari* (president) of the regional government by his own party, being replaced by the much more moderate José Antonio Ardanza. The new *lehendakari* reached an agreement with the PSOE in January 1985 which ushered in a new strategy, that of 'co-managed nationalism', the aim of which was to consolidate the dominance of the PNV within the nationalist community while marginalizing *Herri Batasuna* and ETA with the aid of the socialists. The strategy culminated in the formation of a coalition government of the PNV and the PSOE following the autonomous elections of 1986.

Spain's far-reaching territorial, administrative, and political overhaul produced a much more fragmented and exclusive society. A striking example is the Catalanization of the educational system in Catalonia, which greatly reduced teaching not only in Spanish, but also in the culture, literature, and history of Spain. Another move towards exclusivity was the creation of public-sector jobs that required a regional language, which effectively excluded the overwhelming majority of Spaniards. Nonetheless, the popularity of the autonomous communities was undeniable, a survey of 1986 revealing that 55 per cent of Spaniards approved of the new system in comparison with only 22 per cent who preferred a centralized system, while 5 per cent aspired to independence for their particular region.

## THE EEC AND THE NATO REFERENDUM

For the socialists, the consolidation of Spanish democracy was inextricably linked to the country's membership of the EEC, as this would mark its arrival as a Western European democracy. Due to the obstructionism of the French, who harboured doubts over the viability of the Community's expansion, only six of sixteen policy areas had been negotiated with the EEC by the end of 1982. The Spaniards therefore made a concerted effort to overcome French antagonism, which included a head-to-head meeting between Felipe González and French premier François Mitterrand in December 1983. The outcome was that at the meeting of the European Council in June 1984 Mitterrand announced that Spain would formally enter the EEC on 1 January 1986. On 12 June 1985 Spain signed the Treaty of Adhesion to the EEC, the country's 'most important event' of the decade.[11]

The other main plank of the PSOE's foreign policy platform was to abandon NATO by means of a national referendum. While in opposition, the socialists had treated NATO and the EEC as two separate issues. Once in power, the socialists underwent what the prime minister later described as 'a brutal process of adaptation to reality'.[12] They came to realize how powerful the overlap was between the two bodies, both being central to the Western alliance (nine members of the EEC were also in NATO). They also reached the conclusion that Spain's interests were best served within, rather than outside, the transatlantic organization. An early sign of the way the wind was blowing was the ratification by the Congress of Deputies of the General Agreement on Friendship, Defence, and Cooperation with the United States by an overwhelming majority in April 1983. A month later, González boosted his credentials as a 'pragmatic and responsible partner' of the US by supporting NATO's decision to install nearly 600 cruise and Pershing II missiles in Western Europe.[13] The prime minister's 'calculated ambiguity' over Spanish membership of NATO was finally dispelled in October 1984 during the debate on the state of the nation, when he defended Spain's permanence in NATO, a volte-face that was approved by the Thirtieth Congress of the PSOE a few weeks later.[14] As the foreign minister explained, 'it's very difficult to be an active, loyal, and efficient minister of the Community and not be in the Atlantic Alliance', while the prime minister invoked the 'psychological connection' between the two organizations.[15]

Capitalizing on the climate of celebration following Spain's entry into the EEC, the government held the NATO referendum on 12 March 1986. It left little to chance, especially as a survey of November 1985 had shown that 49 per cent of Spaniards were opposed to NATO and only 19 per cent in favour. Indeed, in the build-up to the referendum, anti-NATO marches were held throughout Spain, a demonstration of February 1986 in Madrid attracting 750,000 people and being addressed by, amongst others, the British historian and CND activist E. P. Thompson. The question posed in the referendum was as restrictive as possible, the 'yes' affirming that Spain would abstain from joining NATO's full military structure, that it would oppose the introduction, installation, or storage of nuclear arms on national territory, and that the US military presence within the country would be gradually reduced. If the 'no' triumphed, González announced, he would step down as prime minister, leaving someone else to manage the result. The electorate was effectively being asked, one minister noted, 'if it was for or against the government'.[16] The socialists' last throw of the dice was to shamelessly exploit their control of the state media by having González address the nation on television the night before the vote. Despite the adverse polls, the government won the referendum by 52 per cent to 39 per cent. In reality, it had been a very close call, but González's gamble had ultimately paid off. He later admitted that the referendum had been 'a trauma' and one of the biggest mistakes of his presidency.[17]

# THE GENERAL ELECTION OF 1986

Shortly afterwards, the prime minister called a general election, taking advantage of not only the government's recent triumphs in joining the EEC and winning the NATO referendum, but also the upturn in the economy, evident since late 1985. The timing of the election also targeted the tumult on the left and the slump in popularity of the right. The PCE's lamentable performance in the 1982 general election had brought its internal tensions to the surface, the pro-Soviets leaving the party in 1983 and Santiago Carrillo being expelled from the Central Committee along with nineteen others in 1985. After nearly fifty years of militancy in the ranks of the PCE, Carrillo abandoned the party that same year. The PCE subsequently forged links with many of the new social movements, such as the ecologists, feminists, and pacifists, which were involved in the anti-NATO campaign. The upshot was the establishment of a new political formation, *Izquierda Unida* (United Left) in April 1986, a heterogeneous coalition centred on the PCE that included a slew of embryonic parties, such as the Progressive Federation led by the ex-Communist Ramón Tamames. On the right, the principal handicap of the Popular Alliance was its excessive dependence on the founder, Manuel Fraga, and its correspondingly limited institutionalization. Defining itself as 'democratic, liberal, conservative, reformist, and interclassist', the party nonetheless failed to convince the electorate that it represented a 'moderate and centrist alternative' to the PSOE, its opposition since 1982 being 'catastrophist and hardly constructive'.[18] Fraga's stunted appeal was reflected in a confidential party survey of 1986, which revealed that he was supported by 25 per cent of Spaniards, but rejected by 60 per cent. The general perception that he was too right-wing to win an election was compounded by his strategic errors, such as the decision to abstain on the NATO referendum, a move that disgusted not only many conservative voters, but also the party's European and American allies.

The PSOE's electoral slogan of 'On the Right Track' alluded not only to the party's achievements, but also to the ongoing nature of its modernizing mission. The electorate concurred insofar as the socialists secured another majority, returning 184 seats with 44 per cent of the ballot (though losing one million votes), while the Popular Coalition returned 105 deputies, having attracted 26 per cent of the ballot (losing 300,000 votes in the process). The other winner was Adolfo Suárez's CDS, which leapt from two deputies to nineteen, while the United Left secured just seven seats with 4.4 per cent of the vote, having failed to win over many disenchanted socialists. The PSOE's overwhelming victory in the Andalusian autonomous elections (held on the same day as the general election), confirmed its hegemony, as it polled 46 per cent of the vote compared to the Popular Coalition's 21 per cent. Manuel Fraga's belief in a 'natural majority' of the right had proved to be unfounded.

The achievement of the socialists between 1982 and 1986 was nothing less than remarkable. In terms of democratic consolidation, these were the most constructive years of Spain's entire history, the socialists having completed the establishment of the autonomous communities, drawn up a new template for local government (by means of the Law on Local Government of 1985), joined the EEC, reaffirmed Spain's presence within NATO, and, last but certainly not least, finally brought the military under civilian control. Moreover, they had overcome the recession, and, by restructuring the economy, helped lay the foundations for the growth of the late 1980s. At the same time they had begun to develop the welfare state and improve other public services. Foremost amongst the socialists' failures were the persistently high unemployment, which stood at 16.5 per cent in 1986, and the alienation of the trade unions, above all the UGT. Micro-managed by Alfonso Guerra, the PSOE had proved effective as an instrument of reform, but insensitive to popular pressure, especially as it was 'more interested in state institutions than citizen empowerment'.[19] Similarly, the socialist attitude to public debate and engagement was disturbingly illiberal. Felipe González – like Adolfo Suárez before him – tended to elude parliament, while the socialist speaker of the Cortes, Gregorio Peces-Barba, resigned in 1986 after being heavily criticized by his colleagues for his impartiality and in particular for his consideration in relation to the opposition. The PSOE's hegemony had induced it, noted Peces-Barba, 'to think that it embodied an indisputable truth about which there could be no debate'.[20] More broadly, the legislature had failed to act as an adequate brake on the executive, a consequence of not only the system established by the Constitution, but also the closed electoral lists (which

allowed party leaders to draw up the slate), as well as the highly centralized nature of the PSOE. A self-serving sectarianism also characterized
the socialists' management of the state media, which they treated as if it
were their own mouthpiece rather than a national resource (journalists
claimed that the state television's daily news agenda had to be approved
by Alfonso Guerra himself). Much the same would later be said of the
regional governments' media outlets. In short, liberalism had its limits in
democratic Spain. Finally, the government had not made much headway
in the struggle against ETA. Admittedly, the cooperation of the French
had been secured in the summer of 1984, but an effort to reach a negotiated solution with the Basque terrorists came to nothing, ETA killing
another 150 people between 1983 and 1986.

The victory of the socialists in the 1986 general election stood out
not only for the margin of its triumph over the right, but also for reinforcing the success of the social-democratic parties in Southern
Europe in comparison with their principal counterparts in the north.
While the British Labour Party and the West German Social Democratic
Party floundered in opposition and the French Socialist Party lost its
majority in 1986, the second electoral victory of the PSOE paralleled
that of the Panhellenic Socialist Movement (PASOK), which won the
elections of 1981 and 1985 in Greece, while the Socialist Party in Italy
headed a coalition government under its leader Bettino Craxi between
1983 and 1987.

## THE PRICE OF ECONOMIC
## RESURGENCE

The overarching goal of the Spanish socialists' second mandate was to
make the economy even more competitive while creating a fully fledged
welfare state. The challenge, observed the finance minister, was to
construct a welfare state 'without producing imbalances and without
impeding economic growth and the creation of employment'.[21] Benefiting from the resurgence of the global markets and Spain's entry into
the EEC, between 1985 and 1992 the economy surged by 3.7 per cent
a year (compared to the Community average of 2.6 per cent), the
'principal motor' being investment.[22] Foreign investment in particular

multiplied fivefold between 1985 and 1990, a development 'without precedent in Spanish economic history'.[23] Unemployment fell to 16.2 per cent by 1989 (nearly two million jobs were generated between 1985 and 1990), while inflation dropped to 4.8 per cent by 1988.

During this period the Spanish economy underwent far-reaching change. For ideological reasons, privatization was pursued in a 'shame-faced and silent' fashion, being dubbed 'rationalization, disinvestment or the downsizing of public holdings'.[24] Still, the policy was of 'great importance', dozens of companies being sold to multinationals, such as the truck business *Enasa* to Fiat.[25] Certain strategic firms were partially privatized in an effort to reduce the deficit, such as *Telefónica* and the energy company *Endesa* in 1988. Foreign trade soon became the dominant sector of the economy. In 1985 exports and imports accounted for just over a third of GDP, but by 1995 they constituted nearly two-thirds, the economy pivoting powerfully towards the European Single Market. In 1985 the EEC accounted for 37 per cent of imports and 52 per cent of exports, but ten years later this had surged to 65 per cent and 72 per cent respectively.

The improvement in the economy encouraged the hitherto marginalized trade unions to seek a greater voice in policy-making. However, Spain's socialist trade unions had far less leverage with their party than those in, for example, West Germany, Austria, and Sweden. Not only was trade-union affiliation in Spain low at 16 per cent, but the UGT in particular had only 630,000 members. Moreover, half its annual budget of 1,000 million pesetas came from the state. The semi-dependent nature of the relationship between the unions and the party does not itself explain why the socialist government 'systematically ignored' the UGT's demands.[26] The PSOE considered that its greatest electoral asset was Felipe González, not the UGT, and that it would be political suicide for the party to fall under the sway of the unions, as occurred with the British Labour Party in the 1970s.

The unions therefore felt betrayed by the socialist government. The final straw was the youth employment plan of 1988, which envisaged short-term contracts at the minimum wage. This formed part of a broader economic strategy whereby employment was to become increasingly 'flexible', that is, low-paid and precarious (the proportion of temporary jobs doubling between 1986 and 1990 from 15 per cent of the workforce to 30 per cent). The unions responded with the first non-revolutionary general strike in Spanish history on 14 December 1988, which brought the country to a complete standstill, the minister of finance recalling that the centre of Madrid 'looked like a cemetery'.[27] An affronted party leadership reacted to the strike with an 'unprecedented mixture of aloofness and arrogance', but nonetheless it met a good many of the unions' demands: in early 1989 public-sector salaries and pensions were tied to the rate of inflation, while unemployment coverage was extended, the proportion of those without work receiving benefits rising from 29 per cent in 1988 to 52 per cent in 1991.[28]

## EXPANDING THE WELFARE STATE

Under the socialists, public spending surged from 42 per cent of GDP in 1985 to 49 per cent in 1993, compared to, say, 51 per cent for West Germany. Much of this was invested in the welfare state, especially pensions, education, and the health system. Pensions received the greatest boost, expenditure rocketing from 1.3 billion pesetas in 1982 to 6.5 billion in 1995, a quarter of all public spending. Not only did the value of the average monthly pension increase from just 19,000 pesetas in 1982 to 52,000 in 1992, but also two million more people were provided with one. The Law on Non-Contributory Pensions of 1990 – a result of the 1988 general strike – provided protection irrespective of a person's contributions, thereby furnishing another 700,000 elderly people with a pension by 1994. Education was also transformed, spending shooting up by 120 per cent between 1982 and 1995. A law of 1990 made school obligatory up to sixteen years of age, reformed and extended vocational training, and brought the non-university sector into line with OECD standards. Expenditure on the national health service multiplied fourfold between 1982 and 1992, thereby covering virtually the entire population. By 1992 the Spanish state spent 5.4 per cent of GDP on health, which was adrift of Italy at 7.6 per cent, but still constituted a massive improvement. By the early 1990s, Spain had therefore established universal coverage in pensions, education, and health, though at a lower benefit level than in the established democracies. State employment under the socialists also expanded, climbing from 1.5 million permanent positions in 1982 to 2.2 million in 1993 (a fifth of all employees), though the socialists lacked the political will to overhaul the notoriously inefficient civil service.

The PSOE's social agenda targeted specific groups, such as women. In 1983 the government established the Institute of the Woman, which promoted research and numerous other projects, as reflected in the Institute's publications. Parental and maternity leave were also introduced, as well as a 1985 law on abortion. The latter was roundly criticized by feminist and other groups for its limited application, as it only permitted abortion in the case of rape or a deformed foetus, or if the mother's life was in danger, but the most ferocious opposition came from the Catholic right, a legacy of the dictatorship's hard line on reproductive rights. Finally, a concerted effort was made to involve women more in the Socialist Party. In 1982 the PSOE was an overwhelmingly masculine entity, as only 10 per cent of its members were female and there was only one woman amongst the leaders. Accordingly, quotas for female electoral candidates were introduced, which rose from just over a quarter in 1989 to nearly half in 2000. The proportion of women actually elected soared from 8 per cent in 1989 to 37 per cent in 2000, compared to 6 per cent and 25 per cent respectively for the quota-less *Partido Popular* or PP (Popular Party), the former Popular Alliance.

The expansion of public provision under the PSOE also embraced the cultural realm, the socialists asserting the state's role in 'protecting, financing, and stimulating cultural production and consumption', while many of the autonomous communities did exactly the same.[29] Between the Ministry of Culture and the regional governments a great deal was done to regenerate the threadbare cultural arena, such as the inauguration of the Reina Sofia Art Centre (Madrid), the National Museum of Roman Art (Mérida), the National Auditorium (Madrid), and the Guggenheim Museum (Bilbao), as well as the restoration of more than forty theatres, including the Teatro Real in Madrid and the legendary Liceu in Barcelona, in addition to the building of public libraries, museums, and theatres. Indeed, 'never had so much been spent on culture'.[30] The socialists transformed the economic, as well as cultural, infrastructure. Spending on roads, railways, ports, airports, and reservoirs surged from 300,000 million pesetas in 1982 to more than 800,000 million in

1991, transport and communications taking up nearly half of all state investment between 1987 and 1991. Major assistance was provided by the EEC, as Spain's surplus with the Community stood at over 3 billion pesetas between 1986 and 1995. The motorway network doubled to 7,000 kilometres, 15,000 kilometres of roads were repaired, airports and ports were upgraded, and reservoir capacity rose by one-fifth. Expenditure on research and development doubled too during the socialists' first ten years in office, reaching 0.9 per cent of GDP in 1992, comparable to other Southern European countries, if well below the 2–3 per cent of Britain, France, and West Germany.

## COMBATING ETA: THE PACT OF AJURIA ENEA AND THE 'DIRTY WAR'

Arguably the most intractable problem of Spanish democracy remained the threat of Basque terrorism. After 1985, ETA carried out most of its attacks outside the Basque region in an effort to force the government to hold negotiations, the terrorists turning to car bombs in order to reap even greater havoc. In June 1987 they killed twenty-one people in the bombing of a Hipercor supermarket in Barcelona and in December slaughtered another eleven people (including five children) in an explosion at the Civil Guard barracks in Zaragoza. The government reacted with a strategy that was designed both to defeat ETA militarily and to isolate its civilian support – that is, *Herri Batasuna* – politically. This process culminated in the Ajuria Enea Pact of January 1988, which was endorsed by all the parties in the Basque Country except *Herri Batasuna*. The Pact recognized the autonomy statute as 'the expression of the majority will of the citizens of the Basque Country', distinguished between the political and the armed struggle, and made it clear that there would be no *political* negotiation with ETA.[31] The result was a sea change within Basque society, as more and more citizens manifested their rejection of political violence and embraced 'the end of silence'; in a 1991 survey, 78 per cent of Basques supported the dissolution of ETA.[32] Following the failure of negotiations with the Spanish government in Algeria in early 1989, the terrorists continued to kill and maim – twenty-five fatalities in 1990 and forty-five in

1991 – in the conviction that this would bring the state back to the negotiating table. However, between 1988 and 1992 a cavernous breach had emerged within Basque society between the defenders of democracy and the advocates of the armed struggle.

A deeply disturbing aspect of the state's anti-terrorist strategy that came increasingly into view was the 'dirty war' waged in France between 1983 and 1987. This claimed twenty-eight victims, including eight French citizens unrelated to the Basque struggle. Articles had first appeared in the Spanish press on the so-called *Grupos Antiterroristas de Liberación* or GAL (Anti-Terrorist Liberation Groups) in 1984, but it was not until July 1988 that two Spanish policemen, José Amedo and Michel Domínguez, were charged with organizing the GAL by means of the 'reserve funds' of the Ministry of the Interior, which were designed for covert operations. The policemen were each given 100-year sentences, but the investigation was unable to establish if they were acting on the direct orders of the Ministry of the Interior, not least because the Ministry refused to allow judicial access to the reserve funds. It was later discovered that 200 million pesetas were paid into a Swiss bank account on behalf of Amedo and Domínguez in order to buy their silence. It is extremely unlikely, if not impossible, that an operation of this magnitude and longevity could have been launched without the knowledge or approval of the government. Felipe González admitted as much by contending that 'one defends the state not only in the meeting rooms and offices, but also in the gutter.'[33]

Despite the mounting scandal over the dirty war in France and the refusal of the UGT to endorse the PSOE ticket, the socialists still managed to scrape a majority in the October 1989 general election, winning 39 per cent of the vote and 175 seats. On the other hand, they had lost 900,000 votes, a decline that was already evident in the municipal elections of 1987, when the party forfeited 1.5 million votes. The general election showed that the PSOE was losing support amongst the young, the self-employed, and the liberal professions, as well as in the big cities. Even so, the Popular Party, now under the youthful leadership of José María Aznar, won 107 seats, failing to surpass the Popular Alliance's electoral peak of 26 per cent of the vote.

## 1992: THE *ANNUS MIRABILIS* OF
## SPANISH DEMOCRACY?

Outside observers would be forgiven for assuming that the year 1992 was the high point of Spanish democracy, as the country hosted not only the Universal Exposition in Seville and the Commemoration of the 500th Anniversary of Columbus' 'discovery' of the Americas, but also the Olympic Games in Barcelona. In a few short years, Spain had leapt from the Western European and transatlantic stage onto the world stage. Spain's outstanding success at the 1992 Olympics – twenty-two medals compared to just five during the entire Franco dictatorship – reflected its new-found prosperity and modernity. The outpouring of nationalist sentiment over the Games also revealed that the sectarian nationalism of Francoism had given way to a more inclusive and pluralistic one.

For the socialist leaders, however, 1992 was a 'catastrophic' year.[34] First, the economy suffered a short but sharp recession, not just the result of the monumental expense engendered by the 1992 global show-pieces, but also the knock-on effect of German reunification, the collapse of Communism, and the Japanese economic crisis. Having grown by a mere 0.7 per cent in 1992, the economy shrank by 1.2 per cent in 1993, as the public deficit reached 6.9 per cent of GDP (not so alarming when placed alongside Italy's 9.9 per cent in 1992) and unemployment surged to 3.5 million (24 per cent of the active population), the economic reforms of the 1980s and 1990s clearly having failed to resolve the structural problem of unemployment. Second, cases of socialist corruption erupted 'almost every day'.[35] The first bombshell involved Juan Guerra, brother of the deputy prime minister, Alfonso. Since 1982, Juan Guerra had occupied an office at the governmental delegation in Seville on the pretext that he was Alfonso's 'assistant'. In reality, he exploited his brother's name and influence to become a mafia-like broker for the private sector in a hoard of construction projects, including luxury ventures on the coast (a far cry from earlier socialist cooperative housing projects), which soon made him fabulously rich. Such rapacious influence-peddling confounded Alfonso Guerra's portrayal of the PSOE as an austere and honourable party, one even 'of the poor and the shirtless'.[36] Breaking in January 1990, the Juan Guerra scandal proved to be merely the tip of the iceberg. Over the following years reams of socialist politicians and public officials were exposed for exploiting their positions for illicit gain in their interactions with the private sector, such as by extracting bribes, furnishing public contracts for family and friends, or syphoning off taxpayers' money into private funds. This was justified by many socialists on the grounds that 'the right was in power for 40 years, so now it's our turn.' The cascade of scandals laid bare not only a far-reaching clientelistic culture within the Socialist Party, but also a highly patrimonial attitude to the public domain (the minister of defence, famously, acquired a grand piano at taxpayers' expense, along with the uninspired moniker of 'The Pianist'). The greater vigilance provided by a free press the judiciary failed to extirpate the clientelism and corruption that had hitherto characterized politics in Spain, making democracy little different in this respect to the other regimes of the twentieth century.

The corruption of the PSOE was not confined to individual members or isolated networks, but enveloped the party apparatus itself. The *Filesa* scandal of May 1991 revealed that the socialists had financed the party illegally by taking 'commissions' from businesses in exchange for undue assistance in relation to the public administrations under their control. As a front company, *Filesa* had been created not only to finance the PSOE, but also to service its family and client networks. An investigation made public by the Ministry of Finance in March 1993 itemized the techniques involved in securing money for the party, such as the payment of 1 billion pesetas for non-existent reports. The torrent of scandals exposed the socialists' disdain for legality and the public trust, while even the 'sins of omission were glaring in a party that was as tightly centralised and hierarchical as the PSOE'.[37] Worse still, the party did not rush to uproot the 'generalised and widespread' corruption, as 'neither the government nor the PSOE seemed particularly anxious to curb [it]'.[38] While the corrosive corruption within socialist ranks did much to taint the party's image, it did not make Spain different insofar as similar scandals befell parties in many other Western European countries during the 1980s and 1990s. What is striking about the Spanish case is the extent to which the scandals were exposed by the press, not the public prosecutors, reflecting the degree to which the judiciary had become politicized. The judiciary's lack of independence, together with the limited accountability of the government, made it clear that the separation of powers in Spain left much to be desired.

## A PARTY DIVIDED

The standing of the PSOE was further weakened by a major schism. For a party that had always prided itself on its unity and discipline, this was a grievous blow. The clashes between the followers of Alfonso Guerra (or *guerristas*) with the *renovadores* (renovators) of Felipe González at the 1990 congress demonstrated the extent to which relations had deteriorated within the party. In reality, the differences between the quasi-radical *guerristas* and the supposedly neo-liberal *renovadores* were few and far between, reflecting above all a struggle for power within the party. The situation worsened considerably once Alfonso Guerra, badly scalded by the Juan Guerra affair, was made to resign as deputy prime minister in January 1991. His presence in the Cabinet had ensured the subordination of the party to the government, as shown by the relatively muted backlash over such potentially divisive issues as the NATO referendum, industrial 'restructuring', pension reform, and the general strike. Guerra's exit from the Cabinet not only exposed it to greater criticism from the party, but also left the government 'defenceless against the increasingly numerous accusations of corruption and the abuse of power'.[39] In addition, the breach between Guerra and González endangered the unity of the parliamentary party, as illustrated by the dispute over a strike bill that the *guerristas* had drawn up in collaboration with the trade unions, but in defiance of the minister of finance. González brought the spiralling discord to an end by dissolving the Cortes and calling a general election for June 1993.

The PSOE fought the 1993 general election not only gravely divided, but also in the midst of a welter of corruption scandals and an economic crisis. Few commentators or pollsters gave them much of a chance. The socialists attempted to combat the wave of discredit by recruiting independent figures of repute as candidates, such as the crusading investigating magistrate Baltasar Garzón or the outspoken judge Juan Alberto Belloch, and by holding out the prospect, in González's words, of a 'democratic boost'.[40] Despite the pessimistic predictions, the PSOE, thanks above all to the charismatic appeal of its leader, won its fourth election in a row, the party reaping 38 per cent of the vote and 159 seats. The Popular Party came second, its 34 per cent of the ballot and 141 seats finally breaching the Popular Alliance's electoral ceiling of 26 per cent. The United Left came third with 9 per cent of the vote and eighteen seats, an improvement of a single deputy on 1989. Faced with a hung parliament, González chose to reach an understanding with the Basque and Catalan nationalists rather than with the United Left, partly because he was averse to reviving memories of the Popular Front, partly because he feared that an alliance might strengthen the Communists at the expense of the socialists, and partly because the United Left's lack of enthusiasm for the newly dubbed European Union could well complicate the government's efforts to comply with the Union's convergence criteria.

## ENGULFED BY SCANDAL

Following the 1993 election, the socialists were in a much more vulnerable position than before not only because they were bereft of a parliamentary majority, but also because they remained divided, as highlighted by the confrontation between *guerristas* and *renovadores* at the 1994 party congress. In any case, the final three years of the PSOE's 'long government' were to be a horror show of scandal after scandal that was to a considerable extent the inevitable denouement of the 'excesses and errors' of the 1980s, principally the widespread malfeasance within the party and the extrajudicial violations of the government.[41] Like the Craxi years in Italy, the latter years of the González era in Spain witnessed 'a radical divorce between politics on the one hand, and morality and the law on the other'.[42]

The corruption scandals that erupted during these years were the worst to date of the democratic era, even tarnishing two of the most venerable institutions of the Spanish state, the Bank of Spain and the Civil Guard. Mariano Rubio, governor of the Bank of Spain, was sent to jail along with Mariano de la Concha, a trustee of the Stock Exchange, for financial irregularities in relation to the Ibercorp bank.

The affair also ensnared the minister of agriculture, Vicente Albero, for committing tax fraud over his Ibercorp investments. A second major scandal involved Luis Roldán, the first civilian director of the Civil Guard. At the end of 1993 the press disclosed that Roldán had extorted unlawful commissions on contracts concerning the Civil Guard, pocketed 'protection money' paid by Basque businessmen to ETA, and pillaged the reserve funds at the Ministry of the Interior for his own enrichment. Despite amassing an illicit fortune of 5 billion pesetas, Roldán was on the verge of being appointed minister of the interior, only to resign as director of the Civil Guard in December 1993 due to the press revelations. He then fled Spain in 1994, was extradited from Laos in 1995, and sent to jail for twenty-eight years in 1998. Hardly surprisingly, both the left- and right-wing opposition, along with much of the media, called on González to resign, especially after the PSOE won only 30.7 per cent of the vote in the European elections of June 1994 (compared to the PP's 40 per cent, the first time that the right-wing party had defeated the socialists in a nation-wide election). Little wonder, too, that the proportion of Spaniards who believed that the government was misusing 'a large part' of their taxes rose from 19 per cent in 1984 to 45 per cent by 1995.[43]

The corruption scandals that engulfed the PSOE and, later, the PP, were far from unusual within Western Europe. Far-reaching scandals surfaced in many Western European countries in the 1980s and 1990s, including France, Belgium, West Germany, Greece, the UK, and Italy. Throughout Europe business people and professionals from the private sector obtained privileged treatment or information from civil servants and politicians in the public sector by means of kickbacks, the line between the two sometimes being crossed, as former politicians joined the boards of major companies (the UK being prominent in this regard) or civil servants entered politics, as in France. The most spectacular scandal of all was that of the *Tangentopoli* ('Bribesville') in Italy, which exploded on the political scene in 1992. At one point, 205 of the 630 national deputies and 81 of the 326 senators were under investigation, the fallout destroying both the Christian Democrat and Socialist parties. The use and abuse of public money was, as the Italian head of state, Oscar Luigi Scalfaro, insisted, 'a very serious misdemeanour; it robs and defrauds the honest citizen who pays his taxes, and undermines severely the faith of citizens in the state: there is no greater evil, no greater danger for democracy than the turbid interlacing of business and politics.'[44]

A second set of scandals concerned the government's extrajudicial operations in the 1980s and 1990s. In 1994, Baltasar Garzón, elected the previous year as a socialist deputy, returned to the judiciary, where he reopened the inquiry into the 'dirty war' on ETA. Having gained the collaboration of the two incarcerated policemen, José Amedo and Miguel Domínguez, Garzón proceeded to jail the former general director of security, Julián Sancristobal, followed by the ex-secretary of state for security, Rafael Vera, and the ex-secretary-general of the PSOE in Vizcaya, Ricardo García Damborenea. By mid-1995, Garzón was ready to charge not only the former minister of the interior, José Barrionuevo, but also the deputy prime minister, Narcís Serra, and the prime minister himself, Felipe González. As all three were *aforados* – that is, protected from prosecution by their parliamentary status – Garzón had to apply to the Supreme Court in order to prosecute them, but the Court only permitted him to indict Barrionuevo, who eventually went to prison in 1998. It was later established that the reserve funds of the Ministry of the Interior had not only financed the Anti-Terrorist Liberation Groups (or GAL), but had also sponsored a life of luxury for its highest-ranking officials, including the purchase of gifts for their wives. González continued to deny any involvement in the GAL, but a survey of July 1995 showed that two-thirds of Spaniards did not believe him. Of all the scandals that discredited the PSOE, the GAL was the one that 'most damaged the credibility of the government, especially that of González himself'.[45] The government's unlawful activities, however, did not stop there. In June 1995 the press exposed the illicit wiretaps carried out by the secret service on a slew of public figures, including the king. The service's deputy director, Colonel Juan Alberto Perote, was then arrested for passing confidential information on to the disgraced banker Mario Conde, who had hoped to use the material to blackmail the government. The scandal had far-reaching repercussions, provoking the resignation of the director of the secret service, the minister of defence, and the prime minister's closest ally, the deputy premier Narcís Serra. In just two years González lost five of his seventeen ministers.

The ongoing political crisis of 1993 to 1996 – less than 10 per cent of the people surveyed during this period regarded the state of politics as 'good' or 'very good' – hampered the ability of the parties to exploit ETA's fragile position following the arrest of its principal leaders at Bidart (France) in March 1992, a time when the organization faced the prospect of defeat at the hands of the police. Indeed, by 1995 the Basque terrorists were attacking Basque and national politicians alike in an endeavour to force the government to negotiate. In January 1995 they assassinated Gregorio Ordóñez, a PP councillor in the Basque Country; in April they nearly killed the PP leader José María Aznar; and in the summer of 1995 they made an attempt on the life of Premier Felipe González. In February 1996, ETA murdered both the socialist Fernando Múgica, brother of the former minister of justice, and Francisco Tomás y Valiente, the highly regarded former head of the Constitutional Court. In the meantime ETA's political allies unleashed a campaign of street violence – the *kale borroka* – with the goal of intimidating Basque society. In short, the unyielding and belligerent nationalism of ETA continued to bedevil Spanish democracy.

## THE END OF AN ERA

The election campaign of 1996 was the most agitated and vituperative since 1936. Thrown on the defensive by the corruption and other scandals, the prime minister went on the attack, even invoking the spirit of the Civil War ('They Shall Not Pass!' he exclaimed dramatically), which sat uneasily with his claim to have modernized Spain. As expected, the right-wing PP won, but only with 38.8 per cent of the vote and 156 seats, while the PSOE managed to secure 37.7 per cent of the ballot and 141 seats. Hoping to make serious inroads on the socialists' support, United Left obtained just 10 per cent of the vote and twenty-one seats, a disappointing return. For the PP, which squeezed home by just 340,000 votes, this was a 'bitter victory', as it had fallen well short of a majority.[46] For the PSOE, the result was unexpectedly good, a 'sweet defeat'.[47] Arguably the single most important reason for the PP's underperformance was that it suffered from a 'certain deficit of legitimacy', as many voters still identified it with the dictatorship (hence González's Civil War rhetoric), though the proportion of those who said that they would *never* vote for the PP had shrunk from 42 per cent in 1989 to 25 per cent in 1996.[48] On the other hand, the PSOE had at last been held accountable for its rapacity and contempt for the rule of law, a sign of democratic vitality. Further, the triumph of the PP strengthened the democratic system, as it signalled the full incorporation of the right and a second ideological change of government.

Looking back over the 'long government' of 1982 to 1996, the socialists had achieved a great deal in consolidating democracy, developing the welfare state, improving public services and the infrastructure, making the economy more competitive, completing the system of autonomous communities, and integrating Spain into the Western system of alliances. On the other hand, they had proven unable to solve the corrosive problem of unemployment or that of Basque terrorism (despite waging a 'dirty war' in the 1980s). Foremost amongst their self-inflicted failings were the untrammelled corruption, the violation of the rule of law, and a certain disdain for the liberal virtues, above all the separation of powers, as shown by the feeble control exercised by the legislature over the executive and the politicization of the judiciary. The faith of Spaniards in democracy was nonetheless stronger, not weaker, at the end of the socialist period, as those declaring democracy to be their preferred system of government had risen from 70 per cent in 1980 to 76 per cent in 1995.

Undoubtedly the rise to power of the conservative Popular Party was a fundamental step in the consolidation of democracy in Spain. Often denounced as Francoists, none of the PP's foremost figures had actually served the dictatorship. In reality, the Popular Party, a reconfiguration of the Popular Alliance, was a liberal, democratic force, not a dictatorial remake, its leaders constituting the first post-transition generation of politicians. Boasting 500,000 members in 1996, the PP was a relatively heterogeneous party comprising conservatives, liberals, Christian democrats, and even some social democrats. The party had been united under the firm leadership of the former tax inspector José María Aznar. Despite his Charlie Chaplinesque moustache, Aznar was somewhat stiff and unsmiling, but he was an efficient administrator and extremely tenacious politician. The early tenor of Aznar's administration was demonstrated by his insistence on securing the backing not only of the Catalan Convergence and Union, but also of the Basque Nationalist

Party for the government's investiture, even though the support of the latter was unnecessary. Aznar considered it essential to overcome the hostility of the regionalists to the Spanish right, an achievement that he acclaimed as a 'historic revolution'.[49] The generational shift on the right was matched by that on the left. In June 2000 the PSOE elected as secretary-general the gangly thirty-nine-year-old José Luis Rodríguez Zapatero, the engaging and enthusiastic leader of 'New Way', a youthful current within the party, which called for a 'political regeneration' that would enhance Spanish democracy. This would be based on the development of social rights and liberties – a 'socialism of the citizens' – and a far greater receptiveness to the demands of the regional nationalists, being open to statutory and even constitutional reform. 'A plural Spain,' as Rodríguez Zapatero put it, 'more secular, of greater solidarity, and more just.'[50]

## BUILDING ON THE SOCIALIST LEGACY

The 'high-stakes polarized politics' which characterized relations between the PP and PSOE for nearly all the 1990s and the 2000s should not distract from the fact that the two parties shared a great deal in common.[51] Like the socialists before them, the conservatives were committed to Spanish integration within the European Union. Thus the Aznar government was determined to meet the criteria in order to join the EU's monetary union. Spurred on much as Felipe González was in his effort to make Spain a member of the EEC, José María Aznar was set on making the country a founding member of the monetary union on 1 January 1999 rather than signing up at a later date. In mid-1996 Spain fulfilled only one of the five criteria, but by the end of 1997 it had achieved four of them, including inflation of less than 2.7 per cent and a deficit of under 3 per cent of GDP. It had still not reached the public debt target of less than 60 per cent of GDP, but the bar was then lowered, as neither France nor Germany had satisfied the debt requirement either. As a result, Spain became a founding member of Europe's monetary union, Aznar's decision proving to be the 'most audacious and correct of his mandate'.[52] Indeed, this was the first time in the twentieth century that Spain had been a founder of a major European enterprise. The Spanish prime minister also fought hard at the Berlin meeting of the European Council in 1999 so as not be overshadowed by Felipe González's performance at Edinburgh in 1992 in relation to the EEC's cohesion funds. A driven Aznar achieved his aim by securing a net balance of 1.2 billion pesetas a year between 2000 and 2006.

The privatization policy launched by the socialists under Felipe González was greatly expanded by the *populares*. Initially, the government sold off those public companies that were already sufficiently attractive to the private sector, such as *Argentaria*, *Endesa*, *Repsol*, and *Telefónica*, and which had been partially privatized by the PSOE. Thereafter, it proceeded to privatize a slew of companies that had hitherto been entirely in public hands, such as *Aceralia*, the *Grupo Potasas*, and *Tabacalera*, the goal being to reach the twenty-first century with a greatly reduced public sector. The policy reaped 4.9 billion pesetas for the Exchequer between 1996 and 1999, as compared to the 2.1 billion pesetas previously raised by the PSOE, while creating 7.5 million new shareholders. A number of the directors of the newly privatized companies were intimates of the prime minister, which allowed him not only to retain a certain control over the enterprises, but also to extend the Popular Party's clientelistic base within the upper echelons of the business world. The PP also did much more than the socialists to deregulate the markets in goods and services. These included the electricity sector in 1997 and telecommunications in 1998, which lowered prices and made possible the development of the mobile phone market. In contrast to the PSOE, the PP reduced income tax (by an average of 11 per cent in 1999), while exempting 1.7 million of the poorest from paying altogether, including 600,000 pensioners. Tax as a proportion of GDP nonetheless rose from 32 per cent in 1996 to 35 per cent in 1999.

Like the socialist administrations of 1982–96, the Popular Party governments oversaw a rise in foreign trade, as exports and imports climbed from 45 per cent of GDP in 1995 to 58 per cent in 1999, which was higher than, say, France (51 per cent) or Italy (48 per cent). A measure of the health of the Spanish economy was a spectacular rise in the number of people in employment from 13.06 million in 1996 to 18.28 million in 2004, which brought unemployment down to 12.08 per cent in 2004 and 8.3 per cent in 2007. Another indicator

was that in 1997 Spanish investment abroad exceeded foreign investment at home for the very first time in the modern era. In fact, by the
end of the 1990s, Spain was the sixth-biggest investor in the world,
ahead even of Japan.

The structure of the workforce changed a great deal during these
years. At the time the Popular Party came to power, its composition
was very different to that of twenty years earlier. In 1976, 21.2 per
cent of the active population worked in agriculture, 27.3 per cent in
industry, and 41.3 per cent in the tertiary sector, but by 1996 agriculture employed only 8.1 per cent, industry 20.5 per cent, while the
service sector had soared to 61.8 per cent, the result not only of the
expansion of the welfare state but also of the creation of the autonomous communities. Under the PP and then the PSOE, this trend was
consolidated, so that by 2008 a mere 4.5 per cent worked in agriculture, 14.1 per cent in industry and over two-thirds (74 per cent) in
services, while 7.1 per cent were employed in the building trade. In
sum, Spain had become a 'society of services'.[53]

The centre-right governments of 1996–2004 also coincided with
the socialists in seeking to consolidate the welfare state, though the PP
differed in seeking to make it 'more rational and efficient'.[54] Thus the
financial underpinnings of the social security system were stream-
lined, while the health sector was subject to a degree of innovation, as
public health foundations were introduced (as in the UK) and tax
breaks were offered for private health insurance. Even so, the amount
spent by the state on health rose from 89,000 pesetas per person in
1995 to 120,000 pesetas by 2000. One sign of the improvement in
public health was the rise in life expectancy from 73.7 years in 1975
to 82.1 years in 2011, one of the highest rates in the world.

Another policy area in which the PP converged powerfully with the
PSOE was the armed forces. Before the 1996 general election, the
socialist premier Felipe González had already decided to take advantage of NATO's post-Cold War restructuring to request Spain's
complete military integration. Once in power, the Popular Party wasted
little time in abandoning Spain's status of, in Aznar's words, a 'reticent
ally', by integrating Spain fully into NATO.[55] The government was also
determined to take on a greater role in the defence of the western Mediterranean and eastern Atlantic, a sub-regional NATO command post

being established at Retamares (Madrid) in 1999. Finally, the vertiginous rise in the number of conscientious objectors after 1993 led the PP to eliminate national service altogether in 2003, a purely professional army emerging that was projected to have 120,000 troops and 48,000 officers. Like full membership of NATO, this decision was essentially a continuation of socialist policy.

## THE CHALLENGE OF REGIONAL NATIONALISM

Despite Aznar's 'historic revolution' of 1996 in forming a parliamentary majority in conjunction with the Catalan regionalists of Convergence and Union, the greatest challenge of the Popular Party's first administration was regional nationalism. In July 1998, regional nationalists from the Basque Country, Catalonia, and Galicia issued the Declaration of Barcelona, which proclaimed that the autonomous model had outlived its usefulness and that the democratic regime had not yet 'resolved the vertebration of the Spanish state as plurinational'.[56] Their goal was 'to supersede the current framework and progress towards the institutional and political elaboration of a plurinational state'.[57] In short, the Constitution had to be revised so that a confederal system could be established. Still, the case for constitutional reform was highly debatable insofar as the regional nationalists did not boast a sizeable hegemony in any of the three regions. The most glaring example was Galicia, where the Popular Party renewed its absolute majority in the autonomous elections of October 1997. In the Catalan elections of October 1999, the socialists won the most votes, though Convergence and Union was able to form a regional government in alliance with the anti-nationalist PP, the inverse of the situation at the national level.

In the Basque regional elections of October 1998, the regional nationalists did win 54 per cent of the vote, but this did not amount to an overwhelming endorsement. On the other hand, ETA had still not been defeated. Like the socialists, the conservatives sought to overcome ETA by a strategy that combined police measures with political ones. The government had leading operatives such as José Luis Urrusolo

Sistiaga arrested, a series of commandos dismantled, and the organization's financial infrastructure crippled. The newspaper *Egin* and the radio station *Egin Irratia* were also shut down as accessories to terrorism. In July 1997 the Civil Guard freed the kidnapped prison officer José Antonio Ortega Lara, who had been held by ETA for 532 days in a minuscule hideout. The terrorists immediately struck back by kidnapping and then executing a young Popular Party councillor from Ermua, Miguel Ángel Blanco. His fate, which attracted enormous public attention, provoked the greatest demonstrations of the entire democratic era, both within and beyond the Basque Country. The operational successes of the police, together with the popular backlash against ETA and its political allies (some *Herri Batasuna* leaders required police protection, ironically), brought the terrorists to the brink of defeat. The prospect of ETA's demise was nonetheless regarded by the Basque Nationalist Party as a disaster for the regional nationalist cause. In August 1998, a month after the Declaration of Barcelona, secret negotiations between the Basque Nationalist Party, *Euzko Alkartasuna* or EA (Basque Solidarity), and ETA led to an agreement whereby the terrorists would declare an indefinite truce in exchange for the establishment of 'a unique and sovereign structure', which would embrace not only the Spanish Basque provinces, but also Navarre and the French Basque provinces.[58] Accordingly, the Basque nationalists would sever all ties with 'the parties whose objective is the destruction of the Basque Country', that is, the PP and PSOE.[59]

On 12 September 1998 the Basque Nationalist Party, Basque Solidarity, and *Herri Batasuna* issued the Declaration of Estella, the 'most important political event' in the Basque Country since the Statute of 1979.[60] The Declaration called for a dialogue without conditions or limits that would be voted on by 'the citizens of *Euskal Herria*' (that is, both the Spanish and French Basque provinces, as well as Navarre) and respected by 'the implicated states', in other words, Spain and France.[61] The proposed 'peace process' excluded all defenders of the Statute, such as the socialists, who had abandoned the regional government during the summer. Four days after Estella, ETA proclaimed an open-ended truce, exultant that after nearly twenty years of autonomy the moderate nationalists had finally realized 'the sterility of this path'.[62] The Declaration of Estella was the greatest coup of the radical nationalists since the dictatorship, as the PNV had deserted the democratic arrangement that had benefited it for nearly two decades in favour of an alliance with the proponents of the armed struggle. Isolated, disoriented, and facing defeat in the summer of 1997, the Basque radicals had reasserted themselves by the autumn of 1998, placing the supporters of the Constitution and the Statute on the defensive.

In the Basque autonomous elections of October 1998 the moderate Basque nationalists lost three seats to the radical left, while the Popular Party's 'spectacular growth' catapulted it from fourth position to second.[63] The regional nationalists had not only failed to secure an overwhelming mandate for their 'peace process' but had also greatly polarized Basque society. In December 1998 the PNV leader Juan José Ibarretxe was invested as *lehendakari* (regional president) with the support of the radical left. Nonetheless, the onward march of the Basque nationalists was 'more apparent than real', as shown by the local elections of June 1999.[64] In Navarre the defenders of the non-nationalist status quo won a towering majority of thirty-nine to eleven. In the Basque provinces the PNV and EA held on to the Bilbao city council, but the PP conquered the city council of the capital Vitoria, while the PSOE retained control of numerous towns and cities, including Baracaldo, Eibar, and San Sebastián. ETA renounced the truce in late 1999, disgusted that the 'process of national construction' had been 'without content', while its murder of the socialist spokesman in the Basque parliament in February 2000 brought the alliance with the moderate nationalists to an end.[65]

The vicissitudes of Basque politics notwithstanding, the Popular Party won an absolute majority in the general election of March 2000, having met the Maastricht criteria, created 1.5 million jobs, upheld the welfare state, and achieved an average growth rate of 3.5 per cent a year between 1997 and 1999. It returned 183 seats, the Socialist Party 125, and the United Left just eight. Between them, the Socialist Party and United Left had lost around 3 million votes, 1 million to the Popular Party and 2 million to abstention. Oddly, the vote of the PP had risen by only 600,000, though it had surpassed the aggregate total of the PSOE and the United Left for the first time.

Later that year the so-called 'constitutionalist' parties of the PP and PSOE took the fight to the Basque nationalists by signing an

Agreement for Liberty and Against Terrorism in December 2000 on the initiative of the socialist leader José Luis Rodríguez Zapatero, which paved the way for the Law on Political Parties, passed by the Cortes in June 2002. This illegalized parties with links to terrorism, which meant that *Batasuna* (the new name for *Herri Batasuna* from June 2001) was banned from future elections. The Law on Political Parties was considered by most Basques to be anti-democratic, but it had an undeniable impact on the radical nationalist movement, which lost a thousand elected representatives and forty-nine local councils, along with all the spoils of local and provincial institutional power. By this stage ETA appeared to be on the wane, as it killed 'only' eight people between 2002 and 2004, while the number of street actions undertaken by its political front (such as assaulting the local branches of the PNV) dropped from 630 in 2000 to just 190 in 2004.

## THE IRAQ WAR

The biggest breach between the PP and PSOE was over foreign policy. Once Spain entered the eurozone in 1999, the EU was replaced as the principal focus of the Popular Party's foreign policy by the United States. In an endeavour to supersede Spain's status as a 'middling regional power', José María Aznar was determined to establish a 'direct line' with Washington, which, it was estimated, would enhance the country's profile not only in Europe, but also in other areas, such as Latin America.[66] In 1998 the prime minister supported the US military intervention in Iraq (Operation Desert Fox), despite the opposition of Spanish public opinion and other European powers. Following the Al Qaeda attacks on New York and Washington DC on 9 September 2001, Aznar's 'unqualified Atlanticism' reached new heights, as he offered his unconditional support for the United States' global war on terrorism, 'despite not possessing either the material or human means necessary to participate in the conflict in a prominent capacity'.[67] He backed America's invasion of Afghanistan in October 2001, and then, in March 2003, took part in the US-led invasion of Iraq, endorsing the US's unfounded thesis that Saddam Hussein's regime was not only in cahoots with Al Qaeda, but also harboured weapons of mass destruction. For Aznar, the alliance was crystallized in the famous (or infamous, according to your point of view) 'Photo in the Azores' in which the Spanish prime minister appeared alongside the American president George W. Bush and the British prime minister Tony Blair. Aznar paid a heavy price for reasserting the transatlantic alliance at the expense of European solidarity, as his alignment with the United States was opposed not only by France and Germany, but also by the majority of his own citizens, as manifested in mass protests throughout Spain. Worse still, Spanish participation in the invasion of Iraq was the principal motive for the Al Qaeda bombing of the Atocha railway station in Madrid on 11 March 2004, which killed 191 people and injured over 1,800, the worst terrorist atrocity in Europe since the Lockerbie tragedy of 1988.

With the general election only three days away, the government rightly feared that the PP might actually lose the election if the Atocha attack was attributed to its involvement in the Iraq war rather than – as expected – win comfortably. In an act of cynical realpolitik, the government insisted – despite all the evidence – that ETA was responsible for the bombing. This provoked a massive backlash, as manifested in the huge demonstrations over the executive's lack of transparency and the intense mobilization of the anti-PP vote. The PP lost the general election to the PSOE by 148 deputies to 164, the socialists winning 3 million more votes than in 2000. Once in power, the PSOE almost immediately withdrew Spain's 1,300 troops from Iraq – a highly popular move – and later closed down the NATO centre at Retamares.

## THE CULTURE WARS

Another major point of rupture between the Socialist Party and the Popular Party in the 1990s and 2000s was cultural policy. Following two decades in which Spanish nationalism had been widely reviled for its association with the Franco dictatorship, the Aznar government was determined to make unabashed patriotism respectable again, unfurling the largest Spanish flag ever in Columbus Square in Madrid on 12 October 2001 (formerly known as 'Columbus Day', that is, the commemoration of the Spanish conquest of the Americas). In the same vein, the PP had proposed that the school history curriculum should highlight Spain's unitary – as opposed to regionally diverse – character, a recommendation that was discarded by the socialists once they took control of the Ministry of Education. In fact, disputes over the past were a prominent feature of the burgeoning culture wars between left and right. In 1999 the PSOE had tabled a motion in the Cortes condemning the Franco dictatorship, but the PP sidestepped the issue, only agreeing in 2002 to condemn all 'totalitarian regimes'.[68] Left and right alike also strove to achieve greater recognition for the victims of their respective ideological camps during the Civil War. On the one hand, groups such as the Association for the Recovery of Historical Memory, founded in 2000, called for the excavation of republican mass graves from the Civil War and for public acknowledgement of the victims of the Franco dictatorship. On the other hand, the Catholic Church had 631 clerical martyrs of the Civil War beatified in 2001 and 2007. The 'memory wars' were exacerbated even further by the passing of the so-called Law of Historical Memory in 2007, which denounced the Franco dictatorship as unlawful and set out to rehabilitate the republican victims of the Civil War. The PP retorted that the law had 'buried the consensus' of the transition.[69] This weaponizing of the past by the politicians was to be expected, but the debate over Spain's recent history has often been further polarized by the historians themselves. Much scholarly work, both Spanish and foreign, has framed Spanish history in terms of the battles of the past, producing politicized and partisan accounts that may have had a strong commercial appeal, but which have done little credit to the profession.

## SOCIAL DIVERGENCES

Relations between the socialists and the conservatives were further antagonized during the Rodríguez Zapatero years by the government's progressive social agenda. In 2005 Spain became one of the first countries in the world to legalize homosexual marriage. The initiative reflected not just the strength of the gay rights movement in Spain, but also majority support within Spanish society for the right of homosexuals to marry. Not surprisingly, the reform was vehemently opposed by the Catholic Church and conservative sectors, the PP contesting the law before the Supreme Court, only for the latter to dismiss the claim in 2012. And, while the PP had passed laws favourable to women, including those between 2001 and 2004 concerning family support, the socialists introduced a whole series of ground-breaking measures, including one against gender violence (2004), another on assisted reproduction (2006), and yet another amplifying the grounds for abortion (2010). A watershed law of 2007 enacted 'effective equality' by stipulating that there should be greater representation of women at the highest levels of government, in the business world, and on the electoral lists. The socialists acted on their principles insofar as Rodríguez Zapatero's Cabinets displayed the greatest gender balance in the history of Spain, women occupying at least 40 per cent of the portfolios, including the first female minister of defence, Carme Chacón. They also created a secretariat of state for Policies of Equality in 2004, and, in 2008, a Ministry of Equality. Such reforms helped reduce the salary gap between men and women from 33 per cent in 1995 to 23 per cent in 2010, though it still remained above the European average.

Other social reforms included a law of 2005 making divorce more straightforward and a ban of 2006 on smoking in bars, restaurants, cinemas, theatres, and other public places, much to the disgust of many conservative politicians, who framed the measure not in terms of public health but as an attack on personal liberty. Arguably the most ambitious reform was the Law of Dependence of 2006, which recognized the rights of the elderly and the physically and mentally disabled. The law sought to provide public assistance for those who required care, which would not only reduce the burden on families, especially women, but also generate greater opportunities for professional carers. An inspired addition to the welfare state, the law failed to live up to expectations, partly because 'it was born without the necessary funds to finance it and without the professional services required' and partly because conservative autonomous communities such as Madrid and Valencia refused to apply it.[70]

## TACKLING REGIONAL NATIONALISM

An era-defining achievement of the Rodríguez Zapatero administrations was the defeat of Basque terrorism. Despite the failure of the Pact of Estella, the Basque Nationalist Party and Basque Solidarity had continued along their 'sovereign path', presenting the 'Ibarretxe Plan' in September 2003, which called for a 'free association' between the (Spanish) Basque provinces and the state, as well as for the right to self-determination.[71] In December 2004 the Plan was approved by the Basque parliament, but rejected for debate by the Cortes in February 2005. In 2008 the Basque parliament attempted to hold a 'popular consultation' on the Plan, but the Constitutional Court overturned the proposal as unconstitutional. The tightening police cordon (305 people being arrested for terrorist-related offences between 2008 and 2010), the hard-hitting restrictions imposed by the Law on Political Parties, and the ever greater opposition within Basque society to the terrorist violence (which even included leaders of *Batasuna*), finally led to ETA's definitive abandonment of the 'armed struggle' in October 2011.

By contrast, the socialists' attempt to resolve the political tensions within Catalonia by means of a greater receptiveness backfired spectacularly. In the 2003 regional elections the moderate Convergence and Union lost control of the *Generalitat* (regional government) after twenty-three years to a left-wing coalition made up of the Republican Left of Catalonia, the Initiative for Catalonia, and the Catalan Socialist Party. The coalition called for a new autonomy statute, which would greatly extend the region's powers vis-à-vis the state and recognize it as a 'nation' (as opposed to a 'nationality'). Presented to the Cortes, the new statute was passed into law in 2006, but to the dismay of the Catalan parties it had been considerably altered. Worse still, the constitutionality of the statute was then challenged by the PP. The ruling of the Constitutional Court in 2010 eliminated fourteen and modified twenty-seven of the statute's original articles, which not only discredited the ruling coalition (that subsequently lost the regional elections of 2010 to Convergence and Union), but also greatly stoked pro-independence sentiment in Catalonia.

The agitated nature of politics in Catalonia and the Basque Country since the 1980s has often been contrasted with the less strident tone of national politics, as reflected in the low levels of party, trade-union, and NGO affiliation, as well as the general lack of a vibrant civil society: a survey of 2005 found that 67 per cent of Spaniards had little or no interest in politics. Admittedly, Spain had not produced the kind of thrumming civil society that then existed in many parts of Northern Europe. On the other hand, 'investment in the electoral system' was consistently high, with turnout in general elections generally ranging between 70 per cent and 80 per cent.[72] Spaniards had also taken to the streets en masse at times of crisis, such as over the assassination of Miguel Ángel Blanco in 1997, the PP's hapless handling of the *Prestige* oil tanker spill in 2002, or the Atocha bombing of 11 March 2004.

## A NEW SOCIETY

The magnitude, rapidity, and depth of the changes that have taken place in Spanish society since the dictatorship 'has no precedent'.[73] By the 2010s the massive expansion of the educational system had transformed the aspirations and opportunities of Spaniards. At the beginning of the twentieth century 47 per cent of children attended primary school, 1–2 per cent secondary school, and a mere 17,363 students, including a sprinkling of women, university. By 2007–8, 99.3 per cent of children went to primary school and 88.6 per cent of sixteen-year-olds to secondary school. In higher education, there were twenty-eight universities by the time of the transition, thirty-five by 1985, and seventy-seven by 2011 (of which fifty were public and twenty-seven private, especially Catholic). The number of university students had skyrocketed from 650,000 during the transition to 1.65 million by the 1999–2000 academic year, the greatest progress being made by women. Virtually excluded at the outset of the twentieth century, by 1986 female students outnumbered male ones, and, by 2008–9, 54.2 per cent of all students were women.

A further transformation within Spanish society came with the spread of secularization. Judging by the number of religious holidays, Catholic schools, and universities, the huge state subsidies paid out to the Church, and the proliferation of streets, squares, schools, businesses, and other entities with Catholic names, as well as the fact that many Spaniards still celebrate their 'saint's day' in addition to their birthday and that ministers are sworn in before a crucifix, one could be forgiven for thinking that Spain remains a deeply Catholic country. But the outward signs and symbols of Catholicism are one thing and the reality of religious practice and faith quite another. Of those Spaniards who defined themselves as Catholic, half in 1984 attended Mass either only a few times a year or not at all, a proportion that had risen to three-quarters by 2012. A study of young people in 2005 found that less than one in five agreed with the teachings of the Church, less than one in ten were practising Catholics, and a mere 2 per cent considered that the Church's views on the contemporary world were important. In the same vein by 2009 the number of civilian marriages had overtaken church weddings.

Yet another seismic shift was the transformation in the role played by women within society. The public profile of women had been on the rise since the 1960s thanks to their involvement in neighbourhood, parent, and other associations, in feminist groups, and in the political and trade-union opposition to the dictatorship. Nevertheless, the change since the transition was far greater, as shown by their evergreater presence within not only education, but also the workforce. In 1986, 29.6 per cent of women had joined the labour market, but by 2011 this had risen to 52.9 per cent, while the proportion of men in employment had dropped from 70.3 per cent to 67.4 per cent during the same period. The mounting presence of women in education and the workforce, together with the sexual revolution, the spread of secularization, and changing gender relations, led to a dramatic fall in the birth rate and a greater diversification in family models, as the traditional paradigm gave way increasingly to the 'modern' family. At the beginning of the 1970s, Spain had, at 2.8 children per woman, one of the highest fertility levels in Europe, but by 1981 this had dropped below the population renewal rate of 2.1, reaching a nadir of 1.16 in 1998, one of the lowest in the world. The fertility rate then rose somewhat, but, following the 2008 recession, had fallen back to 1.33 children per woman by 2015. The fact that a growing number of children were born out of wedlock (rising from 2 per cent in 1976 to over 30 per cent by 2010) is indicative of the reconfiguration of the

Spanish family. By 2007 there were 309,000 single-parent house-holds, 3.52 million couples without children, and 2.86 million couples who chose to live apart; in 2008, 3,549 gay weddings took place. On the other hand, marriage had never been more precarious, as there were 118,939 separations, divorces, or annulments in 2007, which was more than half the number of marriages – 196,613 – for the following year. In sum, the Spanish family of the early twenty-first century was very different from that of only thirty years before.

The rising birth rate during the early twenty-first century was due above all to yet another new and far-reaching social phenomenon: immigration. Between the 1960s and the end of the 1990s Spain had been transformed from a country of emigration to one of immigration. In 1991 the foreign population stood at 400,000, by 2001 it had reached one million, and by 2010 totalled 5.66 million, a larger immigrant population than those found in the United Kingdom (4.36 million), France (4.23 million), or Italy (3.77 million), being surpassed by Germany alone at 7.13 million. The largest single group of foreigners in 2011 were the Romanians at 840,000, followed by the Moroccans at 770,000, and the British at 366,000. By 2009, foreigners accounted for over a fifth of residents in the Balearic Islands and just under that for the regions of Madrid, Catalonia, Valencia, and Murcia. Little wonder that Spain saw the biggest demographic rise of the entire European Union during the first decade of the twenty-first century, leaping from 40.8 million people in 2000 to 46.2 million in 2011.

# FROM THE RECESSION TO
# THE PANDEMIC

The prosperity of the Aznar and early Rodríguez Zapatero years was shattered by the global economic recession of 2008, which had its origin in the collapse of the subprime mortgage market in the United States. The Spanish economy's overdependence on a credit and con-struction boom made it 'tremendously vulnerable' to the American crash.[74] The socialist government badly damaged its public standing by initially denying the gravity of the crisis, repeatedly downplaying it as a mere 'de-acceleration' of the economy. Unable to devalue the currency, as the PSOE had done in 1992–93, and under pressure from the European Union, the International Monetary Fund, the United States, and, above all, the international financial markets, Rodríguez Zapatero, spurred on by the Greek debt crisis, decided to adopt sweeping austerity measures. On 12 May 2010, in a mere 270-word statement to the Cortes, the prime minister unveiled a programme of cuts that amounted to 15,000 million euros, equivalent to 1.5 per cent of GDP. As a result, he had to ditch the government's flagship reforms of the second legislature, such as the promotion of religious liberty and the creation of the Ministry of Equality, as well as some of the measures from the first legislature, such as the Law of Dependence. The cutbacks led to the freezing of state pensions, the axing of support for the long-term unemployed, and a reduction in wages for public employees. The labour market was also made more 'flexible' – that is, job security was undermined – as unemployment reached 20 per cent in 2010, provoking a general strike in September 2010. The savings banks, discredited by their heavy involvement in the building sector, were forced to become regular banks, the result being a series of major fusions, such as the creation of *Bankia* through the merger of *Caja Madrid* and six other entities. The conversion of the savings banks exposed massive corruption, the politicians and trade unionists on many boards of directors having colluded with venal bankers. Another major consequence of the crash was that the PSOE and PP joined forces in peremptorily redrafting article 135 of the Constitution, so that the external deficit was prioritized over and above public services, pensions, and other domestic obligations, a highly controversial measure which did much to tarnish the political establishment's handling of the recession.

The government's faulty crisis management damaged Rodríguez Zapatero's reputation so badly that he did not stand for re-election. The general election of November 2011 was won by the Popular Party under the grey and intensely reserved Mariano Rajoy with a majority of 186 seats, the PSOE collapsing to 110 seats, its worst result under democracy. The austerity measures became even more stringent under the PP. The government managed to avoid a full-scale EU rescue along the lines of Greece, but it did accept a bank bailout of 41,500 million euros in 2012. Growth, which had plummeted to −3.6 per cent in

2009, remained in the black until 2014, while unemployment surged to 26 per cent in 2013. Growth of 1.4 per cent in 2014 signalled the end of the recession, but recovery was incomplete, as employment, disposable income, and social welfare still lagged behind pre-recession levels, making Spain one of the most unequal societies in Europe.

On 15 May 2011 protests were held in sixty towns and cities throughout Spain by young people brought together by the Real Democracy Now network. Two days later, 12,000 people occupied the central square of Madrid, the *Puerta del Sol*, while similar encampments sprung up in thirty other cities, including Barcelona, Bilbao, and Seville. The great majority of those participating in the so-called '15-M' movement were people under thirty years of age who were indignant – hence their moniker of the *indignados* – at the self-interested collusion between the political and financial elites, the political system's lack of accountability, and the pervasive institutional corruption. The movement was a cry of outrage at the bleak future awaiting the younger generations ('Youth without Future'), who appeared to be condemned to a much harder and less prosperous life than that of their parents. The

The '15-M' protest movement in Madrid

15-M was an inspiration to youth elsewhere, such as the 'Occupy Wall Street' movement in the United States, and was backed by two-thirds of the Spanish public for their indictment of the political establishment. The *indignados* gave expression to a growing generation gap within Spanish society, as reflected in the widely supported claim that the state of politics in 2011 was attributable to the incomplete nature of the transition and in particular to its continuities with the Franco dictatorship. In the same vein many young people were convinced that a republic – unlike the monarchy of Juan Carlos I – would engender democratic renewal and social justice.

One of the principal grievances of the 15-M protesters was the self-serving nature of the duopoly created by the PP and the PSOE, the two parties regularly returning around 300 of the 350 seats in parliament. Despite their ideological divergences and public disagreements, the two parties had developed a mutually beneficial modus vivendi over the years. Together they had monopolized the institutional spoils of the state, that is, the political appointments to the higher courts, the Bank of Spain, the savings banks, the state media, and so on. The two parties had also developed a cosy, symbiotic relationship with the 'Ibex 35' (the top companies in Spain), as illustrated by the many politicians, including Felipe González, Narcís Serra, José María Aznar, and Rodrigo Rato, who went on to occupy lucrative positions on company boards, the notorious 'revolving doors' syndrome. One anti-corruption crusader has described the set-up as 'crony capitalism, a parasitical system of the exchange of favours and protection'.[75] In addition, both parties had abused the public trust to a staggering degree, as indicated by the myriad corruption scandals that engulfed them, especially the PP. A deputy new to the Cortes in 2011, Carlos Martínez Gorriarán, recalls that 'to encounter first-hand the depth and extent of the institutional corruption was a real surprise.'[76] Thus the Bárcenas scandal which broke in 2013 revealed that the PP had been running a slush fund for its leading figures for over twenty years. According to the ledger of the party treasurer, Luis Bárcenas, prime minister Mariano Rajoy had received payments of 322,231 euros between 1997 and 2008, while Bárcenas himself had taken advantage of his position to accumulate a fortune of no less than 48 million euros, secreted away in Switzerland and elsewhere. Oddly, Rajoy was never charged by the investigating magistrate, perhaps because, as Martínez Gorriarán claims, 'in the corruption cases which affected the high authorities of state' the public prosecutor was 'too passive'.[77] On the other hand, there was no denying Rajoy's political responsibility, but this was something which – like virtually all ministers in democratic Spain until very recently – he chose to ignore. It was no coincidence, however, that Rajoy was expelled from power in June 2018 following a motion of no confidence that was presented in the Cortes shortly after a court had ruled on the Bárcenas case. The court condemned twenty-nine of the thirty-seven defendants to sentences ranging from five months to fifty-one years in jail, Rajoy's friend and collaborator Luis Bárcenas being sentenced to thirty-three years and four months behind bars and a fine of 44 million euros. The Bárcenas scandal was merely one of many involving the PP – at one point 970 of its members were under investigation for corruption – in embezzlement, fraud, and money laundering, despite the fact that the investigation of corruption cases was constantly hampered by 'the politicization and slowness of the legal system' and the 'shortage of independent newspapers'.[78]

The most sensational socialist scandal of this period was that of the 'Eres' (a payment made to agriculture workers out of season), which resulted in up to 1,000 million euros disappearing from the treasury of the Andalusian Autonomous Community between 2001 and 2009. The accused included half the regional government and two of its former presidents, José Antonio Griñán and Manuel Chaves, an ex-minister and friend of Felipe González. Not that large-scale corruption has been an exclusive preserve of the PP and PSOE. The president of the *Generalitat* for twenty-three years, Jordi Pujol, was put on trial for having allegedly amassed a personal fortune of up to 5,000 million euros thanks to his practice of taking at least a 3 per cent cut on all public contracts. Nor has the Basque Nationalist Party been free of scandal, as shown by tax fraud, money laundering, and embezzlement scandals. Corruption at the strictly local level is, if anything, even more extensive, as revealed by the multitude of scandals involving municipalities throughout Spain. These have been especially common in the tourist areas, as shown by the scandals involving the mayor of Marbella, Jesús Gil, and the mayoress of Mallorca, María Antonia Munar.

The PP and PSOE also blocked investigations which could potentially damage them both, such as that of the train crash of 24 July 2013 outside Santiago de Compostela in northwest Spain in which eighty people (including a pregnant woman) were killed and 152 injured. Officials from both parties, including ministers, were guilty of safety violations in relation to the new high-speed service, but they have connived – the considerable media coverage notwithstanding – to stymie an independent investigation of the crash. In an examination of the circumstances surrounding the accident, the European Railway Agency concluded that the derailment 'has not yet been independently investigated', leaving 'many essential questions unanswered'.[79]

It was not just the self-serving bipartisan political system that has been the target of people's ire, but the monarchy too. In June 2014, Juan Carlos abdicated following a series of all-too-public affairs, a corruption scandal involving the royal family, and a big-game hunting trip to Botswana in the midst of the recession (including a notorious photo of the king next to a slaughtered elephant). Despite the highly laudable performance of his son, Felipe VI, the monarchy's reputation was badly tarnished. In late 2020, Juan Carlos went into voluntary exile following press reports that he had stashed away over 400 million euros in bank accounts in Switzerland and the sensational claim by his former lover, the German princess Corinna zu Sayn-Wittgenstein, that he had given her a 'present' of 65 million euros. The media contended that much of this money derived from the 'commissions' that the king allegedly received for backing the bids of Spanish firms abroad, such as a $100 million 'commission' for helping a Spanish construction company obtain a contract in Saudi Arabia. The king *emeritus* damaged not only his own historical standing, but also the monarchy itself.

The crisis of credibility suffered by the PP and PSOE led to the emergence of new, anti-corruption parties: the centrist *Unión Progreso y Democracia* or UPyD (Union Progress and Democracy), the left-wing *Podemos* (We Can), and the centre-right *Ciudadanos* (Citizens). The Union Progress and Democracy, a socialist breakaway that won five seats in the 2011 general election, has been responsible for uncovering some of the most high-profile corruption cases, such as the *Bankia* and 'Black Card' scandals. The anti-establishment Podemos, founded in January 2014, channelled the spirit of the 15-M movement, making its breakthrough in the May 2014 European elections by winning 8 per cent of the vote and five MEPs. In the December 2015 general election Podemos won fifty-four seats and Citizens forty seats, the Popular Party plunging from a majority of 186 to just 123. Following the June 2016 general election, Podemos, which returned fifty-seven seats, spurned the chance of forming a coalition government with the Socialist Party, but later backed the socialist motion of no confidence that brought down Mariano Rajoy. After the November 2019 election – the fourth in four years – Podemos and the PSOE formed the first coalition government in Spain since the 1930s under the courteous and athletic socialist leader Pedro Sánchez, the first Spanish premier under democracy to speak English. Despite losing seven seats in comparison with the April 2019 election, Podemos still won over 3 million votes, which split the vote of the left far more effectively than the United Left ever did. Having peaked at fifty-seven seats in April 2019, Citizens slumped to only ten seats in November 2019, but another conservative force, the far-right Vox, won fifty-two deputies. This fragmented political landscape meant that the hegemony of the PSOE and PP, which had lasted for nearly four decades, appeared to be finally over, replaced by a new era of hung parliaments and coalition governments. The fracturing of the duopoly fomented greater political instability, but also fostered higher ethical standards, as shown by the resignations of the PP's president of the Community of Madrid, Cristina Cifuentes, in April 2018, and that of the socialist minister of culture, Máxim Huerta, in June of that year.

The new-found instability of national politics was exacerbated by a far-reaching crisis in Catalonia. For over thirty years the Basque region had presented Spanish democracy with its most formidable test, but in the 2010s Catalonia became the principal challenge. There were two initial causes of the Catalan conflict. First, the overturning of core elements of the 2006 Catalan Statute by the Constitutional Court in 2010 caused a furore in Catalonia, the Convergence and Union leader Artur Mas calling it an 'act of betrayal'.[80] Second, the outrage at the decision of the Court was greatly inflamed by the economic recession. Indeed, the protest of many Catalans over the cutbacks, rising unemployment, and the banking collapse was transferred to the regional nationalist cause out of disgust with Madrid and in the belief that an independent Catalonia would provide them with greater security. The situation was made even worse by the ostrich-liked response of the Rajoy government, which, instead of trying to lower tensions by, say, winning over the moderate regional nationalists, stubbornly insisted that this was a legal, as opposed to political, issue; in other words, the unconstitutionality of the Catalan stance left no room for discussion. Small wonder that support within Catalonia for independence, which had stood at under 15 per cent for decades, shot up to 34 per cent in 2012 and 48.5 per cent in 2013.

The watershed moment in this escalating conflict was the illegal 'referendum' of October 2017 on Catalan independence. In reality, this was the third such consultation since 2009, following those of 2009–11 and 2014. The determination of the government to thwart the 'referendum' by sending the national police and Civil Guard into Catalonia was crass and counterproductive, as disturbing images of the police bludgeoning voters shot around the globe. The government not only failed to prevent the 'referendum' – though six out of ten Catalans did not vote – but also lost the public relations battle. On 27 October 2017 the Catalan parliament made a unilateral declaration of independence with the support of seventy of its 135 deputies. The central government, in accordance with article 155 of the Constitution, took over the governance of Catalonia, called a regional election for December 2017 (with the aim of breaking the political stalemate), and arrested a host of nationalist leaders, except for those who had already fled the country, most notably Carles Puigdemont, president of the *Generalitat*.

Convinced that the pressure from other European nations would oblige Madrid to hold a binding vote on independence, the separatist movement was shocked by the lack of international support for its cause in the wake of the 2017 'referendum', especially as the Catalan nationalists had been courting international opinion for years by (illegally) channelling public money into a string of 'embassies', pro-nationalist publications and reports, sympathetic research centres (such as that at the London School of Economics), and so on. The December 2017 regional elections were hailed by the nationalists as a 'plebiscitary ballot', but they came up short yet again, as their share of the vote at 48 per cent stayed the same as in 2015.[81] Worse still, the largest party in the new parliament was the anti-nationalist Citizens. In short, the regional nationalists were still unable to command a credible majority in favour of independence, but the radicalization of Catalan politics since October 2017 made a solution more difficult than ever. The ruling coalition under socialist Pedro Sánchez adopted a much more receptive approach than Mariano Rajoy's government, but by the end of 2022 there was still no solution.

Until 2017, Spain proved to be the European exception insofar as it had not spawned a populist, far-right formation in the mould of, say, the United Kingdom Independence Party or UKIP, the Alternative for Germany (*Alternative für Deutschland* or AfD), or France's National Front (*Front National* or FN). All that changed with the Catalan 'referendum' of 2017. Founded in 2013 by disaffected members of the Popular Party, Vox had won just 0.2 per cent of the vote in the 2016 general election, a resounding failure. By contrast, in the Andalusian regional elections of December 2017 – that is, two months after the Catalan 'referendum' – Vox secured 11 per cent of the vote and twelve of the 109 parliamentary seats. As a result, it became the region's 'political kingmaker', as the Popular Party and Citizens required the votes of Vox in order to form a coalition government.[82] In the general election of November 2019, Vox achieved its greatest triumph so far by winning a staggering fifty-two seats. Distinguished by its xenophobia, hostility to feminism ('feminazis'), and diehard neoliberalism, the quasi-Francoist discourse of Vox is crude and demagogic, redolent of the vituperative political lexicon of the 1930s. Thus Vox repeatedly denounced the Pedro Sánchez coalition government as a 'new Popular Front' for its 'disintegrating and Civil War objectives'.[83]

The tortuous recovery from the recession of 2008 was blown completely off course by the global Covid-19 pandemic of 2020. As in many other parts of the world, the Spanish government reacted late to the onset of the pandemic, though it subsequently imposed the severest lockdown in Europe. Spain was the first European country to reach one million official cases and by the end of 2020 just over 50,000 Spaniards had died from the virus. Even so, by November 2021 Spain had recovered relatively well, as 82 per cent of the population had been vaccinated, one of the highest rates in the world. By April 2022, nearly 103,000 people in Spain had died from the virus, as opposed to 139,000 in France, 160,000 in Italy, and over 175,000 in the United Kingdom. Despite the ravages of the pandemic, Spain today is a stable, prosperous democracy, having become 'just another European democracy', though retaining – like all other European democracies – its own peculiarities.[84]

# Notes

## INTRODUCTION

1. John L. Tone, *War and Genocide in Cuba, 1895–1898* (Chapel Hill, NC, 2006), p. 282.
2. José Álvarez Junco, 'La nación en duda', in Juan Pan-Montojo (ed.), *Más se perdió en Cuba: España, 1898 y la crisis de fin de siglo* (Madrid, 1998), p. 410.
3. *Luces de Bohemia*, scenes VI and XII.
4. Francisco Silvela y de la Vielleuze, *Escritos y discursos políticos: Entre el liberalismo y el regeneracionismo* (Madrid, 2005), p. 194.
5. Antonio Fernández García et al. (eds.), *Documentos de historia contemporánea de España* (Madrid, 1996), pp. 404 and 413.
6. José Luis Gómez-Navarro, *El régimen de Primo de Rivera. Reyes, dictaduras y dictadores* (Madrid, 1991), pp. 129–30.
7. David L. Weber, *The Spanish Frontier in North America* (New Haven, CT, 1992), p. 336.
8. José Álvarez Junco and Adrian Shubert (eds.), *Spanish History since 1808* (London, 2000), p. 8.
9. Tom Buchanan, *The Impact of the Spanish Civil War on Britain: War, Loss and Memory* (Brighton, 2007), p. 5.
10. Ibid., p. 173.
11. Miguel Martorell Linares, 'La pesada losa del fracaso español', in José Álvarez Junco and Mercedes Cabrera (eds.), *La mirada del historiador: Un viaje por la obra de Santos Juliá* (Madrid, 2011), p. 313.
12. Ibid., p. 321.
13. Ibid., p. 319.
14. Ibid., pp. 319 and 320.
15. Raymond Carr, *The New York Review of Books*, 25 November 1965.
16. Leandro Prados de la Escosura, *De imperio a nación. Crecimiento y atraso económico en España (1780–1930)* (Madrid, 1988), pp. 241 and 244.

463

## CHAPTER 1

1. John L. Tone, *War and Genocide in Cuba, 1895–1898* (Chapel Hill, NC, 2006), p. 268.

2. Ibid.

3. Hugh Thomas, *Cuba or the Pursuit of Freedom* (London, 1971), p. 396.

4. Tone, *War and Genocide in Cuba*, p. 286.

5. Ibid., p. 281.

6. María de Echarri Martínez, unpublished diary, 21 September 1898.

7. Ibid.

8. Ibid.

9. José Álvarez Junco, *El Emperador del Paralelo. Lerroux y la demagogia populista* (Madrid, 1990), pp. 177 and 178.

10. Roderick Beaton, *Greece: Biography of a Modern Nation* (London, 2019), p. 169.

11. Jonathan Dunnage, *Twentieth-Century Italy: A Social History* (London, 2002), p. 33.

12. José Álvarez Junco, *Dioses útiles. Naciones y nacionalismos* (Barcelona, 2016), p. 171.

13. José Álvarez Junco, *Mater dolorosa. La idea de España en el siglo XIX* (Madrid, 2000), p. 588.

14. Javier Moreno Luzón, *Modernizing the Nation: Spain during the Reign of Alfonso XIII, 1902–1931* (Brighton, 2012), p. 9.

15. Francisco Silvela y de la Vielleuze, *Escritos y discursos políticos: Entre el liberalismo y el regeneracionismo* (Madrid, 2005), p. 195.

16. Óscar Bascuñan Añover, *Protesta y supervivencia. Movilización y desorden en una sociedad rural: Castilla-La Mancha, 1875–1923* (Valencia, 2008), p. 76.

17. Ibid.

18. Ibid., p. 82.

19. Ibid., pp. 84 and 85.

20. David Cannadine, *Victorious Century: The United Kingdom, 1800–1906* (London, 2018), pp. 340 and 403.

21. Javier Moreno Luzón, *Romanones. Caciquismo y política liberal* (Madrid, 1998), p. 128.

22. Ibid.

23. Joaquín Romero Maura, *'La Rosa de Fuego'. El obrerismo barcelonés de 1899 a 1909* (Barcelona, 1975), p. 95.

24. Nigel Townson, 'Spain: A Land Apart?', in Nigel Townson (ed.), *Is Spain Different? A Comparative Look at the 19th and 20th Centuries* (Brighton, 2015), p. 10.

25. John A. Davis, 'Preface', in John A. Davis (ed.), *Italy in the Nineteenth Century: 1796–1900* (Oxford, 2000), p. vi.

26. Leandro Prados de la Escosura, *De imperio a nación. Crecimiento y atraso económico en España (1780–1930)* (Madrid, 1988), p. 244 and table 1.3, p. 45.

27. Data from Albert Carreras and Xavier Tafunell (eds.), *Estadísticas históricas de España. Siglos XIX–XX*, 2nd ed. (Bilbao, 2005), p. 256, table 4.3. Quote from Pamela Beth Radcliff, *Modern Spain: 1808 to the Present* (Malden, MA, 2017), p. 115.

28. Carreras and Tafunell (eds.), *Estadísticas históricas de España*, p. 360, table 5.1.

29. Radcliff, *Modern Spain*, p. 107.

30. Edward Malefakis, 'Southern Europe in the 19th and 20th Centuries: An Historical Overview', *Instituto Juan March de Estudios e Investigaciones*, Estudio/Working Paper 1992/35, January 1992, p. 3.

31. Ramiro Reig, *Blasquistas y clericales. La lucha por la ciudad en la Valencia de 1900* (Valencia, 1986), p. 195.

32. Romero Maura, '*La Rosa de Fuego*', p. 18.

33. Carlos Dardé, 'La larga noche de la Restauración, 1875–1900', in Nigel Townson (ed.), *El republicanismo en España (1830–1977)* (Madrid, 1994), p. 123.

34. Manuel Suárez Cortina, 'La quiebra del republicanismo histórico, 1898–1931', in Townson (ed.), *El republicanismo en España*, p. 143.

35. Dardé, 'La larga noche de la Restauración', p. 122.

36. Juan Díaz del Moral, *Historia de las agitaciones campesinas andaluzas* (Madrid, 1995), p. 132.

37. Romero Maura, '*La Rosa de Fuego*', p. 32.

38. Ibid., pp. 24, 75 (note 33), and 39.

39. Ibid., p. 95.

40. Reig, *Blasquistas y clericales*, p. 269.

41. Ibid., p. 214.

42. Ibid.

43. Vicente Blasco Ibáñez, *¡Diputado Blasco Ibáñez! Memorias parlamentarias* (Madrid, 1999), p. 248.

44. Reig, *Blasquistas y clericales*, p. 221.

45. Ibid., p. 243.

46. Ibid., p. 215.

47. Ibid., p. 287.

48. Ibid., p. 275.

49. Blasco Ibáñez, *¡Diputado Blasco Ibáñez!*, p. 222.

50. Alejandro Lerroux, *De la lucha* (Barcelona, 1909), p. 119.
51. Álvarez Junco, *El Emperador del Paralelo*, p. 396.
52. Marta del Moral Vargas, *Acción colectiva femenina en Madrid (1909–1931)* (Santiago de Compostela, 2012), p. 93.
53. Ibid., p. 104.
54. Ibid., p. 86.
55. Marta del Moral Vargas, 'La *militancia familiar* como forma de compromiso político: el liderazgo de las hermanas García Pérez (1918–1931)', in *Arbor*, 196:796, (April–June 2020), p. 6.
56. Álvarez Junco, *El Emperador del Paralelo*, p. 396.
57. Ibid., p. 309.
58. Ibid., p. 310.
59. Ibid., p. 309.
60. Ibid., fn. 111.
61. Ibid., p. 306.
62. Salvador Forner Muñoz, *Canalejas y el Partido Liberal Democrático (1900–1910)* (Madrid, 1993), p. 110.
63. Reig, *Blasquistas y clericales*, pp. 153–4.
64. Ibid., p. 92.
65. Ibid.
66. Ibid., pp. 269 and 92.
67. Joseba Louzao Villar, *Soldados de la fe o amantes del progreso. Catolicismo y modernidad en Vizcaya (1890–1923)* (Madrid, 2011), p. 315.
68. Ibid., p. 317.
69. Ibid., p. 220.
70. Ibid.
71. Ibid., p. 326.
72. Ibid., p. 331.
73. Ibid., p. 335.
74. Romero Maura, *'La Rosa de Fuego'*, p. 217, n. 2.
75. Xavier Cuadrat, *Socialismo y anarquismo en Cataluña (1899–1911): los orígenes de la CNT* (Madrid, 1976), p. 88.
76. Ibid., p. 89.
77. Díaz del Moral, *Historia de las agitaciones campesinas*, p. 142.
78. Bascuñán Añover, *Protesta y supervivencia*, p. 42.
79. Ibid., p. 34.
80. Ibid., p. 35.
81. Ibid., p. 41.
82. Ibid., p. 65.
83. Ibid., p. 72.

84. Ibid., pp. 79 and 80.
85. Ángel Herrerín López, *Anarquía, dinamita y revolución social. Violencia y represión en la España de entre siglos (1868–1909)* (Madrid, 2011), p. 56.
86. Ibid., p. 59.
87. Julio Aróstegui (ed.), *Miseria y conciencia del campesino castellano ('Memoria acerca de la información agraria en ambas Castillas')* (Madrid, 1977), p. 135.
88. Ibid., p. 128.
89. Ibid., p. 157.
90. Ibid., p. 117.
91. Ibid., p. 156.
92. Ibid., p. 19.
93. Edward E. Malefakis, *Agrarian Reform and Peasant Revolution in Spain: Origins of the Civil War* (New Haven, CT, 1970), p. 141.
94. Fernando del Rey Reguillo, *Propietarios y patronos. La política de las organizaciones económicas en la España de la Restauración (1914–1923)* (Madrid, 1992), p. 349.
95. Ibid., p. 350.
96. Ibid., p. 351.
97. Ibid., pp. 344–5.
98. Santos Juliá, *Un siglo de España. Política y sociedad* (Madrid, 1999), p. 26.
99. Miguel Martorell and Santos Juliá, *Manual de historia política y social de España (1808–2011)* (Barcelona, 2012), p. 199.
100. Moreno Luzón, *Modernizing the Nation*, p. 128.
101. Carolyn Boyd, *Praetorian Politics in Liberal Spain* (Chapel Hill, NC, 1979), p. 14.
102. Juliá, *Un siglo de España*, pp. 18 and 26.
103. Ibid., p. 26.
104. Ibid.
105. Martorell and Juliá, *Manual de historia*, p. 199.
106. Albert Carreras and Xavier Tafunell, *Historia económica de la España contemporánea* (Barcelona, 2004), p. 196.
107. Juliá, *Un siglo de España*, p. 34.
108. Ibid., p. 35.
109. Ibid.
110. Forner Muñoz, *Canalejas*, p. 113.
111. Ibid., p. 71.
112. Del Rey Reguillo, *Propietarios y patronos*, p. 349.

113. Forner Muñoz, *Canalejas*, p. 81.

114. Juan Pablo Fusi and Jordi Palafox, *España: 1808–1996. El desafío de la modernidad* (Madrid, 1997), p. 185.

115. Forner Muñoz, *Canalejas*, p. 113.


CHAPTER 2

1. Santos Juliá, 'La nueva generación: de neutrales a antigermanófilos pasando por aliadófilos', *Ayer*, 91:3 (2013), p. 130.

2. Francisco Romero, 'Spain and the First World War', in Sebastian Balfour and Paul Preston (eds.), *Spain and the Great Powers in the Twentieth Century* (London, 1999), p. 32.

3. Ibid.

4. Carolyn P. Boyd, *Praetorian Politics in Liberal Spain* (Chapel Hill, NC, 1979), p. 46.

5. Juliá, 'La nueva generación', p. 133.

6. Ibid., p. 131.

7. Ibid., p. 132.

8. Ibid., p. 137.

9. Ibid., p. 138.

10. Romero, 'Spain and the First World War', p. 39.

11. Shlomo Ben-Ami, *Fascism from Above: The Dictatorship of Primo de Rivera in Spain, 1923–1930* (Oxford, 1983), p. 2.

12. Gerald H. Meaker, *The Revolutionary Left in Spain, 1914–1923* (Stanford, CA, 1974), p. 35.

13. Fernanda Romeu Alfaro, *Las clases trabajadoras en España, 1898–1930* (Madrid, 1970), p. 115.

14. Ibid., p. 97.

15. Meaker, *The Revolutionary Left*, p. 34.

16. Ana Aguado and María Dolores Ramos, *La modernización de España (1917–1939). Cultura y vida cotidiana* (Madrid, 2002), p. 94.

17. Meaker, *The Revolutionary Left*, p. 36.

18. Romeu Alfaro, *Las clases trabajadoras*, p. 97.

19. Meaker, *The Revolutionary Left*, p. 37.

20. Romeu Alfaro, *Las clases trabajadoras*, p. 117.

21. Ibid., p. 130.

22. Ibid., p. 131.

23. Ángel Pestaña, *Lo que aprendí en la vida* (Madrid, 1933), p. 57.

24. Meaker, *The Revolutionary Left*, p. 48.

25. Romero, 'Spain and the First World War', p. 41.

26. Boyd, *Praetorian Politics*, p. 51.

27. Ibid.

28. Meaker, *The Revolutionary Left*, p. 55.

29. Ibid.

30. Boyd, *Praetorian Politics*, p. 50.

31. Alejandro Lerroux, *Al servicio de la República* (Madrid, 1930), p. 115.

32. Boyd, *Praetorian Politics*, p. 64.

33. Ibid., p. 69.

34. Meaker, *The Revolutionary Left*, p. 78.

35. Boyd, *Praetorian Politics*, p. 71.

36. Ibid., p. 81.

37. Antonio Fernández García et al. (eds.), *Documentos de historia contemporánea de España* (Madrid, 1996), pp. 393 and 394.

38. Ibid., p. 394.

39. Ibid., p. 395.

40. Meaker, *The Revolutionary Left*, p. 71.

41. Ibid.

42. Boyd, *Praetorian Politics*, p. 79.

43. Meaker, *The Revolutionary Left*, p. 72.

44. Ibid., p. 73.

45. Francisco Cambó, *Memorias (1876–1936)* (Madrid, 1987), pp. 254 and 252.

46. Boyd, *Praetorian Politics*, p. 79.

47. *La Libertad*, *Diario de la huelga* ('The Strike Diary'), 13 August 1917. I should like to thank Marta del Moral Vargas for drawing my attention to this document.

48. Ibid.

49. Ibid.

50. Boyd, *Praetorian Politics*, p. 71.

51. Meaker, *The Revolutionary Left*, p. 91.

52. Ibid., p. 80.

53. Marta del Moral Vargas, *Acción colectiva femenina en Madrid (1909–1931)* (Santiago de Compostela, 2012), p. 253.

54. Ibid., p. 252.

55. 'Relato verídico de los sucesos de Agosto en los Cuatro Caminos', Largo Caballero Foundation Archive (Madrid, 1917).

56. Del Moral Vargas, *Acción colectiva femenina*, p. 254.

57. Francisco Largo Caballero, *Escritos de la República* (Madrid, 1985), p. 6.

58. 'Relato verídico de los sucesos de Agosto en los Cuatro Caminos', Largo Caballero Foundation Archive.

59. Ibid.
60. Ibid.
61. Ibid.
62. Boyd, *Praetorian Politics*, p. 100.
63. Ibid., p. 97.
64. Ibid., p. 112.
65. Sebastian Balfour, *Deadly Embrace: Morocco and the Road to the Spanish Civil War* (Oxford, 2002), p. 49.
66. Ibid.
67. Romero, 'Spain and the First World War', p. 46.
68. Juan Díaz del Moral, *Historia de las agitaciones campesinas andaluzas* (Madrid, 1995), p. 343, n. 78.
69. Meaker, *The Revolutionary Left*, p. 141.
70. Díaz del Moral, *Historia de las agitaciones*, p. 312.
71. Ibid., p. 285.
72. Meaker, *The Revolutionary Left*, p. 143.
73. Ibid., p. 152.
74. Ibid., p. 159.
75. Ibid., p. 165.
76. Ibid., p. 167.
77. Ibid., pp. 186 and 187.
78. Ibid., pp. 167 and 187.
79. Ibid., p. 175.
80. Pestaña, *Lo que aprendí*, p. 186.
81. Meaker, *The Revolutionary Left*, p. 330.
82. Ibid., p. 319.
83. Fernando del Rey Reguillo, *Propietarios y patronos. La política de las organizaciones económicas en la España de la Restauración (1914–1923)* (Madrid, 1992), p. 622.
84. Meaker, *The Revolutionary Left*, p. 331.
85. Del Rey Reguillo, *Propietarios y patronos*, p. 535.
86. Meaker, *The Revolutionary Left*, p. 460.
87. The data are from Del Rey Reguillo, *Propietarios y patronos*, pp. 619–26.
88. Balfour, *Deadly Embrace*, p. 72.
89. Arturo Barea, *The Forging of a Rebel* (London, 2018), p. 329.
90. Indalecio Prieto, *Discursos fundamentales* (Madrid, 1975), p. 65.
91. Boyd, *Praetorian Politics*, p. 190.
92. Ibid., p. 62.
93. Ibid., p. 239.

94. Miguel Martorell and Santos Juliá, *Manual de historia política y social de España (1808–2011)* (Barcelona, 2012), p. 237.
95. Ibid., p. 238.
96. Prieto, *Discursos fundamentales*, p. 129.
97. Javier Moreno Luzón, *Modernizing the Nation: Spain during the Reign of Alfonso XIII, 1902–1931* (Brighton, 2012), p. 141.
98. Boyd, *Praetorian Politics*, p. 258.
99. Ibid., p. 259.
100. Ibid., p. 273.
101. Ibid., p. 271.

## CHAPTER 3

1. Gerald H. Meaker, *The Revolutionary Left in Spain, 1914–1923* (Stanford, CA, 1974), p. 475.
2. Carolyn Boyd, *Praetorian Politics in Liberal Spain* (Chapel Hill, NC, 1979), p. 272.
3. Antonio Fernández García et al. (eds.), *Documentos de historia contemporánea de España* (Madrid, 1996), p. 9.
4. José Luis Gómez Navarro, *El régimen de Primo de Rivera. Reyes, dictaduras y dictadores* (Madrid, 1991), pp. 129–30, and Shlomo Ben Ami, *Fascism from Above: The Dictatorship of Primo de Rivera in Spain, 1923–1930* (Oxford, 1983), p. 176.
5. Ibid.
6. Ibid., p. 192.
7. José Calvo Sotelo, *Mis servicios al estado. Seis años de gestión. Apuntes para la historia* (Madrid, 1931), pp. 331–2.
8. Ben Ami, *Fascism from Above*, p. 72.
9. Ibid., p. 88.
10. Ibid., p. 144.
11. Ibid., p. 179.
12. Ibid., p. 176.
13. Ibid., p. 178.
14. Ibid., p. 167.
15. Fernando Díaz-Plaja (ed.), *La historia de España en sus documentos. El siglo XX. Dictadura ... República (1923–1936)* (Madrid, 1964), p. 32.
16. Ibid., p. 31.
17. Ben Ami, *Fascism from Above*, p. 104.
18. Ibid., p. 103.

19. See tables 2.1 and 2.2 in Guadalupe Gómez-Ferrer Morant and Marta del Moral Vargas, 'Las pioneras en la gestión local: Concejalas y alcaldesas designadas durante la dictadura de Primeo de Rivera y el gobierno Berenguer (1924–1930)', in Gloria Nielfa Cristóbal (ed.), *Mujeres en los Gobiernos locales. Alcaldesas y concejalas en la España contemporánea* (Madrid, 2015), pp. 69–71.
20. Ben Ami, *Fascism from Above*, p. 282.
21. Ibid., p. 284.
22. Ibid., p. 283.
23. Ibid.
24. *Partido Socialista Obrero Español, Convocatoria y orden del día para el XII congreso ordinario* (Madrid, 1927), p. 104.
25. Ben Ami, *Fascism from Above*, p. 294.
26. Ibid., p. 300.
27. Ibid., p. 258.
28. Ibid., p. 152.
29. Calvo Sotelo, *Mis servicios al estado*, p. 24.
30. Ben Ami, *Fascism from Above*, p. 93.
31. Ibid., p. 99.
32. Ibid., p. 100.
33. Ibid., p. 101.
34. Ibid., pp. 101–2.
35. Ibid., p. 116.
36. Ibid., p. 111.
37. Sebastian Balfour, *Deadly Embrace: Morocco and the Road to the Spanish Civil War* (Oxford, 2002), p. 101.
38. Ben Ami, *Fascism from Above*, p. 113.
39. Ibid., p. 115.
40. Balfour, *Deadly Embrace*, p. 117.
41. Ben Ami, *Fascism from Above*, p. 119.
42. Ibid., pp. 120, 121, and 122.
43. Ibid., p. 212.
44. Ibid., p. 232, and Fernández García et al. (eds.), *Documentos de historia*, p. 413.
45. Ben Ami, *Fascism from Above*, p. 233.
46. Ibid., p. 241.
47. Ibid., pp. 242 and 241.
48. Ibid., p. 264.
49. Ibid., p. 241.
50. Ibid., p. 247.

51. Ibid., p. 245.
52. Ibid., p. 268.
53. Calvo Sotelo, *Mis servicios al estado*, p. 124.
54. Ibid., p. 123.
55. Ben Ami, *Fascism from Above*, p. 310.
56. Arturo Barea, *The Forging of a Rebel* (London, 2018), p. 427.
57. Ben Ami, *Fascism from Above*, p. 321.
58. Ibid., p. 323.
59. Ibid., pp. 330 and 331.
60. Rafael Salazar Alonso, *La justicia bajo la dictadura* (Madrid, 1930), p. 265.
61. Ben Ami, *Fascism from Above*, p. 350.
62. Ibid., p. 370.
63. Calvo Sotelo, *Mis servicios al estado*, p. 354.
64. Ibid., p. 238.
65. Ben Ami, *Fascism from Above*, p. 365.
66. Ibid., p. 377.
67. Ibid.

## CHAPTER 4

1. Gabriele Ranzato, *El eclipse de la democracia. La Guerra Civil española y sus orígenes, 1931–1939* (Madrid, 2006), p. 116.
2. Manuel Azaña, *Obras completas*, Santos Juliá (ed.) (Madrid, 2007), vol. 4, pp. 36 and 37.
3. Nigel Townson, 'A Third Way? Centrist Politics under the Republic', in Manuel Álvarez Tardío and Fernando del Rey Reguillo (eds.), *The Spanish Second Republic Revisited: From Democratic Hopes to Civil War (1931–1936)* (Brighton, 2012), p. 98.
4. Shlomo Ben-Ami, *Fascism from Above: The Dictatorship of Primo de Rivera in Spain, 1923–1930* (Oxford, 1983), p. 334.
5. Juan Pablo Fusi and Jordi Palafox, *España: 1808–1996. El desafío de la modernidad* (Madrid, 1997), p. 280.
6. Albert Carreras and Xavier Tafunell, *Historia económica de la España contemporánea* (Barcelona, 2004), p. 258.
7. Fusi and Palafox, *España: 1808–1996*, p. 285.
8. Ibid., p. 282.
9. Ángel Herrerín, *The Road to Anarchy: The CNT under the Spanish Second Republic (1931–1936)* (Brighton, 2020), p. 9.
10. Ibid., p. 35.

NOTES TO PP. 118–27

11. Ibid., p. 14.
12. Ibid., p. 18.
13. Ibid.
14. Ibid., p. 23.
15. Ibid., p. 51.
16. Ibid., p. 22.
17. Ángel Herrerín, *Camino a la anarquía: La CNT en tiempos de la Segunda República (1931–1936)* (Madrid, 2019), p. 108.
18. Herrerín, *The Road to Anarchy*, p. 12.
19. Ibid., p. 51.
20. Manuel Ramírez Jiménez, *La legislación de la Segunda República Española (1931–1936)* (Madrid, 2005), pp. 47–9.
21. Herrerín, *The Road to Anarchy*, p. 61.
22. Sebastian Balfour, *Deadly Embrace: Morocco and the Road to the Spanish Civil War* (Oxford, 2002), p. 239.
23. Mercedes Samaniego Boneu, *La política educativa de la Segunda República durante el bienio azañista* (Madrid, 1977), p. 224, quote between pls. 16 and 17.
24. Sandie Holguín, *Creating Spaniards: Culture and National Identity in Republican Spain* (Madison, WI, 2002), pp. 51 and 146, and Samaniego Boneu, *La política educativa*, p. 98.
25. Ibid.
26. Holguín, *Creating Spaniards*, p. 52.
27. Samaniego Boneu, *La política educativa*, p. 224, and Holguín, *Creating Spaniards*, p. 55.
28. Ibid., p. 56.
29. Samaniego Boneu, *La política educativa*, pp. 218 and 221.
30. Ibid., p. 192.
31. Diego Martínez Barrio, *Memorias* (Barcelona, 1983), p. 37.
32. Stanley G. Payne, *Alcalá Zamora and the Failure of the Spanish Republic, 1931–1936* (Brighton, 2017), p. 33.
33. Nigel Townson, *The Crisis of Democracy in Spain: Centrist Politics under the Second Republic, 1931–1936* (Brighton, 2000), p. 46.
34. Ibid., p. 42.
35. Ibid., p. 44.
36. Azaña, *Obras completas*, vol. 3, p. 23.
37. Nigel Townson, 'La vieja política bajo la II República: Caciquismo, clientelismo y control electoral', in Mercedes Gutiérrez Sánchez and Diego Palacios Cerezales (eds.), *Conflicto político, democracia y dictadura: Portugal y España en la década de 1930* (Madrid, 2007), p. 165.

38. Townson, *The Crisis of Democracy in Spain*, pp. 104–5.
39. Miguel Maura, *Así cayó Alfonso XIII: De una dictadura a otra*, Joaquín Romero Maura (ed.) (Madrid, 2007), p. 355.
40. Ibid.
41. Ibid., pp. 353 and 354.
42. Ibid., p. 354.
43. Townson, 'La vieja política bajo la II República', p. 164.
44. Townson, *The Crisis of Democracy in Spain*, p. 71.
45. Ibid., p. 72, and Fernando Díaz-Plaja (ed.), *La historia de España en sus documentos: El siglo XX Dictadura ... República (1923–1936)* (Madrid, 1964), p. 378.
46. Díaz-Plaja (ed.), *La historia de España en sus documentos*, p. 387.
47. *Diario de sesiones de las Cortes Constituyentes* (DSCC), 1 October 1931.
48. Ana Aguado, 'Entre lo público y lo privado: sufragio y divorcio en la Segunda República', *Ayer*, 60:4 (2005), p. 116.
49. DSCC, 30 September 1931.
50. Ibid., 1 October 1931.
51. Ibid.
52. Ibid.
53. Ibid., 13 October 1931.
54. Díaz-Plaja (ed.), *La historia de España en sus documentos*, p. 383.
55. José María Gil Robles, *Discursos parlamentarios* (Madrid, 1971), p. 63.
56. Díaz-Plaja (ed.), *La historia de España en sus documentos*, p. 388.
57. Gil Robles, *Discursos parlamentarios*, p. 63.
58. Townson, 'A Third Way? Centrist Politics under the Republic', p. 102.
59. Gil Robles, *Discursos parlamentarios*, p. 63.
60. Azaña, *Obras completas*, vol. 3, p. 1043 (diary entry for 6 August 1932).
61. Timothy Rees, 'Agrarian Society and Politics in the Province of Badajoz under the Spanish Second Republic' (Oxford University DPhil, 1990), p. 157.
62. Herrerín, *The Road to Anarchy*, p. 82.
63. Ibid., p. 76.
64. Ibid., p. 92.
65. Aguado, 'Entre lo público y lo privado', p. 123.
66. Ibid., p. 114.
67. Ibid., p. 121.
68. Ibid., p. 124.
69. Alberto González González, 'La primera secularización y la Segunda República. El caso de la provincia de Toledo', in Julio de la Cueva,

Miguel Hernando de Larramendi, and Ana I. Planet (eds.), *Encrucijadas del cambio religioso en España: Secularización, cristianismo e islam* (Granada, 2018), p. 68.

70. Aguado, 'Entre lo público y lo privado', p. 130.
71. Gloria Nielfa Cristóbal and Rosario Ruiz Franco, 'La nueva ciudadanía de las mujeres en el ámbito municipal: Alcaldesas y concejalas en la Segunda República (1931–1939)', in Gloria Nielfa Cristóbal (ed.), *Mujeres en los Gobiernos locales: Alcaldesas y concejalas en la España contemporánea* (Madrid, 2015), table 3.1, pp. 119–21, and table 3.3, pp. 122–4.
72. Townson, *The Crisis of Democracy in Spain*, p. 111.
73. Ibid.
74. Ibid., p. 170.
75. Townson, 'A Third Way? Centrist Politics under the Republic', p. 101.
76. Townson, *The Crisis of Democracy in Spain*, p. 127.
77. Martínez Barrio, *Memorias*, p. 139.
78. Townson, *The Crisis of Democracy in Spain*, p. 131.
79. Niceto Alcalá Zamora, *Memorias (Segundo texto de mis memorias)* (Barcelona, 1977), p. 232.
80. Townson, *The Crisis of Democracy in Spain*, p. 144.
81. Ibid., p. 146.
82. Ibid., p. 149.
83. Herrerín, *The Road to Anarchy*, p. 110.
84. Jerome R. Mintz, *The Anarchists of Casas Viejas* (Chicago, IL, 1982), p. 218.
85. Townson, *The Crisis of Democracy in Spain*, p. 154.
86. Ibid., p. 155.
87. Azaña, *Obras completas*, vol. 4, p. 615 (diary entry 21 February 1933).
88. José María Gil Robles, *No fue posible la paz* (Barcelona, 1968), p. 79.
89. Townson, *The Crisis of Democracy in Spain*, p. 161.
90. Ibid., p. 162.
91. Ibid., p. 167.
92. Ibid., p. 171.
93. Ibid., p. 173.
94. José Manuel Macarro Vera, 'Sindicalismo y política', in Santos Juliá (ed.), *Ayer*, no. 20 (1995), p. 158.
95. Townson, *The Crisis of Democracy in Spain*, p. 174.
96. Ibid., p. 175.
97. Ibid.
98. Ibid.

99. Ibid.

100. Ibid., p. 178.

101. Ibid., p. 180.

102. Martínez Barrio, *Memorias*, p. 191.

103. Alejandro Lerroux, *La pequeña historia* (Madrid, 1963), p. 151.

104. Nigel Townson, 'De Oviedo a la Puerta del Sol. Manuel Rico Avello en la Segunda República, 1931–1933', in Juan Pan-Montojo (ed.), *El sueño republicano de Manuel Rico Avello (1886–1936)* (Madrid, 2011), p. 99.

105. Ibid., pp. 98–9.

106. William J. Irwin, *The 1933 Cortes Elections: Origin of the Bienio Negro* (New York, 1991), p. 258.

107. Fernando del Rey, *Paisanos en lucha: Exclusión política y violencia en la Segunda República española* (Madrid, 2008), p. 312.

108. Rees, 'Agrarian Society and Politics', p. 247.

109. Townson, *The Crisis of Democracy in Spain*, p. 187.

110. Michael Seidman, *The Victorious Counterrevolution: The Nationalist Effort in the Spanish Civil War* (Madison, WI, 2011), p. 17.

111. Herrerín, *Camino a la anarquía*, pp. 252–3.

112. Townson, *The Crisis of Democracy in Spain*, p. 194.

113. Ibid., p. 187.

114. Rees, 'Agrarian Society and Politics', p. 246.

115. Alcalá Zamora, *Memorias*, pp. 259 and 260, and Martínez Barrio, *Memorias*, p. 211.

116. Townson, *The Crisis of Democracy in Spain*, p. 199.

117. Herrerín, *The Road to Anarchy*, p. 145.

118. Murray Bookchin, *The Spanish Anarchists: The Heroic Years, 1868–1936* (New York, 1977), p. 257.

119. Julián Casanova, *De la calle al frente. El anarcosindicalismo en España (1931–1939)* (Barcelona, 1997), p. 123.

120. Herrerín, *The Road to Anarchy*, p. 148. The loss of membership is on p. 201.

## CHAPTER 5

1. *Diario de las sesiones de Cortes* (DSC), 19 December 1933.

2. José María Gil Robles, *No fue posible la paz* (Barcelona, 1968), p. 164.

3. Manuel Álvarez Tardío, *Anticlericalismo y libertad de conciencia: Política y religión en la Segunda República Española (1931–1936)* (Madrid, 2002), p. 293.

4. Nigel Townson, *The Crisis of Democracy in Spain: Centrist Politics under the Second Republic, 1931–1936* (Brighton, 2000), p. 198.

5. Gerald Brenan, *The Spanish Labyrinth: An Account of the Social and Political Background of the Spanish Civil War* (Cambridge, 1960), p. 280.

6. Edward E. Malefakis, *Agrarian Reform and Peasant Revolution in Spain: Origins of the Civil War* (New Haven, CT, 1970), p. 328.

7. Helen Graham, *The Spanish Civil War: A Very Short Introduction* (Oxford, 2005), p. 15.

8. Fernando del Rey, *Paisanos en lucha. Exclusión política y violencia en la Segunda República española* (Madrid, 2008), p. 356.

9. José Manuel Macarro Vera, *Socialismo, República y revolución en Andalucía (1931–1936)* (Seville, 2000), p. 320.

10. Mercedes Cabrera, *La patronal ante la II República: Organizaciones y estrategia (1931–1936)* (Madrid, 1983), p. 259.

11. Ibid.

12. Santos Juliá, *Madrid, 1931–1934. De la fiesta popular a la lucha de clases* (Madrid, 1984), p. 346.

13. Cabrera, *La patronal*, pp. 238 and 260 n. 11.

14. Townson, *The Crisis of Democracy in Spain*, p. 261.

15. Ibid.

16. María del Mar del Pozo Andrés, 'La construcción de la identidad nacional desde la escuela: el modelo republicano de educación para la ciudadanía', in Javier Moreno Luzón (ed.), *Construir España: nacionalismo español y procesos de nacionalización* (Madrid, 2007), p. 225.

17. Townson, *The Crisis of Democracy in Spain*, p. 205.

18. Ibid., p. 208.

19. DSC, 19 December 1933.

20. Álvarez Tardío, *Anticlericalismo y libertad de conciencia*, p. 302.

21. Nigel Townson, '¿Vendidos al clericalismo? La política religiosa de los radicales en el segundo bienio, 1933–1935', in Julio de la Cueva and Feliciano Montero (eds.), *Laicismo y Catolicismo: El conflicto político-religioso en la Segunda República* (Alcalá de Henares, 2009), p. 81.

22. Townson, *The Crisis of Democracy in Spain*, p. 259.

23. Stanley G. Payne, *Alcalá Zamora and the Failure of the Spanish Republic, 1931–1936* (Brighton, 2017), p. 74.

24. Townson, *The Crisis of Democracy in Spain*, pp. 228 and 229.

25. Ibid., p. 235.

26. Ibid., p. 242.

27. Malefakis, *Agrarian Reform*, p. 337.
28. Ibid., p. 338.
29. Juan-Simeón Vidarte, *El bienio negro y la insurrección de Asturias* (Barcelona, 1978), p. 155.
30. Ibid.
31. DSC, 24 June 1934.
32. Sandra Souto Kustrín, 'Y ¿Madrid? ¿Qué hace Madrid?': Movimiento revolucionario y acción colectiva (1933–1936) (Madrid, 2004), p. 173.
33. Santos Juliá, *Historia del socialismo español (1931–1939)* (Barcelona, 1989), p. 79.
34. Manuel Azaña, *Obras completas*, Santos Juliá (ed.) (Madrid, 2007), vol. 6, p. 363 (diary entry 1 July 1937).
35. Ibid., p. 362.
36. Ibid.
37. Townson, *The Crisis of Democracy in Spain*, p. 212.
38. Ibid., p. 269.
39. Norman Lewis, *The Tomb in Seville* (London, 2004), pp. 42 and 45.
40. Souto Kustrín, 'Y ¿Madrid?', pp. 254 and 283.
41. Ibid., p. 286.
42. Payne, *Alcalá Zamora*, p. 84.
43. Paco Ignacio Taibo II, *Asturias, octubre 1934* (Barcelona, 2013), pp. 541–2.
44. Souto Kustrín, 'Y ¿Madrid?', p. 221.
45. Townson, *The Crisis of Democracy in Spain*, p. 277.
46. César Jalón, *Memorias políticas: periodista, ministro, presidiario* (Madrid, 1973), p. 186.
47. Townson, *The Crisis of Democracy in Spain*, p. 284, and Payne, *Alcalá Zamora*, p. 88.
48. Jalón, *Memorias políticas*, p. 184.
49. Ibid., p. 182.
50. Townson, *The Crisis of Democracy in Spain*, p. 306.
51. Ibid., p. 280.
52. Del Rey, *Paisanos en lucha*, p. 423.
53. Townson, *The Crisis of Democracy in Spain*, p. 281.
54. Ibid.
55. Ibid., p. 299.
56. Ibid., p. 286.
57. Ibid., and Leandro Álvarez Rey, *La derecha en la II República: Sevilla, 1931–1936* (Seville, 1993), p. 423.

58. Cabrera, *La patronal*, p. 223.
59. Townson, *The Crisis of Democracy in Spain*, p. 304.
60. Gil Robles, *No fue posible*, pp. 325–6.
61. Townson, *The Crisis of Democracy in Spain*, pp. 301 and 302.
62. Gil Robles, *No fue posible*, p. 146.
63. Townson, *The Crisis of Democracy in Spain*, p. 307.
64. Ibid., p. 313.
65. Gil Robles, *No fue posible*, p. 171.
66. Ibid., p. 290.
67. Townson, *The Crisis of Democracy in Spain*, p. 311.
68. Ibid., p. 312.
69. Ibid., p. 296.
70. Alcalá Zamora, *Memorias*, p. 338.
71. Ibid., p. 320.
72. Gil Robles, *No fue posible*, p. 297.
73. Joaquín Chapaprieta, *La paz fue posible: memorias de un político* (Barcelona, 1971), p. 266.
74. Gil Robles, *No fue posible*, p. 363.
75. Paul Preston, *The Spanish Civil War, 1936–39* (London, 1990), p. 34.
76. Gil Robles, *No fue posible*, p. 431.
77. Santos Juliá, *Los socialistas en la política español, 1879–1982* (Madrid, 1997), p. 229.
78. Malefakis, *Agrarian Reform*, p. 373.
79. Del Rey, *Paisanos en lucha*, p. 502.
80. Ibid., p. 525.
81. Ibid., p. 527, and Macarro Vera, *Socialismo, República y revolución*, p. 451.
82. Del Rey, *Paisanos en lucha*, p. 510.
83. Ibid., p. 516.
84. Stanley G. Payne, *Spain's First Democracy: The Second Republic, 1931–1936* (Madison, WI, 1993), p. 319.
85. Clara Campoamor, *La revolución española vista por una republicana* (Seville, 2005), p. 45.
86. Del Rey, *Paisanos en lucha*, p. 497.
87. Ibid., pp. 527 and 493.
88. Macarro Vera, *Socialismo, República y revolución*, p. 431.
89. Azaña, *Obras completas*, vol. 5, p. 645.
90. Del Rey, *Paisanos en lucha*, p. 533.
91. Azaña, *Obras completas*, vol. 5, p. 634.
92. Ibid., p. 640.

93. Ibid., p. 641.
94. Del Rey, *Paisanos en lucha*, p. 500.
95. Miguel Martorell and Santos Juliá, *Manual de historia política y social de España (1808–2011)* (Barcelona, 2012), p. 297.
96. Ibid., p. 298.
97. Santos Juliá, '¿Qué habría pasado si Indalecio Prieto hubiera aceptado la presidencia del gobierno en mayo de 1936?', in Nigel Townson (ed.), *Historia virtual de España (1870–2004) ¿Qué hubiera pasado si . . .?* (Madrid, 2004), p. 199.
98. Payne, *Spain's First Democracy*, p. 327.
99. Martorell and Juliá, *Manual de historia*, p. 298.
100. Payne, *Spain's First Democracy*, p. 359.
101. Ibid., p. 350.
102. Miguel Maura, *Así cayó Alfonso XIII: De una dictadura a otra*, Joaquín Romero Maura (ed.) (Madrid, 2007), pp. 525, 526, 529, and 534.
103. Gabriele Ranzato, *El eclipse de la democracia. La Guerra Civil española y sus orígenes, 1931–1939* (Madrid, 2006), p. 248.

## CHAPTER 6

1. Francisco Alía Miranda, *Julio de 1936. Conspiración y alzamiento contra la Segunda República* (Barcelona, 2011), p. 140.
2. Ibid.
3. Ibid.
4. Ibid., p. 141.
5. Ibid.
6. Ibid., p. 142.
7. Diego Martínez Barrio, *Memorias* (Barcelona, 1983), p. 364.
8. Ibid., p. 361.
9. Ibid.
10. Federico Escofet, *De una derrota a una victoria: 6 de octubre de 1934–19 de julio de 1936* (Barcelona, 1984), p. 365.
11. Arturo Barea, *The Forging of a Rebel* (London, 2018), p. 545–6.
12. *El Socialista*, 9 August 1936.
13. Francisco Alía Miranda, *Historia del Ejército español y de su intervención política. Del desastre del 98 a la Transición* (Madrid, 2018), p. 124.
14. Sebastian Balfour, *Deadly Embrace: Morocco and the Road to the Spanish Civil War* (Oxford, 2002), p. 271.
15. Miguel Martorell and Santos Juliá, *Manual de historia política y social de España (1808–2011)* (Barcelona, 2012), p. 299.

16. José Álvarez Junco, *Dioses útiles: Naciones y nacionalismos* (Barcelona, 2016), p. 185.

17. Emilio Mola Vidal, *Obras completas* (Valladolid, 1940), p. 1,176 (the edict of 19 July 1936).

18. Álvarez Junco, *Dioses útiles*, p. 185.

19. Xosé M. Núñez Seixas, ¡*Fuera el invasor! Nacionalismos y movilización bélica durante la guerra civil española (1936–1939)* (Madrid, 2006), p. 40.

20. Álvarez Junco, *Dioses útiles*, p. 185.

21. Ibid., p. 185, and Santos Juliá, 'De "guerra contra el invasor" a "guerra fratricida"', in Santos Juliá (ed.), *Víctimas de la guerra civil* (Madrid, 1999), p. 24.

22. David Wingeate Pike, *France Divided: The French and the Civil War in Spain* (Brighton, 2011), p. 35.

23. George Orwell, *Homage to Catalonia* (London, 1959), p. 2.

24. Clara Campoamor, *La revolución española vista por una republicana* (Seville, 2005), p. 102.

25. Ronald Fraser, *Blood of Spain: The Experience of Civil War, 1936–1939* (London, 1981), p. 143.

26. Ibid., p. 138.

27. Ibid.

28. Ibid., p. 141.

29. Santos Juliá, *Los socialistas en la política español, 1879–1982* (Madrid, 1997), p. 240.

30. Fraser, *Blood of Spain*, pp. 137 and 143.

31. Stanley G. Payne, *The Spanish Civil War* (New York, 2012), p. 95.

32. Mary Nash, 'Republicanas en la Guerra Civil: el compromiso anifascista', in Isabel Morant (ed.), *Historia de las mujeres en España y América Latina*, vol. IV: *Del siglo XX a los umbrales del XXI* (Madrid, 2006), p. 128.

33. Ibid., p. 130.

34. Ibid., p. 139.

35. Ibid., p. 143.

36. John Lukacs, *Budapest 1900: A Historical Portrait of a City and its Culture* (New York, 1988), p. 212.

37. Juliá, *Los socialistas*, pp. 242–3.

38. Ibid., p. 243.

39. Carlos Morla Lynch, *España sufre. Diarios de guerra en el Madrid republicano, 1936–1939*, prologue by Andrés Trapiello (Seville, 2008), p. 57 (diary 27 August 1936).

40. Payne, *The Spanish Civil War*, p. 174.
41. The term is taken from Burnett Bolloten's classic study *The Spanish Civil War: Revolution and Counter-Revolution* (Chapel Hill, NC, 1991). Indeed, the first edition of the book (1961) was called *The Grand Camouflage: The Communist Conspiracy in the Spanish Civil War*.
42. Fraser, *Blood of Spain*, p. 148.
43. Miquel Mir, *Diario de un pistolero anarquista* (Barcelona, 2006), p. 184.
44. Fraser, *Blood of Spain*, pp. 149 and 146.
45. Campoamor, *La revolución española*, p. 108.
46. Ibid.
47. Tim Rees, 'Battleground of the Revolutionaries: The Republic and the Civil War in Spain, 1931–39', in Moira Donald and Tim Rees (eds.), *Reinterpreting Revolution in Twentieth-Century Europe* (Basingstoke, 2001), p. 127.
48. Ibid.
49. Payne, *The Spanish Civil War*, p. 225.
50. José Luis Ledesma, *Los días de llamas de la revolución. Violencia y política en la retaguardia republicana de Zaragoza durante la guerra civil* (Zaragoza, 2003), p. 138.
51. Julián Casanova, 'Rebelión y revolución', in Juliá (ed.), *Víctimas de la guerra civil*, p. 121.
52. Julius Ruiz, *'Paracuellos': The Elimination of the 'Fifth Column' in Republican Madrid during the Spanish Civil War* (Brighton, 2017), p. 65.
53. Ibid., p. 1.
54. Ibid., p. 190.
55. Barea, *The Forging*, p. 562.
56. Fernando del Rey, *Retaguardia roja. Violencia y revolución en la guerra civil española* (Barcelona, 2019), p. 375.
57. Ibid., p. 371.
58. Ibid.
59. Gabriele Ranzato, *El eclipse de la democracia. La Guerra Civil española y sus orígenes, 1931–1939* (Madrid, 2006), p. 392.
60. Ibid., p. 397.
61. Ruiz, *'Paracuellos'*, p. 189.
62. Martínez Barrio, *Memorias*, p. 375.
63. Ruiz, *'Paracuellos'*, p. 66.
64. Del Rey, *Retaguardia roja*, p. 541.

65. Julio de la Cueva, 'Religious Persecution, Anticlerical Tradition and Revolution: On Atrocities against the Clergy during the Spanish Civil War', *Journal of Contemporary History*, 33:3 (1998), p. 356.
66. Payne, *The Spanish Civil War*, p. 118.
67. Martorell and Juliá, *Manual de historia*, p. 319.
68. Casanova, 'Rebelión y revolución', p. 159, and Martorell and Juliá, *Manual de historia*, p. 319.
69. Julius Ruiz, *El Terror Rojo. Madrid, 1936* (Barcelona, 2012), p. 375.
70. Ranzato, *El eclipse de la democracia*, p. 390.
71. Francisco Pilo Ortiz, *La represión en Badajoz (14–31 de agosto de 1936)* (Badajoz, 2001), p. 37.
72. Casanova, 'Rebelión y revolución', pp. 174–5.
73. Ibid., pp. 171–2.
74. Del Rey, *Retaguardia roja*, p. 537.
75. Ruiz, *El Terror Rojo*, p. 376.
76. Del Rey, *Retaguardia roja*, p. 232, table 9.1.
77. Ruiz, *El Terror Rojo*, p. 379.
78. Ruiz, *'Paracuellos'*, p. xv.
79. Martin Amis, *Koba the Dread* (London, 2002), p. 239.
80. Del Rey, *Retaguardia roja*, p. 19.
81. Francisco Romero Salvadó, *The Spanish Civil War* (London, 2005), p. 65.
82. Ibid.
83. Morla Lynch, *España sufre*, p. 62 (diary entry for 4 September 1936).
84. Mijail Koltsov, *Diario de la guerra española* (Madrid, 1978), p. 45 (diary entry for 19 August 1936).
85. Juliá, *Los socialistas*, p. 249.
86. Ibid., p. 251.
87. Michael Seidman, *Republic of Egos: A Social History of the Spanish Civil War* (Madison, WI, 2002), p. 146.
88. Martorell and Juliá, *Manual de historia*, p. 323.
89. Ramón Serrano Suñer, *Entre el silencio y la propaganda, la Historia como fue: Memorias* (Barcelona, 1977), p. 245.
90. Javier Tusell, *Franco en la guerra civil. Una biografía política* (Barcelona, 1992), p. 110.
91. José Manuel Sabín Rodríguez, *La dictadura franquista (1936–1975). Textos y documentos* (Madrid, 1997), p. 21.
92. Juliá, *Un siglo de España*, p. 121.
93. Martorell and Juliá, *Manual de historia*, p. 327.
94. Koltsov, *Diario de la guerra española*, p. 354 (diary entry for 5 February 1937).

95. Juliá, *Los socialistas*, p. 253.
96. Palmiro Togliatti, *Escritos sobre la guerra de España* (Barcelona, 1980), p. 174.
97. Ruiz, *'Paracuellos'*, p. 190.
98. Ibid., p. 189.
99. Seidman, *Republic of Egos*, p. 68.
100. Manuel Azaña, *Obras completas* (Mexico, 1990), vol. 3, pp. 502 and 503.
101. Seidman, *Republic of Egos*, p. 68.
102. Juan Pablo Fusi, *Franco: A Biography* (London, 1987), p. 172.
103. Martorell and Juliá, *Manual de historia*, p. 328.
104. María Teresa Gallego Méndez, 'Mujeres azules en la Guerra Civil', in G. Gómez-Ferrer, G. Cano, D. Barrancos, and A. Lavrin (eds.), *Historia de las mujeres en España y América Latina*, vol. IV, *Del siglo XX a los umbrales del XXI* (Madrid, 2006), p. 155.
105. Michael Seidman, *The Victorious Counterrevolution: The Nationalist Effort in the Spanish Civil War* (Madison, WI, 2011), p. 161.
106. Gallego Méndez, 'Mujeres azules en la Guerra Civil', p. 165.
107. Martorell and Juliá, *Manual de historia*, p. 322.
108. Ibid.
109. Payne, *The Spanish Civil War*, p. 140.
110. Mario Ojeda Revah, *Mexico and the Spanish Civil War: Political Repercussions for the Republican Cause* (Brighton, 2016), pp. 99 and 133.
111. Gerald Howson, *Arms for Spain: The Untold Story of the Spanish Civil War* (London, 1998), pp. 250 and 251.
112. Ibid., p. 80.
113. Daniel Kowalsky, *La Unión Soviética y la guerra civil española. Una revisión crítica* (Barcelona, 2004), p. 52.
114. Ibid.
115. Ibid., p. 50.
116. Ibid., p. 64.
117. Ibid., p. 53.
118. Ali Al Tuma, 'The Reds and the Greens: Encounters between Moroccan and Republican Enemies during the Spanish Civil War', in James Matthews (ed.), *Spain at War: Society, Culture, and Mobilization, 1936–44* (London, 2019), p. 90.
119. Héctor Colmegna, *Diario de un médico argentino en la guerra de España, 1936–1939* (Córdoba, 2019), p. 54.
120. Seidman, *Republic of Egos*, p. 95.
121. Ibid., p. 94.
122. Ibid., p. 96.

123. Colmegna, *Diario de un médico*, p. 64.
124. Michael Seidman, 'The Spanish Civil War: A Unique Conflict?', in Nigel Townson (ed.), *Is Spain Different? A Comparative Look at the 19th and 20th Centuries* (Brighton, 2015), p. 127.
125. Payne, *The Spanish Civil War*, p. 129.
126. Seidman, *Republic of Egos*, p. 97.
127. Ibid., p. 69.
128. Seidman, *The Victorious Counterrevolution*, p. 80.
129. Seidman, *Republic of Egos*, p. 150.
130. Morla Lynch, *España sufre*, p. 74 (diary entry for 19 September 1936).
131. Ibid., p. 92 (diary entry for 20 October 1936).
132. Carmen and Laura Gutiérrez Rueda, *El hambre en el Madrid de la Guerra Civil (1936-1939)* (Madrid, 2003), p. 9.
133. Seidman, *Republic of Egos*, p. 130.
134. Payne, *The Spanish Civil War*, p. 129.
135. Juliá, *Los socialistas*, p. 254.
136. Koltsov, *Diario de la guerra española*, p. 352 (diary entry for 7 February 1937).
137. Ibid., p. 353 (diary entry for 7 February 1937).
138. Juliá, *Los socialistas*, p. 256.
139. Ibid., p. 257.
140. Azaña, *Obras completas*, vol. 6, p. 316 (diary entry for 20 May 1937).
141. Ibid., p. 317 (diary entry for 31 May 1937).
142. Ibid.
143. Togliatti, *Escritos*, pp. 127 and 128.
144. Mariano Ansó, *Yo fui ministro de Negrín* (Barcelona, 1976), p. 207.
145. Togliatti, *Escritos*, p. 140.
146. Ibid., p. 196.
147. Julius Ruiz, '"Work and Don't Lose Hope": Republican Forced Labour Camps during the Spanish Civil War', *Contemporary European History*, 18:4 (2009), p. 423.
148. Ibid., p. 439.
149. Ibid., p. 429.
150. Ibid., p. 424.
151. Joseph M. Solé and Joan Villarroya, 'Mayo de 1937-abril de 1939', in Juliá (ed.), *Víctimas de la guerra civil*, p. 257.
152. Ibid., p. 185.
153. Centro Documental de la Memoria Histórica, Causa General, C614, Expediente 1. I am grateful to Julius Ruiz for having drawn my attention to this document.

NOTES TO PP. 243–50

154. Colmegna, *Diario de un médico*, p. 84.
155. Payne, *The Spanish Civil War*, p. 192.
156. Seidman, *Republic of Egos*, p. 155.
157. Gutiérrez Rueda, *El hambre en el Madrid*, pp. 129–31.
158. Interview conducted by Nigel Townson in Madrid on 19 June 2009 as part of the international research project 'Around 1968: Activism, Networks, Trajectories' (2007–2011).
159. Gutiérrez Rueda, *El hambre en el Madrid*, p. 65.
160. Seidman, *Republic of Egos*, p. 199.
161. Ibid., p. 212.
162. Seidman, *The Victorious Counterrevolution*, p. 236.
163. Seidman, *Republic of Egos*, pp. 178 and 177.
164. Ibid., p. 177.
165. Togliatti, *Escritos*, p. 190.
166. Ansó, *Yo fui ministro*, p. 218.
167. Martorell and Juliá, *Manual de historia*, p. 315, and Juliá, *Los socialistas*, p. 273.
168. Ibid., p. 275.
169. Ansó, *Yo fui ministro*, p. 224.
170. Ibid.
171. Chris Henry, *The Ebro 1938: The Death Knell of the Republic* (Oxford, 1999), p. 32.
172. Ansó, *Yo fui ministro*, p. 220.
173. Seidman, *The Victorious Counterrevolution*, p. 77.
174. Juliá, *Los socialistas*, p. 275.
175. Ibid., p. 277.
176. Bill Alexander, *British Volunteers for Liberty: Spain 1936–39* (London, 1986), p. 240.
177. Jason Gurney, *Crusade in Spain* (Newton Abbot, 1976), pp. 73 and 74.
178. Payne, *The Spanish Civil War*, pp. 186–7.
179. Juliá, *Los socialistas*, p. 279.
180. Ibid., p. 280.
181. Ansó, *Yo fui ministro*, p. 242.
182. Juliá, *Los socialistas*, p. 280.
183. Manuel Aguilera, *Compañeros y Camaradas. Las luchas entre antifascistas en la Guerra Civil española* (Madrid, 2012), p. 333.
184. Ansó, *Yo fui ministro*, p. 252.
185. Fernando Díaz-Plaja (ed.), *La posguerra española en sus documentos* (Barcelona, 1970), p. 11.

186. Seidman, 'The Spanish Civil War: A Unique Conflict?', pp. 133–4.
187. Paul Preston, *The Spanish Civil War: Dreams and Nightmares* (London, 2001), p. 5.
188. George Woodcock, *Writers and Politics* (Quebec, 1990), p. 180.
189. Paul Preston, *The Spanish Civil War, 1936–39* (London, 1990), p. 7.
190. Pedro Corral, 'Desertion and Shirking in the Spanish Civil War: Man versus Propaganda', in Matthews (ed.), *Spain at War*, p. 71.
191. Seidman, *Republic of Egos*, p. 38.
192. Corral, 'Desertion and Shirking', p. 71.
193. Seidman, *The Victorious Counterrevolution*, p. 26.
194. Corral, 'Desertion and Shirking', p. 72.
195. Ibid., p. 74.

## CHAPTER 7

1. Manuel Tuñon de Lara (ed.), *Textos y documentos de Historia Moderna y Contemporánea (Siglos XVIII–XX)* (Barcelona, 1985), p. 557.
2. Enrique Moradiellos, *La España de Franco (1939–1975): Política y sociedad* (Madrid, 2000), pp. 72–3.
3. Ibid., p. 73.
4. Ibid.
5. José Manuel Sabín Rodríguez, *La dictadura franquista (1936–1975). Textos y documentos* (Madrid, 1997), p. 79.
6. Santos Juliá, *Un siglo de España. Política y sociedad* (Madrid, 1999), p. 154.
7. Sabín Rodríguez, *La dictadura franquista*, p. 83.
8. Ibid., p. 84, and Moradiellos, *La España de Franco*, p. 74.
9. William J. Callahan, 'The Spanish Church: Change and Continuity', in Nigel Townson (ed.), *Spain Transformed: The Late Franco Dictatorship, 1959–75* (London, 2010), p. 183.
10. Moradiellos, *La España de Franco*, pp. 75–6.
11. Callahan, 'The Spanish Church', p. 183.
12. Moradiellos, *La España de Franco*, p. 76.
13. Ibid., p. 72.
14. Ibid., p. 76.
15. Callahan, 'The Spanish Church', p. 184.
16. Fernando Díaz-Plaja (ed.), *La posguerra española en sus documentos* (Barcelona, 1970), p. 26 (law of 5 October 1939).
17. Ibid., p. 23 (the law of August 1939, 'Reinforcing the Authority of the Head of State').

18. The phrase was coined by Juan Linz in his article 'An Authoritarian Regime: Spain', in Eric Allardt and Yrjö Littunen (eds.), *Cleavages, Ideologies and Party Strategies: Contributions to Comparative Political Sociology* (Helsinki, 1964), pp. 291–341.
19. Carme Molinero and Pere Ysàs, *La anatomía del franquismo: De la supervivencia a la agonía, 1945–1977* (Barcelona, 2008), p. 22.
20. Ibid., p. 23.
21. Sabín Rodríguez, *La dictadura franquista*, p. 85 (the Law on the Cortes of 17 July 1942).
22. Sir Samuel Hoare, *Ambassador on Special Mission* (London, 1946), p. 271.
23. Ibid., pp. 78, 79, and 271.
24. Jean Grugel and Tim Rees, *Franco's Spain* (London, 1997), p. 49.
25. Sabín Rodríguez, *La dictadura franquista*, p. 81.
26. Albert Carreras and Xavier Tafunell, *Historia económica de la España contemporánea* (Barcelona, 2004), p. 274.
27. Carlos Barceló, 'El mercado negro de productos agrarios en la posguerra, 1939–1953', in Josep Fontana (ed.), *España bajo el franquismo* (Barcelona, 2000), p. 196.
28. Julius Ruiz, *Franco's Justice: Repression in Madrid after the Spanish Civil War* (Oxford, 2005), p. 165.
29. Hoare, *Ambassador*, pp. 30 and 35.
30. Moradiellos, *La España de Franco*, p. 89.
31. Antonio Cazorla Sánchez, *Fear and Progress: Ordinary Lives in Franco's Spain, 1939–1975* (Oxford, 2010), p. 64.
32. Richard Wright, *Pagan Spain* (New York, 2008), p. 219.
33. Gerald Brenan, *The Face of Spain* (London, 1987), p. 11.
34. Ibid., p. 24.
35. Ibid., p. 71.
36. Ibid., p. 123.
37. Javier Rodríguez González, *León bajo la dictadura franquista (1936–1951)* (León, 2003), p. 269.
38. Wright, *Pagan Spain*, p. 274.
39. Ibid., p. 178.
40. Vicente Pérez Moreda, David-Sven Reher, and Alberto Sanz Gimeno, *La conquista de la salud. Mortalidad y modernización en la España contemporánea* (Madrid, 2015), p. 51, table 2.1.
41. Ibid., p. 163.
42. Keith Lowe, *Savage Continent: Europe in the Aftermath of World War II* (London, 2013), p. 34.

43. Ibid., p. 35.
44. Ibid., p. 37.
45. Ibid.
46. Miguel Martorell and Santos Juliá, *Manuel de historia y social de España (1808–2011)* (Barcelona, 2012), p. 335.
47. Ibid.
48. Carreras and Tafunell, *Historia económica*, p. 291.
49. Ibid., pp. 288 and 287.
50. Tuñon de Lara (ed.), *Textos y documentos*, p. 556.
51. *Fundamentos del Nuevo Estado* (Madrid, 1943), p. 324 (preamble to the Law of Political Responsibilities).
52. Tuñon de Lara (ed.), *Textos y documentos*, p. 558.
53. Nigel Townson, 'Catholicism and Citizenship under the Franco Dictatorship', in Tamar Groves, Nigel Townson, Inbal Ofer, and Antonio Herrera, *Social Movements and the Spanish Transition: Building Citizenships in Parishes, Neighbourhoods, Schools and the Countryside* (London, 2017), p. 21.
54. Díaz-Plaja (ed.), *La posguerra*, p. 12.
55. Ruiz, *Franco's Justice*, p. 25.
56. Ramón Serrano Suñer, *Entre el silencio y la propaganda, la Historia como fue: Memorias* (Barcelona, 1977), p. 245, and Ruiz, *Franco's Justice*, p. 53.
57. Ruiz, *Franco's Justice*, p. 61.
58. *Fundamentos del Nuevo Estado*, pp. 324, 326, and 327.
59. Ruiz, *Franco's Justice*, p. 139, and *Fundamentos del Nuevo Estado*, p. 326.
60. Ángela Cenarro, 'La Ley de Responsabilidades Políticas', in Julián Casanova and Ángela Cenarro (eds.), *Pagar las culpas: La represión económica en Aragón (1936–1945)* (Barcelona, 2014), p. 36.
61. Estefanía Langarita, Nacho Moreno, and Irene Murillo, 'Las víctimas de la represión económica en Aragón', in Casanova and Cenarro (eds.), *Pagar las culpas*, p. 68.
62. Cenarro, 'La Ley de Responsabilidades Políticas', p. 37.
63. Ruiz, *Franco's Justice*, pp. 151–2.
64. Cenarro, 'La Ley de Responsabilidades Políticas', p. 27.
65. Langarita, Moreno, and Murillo, 'Las víctimas de la represión económica en Aragón', p. 58.
66. Ruiz, *Franco's Justice*, p. 171.
67. Brenan, *The Face of Spain*, p. 228.
68. Ruiz, *Franco's Justice*, p. 172.

69. Ibid., p. 183.

70. José Álvarez Junco, *Dioses útiles. Naciones y nacionalismos* (Madrid, 2016), p. 189.

71. *Fundamentos del Nuevo Estado*, p. 393.

72. Jakin Boor, *Masonería* (Madrid, 1981), p. 75.

73. Javier Domínguez Arribas, *El enemigo judeo-masónico en la propaganda franquista (1936–1945)* (Madrid, 2009), pp. 111–12.

74. Boor, *Masonería*, p. 101.

75. Ibid., pp. 21, 24, 80, and 206.

76. Ruiz, *Franco's Justice*, p. 209.

77. Ibid.

78. Ibid., p. 217, table 6.3.

79. Ibid., pp. 72–3 and 74.

80. Ibid., p. 85.

81. Ibid., p. 127.

82. Ibid., p. 120.

83. Ibid., p. 113.

84. Ibid., pp. 99–100.

85. Ibid., p. 116.

86. Ibid., p. 128.

87. Ibid., p. 228.

88. Álvarez Junco, *Dioses útiles*, p. 187.

89. Tuñón de Lara (ed.), *Textos y documentos*, p. 556.

90. Ibid.

91. Álvarez Junco, *Dioses útiles*, p. 188.

92. Ibid., p. 189.

93. José Luis de la Granja et al., *La España de los nacionalismos y las autonomías* (Madrid, 2001), p. 317.

94. Ibid., p. 316.

95. Agustín del Río Cisneros (ed.), *Pensamiento político de Franco* (Madrid, 1964), p. 154.

96. Sabín Rodríguez, *La dictadura franquista*, p. 97.

97. Ibid., pp. 76 and 72.

98. Moradiellos, *La España de Franco*, p. 73, and Sabín Rodríguez, *La dictadura franquista*, p. 99.

99. Sabín Rodríguez, *La dictadura franquista*, p. 66, and Díaz-Plaja, *La posguerra*, pp. 24–5.

100. Hoare, *Ambassador*, p. 265.

101. Ibid., p. 25.

102. Ibid., p. 57.

103. Paul Preston, *Franco: A Biography* (London, 1995), p. 399.
104. Hoare, *Ambassador*, p. 217.
105. Ibid., p. 285.
106. Carlton J. H. Hayes, *Wartime Mission in Spain 1942–1945* (New York, 1945), p. 301.
107. Juliá, *Un siglo de España*, p. 155.
108. Moradiellos, *La España de Franco*, p. 77.
109. Laureano López Rodó, *La larga marcha hacia la Monarquía* (Barcelona, 1977), pp. 43–4.
110. Hoare, *Ambassador*, p. 293.
111. Hayes, *Wartime Mission*, p. 242.
112. Hoare, *Ambassador*, p. 268.
113. Ibid., p. 269.
114. Ibid., p. 268.
115. Hayes, *Wartime Mission*, ch. VIII, 'Spain's Benevolent Neutrality'.
116. Ángel Herrerín, *La CNT durante el franquismo. Clandestinidad y exilio (1939–1975)* (Madrid, 2004), p. 17.
117. Ibid., p. 25.
118. Harmut Heine, *La oposición política al franquismo. De 1939 a 1952* (Barcelona, 1983), p. 248.
119. Ibid., p. 423.
120. Ibid., pp. 432 and 435.
121. Ibid., p. 214.
122. Ibid., p. 442.
123. Ibid., p. 444.
124. Antonio Fernández García et al., *Documentos de historia contemporánea de España* (Madrid, 1996), p. 563.
125. Ibid., p. 564.
126. Ibid.
127. Hayes, *Wartime Mission*, pp. 251 and 287.
128. Sabín Rodríguez, *La dictadura franquista*, p. 95.
129. Ibid.
130. Ibid., p. 52.
131. Ibid., p. 96.
132. Juliá, *Un siglo de España*, p. 165.
133. Sabín Rodríguez, *La dictadura franquista*, pp. 96 and 93.
134. Juliá, *Un siglo de España*, p. 163.
135. Sabín Rodríguez, *La dictadura franquista*, p. 96.
136. Ibid., p. 97.
137. US Department of State, 4 March 1946.

138. José Borras, *Políticas de los exiliados españoles 1944–1950* (Paris, 1976), p. 67.
139. Hayes, *Wartime Mission*, p. 304.
140. Borras, *Políticas de los exiliados*, p. 66.
141. Heine, *La oposición política*, p. 438.
142. Ibid., p. 433.
143. Ibid., p. 434.
144. Ibid., p. 466.
145. Ibid.
146. Sebastián Balfour, *Dictatorship, Workers, and the City: Labour in Greater Barcelona since 1939* (Oxford, 1989), p. 25.
147. Herrerín, *La CNT durante el franquismo*, p. 30.
148. Ibid., p. 27.
149. Ibid., p. 155, table 3.
150. Ibid., p. 153.
151. Ibid., p. 154.
152. Ibid., p. 146.
153. Heine, *La oposición política*, p. 473.
154. George C. Herring, *From Colony to Superpower: U.S. Foreign Relations since 1776* (Oxford, 2008), p. 595.
155. Ibid., p. 615.
156. Ibid., p. 616.
157. Ibid., p. 600, and Hayes, *Wartime Mission*, p. 287.
158. Charles Powell, *El amigo americano. España y Estados Unidos: de la dictadura a la democracia* (Barcelona, 2011), p. 23.
159. Carreras and Tafunell, *Historia económica*, pp. 302 and 303.
160. Tuñón de Lara (ed.), *Textos y documentos*, p. 556.
161. Wright, *Pagan Spain*, p. 262.
162. Carreras and Tafunell, *Historia económica*, p. 305.
163. Francisco Franco, *Discursos y mensajes del Jefe del Estado 1955–1959* (Madrid, 1960), p. 131.

## CHAPTER 8

1. Carme Molinero and Pere Ysàs, *La anatomía del franquismo. De la supervivencia a la agonía, 1945–1977* (Barcelona, 2008), p. 20.
2. Ibid., p. 26.
3. Carme Molinero and Pere Ysàs, *De la hegemonía a la autodestrucción. El Partido Comunista de España (1956–1982)* (Barcelona, 2017), p. 22.

4. Ibid.
5. Jean Grugel and Tim Rees, *Franco's Spain* (London, 1997), p. 86.
6. Ibid.
7. Ibid., p. 74.
8. Molinero and Ysàs, *La anatomía del franquismo*, p. 26.
9. Ibid., p. 18.
10. Ibid., p. 19.
11. Ibid.
12. Ibid., p. 29.
13. Ibid.
14. Grugel and Rees, *Franco's Spain*, p. 61.
15. Molinero and Ysàs, *La anatomía del franquismo*, p. 38.
16. Ibid., p. 27.
17. Opus Dei card on 'San Josemaría Escrivá. Fundador del Opus Dei'.
18. Molinero and Ysàs, *La anatomía del franquismo*, p. 36.
19. Grugel and Rees, *Franco's Spain*, p. 59.
20. Francisco Franco, *Discursos y mensajes del Jefe del Estado 1955-1959* (Madrid, 1960), p. 725.
21. Albert Carreras and Xavier Tafunell, *Historia económica de la España contemporánea* (Barcelona, 2004), p. 322
22. Ibid., p. 336.
23. Ibid., p. 338.
24. Pablo Martín Aceña and Elena Martínez Ruiz, 'The Golden Age of Spanish Capitalism: Economic Growth without Political Freedom', in Nigel Townson (ed.), *Spain Transformed: The Late Franco Dictatorship, 1959-75* (Basingstoke, 2010), p. 34.
25. Carreras and Tafunell, *Historia económica*, pp. 344-5.
26. Alejandro J. Gomez-del-Moral, 'Buying into Change: Consumer Culture and the Department Store in the Transformation(s) of Spain, 1939-1982', *Enterprise & Society*, 16:4 (December 2015), p. 802.
27. Ibid., p. 804.
28. Ibid., p. 794.
29. Ibid., p. 805.
30. Carreras and Tafunell, *Historia económica*, p. 343.
31. Ibid., pp. 343 and 344.
32. Ibid., p. 344.
33. Gabriel Tortella, *The Development of Modern Spain: An Economic History of the Nineteenth and Twentieth Centuries* (Cambridge, MA, 2000), p. 331.
34. Grugel and Rees, *Franco's Spain*, p. 119.

35. Ibid.
36. Martín Aceña and Martínez Ruiz, 'The Golden Age of Spanish Capitalism', p. 41.
37. Carreras and Tafunell, *Historia económica*, p. 362.
38. Tom Buchanan, *Europe's Troubled Peace, 1945–2000* (Oxford, 2006), p. 95.
39. Carreras and Tafunell, *Historia económica*, p. 341.
40. José Babiano Mora, *Emigrantes, cronómetros y huelgas: un estudio sobre el trabajo y los trabajadores durante el franquismo (Madrid, 1951–1977)* (Madrid, 1995), p. 13.
41. Sasha D. Pack, *Tourism and Dictatorship: Europe's Peaceful Invasion of Franco's Spain* (New York, 2006), p. 51, table 2.1, and p. 91, table 4.2.
42. Sasha D. Pack, 'Tourism and Political Change in Franco's Spain', in Townson (ed.), *Spain Transformed*, p. 54.
43. Pack, *Tourism and Dictatorship*, p. 108, table 5.1.
44. Carreras and Tafunell, *Historia económica*, p. 340.
45. Pack, 'Tourism and Political Change', p. 57.
46. Carreras and Tafunell, *Historia económica*, p. 359.
47. Ibid.
48. Neal M. Rosendorf, 'Spain's First "Re-Branding Effort" in the Postwar France Era', in Francisco Javier Rodríguez Jiménez, Lorenzo Delgado Gómez-Escalonilla, and Nicholas J. Cull (eds.), *US Public Diplomacy and Democratization in Spain: Selling Democracy?* (New York, 2015), p. 173.
49. Ibid., p. 163.
50. Ibid., p. 166.
51. Pack, 'Tourism and Political Change', p. 56.
52. Gomez-del-Moral, 'Buying into Change', p. 801.
53. Pack, 'Tourism and Political Change', p. 60.
54. Ibid., p. 61.
55. Ibid., p. 60.
56. Buchanan, *Europe's Troubled Peace*, p. 150.
57. Mary Fulbrook, *The Fontana History of Germany, 1918–1990: The Divided Nation* (London, 1991), p. 227.
58. Rafael Vallejo, 'La ciudadanía social', in Manuel Pérez Ledesma (ed.), *De súbditos a ciudadanos* (Madrid, 2007), p. 570, table 5.
59. Grugel and Rees, *Franco's Spain*, pp. 152–3.
60. Pamela Radcliff, 'Associations and the Social Origins of the Transition during the Late Franco Regime', in Townson (ed.), *Spain Transformed*, p. 150.
61. Ibid., p. 148.

62. Ibid.
63. Ibid., p. 151.
64. Ibid., p. 149.
65. Pere Ysàs, *Disidencia y subversión. La lucha del régimen franquista por su supervivencia, 1960–1975* (Barcelona, 2004), pp. 124–5.
66. Ibid., p. 126.
67. Ibid., pp. 126, 127, and 128.
68. Ibid., p. 127.
69. Elena Hernández Sandoica, Miguel Ángel Ruiz Carnicer, and Marc Baldó Lacomba, *Estudiantes contra Franco (1939–1975). Oposición política y movilización juvenil* (Madrid, 2007), pp. 158 and 171.
70. Ysás, *Disidencia y subversión*, p. 43.
71. Ibid., pp. 4 and 24.
72. Ibid., p. 5.
73. Ibid.
74. Sandoica, Ruiz Carnicer, and Baldó Lacomba, *Estudiantes contra Franco*, p. 172.
75. Ysás, *Disidencia y subversión*, p. 14.
76. Ibid.
77. Francisco Franco Salgado-Araujo, *Mis conversaciones privadas con Franco* (Barcelona, 1976), pp. 517, 525, and 526.
78. Ysás, *Disidencia y subversión*, pp. 26 and 28.
79. Luis Carrero Blanco, *Discursos y escritos 1943–1973* (Madrid, 1974), pp. 220, 221, and 222.
80. Ibid., p. 221.
81. Ibid.
82. Ysás, *Disidencia y subversión*, p. 39.
83. Ibid., p. 46.
84. Marcelino Camacho, *Memorias. Confieso que he luchado* (Madrid, 1990), p. 165.
85. Ibid., p. 167.
86. Antonio Cazorla Sánchez, 'Order, Progress, and Syndicalism? How the Francoist Authorities Saw Socio-Economic Change', in Townson (ed.), *Spain Transformed*, p. 112.
87. Ysàs, *Disidencia y subversión*, pp. 77 and 78.
88. Franco Salgado-Araujo, *Mis conversaciones*, pp. 338 and 340.
89. Ysàs, *Disidencia y subversión*, p. 82.
90. Ibid., pp. 82 and 83.
91. Sebastian Balfour, *Dictatorship, Workers and the City: Labour in Greater Barcelona since 1939* (Oxford, 1989), p. 30.

92. Camacho, *Memorias*, p. 168.
93. Ibid., p. 192.
94. Balfour, *Dictatorship, Workers and the City*, p. 74.
95. Ysàs, *Disidencia y subversión*, p. 89.
96. Ibid., p. 90.
97. Ángel Herrerín López, *La CNT durante el franquismo. Clandestinidad y exilio (1939–1975)* (Madrid, 2004), p. 280.
98. Camacho, *Memorias*, p. 176, and Ysàs, *Disidencia y subversión*, p. 92.
99. Ibid.
100. Ibid., p. 88.
101. Ibid., p. 93.
102. Balfour, *Dictatorship, Workers and the City*, p. 89, and Ysàs, *Disidencia y subversión*, p. 93.
103. Camacho, *Memorias*, p. 209.
104. Ysàs, *Disidencia y subversión*, p. 93.
105. Ibid., p. 94.
106. Ibid., p. 95.
107. Ibid.
108. Balfour, *Dictatorship, Workers and the City*, p. 97.
109. Ibid., p. 105.
110. Camacho, *Memorias*, p. 215.
111. Balfour, *Dictatorship, Workers and the City*, p. 143, table 4.
112. Carrero Blanco, *Discursos y escritos*, p. 266, and Ysàs, *Disidencia y subversión*, p. 84.
113. Ibid., p. 176.
114. Ysàs, *Disidencia y subversión*, pp. 96–7.
115. Ibid., p. 116.
116. Cazorla Sánchez, 'Order, Progress, and Syndicalism?', p. 108.
117. Guy Hermet, *Los católicos en la España franquista. I. Los actores del juego político* (Madrid, 1985), p. 301.
118. Nigel Townson, 'Catholicism and Citizenship Under the Franco Dictatorship', in Tamar Groves, Nigel Townson, Inbal Ofer and Antonio Herrera, *Social Movements and the Spanish Transition: Building Citizenship in Parishes, Neighbourhoods, Schools and the Countryside* (Cham, Switzerland, 2017), p. 32.
119. Ibid., p. 33.
120. Ibid., p. 30.
121. Ibid.
122. Ibid.

123. Rebecca Clifford and Nigel Townson, 'The Church in Crisis: Catholic Activism and "1968"', *Cultural & Social History*, vol. 8, issue 4 (December 2011), p. 535.

124. Townson, 'Catholicism and Citizenship Dictatorship', pp. 28 and 29.

125. Ibid., p. 29.

126. Sara Martín Gutiérrez, 'Obreras y católicas. De la formación a la movilización. Roles de género y compromiso temporal de la Hermandad Obrera de Acción Católica Femenina (HOACF) en España (1946–1970)', doctoral thesis (Complutense University of Madrid, 2017), p. 389.

127. Óscar Martín García and Damián González Madrid, 'Movimientos católicos, ciudadanía y construcción de enclaves democráticos en la provincia de Albacete durante el franquismo final', *Ayer*, 91:3 (2013), p. 200.

128. Ibid., p. 202.

129. Ibid., p. 204.

130. Townson, 'Catholicism and Citizenship', pp. 35–6.

131. William J. Callahan, 'The Spanish Church: Change and Continuity', in Townson (ed.), *Spain Transformed*, p. 187.

132. Péter Apor, Rebecca Clifford, and Nigel Townson, 'Faith', in Robert Gildea, James Mark, and Anette Warring (eds.), *Europe's 1968: Voices of Revolt* (Oxford, 2013), p. 217.

133. *Vasconia: Estudio dialéctico de una nacionalidad*, 2nd ed. (Buenos Aires, 1973), pp. 9 and 327.

134. Robert P. Clark, *The Basque Insurgents: ETA, 1952–1980* (Madison, WI, 1984), p. 56.

135. Julen Agirre, *Operation Ogro: The Execution of Admiral Luis Carrero Blanco* (New York, 1974), p. 189.

136. Clark, *The Basque Insurgents*, p. 133, table 5.6. I have added three deaths to Clark's total of 11 for 1974, as 12 people died during the bombing of the Cafetería Rolando in September 1974, not 9.

137. James Mark, Nigel Townson, and Polymeris Voglis, 'Inspirations', in Gildea, Mark, and Warring (eds.), *Europe's 1968*, p. 73.

138. Ibid., p. 74.

139. Ibid., p. 80.

140. Ibid., p. 75.

141. Ibid., p. 89.

142. Ibid.

143. Ibid.

144. Ibid., p. 95.

145. Ibid., p. 94.
146. Ibid., p. 95.
147. Ibid., p. 97.
148. Ibid., p. 96.
149. Ibid., p. 99.
150. Ibid., p. 98.
151. Ibid., p. 99.
152. Balfour, *Dictatorship, Workers and the City*, p. 148.
153. Juan Pablo Fusi, *Un siglo de España. La cultura* (Madrid, 1999), pp. 109, 115, 116, and 125.
154. Elisa Chuliá, 'Cultural Diversity and the Development of a Pre-Democratic Civil Society in Spain', in Townson (ed.), *Spain Transformed*, p. 169.
155. Ibid., p. 174.
156. Louie Dean Valencia-García, *Anti-Authoritarian Youth Culture in Francoist Spain: Clashing with Fascism* (London, 2018), p. 111.
157. Ibid., pp. 101, 105, and 106.
158. Ibid., p. 109.
159. Edward Malefakis, 'The Franco Dictatorship: A Bifurcated Regime?', in Townson (ed.), *Spain Transformed*.
160. Robert Gildea, *France since 1945* (Oxford, 2002), p. 34.
161. Tom Buchanan, 'How "Different" was Spain? The Later Franco Regime in International Context', in Townson (ed.), *Spain Transformed*, p. 88.
162. José Manuel Sabín Rodríguez, *La dictadura franquista (1936–1975). Textos y documentos* (Madrid, 1997), pp. 101 and 102.
163. Ibid., p. 104.
164. Ibid., p. 102.
165. Franco, *Discursos y mensajes* (Address before the National Council of the Movement, 17 July 1956), p. 215.
166. Manuel Fraga Iribarne, *El desarrollo político* (Barcelona, 1971), p. 40.
167. Ibid., pp. 40 and 41.
168. Ibid., pp. 41, 42, and 43.
169. Ibid., p. 40.
170. Molinero and Ysàs, *La anatomía del franquismo*, p. 185.
171. Grugel and Rees, *Franco's Spain*, p. 76.
172. Stanley G. Payne, *The Franco Regime, 1936–1975* (London, 2000), pp. 546 and 545.
173. Carrero Blanco, *Escritos y discursos*, p. 247.
174. Molinero and Ysàs, *La anatomía del franquismo*, p. 144.
175. Ibid., p. 146.

176. Ibid., p. 155.
177. Ibid., pp. 156–7.
178. Ibid., p. 158.
179. Ibid., p. 156.
180. Ibid., p. 157.
181. Ibid., p. 151.
182. Ibid., p. 156.
183. Carrero Blanco, *Escritos y discursos*, p. 256.
184. Ibid., pp. 256 and 262.
185. Ibid., p. 262.
186. Ibid., p. 267.
187. Payne, *The Franco Regime*, p. 586.
188. Paul Preston, *Franco: A Biography* (London, 1995), p. 762.
189. Juan Pablo Fusi and Jordi Palafox, *España: 1808–1996. El desafío de la modernidad* (Madrid, 1997), p. 321.
190. Ibid.
191. Molinero and Ysàs, *La anatomía del franquismo*, p. 186.
192. Ibid., p. 187.
193. Payne, *The Franco Regime*, p. 594.
194. Ibid., p. 580.
195. Molinero and Ysàs, *La anatomía del franquismo*, p. 189.
196. Ibid., p. 190.
197. Payne, *The Franco Regime*, p. 604.
198. Molinero and Ysàs, *La anatomía del franquismo*, p. 221.
199. Ysàs, *Disidencia y subversión*, p. 151.
200. Ibid., p. 156.
201. Molinero and Ysàs, *La anatomía del franquismo*, p. 183.
202. Ysàs, *Disidencia y subversión*, p. 150, and Santos Juliá, *Los socialistas en la política española, 1879–1982* (Madrid, 1996), p. 447.
203. Malefakis, 'The Franco Dictatorship: A Bifurcated Regime?', p. 249.

## CHAPTER 9

1. Charles Powell, *España en democracia, 1975–2000* (Barcelona, 2001), p. 145.
2. Ibid.
3. Ibid., p. 146.
4. Carme Molinero and Pere Ysàs, *La Transición. Historia y relatos* (Madrid, 2018), p. 66.
5. *Diario de sesiones de las Cortes*, 28 January 1976.

6. Ibid.

7. Ibid.

8. Ibid.

9. Santos Juliá, *Un siglo de España. Política y sociedad* (Madrid, 1999), p. 215.

10. Molinero and Ysàs, *La Transición*, p. 71, note 19.

11. Javier Tusell and Genoveva G. Queipo de Llano, *Tiempo de incertidumbre: Carlos Airas Navarro entre el franquismo y la Transición (1973–1976)* (Barcelona, 2003), p. 261.

12. Molinero and Ysàs, *La Transición*, p. 74.

13. Ibid., p. 77.

14. Powell, *España en democracia*, p. 153.

15. Molinero and Ysàs, *La Transición*, p. 80.

16. Ibid.

17. Ibid., p. 83.

18. Pamela Radcliff, 'The Transition: A Global Model?', in Nigel Townson (ed.), *Is Spain Different? A Comparative Look at the 19th and 20th Centuries* (Brighton, 2015), p. 157.

19. Pamela Radcliff, *Making Democratic Citizens: Civil Society and the Popular Origins of the Transition, 1960–78* (Basingstoke, 2011), p. 262.

20. Ibid., p. 268.

21. Ibid., p. 325.

22. Molinero and Ysàs, *La Transición*, p. 85.

23. Ibid., p. 86.

24. Ibid., p. 87.

25. Tusell and Queipo de Llano, *Tiempo de incertidumbre*, p. 263.

26. Paul Preston, *The Triumph of Democracy in Spain* (London, 1986), p. 88, and Powell, *España en democracia*, p. 159.

27. Molinero and Ysàs, *La Transición*, p. 63.

28. Powell, *España en democracia*, p. 159.

29. Ibid., and Molinero and Ysàs, *La Transición*, p. 98.

30. Powell, *España en democracia*, p. 159.

31. Juliá, *Un siglo de España*, p. 219.

32. Molinero and Ysàs, *La Transición*, p. 100.

33. Powell, *España en democracia*, p. 161, and Molinero and Ysàs, *La Transición*, p. 100.

34. Powell, *España en democracia*, p. 161.

35. Ibid., p. 151.

36. Molinero and Ysàs, *La Transición*, p. 100.

37. Powell, *España en democracia*, p. 172.

38. Molinero and Ysàs, *La Transición*, p. 112.
39. Ibid.
40. Antonio Fernández García et al. (eds.), *Documentos de historia contemporánea de España* (Madrid, 1996), p. 664.
41. Ibid.
42. Powell, *España en democracia*, p. 165.
43. Molinero and Ysàs, *La Transición*, p. 112.
44. Ibid., p. 113.
45. Ibid., p. 116.
46. Powell, *España en democracia*, p. 168.
47. Ibid.
48. Molinero and Ysàs, *La Transición*, p. 114.
49. Powell, *España en democracia*, p. 173.
50. Molinero and Ysàs, *La Transición*, p. 123.
51. Ibid., p. 125.
52. Powell, *España en democracia*, p. 177.
53. Santiago Carrillo, *Memorias* (Barcelona, 1993), p. 652.
54. Ibid., p. 653.
55. Molinero and Ysàs, *La Transición*, p. 130.
56. Powell, *España en democracia*, p. 177.
57. Molinero and Ysàs, *La Transición*, p. 131.
58. Powell, *España en democracia*, pp. 179 and 180, and Molinero and Ysàs, *La Transición*, p. 131.
59. Carrillo, *Memorias*, p. 660.
60. Powell, *España en democracia*, p. 180.
61. Ibid., p. 182.
62. *Constitución española 1978* (Madrid, 1994), p. 21.
63. Powell, *España en democracia*, p. 192.
64. Molinero and Ysàs, *La Transición*, p. 141.
65. Powell, *España en democracia*, p. 192, note 64.
66. Miguel Ángel Ruiz Carnicer, 'The Blue Factor: Falangist Political Culture under the Franco Regime and the Transition to Democracy, 1962–1977', in Miguel Ángel Ruiz Carnicer (ed.), *From Franco to Freedom: The Roots of the Transition to Democracy in Spain, 1962–1982* (Brighton, 2019), p. 63.
67. Powell, *España en democracia*, p. 193.
68. Carme Molinero and Pere Ysàs, *De la hegemonía a la autodestrucción. El Partido Comunista de España (1956–1982)* (Barcelona, 2017), p. 212, and Santos Juliá, *Los socialistas en la política española, 1879–1982* (Madrid, 1997), p. 483.

69. Ibid., p. 482.
70. Powell, *España en democracia*, p. 198.
71. Juliá, *Un siglo de España*, p. 234.
72. Ibid., p. 233.
73. Molinero and Ysàs, *La Transición*, p. 153.
74. Ibid., p. 151.
75. Ibid., p. 144.
76. Powell, *España en democracia*, p. 223.
77. Ibid.
78. Ibid., p. 212.
79. Ibid.
80. Molinero and Ysàs, *La Transición*, p. 181.
81. Powell, *España en democracia*, p. 215.
82. Molinero and Ysàs, *La Transición*, p. 185.
83. *Constitución española 1978*, p. 19.
84. Molinero and Ysàs, *La Transición*, pp. 160, 185, and 161–2.
85. Ibid., p. 184.
86. Ibid., pp. 185–6.
87. Ibid., p. 186.
88. *Constitución española 1978*, p. 26.
89. Ibid., p. 25.
90. Ibid., pp. 19–20.
91. Powell, *España en democracia*, p. 228.
92. *Constitución española 1978*, pp. 33, 42, and 85.
93. Ibid., p. 22.
94. Ibid., pp. 41 and 40.
95. Radcliff, *Making Democratic Citizens*, p. 325.
96. Molinero and Ysàs, *La Transición*, p. 165.
97. Ibid., p. 178.
98. Powell, *España en democracia*, p. 201.
99. Juliá, *Un siglo de España*, p. 247.
100. Ibid.
101. Ibid.
102. Radcliff, *Making Democratic Citizens*, p. 267.
103. Ibid.
104. Ibid., p. 326.
105. Ibid.
106. *Constitución española 1978*, p. 91.
107. Molinero and Ysàs, *La Transición*, p. 239.
108. Radcliff, *Making Democratic Citizens*, p. 269.

109. Robert P. Clark, *The Basque Insurgents: ETA, 1952–1980* (Madison, WI, 1984), p. 256.
110. Ibid., p. 273.
111. Ibid., p. 133, table 5.6.
112. Powell, *España en democracia*, pp. 269–70.
113. Juliá, *Un siglo de España*, p. 249.
114. Powell, *España en democracia*, p. 286.
115. Ibid.
116. Ibid., p. 289.
117. Ibid., p. 293.
118. Molinero and Ysàs, *La Transición*, p. 209.
119. Charles Powell, *El amigo americano. España y Estados Unidos: de la dictadura a la democracia* (Barcelona, 2011), p. 561.
120. Powell, *España en democracia*, p. 305.
121. Ibid., p. 310.
122. Ibid., p. 275.
123. Ibid., p. 313.
124. Ibid., p. 320.
125. Ibid., p. 326.
126. Radcliff, 'The Transition: A Global Model?', p. 159.
127. Ibid., p. 160.
128. Neal M. Rosendorf, 'Spain's First "Re-Branding Effort" in the Postwar France Era', in Francisco Javier Rodríguez Jiménez, Lorenzo Delgado Gómez-Escalonilla, and Nicholas J. Cull (eds.), *US Public Diplomacy and Democratization in Spain: Selling Democracy?* (New York, 2015), p. 155.
129. José Álvarez Junco, 'Recuerda que eres mortal', *El País*, 9 August 2020.
130. Radcliff, 'The Transition: A Global Model?', p. 180.

CHAPTER 10

1. Santos Juliá, 'The Socialist Era, 1982–1996', in José Álvarez Junco and Adrian Shubert (eds.), *Spanish History since 1808* (London, 2000), p. 333, and Charles Powell, *España en democracia, 1975–2000* (Barcelona, 2001), p. 381.
2. Charles Powell, *El amigo americano. España y los Estados Unidos: de la dictadura a la democracia* (Barcelona, 2011), p. 590.
3. Marcelino Camacho, *Memorias. Confieso que he luchado* (Madrid, 1990), p. 477.

4. Powell, *España en democracia*, p. 353.
5. Camacho, *Memorias*, pp. 478–9.
6. Juliá, 'The Socialist Era, 1982–1996', p. 338.
7. Camacho, *Memorias*, p. 481.
8. Powell, *España en democracia*, p. 373.
9. Ibid., p. 374.
10. Pamela Radcliff, *Modern Spain: 1808 to the Present* (Malden, MA, 2017), p. 271.
11. Powell, *España en democracia*, p. 363.
12. Ibid., p. 357.
13. Powell, *El amigo americano*, p. 594.
14. Ibid., p. 605.
15. Powell, *España en democracia*, pp. 368 and 360.
16. Ibid., p. 369.
17. Powell, *El amigo americano*, p. 622.
18. Powell, *España en democracia*, pp. 417 and 422.
19. Radcliff, *Modern Spain*, p. 270.
20. Powell, *España en democracia*, p. 412.
21. Ibid., p. 456.
22. Albert Carreras and Xavier Tafunell, *Historia económica de la España contemporánea* (Barcelona, 2004), p. 405.
23. Powell, *España en democracia*, p. 426.
24. Carreras and Tafunell, *Historia económica*, p. 432.
25. Ibid.
26. Powell, *España en democracia*, p. 431.
27. Ibid., p. 433.
28. Ibid.
29. Radcliff, *Modern Spain*, p. 273.
30. Fernando Sánchez Marrayo, *La España del siglo XX. Economía, demografía y sociedad* (Madrid, 2003), p. 665.
31. Powell, *España en democracia*, p. 493.
32. Ibid., p. 494.
33. Ibid., p. 508.
34. Juliá, 'The Socialist Era, 1982–1996', p. 341.
35. Ibid.
36. Powell, *España en democracia*, p. 509.
37. Radcliff, *Modern Spain*, p. 274.
38. Juliá, 'The Socialist Era, 1982–1996', p. 340.
39. Powell, *España en democracia*, p. 514.
40. Ibid., p. 517.

41. Ibid., p. 507.

42. Paul Ginsborg, *Italy and its Discontents: Family, Civil Society, State 1980–2001* (London, 2003), p. 150.

43. Powell, *España en democracia*, pp. 552–3, n. 44.

44. Ginsborg, *Italy and its Discontents*, p. 260.

45. Powell, *España en democracia*, p. 537.

46. Ibid., p. 553.

47. Ibid., p. 550.

48. Ibid., p. 554.

49. Ibid., p. 574.

50. Miguel Martorell and Santos Juliá, *Manual de historia y social de España (1808–2011)* (Barcelona, 2012), p. 472, and Xosé M. Núñez Seixas, 'Parte I: Evolución sociopolítica', in idem. (ed.), *Historia de España. Espana en democracia, 1975–2011* (Barcelona, 2017), p. 234.

51. Radcliff, *Modern Spain*, p. 275.

52. Powell, *España en democracia*, p. 577.

53. Martorell and Juliá, *Manual de historia*, p. 482.

54. Powell, *España en democracia*, p. 588.

55. Powell, *El amigo americano*, p. 640.

56. Martorell and Juliá, *Manual de historia*, p. 461.

57. Ibid.

58. Ibid., p. 462.

59. Ibid.

60. Powell, *España en democracia*, p. 604.

61. Ibid.

62. Ibid.

63. Ibid., p. 606.

64. Ibid., p. 607.

65. Ibid., p. 609.

66. Martorell and Juliá, *Manual de historia*, p. 471.

67. Powell, *España en democracia*, p. 585, and *El amigo americano*, p. 642.

68. Radcliff, *Modern Spain*, p. 276.

69. Ibid.

70. Lina Gálvez Muñoz, 'Parte II: Economía y sociedad', in Núñez Seixas (ed.), *Historia de España. España en democracia, 1975–2011* (Barcelona, 2017). p. 484.

71. Núñez Seixas, 'Parte I: Evolución sociopolítica', pp. 313 and 315.

72. Radcliff, *Modern Spain*, p. 278.

73. Martorell and Juliá, *Manual de historia*, p. 473.

74. Gálvez Muñoz, 'Parte II: Economía y sociedad', p. 424.

75. Carlos Martínez Gorriarán, *La democracia robada. Éxito y fracaso de UPyD* (Seville, 2019), p. 107.
76. Ibid., p. 105.
77. Ibid., p. 149.
78. Ibid., p. 105.
79. ERA/ADV/2015-16, p. 4.
80. Tobias Buck, *After the Fall: Crisis, Recovery and the Making of a New Spain* (London, 2019), p. 23.
81. Ibid., pp. 24-5.
82. Ibid., p. 240.
83. *Vive Pozuelo*, no. 175, December 2019, p. 46.
84. Radcliff, *Modern Spain*, p. 266.

# Bibliography

## GENERAL WORKS

Álvarez Junco, José, *Dioses útiles. Naciones y nacionalismos* (Barcelona, 2016).

Álvarez Junco, José, *Spanish Identity in the Age of Nations* (Manchester, 2011).

Álvarez Junco, José, and Adrian Shubert (eds.), *Spanish History since 1808* (London, 2000).

Balfour, Sebastian, and Paul Preston (eds.), *Spain and the Great Powers in the Twentieth Century* (London, 1999).

Barea, Arturo, *The Forging of a Rebel* (London, 2018).

Boyd, Carolyn, *Historia Patria: Politics, History and National Identity in Spain, 1875–1975* (Princeton, NJ, 1997).

Callahan, William J., *The Catholic Church in Spain, 1875–1998* (Washington DC, 2000).

Carr, Raymond, *Spain 1808–1975* (Oxford, 1982).

Carreras, Albert, and Xavier Tafunell, *Historia económica de la España contemporánea* (Barcelona, 2004).

Casanova, Julián, and Carlos Gil Andrés, *Twentieth-Century Spain: A History* (Cambridge, 2012).

Enders, Victoria Lorée, and Pamela Beth Radcliff (eds.), *Constructing Spanish Womanhood: Female Identity in Modern Spain* (Albany, NY, 1999).

Fusi, Juan Pablo, and Jordi Palafox, *España: 1808–1996. El desafío de la modernidad* (Madrid, 1997).

Juliá, Santos, *Historias de las dos Españas* (Madrid, 2004).

Juliá, Santos, *Hoy no es ayer: Ensayos sobre la España del siglo XX* (Barcelona, 2010).

Juliá, Santos, *Los socialistas en la política española, 1879–1982* (Madrid, 1997).

Juliá, Santos (ed.), *Memoria de la guerra y del franquismo* (Madrid, 2006).

Juliá, Santos, *Un siglo de España. Política y sociedad* (Madrid, 1999).

Juliá, Santos (ed.), *Violencia política en la España del siglo XX* (Madrid, 2000).

Lannon, Frances, *Privilege, Persecution, and Prophesy: The Catholic Church in Spain, 1875–1975* (Oxford, 1987).

Lannon, Frances, and Paul Preston (eds.), *Elites and Power in Twentieth-Century Spain* (Oxford, 1990).

La Parra, Emilio, and Manuel Suárez Cortina (eds.), *El anticlericalismo español contemporáneo* (Madrid, 1998).

Martorell, Miguel, and Santos Juliá, *Manual de historia política y social de España (1808–2011)* (Barcelona, 2012).

Morales Moya, Antonio, Juan Pablo Fusi Aizpurúa, and Andrés de Blas Guerrero (eds.), *Historia de la nación y del nacionalismo español* (Barcelona, 2013).

Moreno Luzón, Javier (ed.), *Construir España: nacionalismo español y procesos de nacionalización* (Madrid, 2007).

Moreno Luzón, Javier, and Xosé M. Núñez Seixas (eds.), *Metaphors of Spain: Representations of National Identity in the Twentieth Century* (London, 2017).

Payne, Stanley G., *Fascism in Spain, 1923–1977* (Madison, WI, 1999).

Payne, Stanley G., *Spain: A Unique History* (Madison, WI, 2011).

Prados de la Escosura, Leandro, *De imperio a nación. Crecimiento y atraso económico en España (1780–1930)* (Madrid, 1988).

Preston, Paul, *The Politics of Revenge: Fascism and the Military in 20th-Century Spain* (London, 1990).

Radcliff, Pamela, *Modern Spain: 1808 to the Present* (Malden, MA, 2017).

Sánchez-Albornoz, Nicolás (ed.), *The Economic Modernization of Spain, 1830–1930* (New York, 1987).

Shubert, Adrian, *A Social History of Modern Spain* (London, 1990).

Shubert, Adrian, and José Álvarez Junco (eds.), *The History of Modern Spain: Chronologies, Themes, Individuals* (London, 2018).

Simpson, James, *Spanish Agriculture: The Long Siesta, 1765–1965* (Cambridge, 1996).

Suárez Cortina, Manuel (ed.), *Las máscaras de la libertad: el liberalismo español, 1808–1950* (Madrid, 2003).

Tortella, Gabriel, *The Development of Modern Spain: An Economic History of the Nineteenth and Twentieth Centuries* (Cambridge, MA, 2000).

Townson, Nigel (ed.), *El republicanismo en España (1830–1977)* (Madrid, 1994).

Townson, Nigel (ed.), *Historia virtual de España (1870–2004) ¿Qué hubiera pasado si . . . ?* (Madrid, 2004).

Townson, Nigel (ed.), *Is Spain Different? A Comparative Look at the 19th and 20th Centuries* (Brighton, 2015).

Vincent, Mary, *Spain 1883–2002: People and State* (Oxford, 2007).


## THE RESTORATION (1898–1923)

Álvarez Junco, José, *La ideología política del anarquismo español (1868–1910)*, 2nd ed. (Madrid, 1991).

Álvarez Junco, José, *The Emergence of Mass Politics in Spain: Populist Demagoguery and Republican Culture, 1890–1910* (Brighton, 1990).

Balfour, Sebastian, *The End of the Spanish Empire, 1898–1923* (Oxford, 1997).

Bascuñan Añover, Óscar, *Protesta y supervivencia. Movilización y desorden en una sociedad rural: Castilla-La Mancha, 1875–1923* (Valencia, 2008).

Ben-Ami, Shlomo, *The Origins of the Second Republic in Spain* (Oxford, 1978).

Boyd, Carolyn, *Praetorian Politics in Liberal Spain* (Chapel Hill, NC, 1979).

Cabrera, Mercedes (ed.), *Con luz y taquígrafos. El Parlamento en la Restauración (1913–1923)* (Madrid, 1998).

Cambó, Francisco, *Memorias (1876–1936)* (Madrid, 1987).

Culla i Clara, Joan, *El republicanisme lerrouxista a Catalunya (1901–1923)* (Barcelona, 1986).

Del Moral Vargas, Marta, *Acción colectiva femenina en Madrid (1909–1931)* (Santiago de Compostela, 2012).

Del Rey Reguillo, Fernando, *Propietarios y patronos. La política de las organizaciones económicas en la España de la Restauración (1914–1923)* (Madrid, 1992).

Díaz del Moral, Juan, *Historia de las agitaciones campesinas andaluzas* (Madrid, 1995).

Forner Muñoz, Salvador, *Canalejas y el Partido Liberal Democrático (1900–1910)* (Madrid, 1993).

González Hernández, María Jesús, *Ciudadanía y acción. El conservadurismo maurista, 1907–1923* (Madrid, 1990).

Herrerín López, Ángel, *Anarquía, dinamita y revolución social. Violencia y represión en la España de entre siglos (1868–1909)* (Madrid, 2011).

Lacomba, Juan Antonio, *La crisis española de 1917* (Madrid, 1970).

Louzao Villar, Joseba, *Soldados de la fe o amantes del progreso. Catolicismo y modernidad en Vizcaya (1890–1923)* (Madrid, 2011).

Meaker, Gerald H., *The Revolutionary Left in Spain, 1914–1923* (Stanford, CA, 1974).

Moreno Luzón, Javier, *Modernizing the Nation: Spain during the Reign of Alfonso XIII, 1902–1931* (Brighton, 2012).

Moreno Luzón, Javier, *Romanones. Caciquismo y política liberal* (Madrid, 1998).

Pabón, Jesús, *Cambó*, 3 vols. (Barcelona, 1952 and 1969).

Radcliff, Pamela, *From Mobilization to Civil War: The Politics of Polarization in the Spanish City of Gijón, 1900–1937* (Cambridge, 1996).

Reig, Ramiro, *Blasquistas y clericales. La lucha por la ciudad en la Valencia de 1900* (Valencia, 1986).

Romero Maura, Joaquín, *'La Rosa de Fuego'. El obrerismo barcelonés de 1899 a 1909* (Barcelona, 1975).

Romero Salvadó, Francisco, *Spain 1914–18: Between War and Revolution* (London, 1999).

Romero Salvadó, Francisco, and Ángel Smith (eds.), *The Agony of Spanish Liberalism: From Revolution to Dictatorship, 1913–1923* (Basingstoke, 2010).

Suárez Cortina, Manuel, *El gorro frigio. Liberalismo, Democracia y Republicanismo en la Restauración* (Madrid, 2000).

Suárez Cortina, Manuel, *El reformismo en España* (Madrid, 1986).

Suárez Cortina, Manuel (ed.), *La Restauración entre el liberalismo y la democracia* (Madrid, 1997).

Tone, John L., *War and Genocide in Cuba, 1895–1898* (Chapel Hill, NC, 2006).

Winston, Colin, *The Workers and the Right in Spain, 1900–1936* (Princeton, NJ, 1985).

## THE PRIMO DE RIVERA DICTATORSHIP (1923–1930)

Andrés Gallego, José, *El socialismo durante la Dictadura, 1923–1930* (Madrid, 1977).

Balfour, Sebastian, *Deadly Embrace: Morocco and the Road to the Spanish Civil War* (Oxford, 2002).

Ben-Ami, Shlomo, *Fascism from Above: The Dictatorship of Primo de Rivera in Spain, 1923–1930* (Oxford, 1983).

Calvo Sotelo, José, *Mis servicios al estado. Seis años de gestión. Apuntes para la historia* (Madrid, 1931).

García Queipo de Llano, Genoveva, *Los intelectuales y la dictadura de Primo de Rivera* (Madrid, 1988).

Gómez-Navarro, José Luis, *El régimen de Primo de Rivera. Reyes, dictaduras y dictadores* (Madrid, 1991).

González Calbet, Teresa, *La Dictadura de Primo de Rivera. El Directorio Militar* (Madrid, 1987).

González Calleja, Eduardo, *La España de Primo de Rivera. La modernización autoritaria, 1923–1930* (Madrid, 2005).

Quiroga, Alejandro, *Making Spaniards: Primo de Rivera and the Nationalization of the Masses, 1923–1930* (Basingstoke, 2007).

Tusell, Javier, *La crisis del caciquismo andaluz (1923–1931)* (Madrid, 1977).

## THE SECOND REPUBLIC (1931–36)

Alcalá-Zamora, Niceto, *Memorias (Segundo texto de mis memorias)* (Barcelona, 1977).

Álvarez Tardío, Manuel, *Anticlericalismo y libertad de conciencia: Política y religión en la Segunda República Española (1931–1936)* (Madrid, 2002).

Álvarez Tardío, Manuel, and Fernando del Rey Reguillo (eds.), *The Spanish Second Republic Revisited: From Democratic Hopes to Civil War (1931–1936)* (Brighton, 2012).

Azaña, Manuel, *Obras completas*, 7 vols., Santos Juliá (ed.) (Madrid, 2007).

Blinkhorn, Martin, *Carlism and Crisis in Spain (1931–1939)* (Cambridge, 1975).

Blinkhorn, Martin (ed.), *Spain in Conflict, 1931–1939: Democracy and Its Enemies* (London, 1986).

Brenan, Gerald, *The Spanish Labyrinth: An Account of the Social and Political Background of the Spanish Civil War* (Cambridge, 1950).

Cabrera, Mercedes, *La patronal ante la II República: organizaciones y estrategia (1931–1936)* (Madrid, 1983).

Casanova, Julián, *Anarchism, the Republic and Civil War in Spain, 1931–1939* (London, 2004).

Cruz, Rafael, *El Partido Comunista de España en la Segunda República* (Madrid, 1987).

Cruz, Rafael, *En el nombre del pueblo. República, rebelión y guerra en la España de 1936* (Madrid, 2006).

De la Cueva, Julio, and Feliciano Montero (eds.), *Laicismo y Catolicismo: El conflicto político-religioso en la Segunda República* (Alcalá de Henares, 2009).

Del Rey, Fernando, *Paisanos en lucha. Exclusión política y violencia en la Segunda República española* (Madrid, 2008).

Del Rey Reguillo, Fernando (ed.), *Palabras como puños. La intransigencia política en la Segunda República Española* (Madrid, 2011).

Fusi, Juan Pablo, *El problema vasco en la II República* (Madrid, 1979).

Gil Pecharromán, Julio, *La Segunda República española (1931–1936)* (Madrid, 1995).

Gil Robles, José María, *No fue posible la paz* (Barcelona, 1968).

González Calleja, Eduardo, *Contrarrevolucionarios. Radicalización violenta de las derechas durante la Segunda República, 1931–1936* (Madrid, 2011).

González Calleja, Eduardo, *En nombre de la autoridad: la defensa del orden público durante la Segunda República española, 1931–1936* (Granada, 2014).

Herrerín, Ángel, *The Road to Anarchy: The CNT under the Spanish Second Republic (1931–1936)* (Brighton, 2020).

Holguín, Sandie, *Creating Spaniards: Culture and National Identity in Republican Spain* (Madison, WI, 2002).

Juliá, Santos, *Historia del socialismo español (1931–1939)* (Barcelona, 1989).

Juliá, Santos, *Madrid, 1931–1934. De la fiesta popular a la lucha de clases* (Madrid, 1984).

Juliá, Santos, *Vida y tiempo de Manuel Azaña (1880–1940)* (Madrid, 2008).

Lerroux, Alejandro, *La pequeña historia* (Madrid, 1963).

Macarro Vera, José Manuel, *Socialismo, República y revolución en Andalucía (1931–1936)* (Seville, 2000).

Malefakis, Edward E., *Agrarian Reform and Peasant Revolution in Spain: Origins of the Civil War* (New Haven, CT, 1970).

Martínez Barrio, Diego, *Memorias* (Barcelona, 1983).

Maura, Miguel, *Así cayó Alfonso XIII: De una dictadura a otra*, Joaquín Romero Maura (ed.) (Madrid, 2007).

Mintz, Jerome R., *The Anarchists of Casas Viejas* (Chicago, IL, 1982).

Montero, José Ramón, *La CEDA: el catolicismo social y político en la II República*, 2 vols. (Madrid 1977).

Payne, Stanley G., *Alcalá Zamora and the Failure of the Spanish Republic, 1931–1936* (Brighton, 2017).

Payne, Stanley G., *Spain's First Democracy: The Second Republic, 1931–1936* (Madison, WI, 1993).

Preston, Paul (ed.), *Revolution and War in Spain, 1931–1939* (London, 1984).

Preston, Paul, *The Coming of the Spanish Civil War: Reform, Reaction and Revolution in the Second Republic*, 2nd ed. (London, 1994).

Ranzato, Gabriele, *El eclipse de la democracia. La Guerra Civil española y sus orígenes, 1931–1939* (Madrid, 2006).

Seidman, Michael, *Workers against Work: Labor in Paris and Barcelona during the Popular Fronts* (Berkeley, CA, 1991).

Shubert, Adrian, *The Road to Revolution: The Coal Miners of Asturias, 1860–1934* (Urbana and Chicago, IL, 1987).

Simpson, James, and Juan Carmona, *Why Democracy Failed: The Agrarian Origins of the Spanish Civil War* (Cambridge, 2020).

Townson, Nigel, *The Crisis of Democracy in Spain: Centrist Politics under the Second Republic, 1931–1936* (Brighton, 2000).

Varela, Santiago, *Partidos y parlamento en la II República española* (Barcelona, 1978).

Vincent, Mary, *Catholicism in the Second Spanish Republic: Religion and Politics in Salamanca, 1930–1936* (Oxford, 1996).

## THE CIVIL WAR (1936–39)

Anderson, Peter, *Friend or Foe? Occupation, Collaboration and Selective Violence in the Spanish Civil War* (Brighton, 2016).

Beevor, Anthony, *The Battle for Spain: The Spanish Civil War, 1936–1939* (London, 2006).

Bolloten, Burnett, *The Spanish Civil War: Revolution and Counterrevolution* (Chapel Hill, NC, 2015).

Buchanan, Tom, *Britain and the Spanish Civil War* (Cambridge, 1997).

Buchanan, Tom, *The Impact of the Spanish Civil War on Britain: War, Loss and Memory* (Brighton, 2007).

Campoamor, Clara, *La revolución española vista por una republicana* (Seville, 2005).

Casanova, Julián, *The Spanish Republic and Civil War* (Cambridge, 2010).

Del Rey, Fernando, *Retaguardia roja. Violencia y revolución en la guerra civil española* (Barcelona, 2019).

Esdaile, Charles J., *The Spanish Civil War: A Military History* (Abingdon, Oxon., 2019).

Fraser, Ronald, *Blood of Spain: The Experience of Civil War, 1936–1939* (London, 1981).

Graham, Helen, *The Spanish Republic at War, 1936–1939* (Cambridge, 2002).

Hernández, Fernando, *Guerra o revolución. El Partido Comunista de España en la guerra civil* (Barcelona, 2010).

Howson, Gerald, *Arms for Spain: The Untold Story of the Spanish Civil War* (London, 1998).

Jackson, Gabriel, *Juan Negrín: Physiologist, Socialist and Spanish Republican War Leader* (Brighton, 2010).

Jackson, Gabriel, *The Spanish Republic and the Civil War* (Princeton, NJ, 1965).

Juliá, Santos (ed.), *Víctimas de la guerra civil* (Madrid, 1999).

Kowalsky, Daniel, *Stalin and the Spanish Civil War* (New York, 2008).

Malefakis, Edward E. (ed.), *La guerra civil española* (Madrid, 2006).

Matthews, James, *Reluctant Warriors: Republican Popular Army and Nationalist Army Conscripts in the Spanish Civil War, 1936–1939* (Oxford, 2012).

Moradiellos, Enrique, *El reñidero de Europa. Las dimensiones internacionales de la guerra civil española* (Barcelona, 2001).

Moradiellos, Enrique, *Negrín. Una biografía de la figura más difamada de la España del siglo XX* (Madrid, 2006).

Núñez Seixas, Xosé M., *¡Fuera el invasor! Nacionalismos y movilización bélica durante la guerra civil española (1936–1939)* (Madrid, 2006).

Ojeda Revah, Mario, *Mexico and the Spanish Civil War: Political Repercussions for the Republican Cause* (Brighton, 2016).

Orwell, George, *Homage to Catalonia* (London, 1959).

Payne, Stanley G., *The Spanish Civil War* (New York, 2012).

Preston, Paul, *The Last Stalinist: The Life of Santiago Carrillo* (London, 2014).

Preston, Paul, *The Spanish Civil War, 1936–39* (London, 1990).

Preston, Paul, *The Spanish Holocaust: Inquisition and Extermination in Twentieth-Century Spain* (London, 2012).

Raguer, Hilari, *Gunpowder and Incense: The Catholic Church and the Spanish Civil War* (London, 2006).

Ruiz, Julius, *'Paracuellos': The Elimination of the 'Fifth Column' in Republican Madrid during the Spanish Civil War* (Brighton, 2017).

Ruiz, Julius, *The 'Red Terror' and the Spanish Civil War* (Cambridge, 2014).

Seidman, Michael, *Republic of Egos: A Social History of the Spanish Civil War* (Madison, WI, 2002).

Seidman, Michael, *The Victorious Counterrevolution: The Nationalist Effort in the Spanish Civil War* (Madison, WI, 2011).

Seidman, Michael, *Transatlantic Antifascisms: From the Spanish Civil War to the End of World War II* (Cambridge, 2018).

Thomas, Hugh, *The Spanish Civil War*, 4th ed. (London, 2012).

Tremlett, Giles, *The International Brigades: Fascism, Freedom and the Spanish Civil* War (London, 2020).

Tusell, Javier, *Franco en la guerra civil. Una biografía política* (Barcelona, 1992).

## THE FRANCO YEARS (1939–75)

Balfour, Sebastian, *Dictatorship, Workers and the City: Labour in Greater Barcelona since 1939* (Oxford, 1989).

Borras, José, *Políticas de los exiliados españoles, 1944–1950* (Paris, 1976).

Brenan, Gerald, *The Face of Spain* (London, 1987).

Buchanan, Tom, *Europe's Troubled Peace, 1945–2000* (Oxford, 2006).

Camacho, Marcelino, *Memorias. Confieso que he luchado* (Madrid, 1990).

Carrero Blanco, Luis, *Discursos y escritos, 1943–1973* (Madrid, 1974).

Cazorla Sánchez, Antonio, *Fear and Progress: Ordinary Lives in Franco's Spain, 1939–1975* (Oxford, 2010).

Cazorla Sánchez, Antonio, *Franco: The Biography of a Myth* (London, 2014).

Cazorla Sánchez, Antonio, *Las políticas de la victoria: la consolidación del nuevo estado franquista, 1938–1953* (Madrid, 2000).

Chuliá, Elisa, *El poder y la palabra. Prensa y poder político en las dictaduras. El régimen de Franco ante la prensa y el periodismo* (Madrid, 2001).

Clark, Robert P., *The Basque Insurgents: ETA, 1952–1980* (Madison, WI, 1984).

Domínguez Arribas, Javier, *El enemigo judeo-masónico en la propaganda franquista (1936–1945)* (Madrid, 2009).

Dowling, Andrew, *Catalonia since the Spanish Civil War: Reconstructing the Nation* (Brighton, 2013).

Fontana, Josep (ed.), *España bajo el franquismo* (Barcelona, 2000).

Franco Salgado-Araujo, Francisco, *Mis conversaciones privadas con Franco* (Barcelona, 1976).

Fusi, Juan Pablo, *Franco: A Biography* (London, 1987).

García Delgado, José Luis (ed.), *Franquismo: el juicio de la historia* (Madrid, 2000).

Gildea, Robert, James Mark, and Anette Warring (eds.), *Europe's 1968: Voices of Revolt* (Oxford, 2013).

Gillespie, Richard, *The Spanish Socialist Party* (Oxford, 1989).

Gómez del Moral, Alejandro J., *Buying into Change: Mass Consumption, Dictatorship and Democratization in Franco's Spain, 1939–1982* (Lincoln, NE, 2021).

Gracia, Jordi, and Miguel Ángel Ruiz Carnicer, *La España de Franco (1939–1975). Cultura y vida cotidiana* (Madrid, 2001).

Groves, Tamar, Nigel Townson, Inbal Ofer, and Antonio Herrera, *Social Movements and the Spanish Transition: Building Citizenship in Parishes, Neighbourhoods, Schools and the Countryside* (Cham, Switzerland, 2017).

Grugel, Jean, and Tim Rees, *Franco's Spain* (London, 1997).

Guirao, Fernando, *Spain and the Reconstruction of Western Europe, 1945–57* (Basingstoke, 1998).

Hayes, Carlton J. H., *Wartime Mission in Spain, 1942–1945* (New York, 1945).

Heine, Harmut, *La oposición política al franquismo. De 1939 a 1952* (Barcelona, 1983)

Hermet, Guy, *Los católicos en la España franquista*, 2 vols. (Madrid, 1985 and 1986).

Hernández Sandoica, Elena, Miguel Ángel Ruiz Carnicer, and Marc Baldó Lacomba, *Estudiantes contra Franco (1939–1975). Oposición política y movilización juvenil* (Madrid, 2007).

Herrerín López, Ángel, *La CNT durante el franquismo. Clandestinidad y exilio (1939–1975)* (Madrid, 2004).

Hoare, Sir Samuel, *Ambassador on Special Mission* (London, 1946).

Jensen, Geoffrey, *Franco: Soldier, Commander, Dictator* (Washington DC, 2005).

López Rodó, Laureano, *La larga marcha hacia la Monarquía* (Barcelona, 1977).

Lowe, Keith, *Savage Continent: Europe in the Aftermath of World War II* (London, 2013).

Maravall, José María, *Dictatorship and Political Dissent: Workers and Students in Franco's Spain* (London, 1978).

Molinero, Carme, and Pere Ysàs, *De la hegemonía a la autodestrucción. El Partido Comunista de España (1956–1982)* (Barcelona, 2017).

Molinero, Carme, and Pere Ysàs, *La anatomía del franquismo. De la supervivencia a la agonía, 1945–1977* (Barcelona, 2008).

Molinero, Carme, and Pere Ysàs, *Productores disciplinados y minorías subversivas. Clase obrera y conflictividad laboral en la España franquista* (Madrid, 1998).

Moradiellos, Enrique, *La España de Franco (1939–1975): Política y sociedad* (Madrid, 2000).

Morcillo, Aurora, *True Catholic Womanhood: Gender Ideology in Franco's Spain* (DeKalb, IL, 2000).

Nielfa Cristóbal, Gloria (ed.), *Mujeres y hombres en la España franquista: sociedad, economía, política y cultura* (Madrid, 2003).

Ofer, Inbal, *Señoritas in Blue: The Making of a Female Political Elite in Franco's Spain* (Brighton, 2009).

Pack, Sasha D., *Tourism and Dictatorship: Europe's Peaceful Invasion of Franco's Spain* (New York, 2006).

Payne, Stanley G., *The Franco Regime, 1936–1975* (London, 2000).

Payne, Stanley G., and Jesús Palacios, *Franco: A Personal and Political Biography* (Madison, WI, 2014).

Preston, Paul, *Franco: A Biography* (London, 1993).

Radcliff, Pamela, *Making Democratic Citizens: Civil Society and the Popular Origins of the Transition, 1960–78* (Basingstoke, 2011).

Richards, Michael, *A Time of Silence: Civil War and the Culture of Repression in Franco's Spain, 1936–1945* (Cambridge, 1998).

Rosendorf, Neil, *Franco Sells Spain to America: Hollywood, Tourism and Public Relations as Postwar Spanish Soft Power* (Basingstoke, 2014).

Ruiz, Julius, *Franco's Justice: Repression in Madrid after the Spanish Civil War* (Oxford, 2005).

Sánchez Cervelló, Josep, *La Segunda República en el exilio (1939–1977)* (Barcelona, 2011).

Serrano Suñer, Ramón, *Entre el silencio y la propaganda, la Historia como fue: Memorias* (Barcelona, 1977).

Townson, Nigel (ed.), *Spain Transformed: The Late Franco Dictatorship, 1959–75* (Basingstoke, 2010).

Treglown, Jeremy, *Franco's Crypt: Spanish Culture and Memory since 1936* (London, 2013).

Tusell, Javier, *Franco y los católicos. La política interior española entre 1945 y 1957* (Madrid, 1984).

Valencia-García, Louie Dean, *Anti-Authoritarian Youth Culture in Francoist Spain: Clashing with Fascism* (London, 2018).

Ysàs, Pere, *Disidencia y subversión. La lucha del régimen franquista por su supervivencia, 1960–1975* (Barcelona, 2004).

## THE TRANSITION

Aguilar, Paloma, *Memoria y olvido de la guerra civil española* (Madrid, 1996).

Barahona de Brito, Alexandra, Carmen González-Enríquez, and Paloma Aguilar (eds.), *The Politics of Memory: Transitional Justice in Democratizing Societies* (Oxford, 2001).

Blanco Valdés, Roberto L., *La Constitución de 1978* (Madrid, 2003).

Carr, Raymond, and Juan Pablo Fusi, *Spain: Dictatorship to Democracy*, 2nd ed. (London, 1981).

Carrillo, Santiago, *Memorias* (Barcelona, 1993).

Foweraker, Joseph, *Making Democracy in Spain: Grass-Roots Struggle in the South, 1955–1975* (Cambridge, 1989).

Gilmour, David, *The Transformation of Spain: From Franco to the Constitutional Monarchy* (London, 1985).

Hopkin, Jonathan, *Party Formation and Democratic Transition in Spain: The Creation and Collapse of the Union of the Democratic Centre* (Basingstoke, 1999).

Juliá, Santos, *Transición. Historia de una política española (1937–2017)* (Barcelona, 2017).

Molinero, Carme, and Pere Ysàs, *De la hegemonía a la autodestrucción. El Partido Comunista de España (1956–1982)* (Barcelona, 2017).

Molinero, Carme, and Pere Ysàs, *La Transición. Historia y relatos* (Madrid, 2018).

Pérez Díaz, Víctor, *The Return of Civil Society: The Emergence of Democratic Spain* (Cambridge, MA, 1993).

Powell, Charles, *El amigo americano. España y los Estados Unidos: de la dictadura a la democracia* (Barcelona, 2011).

Powell, Charles, *Juan Carlos of Spain: Self-Made Monarch* (London, 1996).

Preston, Paul, *Juan Carlos: A People's King* (London, 2004).

Preston, Paul, *The Triumph of Democracy in Spain* (London, 1986).

Quirosa-Cheyrouze y Muñoz, Rafael (ed.), *Historia de la Transición en España: los inicios del proceso democratizador* (Madrid, 2007).

Sartorius, Nicolás, and Alberto Sabio, *El final de la dictadura: la conquista de la democracia en España* (Madrid, 2007).

Suárez, Adolfo, *Fue posible la concordia* (Madrid, 1996).

Tusell, Javier, and Álvaro Soto (eds.), *Historia de la Transición, 1975–1986* (Madrid, 1996).

## DEMOCRACY

Alonso, Gregorio, and Diego Muro (eds.), *The Politics and Memory of Democratic Transition: The Spanish Model* (London, 2011).

Aznar, José María, *Ocho años de gobierno. Una visión personal de España* (Barcelona, 2004).

Balfour, Sebastián (ed.), *The Politics of Contemporary Spain* (London, 2005).

Bernecker, Walter L., and Günther Maihold (eds.), *España: del consenso a la polarización. Cambios en la democracia española* (Madrid, 2007).

Buck, Tobias, *After the Fall: Crisis, Recovery and the Making of a New Spain* (London, 2019).

Burns Marañón, Tom, *Conversaciones sobre el socialismo* (Barcelona, 1996).

Closa, Carlos (ed.), *La europeización del sistema político español* (Madrid, 2001).

González, Juan Jesús, and Miguel Requena (eds.), *Tres décadas de cambio social en España* (Madrid, 2005).

Gunther, Richard, José Ramón Montero, and Joan Botella, *Democracy in Modern Spain* (New Haven, CT, 2004).

Heywood, Paul, *The Government and Politics of Spain* (London, 1995).

Iglesias, María Antonia, *La memoria recuperada. Lo que nunca han contado Felipe González y los dirigentes socialistas* (Madrid, 2003).

Magone, José María, *Contemporary Spanish Politics*, 3rd ed. (London, 2018).

Martínez Gorriarán, Carlos, *La democracia robada. Éxito y fracaso de UPyD* (Seville, 2019).

Morata, Francesc, and Gemma Mateo (eds.), *España en Europa, Europa en España, 1986–2006* (Barcelona, 2007).

Núñez Seixas, Xosé M. (ed.), *Historia de España. España en democracia, 1975–2011* (Barcelona, 2017).

Powell, Charles, *España en democracia, 1975–2000* (Barcelona, 2001).

Royo, Sebastián, *From Social Democracy to Neoliberalism: The Consequences of Party Hegemony in Spain, 1982–1996* (London, 2000).

Threlfall, Monica, Christine Cousins, and Celia Valiente (eds.), *Gendering Spanish Democracy* (London, 2005).

Tremlett, Giles, *Ghosts of Spain: Travels through Spain and its Silent Past* (New York, 2006).

Tusell, Javier (ed.), *El gobierno de Aznar. Balance de una gestión, 1996–2000* (Barcelona, 2001).

# Index

Page references in *italics* indicate images.

521

65–6, 73–6; draft constitution
(1929) and 111; exile xviii, 113;
First World War and 56, 63, 64;
'Hispanism' and 94; Italy visit
(1923) 91–2, 94, 95; juntas and
65–6, 73, 74–5; National
Government formation (1918)
and 74–5, 75; National Assembly
and 102, 103; pacification of
Moroccan Protectorate and 100;
political meddling 40–41, 43, 51,
397; Primo de Rivera dictatorship
and xviii, 88, 89, 91–2, 93, 94–5,
100, 102, 103, 110, 111, 112,
113; revolutionary strike (1917)
and 69; Sacred Heart of Jesus,
dedication of Spain to 87; Tragic
Week and 47; Vatican address
(1923) 94, 95
Algeciras Conference (1906) 46
Algeria 15, 311, 324, 343, 347, 348,
353, 431
Al Hoceima Bay landing (5
September 1925) 101–2
*Alianza Nacional de Fuerzas
Democráticas* (ANFD) (National
Alliance of Democratic Forces)
288–9, 296
*Alianza Popular* (AP) (Popular
Alliance) 377–8, 382, 385, 386–7,
388, 391, 393, 398–9, 400, 401,
406, 412, 413, 414, 417, 421,
425, 430, 432, 436, 440
*Alianzas Obreras* (Workers'
Alliances) 171
Almería *xiii*, 60–61, 178, 311, 316,
336, 406
Alonso Vega, General Camilo 326,
330, 360
Al Qaeda 447, 448

Altamira, Rafael 55
Álvarez, Basilio 175, 176
Álvarez, Consuelo 20
Álvarez del Vayo, Julio 347
Álvarez Junco, José 351
Álvarez, Melquíades 33, 56, 66–7,
70, 209, 213
Álvarez Valdés, Ramón 213
*AMA* 309
Amedo, José 432, 438
American Civil War (1861–5) 269
American Red Cross 264
*¡A mi la Legion!* (film) 278
amnesties, political xx, 159, 165,
183, 184, 190, 246, 290, 297,
366–8, 374–5, 379, 381, 384,
389–91
Amnesty International xx, 354
Amnesty Law (1934) 165
anarcho-syndicalist movement;
*Alianzas Obreras* (Workers'
Alliances), origins of and 171;
*blasquistas* backing of 17;
Bolshevik Triennium launched by
77–8; Canalejas assassination and
50–51; CEDA entry into
government (1934), reaction to
169; Civil War and 209, 210, 211,
220, 235, 237–8; CNT and *see
Confederación Nacional del
Trabajo* (CNT) (National
Confederation of Labour);
destruction of state 207–8;
entryism and 330–31; Fígols
miners' strike (1932) and 138;
First World War and 55; Francoist
opposition and 295–6; general
election (1933) and 183; general
election (1936) and 388; general
election (1977) and 183, 388;

INDEX

37–8; urban working class and 30–32

regional nationalists. *See individual region name*

Reig, Joan 209

Reina Sofia Art Centre (Madrid) 430

RENFE 266

*Renovación* 174

*Renovación Española* (Spanish Renovation) 143

Repression of Terrorism bill (1908) 45

Republican Action 124, 125–6, 127, 129, 130–31, 169

Republican Left 169, 183, 192

Republican Left of Catalonia 129, 232, 388, 451

republicans: Alfonso XIII assassination attempts and 21–2; anti-Francoist opposition and 293–8; *antisolidarios* (enemies of Solidarity) 43; Black Legend and xx; *blasquismo* 15–18; Civil War and *see* Civil War; 'Disaster' (1898) and 10–12; elections and *see* elections; First World War and 55–6, 62, 63–4; government-in-exile and 293–4, 297; Left-wing Bloc 45; *lerrouxistas*, Barcelona 18–23, 24; Primo de Rivera dictatorship and 90, 110, 113; repression of, post-Civil War 267–72; Republican-Socialist Conjunction 47–8; resurgence of, post-Civil War 287–90, 293; revolutionary strike (1917) and 70, 72, 74; Second Republic and *see* Second Republic; *solidarios* (supporters of Solidarity) 43;

strikes and *see* strikes; Valencia and 14–18. *See individual party and group name*

Republican-Socialist Conjunction 47–8

Republican Union 23, 43, 183, 195

Requena, Pedro 339

research and development 319, 431

Restoration (1875–1923) xviii, 1–89; Alfonso XIII assassination attempts and plan to overthrow 21–2; *caciquismo*/vote-rigging and 6–7, 32–3, 39, 43, 44–5, 52, 86; Catalan regionalism and 29; *¡Cu-Cut!* incident (1905) 41–2; founding of 11; governments divorced from public opinion 12, 13; mobilization of masses and decline of 14; political system 5–7, 38–41, 52; Primo de Rivera coup overthrows 88–9, 90, 91, 93; Regenerationism reveals limits to 52; revolutionary strike (1917) and 69–77; Second Republic and 114, 115, 121, 125, 126–7, 128, 129, 130, 146–7, 181; 'Tragic Week' and 83–4

Retamares, Madrid, NATO centre at 444, 448

revolutionary committees 70, 204, 211, 213, 220

Revolutionary Federation 23

revolutionary general strike (1917) 69–77

Rico Avello, Manuel 152, 209, 213

Ridruejo, Dionisio 255

Riego, Colonel Rafael del 6

Río, Cirilo del 270

Ríos, Fernando de los 96

Rio Tinto 9

strikes – *cont'd*.

Fígols miners' strike 138, 144;
(1933) mass mobilization 148–9;
(1933–4) Madrid strikes, Radical
response to 149; (1934) 'abusive
strike' decree 173–4; (1934)
Basque Country 167–8; (1934)
FNTT agrarian 166–7, 171, 207;
(1934) general 169–75, *171*;
(1934) *Generalitat* 167; (1936)
increase in 185–6, 189, 190;
(1946) Barcelona textile industry
295; (1947) metalworkers in
Basque Country 295; (1951)
Barcelona general strike 295;
(1962) Asturias coalfield 328–9,
341; (1971) SEAT strike 334;
(1974) Baix Llobregat general
strike 335; (1975) decree 334;
(1976) general strike 375–6;
(1976) Vitoria industrial clash
367, 368; (1985) general strike
420; (1988) general strike 429,
435; (2010) general strike 455;
Francoist labour policy collapse
and 333–4; legislation *see*
*individual law name*; Moncloa
Pacts and 392; women within
ACE and 341; worker-priests
and 340

students 110, 258, 292, 336–7,
338, 343, 353, 357, 361, 381;
numbers of increase 452;
rebellion (1956) 301–6; revolt
(1960s) 324–7, 328, 353;
student unions 255, 302, 326–7,
337, 338

Suanzes, General Juan Antonio 265

Suárez, Adolfo 372–5, 376, 377–80,
381–3, 385, 386, 387, 389, 390,

391–2, 393, 394, 396, 400,
403–7, 409, 412, 414, 417, 426

Superior Junta of the Infantry 66, 68

*Superman* 351–2

supermarkets 309, 318, 431

Supreme Council of Military
Justice 381

Supreme Court 405, 409, 438, 450

Supreme Court of the Treasury 99

Syndical Law: (1971) 334, 360;
(1977) 384

Syndical Organization 372, 384, 385

Syndicalist Party 182

syndicates 327; elections (1966)
358–9; state 331, 332, 335, 337,
372, 384, 385; vertical 256, 274,
281, 282, 292, 295–6, 330, 337

syphilis 264

*Tabacalera* 442

Taboada, Juana 21

Tamames, Ramón 371, 425

Tangiers 56–7, 102, 284, 285, 287

Tarradellas, Josep 394

tax: Alba bill of 'national
reconstruction' (1916) and 61;
*blasquistas* and 18; *cacique* and 7;
Chambers of Commerce and 12,
13; Civil War and 226, 235, 237,
250; consumer tax 34, 50; income
tax 105, 117, 262, 318, 442; Law
for the Development of Industry
and 44; Popular Party and 442,
443; Primo de Rivera dictatorship
and 99–100, 105, 117; PSOE and
418, 437–8; riots 32, 34; Second
Republic and 117, 141, 226, 235,
237, 250; shipping tax 99; tax
collector assaults 33; tax strike,
Barcelona (1899) 13

ALLEN LANE
*an imprint of*
PENGUIN BOOKS

# Also Published

Scott Shapiro, *Fancy Bear Goes Phishing: The Dark History of the Information Age, in Five Extraordinary Hacks*

Elizabeth-Jane Burnett, *Twelve Words for Moss*

Serhii Plokhy, *The Russo-Ukranian War*

Martin Daunton, *The Economic Government of the World: 1933-2023*

Martyn Rady, *The Middle Kingdoms: A New History of Central Europe*

Michio Kaku, *Quantum Supremacy: How Quantum Computers will Unlock the Mysteries of Science – And Address Humanity's Biggest Challenges*

Andy Clark, *The Experience Machine: How Our Minds Predict and Shape Reality*

Monica Potts, *The Forgotten Girls: An American Story*

Christopher Clark, *Revolutionary Spring: Fighting for a New World 1848-1849*

Daniel Chandler, *Free and Equal: What Would a Fair Society Look Like?*

Jonathan Rosen, *Best Minds: A Story of Friendship, Madness, and the Tragedy of Good Intentions*

Nigel Townson, *The Penguin History of Modern Spain: 1898 to the Present*

Katja Hoyer, *Beyond the Wall: East Germany, 1949-1990*

Quinn Slobodian, *Crack-Up Capitalism: Market Radicals and the Dream of a World Without Democracy*

Clare Carlisle, *The Marriage Question: George Eliot's Double Life*

Matthew Desmond, *Poverty, by America*

Sara Ahmed, *The Feminist Killjoy Handbook*

Bernard Wasserstein, *A Small Town in Ukraine: The place we came from, the place we went back to*

Mariana Mazzucato and Rosie Collington, *The Big Con: How the Consultancy Industry Weakens our Businesses, Infantilizes our Governments and Warps our Economies*

Carlo Rovelli, *Anaximander: And the Nature of Science*

Bernie Sanders, *It's OK To Be Angry About Capitalism*

Martin Wolf, *The Crisis of Democractic Capitalism*

David Graeber, *Pirate Enlightenment, or the Real Libertalia*

Leonard Susskind and Andre Cabannes, *General Relativity: The Theoretical Minimum*

Dacher Keltner, *Awe: The Transformative Power of Everyday Wonder*

William D. Cohan, *Power Failure: The Rise and Fall of General Electric*

John Barton, *The Word: On the Translation of the Bible*

Ryan Gingeras, *The Last Days of the Ottoman Empire*

Greta Thunberg, *The Climate Book*

Peter Heather, *Christendom: The Triumph of a Religion*

Christopher de Hamel, *The Posthumous Papers of the Manuscripts Club*

Ha-Joon Chang, *Edible Economics: A Hungry Economist Explains the World*

Anand Giridharadas, *The Persuaders: Winning Hearts and Minds in a Divided Age*

Nicola Rollock, *The Racial Code: Tales of Resistance and Survival*

Peter H. Wilson, *Iron and Blood: A Military History of German-speaking Peoples since 1500*

Ian Kershaw, *Personality and Power: Builders and Destroyers of Modern Europe*

Alison Bashford, *An Intimate History of Evolution: The Story of the Huxley Family*

Lawrence Freedman, *Command: The Politics of Military Operations from Korea to Ukraine*

Richard Niven, *Second City: Birmingham and the Forging of Modern Britain*

Hakim Adi, *African and Caribbean People in Britain: A History*

Jordan Peterson, *24 Rules For Life: The Box Set*

Gaia Vince, *Nomad Century: How to Survive the Climate Upheaval*

Keith Fisher, *A Pipeline Runs Through It: The Story of Oil from Ancient Times to the First World War*

Christoph Keller, *Every Cripple a Superhero*

Roberto Calasso, *The Tablet of Destinies*

Jennifer Jacquet, *The Playbook: How to Deny Science, Sell Lies, and Make a Killing in the Corporate World*

Frank Close, *Elusive: How Peter Higgs Solved the Mystery of Mass*

Edward Chancellor, *The Price of Time: The Real Story of Interest*

Antonio Padilla, *Fantastic Numbers and Where to Find Them: A Cosmic Quest from Zero to Infinity*

Henry Kissinger, *Leadership: Six Studies in World Strategy*

Chris Patten, *The Hong Kong Diaries*

Lindsey Fitzharris, *The Facemaker: One Surgeon's Battle to Mend the Disfigured Soldiers of World War 1*

George Monbiot, *Regenesis: Feeding the World without Devouring the Planet*

Caroline Knowles, *Serious Money: Walking Plutocratic London*

Serhii Plokhy, *Atoms and Ashes: From Bikini Atoll to Fukushima*

Dominic Lieven, *In the Shadow of the Gods: The Emperor in World History*

Scott Hershovitz, *Nasty, Brutish, and Short: Adventures in Philosophy with Kids*

Bill Gates, *How to Prevent the Next Pandemic*

Emma Smith, *Portable Magic: A History of Books and their Readers*

Kris Manjapra, *Black Ghost of Empire: The Long Death of Slavery and the Failure of Emancipation*

Andrew Scull, *Desperate Remedies: Psychiatry and the Mysteries of Mental Illness*

James Bridle, *Ways of Being: Beyond Human Intelligence*

Eugene Linden, *Fire and Flood: A People's History of Climate Change, from 1979 to the Present*

Cathy O'Neil, *The Shame Machine: Who Profits in the New Age of Humiliation*

Peter Hennessy, *A Duty of Care: Britain Before and After Covid*

Gerd Gigerenzer, *How to Stay Smart in a Smart World: Why Human Intelligence Still Beats Algorithms*

Halik Kochanski, *Resistance: The Undergroud War in Europe, 1939-1945*

Joseph Sassoon, *The Global Merchants: The Enterprise and Extravagance of the Sassoon Dynasty*

Clare Chambers, *Intact: A Defence of the Unmodified Body*

Nina Power, *What Do Men Want?: Masculinity and Its Discontents*

Ivan Jablonka, *A History of Masculinity: From Patriarchy to Gender Justice*

Thomas Halliday, *Otherlands: A World in the Making*

Sofi Thanhauser, *Worn: A People's History of Clothing*

Sebastian Mallaby, *The Power Law: Venture Capital and the Art of Disruption*

David J. Chalmers, *Reality+: Virtual Worlds and the Problems of Philosophy*

Jing Tsu, *Kingdom of Characters: A Tale of Language, Obsession and Genius in Modern China*

Lewis R. Gordon, *Fear of Black Consciousness*

Leonard Mlodinow, *Emotional: The New Thinking About Feelings*

Kevin Birmingham, *The Sinner and the Saint: Dostoevsky, a Crime and Its Punishment*

Roberto Calasso, *The Book of All Books*

Marit Kapla, *Osebol: Voices from a Swedish Village*

Malcolm Gaskill, *The Ruin of All Witches: Life and Death in the New World*

Mark Mazower, *The Greek Revolution: 1821 and the Making of Modern Europe*

Paul McCartney, *The Lyrics: 1956 to the Present*

Brendan Simms and Charlie Laderman, *Hitler's American Gamble: Pearl Harbor and the German March to Global War*

Lea Ypi, *Free: Coming of Age at the End of History*

David Graeber and David Wengrow, *The Dawn of Everything: A New History of Humanity*

Ananyo Bhattacharya, *The Man from the Future: The Visionary Life of John von Neumann*

Andrew Roberts, *George III: The Life and Reign of Britain's Most Misunderstood Monarch*

James Fox, *The World According to Colour: A Cultural History*

Clare Jackson, *Devil-Land: England Under Siege, 1588-1688*

Steven Pinker, *Rationality: Why It Is, Why It Seems Scarce, Why It Matters*

Volker Ullrich, *Eight Days in May: How Germany's War Ended*

Adam Tooze, *Shutdown: How Covide Shook the World's Economy*

Tristram Hunt, *The Radical Potter: Josiah Wedgwood and the Transformation of Britain*

Paul Davies, *What's Eating the Universe: And Other Cosmic Questions*

Shon Faye, *The Transgender Issue: An Argument for Justice*

Dennis Duncan, *Index, A History of the*

Richard Overy, *Blood and Ruins: The Great Imperial War, 1931-1945*

Paul Mason, *How to Stop Fascism: History, Ideology, Resistance*

Cass R. Sunstein and Richard H. Thaler, *Nudge: Improving Decisions About Health, Wealth and Happiness*

Lisa Miller, *The Awakened Brain: The Psychology of Spirituality and Our Search for Meaning*

Michael Pye, *Antwerp: The Glory Years*